Smolensk under Soviet Rule

CLASSICS IN RUSSIAN AND SOVIET HISTORY

Additional titles in preparation

Smolensk

under

Soviet Rule

MERLE FAINSOD

Boston
UNWIN HYMAN
London   Sydney   Wellington

Unwin Hyman, Inc.
8 Winchester Place, Winchester, Mass. 01890, USA

Published by the Academic Division of
Unwin Hyman Ltd
15/17 Broadwick Street, London W1V 1FP, UK

Allen & Unwin (Australia) Ltd,
8 Napier Street, North Sydney, NSW 2060, Australia

Allen & Unwin (New Zealand) Ltd in association with the
Port Nicholson Press Ltd,
Compusales Building, 75 Ghuznee Street, Wellington 1, New Zealand

First published in 1958
This edition published in 1989

Library of Congress Cataloging-in-Publication Data

Fainsod, Merle, 1907–1972.
   Smolensk under Soviet rule / Merle Fainsod.
      p. cm. – (Classics in Russian and Soviet history: 2)
   Bibliography: p.
   Includes index.
   ISBN 0–04–445389–2
   1. Smolenskaia oblast' (R.S.F.S.R.) – Social conditions.
2. Smolenskaia oblast' (R.S.F.S.R.) – Politics and government.
3. Smolenskiĭ obkom KPSS – History.
4. Communism – Russian S.F.S.R. – Smolenskaia oblast'.
I. Title.   II. Series.
HN530.S63F3 1989
947-dc19   88-38371
                                                          CIP

British Library Cataloguing in Publication Data

Fainsod, Merle
   Smolensk under Soviet rule. – (Classics in Russian and Soviet history)
1. Soviet Union. Local government, history
I. Title   II. Series
352.047
ISBN 0-04-445389-2

Printed in Great Britain at the University Press, Cambridge

TO ARNOLD J. LIEN
Devoted teacher, wise counsellor, and friend

Acknowledgments

This book could not have been written without the helpful offices of The RAND Corporation in arranging access to the Smolensk Archive and in generously supporting the enterprise from its inception to its conclusion. I owe a special debt of gratitude to Dr. Hans Speier, the Chief of the Social Science Division of RAND, to his associates Robert Tucker and Myron Rush for their exceedingly useful criticism of the manuscript, and to Mrs. Anne M. Jonas for her assistance in locating the maps which are included in this volume. The Departmental Records Branch, Office of the Adjutant General, United States Army, kindly provided the documents upon which the study is based. As always, I remain deeply grateful to the Russian Research Center of Harvard University, both for the stimulation which it provides and for the time which it makes available for continuing research. The completion of this manuscript was also greatly facilitated by my tenure as a Ford Research Professor during the academic year 1956–57. I should like to take this opportunity to pay tribute to the imaginative leadership of the Ford Foundation in establishing such professorships and to thank the Harvard authorities for designating me as a recipient.

This volume also owes much to a group of collaborators who provided invaluable assistance during the crucial research stage in sifting, analyzing, and translating the documents. Merely to mention their names — Professor Zbigniew Brzezinski, Mrs. Alla Emerson, Mr. Gregory Grasberg, Mr. Gregory J. Massell, Mr. Walter J. Vickery, and Mrs. Lois Weinert — can be only the smallest token of my gratitude. I am also greatly indebted to Mr. Glenn G. Morgan, Mr. Donald Blackmer, Miss Anna Dickason, and Miss Nancy Whittier, whose seminar papers on various topics drawn from the Smolensk Archive proved extremely helpful to me in guiding my own researches. Finally, but not least importantly, I should like to express my appreciation of the devoted services of my secretary, Mrs. Ruth Levine, who has borne most of the heavy burden of preparing this manuscript for the press.

Contents

Charts

Tables

Documents

Maps

The reappearance of Merle Fainsod's study of politics and people in the Smolensk region in the 1920s and 1930s is a welcome event. Thirty years after its publication, this work remains a unique effort to understand the transformation of the Soviet Union from the perspective of one particular region. Its strengths are the result of its rich documentary source, the Smolensk Archives, and of the perceptive interpretation of those materials by Merle Fainsod, perhaps the most influential Soviet specialist of the postwar years. The totalitarian model provides Fainsod with the conceptual tools by which to select, organize, and interpret the archival materials. Although that view of Soviet power has been seriously challenged in recent decades, this book remains an indispensable work on Soviet history.

The Smolensk region shared in the tumultuous transformation of the country under Communist dictatorship. Fainsod pays considerable attention, in the early chapters, to the historical context within which to situate what he terms the "life of a typical region during the first two formative decades of Soviet rule" (p. 12). As did other parts of the country, Smolensk experienced the slow recovery from war and civil war within the framework of the New Economic Policy (NEP). The institutions and practices of Communist single-party control extended into the districts of that largely rural area, where as elsewhere in the country it confronted, in Robert Tucker's words, a "scarcely sovietized Russian culture."[1] The restructuring of economic and social relations under the First Five-Year Plan brought Soviet rule into the villages and households of Smolensk. The "revolutionary vigilance" of the secret police made its oppressive weight felt on the population and the Party, for whom 1937 was as cruel a time as it was in other parts of the land. In these and other ways, the story of the country at large is encapsulated within the administrative borders of Smolensk province. Fainsod's approach in this work is both familiar—reiterating topics found in survey histories of the period—and unusual in the sense that textbook generalizations regarding historical trends and forces are embodied in the lives of ordinary individuals and typical events. This book can thus play an important part in making understandable to students of Soviet history the human dimensions of the dramatic events of those years.

The distinctive shape that historical events assume in the Smolensk story is determined largely by the archival source on which this study is based. Soviet zeal in the preservation of documents at the regional (and national) level duplicated practices that are familiar to any researcher who has had the opportunity to explore the vast archival holdings of imperial Russia. The latter have since the 1950s been accessible to Western historians; Soviet archives have only in recent years been opened on a limited, and controlled, basis. The Smolensk Archives went first to Nazi Germany, then to the United States, as war booty. They remain in the possession of the National Archives in the absence of a formal request from the Soviet Archival Administration for their repatriation. Duplicated on microfilm, they are readily available to the public.[2] They contain a vast array of documents, thrown together in folders in somewhat helter-skelter fashion, on social and economic conditions in the region; on the objectives, obstacles, and conflicts of Party rule; and on central state and Party views and instructions regarding local affairs. In Fainsod's hands, they become the substance of what we might term a local history. Their random character assumes a coherent pattern through Fainsod's search for "political processes," by which he means "the organization of authority in the region, the way in which controls operated, and their impact on the people who lived under their sway" (p. 5).

This approach to local history subordinates events in Smolensk to the dictates and controls of Moscow. The region's provincial status places it in a position inferior to central Party organs and to central (Russian Republic and federal) commissariats and other state agencies. Fainsod's interest in Soviet power relations situates the historical events of that area on the periphery of a story whose locus is the Kremlin. The relations among provincial Party organs and local officials and the people of the area duplicate on a regional level the situation between Smolensk and the capital. The archives fit this conceptual structure well, for they contain many instructions, resolutions, and reports sent from Moscow to all of the country's administrative regions.

Fainsod's study is in some respects a view "from below" of the political history of the Party leadership and of state policies. The secret Party documents he analyzes, such as the 1933 "instructions" calling for the relaxation of forced collectivization and of police repression (pp. 185–88), were until Fainsod's work unknown to the West. Many remain unmentioned to this day in Soviet historical studies. If, for example, one reads Fainsod's version of the history of collectivization in Smolensk and then reads of it in Soviet works, one is left with the impression of having read two quite different stories. Fainsod by necessity cites only a small fraction of the pertinent documentation, but his selection appears remarkably judicious and balanced. Scholars may disagree with his interpretation of the documents, but they can find in his book essential materials, in lengthy quotes from sources and in footnote references to archival files, for their own work. Thus Smolensk history remains an invaluable point of departure for research into Soviet history of the interwar years.

Though Fainsod came to understand that the archives tell a "tale of infinite complexity" (p. 447), his history adheres carefully to the conceptual guidelines of totalitarian theory. He had previously completed a comprehensive study of the Soviet system of rule, which presented his readers with a historical–political explanation of "Communist totalitarianism." He found the origins of this system in the Russian past as well as in Marxism–Leninism and in what he termed Stalin's complex "formula of totalitarian rule."[3] The Smolensk Archives offered him a unique opportunity to test his theory against historical reality, albeit in the shape of one relatively minor rural province.

Not surprisingly, the book that resulted from his archival investigation confirms the correctness of the totalitarian model. Behind the diversity and complexity of the life histories and political conflicts revealed in the archives, his history discerns a "totalitarian machine," even if it was "far from perfect" (pp. 449–50). The book is organized by the principal elements that political scientists believed to constitute that "machine." The Party, in its various organizational roles, constitutes the key agent of "control," alongside of which are the agencies of repression, notably the secret police. Their actions largely determine the "impact of authority" upon various segments of the population. The full extent of totalitarian control came only in the 1930s, yet according to Fainsod's account of events of earlier years, no other outcome appears possible or conceivable.

He is aware that the archives tell of a "struggle between the old and the new," but this conflict appears in his view to take the form of chaos versus order. History is a unilinear process. Out of the ruins of war and revolution a new, powerful political system emerges, blending some traits from the past (including a "tradition of servility"), new instruments of repression ("force, terror, and organization"), and a new ruling group (pp. 450–52). Fainsod's conclusion is predictable from the totalitarian theory he had previously applied to Soviet politics and from his premise that the Smolensk Archive is a "mirror of Soviet reality." However improbable, Smolensk is turned into another historical site for the enactment of George Orwell's novel *1984*.

In the decades since Fainsod published his survey of Soviet politics and his study of the Smolensk region, the totalitarian model has ceased to dominate Soviet political history. Its decline has been encouraged by destalinization and the emergence of Soviet political practices which, to a substantial body of scholars, defy fundamental tenets of that model.[4] It has resulted as well from the expansion of historical studies of the interwar years. Some of these works have explored Smolensk archival materials and have addressed issues at the center of Fainsod's view of the Smolensk story. They provide alternative readings of documents and important reinterpretations of events in Smolensk directly relevant to our understanding of Soviet rule.

Despite these efforts, the problem of the uniqueness of the Soviet political experience during Stalin years remains a key historiographical issue. To this extent the question of totalitarianism constitutes a sort of touchstone by which to situate interpretations of the Soviet historical experience in that period. Fainsod's Smolensk study has a vital part to play in that debate. In other words, we can reread the Smolensk study to find answers to new questions and to test the validity of new approaches to Soviet history.

The major question in this reexamination of the interwar years focuses on the continuity of Soviet political development from the Civil War to the period of the Great Terror. Fainsod chooses to organize the Smolensk story thematically, implicitly suggesting that the grouping of events by the customary chronological units of New Economic Policy, First Five-Year Plan, and the Terror is less meaningful than the overall trend. In his telling of the story, issues as diverse as purges, collectivization, and Party rule are all part of one panoramic picture of the totalitarian machine.

The documentary evidence that Fainsod uses to buttress his totalitarian theory is still very germane to current debates on central Party policy and police repression in the 1930s. He devotes particular attention to the Terror, yet it too is subsumed under a general discussiuon of "purges and people." Was terror a constant feature of the 1930s? The issues are complex and have given rise to a debate centered on the revisionist view of J. Arch Getty, who challenges Fainsod's interpretation of Party and police controls in Smolensk.[5] Fainsod cites one Party–state document of 1933, mentioned above, whose explicit purpose was to end indiscriminate arrests and the massive deportation of peasants, and to reduce the numbers of prisoners (p. 186). To him, the facts it contains illustrate the functioning of Party controls over the population. A different reading points to the temporary abandonment of repressive policies, suggesting a moderation of Politburo leadership and even resistance there to Stalin's pursuit of "class enemies."[6] If so, perhaps the theory of totalitarianism is best fitted, as some scholars would argue, to the "horrors of high Stalinism" of the post-1934 years.[7]

The issue of continuity or change is particularly prominent in studies of the transition from NEP to the First Five-Year Plan period. It raises basic questions of the nature and viability of the policies and leadership of NEP, and of the roots of Stalinism. Renewed attention to that historical moment is to some extent a reflection of increased interest in NEP and of the growing condemnation of the Stalinist legacy by the new Soviet leadership of the late 1980s. As well, thoughtful historical studies have presented challenging new interpretations of these topics. Sheila Fitzpatrick has extended the period of "Russian Revolution" from 1917 through the early 1930s. From this point of view NEP occupies a transitory place in a process of fundamental political, social, and economic transformation, in large measure complete only at the end of the First Five-Year Plan.[8] From a very different perspective, Stephen

Cohen finds fault with the totalitarian assumption of continuity, since in his opinion "failure to distinguish between Soviet authoritarianism before and after 1929 means obscuring the very nature of Stalinism."[9] The implication in this reasoning, spelled out clearly in his biography of Bukharin, is that NEP, under that leader's guidance, represented a creative and human path to socialism.[10]

As told by Fainsod, the Smolensk story takes little account of the political transition to Stalinism. For one thing, the controversies that erupted at the Party congresses between "Left" and "Right" Communist leaders did not play an important part in the political activities of provinces such as Smolensk. More important Fainsod had no conceptual basis on which to draw a meaningful distinction between the two periods, which constituted for him integral parts in the unfolding of the "totalitarian process." He judged the problems created by the isolation of Party cadres at the local level to be minor obstacles in the trend toward party dictatorship, and viewed peasants and workers as a largely undifferentiated mass of indifferent or hostile subjects. An alternative perspective emerges when scholars search for explanations for the difficulties confronting the Party in reconciling its ideological commitment to proletarian revolution with its role as revolutionary "vanguard."[11] The historical drama inherent in the confrontation between Marxist dreams and Russian reality is not relevant to Fainsod's structural analysis of Soviet rule. Still, he is aware of the complexity of the daily encounters of Party and people. If we read the material carefully, his book presents a story of utopian visions and political compromises.

The end of NEP and the emergence of Stalinist rule touched Smolensk most visibly and forcefully in the events surrounding the agricultural crisis of 1928 and the subsequent collectivization, and in the form of a Party purge, termed by contemporaries the "Smolensk abscess" and by Fainsod the "scandal." To him, the imposition of collectivized farming in the region represented a major step in the process of carrying the "impact of authority" to the level of the village itself. In his telling, the scandal constituted no more than a typical affair of corruption and "family circles" within regional state and Party organs. One might ask, however, if the procurement crisis and the Smolensk Party affair were not, each in its own way, indications of a moment of reckoning for NEP policies and the moderate leadership. In this light, events in Smolensk become a "local history" illuminating a vital moment of decision in Soviet history. Archival documents, some of which are cited at various points in Fainsod's book, provide insight into public debates and secret factional strife, revealing the depths of the controversy over the policies and ideological principles which had guided NEP.[12] Events that appear to Fainsod as an ongoing process of concentration of power can also be seen as part of the uncertainties and struggles attending a transition of unknown outcome.

The revision of Soviet interwar history during the past several decades has enriched our understanding of that period. It has enlarged our appreciation for the complexity of political and social developments and raised new historical issues. The comprehensive scope and conceptual certainty that the totalitarian theory provided Merle Fainsod in his study of the Smolensk region have disappeared, but no comparable theory has taken its place. A new historical consensus may ultimately emerge out of the debates of recent years. At present, one can only point to new directions that Soviet historical studies appear to be taking. Sheila Fitzpatrick has called for a study of the social history of the Stalin years. The inquiry she proposes would search for the "social dynamics" of that period—and by necessity of the previous years as well—to uncover class structure, interaction, and "the grass-roots viewpoint of ordinary lower-class citizens."[13] All three topics, and especially the last, point to a reexamination of the Smolensk materials, both in Fainsod's book and in the archives. The premises and objectives of this project are the subject of a considerable debate that raises conceptual problems and questions fundamental assumptions of her social history.[14] Judging by recent studies of Nazism, however, we can anticipate that social perspectives on Stalinism will become increasingly pertinent to the history of those times. In this area, the Smolensk materials can make a major contribution.

Another approach that is pertinent to our rereading of the Smolensk story uses the concept of culture to focus attention on the conflict of ideas and values that accompanied the establishment of Soviet rule. Robert Tucker has suggested that the radical reconstruction of the country can be seen as an "effort to refashion the society's culture or habitual mode of life—its institutions, symbol-systems, behavioral patterns, rituals, art forms, values." The Communist Party can be studied, he argues, as a "culture-transforming movement," utopian as well as power-seeking, divided internally by conflicting visions of the future, claiming sweeping authority, but confronting the deeply embedded customs and values of the existing culture.[15]

Seen in this light, Soviet rule did not necessarily have to culminate in Stalinist revolution. The cultural approach supposes that we look carefully at other groups and listen to other voices besides the Communists who were engaged in this "refashioning" of the dominant values and practices of governance and social relations. One collective work has already introduced the concept of cultural revolution to reexamine the NEP years; another has used it to reevaluate the forces and ideals at work during the First Five-Year Plan period.[16] In my opinion, the cultural approach is another promising perspective from which to rethink the Smolensk experience and to reread Fainsod's book. Despite his conviction that the totalitarian model best explains the history of Smolensk as revealed in the archives, he recognizes throughout his account the presence of "ordinary human beings trying desperately to lead normal lives in the midst of extraordinary and abnormal events" (p. 446). This human face to the revolutionary turmoil, which he finds within the Party as well as among the population, cannot be compressed into one neat theoretical package and does not fit the image of the brainwashed denizens of Orwell's nightmarish world of *1984*. What we lose by abandoning the neat certainties of totalitarianism, we gain by opening our eyes to the presence of multitudes of people whose experiences constitute perhaps the key to understanding Soviet rule. If this is so, then Fainsod's work is as meaningful now as it was when first published.

Daniel Brower
University of California–Davis

Notes

1 Robert Tucker, "Stalinism as Revolution from Above," in R. Tucker (ed.), *Stalinism: Essays in Historical Interpretation* (New York, 1979), p. 80.

2 "Records of the Smolensk Oblast of the All-Union Communist Party of the Soviet Union, 1917–41," National Archive, Microfilm Publication T-84, T-87, T-88; Fainsod prepared an incomplete, annotated index following his chapter topics, duplicated on roll 1 of T-87. Another, unannotated index encompassing the entire archive is *Guide to the Records of the Smolensk Oblast of the All-Union Communist Party* (National Archives, Washington, D.C. 1980).

3 Merle Fainsod, *How Russia Is Ruled* (Cambridge, Mass., 1953), pp. 3–4, 59, 109–10.

4 For a succinct history of totalitarianism's place in Soviet studies, see Abbott Gleason, "'Totalitarianism' in 1984," *The Russian Review*, v. 43 (1984), pp. 145–59.

5 J. Arch Getty, "Party and Purge in Smolensk: 1933–1937," *Slavic Review*, v. 42 (Spring, 1983), pp. 60–96. Getty's views are spelled out at greater length in *Origins of the Great Purges: The Soviet Communist Party Reconsidered, 1933–1938* (Cambridge, Mass., 1985).

6 This question is explored in B. Brower, "Collectivized Agriculture in Smolensk," *The Russian Review*, v. 36 (April, 1977), pp. 151–66.

7 Gleason, p. 155.

8 Sheila Fitzpatrick, *The Russian Revolution* (New York, 1982).

9 Stephen Cohen, "Bolshevism and Stalinism," in R. Tucker (ed.), *Stalinism*, p. 12.

10 S. Cohen, *Bukharin and the Bolshevik Revolution: A Political Biography* (New York, 1973); Cohen's new introduction to the Oxford paperback edition presents his defense against the critics of his book (New York, 1980).

11 See William Rosenberg, "Smolensk in the 1920s: Party–Worker Relations and the 'Vanguard' Problem," *The Russian Review*, v. 36 (April, 1977), pp. 127–50.

12 See D. Brower, "The Smolensk Scandal and the End of NEP," *Slavic Review*, v. 36 (Winter, 1986), pp. 689–706.

13 Sheila Fitzpatrick, "New Perspectives on Stalinism," *The Russian Review*, v. 45 (October, 1986), p. 367.

14 Ibid., pp. 375–414; and ibid., v. 46 (October, 1987), pp. 375–431.

15 Robert Tucker, "Stalinism as Revolution from Above," in Tucker (ed.), *Stalinism*, p. 79; also, R. Tucker, *Political Culture and Leadership in Soviet Russia: From Lenin to Gorbachev* (New York, 1987).

16 Abbott Gleason, Peter Stites, Peter Kenez (eds.), *Bolshevik Culture: Experiment and Order in the Russian Revolution* (Bloomington, Ind., 1985); Sheila Fitzpatrick (ed.), *Cultural Revolution in Russia, 1928–1931* (Bloomington, Ind., 1978).

PART ONE

The Background

Introduction — The Nature and Significance of the Smolensk Archive

In mid-July 1941, less than a month after Hitler launched his invasion of the Soviet Union, German army units swept into the city of Smolensk. The local authorities were presumably under instructions to destroy or withdraw their records, but in the general confusion of the evacuation, arrangements went awry. At Party headquarters in Smolensk, where current files were kept, Party officials apparently managed to burn or remove all important documents; at least none of any real significance was found for the period 1939–1941. The back files, however, covering the period 1917–1938, were stored in another building far from Party headquarters, and these remained largely intact. German intelligence officers, who discovered the collection, found it in a state of great disarray and made a rather random selection of more than 500 files containing approximately 200,000 pages of documents which were shipped back to Germany for examination. There at the end of the war they fell into American hands.

This collection, usually described as the Smolensk Archive, is in many respects unique.* Its analogues can, of course, be found in every section of the Soviet Union itself, but access to Party archives of this type has long been denied to Western non-Communist scholars, and there is no imminent likelihood that these bans will be removed. So far as this writer has been able to ascertain, no comparable local or regional Soviet archival collections are available in the West. While the Smolensk documentation is limited to a particular region, the illumination which it sheds extends well beyond the boundaries of Smolensk. The Archive provides an unparalleled opportunity to view the processes of regional and local government in the Soviet Union from the inside.

The contents of the Archive reflect the changing jurisdiction of the Smolensk Party headquarters over the years. From 1917 until 1929 the records are limited largely to Smolensk guberniya (see back endpaper map). From 1929 to 1937 they broaden out to embrace the Western Oblast (see front endpaper map). After September 1937, with the split-up of the Western Oblast, they narrow down to the newly created Smolensk

* See Bibliographical Note, p. 456, for location and availability of documents.

Oblast which marked the reappearance of the old guberniya in a somewhat altered guise.

In terms of bulk as well as of significance, the largest part of the Archive consists of Party records of all types. They include directives from Moscow to Smolensk and reports from Smolensk to the center, protocols of Party and Komsomol committee meetings at every level of organization from the guberniya and oblast down to primary Party cells, and the orders, reports, and correspondence of Party secretaries at corresponding stages of the Party hierarchy. But the Archive is in no sense limited to records of internal Party life. Because the Party served as the fountainhead of authority in the region and its controls reached out in many directions, the documentation in the Party archives touches on almost every aspect of regional existence. It incorporates proceedings of governmental bodies at various levels and reports of the security police, the procuracy, the courts, and the militia. It contains a large body of material on agriculture, including extensive records of the collectivization process and many specific reports on the experience of kolkhozes, state farms, and machine-tractor stations. It embraces a considerable variety of miscellaneous material on trade unions, Party relations with the armed forces, education, censorship, and religion. Scattered through the Archive are also many hundreds of anguished letters from ordinary Soviet citizens addressed to the press and to Party authorities, which do much to bring home the human impact of Soviet policies.

As might perhaps be expected, the Archive has its strengths and its weaknesses. There are certain areas where the Archive is particularly rich. There is a profusion of material on the work of regional and district Party committees and their secretariats, on the organs of State Security — the Cheka, the OGPU, and the NKVD — on the Purges, and the grassroots history of collectivization. Similarly, there are impressive collections of data on censorship, on police reports of crime in the area, and on Party controls of higher education, which provide a great deal of information that is unavailable in open sources.

The Archive is, however, uneven in its coverage. Industry played a minor role in the economic life of the region, and the Archive reflects this in the rather scanty accounts of Party life in the factories and in the trade unions. The armed forces come in for only occasional mention; such documents as survive relate largely to Party work in army units. References to church activities are scattered and fragmentary.

Perhaps the most important weakness of the Archive involves the absence of adequate documentation on the decision-making processes of the central authorities in Moscow. While the Archive contains many important and hitherto unpublished central directives of top Party and governmental leaders, there are no records of the proceedings of top policy-making bodies with the exception of one file of protocols of joint sessions of the Presidium of the Central Control Commission and the collegium of the Commissariat of Workers' and Peasants' Inspection for the period November 1929–June 1930. Receipts found in the files clearly indicate that numbered copies of stenographic reports of Central Committee sessions were circulated to all first secretaries of district Party committees, but under the rules then in force they had to be returned to Moscow after a few days. Since no copies were found in the Archive, it can be assumed that these rules were rigidly enforced.

Another serious deficiency of the Archive is its random character. There are frequent gaps in the chronological sequence of the records of many important Party and governmental agencies in the region. An example may, perhaps, illustrate the problem. There are protocols of meetings of the gubkom, or Party committee of Smolensk guberniya, for the years 1920, 1922, and 1928, but not for the years in between. There are similar protocols for the Western obkom, or oblast Party committee, for the years 1929, 1936, and 1937, but not for the intervening period. Fortunately, some of these gaps can be filled by other Party reports or documentation in the Archive which make it possible to reconstruct the main lines of development. Yet many irritating lacunae remain for which neither the Archive nor any outside source provides a solution.

Any effort to exploit the resources of the Archive must therefore adjust to both its strengths and its weaknesses. The nature of the material imposes its own limitations and opportunities. The array of documents in the Archive ramifies over so many diverse fields as inevitably to pose a serious problem of organization, selection, and emphasis. The vantage point which has been chosen for this volume puts major stress on political processes. The emphasis is on the organization of authority in the region, the way in which controls operated, and their impact on the people who lived under their sway. The study is divided into two parts. The first is devoted to the structure of power in the area. A history of the Smolensk Party organization is followed by an examination of the manner in which Party and governmental organs functioned at the regional, district, and village levels and by an analysis of the roles of the agencies of state security, the courts, the procuracy, and the militia. The second part of the book stresses the effect of controls on the people. Police records are utilized to portray the range and incidence of crime in the region. Next the purge files lay bare their own tragic evidence of lives and careers that were wrecked and destroyed. Then comes a series of chapters on the peasant — the story of collectivization in the region, and the impact of collective farms, state farms, and machine-tractor stations on life in the countryside. Succeeding chapters are dedicated to the industrial worker, the army, the university and higher education, censorship, letters to the press and to Party headquarters, the Komsomol, and religious activity. The choice of topics, while determined largely by the availability of archival material, also serves to register the wide-ranging incidence of Party controls.

To see the Smolensk Archive in perspective, one must view its contents against the broader background of the evolution of the Soviet system during the period 1917–1939. While there is no lack of books which outline these developments, it may be helpful to the general reader, if not to the Soviet specialist, to recapitulate some of the main trends before plunging into the story of Smolensk.*

The time span covered by the Archive is ordinarily divided by historians of the Soviet regime into three periods: 1917–1921, The years of Civil War and War Communism; 1921–1928, The Era of the New Economic Policy (NEP); and 1928–1939, The Pre-World War II Decade of Collectivization and Industrialization. Each of these periods had its distinctive characteristics, and together they left their successive imprints on life in Smolensk.

During the first period the Bolsheviks were engaged in a desperate battle for survival. After seizing power in November 1917, they found themselves manning a beleaguered fortress, threatened first by a German advance, and fighting off a succession of challenges from White Generals, the Allied Intervention armies, the Poles, peasant revolts, and rebellious anti-Bolshevik nationalist movements in the borderlands. Smolensk was never far from the swirling lines of battle, and for much of the time it took on the character of an armed camp in which men and resources were constantly being mobilized to strengthen the Red Army at the front.

From the beginning the Bolsheviks, who were a small minority in the country, concentrated all their efforts on building firm instruments of power. They occupied the commanding positions in state administration, controlled the army and the Cheka (secret police), and asserted the paramount position of the Party in every walk of life. Nevertheless, the machinery of control fell far short of the tightly centralized bureaucratic structure into which the Soviet regime later developed. Under the impact of the Civil War, the trend toward domination of the Party by its central organs was strongly reinforced, but the Party remained a battleground of competing factions, and the authority of the top Party leadership was still subject to challenge from below. As the Smolensk Archive makes clear, localism flourished, and the effectiveness of Communist controls diminished in direct relationship to the distance from the great urban centers. The first years of Soviet power were uniquely a period

---

* The following account is a condensation of material contained in my earlier volume, *How Russia Is Ruled* (Harvard University Press, 1953).

when the spontaneous and anarchic forces of the Revolution had their way. The flood of decrees from the center bore little relation to the actual sequence of developments in the localities. The breakdown of supply and communications, the shifting lines of battle, and the initial inexperience of the regime combined to create a situation in which authority was dispersed and broken into fragments. It required the most strenuous efforts of the Party to impose even a semblance of direction on the course of events.

The desperate struggle for survival compelled equally desperate expedients. Policy toward the peasants was a by-product of the problem of supplying the Red Army. The Soviet regime faced the task of extracting grain from the peasants without being able to provide them with consumers' goods in exchange. It met the problem by forcible requisitions and alienated the peasantry in the process. The industrial policy of the Bolsheviks reflected the same overriding concern with immediate military considerations. During the first months of the Revolution, Lenin tried to confine nationalization to the commanding industrial heights and to smooth the transition by retaining the services and tapping the skills of former factory owners and bourgeois technical specialists. These measures revealed themselves as largely abortive. In mid-1918 virtually every important branch of industrial life was nationalized, but efforts to revive production encountered frustrating obstacles. Failures of communication and transport, as well as shortages of raw material, led to work stoppages, and industrial breakdowns were contagious and cumulative. The cities suffered from cold and hunger, and workers abandoned the factories in large numbers. The output of those factories that continued to operate was reserved almost entirely for the Red Army; supplies that might be useful at the front were simply requisitioned. Shortages became so extreme as to render price and rationing controls meaningless. Money lost all value. Workers had to be paid in kind, and a rapidly expanding black market largely displaced the official channels of trade. By the end of the Civil War, want and hunger were general. Even after the White armies were beaten off, internal discontent continued to express itself in a swelling tide of sporadic peasant risings, strikes of factory workers, and the revolt of the Kronstadt garrison in March 1921, with its call for a third revolution to throw off the yoke of the Communists. Although the Kronstadt revolt and other risings were bloodily suppressed, their meaning was not lost on the Communist high command. Steps were taken to ameliorate the dissatisfaction of the mass of peasants and workers.

The NEP, or New Economic Policy, on which the regime embarked in 1921, embraced a series of measures designed to placate mass unrest and to stimulate a revival of the productive forces of the nation. The most important concession to the peasantry was the abandonment of the policy of forced requisitions in favor of a fixed tax in kind, which left the peasants free to dispose of such surpluses as remained after the tax assessment had been met. In order to persuade the peasants to part with their surpluses, incentives had to be provided in the form of increased supplies of consumers' goods. This made an increase in industrial production imperative. The NEP industrial policy put initial emphasis on the development of small industries, whether in the form of private enterprise or of industrial coöperatives, in the hope that they would most readily increase the flow of consumers' goods. New enterprises were promised freedom from nationalization. Small enterprises which had been nationalized were leased to their former owners or industrial artels (producers' coöperatives) for fixed terms with the proviso that rentals were to be paid in the form of a definite proportion of the output of the enterprise. The so-called "commanding heights" of large-scale industry remained under state administration, though even these enterprises, organized in the form of trusts, were to be operated on commercial principles with substantial freedom to buy and sell on the open market, and with the obligation to operate on a basis of profitability. Private trade was restored, and a new generation of so-called Nepmen arose to carry on the function of middlemen in the Soviet economy. The Soviet leadership sought to attract foreign capital by offering "concessions" to capitalist entrepreneurs, but the bait proved unalluring, and in all but a few cases negotiations collapsed.

The Party, meanwhile, compensated for its concessions to the peasantry and the private trader by utilizing the interval of the NEP to tighten its hold on the political instruments of power. After 1922 any form of Menshevik, Socialist-Revolutionary, or other anti-Communist political activity was treated as counterrevolutionary and ruthlessly extirpated. While the battle for the succession which set in even before Lenin's death produced a major Party crisis — in the course of which first the left-wing opposition of Trotsky, Zinoviev, and Kamenev, and later the right-wing opposition of Bukharin, Tomsky, and Rykov were eliminated — the outcome of the struggle was a strengthening of the power of the central apparatus and the emergence of Stalin as the undisputed ruler of the Party's destinies. Stalin and his faithful Party lieutenants maintained a firm grip on the army, the secret police, and the administrative and trade union apparatus. While the Party remained weakly represented in the countryside, it strengthened its position in the major urban areas. No organized force appeared to challenge its dominating position on the Soviet political scene.

The initial recuperative effects of NEP policies fortified the position of the Party leadership. With the introduction of the tax in kind, peasant disorders died down; and after the disastrous harvest of 1921, a steady improvement in agricultural production was evident. A marked revival of light industry took place, and consumers' goods became somewhat more plentiful. Although there was a lag in heavy industry accompanied by considerable unemployment and worker dissatisfaction, a modicum of relief was provided by unemployment benefits and the perceptible improvement in economic conditions generally.

The Communist leadership, nevertheless, faced a dilemma for which there was no easy resolution. However firmly it controlled the state machinery, it remained essentially an army of occupation in an overwhelmingly peasant country. In the first trial of strength, the peasantry had been able to extract substantial concessions from the Soviet regime, despite the fact that the Communists retained their hold on the strategic instruments of power. Given the socialist and industrial orientation of Communism, the NEP could at best be defended as a necessary but dangerous compromise. Both the logic of long-term survival and the dogmas of inherited ideology appeared to dictate a program of industrialization and collectivization.

In the situation in which the Soviet regime found itself in the twenties, the only important source from which capital could be accumulated was the peasantry. Long-term foreign loans, the historic instrument of industrial development in backward countries, were not available. The concessions policy of the Soviet regime met almost complete frustration. The only remaining alternative was aptly described by V. M. Smirnov and E. A. Preobrazhensky as "primitive socialist accumulation," the diversion of the output of the peasantry and the private sector of the economy to finance investment in socialized heavy industry.

The NEP provided no ready expedients for securing a large-scale diversion of peasant production to subsidize industrialization. The introduction of the tax in kind stimulated a considerable increase in agricultural output; but it was accompanied by a substantial reduction in agricultural exports as compared with pre-World War I days when the surpluses extracted from the peasants were used to finance a considerable inflow of foreign capital goods and luxury items. Under NEP, the peasant, after paying his tax in kind, could dispose of his remaining output in any way that pleased him. Since the terms of trade with the towns after 1922 were unfavorable to the peasantry and the rural population continued to mount rapidly, the small peasant demonstrated an increasing propensity to consume his own output. The kulaks, or well-to-do farmers, produced a far larger share of their output for the market, but when price relationships were unfavorable, they withheld their grain in order to drive a hard bargain to safeguard their own interests. As the NEP developed, moreover, social differentiation in the countryside intensified; the less efficient peasant households fell back into the status of poor peasants and hired laborers, and the position of the kulaks was strengthened.

The industrialization problem and its implications for the peasantry posed difficult choices for the Party leadership. One position, which expressed the program of Bukharin and the Right Opposition of 1928–29, counseled avoidance of repressive measures in dealing with the peasantry. The Bukharin group was prepared to offer price concessions to the peasants in order to encourage production for market. It saw no danger in tolerating and even encouraging the emergence of strong peasant holdings which would direct larger proportions of their output to the market. As long as the Party maintained its control of the instruments of power, the Right Opposition believed that the road to socialism was safeguarded. While it was prepared to squeeze the kulak through increased taxation, it also recognized that in order to obtain large grain deliveries, more and cheaper consumers' goods would have to be made available to the rural population. The implications of this position were twofold: (1) a substantial part of the burden of industrialization would be shifted to the urban population, and (2) industrialization would have to proceed at a relatively slow pace.

The opposing position, ultimately incorporated by Stalin in the First Five Year Plan (1928–1933), started from the assumption that a program of rapid industrialization was imperative and that nothing short of a wholesale reconstruction of Soviet agriculture could guarantee the grain reserves to carry it forward. The Stalinist plan, borrowed in many of its aspects from the proposals of the Left Opposition which he had earlier repudiated, involved the preliminary application of "emergency measures" against the kulaks in order to expropriate the surpluses which they were allegedly hoarding and the subsequent liquidation of the kulaks as a class opposed to collectivization. In order to increase the productivity of agriculture, mechanized grain factories or state farms were to be extended, and the poor and middle peasants were to be enrolled in collective farms which would be served by machine-tractor stations equipped with modern agricultural implements. This grandiose scheme, as later events were to disclose, also carried its hidden implications. The main burden of accumulating an industrialization fund was to be transferred to the countryside.

Fundamentally, the Stalinist program meant a revival of the Civil War policy of forced requisitions under conditions giving the state much more powerful weapons to enforce its demands. By herding the agricultural population into state and collective farms, the regime would be able to operate through a relatively limited number of controlled collective units instead of dealing individually with millions of peasant households. Although the advocates of this plan professed to believe that rapid industrialization could be combined with an immediate increase in consumption, as the result of the application of modern technical methods to agriculture, in practice this hope was shown to be illusory. Mechanization could only be introduced slowly, and meanwhile the state faced the problem of extracting the grain from the collective and state farms to pay for the industrial base on which the production of tractors and other agricultural implements depended. Stripped of its propaganda verbiage, the Stalinist program foreshadowed a profound extension of the scope of totalitarian power. The peasantry was to be brought to heel and harnessed to state ends. The surpluses extracted from the peasantry were to provide the wherewithal to create a powerful industrial structure which would render the Soviet citadel impregnable.

As Stalin consolidated his position in the Party, he pressed forward with the realization of his program. The NEP was liquidated; the era of Five Year Plans began; and the program of collectivization was imposed on the countryside. The new phase in the development of the Soviet system marked a Third Revolution, far more important in its long-term consequences than the February and October Revolutions of 1917 which were its entr'actes. It represented a determined effort to destroy the petty-bourgeois peasant revolution which had been achieved in 1917 and to seize the positions which the peasantry had occupied during the NEP. It launched the Soviet Union on a course of industrialization that transformed it into a first-class military power. It was also accompanied by Stalin's emergence as the nation's unchallenged dictator.

The Stalinist impact on Soviet society was many-sided. In the economic sphere the driving thrust was rapid industrialization and the exertion of constant pressure on the countryside to mobilize the capital necessary to support the industrialization drive. Heavy industry and the armed forces enjoyed a prior claim on all economic resources; the result was a lopsided economic development in which the consumption sector of the economy was sacrificed to strengthen the sinews of industrial and military might. Power took precedence over welfare, and the great mass of rank-and-file collective farmers and workers was confronted with a chronic shortage of food, consumers' goods, and housing. At the same time industrialization unleashed its own imperatives. The crying need for engineers and technicians to man the new industrial plants led to an overhauling of the educational system, an emphasis on technical training, and the growth of a new Soviet-trained technical intelligentsia, which played an essential role in managing an increasingly complex economy. Technical dynamism was built into the system, not only by the emphasis on technical education, but also by surrounding the career of the engineer and the manager with special privileges, perquisites, and status in order to attract talent. Egalitarianism was repudiated as "petty-bourgeois nonsense"; the new state élite that emerged under Stalin largely monopolized the rewards of Soviet society.

In the political sphere, Stalinism spelled the development of a full-blown totalitarian regime in which all the lines of control ultimately converged in the hands of the supreme dictator. The Party became a creature of Stalin's will and lost such policy-determining functions as it once possessed. Its role was reduced to that of a transmission belt, which Stalin used to communicate his directives, to mobilize support for them by propaganda and agitation, and to check on their execution. As the purges of the mid-thirties approached their apogee, terror itself became a system of power, and the secret police flourished and multiplied. The fear which its agents inspired provided the foundation of Stalin's own security; through them he guarded the loyalty of the Party, the armed forces, the bureaucracy, the intellectuals, and the mass of the population generally.

Stalinism also left its impress on social and intellectual life. The schools were transformed into an authoritarian instrument to instill devotion to the regime and to prepare youth for its appointed place in the Soviet hierarchical structure. The family was visualized as a species of human machine-tool which could be stimulated to Stakhanovite productivity by outlawing divorces, imposing restrictions on abortions, and holding out special premiums for overquota child-bearing. A strange brew labeled Soviet patriotism was concocted to demonstrate that the Soviet regime was the legitimate custodian of Russian historical traditions and national interests. Infused with a strong Great Russian content, it was to operate as a powerful cohesive force during World War II. Intellectual life was increasingly permeated by the atmosphere of Byzantine fawning and servility that surrounded Stalin's every word. His pronouncements were treated as Holy Writ, and ideological discussion reduced itself to parroting his latest sentences. Except in the area of technology and science, and in some cases even there, such fragments of freedom as persisted from an earlier period were almost wholly obliterated.

The story of Smolensk as it emerges from the Archive is part of this larger tale. It provides an unforgettable record of Russian experience as reflected in the life of a typical region during the first two formative decades of Soviet rule. Mirrored in the documents are whole galleries of Soviet provincial types — the little Stalins who ruled the oblast and the raions, the local Party aristocracy who surrounded and supported them; the police officials and the army officers, the old regime professors and the eager students at the university, the chairmen of kolkhozes and the MTS directors, and the lowly kolkhozniks and workers fresh from the countryside who still spoke in a servile idiom that reached far back into tsarist times. To immerse oneself in the story of Smolensk is to capture the "feel" and texture of Soviet life — the constant pressure from the center for ever greater production and the difficulty of transmitting this pressure down to the grass roots; the struggle of ordinary people to survive at the barest margin of subsistence and the desperate expedients to which they were driven to make both ends meet; the militant fervor of the occasional Party or Komsomol zealot and the more cynical and ruthless machinations of the ambitious careerists determined to rise above the common herd; the nightmarish quality of the worst of the purge period and the, in some ways, even more trying problem of adjusting to a daily routine in which it was dangerous to speak frankly even to one's intimate friends; the tensions of living in a society in which human beings were means and not ends, where both local officialdom and the mass of the population were caught up in the same web of suspicion and insecurity, and where indeed the higher one rose, the more precarious life became.

Much of what the Archive contains is not unknown to us on the basis of scattered reports and reminiscences of former Soviet citizens who have fled their native land. But the difficulty of verifying the testimony of refugees has led many cautious scholars to treat their stories with circumspection and to ask for supporting documentary evidence which most refugees were in no position to supply. Not the least of the values of the Archive is that it provides such documentation on an unparalleled scale. Many a surmise or revelation that could previously be attributed only to a refugee informant can now be documented by citing official material of unimpeachable authenticity.

In this and other respects an investigation of the Smolensk Archive yields important insights into the functioning of the Soviet system, which transcend its apparent limitations as a mere record of the history of Smolensk.

The documents add substantially to our knowledge of the processes of regional and local government on an all-Union scale, and the wealth of material on the organization, functions, and activities of Party organizations at local levels can properly be described as unique. The information which the Archive contains on methods of recruiting the security police, on its composition, and on Party-police relationships supplies a new dimension of authoritative verification in an area that was previously obscure. The history of the purges has not hitherto gone unnoticed, but here again the Archive provides a range of documentation and many illustrative case studies which should enrich our knowlege of their impact on the countryside. The story of collectivization is familiar in its broad outlines; the contribution of the Archive is to provide vivid and novel supporting detail in the form of Party directives on dekulakization and deportation, Party and governmental reports on the collectivization experience, police accounts of peasant attitudes, and the views of the peasants themselves as preserved in their surviving letters. In similar fashion, the contents of the Archive yield fresh data on life in the kolkhozes, the machine-tractor stations, and the state farms; provide new material on the operations of the censorship and the universities; reveal the range and incidence of crime at the local level; document the grievances of industrial workers; and illumine the attitudes of believers, of youth, and of many other groups in the Soviet population. In short, the Archive offers a mirror of Soviet reality as it manifested itself at the provincial level.

One of the most significant aspects of the Smolensk story is the light it sheds on post-Stalinist developments. To read the Archive is to sense anew the legacy of suppressed aspirations which Stalin bequeathed to his heirs and with which they have had to reckon. Manifest in the Archive is a widespread desire for a higher standard of life — for more food and consumers' goods, for better housing, for more leisure, and for more adequate provision for old age and other disabilities. The most disadvantaged groups are the collective farmers and unskilled workers, but the urge to improvement extends well beyond these groups into the middle and even relatively privileged strata of Soviet provincial society. There is the desire for greater security, for a life of more stable expectations, for liberation from the threat of the concentration camp and the numbing uncertainties of constant surveillance and denunciation. Perhaps not altogether paradoxically, the resentment against Stalin's system of calculated insecurity is most intense among those who have most to lose as a result of arbitrary arrest and removal, though the cloud of fear which Stalin projected cast its shadow over the whole of Soviet society. There is a palpable reaching out for greater freedom, not necessarily freedom in the Western political sense, but freedom from the excessively centralized controls of a suspicious despot, freedom to exercise initiative without fearing the consequences, and freedom to transcend the Stalinist doctrinal rigidities in thinking and writing about Soviet realities. Suppressed though these aspirations were during the Stalinist era, the Archive reveals them fermenting behind the façade of Stalinist enforced conformity.

The course of events since Stalin's death makes clear that his successors have not been unaware of these aspirations and that they have found it advisable to go at least part way to meet them. The recent efforts to improve living standards, the curbs on the powers of the security police, the curtailment of forced labor, the moves in the direction of administrative decentralization and economic regionalization — these and other reforms of the post-Stalinist era may be viewed in part, at least, as a belated response to popular and official grievances that find expression in the Archive. The ultimate importance of the Smolensk story may well be, not what it discloses about the past, but the future transformations in Soviet society which it portends.

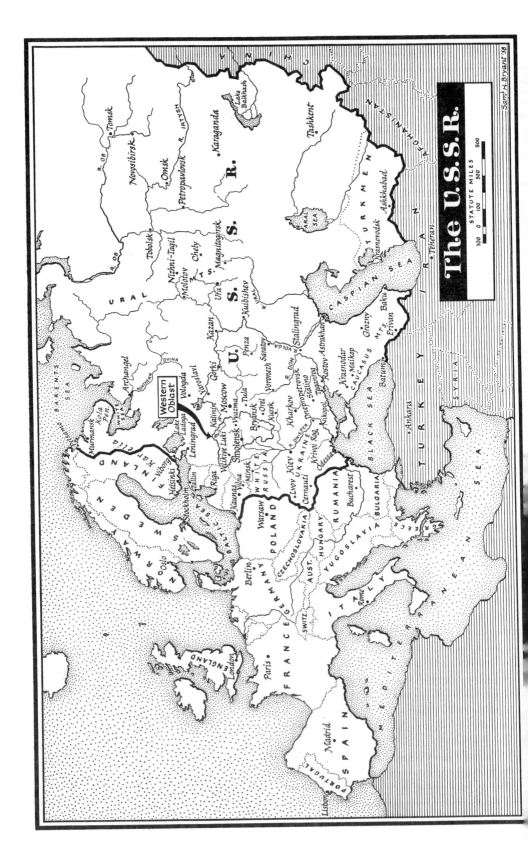

The U.S.S.R.

STATUTE MILES
100   0   100   300   500

Sam'l H. Bryant '58

1 Smolensk — Land, People, and History

Some 418 kilometers to the southwest of Moscow on the railroad trunk line which leads to Minsk and Warsaw lies the ancient and much fought-over fortress city of Smolensk. Remnants of its once imposing walls still stand in the old town, which is perched on the south bank of the river Dnieper; the newer industrial areas of Smolensk spill over to the flatter land on the north side of the stream. Long a center of provincial administration under the Tsars, Smolensk retained that role under the Bolsheviks. Until 1929 it was the capital of Smolensk guberniya, a province with a population of more than 2,300,000 in 1926. From 1929 to 1937, the city of Smolensk served as the center of the Western Oblast, a region with over 6,500,000 people which absorbed Smolensk, Bryansk, and Kaluga guberniyas as well as parts of the present Velikiye Luki and Kalinin oblasts. In September 1937 the Western Oblast was dissolved, and Smolensk became the chief city of Smolensk Oblast, a change which merely marked the reëmergence of the old guberniya in a new guise.

Economic Resources

The countryside around Smolensk presents the aspect of a rolling plateau with a few low hills and numerous marshy depressions in which peat bogs abound. The land is intersected by deep river valleys and ravines with dense forests scattered over parts of the region. The combination of rather poor clay soils and cool, moist summers offers particularly favorable conditions for the cultivation of flax, and with interruptions during the years after the Revolution, this has remained one of the agricultural specialties of the region. Flax, together with fodder crops, potatoes, dairy farming, hog-raising, and the sowing of rye and oats, dominates the region's agricultural profile. Mineral resources are of very subsidiary importance. The most important deposits are clay, which is used for building material, and peat, which serves as the principal local fuel.

During the period covered by the Archive (1917–1939) the Smolensk area was still a predominantly agricultural region. On January 1, 1925, only 8.8 per cent of the inhabitants of Smolensk guberniya were classified as urban; in 1932 only 12.2 per cent of the population of the Western Oblast lived in cities.[1] By 1939 the proportion of city dwellers in Smolensk Oblast had climbed to 17 per cent, while the population of the city of Smolensk itself mounted from 86,000 in 1931 to 156,700 in 1939.[2] Nevertheless, compared with such nearby regions as Moscow and Leningrad, the industrial development of the Smolensk area was clearly retarded. Aside from a few metallurgical and machine-building works, there was relatively little in the way of heavy industry in the region. With the exception of the machinery and cotton-textile factories, the industrial life of the area was based largely on locally produced agricultural and mineral resources. Processing industries engaged in the retting, spinning, and weaving of flax, butter- and cheese-making, meat-packing, flour-milling, bread-baking, distilling, and the tanning and working of leather. The mineral resources of the area furnished a basis for the production of construction materials, glass, porcelain, chemical fertilizer, and electrical power. Timber resources supplied raw material for sawmills and plywood mills, wood-working industries, paper and match factories. While the size of industrial plants and the value of their output increased considerably as compared with the pre-World War I period, on the eve of World War II the Smolensk region was still industrially weak, and as late as 1940, the total factory labor force numbered only 82,200 in an oblast with a population of more than 2.5 million.[3]

History

A brief review of the history of Smolensk may help shed light on its development during the Soviet period.[4] Smolensk makes its first appearance on the historical scene as the chief town of one of the aboriginal Slavic tribes known as the Krivichians. The precise date of its founding has not been established, but by the ninth century it was already known as an important settlement on the Dnieper waterway — the "road from the Varangians to the Greeks" — and early annals describe the merchants of Smolensk as playing a significant role in the trade between Kiev and Novgorod. Subordinated first to Kiev and then to Novgorod, during the twelfth century Smolensk established its independence under its own prince Rostislav and greatly extended its domains. By the beginning of the thirteenth century Smolensk had emerged as one of the important centers of Russian trade with Western Europe. Dutch, German, and other foreign merchants regularly visited Smolensk, and the population of the city and its outskirts mounted to more than 50,000 to make it one of the large European cities of the period.

But the glory of Smolensk was short-lived. For the next century and a half the Smolensk region was transformed into a battleground. Lithuanian and German invasions from the west were followed by a long series of Tatar marauding expeditions from the east, and for many decades Smolensk was compelled to pay tribute to the Tatar hordes. In the early fourteenth century, the Princes of Moscow began to encroach on Smolensk land, and Smolensk turned to the Lithuanian princes to defend it against Muscovite incursions. As a result Smolensk fell under the power of the Lithuanians, who maintained their rule with only minor interruptions from 1395, when they seized the fortress of Smolensk, until the beginning of the sixteenth century. During this period there were two bloody risings in Smolensk, one in 1401 when the people of Smolensk successfully ejected the Lithuanians only to fall victim to a long siege which restored Lithuanian rule in 1404, and another in 1440 which was brutally suppressed by the Lithuanian conquerors. Step by step Smolensk was transformed into a province of the Lithuanian State; many of its Russian inhabitants were deported and replaced by Lithuanians and Poles. The Russians that remained in the city were largely traders, artisans, and laborers who served as hewers of wood and drawers of water for the Polish-Lithuanian aristocracy who ruled the city. Smolensk itself was transformed into a fortress to ward off Muscovite attack; it remained impregnable until 1514 when it finally yielded to Moscow's siege.

From 1514 to 1611, through the various wars with Poland, Moscow held Smolensk. Its defenses were greatly strengthened; the fortress city of Smolensk was generally recognized as "the key to Moscow." During this period Smolensk underwent a second Golden Age of development. Its fortunes as a great trading center revived, and it again became one of the important links with the West. Many artisans and traders settled in Smolensk, and foreign merchants also established headquarters in the city. By 1581–82 its population was estimated at 70,000, more than three times the size of such important European centers as Strasbourg and Nuremberg. With the restoration of Russian rule, the population was also Russified and many of the Poles and Lithuanians expelled.

In 1611 Smolensk fell to the Poles, after a bitter siege of more than two years. Polish rule lasted for the next forty-three years and was attended by a considerable degree of Polonization of the city and a decline in its commercial importance. The recapture of Smolensk by the Russians in 1654 stimulated an economic revival of sorts. Smolensk was restored as a strong point, was heavily garrisoned, and regained a measure of its former economic importance. In 1708 it became a guberniya center with a resulting influx of administrative personnel.

The eighteenth century was not kind to Smolensk. With the extension of Russian power to the Baltic, the transformation of Riga into a Russian port, and the building of St. Petersburg, Smolensk lost both its military and commercial importance. Its garrison was greatly reduced; its trade shifted to Riga; and the trade routes from west to east moved north of Smolensk. The city receded to a small guberniya center with a rather weak local market and with little perspective for commercial and industrial development. By 1780 its population had declined to 11,490, and for the balance of the century it stagnated. Yet in one respect this was the period of Smolensk's greatest good fortune. For more than 150 years (1654–1812), it was spared being fought over; its walls were not stormed, and it had no sieges to endure.

The long era of peace came to an end with the Napoleonic invasion of 1812. The war dealt Smolensk a heavy blow. The destruction was great, and the population fell to below 10,000. After the war the restoration of Smolensk lagged badly; as late as 1850 its population of 11,000 had still to attain the level of 1780. Its trade also languished and even fell behind such relatively insignificant neighboring market towns as Gzhatsk and Belsk.

After 1860 Smolensk embarked on another impressive period of economic revival. Its strategic location on the trunk line between Moscow and Warsaw and its importance as the center of a local rail network helped to stimulate a renewed flow of trade. The building of the railroads also induced a sharp change in the character of the agricultural economy of the region. The raising of grain in the guberniya was no longer advantageous, since it had to compete with the much cheaper grain which could be imported by rail from the Ukraine and the Black Earth regions. As a result the Smolensk area began to shift to flax, potatoes, dairy farming, and the production of meat. Before the abolition of serfdom, flax accounted for only two per cent of the sown area; by the end of the century it was estimated that 20 per cent of the land under cultivation was devoted to flax. Since by far the greater part of the flax was exported, this too gave a strong impetus to Smolensk's economic revival. While industry was slow to come to Smolensk, there was a very substantial increase in the number of merchants, of small shops and artisan establishments. By 1901 the population of Smolensk had climbed to 57,700, more than five times the 1850 figure.

The Condition of the Peasantry

Smolensk historically had the reputation of being one of European Russia's poorer agricultural provinces. The scarcity of allotment land at the time of emancipation left a legacy of continuing peasant land hunger. Despite the fact that the noblemen of the province sold more than half their land between 1877 and 1916 and that the land in peasant ownership increased one and a half times between 1877 and 1912, the average acreage owned per peasant household actually decreased during the same period.[5] Rural overpopulation and backward agricultural practices conspired to hold back improvement in the lot of the peasants.

Yet one must be on guard against painting too dark a picture of rural Smolensk in the era between the agrarian reforms and the revolution of

1917. Mackenzie Wallace, the distinguished British observer, who visited the province of Smolensk in the summer of 1903, came expecting to find complete impoverishment. Instead, he reported:

What I saw around me seemed to contradict the sombre accounts I had received. The villages through which I passed had not at all the look of dilapidation and misery which I expected. On the contrary, the houses were larger and better constructed than they used to be, and each of them had a chimney! That latter fact was important, because formerly a large proportion of the peasants of this region had no such luxury, and allowed the smoke to find its exit by the open door. In vain I looked for a hut of the old type, and my *yamstchik* [driver] assured me I should have to go a long way to find one. Then I noticed a good many new ploughs of the European model, and my *yamstchik* informed me that their predecessor, the *sokha* [wooden plow], with which I had been so familiar, had entirely disappeared from the district. Next I noticed that in the neighborhood of the villages flax was grown in large quantities. That was certainly not an indication of poverty, because flax is a valuable product which requires to be well-manured, and plentiful manure implies a considerable quantity of livestock. Lastly, before arriving at my destination, I noticed clover being grown in the fields. This made me open my eyes with astonishment, because the introduction of artificial grasses into the traditional rotation of crops indicates the transition to a higher and more intensive system of agriculture. As I had never seen clover in Russia except on the estates of very advanced proprietors, I said to my *yamstchik*: —

"Listen, little brother! That field belongs to the landlord?"

"Not at all, Master; it is muzhik-land."

On arriving at the country-house, I told my friends what I had seen, and they explained it to me. Smolensk is no longer one of the poorer provinces; it has become comparatively prosperous. In two or three districts large quantities of flax are produced and give the cultivators a big revenue; in other districts plenty of remunerative work is supplied by the forests. Everywhere a considerable proportion of the younger men go regularly to the towns and bring home savings enough to pay the taxes and make a little surplus on the domestic budget. A few days afterwards the village secretary brought me his books, and showed me that there were practically no arrears of taxation.[6]

As this report indicates, there were a number of ameliorating factors at work in the Smolensk area which combined to ease the situation of part of the peasantry. The shift to flax culture represented a source of added income for some, at least as long as the export demand remained brisk and prices were rising. Village crafts also provided extra compensation for a number of peasants in wooded areas. In 1914 there were more than 14,000 village craftsmen in the guberniya who were engaged in making sleighs, carts, shovels, and other products made of wood, which were sold chiefly to the local peasantry.[7] In these same areas other peasants supplemented their income by work in the expanding lumber industries. Many peasants also eked out extra earnings as migratory workers. In the year 1898, for example, 9.8 per cent of the male population and 3.2 per cent of the female obtained passports as *otkhodniki,* or migratory workers.[8] Some hired out as railroad workers. Many went into domestic service in St. Petersburg and Moscow, and increasing numbers flowed into industry, sometimes departing for far away areas of Russia. It is perhaps not without significance that in the revolution of 1905, Smolensk was among the areas least affected by peasant disorders.[9]

But this did not mean that the Smolensk peasantry was satisfied; indeed the very fact that some were driven to seek subsistence off the land is a measure of the pressure with which they had to reckon. Within the ranks of the peasantry, nevertheless, a process of internal differentiation was at work. The more enterprising and energetic minority, later to be termed kulaks, gradually gathered more land to themselves and emerged as a relatively prosperous peasant stratum. By 1915 under the impact of the Stolypin reforms 14.6 per cent of the Smolensk land originally allotted to the peasants under the agrarian reforms had been separated out to individual peasant households.[10] The separators were usually the more well-to-do peasants, the so-called "strong" peasants on whom Stolypin relied to provide a barricade against a revolutionary explosion in the villages. At the other extreme from the new "Stolypin landowners" there remained many relatively poverty-stricken peasant households in the Smolensk area. On the eve of the Revolution 13.3 per cent of all peasant households in the region were horseless.[11] The land holdings of poor peasants were contracting. Meanwhile, the nobility of the province still owned 20.2 per cent of the land under cultivation and merchants and tradesmen an additional 12.6 per cent.[12] Much of this land was leased to the peasants, and because of the shortage of land, land values were driven up, and the money payments for leased land mounted accordingly. The land hunger of the bulk of the peasantry provided the combustible material on which the Revolution was destined to feed.

The Grievances of the Workers

Compared with the peasantry, the factory proletariat played an insignificant role in the economic life of the guberniya. The retarded industrial development of the Smolensk area was reflected both in the minute size of its factory labor force and the small scale of its industrial enterprises. At the end of the nineteenth century the only large-scale factory in the guberniya was the Yartsevo textile mill, which employed 4,190 workers in 1898.[13] At that time the total industrial labor force of the guberniya totaled 13,230, and by 1914 it had increased to only 23,242.[14] The city of Smolensk itself at the end of the nineteenth century had less than a thousand factory workers.[15]

Both the nobility and merchant class far outnumbered the factory proletariat. As a result of Smolensk's rising importance as a trading center the number of merchants in the city increased from 495 in 1846 to

2,973 in 1899.[16] During the same period the nobility resident in the city of Smolensk multiplied more than eightfold, from 876 in 1846 to 7,273 in 1899.[17] This startling increase registered the sale of many small landed estates in the post-emancipation period and a movement of impoverished noblemen to the city where they were attracted by the opportunities for employment which Smolensk held out as a guberniya center. Altogether, the social composition of Smolensk seemed to offer poor soil for revolutionaries who looked to the industrial proletariat for their mass base.

But appearances were deceptive. If the industrial labor force of Smolensk was weak in numbers, it nevertheless had powerful grievances. Most of the workers were employed in small shops where the working conditions bordered on the worst kind of exploitation. Toward the end of the 1890's working hours averaged nearly thirteen hours a day, and in extreme cases ran to fifteen and even sixteen hours.[18] Wages were low, running from eight to sixteen rubles per month, and the housing to which workers were consigned was frequently deplorable. As a result the justified complaints of the workers provided rich fuel for revolutionaries to ignite.

Revolutionary Stirrings: 1902–1917

The Smolensk Archive contains a folder of materials collected by the Smolensk Istpart, or Party History section, for the period 1902–1907 which gives some indication of the scope of Social-Democratic activity in the guberniya at that time.[19] The items ordinarily make no distinction between Bolsheviks and Mensheviks; both are lumped together as members of the Social-Democratic Labor Party, and indeed, from local evidence elsewhere as well as in Smolensk, there is reason to believe that the line between them was blurred during the revolution of 1905. As early as April 1902 there are reports of police arrests of various individuals who were found in possession of illegal Social-Democratic literature or were caught distributing it in the guberniya. An item in *Iskra* (November 1, 1902) mentions the establishment of a Smolensk Committee of the Russian Social-Democratic Labor Party in August 1902 and refers to a proclamation which it addressed to the shop clerks. In addition, Roslavl is listed as the center of another Social-Democratic organization. There are also scattered references to strikes by tailors, shop clerks, and cabmen, primarily of an economic character and ending in some cases with a victory of the employees. There is only one entry for the years 1903 and 1904, an item dated May 13, 1904, reporting a police raid on an apartment in Smolensk which yielded a cache of Social-Democratic literature.

The revolutionary year 1905 was marked by a very considerable intensification of Social-Democratic activity in the guberniya. Despite a number of arrests of persons distributing Social-Democratic proclamations, revolutionary literature was widely circulated, and mass meetings and demonstrations organized. On May 18, 1905, a group of youths demonstrated in a Smolensk park and sang revolutionary songs. On May 29 two thousand persons participated in a popular demonstration and shouted, "Down with Nikolai," "Down with Autocracy," "Down with the Police," and "Greetings to the Revolution," until they were finally dispersed by the police. On June 11 the police raided a Social-Democratic meeting at which about one hundred persons were present, arrested the leaders, and confiscated the proclamations which were being distributed. On November 11 a meeting sponsored by the Social-Democrats attracted an audience of eight hundred persons.

The year 1905 was also a time of strikes and trade union organization in Smolensk. On March 28 the Yartsevo textile workers walked out and demanded a nine-hour working day, a 10 per cent increase in wages, and a lowering in the rent for their living quarters. The strike must have made a considerable impression on the authorities; on March 29 the governor himself left for Yartsevo with a battalion of soldiers. Between May 22 and May 30 a strike took place in the artisan workshops in Roslavl. The strikers achieved a twelve-hour working day, including a two-hour break for meals. Typical of many similar actions was a strike of workers in the meat trade on November 24. Included among their demands was a twelve-hour working day with two hours off for meals, a 25 per cent increase in wages, better housing, and the formation of a commission to examine their grievances.

Smolensk had its own Soviet of Workers' Deputies, and on November 10 it issued a call for a general political strike. According to one report quoted in the Archive: "Typographies, factories and plants, artisan shops, bakeries and employees . . . interrupted their work. Streets are filled with people." On December 12 the soviet again called for a general political strike as a symbol of solidarity with the Moscow uprising, but the strike was ordered discontinued on December 15 after attracting considerable initial support.

The Archive also contains some evidence of peasant restiveness in 1905. There are occasional references to Social-Democratic proclamations which found their way to the villages, but no indications that they had any marked effect. The initiative in the villages lay with the peasants themselves, and there are numerous reports of peasant meetings, chiefly in November and December 1905, which drafted resolutions calling for the distribution of land to the peasantry, and in some cases, demanding a Duma, or Constituent Assembly elected in a democratic manner, and even threatening not to pay taxes until the land had been allotted to the peasants. But unlike peasants in some other areas, the Smolensk peasantry largely refrained from direct action and violence, despite the efforts of "outsiders" to induce them to rise against absolutism and to seize the landowners' land by force.

During the next two years (1906 and 1907) the local authorities embarked on increasingly repressive measures to stamp out revolutionary activity. On January 4, 1906, both the Social-Democratic and Socialist-Revolutionary clubs in Smolensk were surrounded by police and their premises raided. At the Social-Democratic club ninety-seven men and sixty-five women were arrested; at the SR club the police apprehended eighty-five men and fifty-seven women. In succeeding months there were many searches of houses of suspected revolutionaries; a considerable quantity of illegal literature was confiscated. On December 21, 1906, there is a report of a police raid on a meeting of the "Social-Democratic Jewish Revolutionary Party"; all nine participants were arrested. Despite constant searches and seizures, revolutionary literature continued to be distributed. There are also a number of references which indicate that trade unions remained active, though they operated under increasing difficulties. A meeting of the bakery workers was dispersed by the police. The strike of the weavers in the Yartsevo textile factory in June 1906 met stiffened resistance from management, and the strikers were informed that they would have to vacate their living quarters. The strike ended without yielding any satisfaction to the workers' demands.

The year 1906 brought an upsurge of sporadic acts of violence in the Smolensk countryside. To be sure, the incidents were isolated rather than general; nevertheless, they provided a sharp contrast with the preceding year. Peasant meetings continued to echo the demand for land, and the resolutions addressed to Duma members displayed a sharper tone. The Roslavl area was a particular center of unrest and direct action. In January peasants from the village of Budy seized 150 dessyatins of forest from a landowner. In the same month peasants from another village felled 3,000 trees on an estate without permission. In order to stop them, "armed force" was used. In the same month there were two clashes between police and peasants, one of serious proportions in which eight peasants were killed and nine wounded. In June in the village of Shelebitse mounted police killed two peasants. In the same month agricultural workers on the estate "Vysokoe" in Sychevka uyezd proclaimed a strike, and peasants in neighboring villages joined in sympathy. A platoon of Cossacks was dispatched to the estate on July 2 to arrest the leaders of the strike. During the remainder of the year, there were few reported incidents of violence, but smoldering unrest persisted among the peasantry.

The material in the Archive for the year 1907 is scanty, but there is evidence to indicate that the Smolensk Social-Democratic Committee still remained alive, and its hectographed literature appeared in various districts of the guberniya despite police efforts to hunt down and root out the activists. But the revolutionary tide had definitely receded. In the words of a letter quoted in the Archive: "nothing new was occurring; the Bolsheviks continued to rage, and the Mensheviks continued to do nothing."

The organizing focus for the upsurge of revolutionary activity in the Smolensk area during the 1905 period was provided by a relatively tiny minority made up largely of students, members of the professional classes, and an occasional worker. They had relatively little effect on the countryside, but in Smolensk, Yartsevo, and other towns of the guberniya they were able to capitalize existing discontents, to organize demonstrations, and to provide leadership for the strike movements which engulfed the handful of industrial workers in the province. The Archive testifies to the vigilance of the police, but despite numerous arrests, searches, and seizures, a tradition of revolutionary organization survived which was to become the stepping stone to 1917.

The Revolution of 1917

The Archive contains only fragmentary material on the revolutionary events of 1917 in Smolensk.[20] One file of miscellaneous notes based on local newspaper and other sources appears to have been collected as data for a history, which, if written, did not find its way into the Archive. The notes are far from complete, but they nevertheless help to illuminate the stormy events of that crucial year.

The wave of labor and peasant unrest which swept through Russia after the downfall of the Tsar did not leave the Smolensk area untouched. Labor unions rapidly spread among the industrial workers, and their demands for higher wages and an eight-hour working day soon involved them in sharp conflicts with their employers. The Archive contains references to union organization among the hat-makers, the tailors, the cigarette makers, and virtually every craft represented in the industrial life of Smolensk. Delegates were quickly elected to the local Soviet of Soldiers' and Workers' Deputies, which, like its counterpart in Petrograd, became powerful enough to challenge the authority of the local duma. As the cost of living mounted and the pressure for higher wages intensi-fied, strikes became more and more frequent, and they took on an increasingly political character. By June 1917 the Union of Metal Workers was already demanding that the workers take over the production process. By October militia reports listed a number of instances where striking workers were "expropriating" factories.

The Archive is unclear about the precise character of the political leadership of the unions, but such evidence as is available points to increasing Bolshevik influence over the year. On June 30, 1917, for example, when the Executive Committee of the Roslavl Soviet, in which railroad workers were particularly influential, established a newspaper, the three-man collegium which was chosen to edit it was recruited from the "Menshevik bloc." By September 30 the same soviet had moved much further to the left. It was attacking the Provisional Government for its broken promises and pressing for a railroad strike as a "political weapon" in the class struggle. But there were also exceptions. The Yartsevo textile factory, the largest in the guberniya, participated in the general strike movement, but as late as October 21, 1917 (old style), the workers of the Yartsevo factory district voted to disregard the national textile union congress' call to proletarian revolution on the ground that it "would only help the reaction and drown Russia in the blood bath of civil war."

Peasant disorders in Smolensk were slower to develop, but once launched they gathered a momentum that rivaled the violence of the urban workers. The peasants began cautiously. They elected their own township, or volost, committees and delegates to the local soviets of peasants' deputies. By May there were reports of peasants sending their cattle to feed on estate meadows. By June they were occupying the meadows. Landowners sought vainly to collect fees from them and addressed complaints to the guberniya commissars representing the Provisional Government. In July the Kerensky regime appointed land committees to impose orderly legal processes on the encroachments of the peasants. The land committees in turn established mediation chambers to adjudicate disputes between peasants and landowners. The mediation chambers ruled that the owners whose land had been occupied by the peasants were entitled to just compensation, but there was no way to enforce these decisions. The peasants proceeded to detach more land from the estates and by the end of July they were already harvesting the land which they had seized. When mediation chambers complained that local governments refused to carry out the decisions of the mediation chambers, the local authorities replied by labeling the decisions of the mediation chambers as "incorrect." On July 2 the Roslavl Mediation Chamber, for example, pressed for action against "arbitrary occupation of landed estates by peasants." The local executive committee retorted that it was acting in accordance with "the true interests of the peasants" and that the guberniya commissar and the land committees ought to cease paying attention to the "false tears" of the "wealthy."

As peasant land seizures became epidemic, there were mounting demands from property owners that the guberniya land committee take action. On June 30 it "suggested" to its local land committees that they stop the "arbitrary" and illegal occupation of church lands and that they consider the priests as "petty property owners" who should be permitted to gather their own harvests. But these appeals were in vain, and on October 4, 1917, the Smolensk Religious Consistory again addressed an anguished appeal to the guberniya land committee to look into the "unjust action" of peasants in appropriating land and woods belonging to a monastery. The peasant hunger for land could not be denied. As elsewhere in Russia, the efforts of the local representatives of the Provisional Government to "regularize" the process and to postpone a land settlement until after the convocation of the Constituent Assembly served only to alienate the peasants. Meanwhile, the Bolsheviks and the Left SR's identified themselves with the grievances of the peasants, urged them to take the estates without compensation, and rallied increasing support under the appealing banner of "Land to the Peasants."

The Smolensk reaction to the Kornilov affair also finds reflection in the Archive. The organization of a "Committee for Struggle with Counterrevolution" in Petrograd had its reverberations in Smolensk in the establishment of a so-called "Revolutionary Committee" to defend the Provisional Government against Kornilov's effort to establish a military dictatorship. The committee began its work on August 31 (old style) by distributing rifles to its own militia ("without bullets!"), by forbidding gatherings in the street, and by entrusting the defense of Smolensk to a general of the local garrison who took an oath of loyalty to the Provisional Government.

At first the Revolutionary Committee refused to have anything to do with the Bolsheviks. It rebuffed a demand of workers of the local railroad car repair shop to release a confiscated brochure of Lenin on the ground that the speech was not "objective" enough with regard to the War. But, faced with the necessity of rallying maximum mass support against Kornilov, it soon reversed itself and included Bolsheviks in its ranks. The Smolensk Soviet of Soldiers', Workers' and Peasants' Deputies voted support for Kerensky against Kornilov. The Yartsevo garrison also proclaimed its loyalty to Kerensky.

But the sentiment for Kerensky was by no means unanimous. "Alarming" reports from Viazma indicated that Cossack supporters of Kornilov were at odds with the rest of the garrison and with the local Soviet. The Smolensk post office declared its "neutrality" in the "struggle for power" between Kornilov and Kerensky. Despite this, the Revolutionary Committee managed to stop all telegrams "of advantage" to Kornilov's rebellion and to suspend rail movements which might conceivably assist the rebels. The ignominious collapse of the Kornilov uprising was in no small degree due to the ability of groups such as the Smolensk Revolutionary Committee to improvise measures which paralyzed the revolt almost at its inception. One of the unintended consequences, in Smolensk as elsewhere, was a sharp upsurge in Bolshevik support.

By the fall of 1917 Bolshevik power was already on the rise, in town and country alike. Trotsky, in his *History of the Russian Revolution,* notes:

In Smolensk province towards the end of August, according to the peasant Kotov, "We began to interest ourselves in Lenin, began to listen to the voice of Lenin . . ." In the village zemstvo, however, they were still electing an immense majority of Socialist Revolutionaries . . . In Smolensk province, according to the recollection of Ivanov, "Bolsheviks were very rare in the villages. There were very few of them in the counties. There were no Bolshevik papers. Leaflets were very rarely given out . . . And nevertheless the nearer it came to October, the more the villages swung over to the Bolsheviks." [21]

The same increase in Bolshevik influence was noticeable in the towns. By the middle of October, the Bolsheviks together with the Left SR's had gained a majority in the Smolensk election of delegates to the All-Russian Congress of Soviets. During September and October a new wave of strikes engulfed Smolensk. Strikers were increasingly militant, expropriating factories and even attacking the police and confiscating their arms.

On October 26, 1917, the chief of the Smolensk militia received a telegram from his superiors in Petrograd informing him that part of the Petrograd garrison had revolted against the Provisional Government and that the Bolsheviks were attempting to seize power. On that same date the Smolensk City Duma assembled and issued a call to the citizenry to support the Provisional Government. Its ringing manifesto branded the Bolsheviks as traitors whose actions threatened both Russia and revolutionary freedom. For the next few days Smolensk was still officially "loyal" to the Provisional Government. On October 27–29 came the announcement of the organization of a "Committee to Save the Revolution" from the Bolsheviks. Its membership embraced SR's, Mensheviks, Polish and Jewish socialists, representatives of the Soviet of Peasants' Deputies, officers of the military district, and officials of the city and guberniya governments. The committee addressed a special appeal to the peasantry not to believe in Bolshevik promises of free land. It claimed control of the countryside and called for the creation of local Committees to Save the Revolution throughout the guberniya.

Meanwhile, the Bolsheviks organized their own contingents of soldiers and workers to take power. There were armed clashes between the rival groups and some casualties. On October 30–31 the shooting in Smolensk caused the post office and telegraph workers as well as other government employees to suspend work. On October 30 the guberniya commissar representing the Provisional Government telegraphed his superiors that "all is grief," except in Vyazma and Roslavl where the situation was "undetermined." On November 1 a militia district headquarters in

Smolensk reported that a group of armed men had raided the militia station, confiscated all arms and ammunition, and disappeared. Shooting continued.

Finally in early November an agreement was reached among the "different groups" to stop the armed struggle. A Committee of Public Safety was established consisting of representatives of the city duma, the soviet, the army, the trade unions, as well as Bolshevik, Menshevik, SR, and Bund delegates. The committee issued an appeal for the restoration of order and called upon all "civic organizations" to prevent plunder and the destruction of the estates. Meanwhile, effective power passed to the Soviets, in which the Bolsheviks and Left SR's commanded a majority. The elections to the Constituent Assembly which followed shortly thereafter yielded a clear majority for the Bolsheviks. The vote in Smolensk guberniya was reported as follows:[22]

Bolshevik	361,062
SR	250,134
Menshevik	7,901
Other minor socialist parties	2,210
Kadets	29,274
Other nonsocialist parties	5,300
Other nationality parties	1,708
Unclassified	645
Total	658,234

The tremendous vote rolled up by the Bolsheviks in Smolensk was all the more astounding because it was obtained in an area which even the Bolsheviks themselves classified as a "backward province" that was likely to be particularly resistant to their propaganda.[23] The triumph, moreover, was registered by a party whose total guberniya membership, while not precisely known, was probably not much more than a thousand. Altogether, the Bolshevik victory in Smolensk was an impressive testimonial to the ability of the Bolshevik minority to identify itself with mass grievances, to mobilize them, and to use them as a catapult to power.

Given the economic complexion of Smolensk guberniya, it was clear that Bolshevik success in the elections to the Constituent Assembly would have been impossible without a very substantial degree of peasant support. As future events were to disclose, that support rested on a peasant misunderstanding, the assumption that when the Bolsheviks promised land to the peasants, they would distribute the land and then leave the peasants to their own devices. But such was not to be the course of events. With the outbreak of civil war and the worsening food situation in the army and the cities, armed detachments of Red Guards and

Communist commissars were soon roaming the villages in quest of bread and confiscating grain wherever they could lay hands on it. The peasants were subjected to the first of what was to prove a series of rude awakenings. By that time, however, it was too late; there was no longer any election machinery available to oust the Bolsheviks. A new era of Communist rule had begun in Smolensk.

PART TWO

The Pattern of Controls

2 The Smolensk Party Organization — A

History of Growth and Crisis

The material the Archive contains on the early history of the Smolensk Party organization is scattered and fragmentary, and putting it together has all the fascination and difficulty of assembling a puzzle when many of the key pieces are missing. What is quickly apparent is the numerical weakness of the Bolshevik organization in Smolensk. Although exact figures on the number of Bolsheviks in the region in 1917 are unavailable, the small size of the "revolutionary vanguard" is indicated by the fact that when a count of the guberniya Party organization was made on January 1, 1924, only 128 members were discovered who had joined the Party prior to 1917 and only 366 more who became members during 1917.[1]

First Organizational Steps

After the Bolshevik *coup d'état,* Party ranks swelled greatly, and by March 1919 the Smolensk guberniya organization claimed a membership of 12,000.[2] But Party records during this period were notoriously chaotic and unreliable, and when the Party Central Committee ordered a re-registration in 1919 both to set the membership records straight and to weed out "undesirable" elements, nearly four-fifths of the claimed membership evaporated. As of November 1, 1919, the Smolensk Party organization announced a total strength of 2,566, consisting of 1,905 members and 661 candidates and sympathizers.[3] During November and December 1919, the Smolensk Party organization launched a drive to recruit new members; it was announced that 8,498 persons joined the Party in the course of the campaign.[4] On the eve of the 1921 Party purge, the Smolensk organization boasted a total membership of 10,657 in a guberniya with a population of more than 2,000,000.[5]

The Smolensk Party group at first was attached to the Moscow organization and was directly subordinate to it. In 1918 Smolensk guberniya was made part of the Western Oblast, despite a protest of the Smolensk guberniya ispolkom (executive committee of the guberniya soviet) against separation from Moscow.[6] A Party conference of the new Western Oblast Party organization was held in Smolensk September

1–4 and included representation from Vitebsk, Mogilev, and Chernigov guberniyas as well as from Smolensk itself.[7] The Party hierarchy established at the conference led down from the oblast through the guberniyas, raions, uyezds, sub-raions, volosts, and village organizations. Until uyezd organizations were established, town committees were authorized to exercise the authority of uyezd committees.

From the very beginning the principle of Party organization proclaimed was one of "the most strict centralization."[8] All local organizations were required to render weekly reports on their activities to their superiors in the hierarchy, to assume leadership in soviet, trade union, and other organizations, and to make special efforts to sink roots in the villages. The volost and uyezd organizations were especially enjoined to establish cells in every rural settlement, if only of two or three sympathizers among poor peasants. Party organizations were also commanded to exercise the strictest control over the issue of arms in order to prevent them from falling into the hands of enemies of the revolution. At the same time they were also required to master the use of arms themselves in order to defend the revolution. Five per cent of the monthly income of each Party organization was to go to the oblast, 10 per cent to the Central Committee. Every Party Committee was also instructed to release at least one member for full-time Party work and to put on him the responsibility for maintaining communications with the oblast center. There was a questionnaire provided for weekly reports. Included in the information to be furnished were data on Party members, admissions and exclusions, reasons for exclusions, members' dues, reports on lectures, meetings, and concerts, lists of prominent members of the Party organization, Party activity in the soviets and in military units, reports on opposition elements and on the attitude of the population toward the Bolsheviks.[9]

A penchant for organizational blueprints was visible early in the history of the Smolensk organization. The records of the uyezd Party Committee in Yelnya for 1919, for example, unfold an ambitious plan of subdividing responsibilities.[10] The Yelnya uyezd partkom was divided into the following seven sections:

1. The Secretariat — to handle correspondence and visitors and to control and coördinate other sections and to report on their activities.

2. The Information Section — to communicate with higher and lower Party organizations, to supply material to the newspapers, and to report on the organization's activities.

3. The Organization Section — to maintain membership and personnel files, to instruct primary cells and to organize, control, and account for communes.

4. The Agitation Section — to carry on agitation and propaganda and to organize and supervise Party schools.

5. The Inspection and Investigation Section — to inspect Party organizations and to investigate malpractices.

6. The Literary Section — to organize libraries and associated activities.

7. The Financial Section — to collect dues and to maintain the accounts of the organization.

Actually most of these blueprints remained on paper. This was a period when the Party was fighting for its life, and in Yelnya itself the most immediate concern was the attempted assassination of the Yelnya Party chairman.[11] With Kolchak advancing from Siberia to the Volga, all Party organizations were placed on a wartime footing, and the great majority of Party members were mobilized for the front. Communists who were not mobilized had to spend a large part of their time on military training, on local defense assignments, on requisitioning grain from the peasants, and other emergency activities. The Yelnya Party records give some sense of the chaos which actually prevailed, with the soldiers of Yelnya's First Infantry regiment roaming the countryside, begging for bread and finally rebelling "owing to severe hunger in the unit." [12] In the "critical moment" when Party people were needed to deal with the rebellion, few were present or willing to fight, and the Party Committee had to address a special appeal to the military authorities in Smolensk to transfer the regiment to some other area where bread was more available.

The Grim Struggle for Survival

After 1919 Party records begin to become more plentiful, and though there are still many gaps, there are also rich runs such as a more or less complete set of minutes of meetings of the Smolensk gubkom (Guberniya Party Committee) for the year 1920 which provides interesting material for analysis.[13] From these reports it becomes possible to reconstruct a picture of the activities and problems of the Smolensk Party organization in that fateful year.

This was, of course, one of the grimmest years in Soviet history, and Smolensk had more than its share of grimness. The War against Poland transformed the guberniya into an armed camp, and the overriding priority became survival itself. The ravages of revolution and war, of hunger and disease were evident on every side. At a meeting of the bureau of the Smolensk gubkom on February 11, 1920, it was reported that there were 2,500 cases of typhus in Smolensk alone with the epidemic still spreading.[14] The food shortage was little short of catastrophic; army units and even the most essential factory workers frequently went unfed. Banditry was rife, and army deserters roamed the countryside begging for food. Industrial production was virtually at a standstill. Labor productivity was reported (July 23, 1920) as having fallen to 8 to 10 per cent of normal.[15] White-collar workers in Soviet enterprises were said to be completely demoralized by hunger and cold, working only one to two hours a day.[16] Workers in the important textile factory of Yartsevo went out on strike after failing to receive wages and rations for two whole months.[17] The military units stationed in the guberniya were restive. A revolt broke out in Roslavl, and on September 3, 1920, the gubkom was informed that there was real danger that the uprising would spread to Smolensk.[18] The impression derived from the Archive is one of almost chaotic disorganization, with the Party itself more a helpless victim than master of the whirlwinds which it had helped unleash. Indeed, as one studies the record, the wonder is, not merely that the Party was victorious, but that it managed to survive at all.

From the beginning the Party organization faced a crying shortage of qualified personnel. Such leadership material as was available was periodically raided by the Central Committee and transferred to more urgent Party assignments in Moscow, the Ukraine, and the military fronts. The membership of the bureau of the gubkom (the directing body of the organization) went through a process of constant turnover and turmoil. At a meeting of the gubkom on February 23, 1920, its first secretary, Remizov, reported the transfer of five bureau members to the Ukraine and the loss of three successive Party secretaries in a period of five weeks.[19] The membership itself was periodically decimated by successive mobilizations for duty at the front.

In these circumstances it was all but impossible to keep a functioning organization together. We see the guberniya leadership constantly protesting to Moscow against the commandeering of personnel for the center, pleading that particular individuals be permitted to remain, and sometimes, in desperation, defying the Central Committee by ordering these individuals to remain despite the commands from above.[20] Faced with the loss of valuable personnel to the center, the Smolensk authorities in turn sought to repair the deficiency by raiding the uyezds, only to meet the same outraged cries of indignation and occasional defiance with which Smolensk confronted Moscow.[21] In at least one case the gubkom even decreed that draft postponements be granted to certain Party officials, despite an order of the Council of Defense specifically annulling all draft postponements.[22] A letter was sent to the Central Committee explaining that the draft would destroy the Smolensk Party and governmental organization, and that the gubkom was therefore taking it upon itself to instruct the officials to stay at their posts until the matter had been cleared with the Central Committee. The Orgbureau of the Central Committee replied with a sharp rebuke to which the Smolensk gubkom responded that, while it was probably not authorized to grant draft postponements, nevertheless it felt that its action was justified by "revolutionary considerations." [23]

The staff difficulties under which the Smolensk Party leadership labored are vividly illustrated by a report from Remizov to the gubkom on February 23, 1920. According to Remizov, the apparatus of the gubkom bureau was in a state of "utter confusion." [24] There was only one typist to man the office; all others had either been mobilized or were ill with typhus. Remizov was the only member of the bureau who was able to devote himself exclusively to Party affairs and even he had been threatened with arrest for neglecting his duties as a member of the Communist Military Unit of Special Assignment.[25] In answer to the anguished plea of Remizov, the gubkom decided to make two other members of the bureau available for Party work, but whether in fact this happened is extremely doubtful, since the protocols of meetings disclose bureau members constantly being diverted from Party work by a crisis of one sort or another.[26] As a result of the acute shortage of qualified Party personnel, the guberniya and city Party and governmental organizations were combined, though the uyezds remained as independent organizational units.

The situation in the countryside was even more critical. There was only one Party instructor for every three volosts, and the head of the guberniya department for village work acknowledged openly that the Party had virtually no influence in the rural coöperatives and sovkhozes, which, according to him, were dominated by kulaks and priests.[27] The prestige of the gubkom sank to an almost ridiculous point in October 1920 when "military comrades" from the Staff of the Front in search of office space evicted gubkom families from their living quarters.[28] The protest of Remizov against this "barbaric action" was of no avail; the only action of the gubkom was a resolution reproving the Guberniya Housing Commission for participating in the raids on gubkom apartments. The army itself went unmentioned.

Despite all these handicaps, the Party maintained itself and even sought to extend its organizational net. In the midst of the war crisis, special Party schools were established to train new recruits and active Party workers.[29] The shortage of Party personnel was so desperate that even sympathizers and non-Party people were accepted in the Party schools, provided that they were recommended by Party, Komsomol, trade union, or soviet organizations. Special emphasis was placed on Komsomol work, though here again there was the same old complaint of lack of qualified cadres, and the assistance of the Central Committee was invoked to release young Red Army members for work in the Komsomol cells. Particularly strenuous efforts were made to win peasant youth to the cause, though the gubkom discussions revealed the strongest doubts about the reliability of the peasant Komsomol organizations.[30]

Weak as the Party was, it managed to occupy the center of the stage because no rival force was powerful enough or sufficiently organized to challenge its position. Individual Mensheviks were still influential in the trade unions and coöperatives, but by infiltrating Party candidates into leading posts in these organizations, the Party maintained a precarious hold on them.[31] In rural areas the Party was far weaker, and it faced a constant threat from spontaneous peasant organizations which sprang up on the local level "to defend their interests." At the February (1920) plenum of the gubkom, Ivanov, the Chairman of the gubispolkom, expressed his alarm at the rise of "kulak and middle-peasant dominated" peasant unions along lines "that are far from favorable for party objectives in the long run." [32] The plenum determined that it could not for the moment stop these conferences, but decided to move toward their liquidation by seeking to divert peasant energies into the soviets and coöperatives where Party influence was stronger.

Given the situation which confronted it in 1920, the Smolensk Party had no recourse except to move from crisis to crisis, improvising as best it could in the face of difficulties. The mobilization of Party members for the front provided a constantly recurring challenge. Indeed, at one point of extreme crisis in the Polish war, Remizov proposed the abandonment of all Party activities in favor of sending all Party forces, including the gubkom, to hold the front.[33] Remizov was overruled, on the ground that the Party organization could make its most effective contribution by strengthening the rear and by concentrating its energy on providing food, clothing, and armaments for the army, but the line which divided Party from military work was never an easy one to draw. All Party members and candidates, regardless of age or sex, were required to register with the military authorities, to engage in military training, and to become members of so-called Units of Special Assignment which were organized to suppress banditry, to stiffen wavering troop units, to guard vital installations, and for other emergencies.[34]

One of the most difficult problems which the gubkom faced was the struggle against banditry and deserters. While the actual operations were conducted by special Cheka battalions and military units of the Western Sector, the gubkom attempted to coördinate their activity. Rivalry between the Cheka and the army was serious. The Cheka complained that its troops received the worst barracks, and that officers of Cheka units operating near the front line under army command had a way of "simply disappearing" into army formations.[35] The gubkom sought to assign the leading role to the Gubcheka and recommended that the Cheka be authorized to borrow Sector troops where necessary.[36] Whether the intervention in favor of the Cheka was successful, the record does not disclose. From March to July, according to one gubkom report, some 30,000 deserters and 313 bandits were caught in Smolensk, Vitebsk, Gomel, and Chernigov guberniyas, but despite these numerical triumphs, the problem of banditry continued to plague the regime and at least during 1920 was far from stamped out.[37]

The catastrophic food situation presented a perennial problem. At one point (August 7, 1920) the gubkom was frank to admit that there was not even enough food to feed the troops stationed in the guberniya.[38] The situation was further complicated by a fire which destroyed Viazma's food warehouse.[39] The response of the central authorities was drastic. Many of Viazma's leading Communists were arrested for negligence and sentenced to death or long prison terms by the Revolutionary Tribunal of the republic. In this case the gubkom intervened to plead for a mitigation of the sentences on the ground that many of the condemned had long histories of devotion to the revolutionary cause. Ivanov, the chairman of the gubispolkom, even made a special trip to Moscow to plead for mercy. Moscow, on the whole, was adamant, though it did permit a few of the condemned culprits to continue to occupy responsible posts for which they had indispensable qualifications.

As a result of the stringency of the food situation, unrest spread in the barracks and factories. The revolt of the Roslavl garrison had to be put down by force of arms. At a meeting of the gubkom on September 3, 1920, the alarming situation in the military units came in for a full-dress review.[40] The discussion revealed "intensive" agitation against the Soviet regime in the reserve units. Desertions were on the increase (especially of the last draft of 1901), and a revolt in Yelnya was averted only by breaking into the last food reserves of the district. One gubkom member described the "terrifying condition" in which Red Army men lived in his raion. There was a need to get them to the front, but clothing was lacking to outfit them. To allow the units to remain in the villages was completely "to demoralize them." The situation in Smolensk itself was dangerous. The gubkom argued that the army had to be fed, but this was more easily said than done. Meanwhile, the gubkom called for the forced collection of clothing from the civilian population, an improvement of political work in the units, the distribution of Communists among them to stiffen morale, special attention to the artillery units to reinforce their loyalty, and the placing of the Communist Units of Special Assignment on a war footing in order to be prepared to deal with emergency outbreaks.

The situation in the factories was no less tense. A threatened strike of the Yartsevo workers in March was temporarily averted when the gubkom ordered the guberniya financial department to pay two months' back wages.[41] But in June the workers went out on strike demanding higher pay and larger rations. A special commission was designated by the gubkom to use "all means" to get the workers back to work, but the commission was also instructed "not to promise anything — so as to avoid making the workers aware that striking gets results." [42] Among other things, the commission was told to investigate the role of Yartsevo Communists in the strike, "if indispensable" even to arrest those who participated, and to try to strengthen the Yartsevo Party organization.[43] The gubkom sought to do what it could to overcome "the negativism" of the trade unions, but the food problem remained critical, and production continued to decline. Meanwhile, the Party organization improvised as best it could, maintaining a precarious foothold in the guberniya, and adjusting its activities to give maximum support to the Front.

The Problems of NEP

With the end of the Civil War and the adoption of the New Economic Policy the Smolensk Party organization turned hopefully to the task of peaceful reconstruction. The problem of the Party was to stabilize its position in the guberniya, to extend its control from the cities and towns into the rural areas, to guide and direct the economic recovery of the guberniya, and at the same time to safeguard the dominance of the Party against all the antagonistic forces which the NEP unleashed.

But the healing effect of the NEP concessions was slow to take hold in Smolensk. Owing to bad weather, the 1921 harvest was even worse than that of 1920, and except for potatoes, agricultural production fell short of the very low 1920 output.[44] State industry was in an even more parlous condition, and discontent among workers was widespread. The top-secret reports of the Cheka on the mood of the population, which are available for the Roslavl area for 1922, give a sense of the underlying grievances. On January 13, 1922, the Cheka reported dissatisfaction among the workers of the Smolensk railroad station because the food rations for November and December had not been issued nor had salaries been paid.[45] Many workers did not appear at work because of lack of proper shoes and clothing. Some criticized the NEP and said the government had retreated from its program and was leaning toward the tsarist order.[46] There was grumbling because of the privileged position of the Communist Party. People said there should be no preferential treatment in Soviet Russia. If difficult times had to be experienced, everyone should experience them equally. On February 1 the Cheka noted discontent among workers at the Roslavl railroad shops because of insufficient wages, shortages of food stuffs, and extreme price rises on products of primary necessity. For the period from February 1 to March 1 the Cheka reported that the mood of the workers was still "bad." "The workers, especially those with large families, must endure such critical circumstances that they completely lose heart and cannot think of work at all, and they are only concerned with an escape from such a critical position. All this aggravates the workers so greatly that they are now no longer interested in the least in work, which acutely influences [their] productivity . . ." [47] On March 1 the Cheka recorded a strike in one factory due to poor salaries, but noted that it was now settled. [48] For the period March 1–15 the Cheka reported continued worker dissatisfaction. "Every worker seeks illegal means to escape from his critical position. Some steal materials . . . The workers say that when the Soviet government was in bad straits, it promised the workers good food and salaries, but when it escaped from its critical situation, it forgot to think about the worker. The workers say the Soviet government feeds them with promises only." [49]

The Cheka also reported grumbling among the peasants inspired by the unavailability of manufactured goods and the confiscation of church valuables. [50] At the same time the Cheka was instructed to handle the peasantry cautiously. "In the campaign to collect the tax," a Cheka order read, "avoid administrative pressure on the population and make only a minimum of arrests of people who do not pay, for this will reflect poorly on the mood of the masses, undermining the foundation of the political well-being of the uyezd. Do not sentence to imprisonment those who do not pay, except in the case of millers. Treat the poor peasants with the most skillful diplomacy. Make the wealthiest people carry the main tax burden." [51] Despite this injunction, the Cheka noted much complaining among the poor peasants. "The poor peasants consider themselves even poorer under the NEP because they don't have enough money to buy the equipment they need to keep up their enlarged households." [52] In a report for the period May 15–31, 1922, the Cheka stated, "Among the peasants there are no limits to the grumbling against the Soviet Government and the Communists. In the conversation of every middle peasant and poor peasant, not to speak even of the kulak, the following is heard, 'They aren't planning freedom for us, but serfdom. The time of Godunov has already begun, when the peasants were attached to the landowners. Now we [are attached] to the Jewish bourgeoisie like Modkowski, Aronson, etc.'" [53]

The period 1921–22, however, represented one of the low points in the economic fortunes of Smolensk guberniya. During the next year a gradual improvement became manifest. By 1923 the area sown to food crops increased 14.8 per cent compared with 1920, and while industry was slower to recover, in Smolensk guberniya it played a relatively minor role. The report of the Smolensk gubkom for the period from March 1, 1923, to March 1, 1924, claimed a real increase in the authority of the Party and the "Soviet power" among the inhabitants of the guberniya.[54] Banditry had been substantially eliminated. The "political-economic" position of the workers was reported as "in general satisfactory" and "improving," but the material situation of the unemployed, of whom there were more than 12,500 in the guberniya, was pronounced "exceptionally unsatisfactory." The "mood" of the peasants was also declared to be "better," although anti-Soviet elements were still "active" in the villages, and the countryside was disturbed by rumors of the imminent outbreak of war. The attitude of state employees to the "Soviet power" was described as "passively loyal," and a "swing" of the intelligentsia toward the Party and government was definitely noticeable. The gubkom was also pleased to report that the Mensheviks had now formally liquidated their Party organizations, and that many former Mensheviks were actually working to help the Party and government. Some Socialist-Revolutionaries, while not organized, continued to conduct agitation against "Soviet power" in the villages.

The Communist Party itself still represented a tiny vanguard. More than 30 per cent of the members were eliminated in the course of the 1921 purge; on its completion the Smolensk organization was left with a total membership of 7,425.[55] During 1922 membership continued to decline. At the end of 1922 the size of the guberniya Party organization totaled 5,925.[56] By March 1923 it shrank further to a total of 5,655, made up of 4,829 members and 826 candidates.[57] During the next year (as of April 1, 1924) the number of candidates mounted to 1,720, but the number of full members dropped to 3,696. The decline, however, was largely a result of a change in accounting, since the Party members in army units in the guberniya were shifted from the rolls of the territorial Party organizations to the political organs of the Red Army.

Even more striking than the small size of the Party was its distribution between town and country. Out of a total of 5,416 members and candidates on April 1, 1924, 3,704 were concentrated in the towns, and only 1,712 were spread through the rural areas.[58] There were only sixteen Communists for every 10,000 rural inhabitants of working age, or approximately one Party member for every ten villages. Since over 90 per cent of the population of the guberniya was located in rural areas, the extreme weakness of the Party in the countryside becomes readily apparent.[59]

The social composition of the Party reflected the predominantly peasant character of the guberniya. As of January 1, 1924, 44.5 per cent of the membership was of peasant origin compared with 33.2 per cent classified as workers and 19.4 per cent as employees.[60] A determined drive was launched, coinciding with Lenin's death, to increase the proportion of workers, and by March 1 their percentage had mounted to 42 per cent while the peasant and employee components in the Party declined to 39 and 17 per cent respectively.[61] But the directive of the Thirteenth Party Conference to induct at least 10 per cent of all workers at the bench into the Party was only imperfectly fulfilled in Smolensk.[62] Nineteen out of every twenty workers engaged in physical labor remained outside of Party ranks.

The nationality composition of the Smolensk Party organization registered the predominance of Great Russians in the guberniya, though the proportion of Latvians and Jews was high here as well as in other areas of Western Russia. The Great Russians accounted for 78 per cent of the membership, Latvians 7.8, Jews 7.7, Poles 2.0, Belorussians 1.2, and Lithuanians 1.0 per cent, while a sprinkling of other nationalities made up the remainder.[63]

One of the most poignant sections of the 1924 report is devoted to the health and material situation of Party members. The shattering effects of the revolutionary and Civil War years can be observed in the official statistics. A sample analysis of 963 members of the Smolensk city organization revealed that 17 per cent were ill with tuberculosis, and that a total of 90.1 per cent had illnesses of one kind or another.[64] The situation of the village Communists, the majority of whom were classified as poor peasants, was described as equally deplorable. Many of them were illiterate or semiliterate, and exercised little influence on their neighbors. Indeed, the report for the year 1924 noted a decline in the number of village Party cells and a loss of eighty-eight members.

The Party apparatus itself was still modest in scope. At the guberniya level it consisted on March 1, 1924, of only twenty-eight responsible workers and sixteen technical workers; at the uyezd and raion levels it numbered 128 responsible workers and 132 technical workers.[65] Included in the nomenklatura of the gubkom (appointments subject to its confirmation) were 695 responsible state and Party workers, of whom 120 operated at the guberniya and 575 at the uyezd level. This group, which constituted the effective government of the guberniya, consisted predominantly of Communists who had joined the Party during the Civil War or earlier. It was through them that the Party sought to project its control into the farms and factories of the guberniya.

Under the conditions of NEP the task was far from easy. Smolensk remained an overwhelmingly agricultural guberniya, and, as has already been noted, Party controls were weakest in the countryside. The bulk of the peasants tended to go their own way, grumbling about taxes, high prices, and scarcity of goods, and adjusting as best they could to the Soviet power which stood over them. As late as 1926–27 the private sector in agriculture accounted for 98.7 per cent of the gross output.[66] Pressed by a high rural birth rate and unfavorable terms of trade with industry, the peasants cut down on their production of technical crops (flax and hemp), and increased their output of grain, potatoes, vegetables, and livestock. Peasant conservatism was strongly entrenched in the guberniya. The bulk of the peasantry adhered to traditional practices, tilled their fields according to the old three-field system, and remained loyal to the mir, or communal form of land tenure, which still accounted for 64.8 per cent of all cultivated land. The province, however, was far from prosperous. Less than 5 per cent of the peasants fell into the category of wealthy or kulak households, and no less than 25 per cent of all the households were described in an official 1926 report as falling into "the category of absolute poverty." [67]

The problems of the Smolensk Party leadership were further complicated by a succession of bad harvests in 1926 and 1927.[68] The poor harvest of 1926 created a deficit in the grain market of 1,800,000 puds of rye and 1,650,000 puds of wheat. Efforts to make up the deficit by drawing on central reserves proved abortive, and the result was a grain crisis. In the words of Pavlyuchenko, the first secretary of the gubkom, "Rumors of the possibility of war, [rumors] that the state was hoarding stocks for the satisfaction of the needs of the Red Army and others, created a mood of panic in the grain market. The population, drawing on the experience of the last war, tried to hoard grain, and the surpluses on hand were not put into the market." [69] Instances of violence were not uncommon. According to Pavlyuchenko:

In Roslavl, owing to insufficient supplies of flour in the Central Workers' Coöperative, the local populace and some of the peasants broke the doors and counters of two shops of the Central Workers' Coöperative. The interference of the police was necessary. In Smolensk in one of the meal shops of the Grain Products Organization up to 700 peasants assembled to buy oats, and all kinds of indignant outbursts and complaints were made against the employees of the meal shop . . . In connection with the rumors about war and the grain crisis the anti-Soviet elements of the city and the country became noticeably more active. . . . There were completely inadmissible actions also on the part of individual farmers, for example, cases of refusal to deliver grain because of the disadvantageous selling conditions, which also made the situation worse.[70]

Because of excessive rainfall the 1927 harvest also proved disappointing, yielding only 92 per cent of the grain and 87.8 per cent of the potatoes produced in 1924. The result was another grain crisis and hoarding of grain by the more well-to-do farmers. A gubkom report of April 10, 1928, noted that kulaks were openly toasting the forthcoming liquidation of all Communists, and that some poor and middle peasants had fallen under their sway.[71] The local authorities in rural districts encountered great difficulty in collecting taxes. Indeed, in the case of the self-obligation tax (imposed to pay for local services such as schools and roads), two volost Party committees joined in the general peasant opposition. The gubkom noted sorrowfully that the lower the Party and administrative level, the worse the performance. Under the stress of crisis the grass-roots weakness of the Party was made patently manifest.

Faced with these problems, the gubkom sought to strengthen both its leadership and its base of support in the villages. Where possible, responsible Party workers from the towns were dispatched to rural centers to reinvigorate the local Party organizations. An effort was also made to increase rural Party membership; the total number of members and candidates in the countryside increased from 1,712 on April 1, 1924, to 2,672 on January 1, 1926.[72] But even this number still represented a pitiful handful, and of the 2,672 total, 1,291 were Party candidates of uncertain quality and reliability. The gubkom also stressed the importance of organizing the poor peasants as a bulwark of Party support, though it also complained that "a number of directives of the Central Committee and the Gubkom on this problem still remain unfulfilled."[23] The basic difficulty remained the weakness of Party organization in rural areas.

In the cities and towns, the position of the Party was much stronger, though here too there were problems. The industry of Smolensk guberniya was poorly developed and consisted largely of textile, food, and other types of light industry. In terms of value of output state industry was predominant (73.6 per cent of the total), but private industry, including artisans and handicraftsmen, accounted for 69.8 per cent of the number of employed workers.[74] As late as January 1, 1928, 20,123 people were listed as unemployed, and the gubkom reported that 300 daily free lunches were being made available to the poorest among them.[75] Housing was desperately inadequate, and in 1927 the living area per individual dropped to 6.14 square meters per person compared with 6.25 square meters in the preceding year.[76] The effects of the grain crisis have already been noted; under the conditions of NEP they were felt as sharply in the towns as they were in the villages. The picture which emerges is essentially a rather static one. The Smolensk area was an industrial backwater and it tended to be neglected by the center. The local Party leadership sought to hold on to and restore such industry as the guberniya possessed, but it exercised hardly any initiative, and it did little to develop the resources of the guberniya. The industrial face of the guberniya was largely unchanged during the period of the NEP.

Meanwhile, the Party organization itself underwent a process of slow growth. From a total of 5,416 members and candidates on April 1, 1924, it increased to 9,076 members and candidates on October 1, 1927.[77] Under the impetus of the drive to increase the proletarian base of the

Party, the percentage of workers mounted to 49.1 per cent, while the peasant component declined to 29.2 per cent. Indeed, the gubkom now complained that the local Party organizations were paying inadequate attention to the recruitment of rural cadres, and the failure to attract batraks (farm laborers) into the Party was singled out as especially unsatisfactory.

The Smolensk Party organization seems to have been relatively little affected by the intra-Party struggles of the mid-NEP years. Judging by the discussions and types of questions put at local Party meetings, the issues were far from clear to the Party rank and file. While there were isolated expressions of sympathy for the views of Trotsky, Zinoviev, and Kamenev, in virtually all cases the local Party organizations took their cue from the gubkom leaders and condemned the left wing by over-whelming votes. The Stalinist forces appeared to be in full control in Smolensk.

In non-Party circles there was a tendency to regard the whole debate as essentially a struggle for power at the top of the Communist hier-archy, of little concern to the ordinary Soviet citizen. Occasionally popu-lar reactions to the intra-Party contest took on distinct anti-Semitic over-tones.[78] A typical peasant utterance is quoted in a Party report (1926) as follows: "Our good master, Vladimir Ilich had only just passed away when our Commissars began to fight among themselves, and all this is due to the fact that the Jews became very numerous, and our Russians do not let them have their way, but there is nobody to suppress them, and each one considers himself more intelligent than the others." The OGPU reported that some "unconscious" workers in Bryansk were say-ing that Trotsky, Zinoviev, Kamenev, and others were Jewish by origin and that when Lenin died, Trotsky wanted to lead the state, that is, to take Lenin's place and put Jews in all the responsible positions, but Trotsky and his opposition were unable to do this, and that is why they were fighting against the Central Committee of the Party.[79]

The Smolensk Scandal of 1928

Not only did the Smolensk Party organization remain largely un-touched by the ideological struggles of the mid-twenties; it also fell victim to corruption in high places. The so-called Smolensk Scandal of 1928 shook the guberniya to its foundation. In the background and pro-viding the organizational preconditions for the scandal was that familiar Soviet institution, the entrenched family circle embracing the leading Party and governmental officials of the guberniya who did their best to protect each other from exposure of their sins of commission and omission. During the mid-twenties this circle was headed by the gubkom first secretary D. Beika, of whom it was said that he had a wife in every town in the guberniya.[80] In 1926 Beika was transferred to Moscow, but his successor D. A. Pavlyuchenko, a former worker and Party member since 1918, who had been in charge of Party cadres under Beika, continued Beika's practices. As a result the Smolensk Party organization was riddled with corruption and drunkenness. As one witness later put it, "Every one in the Party organization drinks — from the top to the bottom there's drinking. Guberniya Party conferences were just one big drinking party."[81]

The demoralization of the organization finally reached a point where the central authorities determined to intervene. In the spring of 1928 two investigators of the Central Control Commission, Tseitlin and Lyakoutkin, were dispatched to Smolensk to look into the situation.[82] The "dung heap" which they uncovered in the course of their two-month stay in the guberniya convinced the central authorities that drastic action was necessary. Pavlyuchenko and his leading associates were summoned to Moscow for a hearing before the Central Control Commission. Their pleas for mercy went unheeded, and the decision was made to demote them to "industrial work according to specialization, with a prohibition on holding responsible posts." The resolution of the Presidium of the CCC on the Situation in the Smolensk Organization, adopted on May 9, was published in *Pravda* on May 18, 1928. Although denouncing the corruption, drunkenness, and sexual degeneracy in the Smolensk apparatus, its treatment of Pavlyuchenko and the "leading organs of the guberniya" was relatively mild.

Acting on the basis of the resolution, A. Yakovlev, a respected member of the Presidium of the CCC and deputy commissar of RKI (the Commissariat of Workers' and Peasants' Inspection), proceeded to Smolensk to purge the Party of its "unhealthy" elements. On May 18, 1928, a joint plenum of the gubkom, the Guberniya Control Commission, and the uyezd and volost aktiv was assembled to listen to Yakovlev's report.[83] The meeting lasted two days, and it was attended by 1,100 Party members of whom 40 per cent were production workers. The story which Yakovlev unfolded was unsavory in the extreme. The Katushka factory, which was one of the proletarian strongholds of the province and enlisted 50 per cent of its workers in either the Party or the Komsomol, was revealed as a nest of bribery and promiscuity. Female workers were taken advantage of by the foremen. In the Yartsevo factory there had been seven suicides of workers, because of the indifference of the Party leadership to their grievances. Old revolutionaries had turned into drunkards and indulged in sexual license. One volkom secretary had had five wives in the course of one year. Yakovlev revealed that sixty persons had already been placed under arrest and that while the ex-gubkom secretary and the ex-guberniya executive committee chairman had not been formally charged with criminal responsibility, they had been removed from their positions and would be used on low level work where they might have a chance to redeem themselves. He added that their attempts at explanation had only made the CCC wish to punish them more severely. He then announced that the Central Committee had "imported" new elements into the guberniya to strengthen the organization. Comrade Borisov, who was to replace Pavlyuchenko as gubkom secretary, had previously served as secretary of the Orlov gubkom, had been a Party member since 1908, and had served five years in tsarist prisons. Comrade Egorov, who was to become the new chairman of the guberniya control commission, had previously served as a gubkom secretary and chairman of a guberniya executive committee. He was a Leningrad worker who had also spent two and a half years in a tsarist prison.

Yakovlev's statement was followed by a general discussion which expanded the indictment and provided a detailed documentation of the abuses and shortcomings of the previous leadership. Indeed, when the discussion was finished, Yakovlev observed that only the "first steps" had been taken to cleanse the "dung heap." "So far," said Yakovlev, "we have cleaned up one-tenth of the Party organization; but the whole organization must be cleaned up. So far sixty people have been arrested. On the basis of what has been said here, it appears not enough." He promised that a new aktiv would be put together, and the Smolensk organization would emerge all the stronger as the result of its trials.

The first reaction to Yakovlev's speech was a mood of panic among responsible Party workers. Many felt correctly that their own positions were in danger; indeed in the preliminary discussion they urged that the CCC resolution not be published on the ground that the authority of the Party would be discredited. Yakovlev and the task force from the center nevertheless proceeded with their revelations, and a series of meetings were held throughout the guberniya at which the sins of the old leadership were discussed and denounced. An Informational Report contained in the Archive provides a frank summary of the result of these discussions.[84] In general, the reaction of the Party masses was described as "healthy"; there was great indignation and relief that the scandal had been unmasked. Many workers, however, demanded even more severe treatment for the leaders. They were reported as not liking the idea of demoting Party leaders to industrial work — "industry is not Katorga (exile)." They demanded that the leaders be expelled from the Party. Some felt that what had happened was the result of suppression of criticism, and there were occasional demands that other parties ought to be legalized, and that there ought to be a free press. One worker in Verkhni-Gorod raion was even elected to the RKI after stating, "Give me three days in Smolensk, and I will liquidate all Communists and Jews, and establish order."

The uyezd and especially the guberniya Party aktiv were reported as silent and worried. Some said that the conditions which had been revealed were a more widespread phenomenon, not restricted to Smolensk alone, and that Smolensk was being made a scapegoat. Others tended to blame their troubles on the unsatisfactory leadership of the Central Committee; "things are probably far worse in the CC."

Meanwhile, the purge of the Smolensk organization proceeded steadily. The bureau of the gubkom was reorganized to include a predominance of worker members; new cadres were promoted to leading positions. According to *Izvestia TsK* (no. 4, August 1928), these new cadres constituted 66 per cent of the gubkom bureau, 76.6 per cent of the volkom-raikom bureaus, 48 per cent of the volkom secretaries, and 44 per cent of all secretaries of primary Party cells. The new leadership took steps to alleviate underlying economic difficulties. On June 1, 1928, Borisov, the new gubkom first secretary, reported on the results of an interview with Stalin at the center.[85] He informed the gubkom bureau that Stalin had promised help on the bread question and had requested Borisov to approach Narkomtorg (the People's Commissariat for Trade) for relief. He also reported that he had called Stalin's attention to the urgent need of new workers in the guberniya, and that they would arrive shortly. The Politburo, he said, had approved the actions of the gubkom, had raised the question of proceeding further with the screening of guberniya Party organizations, and had instructed the CCC to reëxamine its decisions concerning the former leaders with a view to increasing their severity.

Meanwhile, the new leadership began to experience its own difficulties. The installation of a third shift and an increase in the work norms at the Yartsevo textile plant aroused great dissatisfaction among the workers, and a special workers' delegation was dispatched to Moscow to get the order rescinded. Moscow refused, and dissatisfaction mounted. Yakovlev and Borisov then went to Yartsevo to still the discontent. They met a stormy reception, and even Borisov found it impossible to finish his speech. Angry workers shouted, "We cannot hold the Party dear with the dictatorship of the CC and the Gubkom."[86] They bitterly criticized the action of the new leadership in removing the Yartsevo ukom secretary, Kartyshev, without consulting the Yartsevo organization. Borisov's effort to postpone all voting was swept aside, and another motion to liquidate the third shift and the new norms was adopted. Party members remained largely silent during the meeting; presumably their sympathy was with the workers.

The meeting of the seamstresses was a repetition of the Yartsevo affair on a smaller scale.[87] Comrade Anshin, the head of the Seamstress Union, had been one of the victims of the Smolensk affair, and the resolution of the CC and the CCC forbade him to occupy a responsible post in the trade union apparatus for one year. But the Party fraction of the Seamstress Union repudiated the decision of the central authorities, appointed its own subgroup to study the materials on Anshin, and then renominated him for the chairmanship of the Seamstress Union. The restiveness in the trade unions took on anti-Soviet overtones. There were demands for freedom of speech and the press. One worker was cited as saying, "Formerly there was one Tsar — now a whole lot of them — every Communist is a Tsar." [88]

Meanwhile, the new leadership carried forward its efforts to obtain a firm grip on the guberniya Party organization. The operation was described as a screening, rather than a purge, but in any event 13.1 per cent of the total membership was expelled in the wake of the Smolensk scandal.[89] Slowly but inexorably resistance was being stamped out, and Smolensk, along with other Party organizations, was beaten into the obedient Stalinist amalgam into which the Party was being transformed.

New Leadership and New Plans

The next step in the history of the Smolensk Party organization involved a major territorial reorganization, the creation of the Western Oblast. This measure, which was announced to Party members on March 15, 1929, merged the Bryansk, Smolensk, and Kaluga guberniyas, the Rzhev and Ostashkovsky uyezds of Tversk guberniya, and Velikiye Luki okrug of the Leningrad Oblast, into a new administrative unit with a population of approximately 6,500,000 and with headquarters in Smolensk.[90] The old guberniyas were abolished and replaced by eight okrugs, which were further subdivided into raions. This reorganization had barely been completed when a resolution of the Sixteenth Party Congress in the spring of 1930 ordered the abolition of the okrugs. As a result the size of the raions was somewhat enlarged, but when the reorganization was completed, the authorities in Smolensk found themselves charged with the direct supervision of three cities — Smolensk, Bryansk, and Bezhitsa — and 110 raions.

Needless to say, these successive reorganizations sowed their own special seeds of confusion. Coming hard on the heels of the Smolensk Scandal, their effect for a time was merely to compound the chaos. No sooner had the guberniya staffs been distributed among the new okrugs than they had largely to be redistributed again among the raions. The resentment of those who found themselves forced down two steps in the hierarchy cannot only be imagined; it can be documented.[91] The directive of the government provided that not less than 90 per cent of all former okrug workers were to be assigned to the raions. Most went where they were sent, but some refused and were dismissed from the service. Meanwhile, there were many problems to be resolved until the raions adjusted to their new responsibilities and the Western Oblast authorities in turn developed effective techniques of supervising their sprawling and numerous organizational subdivisions.

The creation of the Western Oblast brought new Party leadership to the forefront. Borisov, who had been "imported" to clean up the "dung-heap," was apparently not considered strong enough for the number one Party post, and Ivan Petrovich Rumyantsev, an Old Bolshevik who had joined the Party in 1905, was sent in to become the responsible first secretary of the new oblast. For a brief period Borisov served as his second secretary and was then dispatched elsewhere. The new team which now took over and remained at the helm until the Great Purge of 1937 consisted of Rumyantsev as first secretary, Shilman as second secretary in charge of organizational matters, and Rakitov, who served as chairman of the Zapoblispolkom (the executive committee of the Western Oblast Soviet.)

The mission with which the new leadership was charged was nothing less than the transformation of an overwhelmingly agrarian oblast into an industrial-agricultural one. The first task in agriculture was collectivization; its history will be separately treated in Chapter 12.[92] But within the framework of collectivization the agriculture of the oblast was to be reorganized around specialization in flax and hemp production and live-stock breeding. The First Five Year Plan designated the Western Oblast as the primary flax-raising and flax-industry region of the RSFSR.

The industrial development plan of the oblast contemplated the creation of a "powerful base" drawing on the rich peat resources of the area and the establishment of a number of new factories based on locally available raw materials. These new enterprises were to be concerned largely with the processing of flax, the manufacture of twine, forest products, glass, cement and bricks, phosphate fertilizer, and similar products. This plan, which largely reflected the initiative of the new Party leadership of the oblast, was to guide its activity over the next years.[93] Despite setbacks and difficulties, particularly in the early period, the industrialization drive began to leave its imprint on the oblast. The pace of development, however, was slow compared with the newer industrial areas, and the great majority of the population during the thirties continued to be engaged in agricultural pursuits.

At the same time, beginning with the Five Year Plans and collectivization, there was a significant shift in the locus and character of Party activity. To a far greater extent than before, economic problems engaged the primary attention of the oblast Party leadership. Economic questions dominated the agendas of Party meetings and the correspondence of Party organs. The fulfillment of plans became a central concern of Party workers at every level of the Party hierarchy. The priorities of the center found their reflection in the tempo and direction of local Party life.

Yet it would be a mistake to assume that the local Party workers were thereby transformed into automatons doing little more than executing the will of their superiors. The succession of purges which engulfed the Party organization of the Western Oblast testifies to the refractory character of its human material and the problems which are inevitably encountered when one seeks to pour even Communist man into a monolithic mold.

Peasant Moods and the Right-Wing Opposition

Every Party organization has its own special characteristics, which are determined by the nature of its membership and by its roots in the local scene. The Party organization of the Western Oblast was no exception. It operated in a predominantly rural area, and it was therefore particularly sensitive to the grievances of the countryside. Its rural recruits manifested a peasant outlook which not even a Party card could dissipate. Even in the cities and towns many so-called worker Communists were still relatively fresh from the land, had relatives in the villages, and looked at the world through peasant eyes. Many worker Communists were dispersed among numerous small enterprises and preserved the outlook of the artisan threatened by large-scale industrialization. For these reasons, the right-wing opposition with its challenge to hasty collectivization and the rapid development of heavy industry found a sounding-board of support in the Smolensk area which the left-wing opposition of Trotsky, Zinoviev, and Kamenev was never able to develop.

The purge of the Party organization of the Western Oblast in 1929–30 revealed the strength of right-wing sympathies among the membership. Some extracts from the Report of the Control Commission of the Western Oblast on the result of the purge will help convey the character of these sentiments.[94] "In the factories of the Western Oblast," noted the report, "there are many Communists who have not entirely broken their ties with the country and who [still] have their own farms . . . there are many cases where these Communists are not members of the kolkhozes, sometimes come out against the kolkhoz, sometimes earn much money in the factory, become kulaks in the country, and resolutely hold onto their individual farms." "As a clear example of rightist opportunism," the report cited the Party cell of the administration and supply section of the factory "Red Profintern." Eighty per cent of its membership were Communists connected with agriculture, and the cell had pursued "a kulak policy in practice." The leadership of the cell was headed by "well-to-do

'Communists' "; the majority were people from the same locality and relatives. The suppression of self-criticism in the cell was truly "exemplary." Everyone who dared to criticize "his fellow countrymen" received a sharp rebuff from the bureau of the cell.

The investigation of rural Party cells proved even more revealing:

> In Klintsovsk okrug it is observed that Communists dread going into the kolkhoz and do not believe in the success of kolkhoz construction . . . In Churovyachsk raion the questions of the collectivization of agriculture and the organization of kolkhozes were discussed in the majority of the cells, but almost no Communists participated in the kolkhozes and their organization. Some Communists not only were not leaders of kolkhoz construction, but when kolkhozes were organized by Komsomol members and the poor-peasant element of the countryside, they tried to get out of entering the kolkhoz, preferring to have an individual farm . . . In Rzhev okrug also there is observed passivity on the part of rural Communists in regard to collectivization, extending in some cases to opposition to the kolkhoz structure . . . In the Karmanovsk Party organization most of the Communists live on individual farms . . . When they are asked about entering the kolkhoz, they answer that their families are not prepared, that their mother-in-law prevents, or that conditions are not ripe in our rural areas. Out of the whole organization, only one Party member belongs to the kolkhoz . . .

These examples, which are largely chosen at random and which could be multiplied many fold, point to the difficulties which the Smolensk leadership faced in building reliable cadres that could be trusted to carry out the commands of the center.[95] With time and the influx of new members, some of these difficulties were overcome, but the purges of the thirties were also to make clear that they were far from resolved.

By the time the Sixteenth Party Congress assembled in June 1930, the Party organization of the Western Oblast totaled 45,610, of whom 31,510 were members and 14,100 candidates.[96] During the next few years growth was rapid, and an especially determined effort was made to increase the proportion of worker membership. By July 1, 1932, the total reached 66,895 of whom 42.3 per cent were candidates. In terms of social origin 61.7 per cent of the Party organization were classified as workers, 32.1 per cent as peasants, and 6.0 per cent as employees. However, only 41.7 per cent were engaged in physical labor while 29.2 per cent were actually serving as employees.[97]

The Continuous Purge, 1933–1937

From 1933 until 1938 the Party organization of the Western Oblast, even more than most organizations, was subjected to an almost continuous purge. By early 1936 the total number of members and candidates declined to approximately 42,000.[98] While no figures were released the next year, which represented the height of the purge, the probabilities are that membership continued to shrink. Indeed one of the charges leveled against Rumyantsev when he was finally purged in 1937 was that the last two years of his reign were marked by the liquidation of seventy-one kolkhoz Party organizations and 345 candidate groups.[99]

The 1933 purge, which was inaugurated nationally by a joint CC-CCC decree of April 28, 1933, was designed to accomplish two primary purposes: (1) to eliminate so-called class-alien and careerist elements who had "wormed" their way into the Party in the preceding period of stormy growth, and (2) to serve as a spur to "honest" but "politically illiterate" comrades to improve their qualifications by demoting them to the stage of candidates for a year's trial, after which they were to be readmitted as Party members if they succeeded in raising their "political literacy" to the required level.[100] The effect of the 1933 purge on the Western Oblast was felt largely in the loss of recently recruited worker and, especially, peasant contingents who failed to meet the standards of ideological sophistication which the purge commissions imposed.[101] Here and there, however, so-called opportunistic and kulak elements, Party members who had managed to conceal their "bourgeois" origins, self-seekers who had used their Party cards to line their own pockets, and other violators of Party discipline were also exposed and expelled.

Despite these actions the situation in the oblast Party organization left much to be desired. On July 9, 1934, Rumyantsev dispatched a closed letter to all Party and Komsomol organizations in which he called on them "to liquidate unhealthy and disgraceful symptoms in a number of organizations: mass violations of revolutionary legality, administrative excesses in regard to individual farmers and kolkhozniks, cheating in workers' wages, embezzlement and peculation in the coöperative trade network, and what is most important, the insensitive reaction of many Party organizations to these disorders and crimes." [102] The letter spelled out these charges in detail, pointed out that "cases where peculations and embezzlements are committed by Communists and Komsomols are not rare," and called upon the local Party organizations to improve their work as rapidly as possible. After the letter came a number of show trials, one of the most dramatic disclosing large-scale embezzlement in Zagotlen (the Association for the Procurement and Marketing of Flax, Hemp, and Clover Seeds).[103] Of the embezzling group of thirty-six, ten were Party members or candidates, including seven kolkhoz chairmen.

The worst period of storm and stress for the oblast Party was ushered in by the assassination of Kirov in December 1934. A closed letter of the Central Committee, entitled "Lessons of the Events Bound Up with the Evil Murder of Comrade Kirov," was circulated to all Party committees and in effect invited them to hunt out, expel, and arrest all former oppositionists who remained in the Party.[104] Toward the end of December 1934 the letter was discussed in all Party organizations and was followed by a hailstorm of indiscriminate denunciations in which listening to an anti-Soviet anecdote or even passivity in the performance of Party duties was assimilated to membership in an opposition group. The main target ostensibly was former members of the Zinoviev-Kamenev-Trotsky opposition, but the net was spread wide, and many who were caught in it found themselves the victims of inventive busybodies who saw an opportunity to prove their devotion and improve their fortunes by zealously denouncing their colleagues. Buried in the Smolensk Archive are long lists of the denounced, with brief references to their alleged crimes, the Party official charged with the investigation, and the records of actions taken.[105] At this period the Great Purge was still in its early phases, and though the denunciations were already irresponsible, there is evidence of discrimination in acting on them. Thus friendship with an excluded Trotskyite was still the occasion for a stern rebuke, rather than exclusion from the Party or arrest. (Only a few years later such mild punishment would come to be regarded not merely as extreme liberalism, but as clear indication of the complicity of the judges in counterrevolutionary activity.)

As the year 1935 wore on, the heresy hunt gathered momentum. This time the pressure from the center came in the form of a closed letter from the Central Committee dated May 19, 1935, and entitled "On Disorders in the Registration, Issuance, and Custody of Party Cards, and on Measures for Regulating this Matter." [106] According to the letter, a "special investigation" had established that "enemies of the Party and the working class enjoyed access to Party documents, received Party cards and protected themselves with them in their infamous work of undermining the cause of the Party and the Soviet State." The letter then cited cases of alleged spies and scoundrels who operated under the immunity of Party documents and blamed this on "extreme neglect and disorganization in the registration of Communists and lack of study of the members of the Party who have recently come into the organization." The local Party organizations were instructed to check the authenticity of Party and registration cards, and members of all primary Party organizations were required to appear personally at the raikom, and to be examined by the raikom secretary, or in the case of large raions, by members of the raikom bureau.

The Party leadership of the Western Oblast apparently failed to take this letter with becoming seriousness. Of the documents checked, only 4.3 per cent were challenged. The formal manner in which the investigation was conducted aroused the ire of the central Party authorities, and on June 27, 1935, a special Central Committee resolution on the Western Oblast reprimanded Shilman, the oblast second secretary, and Kiselev, the head of the Division of Leading Party Organs; expelled the Secretary of the Pochinkovsk raion from the Party for failing to give the matter personal supervision; and ordered that a second check-up of Party documents in the Western Oblast be promptly launched.[107] This time there was no lack of zeal. Indeed a report on the progress of the investigation, signed by Yezhov and Malenkov and dated August 8, 1935, noted that up to August 1 the Western Oblast had finally taken away 7.4 per cent of all Party cards checked and was holding an additional 15.6 per cent for further examination.[108] The 23 per cent total of cards either taken away or in doubt represented a figure far in excess of that of any other Party organization in the Soviet Union. Among the bizarre Western Oblast situations allegedly revealed by the investigation and cited in the Yezhov-Malenkov reports were the cases of a Party secretary in a tekhnikum (technical school) who managed to conceal the fact that he had previously been twice expelled from the Party for embezzling funds, the manager of a raikom who had set up a business of forging Party documents, the organizer of a religious sect, a suspected spy for Latvia, former volunteers in the White Army, and of course, many former members of opposition groups who had succeeded in hiding their earlier affiliations.

During the year 1936 tension in the Party mounted. On January 14, 1936, the Central Committee sent instructions requiring all Party members and candidates to turn in their old Party documents for new ones. This exchange of documents, which was to take place between February 1 and May 1, was designed to provide still another screening of the Party membership, this time to eliminate not only so-called "enemies of the people" but also "passive elements, accidentally taken into the ranks of the Party, and not justifying the high title of Party member." [109] This screening had hardly been completed when the Party organizations of the Western Oblast found themselves the recipient of still another top-secret Central Committee letter dated July 29, 1936, and spelling out details "On the Terrorist Activity of the Trotskyite-Zinovievite Counterrevolutionary Bloc." [110] The letter pointed out that "some of the arrested participants . . . were passed in the check of Party documents and were left in the ranks of the Party." Calling for a renewal of "revolutionary vigilance," the Central Committee ended its letter with the following statement: "The inalienable quality of every Bolshevik under present conditions should be the ability to recognize an enemy of the Party, no matter how well he may be masked."

The new wave of denunciations which this letter unleashed finds its reflection in the Smolensk Archive in long lists of so-called anti-Soviet elements who were presumably slated for arrest by the NKVD.[111] By the end of 1936 a mood of panic and hysteria was beginning to sweep through Party ranks, and this time not even the leadership of the oblast

was immune. At a top-secret meeting of the bureau of the Western obkom, Rumyantsev, the first secretary, acknowledged his guilt in having
earlier defended and expressed confidence in one Klyavin, who had just
been expelled from the Party as a "Trotskyite double-dealer." [112] Although the matter was passed over at this time, there were beginning
to be indications that the end of the long reign of Rumyantsev in the
Western Oblast was in sight.

Signs of Rumyantsev's increasingly shaky position became evident
at the Fifth Oblast Party Conference in June 1937.[113] Although the conference acknowledged that the political line of the obkom was satisfactory, it also noted "serious shortcomings" of the obkom's leadership.
Among these it listed mistakes which had already been censured by the
Central Committee in connection with the investigation of Party documents, the "dulling of vigilance" and the failure to prevent "enemies of
the people" from worming their way into responsible posts, neglect of
political education of the masses, poor economic leadership, and other
equally reprehensible crimes.

The day of reckoning was quick to follow. It came hard on the heels
of the *Pravda* announcement on June 10, 1937, of the execution of Marshal Tukhachevsky and seven other prominent generals of the Red Army
"for espionage and treason to the Fatherland." One of the executed was
General Uborevich, the Commander of the Western Military District,
whose assignment brought him into close working relations with Rumyantsev and other leaders of the Western Oblast. This was to prove a
convenient connection. This time Kaganovich was the chief executioner.
Toward the end of June 1937, he appeared in Smolensk before a hastily
summoned special session of the Western obkom and announced the decision of the Central Committee to purge the obkom leadership.[114] Rumyantsev, Shilman, Rakitov, and their associates were coupled with Uborevich as "traitors" and "spies" of German-Japanese fascism," as members
of the "right-Trotskyite band of enemies of the people . . . who committed infamous counterrevolutionary crimes directed toward the preparation of the military defeat and the restoration of capitalism in the
USSR . . ." Presumably, Rumyantsev and company were arrested and
either executed or sent to forced-labor camps. In any case, they left no
traces behind.

What the real crimes of Ivan Petrovich Rumyantsev were, if any,
must remain a matter of speculation on which the Archive throws little
light. Like many another obkom secretary who fell victim to the Great
Purge, Rumyantsev had been a Party stalwart, faithful to Stalin through
all the opposition struggles, and indeed rewarded with his post as leader
of the Western Oblast because of his presumed loyalty and dependability.
But Rumyantsev had been long in one place, and borrowing a page from

his master's book, he had made himself something of a little Stalin in his home territory. His intimates were entrenched in leading posts; his portraits and photographs were everywhere; and there were even factories in the oblast which were named after him and his second secretary, Shilman. In the flood of recriminations released by his arrest, it was charged that he ruled with an iron hand and that his subordinates did not dare contradict him. Even more unsavory details came to light. There were stories of high living and great drinking parties at the obkom rest home at Vonlyarovo and the trade union retreat at Gniezdovo in which Rumyantsev and his associates played a leading role.[115] There were tales of lordly processions through the countryside during which Rumyantsev scattered kopecks to be scrambled for by the children and peasants. It may be that Stalin looking on from afar began to believe that Rumyantsev was feeling too secure, and that the time had come for a change.

Meanwhile, there were real grievances in the Western Oblast for which Rumyantsev provided a convenient and available scapegoat. Accomplishments in both industry and agriculture left much to be desired. According to Pliusnin, a former chairman of the gorsoviet, the housing space available in Smolensk had fallen to the incredible figure of three square meters per inhabitant.[116] There was a substantial loss of Party strength in the countryside; as has already been noted, many kolkhoz Party organizations and candidate groups simply disappeared. All this may have contributed to the decision of the center to liquidate the Rumyantsev group.

Rumyantsev's successor as first secretary of the Western Oblast was D. Korotchenkov, who had served earlier as first secretary of the Bauman raion in Moscow and as one of the secretaries of the Moscow obkom under the name of Korotchenko. He was to become even more famous later as chairman of the Ukrainian Council of Ministers, Ukrainian Party secretary, chairman of the Ukrainian Supreme Soviet, deputy chairman of the Presidium of the USSR Supreme Soviet, and both member and candidate member of the Party Presidium. Under Korotchenkov's aegis, the purge of the Rumyantsev leadership spread out in ever widening circles, spurred on by a fever of denunciations as those who had risen with Rumyantsev tried to save their skins. Less than three months after coming to office, Korotchenkov reported in *Partiinoe Stroitelstvo* that "according to incomplete data," about 1,000 new people had been promoted to various leading posts, including 188 to leading Party work, 37 to Komsomol duties, and about 500 to various Soviet assignments.[117] Thus what was catastrophe for the Rumyantsev entourage represented opportunity and an undreamed of rapid rise for younger cadres who now came to the fore. The files of the Archive contain long lists of people previously occupying junior posts who found themselves lifted by the Purge of 1937–38 to positions of far greater responsibility.[118]

At the same time a determined effort was made to use the Komsomol to bring new talent and energy to the disposal of the Party leadership. In addition, many hundreds of cases of Komsomols who had been "mistakenly" excluded during the purge were now reëxamined and readmitted to swell the ranks. To some extent the same process was repeated in local Party organizations where excluded Party members who still survived now found it possible to gain readmission by demonstrating that they had been the victims of "excesses." [119]

At this point the Smolensk Archive stops, and the history of the Western Oblast comes to an end. Originally an amalgamation of a number of guberniyas, it was now condemned as unwieldy and again subdivided. The new Smolensk Oblast, which was organized on September 27, 1937, with its own Party organization, represented the reappearance of the old guberniya in a new form. Since 1937, it has had its own checkered history, but the telling of that tale requires access to archives which still remain closed.

3 Party Organization and Controls
at the Oblast Level

The Smolensk Archive is particularly valuable for the light which it throws on the problems of regional administration in the Soviet system. The intermediate layers of administration in the Soviet Union — what are now known as the oblasts and raions — have been little studied; the tendency in the past was to dismiss them as of little significance on the general assumption that the Soviet system was so highly centralized as to allow little or no discretion to regional or local governing bodies. While the assumption that the Soviet system is highly centralized is a correct one, it does not follow that regional and local administrators do not have an important role to play. The Soviet Union is a vast empire; all-powerful as the leaders in Moscow may seem to be, their authority in the final analysis rests on the effectiveness with which regional and local administrators exercise their responsibilities throughout the length and breadth of the land.

The Organization and Functions
of the Oblast Party Apparatus

A concrete description of the organization and functions of the oblast Party apparatus in the Smolensk area may help to convey a sense of its wide-ranging activities. Chart I outlines the structure of the Western Oblast Party secretariat as it was approved by the obkom bureau on October 19, 1936.[1] While the pattern of organization has varied greatly over the years, in 1936, as at present, it sought to parallel the governmental and economic structure as well as to provide for the needs of internal Party administration. As the chart indicates, the basic work of the Secretariat was performed through seven main divisions: (1) Leading Party Organs, (2) Industrial-Transport, (3) Agricultural, (4) Soviet-Trade, (5) Party Propaganda, Agitation, and the Press, (6) Schools and Scientific Institutions, (7) Cultural and Educational Work.

The Division of Leading Party Organs had as its primary responsibility the supervision of the raion, city, and town Party organizations and the oblast Komsomol group. In addition, it exercised jurisdiction over all important appointments in the oblast Party apparatus and served as

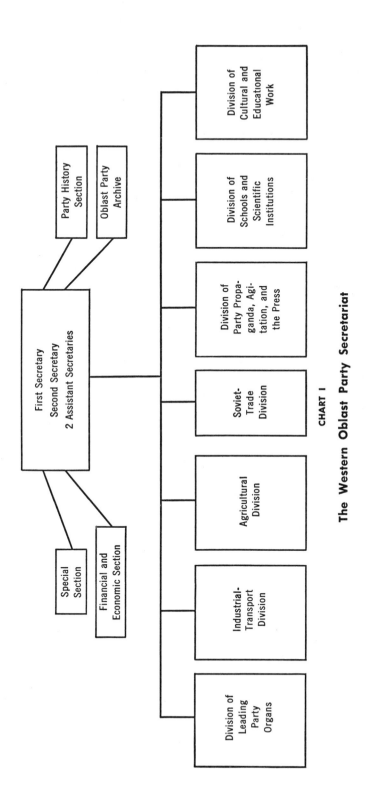

CHART I

The Western Oblast Party Secretariat

Party History Section

Oblast Party Archive

First Secretary
Second Secretary
2 Assistant Secretaries

Special Section

Financial and Economic Section

Division of Leading Party Organs

Industrial-Transport Division

Agricultural Division

Soviet-Trade Division

Division of Party Propaganda, Agitation, and the Press

Division of Schools and Scientific Institutions

Division of Cultural and Educatonal Work

the channel of communication with the Party Central Committee on all matters involving Party records, membership questions, appointments to leading Party posts in the oblast, and other organizational problems. On the staff of this division were eight responsible instructors, each of whom supervised a group of approximately ten raion Party organizations. Each instructor was supposed to visit his raion Party organizations periodically, to study the protocols of all meetings of their raikoms, to acquaint himself with their activities, to rectify incorrect decisions, to follow through on problems requiring the action of other divisions of the oblast secretariat, and to check on the fulfillment of decisions of the Central Committee and the obkom by the raikom and gorkom organizations. The nomenklatura, or appointment responsibilities, of the Division of Leading Party Organs, included a total of 596 raikom and gorkom jobs: 83 first secretaries, 52 second secretaries, 31 deputy secretaries, 2 heads of Party cadre divisions, 345 instructors, and 83 heads of registration divisions.[2] With respect to first and second secretaries and in other important cases, the consent of the Central Committee was also necessary to make these appointments official. In addition, the division was charged with the task of keeping the Central Committee Secretariat informed on all oblast Party activities. It was required to render biannual reports to the Central Committee, to forward informational-accounting materials every two months, and to make certain that all obkom protocols were forwarded to Moscow within three days after the completion of the session.[3]

The jurisdiction of the Industrial-Transport Division embraced, as its name implied, all the industrial and transportation enterprises of the oblast, including communications, road construction, building, communal economy, and the trade unions operating in these areas. It did not include enterprises of all-Union significance which were directly subordinate to the Central Committee Secretariat. The nomenklatura, or appointment responsibilities, of the division numbered 322 positions, chiefly managers or directors of enterprises, but also including secretaries of factory Party committees and trade union heads.[4] In the case of factory managers, or directors, the appointment initiative ordinarily was exercised by the commissariat within which the enterprise was located, but the appointment had to be cleared through the Industrial-Transport Division of the oblast secretariat before becoming official. The personnel of the division comprised a chief, a deputy chief, and four responsible instructors. It was their duty not only to supervise Party activities in the enterprises which fell under their jurisdiction, but also to check and report on the state of plan fulfillment to higher Party authorities.

The Agricultural Division, which was of key importance because of the rural character of the oblast, exercised jurisdiction over the Oblast Land Division, the raion agricultural divisions, the machine-tractor stations, the sovkhozes, the agricultural procurement organizations, the experiment stations, the agricultural schools, and the trade unions of agricultural workers. In all, 832 positions were listed on the nomenklatura of this division.[5] Of particular importance in the Party chain of command were the 132 deputy directors for Political Affairs of the MTS's and the forty-two chiefs of the Political Divisions of the sovkhozes. In these cases the Agricultural Division took an active role in initiating appointments; in the case of sovkhoz and MTS directors and other officials of the Commissariat of Agriculture, the division merely cleared or ratified appointments which were the primary responsibility of the appropriate government department. The staff of the Agricultural Division contained eleven full-time officials, a director, a deputy director, six responsible instructors, and three members of a special sector for sovkhoz affairs. In addition, from time to time, a supplementary staff of unpaid instructors was made available to this division, as well as to others, to provide emergency assistance. In 1936 this supplementary staff of the Agricultural Division included thirty-seven individuals who were specially recruited to assist in its activities. While the primary responsibility of the Agricultural Division was to direct and supervise Party activities in agricultural enterprises, a reading of the protocols of the obkom bureau makes clear that the division was deeply involved in managerial responsibilities which were almost indistinguishable from those vested in the agricultural commissariat itself.

The Soviet-Trade Division was responsible for supervising a vast miscellany of activities. Its jurisdiction embraced both the oblast and raion executive committees and the city soviets; all legal and punitive organs including the oblast and peoples' courts; the oblast and raion procuracies; the oblast, raion, and city branches of the NKVD; the oblast planning commission; the oblast and raion financial and credit organs; the coöperatives and trading organizations of the oblast; and the trade unions associated with these diverse activities. The nomenklatura of this division totaled 742 positions, though an overwhelming majority of them represented appointments which were initiated through various government departments and merely submitted to the division for approval.[6] The staff of the division was small, including only two responsible instructors in addition to the head of the division. Given its staff limitations, it is difficult to visualize the Soviet-Trade Division as more than a clearing house which received reports from its diverse constituents, processed them to the best of its ability, and injected itself into an occasional troubled situation where an investigation was required.

The Division of Party Propaganda, Agitation, and the Press concerned itself with agitprop activities within the Party, Party schools, and with supervision of the oblast and raion press and other publishing activities centered in Smolensk. Its nomenklatura included 286 positions, of which 128 represented raikom and gorkom heads of Culture and Propaganda and Party Cabinets, another 79 editors of raion newspapers, while the rest were scattered among a variety of Party educational and publishing activities.[7] The staff of the division comprised a director and five responsible instructors. They planned agitprop campaigns for the area, supervised the work of corresponding organs at lower levels, made arrangements for Party schools, assigned lecturers to their faculties, and designated students to attend them. It was also their function to read the raion and oblast press, to criticize its content, to provide guidance for editors, and to consult with them when problems arose.

The Division of Schools and Scientific Institutions had as its area of responsibility the oblast, raion, and city departments of public education, the higher educational institutes of the region, the tekhnikums, the middle schools, the kindergartens, and the trade unions associated with these institutions. The nomenklatura of the division embraced 281 positions, including 81 heads of city and raion departments of public education, 55 directors of tekhnikums, 35 school directors, 59 kindergarten heads, and the directors, Party secretaries, chiefs of curriculum, and holders of chairs in the social and economic disciplines in all higher educational institutes in the region.[8] The head of the division was assisted by two responsible instructors. As in other areas, the degree of control which the division exercised over appointments varied with the job. Where the appointment involved Party responsibilities or was closely related thereto, the division played a leading role. In other cases, the initiative lay with the educational authorities, and the function of the division was to ratify or disapprove. Above all, the function of the division was to insure that the spirit of partiinost, of devotion to the Party cause, prevailed in the selection of personnel, in the content of the curriculum, and in the teaching which took place in the educational institutions of the oblast.

The Division of Cultural and Educational Work was charged with supervising a miscellany of assorted functions. In addition to public health, its jurisdiction included the oblast Union of Soviet Writers, workers in the pictorial arts, films, the theater, radio broadcasting, Osoaviakhim, the Red Cross, the League of Militant Atheists, and the oblast Committee of Physical Culture. Its nomenklatura included only twenty-six positions, but because of the variety of activities over which it exercised jurisdiction, the staff of the division consisted of a director and three responsible instructors.[9]

In reviewing the activities of the various divisions of the oblast Party secretariat, one cannot help but be struck by the all-embracing character of their interests. The Party Secretariat sought to contain the whole life of the oblast. One searches in vain for any aspect of oblast activity which does not find its reflection and point of control in one or another division of the secretariat.

Directing the work of the oblast Party secretariat were a first secretary, a second secretary, and two deputy or assistant secretaries, all of whom, theoretically at least, were responsible to the bureau of the obkom. Immediately attached to the secretaries were a Special Section, which was charged with problems of internal security within the secretariat, including the handling of secret files and communications; a Financial and Economic Section, which as its name implies was responsible for the budget and finances of the oblast Party organization; and two small sections devoted to Party History and the Oblast Party Archives.[10] The actual division of responsibility among the secretaries varied in particular cases, although in the mid-thirties the second secretary ordinarily dealt with Party organizational questions. The only formal record in the Archive of a division of duties between the first and second secretaries dates back to 1929 when the Western Oblast was first organized.[11] In that case Rumyantsev, the first secretary, in addition to exercising general leadership over Party work in the oblast, took special responsibility for relationships with the center, and directly handled problems involving the OGPU, the oblast newspaper, the political administration of the okrugs, and economic, railroad, financial, and agricultural questions. Borisov, then second secretary, watched over the Smolensk gorkom, mobilization work, the coöperatives, contacts with the oblast Control Commission, and all other Soviet and public organizations which did not come under Rumyantsev's direct jurisdiction.

What has been described so far is largely formal structure, the institutional fabric through which the oblast Party leadership exercised its control. Actually, over most of the period from 1929 through mid-1937, the direction of affairs in the oblast was in the hands of the so-called Big Three: Rumyantsev, the first secretary; Shilman, the second secretary; and Rakitov, the chairman of the oblispolkom. They dominated the obkom and staffed its bureau largely with their close associates and dependents.

The Responsibilities of the Obkom and Its Bureau

The Smolensk Archive contains a complete file of protocols of obkom bureau meetings for the year 1936.[12] From a study of the file it is apparent that the real work of the obkom was carried on by its bureau, which in substantial degree overlapped in membership with the obkom secretariat, so that in a sense the obkom bureau merely represented the secretariat in a somewhat enlarged guise. In addition to the first and second secretary and the heads of important divisions in the obkom secretariat, the membership of the obkom bureau included the chairman of the oblispolkom, the first secretary of the oblast Komsomol organization, the editor of the oblast newspaper *Rabochii Put* (Worker's Path), the head of the obkom NKVD, and the commander of the Western Military District, Uborevich. If the 1936 files can be taken as indicative, Uborevich rarely attended bureau sessions, though he was later to become the link which was used to indict the whole oblast Party leadership as a group of traitors and spies. The hard core of those in regular attendance with voting power consisted chiefly of the secretarial group.

Formal sessions of the bureau during 1936 took place at intervals of approximately eight or nine days. The work of each meeting was organized around an agenda which frequently included more than a hundred items touching upon every facet of oblast life. Each item was customarily presented by a reporter or a group of reporters and discussants within whose jurisdiction or field of interest the item fell. Usually the reporter was a member of the bureau or of the secretariat, but this was not invariably the case. The participants in bureau sessions varied with the nature of the problem discussed. In regular attendance were members and candidates of the bureau, representatives of the oblast Control Commission, and heads of divisions, deputies, and instructors of the obkom secretariat. Others were invited to specific meetings to report on particular problems and activities which were being considered by the bureau. Sometimes this rotating group might consist of raikom secretaries, selected chairmen of kolkhozes, and agricultural experts; at other times, depending on the agenda, enterprise managers or other officials might be represented. The summons to appear before the bureau frequently signaled trouble, but this was not invariably the rule. Sometimes officials appeared in a purely informational or expert capacity to advise the bureau on problems before it and to help make plans for future activity.

Theoretically, at least, the rhythm of obkom activity was carefully regulated by advance planning. Each division of the obkom secretariat was required to prepare a six months' work plan, which required the approval of the obkom bureau.[13] The obkom bureau in turn prepared its own work plan, usually covering a period three or four months in advance.[14] A monthly plan specified the items that the bureau hoped to consider, with about twenty-five items normally allotted to each month. Copies of the work plan were submitted to the Central Committee and were also forwarded to the raikoms in order to enable them to coördinate their work with the obkom schedule.

In actual practice, these plans proved less restrictive and provided for less direction than the commitment to careful planning implied. For one thing, the plans were themselves frequently vague and broad, being little more than lists of topics which the obkom expected to discuss, with no indication of priorities or detailed time schedules. For another, the obkom bureau found itself constantly confronted with demands from the center which it did not or could not anticipate as well as unexpected emergencies in the oblast which could not be foreseen but which nevertheless claimed immediate attention.

A comparison of the work plans prepared in advance with the actual agenda of the obkom bureau for a given period is highly revealing. For example, out of thirty-two items planned for treatment in November 1936 only six actually appeared on the agenda of the November protocols. Not only did most topics in the work plan go untouched; many were treated that did not appear in the work plan at all. The impression conveyed is one of considerable improvisation with the obkom bureau in fact giving priority to immediate problems whose urgency could not be denied.

The business of the obkom as it found reflection in the bureau protocols mirrored the life and problems of the oblast. From year to year there were, of course, variations in emphasis and direction, but there were also persisting themes which registered the long-term priorities of the center and the more or less fixed contours of the local scene. An analysis of the 1936 protocols may serve to illustrate the wide variety of activity in which the obkom bureau was engaged.

As might be expected, a primary preoccupation of the bureau was with Party matters and the state of subordinate Party organizations. A great deal of attention was devoted to their personnel problems — appointments, removals, and shifts of assignments. Repeated concern was expressed over the condition of Party organizations in rural areas, and continuing efforts were made to raise their educational level. Monthly and bimonthly courses were organized for raikom secretaries and instructors, and lectures and readings on specific topics prepared.[15]

Bulking particularly large in the 1936 protocols was the screening of Party documents, which served as an instrument of the continuing Party purge. In the early part of the year the obkom bureau was deeply involved in making arrangements for the exchange of Party cards, in providing necessary instruction to the raikoms, in checking on progress, and finally in seeing to it that the deadline for the completion of the exchange was met. At the same time the obkom bureau agenda was also filled with resolutions approving individual and group expulsions from the Party by lower Party organs. In theory all expulsions were supposed to be individual; in fact, on frequent occasions the Bureau approved entire lists of expulsions running into the hundreds.[16] In a number of cases the bureau acted on appeals for reinstatement by Party members who had been excluded by the raion Party organizations. A sampling of such cases indicates that in from one-fourth to one-third of the appeals, the expulsions were overruled. As 1936 wore on, and more particularly after the Central Committee circular "On the Terrorist Activity of the Trotskyite-Zinovievite Counterrevolutionary Bloc," there was a new accent on political vigilance, and the uncovering of "degenerates" in various Party organizations intensified. This, of course, tended to increase the scale of Party expulsions. By the end of the year the obkom bureau had approved more than 2,980 expulsions from Party ranks.[17]

Second only to matters of internal Party administration in importance were the recurring problems of agricultural production — sowing, harvesting, and fulfilling state delivery quotas. Spurred on by demands from the center, the obkom bureau in turn shifted the pressure to the raions, urging, imploring, and threatening in order to meet the agricultural goals set. There were times when the obkom bureau appeared almost indistinguishable from the Commissariat of Agriculture. In the spring when the sowing was getting under way, the protocols of the bureau were filled with draft proposals for the allocation of seed supplies, plans for spreading fertilizer, projects for tractor repair, and schedules establishing work norms and deadlines for each task.[18] The raikoms were bombarded with instructions to check the MTS's and collective farms under their jurisdiction and were informed that the obkom would closely inspect the measures which they had taken.

Even as the spring sowing was already beginning, the obkom bureau passed a resolution on April 4 demanding a struggle for a higher harvest and setting down specific yields to be obtained from every hectare according to type of crop.[19] A few days later, however, the bureau was forced to note that many of the collective farms were still not ready for sowing, owing to the poor condition of their horses, failure to sort the seeds, and so on. Obkom delegates were sent out to the countryside to investigate and prod.[20] The obkom also took stock of current performance in meat deliveries and observed that the first quarter results were "completely unsatisfactory." The raions were ordered to conduct a thorough investigation and to improve matters within ten days.[21]

In mid-April the bureau began to devote its attention to planning delivery quotas for various agricultural staples. Detailed quotas were set for individual raions for flax, hemp, hay, and milk. However, even as late as mid-May, when the first plans for hay-cutting were already being drafted, the obkom bureau paused to note its dissatisfaction with poor MTS performance in the spring sowing. In a number of areas the spring work was still substantially unfulfilled, and again remedial measures had to be taken.[22]

As the summer wore on, preparations for the harvest overshadowed other concerns. The first stages of the harvesting operation apparently left something to be desired, and soon urgent messages were being sent to raikom secretaries, RIK (raion executive committee) chairmen, MTS directors, RaiZO (raion agricultural) officials and others, reminding them of the "obligations undertaken to Comrade Stalin" and urging them not only to meet their commitments but also to surpass them.[23] There were references to harvesting losses (estimated as running between 10 and 15 per cent), and raion newspapers were alerted by the bureau to organize campaigns to combat this evil.

With the harvesting still in full swing, preparations were already being made for fall plowing and winter sowing. Soon there was a steady , stream of instructions on the storage of food supplies, repairs, veterinary inspections, the disinfection of animals and barns, etc.[24]

As the year's end approached, tension mounted as the obkom became concerned over the failure of some raions to meet their commitments. Frantic telegrams were dispatched demanding that "all measures" be taken to fulfill the plan. A message dated December 8 and addressed to chairmen of village soviets and kolkhozes complained that the flax delivery plan was not being fulfilled, although Kaluga Oblast had met its plan long ago, adding that "we must remind you of the obligations undertaken by the Oblast before the country, the government and the leader of the people STALIN." This message was to be read in all kolkhozes, and "all measures" were to be taken to meet the plan by December 20.[25]

Even while the final stocktaking was in progress and the collective farms were calculating their income, the year 1937 was making its claim on the obkom's attention. As early as September the 1937 meat delivery quotas had already been prepared, and by the time December came around preparations for the coming year's "agricultural battle" were far advanced. MTS cadres were being sent to special courses; political training programs were organized; there were refresher courses for collective farm chairmen; fertilizer plans were drafted; and posters and leaflets printed for the spring sowing campaign.[26]

The battle for agricultural production was a round-the-clock concern of the obkom bureau. Each season had its special tasks and its special problems; but the paramount concern was to fulfill the goals set by the center. Nor was the obkom expected merely to deal with the pressures of the moment. There were also plans for long-range improvements to be prepared, generally within the framework of all-Union plans ordered by the Central Committee and the Council of People's Commissars. One such plan, for example, involved provisions for the purchase of breeding bulls and measures to assure an increase in the number of horses and horned cattle. Another issue which preoccupied the obkom during this time was the question of collective farm reorganization, involving changes in size and jurisdiction, presumably to establish a more rationalized pattern of management and control. These long-range measures, however, were generally overshadowed by the immediate emergencies which cried out for action. As one reads the protocols, one is made increasingly aware of the atmosphere of crisis and urgency which pervades them. In this setting the pressure to devote one's energies to immediate problems was almost irresistible.

Given the nature of the economy in the Western Oblast, it was perhaps inevitable that agriculture was in the forefront of the obkom's attention. In comparison industrial problems received far less consideration. To some extent this registered the relatively retarded industrial development of the region, but it probably also reflected the higher degree of centralized control in the industrial area. In industries of all-Union or republic significance, the major initiative lay in Moscow, rather than in Smolensk. In the case of regional and local industry, however, the protocols make clear that the obkom bureau was far from inactive. Indeed, it participated directly in the planning process, set goals, and checked on their execution. It devoted considerable attention to various construction projects and related problems of brick production, and its repeated intervention in this area may suggest that this was a particularly troublesome problem. Appointments of heads of factories and construction projects and Party secretaries in important enterprises required the approval of the obkom bureau, though, outside of the Party sphere, the bureau merely ratified appointments which were initiated in the hierarchy of the commissariats. The obkom bureau also played an active role in planning meetings and campaigns to popularize the Stakhanovite movement, and it was, of course, constantly giving consideration and direction to Party activities in the factories and enterprises of the oblast.

The dominant position of the obkom bureau in regulating the life of the oblast can be documented in every protocol of its meetings. In its relationship with all oblast governmental organs, the supremacy of the obkom was clearly apparent. The oblispolkom was subordinate to the obkom. Its personnel was "recommended" by the obkom; even the dates of its meetings were set by the obkom.[27] Many important decrees were issued over the joint signature of the obkom first secretary and the chairman of the oblispolkom, but even in such cases the content of the decrees was almost invariably first approved by the obkom bureau. The departments of the oblispolkom reported directly to the obkom bureau as well as to their superiors in their own governmental chain of command.[28] The Party raikoms and gorkoms, of course, operated under the immediate direction of the obkom, but even the raiispolkoms (RIK's) frequently appealed directly to the obkom for funds or for assistance on one matter or another. The obkom bureau designated the individuals it desired to have elected as RIK chairmen; the task of the raikoms was to "arrange" such elections. Indeed, with the possible exception of the army and the NKVD, there was no organized activity in the oblast which was free from the bureau's guidance and direction. A leafing of the protocols unfolds a miscellany of resolutions on such diverse topics as the Atheist League and the Aero Club, a celebration of the Pushkin jubilee, an increase in the print order of a newssheet at a construction project, an authorization of funds for needy students and for the purchase of portraits of Party leaders, vacation leaves for Party and governmental officials in the oblast and the raions, authorization to rename a theater and factory after Rumyantsev, and a host of other matters, large and small.

Generally illuminating as the protocols are, they remain obscure on the relations between the obkom bureau and the military and NKVD officials in the area. While Uborevich, the Commander of the Western Military District, was a member of the obkom bureau, his role in the bureau does not emerge in clear focus. As has already been noted, he rarely attended bureau meetings, and there is no evidence in the protocols of the bureau that it concerned itself with military affairs, aside from assisting in the preparation of mobilization plans and in the annual call-up of recruits for the army. Presumably in this case the lines of Party control ran directly from the Central Committee in Moscow through the Political Administration of the army, which functioned as a branch of the Central Committee secretariat.

In the case of the NKVD the protocols also leave many questions unanswered. The leading officials of the oblast and raion NKVD offices were listed in the nomenklatura of the obkom, but the records of actions taken on NKVD appointments indicate that it was the NKVD itself which proposed appointments or removals, and that it was the obkom bureau which "accepted the proposal." There is clear evidence in the Archive that the Party committees recommended Party members for police work.[29] On occasion, the obkom bureau intervened locally, to secure the removal of a raion NKVD head, but presumably such actions were coördinated with higher NKVD officials, and the replacements in any case were provided by the NKVD itself with Party ratification. There is also evidence that Party officials were forbidden to interfere in NKVD operative work or to detach NKVD employees from their police assignments for other emergency Party or governmental activities.[30] At the same time, the Party cells in NKVD units operated under the direct supervision of the raion and obkom Party authorities. It was also customary for both raion and oblast NKVD officials to supply copies of many

of their reports to the Party leadership in their areas, though almost certainly some reports which would have had unwelcome repercussions in Party circles were dispatched only to NKVD superiors. Altogether, the impression derived from the Archive is that the operative or secret police work of the NKVD in the Western Oblast was largely free from obkom supervision during the mid-thirties. In this case, as with the army, effective control was exercised by Stalin and his secretariat in Moscow rather than by the Party authorities in Smolensk.

Relations with the Center

Relations with the center posed a particularly difficult problem for the Smolensk Party leaders. In the Western Oblast they were little lords, but, like other oblast aristocracy, they had to cringe before the great lords of Moscow. Rumyantsev, the first secretary, was a not unimportant figure in the Party. At the Seventeenth Party Congress in 1934 he had been named a full member of the Central Committee, one of seventy-one similarly honored, but the Great Man of Smolensk was under constant pressure from the center to meet what must at times have seemed unattainable production and delivery goals, and he had more than his share of difficulties in dealing with those who brought the pressure to bear. The Archive contains a rather poignant letter written by Rumyantsev on October 10, 1933, which illustrates the process at work.[31]

I am sending this note to all secretaries in flax raions — and here is why. The other day [October 8] I was with Comrades Chernov and Radchenko in Moscow, and saw the first summaries on the deliveries of flax fiber and seeds in all the oblasts, and I could hardly believe my eyes.

Delivered	Flax seed	Flax fiber
Leningrad Oblast	100.0%	14.1%
Moscow Oblast	98.5%	10.8%
Ivanov Oblast	96.5%	11.8%
Western Oblast	42.6%	0.6%

As you see, Leningrad has already completed deliveries and Moscow and Ivanov will finish in a day or two. But on this date we have delivered 42%. Leningrad has delivered 14% of the flax fiber. Moscow and Ivanov have fulfilled the plan 11–12%, but we have delivered only a few tons. Together with this, all the above oblasts delivered the first portions of flax of a quality higher than their assignments according to grade, while we from the very beginning delivered a grade 1¼ times lower than our assignments.

On the next day [the 9th] I was with Comrades Kaganovich and Molotov, and was forced to hear from them very unflattering warnings in regard to this. Don't think that I have exaggerated one word or laid it on thick. I report this in the most honest way.

In regard to flax, only the Urals, Byelorussia, and Siberia are behind us. But you certainly know that these oblasts do not noise it about in the whole

т. Криницкому-Локтеву

Эту записку послал всем секретарям льняных районов - и вот почему. Был на днях (8 октября) у т.т. Чернова и Радченко в Москве, видел первые сводки по заготовкам льноволокна и семян по всем областям и прямо сам себе не верил.

		ЗАГОТОВЛЕНО ЛЬНОСЕМЯН	ЛЬНОВОЛОКНА
Ленинградская область		100%	14.1%
Западная	-"-	42,6	0,6
Ивановская	-"-	96,5	11,8
Московская	-"-	98,6	10,8

Как видишь, Ленинград уже сдал, Москва и Иваново закончат через день - два. У нас же на это число 42%. Ленинград сдал 14% льноволокна. Москва и Иваново по 11-12% выполнили, а мы всего лишь несколько тонн. Наряду с этим, все упомянутые области первые партии льна сдали по качеству выше своих заданий по номерности, а мы с первых же дней сдали на полтора номера по качеству ниже своих заданий.

На другой день (9-го числа) был у т.т.Кагановича и Молотова, где уже пришлось выслушать от них очень нелестно предупреждения по поводу этого факта. Не подумай, что я хоть одно слово преувеличил или сгустил краски. Самым, что называется честным образом сообщаю это.

По льну сзади нас только Урал, Белоруссия и Сибирь. Но ведь ты знаешь, что эти области и не шумят на весь Союз, что они "льноводная база", пуп земли по льну. Вот в чем дело то.

Вывод по моему тут один. Со льном мы провалили, и сейчас, пока дело не совсем упущено, надо наверстать во что бы то ни стало, иначе для нас, как партийных руководителей, позор, а для государства и колхозов от этого большие убытки.

Где причины? По моему мы преступно затянули с отстилом соломки, все ждали для сушки и обмолота хорошей погоды. Лен долго был под дождями в бабках и как результат этого - не только упустили темпы в обработке и заготовках льна, но навредили здорово качеству волокна. А семя - просто половину сгноили. Это надо признать. Только Ржев, Старица полностью и еще два - три района частично сумели избежать этого.

А как сейчас идет дело с под"емом со стлищ? Тоже ни к чорту негоже. Дифференцированного подхода к этому процессу нет. С под"емом льна уже запаздываем, а где и подняли лен, то не свезли еще его в овины. Обработка же не развернута вовсе. Все еще раскачиваемся.

Что касается пеньки, то тут дело еще хуже.

Можно ли поправить дело ? Конечно можно. Стоит лишь Вам, не теряя ни одного дня, как следует нажать, и если Вы по партийному возьметесь сами спасать положение.

Почему я льняшкам пишу об этом? Очень боюсь за лен. Ведь мы область льняная и ЦК совершенно правильно будет требовать и ценить нашу работу именно на примере успешного выполнения этой работы, и какие бы ни были у нас достижения по хлебу и картошке

A secret letter from Rumyantsev, the oblast first secretary, about the reaction of Molotov and Kaganovich to failures in Western Oblast flax deliveries — October 10, 1933.

Union that they are a "flax cultivation base," the center of the earth in regard to flax. That is the point.

There can be only one conclusion, in my opinion. We have lagged behind with regard to flax, and now since things are not yet lost, it is necessary to make up for lost time in any way possible; otherwise, for you as Party leaders, there will be disgrace, and the state and the kolkhozniks will suffer great losses . . .

Why do I write about this? I am very much afraid about the flax. For we are a flax oblast, and the Central Committee completely correctly will make demands and evaluate our work precisely on the basis of the successful fulfillment of this work, and whatever achievements we show in regard to bread and potatoes (if we still do) everything will be canceled out if there is a failure in the flax sector. The Central Committee will beat us roundly if we do not correct the situation immediately . . .

If I had known about this situation in regard to flax several days earlier, I would on no account have allowed Rakitov and other members of the Bureau to ask the Central Committee for permission for a vacation for me. What the devil kind of a vacation would it be if you were persecuted all the time with the constant thought of failure . . .

I think this is all I wanted to say to all of you. Again I emphasize the great seriousness . . . of the flax situation, and I beg you to harvest as you should and to correct the situation immediately.

P.S. If you have business, write. Get the address from Tikhomirov.

As this letter reveals, the situation of the obkom secretary was far from enviable. The center held him responsible for results, and if he failed to deliver, the price of failure was disgrace, demotion, or even worse. Faced with constant demands from the center, the obkom secretary had no alternative except to shift the pressure to his subordinates in the raions: to cajole, persuade, storm, and threaten in order to extract contributions from them which would make it possible to meet oblast goals.

But there were also times when the obkom secretary had to be a middleman or broker, mediating between the rock-bottom needs of his constituents and the niggardly resources which the center made available to meet them. As a representative of the interests of the oblast, and indeed as a condition of his own survival, the oblast secretary had to press for allocations of supplies to the oblast, for budgetary appropriations which would enable him to fulfill the commitments which the center imposed on him. In periods of distress, such as harvest failures, he had to plead for a lifting of the burden, for special assistance which was infrequently and only grudgingly forthcoming. What was required was negotiating skill of a high order, but it had to be supported by an over-all record of successful performance of function. The long reign of Rumyantsev in Smolensk (1929–1937) testified to his adroitness in navigating between central and local pressures, though when disgrace finally came, it was complete and crushing.

From the point of view of the oblast Party leadership, relations with the center represented both opportunity and threat. On the one hand, the center was the source from which recognition came and blessings flowed. It was the center which conferred promotions and rewards, perquisites and privileges. On the other hand, the center also was a constant menace. Its demands were voracious and ever-increasing. It respected achievement, but it had no patience for excuses. Its conduct frequently seemed, and was, suspicious and capricious. Moscow under Stalin was a jealous and hard taskmaster who brooked no contradiction and whose whims were tantamount to commands.

The pressure of the center was felt in a variety of ways. First, there was the constant bombardment of the oblast by central directives, ordering this or that action and frequently prescribing procedures in excruciating detail. These directives were of all types and varieties. At the most general level there was the problem of keeping the oblast and raion Party leadership informed of changes in the political line and of the guiding priorities of the top leadership. Formal instructions were buttressed by unofficial contacts. During most of the period when Rumyantsev served as a member of the Central Committee, it can be presumed that his relations with Moscow were reasonably good, and that his frequent trips to the capital kept him fairly well in touch with the way the political winds were blowing. But beyond such informal channels, there were also formal communications to the oblast which were designed to provide official guidance. Copies of the protocols of sessions of the Central Committee and of joint plenums of the Central Committee and the Central Control Commission were forwarded both to the obkom and to the secretaries of raikoms, though each copy was numbered and labeled top secret, and had to be returned to Moscow through the NKVD courier service after a few days. (While the Smolensk Archive contains many receipts indicating that the documents had passed through raikom channels, unfortunately there are no copies of the protocols themselves, an indication that in this case at least security precautions apparently operated with air-tight efficiency.) In addition to these protocols, there were occasional top-secret circular letters, also numbered and reaching down to the raikom secretaries, which dealt with transcendent issues of the time. There are a number of such documents in the Archive, including the dramatic Stalin-Molotov letter of May 8, 1933, on arrest and deportation abuses in connection with collectivization and dekulakization and the closed letter of the Central Committee of July 29, 1936, which preceded the Zinoviev-Kamenev trial, on the "Terrorist Activity of the Trotskyite-Zinovievite Counterrevolutionary Bloc." [32] These letters in effect put the lower Party organs on notice of an important impending development, provided guidance as to how to treat it, and enabled the regional authorities to make advance plans for exploiting it in accordance with the wishes of the center.

The central directives in the Smolensk Archive tend to concentrate in two areas: Party affairs and economic problems. Although a few are general in scope and leave room for flexible application in the oblast, the great majority run to explicitness of detail and appear designed to allow a minimum exercise of discretion on the part of lower Party and governmental organs.

Some examples from the Party sphere may serve both to illustrate the rigidity which characterized these directives, the difficulties of enforcement which they created, and the techniques of evasion which they generated. On March 13, 1928, the Central Committee of the Party issued a decree "On the Definition of the Social Position of Communists Admitted into the Party." [33] The decree sought to classify all Party members and candidates in one of three categories — as workers, peasants, or employees — on the basis of their chief occupation or position in production before entrance into the Party. The decree was supplemented by instructions running over many pages which attempted to anticipate all contingencies and to lay down water-tight rules that would insure uniformity of treatment and would require only mechanical application by lower Party organs. At this time and for many years after, admission into the Party was made easier for those who could claim the social position of workers, and local Party organizations were under pressure to increase their worker component. Many local Party organizations responded to this pressure either by manipulating their records to show a higher worker membership than in fact existed, or by permitting Party members to claim worker status when they were not entitled to it. Thus an investigation in the Western Oblast ordered by the Central Committee in 1934 established that

the Roslavl raikom gave information that there were 120 Communist factory workers in the organization and a total of 292 workers by occupation. Actually, after the investigation it turned out that there were only 47 factory workers and a total of 149 workers by occupation. In the Smolensk organization the number of workers according to social status was crudely upped in comparison with the real situation by 10–24 per cent in various organizations. According to type of occupation, instead of the 1,618 Communist workers in production indicated by the city raikom, actually there were 888. The same crude discrepancies occur in information on the Party nucleus in the Komsomol . . .[34]

The obkom blamed this "tendency to exaggerate" on the "formal" attitude of local Party organizations in dealing with the problem; what it could not disclose was that there were built-in pressures to exaggerate deriving from the demands of the center for Party proletarianization. The difficulty of fulfilling these demands led to the evasion of even the most precisely worded directive.

Another example may serve to illustrate that detailed instructions do not necessarily guarantee specific performance. The directives of the Special Section of the Central Committee on the handling of secret documents were precise and inclusive. Only persons who had been checked by the security police could handle such documents. The rules for the storage and the use of secret files, for wrapping and sending secret packages, and for returning them to the point of origin were explicit in the extreme, and penalties for violation were drastic. Yet in fact, human frailty and carelessness being what they are, even among Communists, the actual observance of these conspiratorial restrictions left much to be desired. On April 1, 1931, Rumyantsev addressed a letter to all raikom secretaries which read in part as follows:

In the obkom there is information on cases of the raikoms divulging the secrets . . . of the Central Committee and the obkom and of violation of the rules of secrecy in using . . . materials.

Concretely . . .

1. The rules for preliminary checking by the organs of the GPU of workers of the apparatus who have access to secret correspondence are not observed.

2. Top-secret materials sent by the obkom, series "k" (protocols of closed sessions of the Bureau, protocols of the three-man commission on dekulakization, correspondence on mobilization work) are not received and opened in the raikom personally by the secretary or his deputy, but often by workers of the apparatus, and even by people not investigated and not allowed access to the secret correspondence by the organs of the GPU.

3. Despite the special instructions (in the same document) on forbidding the removal of copies, copies are removed and distributed without an indication of the number of typed copies and [the person] to whom each copy was sent.

4. The rules for safeguarding and return of secret materials are violated. Documents are kept in plain desks (instead of safes), together with ordinary correspondence. They remain on tables when people leave; they are returned to the obkom after much delay and after a number of reminders, and in some cases not through the field communications [of the OGPU], but by regular delivery (although they are "especially important"). There are cases of answers to top-secret requests and directives by open telegrams.

5. Broad layers of Party members are acquainted with some materials (without special obkom permission), sometimes with reference to a decision of the Central Committee and the obkom . . .

The practice of detailed protocoling at closed meetings of the descriptive part of the question, where basic and completely detailed figures and other data are brought in, has not been eliminated, and at closed meetings materials are distributed (draft proposals, numerical and other materials, etc.), without exact control over their return.

In order to insure maximum secrecy in the use of top-secret materials of the Central Committee and the obkom, I order you immediately to eliminate the above shortcomings . . .[35]

In citing these examples, however, the object is not to imply that central directives were regularly flouted, or that there was a direct correlation between the rigidity of the directive and the extent to which it was disregarded in the field. Indeed, the more usual pattern was to try to follow the precise instructions from above so far as that was humanly possible. But there were also many cases where self-interest, sheer human incapacity, or the obdurate realities of the local situation contributed to make rigid adherence to the prescriptions of the center a virtual impossibility.

The difficulties the center created for the oblast received their most vivid illustration in the central directives dealing with economic questions. These directives typically set annual targets which the oblast was supposed to fulfill or overfulfill. Thus in the sphere of agriculture the oblast was given a set of delivery quotas for flax, grain, meat, milk, and other products; in the sphere of industry production norms were set for each factory; and it was the responsibility of the oblast Party authorities to make certain that they were met. Once the delivery quotas in agriculture were established, for example, it was up to the oblast authorities to break them down and redistribute them among the raions. The oblast authorities, in other words, were judged by their success in extracting the necessary supplies from the raions under their jurisdiction. The higher the oblast quotas, the greater were the burdens on the raions and the greater were the difficulties encountered by the oblast leadership in meeting its goals. The drive from the center, moreover, was always in the direction of lifting the quotas, since Moscow itself was under pressure to supply the rapidly growing industrial centers projected by the Five Year Plans.

The Smolensk Archive sheds little light on how exactly the central leadership established its quotas for the Western Oblast. There is evidence to indicate that the oblast planning authorities participated in the process, but the final determinations clearly were made in Moscow, and the tone of Rumyantsev's letters indicates that the center's demands never erred on the low side. Since the Western Oblast was the premier flax-producing province, its performance in this sector was crucial. The record here is one of constantly increasing demands and of great difficulty in meeting them. Rumyantsev's unpleasant interview with Molotov and Kaganovich in October 1933 has already been cited. At the end of the next year, December 31, 1934, a top-secret telegram signed by Stalin and Molotov noted "an impermissible lag in fulfilling the plan for flax collection" and declared that the obkom secretary would be held "personally responsible for checking on the fulfillment by the raikoms and the raion executive committees of the decrees of the Central Committee . . . on flax collection and for severely punishing those guilty of lack of activity in organizing flax collections." [36] A final deadline of February 1, 1935, was established for the fulfillment of the plan, and the obkom secretary was required to report to Moscow every five days "on measures taken and progress in the collection of flax." This telegram was transmitted by Rumyantsev to all raikom secretaries in flax-producing regions, and they in turn were ordered to report at five-day intervals, and to indicate the names of raikom bureau members and members of the presidium of the raion executive committee who had been assigned to each village to check on flax procurement. It should be added that this final demand frcm Rumyantsev came on the heels of a number of earlier pleas, including a personal letter of September 19, 1934, in which he wrote all raikom secretaries, ". . . I earnestly beg you not to delay the important work in flax and hemp . . . Let us deliver the flax by the October holidays, and let us deliver good flax . . ." [37] But despite the cajoling and threats, the flax quotas still were not fulfilled.

Another example may provide even clearer insight into the problem. On September 11, 1934, the obkom leadership received a secret telegram signed by Stalin and Molotov. The telegram read in part,

> In view of the fact that the grain reserves which are at the disposal of the state in accordance with the state grain delivery plan will be significantly smaller in comparison with those of last year . . . and with the growing demand of the country for grain, an exceptionally tense situation has been created in regard to supplying the country with grain during the current year.
> The Central Committee and the Council of People's Commissars emphasize especially that the outcome of supplying the country with grain depends completely upon the successful fulfillment of the minimum plan for purchasing 200,000,000 puds of grain . . . Failure to fulfill the grain purchasing plan will unavoidably lead to catastrophic consequences in supplying the country with food.[38]

In accordance with this directive, the Western Oblast was given its grain purchasing quota, and told to redistribute it among the raions within three days. It was also ordered to report on the progress of the grain purchases at five-day intervals and informed that goods worth 20,500,000 rubles in retail prices would be assigned to the Western Oblast to induce kolkhozniks to sell grain to the state. As usual the oblast leadership was also warned that it would be held responsible for results and "would pay the penalty for failure to fulfill the grain purchasing plan within the time limits established . . ."

On September 17, 1934, the obkom sent copies of this telegram to all raikoms and informed each raion of its quota. The message to the Kozelsk raikom read in part as follows:

> In accordance with the decree of the Central Committee . . . and the USSR Council of People's Commissars "On Purchasing Grain from the Harvest of 1934" . . . the Bureau of the Obkom and the Presidium of the Oblast Executive Committee have determined an obligatory grain purchasing quota

of 1,000 tons for your raion, including 650 tons of food crops (rye and wheat).

The time limit for fulfilling your grain-purchasing quota is set for November 1, with 400 tons to come in September and 600 tons in October.[39]

The raions were ordered to set quotas for each kolkhoz in accordance with their yields, to hold meetings with kolkhozniks to explain the program, and especially to make clear that the government was issuing goods in order to stimulate grain sales. The letter, signed jointly by Rumyantsev and Rakitov, concluded, "Despite the significant size of the grain purchasing assignments, our oblast, which this year has had a good harvest of grain, potatoes, vegetables, and other agricultural crops, is obliged in one way or another to fulfill the established grain-purchasing quota for the state completely and on time." [40]

On September 23, 1934 the Kozelsk raikom and executive committee dispatched an interim report to Smolensk. It reported fulfillment of the plan by twenty-four village soviets out of twenty-eight, but quoted no tonnage or percentage figures. But it also noted difficulties:

We have received no goods for inducing grain purchases except manufactured goods valued at 3,100 rubles. The kolkhozes and kolkhozniks mainly demand the following goods: nails, glass, kerosene, salt, sugar, dry goods, and shoes . . . There are cases where in certain kolkhozes the grain-purchasing plan is either not accepted, or is accepted with reductions. There are cases where individual Communists and Komsomol members have begun to hamper the grain purchasing. In the kolkhoz "Krasnyi Kazak" . . . the secretary of the Komsomol organization . . . openly stated at a general meeting that of the proposed plan of 40 centners, the kolkhoz was in a position to fulfill only 10 centners. In the kolkhoz "Novaya Derevnya" [New Country] . . . the Party organizer . . . spoke out against grain purchases. In the kolkhoz "Pamyat Lenina" [The Memory of Lenin] . . . the chairman of the kolkhoz . . . who was expelled from the Party two years ago, came out with roughly the following speech at a kolkhoz meeting: that the decision of the government on grain purchases was nowhere made public and that there was no decision, that grain purchases were made by the oblast or raion; that in his opinion the raikom and the raion executive committee make grain purchases on their own initiative, and that the Party should make them responsible for this, and . . . that the proposed grain-purchasing plan for this kolkhoz ought not to be fulfilled. Another kolkhoznik . . . stated that we should supply ourselves with grain [and asked] of what concern the general interests of the state are to us. It must be noted that we observed most opposition to carrying out the grain purchases in kolkhozes which are economically stable and in which there is good pay for a working day . . .[41]

This gloomy report was followed on October 25, 1934, by an anguished plea to Rumyantsev and Rakitov to reduce the raion grain-purchasing quota from 1,000 tons to 900 tons.[42] The Archive contains no record of a favorable response to this plea, or indeed of any response. It can be presumed on the basis of other somewhat similar cases that any reply would probably have been in the negative. The pressures under which the oblast itself operated left it no other alternative.

As these examples perhaps make clear, the central directives in the economic area set goals or targets for the oblasts which they were expected to fulfill under threat of severe penalty for failure. Whether they succeeded in fulfilling them depended on the ingenuity with which they were able to marshal the resources available to them in the oblast. The system was one of continuing and unceasing pressure, and the oblast and raion apparatus served as the transmission belt to communicate the pressure to the grass-roots enterprises in the countryside and in the towns. The ultimate arbiters of success or failure were the peasants in the kolkhozes and the workers in the factories, and beyond a certain point they could neither be driven nor cajoled. But weak links in the apparatus of control — in the regional and local Party and governmental organs — could also spell disaster, and consequently one finds the center developing an elaborate network of controls and procedures to check the quality and reliability of its subordinate regional and local organs.

Some of these controls will be analyzed in far greater detail in Chapters 8, 9, and 20, but their general character, in so far as the Archive reveals them, can perhaps usefully be sketched at this point. First, there was the reporting system which the center utilized to keep informed of developments in the oblast. Reports were transmitted to the center through various channels — some Party, some governmental, and some police. The Party reports were ordinarily sent to the Central Committee secretariat, where instructors specializing in the affairs of the Western Oblast collated and digested them. Protocols of obkom bureau sessions had to be dispatched within three days after their conclusion, and similar protocols of plenums of the obkom and other oblast Party conferences were regularly sent to the Central Committee secretariat.[43] The obkom secretary also filed a biannual report on the state of the Party organization in the Western Oblast, and an informational-accounting report on Party organization and membership at intervals of two months. The lines of communication between the obkom and the Central Committee secretariat also ran in specialized channels according to functional interests. Thus the Division of Leading Party Organs in the obkom secretariat corresponded with and reported directly to its opposite number in the Central Committee secretariat, and the Agitprop Division in Smolensk received instructions from and sent reports on its activity to the Agitprop Division of the Central Committee secretariat. Thus too the oblast Party Control Commission in Smolensk reported regularly to the Central Control Commission in Moscow and received periodic instructions from it. From time to time, moreover, oblast Party officials were summoned to Moscow to report orally or to participate in conferences which took place under the aegis of one or another branch of the Central Committee secretariat, and the Central Committee instructors in turn periodically visited the oblast.

In addition to these regular commitments, there was a constant flow of special reports prepared at the instance of one of the Central Committee secretaries or of the branches reporting to them. The scope and character of these reports varied with the paramount preoccupations of the central Party leadership and the nature of the emergencies which it was currently confronting. Frequently the demand for these reports was stimulated by news of deficiencies of performance in particular sectors of the economic or political life of the Western Oblast. The example cited earlier in connection with the oblast failure to meet flax procurement goals is typical. In such cases it was customary for the center to intensify its pressure by requiring the oblast to report at frequent intervals directly to Stalin and Molotov, so that the center could both keep itself well informed of progress and signal its continuing concern.

At the same time there were other channels through which a constant stream of reports flowed in to the center. Every central governmental commissariat which had subordinate enterprises or activities in the Western Oblast had its own special representative at Smolensk, and received reports from him as well as from those more directly in charge of particular enterprises or activities in the oblast. The chairman of the oblispolkom reported on the affairs under his jurisdiction to the Council of People's Commissars of the RSFSR. Of particular importance, at least under Stalin, were the reports which came to the center through the organs of the OGPU, and its successor the NKVD. Since this channel of communication operated more or less free from the control of the oblast Party and governmental authorities, it provided an independent check on the situation in the oblast on which Stalin and his cohorts apparently relied heavily. The police reports which are available in the Archive are wide-ranging in their coverage. Not only do they supply a frank appraisal of the political mood of the oblast and a wealth of specific detail on the utterances and activities of those deemed politically unreliable; they also report extensively on abuses of power by Party and governmental officials and call attention to failures of performance in many sectors of the regional economy. Not infrequently they stimulated drastic intervention by the center in the affairs of the oblast.

In addition to the formal reporting which has already been described, there was also a rich flow of informal reporting from the oblast to Moscow which frequently helped the center to identify trouble spots and to take the necessary action to eliminate or ameliorate them. The

Archive contains many hundreds of letters of complaint written by peasants, workers, and employees in the oblast, most of them addressed to the central press, but also sometimes to Kalinin, Stalin, the Central Committee of the Party, or to various commissariats of the central government. These letters will be discussed in greater detail in Chapter 20; at this point it is perhaps sufficient to note that, though the great majority of them were forwarded to the oblast authorities for disposition, some at least furnished the basis for central investigations which served as a not unimportant checkup on the oblast apparatus. On occasion the follow-up took the form of press exposure based on investigation of the incidents by assigned newspaper correspondents; on other occasions special Party commissions visited the oblast and made recommendations founded on inquiries on the spot. The revelation of the Smolensk scandal of 1928 which led to a complete overturn in the guberniya Party leadership was preceded by a number of letters calling attention to abuses in the guberniya.

Given the existence of this complex network of central controls, one may well wonder how, in the face of it, it was possible to develop the kind of quasi-independent satrapies over which Pavlyuchenko presided in the late twenties and which Rumyantsev consolidated in the period between 1929 and 1937. The Smolensk Archive provides some hints, but it does not yield a completely satisfactory answer. One may infer, first, that the central controls which looked so all-inclusive and deeply penetrating on paper did not in fact operate with the thoroughness and dispatch it is so easy to attribute to them. In the second place, the very multiplication of central controls generated its own local counterpressures, which took the form of strengthening regional and local barricades against intervention by the central authorities. Both the Pavlyuchenko and the Rumyantsev regimes in Smolensk provide vivid examples of that familiar Soviet phenomenon, the so-called family circle with its effort to build an ever-widening entourage that embraces the key points of power in the area and seeks to suppress or regulate the type of criticism on which effective central control depends. Under the cover of such arrangements for mutual protection, it was apparently possible for all kinds of local abuses to flourish for months and even years, simply because the guberniya or oblast leadership had put together an effective machine which at least temporarily maintained its own discipline. In the third place, the regional leaders tended ultimately to be judged in terms of their over-all success or failure in meeting the political and economic goals that the center set for them. As long as the oblast managed a margin of achievement which was roughly satisfactory, the center presumably was not inclined to inquire too closely into the methods used to obtain such results or even into the abuses that attended them.

Yet even under the most favorable conditions, there was always a very considerable element of instability in the reign of the Smolensk satraps. For one thing, one could never be certain that the family circle was complete, or that one or another member might not be tempted to vie for the favor of the center by exposing the sins of his neighbors. For another, there were some channels of communication with the center, notably the NKVD reports and the flow of grass-roots correspondence and denunciation, which could never wholly be controlled or blocked off. And finally, there was an implacable gauntlet that had constantly to be run, the race of production in which, to borrow from Alice, one had always to run twice as fast in order to remain in the same place.

Relations between the Oblast and Raion Party Organizations

If relations with the center posed the kind of problem in which the center was the hunter and the oblast the pursued, the roles were reversed when one turned to relations between the oblasts and raions. Now it was the oblast which was the hunter and the raions which were the pursued. The pressure from the center on the oblast was transmitted from the oblast to the raions, and the same problems of compliance and evasion reappeared in a not dissimilar guise.

One of the central issues in oblast-raion relationships was the control of appointments of key raion Party and governmental personnel. Just as the oblast sought to free itself from effective central control by converting the oblast leadership into a family group, so the raion leadership too tried to protect itself against the oblast by building its own inviolable sanctuary. In this process the appointing power was of prime importance. Legally, all leading Party and governmental workers of the raions were listed on the nomenklatura of the oblast, and indeed in some cases, for example the first and second secretaries of the raikoms, the appointments even required the ratification of the Central Committee of the Party. Nevertheless, the raikom first secretary and the bureau of the raikom exercised considerable influence in designating their subordinate personnel; they made recommendations, urged the merits of particular candidates, and indeed in some cases took actions which virtually confronted the obkom with a *fait accompli*. At the same time the obkom was understandably jealous of its prerogatives. It recognized the strategic importance of controlling raion appointments in order to prevent local cliques from consolidating and therefore sought to make its intervention more than a mere formality.

Some examples from the Archive correspondence may serve to illustrate the tug of war between the oblast and raion Party authorities which appointments precipitated. The rules on the registration and selection of nomenklatura cadres, reiterated in an obkom bureau resolution of October 25, 1936, categorically forbade "the raikoms, gorkoms, and leaders of departments to transfer and remove workers who came under the jurisdiction of the obkom without the approval of the obkom." [44] Yet on November 19, 1936, obkom secretary Shilman found it necessary to address the following message to all raikom secretaries:

A number of raikoms violate the established procedure of appointing workers who come under the obkom nomenklatura. Thus the Novozybkovo raikom recommends a comrade who is being promoted as secretary of the "Revput" factory Party committee *after* this comrade's election at the general Party meeting, placing the obkom before an established fact. The same happened with the Duminichi raikom in the case of the promotion of the "Revolyutsioner" factory Party committee secretary. The Glavk-appointed director of the processing plant "Oster" arrived in Roslavl without previously presenting himself at the obkom.

The obkom recommends that the following procedure be followed:

1. In the case of promotion to a post included in the obkom nomenklatura, the raikom dispatch the nominee to the obkom and formalize the appointment only after receiving obkom sanction.

2. When a Party member arrives from another organization with a nomination from an economic or other organization to a post included in the obkom nomenklatura, the raikom includes him in its roles only *after* being shown an obkom authorization confirming the appointment. In all cases when the new arrival does not have an obkom authorization, the raikom must require him to report immediately to the obkom. [45]

The pressure from the raion to hold on to its team and, where possible, to control its own appointments finds frequent reflection in the Archive. Thus on July 18, 1935, Sorin, the first secretary of the Baryatino raikom wrote Shilman as follows:

Comrade Timoshkov, the head of the NKVD of our raion, has been working here since February 15, 1935, and now it has become known to us that Comrade Timoshkov is being transferred to oblast work. This leaves us with only two bureau members who remain from the last raion Party conference — myself and the RIK chairman . . . I strongly urge — and this is also the firm request of the raikom bureau — that Comrade Timoshkov be left in raion work. [46]

What action was taken on this request is not a matter of record, but in other instances the obkom was quite prepared to reject the preferences of the local leadership, in favor of installing its own candidates. Thus on November 14, 1936, Shilman wrote to Comrade Kovalev, then first secretary of the Belyi raikom:

With reference to the second secretary of the raikom, the situation is as follows: we cannot agree to the candidacy of your kultprop; he does not have experience in Party work; he is superficial; the Central Committee would not approve. We recommend to you for the post of second secretary Comrade

Karpovsky; he has been a member of the Party since 1927; he is a literate person; has been working for about three years in the Yartsevo raikom . . . knows agriculture well, is as a matter of fact the manager of the agricultural otdel of the Yartsevo raikom. Comrade Yakovlev does not want to let him go at all, but I have pushed him to it. A proper nomination, a man with a perspective for growth.

If you agree, we will send him to the Central Committee for confirmation. Until CC confirmation, where the matter may drag out, we will, with your approval, send him to you to work as unconfirmed second secretary (in the capacity of instructor). In this connection, the question of your leave will clearly drag out a little; you probably will not be able to go earlier than mid-October.[47]

On the same day, November 11, 1936, Shilman also found it necessary to dispatch a letter to another raikom secretary, Comrade Tishenkov of Safonovo, who had apparently protested sharply because his second secretary had been promoted to another post and a new second secretary had been named without his knowledge while he was away on vacation. Shilman's reply was placatory but firm:

Your letter surprised me extremely. When we summoned Podporenkov for discussions about promoting him as first secretary in Krasnyi, we suggested in his place a number of nominees. He himself named Comrade Rakhshensky. After talks with Rakhshensky, I sent his name to the CC for confirmation — there were some objections to him, but considering that Rakhshensky was being promoted by the Raikom itself, which knows him best of all, he was finally confirmed. If you were not in agreement with the nomination of Comrade Rakhshensky, you could have come to the Obkom a long time ago or phoned me. We were convinced that you were also backing Comrade Rakhshensky; as to your complaint that you were not consulted, this is why: you were on leave; we had to present a new nomination in the place of Comrade Podporenkov promptly; but we did not want to disturb you while you were on vacation.

Now with respect to the formalization of Comrade Rakhshensky's position — insofar as CC confirmation has not come through yet — it's expected any day now — don't install him yet, but in fact let him do the work formerly performed by Comrade Podporenkov.

As soon as we receive the CC resolution, you will summon the plenum and elect Rakhshensky second secretary. Since he is a member of the plenum, the question of his election can be resolved simply. It won't be necessary to coöpt him, and you can conduct a legal election . . .

With respect to my not wanting to talk with you, that's nonsense. It's I who see and hear you little; you sit quietly and never raise your voice — that's not proper.

Greetings,

SHILMAN[48]

These letters can be read at various levels. At their most obvious, they provide an insight into the procedures actually employed in making raion appointments, and they illustrate the sham character of local "elections" and the dominant role of the obkom in designating raion personnel. But beneath the surface, one also catches a glimpse of the pulling and hauling, with the raikom first secretary seeking to do everything in his power to build his own secure machine, while the obkom secretariat in turn seeks to project its own people into the strategic raikom jobs and to construct a reliable entourage composed of "promoted" Party workers who owe their good fortune to the action of the obkom. Once installed in raion posts, however, the "promoted" Party workers faced the same problems which plagued their predecessors and frequently ended up by building their own barricades against excessive oblast demands.

But obkom supervision over the raikoms was in no sense limited to appointments. It encompassed every activity in which the raikoms were engaged. There was a constant flow of instructions from Smolensk to the raikoms, and the instructions were usually specific and detailed, leaving the raikoms a minimum of discretion to exercise their own initiative. They covered such apparently minute topics as the percentage of women to be elected Selpo (village coöperative) chairmen and the number of collective farmers to be chosen as members of raion soviets; they provided precise rules for organizing mass radio-listening on the occasion of a session of the All-Union Congress of Soviets; they offered exact instructions on how to conduct meetings, what topics to discuss, and how to discuss them. In the all-important agricultural area the directives were frequently even more detailed. They specified when every collective farmer was to begin his work; when brigadiers were to issue their instructions (the evening before); when the sowing, the harvesting, and threshing were to start; what the norms should be for each crop per hectare; and exactly how the work was to be conducted with deadlines for the completion of each phase. This tendency to limit the discretion of the raions and to try to anticipate every contingency with a precise rule registered the centralistic bias of Soviet administration. It also reflected the fact that there was a sharp falling-off in the quality and dependability of the apparatus as one moved toward the grass roots. Lack of confidence in the raions thus reinforced the tendency toward tight controls.

At the same time there were some areas in which the obkom had to allow the raions to exercise a certain degree of initiative. It was manifestly difficult, for example, for the oblast authorities to fix delivery quotas for each collective farm in the oblast, and in this case, the obkom authorities assigned quotas for each raion as a whole, leaving it to the raion officials to subdivide their quotas among the kolkhozes of the raion. As has already been noted, the establishment of raion quotas was frequently the occasion for anguished protests. In the face of these protests, the obkom was almost invariably firm. It had its own quotas to meet, and they could not be met without maximum pressure on the raions. Indeed, the obkom usually arranged matters so that the sum of the quotas of the raions exceeded its own debt to the center. In this way it sought a safety factor to protect it against the possibility that one or another raion might fail to meet its commitments.

Obkom supervision of the raions, theoretically at least, was comprehensive and complete. Instructors on the staff of the obkom secretariat were supposed to keep in intimate touch with the groups of raions which were assigned to them. They visited the raions periodically, and they analyzed their reports. But communications between Smolensk and the raions did not always work as effectively as the rules specified. At a session on October 25, 1936, the obkom bureau noted "that the majority of the raikoms and gorkoms present protocols of the sessions of the bureaus, plenums, raion meetings, and the aktiv to the Obkom of the Party extremely irregularly and not on time and that they often send protocols signed by technical workers . . ." [49] The raikom and gorkom secretaries were ordered to send protocols of these sessions not later than three days after their conclusion. The obkom bureau also demanded that the raikoms and gorkoms present comprehensive reports on their activity once every four months, and additional informational and accounting material once every two months. The resolution read: "The raikoms and gorkoms in their accounts must report on the fulfillment of the directives of the Party and the Government, on the status of Party work, on measures for improving Party work, on their leadership of the economic, political, and cultural life of the raion and the town, on appointments and transfers of leading cadres, and on other aspects of their activity." [50]

Despite these requirements for reporting and periodic check-ups by oblast Party officials, the obkom bureau encountered real difficulty in keeping adequately informed of current developments in the raions. Not infrequently, its intervention did not come until a crisis had erupted. Sometimes the problem was one of breaking up too intimate a family group under the cover of which all manner of abuses were permitted to flourish in the raion. At other times the problem was one of bickering and squabbling raion leaders, whose differences could only be resolved by obkom action. The protocols of the obkom bureau record a number of such interventions. On June 25, 1936, for example, the bureau noted an "unhealthy" situation in the Baryatino raikom as a result of the fact that "the editor of the raion newspaper, Comrade Borobykin, instead of formulating in a businesslike manner before the raikom the question of aid to the newspaper, began to make narrow squabbling attacks on the raikom and on its secretary, Comrade Sorin, accusing the raikom without basis of suppressing self-criticism, of creating cliques among the leading workers of the raion." [51] It pointed out that "the head of the raion division of the NKVD, Comrade Petrovski, taking part in the raikom's decision on the poor work of Comrade Borobykin, at the same time supported Comrade Borobykin in his unfounded accusations against the leaders of the raikom, thus facilitating the rise of dissension." At the same time it accused the raikom of insufficient guidance of the raion newspaper, of having transferred the leadership of the newspaper to the assistant secretary of the raikom, and of having been unable to make the newspaper "a militant organ" of the raikom. It ordered the removal of Borobykin from his position, raised the question of whether the raion NKVD head should not also be removed "because of his poor work and two-faced behavior," and called upon the raikom to improve its "guidance of the newspaper."

Toward the end of the year the obkom bureau faced a somewhat similar crisis in the affairs of the Kardymovo raikom. In this case the raikom secretary found himself at odds with the chairman of the raion executive committee and the head of the raion section of the NKVD. On November 10, 1936, the obkom bureau intervened because the feud had led "to a deterioration of work in the raion and to serious backwardness in the fulfillment of very important agricultural decrees." [52] It noted that the raikom secretary had committed "serious mistakes" in his relationships with other members of the bureau, that he was guilty of "coarseness," not heeding the orders of the bureau, and that he "did not know how to rally the bureau of the raikom for the fulfillment of the tasks facing it, and did not eliminate abnormalities in his personal life." The RIK chairman and NKVD head, on the other hand, were accused of having "followed the incorrect line of shattering the authority of the raikom, of not informing the obkom bureau of the existing abnormal relations, and of not having taken the necessary measures during the vacation of the raikom secretary toward liquidating the backwardness of the raion." In this case the obkom bureau warned the raikom secretary "of the necessity of a radical change in his methods of work," including correction of "his personal shortcomings which discredit him as a raikom secretary"; demanded that the RIK chairman and NKVD head immediately eliminate their "unhealthy relationship" and establish "friendly businesslike work in the raikom bureaus"; and ordered the raikom "to take energetic measures toward the liquidation of the backwardness of the raion." At the same time an instructor of the Division of Leading Party Organs of the obkom was dispatched to the raion to investigate its "leadership situation" and to recommend further measures.

The next month, on December 14, the obkom bureau had to cope with still another Kardymovo feud. [53] This time the problem was one "of unhealthy and squabbling relations" between the director of the MTS and his deputy director for political affairs. The obkom bureau removed the deputy director from his position after finding him guilty of "crude mistakes" and of having made "unfounded accusations" against the director. At the same time it described the work of the MTS as unsatisfactory, ordered the director "to eliminate shortcomings," called upon the Kardymovo raikom to help reorganize the work of the MTS, and instructed the Oblast Agricultural Administration to inspect the financial condition of the MTS and to assist in putting its accounts in order.

As these examples perhaps illustrate, the conflicts that developed in the raions often enabled the obkom to obtain a real insight into raion affairs. Faced with these conflicts, the obkom bureau had no alternative except to investigate, to sit in judgment, and to take such action as seemed calculated to improve matters. In some cases it satisfied itself with a warning or reproof; in others it took the more drastic course of purging the offenders or even of initiating police action. It shifted personnel about to break up established relationships, and it utilized oblast officials to check on whether the difficulties had been eliminated.

But the over-all impression, as one reads the obkom records, is not one of sedate and orderly processes of administration. An all-pervading atmosphere of urgency and tension appears to dominate everything that the obkom undertakes. Over and over again, one gets the sense of a group of men operating under tremendous pressure to realize seemingly impossible objectives, and exercising a similar pressure on their subordinates in lower Party and governmental organs. Like firemen summoned to a blaze, they rush from situation to situation, dealing as best they can with the emergency which confronts them. They try to be sensitive to the ruling priorities of their superiors and to communicate that same sensitivity to their inferiors in the raikoms. The rhythm of their lives is dictated by deadlines and goals; they are almost violently achievement-oriented. They know that success or failure, even life or death may depend on their ability to satisfy the expectations of their chiefs. And yet, behind the fury and the urgency, one also catches a sense of an almost desperate desire for relaxation and security, the kind of yearning which led both Pavlyuchenko and Rumyantsev to try to build their own protective family circles and which ultimately contributed to their undoing. In prewar Smolensk under Stalin, the oblast Apparat was privileged, but it also lived in perpetual fear and in perpetual motion.

4 Governmental Organization and Problems of the Oblast

Analysts of the Soviet political system have always found it difficult to draw a clear dividing line between the spheres of Party and government. The contribution of the Smolensk Archive is to demonstrate that, for the period which it covers, no clear distinctions can be made. Soviet methods of rule were consciously constructed around overlapping, duplication, and parallel functions.

The Dominant Role of the Party

Without question it was the Party which played the dominant role in the Smolensk area. The supreme power in the oblast was concentrated in the hands of the obkom bureau, and within the bureau there existed an interlocking directorate of Party and government. From 1931 to 1937, Rakitov, the chairman of the oblast executive committee, served as a member of the obkom bureau, and together with Rumyantsev, the first secretary, and Shilman, the second secretary, was commonly regarded as one of the Big Three who really ran the oblast. As a member of the obkom bureau, Rakitov participated influentially in the discussions that determined the course of action of the oblispolkom, but he participated as one member of a group, and his authority was definitely subordinate to that of Rumyantsev, who was not only first secretary, but after 1934 also a member of the Central Committee of the Party.

The transcendent position of the obkom bureau vis-à-vis the oblast congress of soviets and the oblispolkom is unmistakable. The obkom bureau laid down the policies and drafted the directives which guided their actions; it initiated the key appointments which were subsequently ratified and approved by the oblast congress of soviets and the oblispolkom. The secretariat of the obkom paralleled the governmental departments; it intervened constantly to direct, scold, and prod the administrative organs subject to its supervision.

Constitutionally, the oblast congress of soviets was the top governmental authority of the region, and the powers of the oblispolkom derived from it. But even the most cursory reading of the Archive makes clear that this was fiction, rather than fact. The congress of soviets met at irregular intervals and for very brief periods largely to ratify measures which had been prepared for it by the oblispolkom, which in turn operated under guiding instructions from the obkom bureau. The agenda for the meetings, the designation of reporters, and the resolutions to be voted all required prior Party approval. Even the delegates to the congress and the members of the oblispolkom who were theoretically "elected" by the congress were chosen under the watchful supervision of the obkom secretariat. Thus we find Shilman, the second secretary of the Western obkom, sending top-secret instructions to all raikom secretries on October 11, 1936, with reference to the coming Fourth Oblast Extraordinary Congress of Soviets on November 20. His letter to the secretary of the Kozelsk raikom read:

The Obkom directs your attention to the necessity of a careful choice of candidates for the Oblast Congress, so that actually the best delegates will be elected, the most authoritative representatives of the raion.

In selecting the candidates, take into consideration the fact that in our opinion there should be 6 delegates from the raion: 1 male or female worker (the best of the Stakhanovites in production); 3 collective farmers, male or female; [blank] representatives of the intelligentsia (engineers, agronomists, teachers, physicians); [blank] men from the Army.

Among the delegates of the raion there should be not less than 3 women, and 45–50% Communists and Komsomols.

We warn that it is not permitted to select more delegates to the Oblast Congress of Soviets than the norm established in the resolution of the Oblast Executive Committee. This resolution will be strictly enforced.[1]

Similarly tight Party controls were exercised over the composition of the oblispolkom. On December 23, 1934, Rumyantsev wrote the following top-secret letter to all raikom secretaries:

In connection with the forthcoming Oblast and All-Union Congress of Soviets, it is necessary to begin to select candidates for promotion to . . . the Oblast Executive Committee. . . . This is necessary so as not to have a repetition of past mistakes, when the candidates were not designated until the Congress was in session, were chosen in a hurry, and this led to cases where insufficiently investigated and authoritative people were promoted . . .

In connection with this, within a narrow circle (members of the bureau of the raikom) designate a group of candidates from the staff of male and female workers, male and female kolkhozniks, and local workers—chairmen of village soviets, chairmen of kolkhozes, Soviet intelligentsia (engineers, agronomists, teachers, physicians etc.). Carefully check each candidate and then prepare for each one a detailed written characterization over your signature and that of the chairman of the Raion Executive Committee.

Send all materials (lists of candidates chosen for promotion and characterizations) not later than January 8, 1935, by special delivery, through the NKVD to the Sovtorgotdel [Soviet-Trade Division] of the Obkom, personally to Comrade Khirkovsky.

On the basis of this, we will be able to choose more carefully from the reserve the best comrades for promotion.[2]

Operating in this fashion, the obkom secretariat in effect determined the composition of the oblispolkom. Since the heads of the various departments of the oblispolkom were also on the nomenklatura of the obkom, their choice too was specified by the obkom bureau. Thus the controlling authority remained in the hands of the Party secretariat.

Oblast Administration

Meanwhile, the routine day-to-day processes of oblast administration were the responsibility of the oblispolkom. Within the oblispolkom guidance was provided by the Presidium (sometimes the so-called small presidium which was a kind of presidium within the Presidium). The Presidium was headed by the chairman of the oblispolkom and consisted ordinarily of nine members and candidates who directed the most important departments of the oblispolkom. Its meetings, which took place at approximately weekly intervals, were attended not only by members and candidates but by various oblast administrative officials or raion executive committee chairmen who had items of business before it or whose presence was required by the nature of the docket.

The Archive contains one reasonably long run of Protocols of the Presidium of the oblispolkom of the Western Oblast — from August 6, 1930, through January 1, 1931.[3] Although these protocols reach back to the formative days of the Western Oblast and therefore have their special time frame, they nevertheless convey a sense of the continuing activities in which the Presidium was engaged.

Broadly speaking, the Presidium served as the coördinating point for all oblispolkom activities. Subject to limitations imposed by the center and guidance from the obkom, the Presidium bore the primary responsibility for ratifying the oblast plan and approving the budget of the oblispolkom and the raion executive committees. It also sanctioned departures from the budget, though in most cases the sums involved were small. It exercised control over the administrative structure of the oblispolkom and the ispolkoms (executive committees) of raion and city soviets. No new positions could be created nor salaries fixed without its approval. Its discretion in this sphere, however, was sharply hedged, since all of its actions had to be in accord with a standard staff and pay schedule for oblast, raion, and city ispolkoms issued by the Council of People's Commissars in Moscow.[4]

In addition to these over-all responsibilities, the Presidium supervised the particular activities of the various departments of the oblispolkom. Agricultural campaigns, trade and supply problems, rationing regulations, road-building, housing construction, taxes, social insurance, education, public health, and a wealth of other matters involving the regional economy find their reflection in the Presidium protocols. In many respects there is a striking similarity between the agenda of the Presidium meetings and the protocols of the obkom bureau which were analyzed in the preceding chapter. But there are also differences. For one thing, the internal problems of Party organization receive little or no treatment in the protocols of the oblispolkom. For another, the oblispolkom protocols contain a wealth of precise administrative instructions which are ordinarily, though not always, missing from the deliberations of the obkom bureau. In this respect, at least, one can differentiate between the two organs — the oblispolkom putting its primary emphasis on operations, the obkom bureau on policy guidance and control.

The Presidium protocols reveal yet another area of specialized concern — the supervision of the activities of raion and city soviets and even of rural soviets. A substantial portion of the agenda of Presidium meetings was devoted to reports on the activities and problems of various raion executive committees, petitions from them for authorizations to act, requests for budgetary assistance, and even appeals from individuals for relief from the allegedly arbitrary action of lower governmental organs.

The indiscriminate character of the agenda is striking — issues of importance are buried in a mass of trivia, and one cannot help wondering how the Presidium members ever found time to address themselves to the problems that really mattered. And pervading the protocols is the same breathless sense of urgency and pressure which has already been noted as one of the hallmarks of oblast Party life.

Operating under the direction of the Presidium were various departments and offices in which the actual responsibility for day-to-day administration was vested. Charts II and III blueprint the administrative organization of the Western Oblast as it existed in 1930 and 1936.[5] They reveal a rather striking continuity in administrative structure. Certain departments — Organization, Finance, Land, Education, Trade, Communal Economy, Roads, Health, Social Security, Archives, Communications, the Planning Commission, and the legal and punitive organizations — retained their identity over the years, although in a few cases there were slight variations of title as, for example, the transformation of the OGPU into the NKVD. Functions, of course, shifted with changing programs, but by and large the scheme of administrative organization itself remained fairly stable.

This was a period of increasing centralization in Soviet life, particularly in the area of heavy industry emphasized by the Five Year Plans, but since the Western Oblast was relatively little affected by the heavy-industry drive, it felt the intrusion of the center in this sphere less than most. Nevertheless, a number of the newer industrial plants which were located in the oblast during the thirties were removed from oblast con-

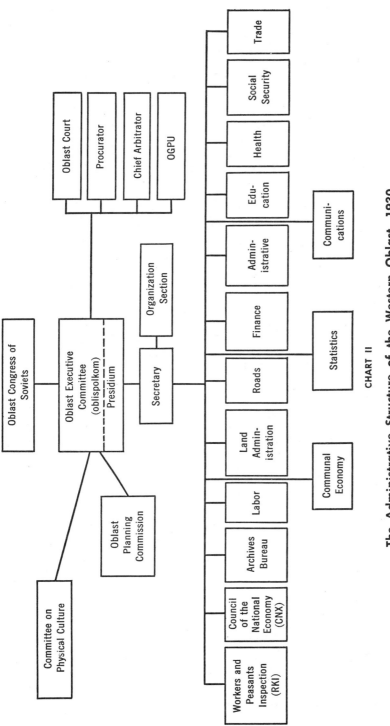

CHART II

The Administrative Structure of the Western Oblast, 1930

Oblast Congress of Soviets

Oblast Executive Committee (oblispolkom) Presidium

Organization Section

Secretary

Oblast Court
Procurator
Chief Arbitrator
OGPU

Committee on Physical Culture

Oblast Planning Commission

Workers and Peasants Inspection (RKI)

Council of the National Economy (CNX)

Archives Bureau

Labor

Land Administration

Roads

Finance

Administrative

Education

Health

Social Security

Trade

Communal Economy

Statistics

Communications

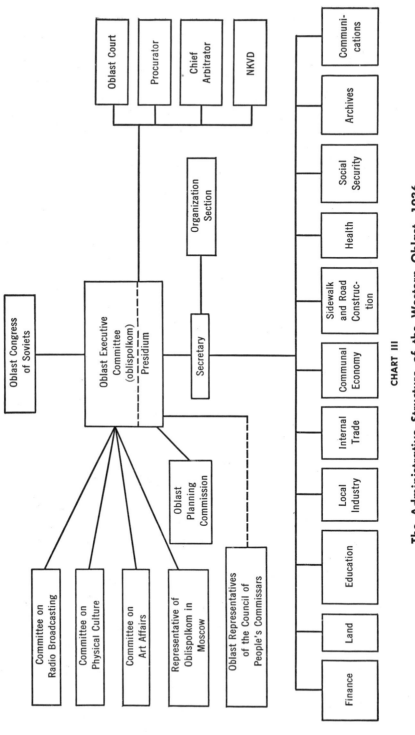

CHART III

The Administrative Structure of the Western Oblast, 1936

trol; its jurisdiction was confined to local industry, and a new department so-named was created to supervise developments in this sphere. The oblast Council of the National Economy which existed in 1930 to supervise the more important plants was abolished, and its functions were transferred to the newly created industrial commissariats which carried out their supervisory responsibilities through their own agents stationed in Smolensk. The Labor Department too was liquidated when its functions were assigned to the trade unions in the early thirties.

The total number of administrative personnel employed by the Western oblispolkom on October 1, 1930, ran between 800 and 900.[6] Of the total, 114 were concentrated in the Land Department alone, an obvious reflection of the central importance of agriculture in the life of the oblast.[7] Unfortunately, the Archive yields no comparable totals or breakdowns for later years, so that it is impossible to venture any observations on the growth of the oblast administrative apparatus. Nor does the Archive contain any very satisfactory material on the recruitment and training of oblast administrative personnel. Promotions from the raion executive committees and other lower organs played an obviously significant role; there are records of such actions galore, including pained protests from below at being raided by the oblast. When the okrug layer of administration (between the oblast and the raions) was liquidated in 1930, a report of the Western oblispolkom indicated that some sixty-seven leading okrug workers and specialists ended up in the employ of the oblispolkom.[8]

The obkom of the Party exercised a decisive influence over all important oblispolkom appointments. The Party nomenklaturas make this clear. The 1929 nomenklatura distinguished between those appointments which required official action of the obkom bureau and those which were made by its secretariat.[9] In the former category were both heads and deputy heads of all departments in the oblispolkom; in the latter, chiefs of sections within the departments. The 1936 nomenklatura made no distinction between the obkom bureau and the secretariat and merely listed positions under the jurisdiction of the obkom.[10] The list, however, included section chiefs as well as heads and deputy heads of all oblispolkom departments. Nor were these listings mere formalities. The obkom records indicate that the leading workers of the oblispolkom were in fact selected and designated through the obkom apparatus. While too little is known of the actual procedures employed, it is clear that the secretariat of the obkom maintained a file of Party members who were judged "suitable" for work at the oblast level. From time to time raikom secretaries and perhaps other leading officials were invited to make recommendations for additions to this file, and it was from this reservoir that the secretariat drew in making its "suggestions" to fill oblispolkom vacancies. At the height of the Great Purge when the Rumyantsev-Rakitov group in the obkom and oblispolkom were decimated, emergency procedures had to be employed to fill the gaps. On that occasion the new obkom secretariat reached far down into junior ranks in order to make replacements, but under more normal conditions it was the so-called "obkom reserve" that provided the source for important oblispolkom appointments.

Distinctions, moreover, need to be drawn between the appointment of so-called leading workers such as RIK chairmen and the designation of technical specialists. In the former case the obkom exercised the major initiative; in the latter the initiative was more likely to lie with the affected commissariat or one of its subordinate institutions with specialized competence in the field. In addition, it should be noted that the oblispolkom had its own personnel agency; in the period under review it was known as the Orgotdel, or Organization Section of the oblispolkom. This section not only had jurisdiction over junior appointments in the oblispolkom and the raion executive committees; it also could suggest the appointment of leading personnel in the oblispolkom and the raions, though in the latter case the obkom was, of course, required to concur. In the period of the early thirties, moreover, the oblast branch of the Commissariat of Workers' and Peasants' Inspection also had an important role to play in the personnel field. The representatives of this commissariat functioned as a kind of organization and methods, or administrative management branch of the oblast government. They established staff limits for each department of the oblispolkom and classified jobs in accordance with model plans devised at the center. They investigated cases of administrative inefficiency and malfeasance, and their recommendations exercised an important influence in shaping the organizational structure and personnel policy of the oblispolkom.

The Oblast Budget

The tempo and scope of oblispolkom activities were also regulated by budget and plan. Of these, the budget was the more precise instrument, though even it sometimes demonstrated unsuspected flexibility and was subject to change from quarter to quarter in accordance with modifications introduced by the central authorities. The protocols of the Presidium of the oblispolkom for late 1930 contain a number of sample oblast budgets as well as a record of the action taken by the Presidium with regard to them.[11] The report of the oblispolkom for 1930 also has a brief section on the budget.[12] An analysis of this material may shed some light on the role of the budget in regulating the administrative activities of the oblast.

From these sources it is clear that the budget of the Western Oblast was beginning to rise sharply in the early thirties, despite the efforts of the center to curtail expenditures. From 63.9 million rubles for 1928–29 the budget shot up to 92.7 million for 1929–30, and the control figures for 1930–31 projected a further increase of 60.6 per cent to 145 million rubles. Of the total, however, only 17.4 per cent was assigned to oblast governmental activities proper. The great bulk, 70.6 per cent, was allotted to the raions, and the remaining 12.2 per cent was divided up among the cities of Smolensk, Bryansk, and Bezhitsa.[13]

As is not uncommon in governments elsewhere, the Western Oblast administrators found it easy to spend the sums allotted to them, but more difficult to collect the taxes which were designed to support their activities. In the words of the oblispolkom report for 1930, "The arrears in state taxes and collections (excluding the agricultural tax) were 1.8 million rubles on October 1, 1929, 17.6 million rubles on May 1, 1930, and 11.1 million rubles on December 1, 1930. This increase in arrears is due to the extremely weak organization of the local finance organs, which do not take into consideration the enormous significance of the mobilization of monetary resources and which display opportunist attitudes in regard to confiscations from kulak and Nepmen groups . . ." [14] These "opportunist attitudes" were to be corrected later. As the report put it, "The Oblast Executive Committee gave oral directives on exposing and taxing the kulak households." [15]

A typical quarterly budget (for the October–December 1930 period)[16] is presented in Table 1. As this budget makes clear, by far the greatest increases in rates of expenditure were planned for industrial expansion and transport. In comparison, the planned increases for agriculture, communal economy, education, and labor protection were relatively modest in scope, and in the case of public health the projected rise was insignificant. The budget met criticism in Moscow; as a result the Presidium of the oblispolkom issued instructions presumably in accordance with a central directive that expenditures on communal economy (housing and public services) be decreased "maximally," that purely "administrative" expenditures be held down to the level of the first quarter of the 1929–30 budgetary year, but that outlays on elementary and polytechnic education were not to be cut.[17]

The actual results as noted in the 1930 report of the oblispolkom underlined the difficulties which the oblast faced in maintaining budgetary discipline. While the report made no mention of what happened to the communal economy sector of the budget, it did reveal that outlays on public health and agriculture (exclusive of kolkhoz construction) fell below the budget projections. On the other hand, expenditures significantly exceeded projections in the following areas: kolkhoz construction, 39 per cent; industrial expansion, 25 per cent; labor protection, 40 per cent; and administrative expenditures, 13 per cent.[18]

TABLE 1

Budget of the Western Oblast for the Quarter October–December, 1930

(In millions of rubles)

Type of expenditure	For the quarter Oct.–Dec., 1930	Per cent increase	Including				
			Oblast budget	City of Smolensk	City of Bryansk	City of Bezhitsa	Raion budgets
Industry...............	1700.0	1453.0	1700.0	—	—	—	—
Electrification..........	98.3	—	—	20.0	1.0	—	77.3
Agriculture............	1182.4	125.0	420.7	—	4.9	0.8	756.0
Water power	—	—	—	—	—	—	—
Forestry...............	87.3	—	—	—	—	—	87.3
Communal economy and housing..............	1867.9	122.4	240.2	543.0	284.3	123.1	677.1
Trade.................	72.8	—	0.8	2.1	0.4	—	69.5
Transport..............	541.4	324.0	486.0	—	—	—	55.4
Public communications..	303.3	—	285.0	—	—	—	18.3
Education.............	12028.4	156.6	901.6	558.5	337.4	110.5	10120.4
Public health..........	2980.2	100.4	347.6	404.2	160.2	137.8	1930.4
Labor protection and social security..........	917.4	148.0	97.0	50.7	15.7	7.2	746.8
Participation in expenditures of the Red Army	447.3	—	120.0	2.0	2.0	1.7	321.6
General administration..	2250.0	141.5	326.4	51.2	18.3	10.1	1844.0
Legal organs..........	452.5	122.8	178.0	8.8	5.9	3.6	256.2
Protection of public order	1133.4	127.3	181.9	102.3	24.0	8.0	817.2
Extra and reserve funds..	68.9	—	23.0	10.0	1.7	1.0	33.2
Expenditures on loans...	1750.2	—	1750.4	—	—	—	—
Various expenditures....	247.1	—	44.0	0.6	0.5	0.5	201.5
Social insurance funds...	1181.6	—	70.0	60.0	32.8	19.8	999.0
Totals...............	29310.4	143.0	7172.6	1813.4	889.1	424.1	19011.2

The paucity of material on later budgets makes it impossible to project trends. Yet a few tentative generalizations may be ventured on the basis of the material that is available. Clearly, there was no precise correspondence between the budget as planned and the actual record of income and outlays. Budgetary discipline was difficult to enforce. This was particularly true of administrative expenditures, which continued to mount despite repeated injunctions to hold them down to previous levels. At the same time the oblast budget reflected the ruling priorities of the center. The great expansion was in the industrial sector, and indeed the crucial importance of meeting central expectations in this area even led to overexpenditures to attain planned goals. Education — and more particularly, polytechnic education which provided essential underpinning for industrial development — was one of the important growing points of the budget. On the other hand, the growth in outlays on other governmental functions was far less impressive. Agriculture was given a back seat, despite the fact that the Western Oblast was a predominantly agricultural area. The bite of budgetary limitations was most deeply felt in restricted outlays on housing, public health, and other communal services. In miniature, the budget of the Western Oblast mirrored the problems of budget-makers everywhere in the Soviet Union. It registered the strains and tensions of the industrialization drive.

The Oblast Plan

The budget itself was in the final analysis merely the monetary expression of the oblast plan. The origins of the Western Oblast plan are outlined in the report of the oblispolkom for 1930, and if the account is to be fully credited, it implies a degree of initiative on the part of the oblast authorities which is in some contradiction to the usual emphasis on the centralized processes of Soviet planning. It will be remembered that the Western Oblast was formed in 1929. According to the report, "Since the Five Year Plan for the national economy of the USSR was approved by the All-Union Congress of Soviets in 1929, it was natural that the Western Oblast, as a newly created economic unit, could not find in this plan a complete reflection of the prospects for its development. Therefore the First Oblast Congress of Soviets ordered the Oblast Executive Committee to present to the Government a reworked draft of a five year plan for the national economy and cultural construction of the Western Oblast and to insist that necessary funds be supplied to raise the level of its development to that of the average republic." [19] The oblispolkom took as its point of departure the fact that flax was the leading crop of the region and instructed the Oblast Planning Commission "to work out the problem of flax and hemp and outline the prospects for the development of this basic branch of the Oblast economy in the five year plan." [20]

The Oblast Planning Commission proposed an increase in the gross output of flax from 79.8 thousand tons (1928–29) to 414 thousand tons in 1933, and in hemp from 17 to 99.2 thousand tons with, of course, corresponding increases in the acreage sown to these crops. The commission also proposed the forced development of a mechanized flax-processing industry with some 300 industrial aggregates to be established by 1933 for the combing, spinning, and weaving of flax. These recommendations were then referred to the Flax and Hemp Committee of the Gosplan of the RSFSR, which adopted a resolution approving the plan and the measures necessary for its fulfillment. The matter was then referred to the USSR Council of People's Commissars which on January 1, 1930, decreed as follows: "Based on the fact that the Western Oblast was organized as a flax-raising oblast, [we] recommend to the RSFSR Economic Council that it concentrate mainly and predominantly in this oblast the organization of flax-raising sovkhozes, the building of flax factories (including experimental ones), and the carrying out of other work aiding the development of flax raising and the improvement of the processing of flax." [21] In a subsequent decree of February 11, 1930, the USSR Council of People's Commissars instructed the USSR Gosplan to present the Council with a plan for the economic development of the oblast for the remaining three years of the First Five Year Plan.

On May 13, 1930, the chairman of the oblispolkom, at the suggestion of the First Oblast Congress of Soviets, reported to the RSFSR Council of People's Commissars on the state of the economy of the oblast and on the prospects for its development. The RSFSR Council of People's Commissars reacted to this report with a resolution adopted on June 2 in which it called upon the Gosplan and People's Commissariats of the RSFSR to draft their plans for the oblast on the following "basic premises":

    a. the necessity of creating in the Western Oblast a powerful energy complex on the basis of its rich peat resources;

    b. the necessity of speeding up the industrialization of the oblast on the basis of the use of significant raw material resources created by flax and hemp raising and other branches of agriculture, and also resources of forest and mineral origin;

    c. the presence in the oblast of a dense railroad network;

    d. the dense population;

    e. the peculiarities of the geographical location of the oblast;

    f. the reorganization of the agriculture of the oblast toward specialization in flax and hemp production and livestock breeding.[22]

Meanwhile, the actual drafting of the plan continued to drag out. A resolution of the oblispolkom Presidium, dated October 6, 1930, directed the various branches of the oblispolkom and the planning commission to meet with appropriate sections of the USSR Gosplan in order to put the plan into final shape.[23] The resolution indicated that the plan was scheduled for discussion by the USSR Council of People's Commissars "in the early days of November." Presumably, after its long travail, the plan was finally approved by the end of the year. The 1930 report of the obispolkom states: "This plan [for the remaining three years of the First Five Year Plan] was worked out by the Oblast Planning Commission, presented to the USSR Gosplan, where it was adopted, was brought in for review by the USSR Council of People's Commissars, and thus the oblast is included in the general system of the plan for the socialist reconstruction of the national economy of the USSR."

Regrettably, this story of the origins of the first long-term plan for the Western Oblast is not duplicated by similarly detailed accounts for later periods. Yet the documents in the Archive make clear that, for the 1930 period at least, the Oblast Planning Commission and the oblast Party and governmental apparatus generally, still had an important role to play, at least within the limits of their jurisdiction and the functions assigned to them. The data which they supplied, the reports which they rendered, and the recommendations which they made formed the basis on which oblast plans had ultimately to be drafted and enacted. To be sure, these recommendations were conditioned by a vivid sensitivity to central priorities; the stress of oblast planners on industrial development and flax production reflected this awareness. For this reason the drive for industrial expansion and the battle for flax were always in the forefront of the oblispolkom's calculations, while housing, trade, public health, and communal economy received only desultory attention. A failure to meet a housing plan might merit a rebuke, but the mortal sin in the Western Oblast was a lapse in flax production or a collapse on the industrial front. It was perhaps not entirely coincidental that when the Rumyantsev-Rakitov leadership was finally liquidated, not the least of its crimes was unsatisfactory plan fulfillment in some of the most important industrial enterprises of the oblast.[24]

The administrative task that confronted the oblispolkom apparatus was not easy. It had to enforce the discipline of the plan and the budget, not only on oblast institutions, but also (as of 1930) on some 110 raion executive committees and three city soviets — Smolensk, Bryansk, and Bezhitsa. The problem of insuring adequate supervision of the work of the raions presented many difficulties, not the least of which, noted the 1930 oblispolkom report, was "the shortage of cadres of instructors, inspection workers, and specialists." [25] The oblispolkom attempted to organize a system of differentiated leadership over the raions by dividing them into nine groups, arranged roughly "in accordance with the economic similarity of the raions." The instructorial staffs of the oblast departments were set up so that each instructor specialized in one or another of these groups of raions. Theoretically, each instructor kept in constant touch with developments in his group of raions by reading protocols of RIK meetings, processing raion reports, and periodic visits to his constituents. In fact, much of the supervision was paper control, and visits to the raions were brief, intermittent, and none too effective. The problem was made even more complex by the marked deterioration in the quality and reliability of administrative personnel as one moved out from Smolensk to the raions and the villages.

Scandals and Abuses

The results were manifest, not only in inefficiency and abuse of power at the raion and local levels, but in a whole series of scandals which shook the oblast. The great Smolensk scandal of 1928, which resulted in a complete overturn of the oblast leadership and a purge of the raions, has already been noted.[26] But the phenomenon was endemic, and hardly a year passed without its revelation of abuses, both great and small. Some examples may serve to illustrate the problem. On July 9, 1934, after a very considerable accumulation of such incidents, Rumyantsev circulated a closed letter to all raikoms calling attention to what he called "unhealthy and disgraceful symptoms which exist in a number of organizations: mass violations of revolutionary legality, administrative excesses in regard to individual farmers and kolkhozniks, cheating in workers' wages, embezzlement and peculation in the coöperative trade network, and what is most important, the insensitive reactions of many Party organizations to these disorders and crimes." [27] Rumyantsev pointed out that the situation in trade and in the system of coöperatives was "especially unfavorable," that in the consumers' coöperatives, "in 1933 there were embezzlements and peculations to the sum of 4,793,000 rubles, which is 35 per cent of the shares collected. In the first quarter of 1934 they ran to 1,160,000 rubles, or fifty per cent of the collected share fees." He listed similar thievery, which had been uncovered in many other trading organizations and emphasized that "cases where peculations and embezzlements are committed by Communists are not rare." He called on the raikoms to wage a sharp struggle to eliminate these abuses and threatened the most drastic sanctions against those caught violating "revolutionary legality."

Despite all of Rumyantsev's threats and warnings, embezzlements continued on a large scale. In March 1935 came the announcement of the discovery of a group of thirty embezzlers in the system of Zagotlen (The Association for the Procurement and Marketing of Flax, Hemp, and Clover Seeds).[28] Of the participants ten were Party members or candidates, and the group included seven employees of Zagotlen and twenty-two chairmen and members of kolkhozes. According to a top-secret bulletin circulated by the NKVD, the thievery proceeded along the following lines:

1. The kolkhoz chairmen were issued fictitious receipts for flax and hemp raw materials which were allegedly received, for which the Zagotlen workers received money and seeds.
2. Kolkhozniks who delivered their flax and hemp raw material were systematically cheated by false weighing.
3. The numbering [indication of quality] of the flax and hemp material received from those delivering them was falsely raised in return for bribes.
4. The state factories were cheated in the weight of the raw material given to them from the storehouse for manufacture.[29]

The NKVD observed in passing that one of the kolkhoz chairmen who had been given fictitious receipts had received a prize of 500 rubles for overfulfilling the plan of flax deliveries and was even chosen as a delegate to the second All-Union Congress of shock-worker kolkhozniks. "It is typical to note," continued the NKVD report, "that the inspector who arrived on the spot to investigate as a representative of the oblast office of Zagotlen (a non-Party man), got drunk together with the Zagotlen workers and of course 'did not notice' the disorders taking place right on the spot." [30] In this case the state suffered the relatively modest loss of 36,131 rubles before the thievery was uncovered. What happened to the culprits the record does not disclose.

On June 4, 1935, Rumyantsev addressed still another letter to all secretaries of Party committees and Party organizers of coöperative trade organizations. Again the theme was "corruption and degeneracy." Rumyantsev wrote:

> The materials show that a number of Party organizations have not seen the disorders being committed before their eyes, or have become reconciled to them. Thus, for example, in Komarichi raion during 1934, embezzlements ran to 150,000 rubles, and 20 Communists and 18 Komsomols were brought to trial; in the Kholm-Zhirkovski raion union, more than 130,000 rubles were embezzled, the Communist leaders had drinking bouts, made personal appropriations, and behaved like hooligans. In Vyazma the leaders of the GORPO took from the stores goods "on credit" without paying, and the heads of the stores and other workers committed robberies with them and embezzlements exceeded 130,000 rubles; in Novozybkov, the trade apparatus was infested with alien elements, with the direct permission of the leader, the Communist K———, as a result of which peculation and embezzlements ran to more than 100,000 rubles. Such situations, although to a smaller degree, are observed in other organizations . . . The bad situation in Party work led to the occurrence in our oblast during 1934 of enormous embezzlements in the trade organizations: in the Western Union [of Coöperatives] they ran to 4,534,000 rubles; in the GORT 720,000 rubles; in Torgsin 260,000 rubles. Many Party organizations did not draw the proper conclusions from the 'Obkom letter sent to them in June 1934 . . .[31]

Again they were enjoined to "take measures for the speedy cleansing of trade organizations of alien, hostile, corrupt, and swindling elements." But despite the stern injunction, "disorders" continued, and examples similar to the above could be multiplied ad nauseam for succeeding as well as prior years.

As these examples illustrate, corruption was particularly rife in the trade network, where the opportunities were greatest, but it was in no sense confined to this sector. There were many other areas — tax collections, agriculture and industry — where similar problems presented themselves. The oblispolkom faced formidable obstacles in making its far-flung oblast and raion administrative apparatus a pliable instrument of its will. The familiar phenomena of family circles and mutual guarantees which have already been noted in the Party organizations spilled over into administration and frequently interposed barriers against effective oblispolkom control of lower governmental organs.

At the same time, numerous and endemic as corruption and other administrative abuses were, there were also periodic campaigns to root them out. These campaigns served as a reminder that flagrant thievery would not be tolerated and that corruption, when it was discovered, would be dealt with drastically. But despite all the presumed resources of the totalitarian machine and the pervasive network of police and Party controls, the processes of discovery were not easy, and the temptations were great. A regime which was exploiting its people to pay the costs of industrialization found itself exploited in turn by some of its own unscrupulous officials who sought an easy, if dangerous, road of escape.

Yet despite the leakages and losses from embezzlement and corruption, the Western oblispolkom served the center not badly. It projected Soviet power into the raions and the villages, and the administrative apparatus which it put together improved with the years. It worked under great handicaps, frequently haltingly and inefficiently. But by and large it did enforce central priorities in the oblast, though sometimes, as with collectivization, at a fearful cost. Like the oblast Party leadership, it operated in an atmosphere of constant strain and pressure, and like the Party leadership too, it found that it was dispensable when it no longer produced results. Failure was its epitaph and survival its greatest triumph.

5 The Role of the Raion in the Soviet Control System

Shortly after the organization of the Western Oblast in 1929, as has already been noted, the oblast was subdivided into some 110 raions and three cities, all directly responsible to the oblast leadership.[1] The raion became the basic unit of governance through which the oblast leadership enforced its control over the countryside. The raion authorities supervised and maintained direct contact with the town and village soviets, the kolkhozes, sovkhozes, and MTS's, the industrial and trading enterprises, the schools and other public services in the area subject to their jurisdiction. The typical raion in the Western Oblast at the time of its formation had a population ranging from 50,000 to 75,000. The raion center, where Party and governmental headquarters were located, was ordinarily an old market town with an average population of around 5,000. The great bulk of the inhabitants lived in rural areas under the direct jurisdiction of one or another of the twenty-five to forty village soviets into which the raion might be divided. Their most immediate contact with Soviet power was through the chairmen of the village soviets, or, if they were kolkhozniks, through the chairmen of their kolkhozes and the MTS which served them.

The Raion Power Structure

At the pinnacle of the power pyramid of the raion was the raikom first secretary, formally elected by the raikom of the Party, but always either designated or approved by the obkom with the consent of the Central Committee of the Party. The raikom first secretary served as the plenipotentiary of the obkom in the raion; his was the primary responsibility for its performance, and he was held directly accountable by the obkom Party leadership if things went wrong. Sharing power with the first secretary, though in lesser degree, were the members of the bureau of the raikom. The raikom bureau included the key Party and governmental figures in the raion; like the obkom bureau, it functioned as an interlocking directorate to bind Party and government together. Its membership was carefully regulated by directives from the oblast, which, it may be assumed, reflected central instructions. The following letter, stamped "secret" and dated February 14, 1934, from Rumyantsev to the secretary of the Kozelsk raikom, illustrates the principle of selection:

On the basis of the statutes of the CPSU(b) established by the 17th Party Congress, the Bureau of the Raikom should have 5 to 7 members. You must immediately and definitely set up the Bureau of the Raikom with not more than 5 members and 2 candidates and present the membership of the Bureau of the Raikom to the Obkom for confirmation. The Bureau of the Raikom should be recruited, on the basis of strict personal selection, from . . . the following categories of workers: (1) the secretary of the raikom, (2) the second secretary, (3) the chairman of the raion executive committee, the Chief of the Political Section (of the MTS, the Sovkhoz, the Railroad, or an army unit), the OGPU, the editor, the secretary of the Raikom of the Young Communist League, the chairman of the Raion Council of Trade Unions. The Obkom warns that no broadening of the staff of the Bureau of the Raikom is permissible . . .[2]

The raikom bureau thus mirrored the structure of authority in the raion. Next to the first secretary, the leading figures within the bureau were usually the second secretary and the RIK chairman, though the actual status of the leaders tended to vary with personality and reputation. The high rate of turnover in raion leadership testified to the fact that authority was easily dissipated. Within the bureau, moreover, there were independent kernels of power which were not wholly responsive to the direction of the raikom first secretary. The raion NKVD chief and the raion representative of the War Commissariat, for example, had their own independent channels of communication and command into which it was not easy for the raikom first secretary to intrude. The watchdog function of the NKVD furthermore contributed an element of built-in rivalry and criticism which the raikom secretary could only hope to meliorate by absorbing the raion NKVD chief into his family circle.

The role of the raikom secretary was a difficult one, full of contradictory pressures and temptations. The pressure from above was for performance, for fulfillment and overfulfillment of the production and delivery quotas set by the oblast leadership. If these quotas were to be met, the raikom secretary had to be a relentless driver, constantly prodding his associates and subordinates to meet the goals which spelled success in the eyes of the oblast. At the same time the secretary had to work in an environment that was heavily saturated with peasant apathy and indifference, with passive and even open resistance to the state's demands. To make matters even worse, the Party and governmental apparatus which the raikom secretary had at his disposal was, to say the least, imperfect. Its own ties with the countryside sometimes made it an undependable instrument; it was often sluggish and inefficient, and not infrequently it was tempted to feather its own nest. Caught between the pressures from above and the resistances from below, the raikom secretaries found themselves in a far from enviable position. Sometimes aided by a favorable conjuncture of management skills and a good harvest, they were able to drive through to victory and to score a resounding success with their superiors. Sometimes the victory was only partial, but at least it was sufficient to insure survival, if it was registered in an area high on the priority list of the center. Sometimes the goals might be missed badly, and the raikom secretary would still win a reprieve, if the calamity was attributable to bad weather or other phenomena beyond the control of the local authorities. But persistent underfulfillment of the plan could have only one result, the removal and disgrace of the raikom secretary.

Within the limits of a situation which always remained precarious, the raikom secretary usually sought such security and stability as was attainable. He endeavored to surround himself with faithful subordinates and to cement loyalty with perquisites and favors. He tried to enlist the key political figures of the raion in his family circle, in order to involve them in a pattern of mutual protection and guaranty which would discourage tale-bearing to the oblast. But "familyness" too had its dangers. The price of its perpetuation was mutual forbearance in overlooking each other's sins and transgressions, but the compact was not easy to maintain in the face of local rivalries and ambitions. It became all the more difficult to enforce when "familyness" sought to conceal major local scandals or serious failures in economic performance from the center. In such cases the ambitious subordinate had much to gain and little to lose by rushing to Smolensk and ventilating the crimes of his superiors. "Familyness" was the mortal enemy of control, and if the temptation to indulge in it was endemic and irresistible, the drive to extirpate it was also remorseless and unyielding.

One of the primary weapons of the obkom in dealing with it was through control of appointments. The 1936 obkom nomenklatura listed the following raion positions as subject to obkom jurisdiction: first secretary, second secretary, assistant secretary, registration head, heads of culture and propaganda and Party cabinets, instructors, newspaper editor, RIK chairmen and deputy chairmen, NKVD head, procurator, heads of the financial, agricultural, and communications divisions, and directors and deputy directors of MTS's and sovkhozes.[3] Thus practically all the key appointments in the raions were subject either to obkom initiation or ratification, and as we have seen, the obkom guarded its jurisdiction in this sphere jealously. The rate of turnover in raikom secretaries was unusually rapid during the thirties; a stay of more than a year or two in the same raion was a fairly unusual phenomenon. While the attrition rate was undoubtedly accelerated by the purges of the mid-thirties, the obkom also followed a conscious policy of not permitting the same raikom secretary to remain too long in the same place. It can be assumed that this was a form of prophylaxis to prevent the crystallization of "familyness" and local satrapies in the raions.

Raion Organization and the Activities of the Raion Functionaries

Chart IV outlines the typical organization of a raikom during the mid-thirties. At that period, judging by such data as are available in the Archive, the total personnel of an average raikom in the Western Oblast rarely exceeded fifteen to twenty full-time Party workers. While the first secretary retained the key directing role, it was customary to divide supervisory responsibilities between the first and second secretary. In Belyi, for example, in 1937 the first secretary took special responsibility for internal Party management and accounting, relations with the raikom instructors and the Party aktiv, the Komsomol, agriculture, Party leadership in the raion soviet, the coöperatives and trade network, and the most important state obligations such as flax and grain deliveries and taxes.[4] The second secretary busied himself with agitation and propaganda, the raion press, help to Party organizers, education, health, industry, the trade unions, the Belyi town soviet, the finances of the raikom, and such state obligations as were not under the direct jurisdiction of the first secretary. As this list indicates, the more important responsibilities remained with the first secretary, and this was the general rule. The actual division of functions varied in detail from raion to raion, depending on the preferences of the first secretary. In addition to the first and second secretaries, each raikom had an assistant secretary, whose concern was primarily with the house-keeping routine of the raikom — the maintenance of files and records, the preparation of protocols of raikom and raikom bureau meetings, and other similar secretarial duties.

The organization of the raikom apparatus underwent many transformations over the span of the Smolensk Archive as the central leadership experimented with various organizational devices designed to secure more effective Party supervision at the local level. Prior to the Seventeenth Party Congress in 1934, the tendency was to organize the raikom apparatus around subject-matter sections — agriculture, industry, trade, etc. — with each section responsible for that sector of raion life assigned to it. This scheme of organization apparently had the defect of failing to provide for adequate raikom leadership of the primary Party organizations of the raion; the Seventeenth Party Congress therefore ordered the abolition of all raikom sections and their replacement by a group of raikom Party instructors, each of whom was supposed to exercise direct supervision of the entire life and activities of a group of primary Party organizations. On February 14, 1934, Rumyantsev communicated this decision to all raikoms in the oblast. He ordered each raikom to "liquidate

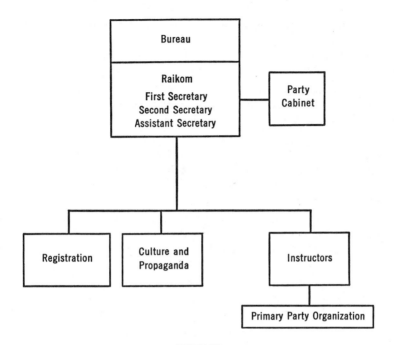

CHART IV

The Organization of a Raikom, 1936

all sections and replace them with separate responsible instructors — members of the raikoms and gorkoms — assigning each of them to a specific group of primary organizations." [5] By 1936, however, the sectional scheme of organization was beginning to reappear. As Chart IV indicates, a section devoted to culture and propaganda reëmerged in order to concentrate attention on the traditional agitprop functions, and a section devoted to registration of Party documents was created to deal with the problems involved in verifying and exchanging Party cards. The next year (1937) rural raikoms reëstablished agricultural sections to focus responsibility in this area of central concern, and at the Eighteenth Party Congress (1939) the new Party rules provided still another pattern of organization built around three sections: (1) Cadres, (2) Propaganda and Agitation, and (3) Organization and Instruction.

Regardless of the precise organizational scheme in vogue at a given time, the actual activities of the raikom apparatus tended to follow a fairly standardized pattern, except for the worst of the purge period when the raikoms, along with other Party organizations, were caught up in a struggle for survival which left little time for anything else. The responsibilities of the raikom reached out to every aspect of the life of the raion, but within this broad mandate there were, of course, certain fields of action which received special emphasis.

First, there was the area of inner-Party work, of supervision of the work of primary Party organizations and Komsomol cells. These activities included the recruitment of new members, admissions to Party candidacy and membership, and exclusions from the Party. While the chief initiative in these fields lay with the primary Party organizations, no final action could be taken without the express approval of the raikom. Then there were the problems of the education of Party members and the training of propagandists and agitators. Here the raikom apparatus played a leading role. It organized schools for political literacy, circles to study the history of the Party and Leninism, and seminars to train members of the Party aktiv to serve as agitators and propagandists. It prepared the programs for meetings to commemorate Soviet holidays and heroes. It drew upon its reservoir of agitators and propagandists to stir interest in Soviet elections, to enlist support for the Stakhanovite movement, to stimulate subscriptions to state loans, and to mobilize the Soviet citizenry behind whatever campaigns were currently being stressed by the center. Each raikom instructor moreover, had a special responsibility for supervising a group of primary Party organizations. He was required to familiarize himself with their work, to read the protocols of their meetings, to approve the appointments of their Party secretaries or organizers, to visit the organizations, to report on their activities to the raikom, and to guide them toward the fulfillment of the demands higher Party authorities made on them. Contact with the Komsomol was maintained through the Komsomol raikom secretary, who was usually also a member of the bureau of the Party raikom. The raikom depended on him to insure Party guidance and control of the work of the Komsomol.

Second, there was the responsibility for Party leadership in agriculture, a field which was, of course, of transcendent importance in rural raions where raikom secretaries were measured by their success or failure in meeting delivery quotas to the state. Formally, management activities in this area were centered in the RIK agricultural section and in the MTS, sovkhozes, and kolkhozes of the raion, but since the raikom secretary was also held responsible for their performance, he was under constant pressure to give the closest attention to their operations. As a result, the protocols of raikom bureau meetings, even more than those of the obkom, read like an agricultural calendar. Each season had its own characteristic preoccupations, with the raikom prodding and threatening, persuading and agitating to get the work done. During the late winter and early spring there were the tools and machinery to be repaired, the seeds to be sorted and delivered. With the spring came plowing and sowing; as the summer approached there was weeding and care of the fields. In late summer the raikom moved toward preparation for the harvest, the struggle to bring it in, and finally the deliveries to the state. Each part of the process found almost frantic reflection in the bureau protocols, though the urgency of the Party directives was not necessarily accompanied by a similar sense of urgency in the fields. The language of the protocols was the vocabulary of battle. Every phase of the agricultural cycle was the occasion for a campaign; when one considers the methods and the stakes involved, perhaps the military analogy was not far wrong. In the eyes of the center what counted were results, and the raikom secretary who failed to deliver was not destined to remain raikom secretary long.

Third, there was a vast miscellany of raikom activities that fell within the general classification of work with Soviet organs and Party-sponsored societies of different types. There were slates to be prepared and approved for the elections to the raion congress of soviets, to its executive committee, and to leading posts in the RIK apparatus. There were similar nominations to be made for such positions as the chairmen of town and village soviets and the chairmen of kolkhozes. There was the raion newspaper to be supervised, the schools to be watched, the coöperatives and trading organizations to be policed, the taxes to be collected, the trade unions to be guided, and the raion military authorities to be assisted in the annual call-up of army conscripts. There were the raion public services — health institutions, roads, communications, housing — for which the raikom also had an over-all responsibility. Finally there was a variety of societies such as Osoaviakhim (to assist the armed forces), MOPR (to aid revolutionary victims abroad), ODGB (The League of Militant Atheists), and many others which the raikom also sponsored and led.

Merely to list these activities is to suggest the all-encompassing jurisdiction of the raikoms, but it tells us little about how these manifold duties were discharged. Indeed, the very multiplicity of tasks heaped on the raikoms militated against the possibility of effective supervision and performance. Faced with responsibilities which were in fact broader than the capacity to discharge them, the raikoms tended to concentrate on those which they deemed most important, or rather on those which they sensed the oblast or central Party leadership considered most important. At the same time they preserved a right of intervention in other areas, a right which all too frequently was exercised only after serious trouble had developed. While the key governmental posts in the raion centers were occupied by Party members who were supposed to maintain effective Party control in the areas assigned to them, they necessarily had to operate through supporting organizations in which Party members were few and far between and where effective Party control was in fact elusive. As one moved out into the countryside — into the village soviets and the kolkhozes — the total absence of Party representation at many important local control points was an unending source of frustration. At the critical spots where policy and directive had to be translated into action, the Party frequently lacked dependable instruments to execute its will. The absence of a widely dispersed but tightly disciplined Party membership at the grass roots was a liability that handicapped the raikoms at every turn.

Necessarily, the raikom had to place considerable reliance on the governmental apparatus in order to achieve its purposes in the raion. Chart V outlines the typical structure of the raion administrative apparatus as it existed in the Western Oblast in 1936. As this chart indicates, the pattern of organization was not greatly different from that of the oblispolkom, except that there were fewer governmental functions represented at the raion level. The major distinctions between the raion and the oblast administrative apparatus derive from the different levels of responsibility at which they operated. The oblispolkom was essentially the regional field office of the RSFSR for the Western Oblast. It transmitted the directives of the central government to the raions, assigned production and delivery quotas to them in accordance with Party directives, checked on their execution, fixed limits on their budgets, and directed administrative activity in the raions. As a supervisory agency, the oblispolkom dealt with lower-level bureaucrats in the RIK's; it had little or no direct contact with ordinary Soviet citizens, except as it exercised its investigatory powers to check on performance at the grass roots. The

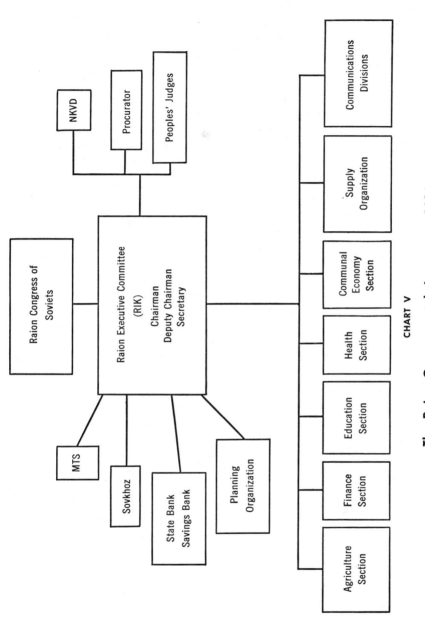

CHART V

The Raion Governmental Apparatus, 1936

RIK or raiispolkom apparatus, on the other hand, was much more directly in touch with the living realities of Soviet life. It had the ungrateful task of actually collecting taxes, of imposing specific production and delivery quotas on each kolkhoz, of doling out such supplies as arrived in the raion to the town and village stores, and of determining what schools, hospitals, roads, and houses could be built with the limited funds which the oblast placed at its disposal. To be sure, it was still one stage removed from direct contact with the Soviet populace itself. It dealt with kolkhozes rather than kolkhozniks, with village soviet chairmen rather than the peasants who were subject to their jurisdiction; with store managers rather than their customers. But it was at least close enough to the point of impact to have a lively appreciation of the reactions which its measures invoked, even when it was more or less powerless to do anything about them. In a period when the peasants were deliberately being made to bear the brunt of rapid industrialization, the role of the raion apparatus was extractive and exploitative. Willingly or unwillingly (and frequently unwillingly), the raion apparatus squeezed what it could from the countryside and enforced the Draconian terms of trade which made it possible for the Center to accumulate its industrialization fund.

Privileges of the Raion Apparatus

If the raion apparatus could do little to meliorate the peasants' lot, it could within limits meliorate its own. There is in the Smolensk Archive an interesting list of members of the raion apparatus who were entitled to preferential supply from central stocks in 1934 when the mass of the population was severely burdened by rationing restrictions.[6] The list included the secretaries and instructors of the raikom, the raikom Komsomol secretary, the editor of the raion newspaper, the directors and workers of the political divisions of the MTS and sovkhozes, the chairman, deputy chairman, and secretary of the RIK, the chairman of the raion planning organization, the heads of the finance, agricultural, education, health, communications, and supply departments of the raiispolkom, the NKVD chief, the procurator, people's investigators and people's judges, the manager of the state bank and the head of the savings bank, the chairman of the raion consumers' union, the raion senior agronomist, veterinarian, zootechnician, and the national economy accountant. In addition, the raikom and RIK were permitted, within the limits of available supplies, to add to this list directors of individual enterprises, physicians, and others performing important functions. In effect, this list was an official recognition of the composition of the raion aristocracy, or to put it into more acceptable Soviet terminology, of the "leading and responsible workers" of the raion who were legally entitled to special care by the state.

Despite this legally privileged supply position, the economic status of the raion aristocracy still left much to be desired, and its members were under constant temptation to use such influence and authority as they possessed to supplement their meager perquisites. A relatively trivial incident illustrates the process at work. In this case a group of raikom workers in Pogarsk arranged with the manager of the raion store to divert dry goods to them which should have been transported directly to the villages for sale. There were complaints to the obkom trade division which in turn asked the raikom secretary for an explanation. The raikom first secretary replied as follows:

On July 15, this year [1936], dry goods came to the raion store. The head of this store, Comrade Sobol, was to have transported all these dry goods on July 16 for sale directly in the village. On the morning of July 16, the assistant secretary of the raikom, Comrade Prudnikov, during the time when Comrade Sobol was on duty in the raikom, asked him to leave a few meters of dry goods for the workers of the raikom, the majority of whom, because of their work, do not have the opportunity or time to stand in line to buy dry goods. When Comrade Prudnikov asked him, Comrade Sobol answered that it was possible to do this.

Comrade Prudnikov collected information on the amount of dry goods to be purchased for 10 people [members and wives of members of the raikom staff], collected 615 rubles, went to the store, paid the above sum and came to an agreement that the dry goods which he bought should be divided in accordance with the orders. A total of 143 meters was bought . . .

I, as secretary of the raikom, personally did not know about the purchase of dry goods. Neither did the second secretary, Comrade Tereshov. I learned about this later when the goods had already been distributed. My wife Kuryanova (she is a Party member) took part in this purchase. I first heard of this through Kuryanova. At first I did not attach much significance to this matter.

After you summoned me, I investigated this matter and let you know how things stood. This problem was discussed at the bureau of the raikom. The raikom made the following decision: for violating the principle of free trade, Comrade Prudnikov, as the organizer, was given a severe reprimand, and all the others were reprimanded . . .[7]

The raikom secretary, Geraskin, attached an explanatory note from Prudnikov. It repeated the facts in more elaborate detail and concluded:

In the first place I consider that I made a profound mistake in that I did not inform you, as raikom secretary, that the workers of the raikom asked me to get dry goods for them . . . I am sure that if I had informed you of this case on time, you, as the leader, would have judged my action as incorrect and thus there would not have been any collective buying of dry goods for the fellow-workers who asked me to buy for them. This case of collective purchase will remain in my memory all my life as a lesson. I never did these things before and this was only the first time, but it will be the last.[8]

While Comrade Prudnikov drew a rebuke in this case as a result of obkom intervention, one can infer from the observation of the raikom secretary ("at first I did not attach much significance to this matter") that the practice in which Comrade Prudnikov engaged was not deemed particularly reprehensible. Compared with other exposures of "disorders" in the raion apparatus recorded in the Smolensk Archive, it was mild indeed. The endemic character of complaints about large-scale pilfering and embezzlement in the coöperative and trade network has already been noted.[9] These abuses persisted over the whole life of the Archive despite the most strenuous efforts to stamp them out.

An analysis of some cases cited in the files of the Kozelsk raikom for the period 1931–1933 may serve to illustrate the degree of self-seeking which was occasionally to be encountered in the lower Party and governmental apparatus.[10] On March 28, 1931, the procurator of the Kozelsk raion reported to the raikom on certain "marauder" activities of gorsoviet (town soviet) members while liquidating kulak households.[11] The actions cited included "feasts" in homes of dekulakized peasants made with "confiscated" foodstuffs and alcohol. Even perfume found in a kulak's house was sprinkled "on all those present" to "make the air more pleasant." The gorsoviet chairman, "instead of stopping such activities," proceeded to appropriate for himself the house and furniture of a dekulakized peasant. Some of the "accused" confessed that their actions constituted "a political error," but others felt that the accusations were exaggerated, that the case did not merit the blown-up attention it was getting. "Instead of investigating," one of the accused commented, "you should rather have given me some boots."

On April 18, 1931, the raikom bureau again discussed the pilfering by Communists of dekulakized property.[12] One of the culprits, a raikom instructor, at first denied that there could be anything "criminal" in appropriating kulak property, but after being condemned by all present, he "confessed" his sins and promised to improve his behavior. The punishment he received was removal from his position as instructor and member of the raikom. On October 15, 1931, still another session of the raikom was devoted to the problem of stealing dekulakized and state property. Among the accused this time was a senior people's judge who "bought" dekulakized property and a chairman of the raion consumers' union who supplied himself with consumers' goods from the warehouse without accounting and allowed other raion officials to do the same.[13] The replies of the accused to these charges were, to say the least, interesting. The "main line of defense" consisted of naming other, higher-up Communists or their wives "who also took things." "If they took [e.g., the raikom secretary's wife], why couldn't I?"[14] The raikom bureau, perhaps understandably, was lenient toward the culprits. It contented itself with a resolution reprimanding them and denouncing the existing state of affairs in the raion Party organization — the absence of self-criticism, "familyness" among Communist functionaries, and the persistence of petty-bourgeois attitudes.

On April 21, 1933, the raikom bureau dealt with another scandal involving high raion officials. This time those involved included raivoyenkomat (raion military department) functionaries, the editor of the raion newspaper, the gorsoviet chairman, the head of the raion store, and the head of the raion financial department.[15] The group was accused of pilfering consumers' goods, of "systematic group drinking," of alcoholic and sexual orgies in which they were joined by "foreign elements" (one of the latter the daughter of a lisheniets, or person deprived of the voting privilege). All this, said the bureau resolution, had been brought about by "familyness" and "krugovaya poruka" (mutual responsibility) which resulted in a "lowering of class vigilance" and the corruption and degeneration of the responsible officials involved. In this case the authorities were more severe. One of the culprits was arrested by the OGPU; a number of others were expelled from the Party, while a few were fortunate to escape with a severe reprimand.

As these cases perhaps illustrate, the raion apparatus of the Western Oblast had its share of careerist and self-serving elements. The reported cases are numerous enough to indicate that these were not isolated incidents; on the other hand, they do not necessarily prove that the whole apparatus was corrupt and venal. Undoubtedly there were many Communist functionaries in key places who were zealously devoted to their cause; indeed it is hard to see how the system could have functioned at all without their presence. Moreover, the perennial battle waged in the Western Oblast to weed out the venal and corrupt testified to a realization on the part of the leadership that at least a minimum standard of administrative integrity had to be maintained if the system were to operate with any degree of efficiency. The struggle was not an easy one. The temptation to enjoy the fruits of power was great, and perhaps nowhere greater than in the raions where even key officials in the apparatus were frequently poorly paid, poorly trained, and poorly indoctrinated. As one ponders the record, the wonder is, not that corruption was rife, but that despite this, the Party could still maintain and extend its hold on the villages.

6 Belyi — A Case Study of a Raion Party Organization

Some 150 kilometers to the northeast of Smolensk lies the raion of Belyi, a remote rural district now a part of Velikiye Luki Oblast. During the early and middle twenties, it was one of the uyezds of Smolensk guberniya; and when the Western Oblast was organized in 1929 it became one of the 110 raions over which the oblast exercised jurisdiction.

The Problem of Party Organization in a Rural Area

Belyi raion in 1933 had a population of 91,044, of which only 5,800 were classified as urban.[1] A predominantly agricultural region, its chief activities were flax raising and dairy farming. Always an area in which peasant individualism ran strong (measured by the high percentage of khutor, or individual, farms both in tsarist and NEP days), as late as January 1, 1934, it was only 53.2 per cent collectivized.[2] At that time the socialized sector of agriculture included one sovkhoz, one MTS station, and 257 kolkhozes. The territory of the raion was divided into forty-two village soviets, with an average of a little more than 2,100 people under each soviet. According to the tax figures for 1933, there were only 1,228 workers in the whole raion, of whom 915 were employed in lumbering, 114 in three flax factories, seventy-eight in the butter and cheese factories, sixty in an artel of sewing workers, and the rest in various small shops and coöperatives.[3] The Communist Party in Belyi had virtually no local industrial proletariat on which to draw. Its problem was the formidable one of building an organization and sinking roots in an overwhelmingly peasant community.

The Smolensk Archive sheds no light on the history of the Belyi Party organization during the Civil War and early NEP days. The first body of material which lends itself to systematic analysis consists of uyezd Party committee reports and protocols of meetings of the bureau of the ukom (uyezd Party committee) for the period 1925–26. These records reveal that on October 1, 1925, the roll of Party members and candidates in the whole of Belyi uyezd totaled only 305, and of this total 82 were concentrated in the town of Belyi itself.[4] The remaining 223 village Communists were spread paper thin over the countryside. There were still many villages where there were no Party members or candidates and such as passed through were regarded as curiosities from a distant outer world. Of the total membership of the Belyi Party organization, only 103 were of peasant background. The rest were of worker or employee origin, frequently imported from beyond Belyi's boundaries to govern and administer its affairs.

If the Belyi Party organization was to grow indigenously, it had to recruit among the peasants, and the Party records show that such efforts were made. The ukom protocols contain brief biographies of all persons admitted to Party candidacy or transferred from candidacy to full membership. The peasant biographies disclose an almost uniformly low level of formal education, but they also indicate that the schools which prepared the peasants for Party membership were either service in the Red Army, Komsomol affiliation, or a leadership role in the village soviet — indeed, not infrequently, a combination of all three. Somewhat surprisingly, in view of the Party's stated preference for poor peasants and batraks (farm laborers), it was not so much this group that pressed for Party membership as it was the more ambitious young middle peasants who saw in the Party an opportunity to make a career. But peasants were still a minority among the candidates recruited in 1926; the bulk of the new recruits were drawn from employees and former workers who occupied posts of greater or lesser responsibility in the uyezd administration.

The Hostility of the Peasantry

To read the Party records of 1925–26 is to catch something of the flavor of an army of occupation in hostile territory. By this time the armed bands of dissident peasants who roamed the countryside during the Civil War and early NEP period had been stamped out, but the uyezd Party leaders still spoke of the Socialist-Revolutionaries as a living force which exercised great influence among the well-to-do and even middle peasants. This was still a period when overnight some fifty posters could appear on the walls of the town of Belyi on market day (April 3, 1926), ending with the roughly inscribed slogans, "Leninism leads to poverty. Down with Leninism. Down with Taxes." [5] And while the ukom in its report to the gubkom could describe the attitude of the peasantry toward the Party and "Soviet Power" as generally "good," it also noted that the peasants were "disturbed" by the slowness of the regime in turning over state lands and forests to them, by the lack of agricultural credits, and by the low price of agricultural products as compared with the high prices of goods produced by state industry.

Indeed, the great event in Belyi uyezd in the year 1926 was the temporary rebuff administered to the Belyi Party leadership in its efforts to control the Selpromsoiuz, or Agricultural-Industrial Credit Union. The local membership of the Selpromsoiuz tended to be dominated by the middle and well-to-do peasants, and the administration of Selpromsoiuz, including its Communist fraction, reflected their interests. Such credit as it was able to extend went to "sound" risks, that is to say, to the more substantial element among the peasantry. The bednyaks, or poor peasants, fared badly under this arrangement, and the Belyi Party leadership, as the ostensible caretaker of the interests of the poor peasants, sought a way to utilize the resources of the Selpromsoiuz to take care of them more adequately. Such efforts were resisted by the Selpromsoiuz administration, on the ground that it would transform an agency based on sound cooperative credit principles into a vehicle of "philanthropy." [6]

Matters came to a head at a meeting of plenipotentiaries of the Belyi Selpromsoiuz on March 8–10, 1926, when the Belyi Party leadership decided to install an administration which would reflect its point of view. But the maneuver was badly planned and ran into unexpected difficulties.[7] The spearhead of the attack was one Tsyganov, the chairman of the executive committee of the uyezd Soviet and a member of the ukom Party bureau. According to one account, some three weeks before the scheduled meeting of the plenipotentiaries, the Communist Party fraction in the administration was called together to prepare for the forthcoming session. At this preparatory meeting Tsyganov suggested that the administration of Selpromsoiuz be increased from four members to seven, in order to tilt the balance of control toward the Party leadership. Tsyganov's proposal, however, was rejected by all those present (Party members working in the Selpromsoiuz apparatus) and when Chekalov, the ukom first secretary, was informed he apparently refrained from direct intervention. On March 6, the Party fraction was again called together, and Tsyganov once more advanced his proposal that the size of the administration be increased to seven, only to be turned down again by all of those present except one. At this meeting the Party fraction chose a bureau, headed by Tsyganov, to direct Party activities at the congress of plenipotentiaries of Selpromsoiuz and at sessions of its soviet.

The dissension in the Party fraction now broke into the open.[8] At a meeting of the soviet of Selpromsoiuz, Chernov and Voronov, the Party members in the administration, openly opposed Tsyganov's call for changes in the structure of Selpromsoiuz, for public ballots, and for a program to activate the bednyak fund. Toward the end of the session Tsyganov called a private meeting attended by the Party fraction and non-Party members of the administration, at which he informed them in the name of the ukom of the Party that the administration had to be increased to seven. Again he was rebuffed by all of those present except one. Then in the name of the gubkom and ukom, he moved that the administration be increased to five members, only once more to meet defeat.

Meanwhile, as the open meeting of the plenipotentiaries began, Secretary Chekalov summoned the Party fraction to his office, called upon them to maintain discipline, and categorically demanded that a fifth member be introduced into the administration in the person of one Comrade Tapeshkin.[9] Tsyganov then assembled a plenum of the soviet and administration, and again raised the fifth member issue. But Chernov and Voronov both defied Party discipline, and the motion was again defeated.

Despite this ominous sign, Tsyganov was determined to push ahead and brought the matter up before the open meeting of the plenipotentiaries. The reception was hostile, and Tsyganov's motion was overwhelmingly rejected by a vote of thirty-nine to nineteen. In his report to the ukom, Tsyganov later commented that "the composition of the meeting was about seventy per cent SR's who masked themselves as non-Party people." [10] Tsyganov then took the drastic step of recalling members of the Party fraction from the administration, meanwhile announcing to the assembled plenipotentiaries that in view of "the negative attitude of the non-Party part of the Selpromsoiuz administration toward the cooperative policy of the Party," the Party fraction had decided that a continuation of the present arrangements "would not serve the cause of Socialist construction." [11] The non-Party fraction replied by denying the charges leveled against it and stating that "the uncompromising attitude of the Party fraction" had made it necessary for the non-Party elements to consider leaving the Selpromsoiuz, though they proposed to continue working in it temporarily.[12]

At this point the chairman declared an intermission, during which another meeting was held between the Party fraction and non-Party representatives in the administration. What transpired at this meeting is not a matter of record, but it can be assumed that Tsyganov brought maximum pressure to bear. In any event when the congress reassembled, it was moved and carried that new elections be held and that five members be named to the administration. This time there were thirty-eight votes in favor of the motion, one against, and eight abstentions. Tsyganov then offered the gathering the slate of the Party fraction, which included two non-Party holdovers from the old administration. After some initial hesitation the latter agreed to run, and the slate was approved by a vote of fifty-four in favor, none opposing, and three abstaining.

The "victory" which Tsyganov finally snatched from the congress turned out to be costly for the Belyi Party leadership. Not only were the majority of peasant representatives in Selpromsoiuz disillusioned and outraged by the high-handed conduct of Tsyganov and his collaborators, but the reverberations of the scandal also reached Smolensk, and the gubkom itself decided to intervene. On April 2, 1926, Beika, the gubkom first secretary, and Pavlyuchenko, then head of the organization section of the gubkom secretariat, dispatched a letter to the Belyi ukom which began: "Dear Comrades, With reference to the decision of the Gubkom bureau of March 25, the Gubkom considers it necessary to draw your serious attention to the following abnormal manifestations in your work." [13] The letter then listed a bill of particulars of six items: (1) The meeting of the Plenipotentiaries of the Selpromsoiuz made clear that the election campaign for the selection of representatives had not been given sufficiently strong Party leadership. (2) At the meeting, Party-Komsomol representation amounted to only seven people or 9 per cent, confirming Point One. (3) The ukom, under these circumstances, pursued an improper line by its categorical insistence on a five-member administration, causing an open and serious rift with the non-Party elements. (4) The attitude of "no matter what" and the tactics of threats and dictates in order to attain a majority in the administration undermined the authority of the Party. (5) The decision to boycott Selpromsoiuz (through the withdrawal of Party members) in an equally objectionable way cut the ukom off from its proper leadership role. (6) Despite the seeming "success" of the Party fraction after that, the character of the non-Party declaration of the former leadership of Selpromsoiuz demonstrated the improper leadership of the ukom bureau.

The letter also pointed out that similarly indefensible tactics had been pursued in the Union of Teachers, and that the situation there had only been mitigated by gubkom intervention. The letter closed with a statement that the gubkom took a serious view of the situation and called for an elimination of the "unhealthy" methods which the Belyi Party leadership had employed.

The Belyi Party leaders were not disposed to take this rebuke lying down. Convinced that they were correct in having done what they did and that the gubkom misunderstood the local situation, they sought both to justify their course of action to the gubkom, and to retaliate against Chernov and Voronov who had broken the discipline of the Party fraction. Disturbed by the self-righteous and defiant attitude of the Belyi leaders, the gubkom decided to remove both Chekalov, the first secretary, and Tsyganov, the chairman of the soviet, from their positions of responsibility in Belyi.

This set off another major explosion in the Belyi Party organization, this time directed against the gubkom. Indeed, the situation became so serious that Chekalov telegraphed Smolensk urging either Beika or Pavlyuchenko to come to Belyi to explain matters.[14] Neither came, but Comrade Zimenkov, a member of the gubkom bureau, was sent instead. On May 10 a special session of the ukom bureau assembled to hear Zimenkov and to meet Chekalov's replacement, Comrade Golik.

The session was stormy. Zimenkov began by reading a gubkom letter of May 8 which announced that Golik was being placed at the head of the Belyi Party organization "to set its house in order." [15] He expressed the hope that, despite disagreement, Belyi would support the gubkom and install Golik as first secretary without incident. He was immediately bombarded with hostile questions. Had the matter of Chekalov's removal been cleared with the Central Committee? Did the gubkom think that it was established that the Belyi leaders had not discharged their work satisfactorily on the basis of the decisions of the Fourteenth Party Conference? Why didn't the gubkom make a careful investigation of the situation in Belyi instead of recalling Chekalov? Did the gubkom think that the old Selpromsoiuz administration was correct in its policy and what did the gubkom propose to do about the Selpromsoiuz apparatus? Zimenkov dealt with these questions as best he could, and then Tsyganov arose. In forthright language he denounced the gubkom decision as incorrect, "as a death verdict on the Party in favor of the SR's." He expressed his disbelief at the report that Molotov had approved Chekalov's recall, and he called for a detailed investigation by a special commission of the gubkom, with Chekalov meanwhile to remain at his post. Most of the others who spoke supported Tsyganov, though one member, Kovalev, who was later himself to become first secretary, after observing that "the measures taken by the gubkom are extraordinarily extreme," nevertheless urged that the gubkom's decisions be carried out. Chekalov himself, after expressing his regret at the absence of advance consultation on the part of the gubkom, nevertheless urged that Golik be approved. "We must agree and do what the gubkom recommends." Zimenkov concluded the discussion by denouncing its "improper tone" and repeating his earlier declaration that the gubkom was adamant in its decision to recall Chekalov. A vote was taken, and by a majority of three to two the gubkom action was approved.

The next day, May 11, the ukom plenum assembled to endorse the action of its bureau. This time the session was, if anything, even more stormy. Zimenkov began by reading the gubkom letter announcing the recall of Chekalov. Again there were indignant outbursts from the floor. Tsyganov repeated his view that the gubkom was "basically wrong." A Comrade Chibisov scored the gubkom's high-handed tactics in confronting the Belyi organization with an ultimatum. "To my mind," said Chibisov, "lower Party organs can discuss and express their opinion on all resolutions of higher Party bodies; but I haven't heard for a long time of a case such as this, where Comrade Zimenkov pronounces, 'once the gubkom decides, that's how it must be.'" Again Chekalov played the role of the disciplined Party apparatchik. He called for active support of the gubkom "in a united front" and offered a resolution expressing agreement with his own removal and his replacement by Golik. His resolution also requested the gubkom to undertake "a detailed study of the question of agricultural coöperation in Belyi uyezd." But Tsyganov refused to go along. Instead he moved a substitute resolution which declared, "In view of the insistent demand of the gubkom for the recall of Comrade Chekalov, we agree to induct Comrade Golik as a member of the ukom and to elect him first secretary instead of Chekalov, thus fulfilling the task of giving him the necessary authority before the organization and good conditions for work. We request the gubkom to study further its accusation of a rupture between the ukom and the peasantry, and once the facts are established, to remove its accusation." [16]

This time a majority of the speakers supported Tsyganov, and the representatives of the gubkom asked for the floor. Kuchinsky, who had accompanied Zimenkov to Belyi, spoke first. He insisted that the gubkom did not demand subordination but agreement, and he called for approval of Chekalov's resolution. Zimenkov added that acceptance of Tsyganov's formula would discredit the gubkom, but nevertheless, by a vote of seven to six it was approved. But disputes continued as to whether Belyi was "subordinating" itself to the gubkom or merely "agreeing" with its actions. Finally Chekalov could stand it no longer. Taking the floor, he shouted: "To the devil with this legalistic terminology of 'subordination' or 'agreement.' The question before us is not one of words, but of fact. I propose to the plenum that it actively support the decision of the gubkom concerning the recall of Comrade Chekalov and the arrival of Comrade Golik." The plenum agreed.

On May 14 the plenum of the ukom assembled formally to elect a new secretary and bureau.[17] This time there were no disputes, and Golik was elected. In the interim Kovalev had replaced Tsyganov as chairman of the uyezd executive committee, although Tsyganov temporarily remained as his deputy. In the elections to the new bureau, Tsyganov was demoted from member to candidate. But he still had one verbal triumph to celebrate, the farewell to Chekalov which the whole bureau endorsed. The tribute read: "Comrade Chekalov, working for a year as the leader of the Belyi uyezd Party organization (as secretary) showed himself before the Party masses as a seasoned, able, and staunch leader, a good comrade and Party member, uniting the organization, strengthening its unity and solidarity and raising its capacity for work. In the period of his labors the organization grew satisfactorily, was strengthened, and prepared itself for further work in the leadership of the worker-peasant masses and the state apparatus, on the basis of the decisions of the Party Congresses and conferences." [18] Whether this expression of appreciation helped Chekalov's career is open to doubt. Restiveness, independence, and insubordination in lower Party organs were not qualities which Party superiors were to value highly in the years to come. But they were also qualities which were never wholly eliminated in Belyi, as will subsequently appear.

The Persisting Weakness of the Belyi Party Organization

The records of the Belyi Party organization for the period 1927–1933 are missing from the Smolensk Archive, and this part of the story must remain an untold tale. It can be assumed that the history of Belyi during the years of dekulakization and collectivization was part of the larger history of the Western Oblast, with the same story of food shortages, kulak deportations, and the tortuous beginnings of kolkhoz construction.[19] One important difference there was. Industrialization left Belyi raion largely untouched, except that a MTS with some thirty-five tractors (January 1934) appeared as a symbol of the mechanization of agriculture.[20] For the rest, Belyi remained a rural stronghold, with few new industrial enterprises to disturb its sylvan quiet. Even collectivization was slow to penetrate Belyi raion, and as late as January 1934 nearly half the land was still tilled by individual farmers. The Party authorities in Smolensk were sufficiently disturbed by this situation to initiate a special investigation of the reasons for the failure of individual farmers to join the kolkhozes. The report from Belyi yielded an interesting reply. It stated:

In analyzing the reasons why whole villages of individual farmers do not enter a kolkhoz we receive the following picture (we cite the most characteristic and typical reasons from the majority of such settlements in the raion): The village of Nivki, Konnovsk village soviet, consists of nineteen farms, four of them prosperous ones. In this village there is an anti-Soviet group who keep the entire village under their thumb. The leader of this group is Roman Chervyakov. A one-time chairman of a village soviet, he enjoys great respect and confidence among his fellow-villagers. His closest assistant is Yegor Kovalev, a fiery agitator against the kolkhozes. He leads five farms. In the spring in this village there were many who wanted to join the kolkhoz, but under the influence of this group the organization of the kolkhoz did not take place. Now among the peasants there is a mutual guarantee (an agreement that no one will join the kolkhoz). Two poor peasants tried to violate this agreement because of a bread shortage, and they wanted to enter the kolkhoz. But [the anti-kolkhoz fraction] bargained with them, hired them to pasture the cattle of the village, gave them as much bread as they asked for, and persuaded them in no case to enter the kolkhoz.

In another village — Galnevo — a group of sectarians read the Bible collectively, predict that "there is not much longer to live; do not succumb to temptation, brothers" (i.e., do not enter the kolkhoz).

We find the same things in a number of other settlements.[21]

It needs to be remembered that the taxes and obligatory deliveries of the individual farmer to the state were far heavier than those of the kolkhoznik. The decision to stay out of the kolkhoz was therefore made at a heavy price. It was in the face of this adamant resistance that the Belyi Party organization sought to carry on its activities.

The Archive contains detailed data on the composition of the Belyi Party organization for the period 1934–1936.[22] An analysis of this material yields some interesting results. The membership of the Belyi organization increased very little compared with the mid-twenties — from 305 on October 1, 1925, to 367 on September 1, 1934. Indeed, by July 12, 1936, after the exchange of Party documents, the membership declined to 241.[23]

Of the total membership of the Belyi Party organization at least half consisted of those employed in so-called "leading work" — that is, raion Party and government officials, directors of flax factories, officials of the MTS, chairmen of village soviets, chairmen of rural consumers' societies, the sovkhoz and kolkhoz chairmen, and others occupying equivalent positions. Out of a total of 257 kolkhozes in the raion, only seven had primary Party organizations, though an additional thirteen had Party-candidate groups, and seven had Party-Komsomol groups.[24] In addition, there were nine village soviet Party organizations of various types with which individual Party members in a nearby kolkhoz could affiliate. But as these figures indicate, the great majority of kolkhozes lacked any form of Party representation. During the mid-thirties in Belyi raion, the projection of Party controls into the kolkhozes was still an operation which had largely to be performed from the outside.

On January 1, 1935, the Belyi Party organization reported on the social composition of its membership.[25] Again the data hold our great interest. Of the total Party membership of 355 on that date, in terms of social origin 273 were peasants, sixty-three were workers, and nineteen employees. When the current occupations of the membership were examined, however, the proportions changed in startling fashion. Of the total of 355, 202 were classified as employees, 144 as kolkhozniks, and only nine as workers. While these figures again stress the dominant role of the Party and governmental apparatus in the membership of the Belyi organization, they also emphasize the extent to which by the mid-thirties this apparatus was being recruited from persons of peasant origin who were using Party membership to lift themselves in the social and political scale. But peasant recruitment exacted its price. A subsequent report noted "the continued existence in the organization of a significant number of semiliterate Communists in regard to political preparation and an even greater number in general education." [26]

On July 12, 1936, Kovalev, the first secretary of the Belyi raikom, delivered a report on the state of the primary Party organizations in the raion in connection with the completion of the exchange of Party documents.[27] The report revealed that there were only twenty-one primary Party organizations in the whole raion, exclusive of Party-candidate and Party-Komsomol groups. Of these twenty-one organizations, only four were located in kolkhozes; the largest consisted of four members and three candidates and the smallest of three members and two candidates. Of the other seventeen primary Party organizations, two were in the lumber industry, one in the MTS, one in the sovkhoz, one in the Prigorodnyi village soviet, one in the raion consumers' union, one in the agricultural tekhnikum, and one under the raikom itself; the remaining nine organizations were located in the RIK, its various departments, and in the city soviet of Belyi. The largest primary organization by far was in the raikom itself. It consisted of nineteen Party members, chiefly members of the raikom apparatus.

The evaluation of these primary Party organizations by the raikom secretary is not without interest. Significantly, since the year was 1936, the primary Party organization of the NKVD, which consisted of seven members and four candidates, was singled out for special praise. It was saluted as "a model for other primary organizations . . . all Party workers who work in the Division of the NKVD take an active part in Party work." On the other hand, perhaps also significantly, the primary Party organizations in the raion consumers' union and in the supply organizations were singled out for special criticism. Here again one encountered the familiar charge of corruption in the trade network. "In a number of selpos [village stores]," noted Kovalev, "there is a shortage of necessary goods; the status of the stores is anticultural . . . Besides . . . embezzlements have been taking place in some selpos." He complained of drunkenness and moral corruption among some Communists in the supply organizations and called for a "radical revamping and improvement of Party work" in these organizations. In the case of most of the other primary organizations Kovalev offered a judicious mixture of praise and reprimand, though at least one kolkhoz, "Putevaya Zvezda," obviously the model kolkhoz of the raion, was especially lauded for its success in achieving a large harvest of flax in 1935 and for developing a Stakhanovite movement among the kolkhozniks. On the other hand, in the kolkhoz misnamed "Vperyod" (Forward), Kovalev noted that Stakhanovites were the victims of "organized persecution by other elements in the kolkhoz," and he called for a quick end to "these disorders."

Meanwhile, the obkom also entered the Belyi picture. Aroused by charges and countercharges of corruption, it sent a special commission to investigate. On September 25, 1936, the obkom bureau passed the following resolution on the situation in Belyi:

Having heard the report of the commission of the obkom . . . on the results of the investigation of the statement of Troinitsky on the situation in Belyi, the bureau of the obkom considers it established that it was correct in bringing Troinitsky to criminal trial. Troinitsky, as head of the accounting and bookkeeping school, allowed stealing and embezzlement of state funds, chose for work in the school a group of clearly hostile people . . . and committed a number of other crimes. And Troinitsky's statement on the corruption of the raion leaders and their badgering of Troinitsky was made by him after his exposure, with the clear aim of avenging his crimes.

Considering Troinitsky's statement about the corruption of the Belyi leaders and the Party organization to be slanderous, the bureau of the obkom reports, however, that . . . a number of serious shortcomings in the work of the legal and investigating organs, of the raion newspaper, and the raion health department, really existed. Besides, a shocking attitude has been revealed by the raion organization in regard to the suicide of the demobilized Red Army man, Machkurov, and others. The raikom of the Party, discussing these questions and taking a narrow attitude toward them, did not impart any political significance to them and did not carry the matter to its conclusion.[28]

The obkom thereupon decreed that all these "disorders" be eliminated. Kovalev, the raikom secretary, was treated rather gently. Not only was he cleared of the charge of corruption, but he managed to escape without even a formal rebuke. His respite, however, was not to be long lasting.

The Great Purge in Belyi

The year 1937 ushered in what was beyond doubt the most traumatic period in the history of the Belyi Party organization. At the beginning of the year the members of the raikom bureau and leading personalities of the raion were Kovalev, the veteran first secretary; Karpovsky, the second secretary, who had just arrived in the raion; Stogov, the chairman of the RIK; Vinogradov, the head of the raion office of the NKVD; Yakushin, the raion military commissar; Kurdenkov, the Komsomol head; Senin, the head of the Politotdel in the Sovkhoz "Shamilovo"; and Frolov, the raion newspaper editor. Kovalev appeared to be in firm control; indeed, if later testimony is to be credited, he operated as a kind of little Stalin in the raion.

The first hint of trouble came on March 15, 1937, when Kovalev delivered a report to the raikom bureau on the resolution of the February Central Committee plenum calling for a revival of intra-Party democracy and strict observance of the Party statute in conducting elections.[29] At this meeting there was much criticism of the work of the raikom, but the attack on Kovalev himself was indirect rather than frontal. The bureau decided to call a general meeting of the raion Party organization on March 19 for further consideration of the problem.

In the interim, the obkom apparently decided to make Kovalev the raion scapegoat for the sins against which the February plenum of the Central Committee had inveighed. His removal as raikom secretary was decreed, but his connections with Rumyantsev and Shilman were still sufficiently close to insure him a line of retreat to Smolensk, where he was given a job in the obkom secretarial apparatus. Meanwhile, however, Kovalev had to be publicly "executed" in Belyi, and the ceremonies, which were attended by 137 members and 83 candidates, stretched over four days, from March 19 through March 22.[30] Golovashenko, a representative of the obkom, presided over the shambles, and indeed had to exercise a restraining hand.

The abuse which was heaped on Kovalev at this marathon session was more than a catharsis for pent-up hatreds. It revealed a group of badly frightened men and women who were seeking to disassociate themselves from their long involvement with a leader who had fallen from grace. Kovalev opened the meeting with a report on the February plenum. The tone of the discussion which followed was set by the first speaker, one Martinov, Director of Accounting Courses, who launched on a diatribe against Kovalev, denouncing him as a dictator who constantly abused his subordinates. He described the report which Kovalev had just delivered as contrary to the Party line and cited past deviations on Kovalev's part, including the allegations that he had quit the Party in 1921 because he did not approve of the NEP, that he had lived with a Trotskyite for a time, and that he shared Trotskyite views. The discussion proceeded in this vein, with one speaker also charging that Kovalev had deserted from the Red Army during the Civil War, and many others piling up additional evidence of his abusive and dictatorial conduct.

As those who had been closest to Kovalev vied with each other in excoriating him, there were some embarrassing questions from the rank and file. "Every one blames Kovalev," said one member, "but what about the other Party bureau members?" A raikom instructor added, "Every one in the bureau approved Kovalev's decisions and praised him for them." And a village soviet chairman put it most pointedly of all, "Every one now blames Kovalev — but why, if it's all true, didn't they do something about it?" Soloviev, the assistant secretary of the Raikom, ventured a lame reply: "Comrades, four years I have been silent, four years I did not participate in Party meetings . . . The reason is I was forbidden to speak. I was a hairbreadth away from expulsion from the Party . . . Kovalev attempted to drive Soloviev out of the raion; not being able to do so, he ordered him to be silent." And then Soloviev too proceeded to blast Kovalev.

The summary speech was delivered by the Obkom representative, Golovashenko. By contrast with some that had preceded it, it was relatively moderate and responsible in tone. He too denounced Kovalev for his poor leadership — pointing out that he had rarely participated in RIK and town soviet meetings, that he had violated democratic centralism by coöpting fifteen out of twenty-five raikom members, and that he had personally removed nine out of eighteen "elected" Party organizers in 1936 alone. He emphasized the major shortcomings of the raikom as flattery of Kovalev, passivity, political blunders, and lack of self-criticism. But he refused to associate himself with the charge that Kovalev was a Trotskyite. "Personally," he said, "I do not have sufficient basis to call Kovalev a Trotskyite. We need to understand what a Trotskyite is — an agent of fascism, a restorer of capitalism, who must be destroyed as an enemy of the working class." The evidence, he added, must be investigated; the immediate task before the Belyi organization was to choose a new secretary.

Kovalev had the last word. The speech of Rumyantsev at the obkom session, he declared, had made him realize his shortcomings, but he had not expected such an onslaught as had here been directed against him. He found it a sad experience to live through — the evidence of lack of faith in him. Nevertheless, he asserted, his record was clear. He had served in the Red Army during the Civil War as a volunteer. He first entered the Party in 1920 and had been "mechanically" removed in 1921 for passivity. He had never been a member of any Trotskyite "group" nor had he had any connection with such groups. He realized that it was wrong to behave as he had done, and he promised to try to remedy his deficiencies.

The meeting concluded with a resolution listing all of Kovalev's shortcomings and ordering his removal from the post of raikom first secretary "for rudeness, the suppression of self-criticism, and non-Bolshevik methods of work." The duties of the first secretaryship were temporarily assigned to Karpovsky, the second secretary.

The problem of a permanent replacement for Kovalev provided the Belyi organization with its next thorny issue. On April 5, 1937, the raikom bureau decided that Karpovsky was too new to the raion and too inexperienced to take over the job. The bureau requested the obkom to send in "an experienced worker who will work better than Kovalev," and at the same time suggested that at least three of its members, Senin, Stogov, and Yakushin, had the necessary authority to discharge the duties of raikom first secretary.[31] Meanwhile, a meeting of the Belyi Party aktiv was called for April 29, 1937, to approve the obkom choice, one Boradulin, who had worked in the obkom apparatus and had previously served as first secretary in Demidov and Krasnyi.[32] Boradulin was not present and had apparently made a bad impression on his earlier visit to the raion. The result was an open revolt at the meeting. Although Karpovsky and one or two others urged that the obkom choice be approved, the majority aired their unfavorable impressions of Boradulin and attacked him as being as bad as or worse than Kovalev.

Sentiment turned toward the retention of Karpovsky ("We might as well leave Karpovsky"), and finally a motion was carried that the obkom be informed that the raion aktiv "oriented" itself toward Karpovsky, Frolov, Zhukov, and Shitov as candidates for the first secretaryship. This was the period when the authority of Rumyantsev, Shilman, and other leaders of the obkom was becoming increasingly shaky; indeed less than two months later they were to be purged. In any case, they apparently accepted the rebuff from Belyi, and in May Karpovsky was designated first secretary and Shitov second secretary.[33] Since Karpovsky had originally been sent into Belyi by the Rumyantsev-Shilman group it can also be assumed that the rebuff was not too severe. This was soon to prove the cause of Karpovsky's undoing.

The next stage in the checkered history of the Belyi organization was signaled by the "unmasking" of the obkom "wreckers" in June. On June 23 Karpovsky informed the raikom bureau of the special plenum of the obkom where Rumyantsev and his followers were purged.[34] The obkom plenum made clear that the "unmasking" at the top was only the beginning and that the "agents" of the "wreckers" in the raions would also be rooted out. Hysteria spread to Belyi, and an ominous chain of denunciations was set in motion. At the meeting of July 23 the hunt began to rid Belyi of the former associates of the "subversive" Kovalev. Frolov, the raion editor, denounced Stogov, the RIK chairman, and Vinogradov, the NKVD head, as Kovalev's allies, and the meeting recommended the removal of the "right-deviationist" Stogov and an investigation of Vinogradov's anti-Party behavior.

On June 26–27 the raikom plenum and Party aktiv assembled to hear Karpovsky's report on the special obkom plenum.[35] At this meeting Stogov tried to save his skin by joining feverishly in the denunciations of Kovalev and Rumyantsev, but in vain. The meeting recommended the removal of Stogov and his deputy Vasiunin and asked the obkom to bring Kovalev to an "accounting." The discussion quickly flared into a fever of mutual denunciations, and all the dirty linen of the raion was spread upon the table. During the next weeks the relentless search for victims gathered increasing momentum, and one by one those who had held high office in the raion under Kovalev found themselves compromised and victimized by the association. Shitov was removed as second secretary and replaced by Frolov, the raion editor.[36]

Now it was to be Karpovsky's turn. On September 18–19, 1937, a raikom plenum, with the obkom representative, Shirozyan, in attendance, met to administer the *coup de grâce*.[37] Frolov presided. The material on Karpovsky was read. He was accused of having been an agent in the raion of the former oblast leadership, of having once been a participant in a bandit gang, of having relatives abroad, of maintaining connections with a sister who had married a former merchant, and of continuing his contacts to the last with "enemies of the people" such as Shilman. Karpovsky tried in vain to counter these accusations. He denied any relationships with enemies of the people. He claimed that instead of having been a member of a band, he had participated in exterminating one and had himself killed two bandits. He admitted receiving a letter from an aunt in Rumania, but insisted that he had never met her since she had left Russia in 1908 when she married a Rumanian. He acknowledged that his sister had married a former merchant, but pointed out that they were both now employed in useful work. One brave friend, a Comrade Moskalev, even rose to Karpovsky's defense and testified that they had participated together in the liquidation of "bands," but all the explanations and denials proved wasted breath. Karpovsky was unanimously excluded from the Party, and Frolov was temporarily charged with the task of performing the duties of first secretary. Again the discussion turned into a series of denunciations, which spilled over with unprecedented virulence into a general meeting of the raion Party organization on September 19–20 attended by 117 members and 63 candidates.

At this meeting speaker after speaker denounced Karpovsky as a bandit, and even the loyal friend who had testified that they fought together against bandits, and who now found himself attacked on all sides, said weakly that he had not known that Karpovsky belonged to a band.[38] Shirozyan, the obkom representative, charged that Karpovsky had been sent into the raion by the old leadership to protect Kovalev's cadres, that there were still many enemies in the raion, and that it was necessary to eliminate them. The meeting obliged with a new hail of denunciations and expulsions. Now the heat turned on Frolov, who was accused of displaying "liberalism" and of having been closely associated with Karpovsky. The obkom was urged to send some one else to serve as first secretary.

The obkom obliged and sent one Comrade Galkin, who had served earlier as raikom secretary in Kozelsk. This time there was no debate, and at a meeting of the raikom plenum on October 21 Galkin was approved.[39] The same day Shirozyan, the obkom instructor, reported to a general meeting of the Belyi Party that the obkom, as requested, had sent Comrade Galkin to serve as Belyi first secretary.[40] Galkin recited his autobiography to the meeting, and in answer to questions, revealed that his father was a factory worker in the Ukraine, that the family had joined a kolkhoz in 1929, that he had received his political education in a Red Army Party school, and that he had been crippled as a result of a kulak attack. This time there was not the slightest disposition to challenge the obkom, and Galkin was unanimously elected to the raikom. Meanwhile, the purge of those who had had any previous connections with the Kovalev leadership pursued its relentless course. Frolov was removed as second secretary but was left temporarily to serve as editor of the raion newspaper while a commission investigated his past. A new second and a new third secretary were chosen, and a new RIK chairman installed. By the end of the year 1937, a completely new team had taken over in Belyi, and they were all strangers to the raion.

At this point, the history of the Belyi Party organization stops, at least so far as the Smolensk Archive is concerned. As this review of the events of 1937 indicates, even a Party organization in as remote a rural backwater as Belyi found itself tragically caught up in the convulsions of the Great Purge. In the course of one year there were three first secretaries, Kovalev, Karpovsky, and Galkin (four if the interim status of Frolov is included), and the ranks of the raion Party and governmental leadership were decimated. By the end of the year the Belyi Party organization had less than 200 members in a raion with a population of more than 90,000.[41] During the next years it would rebuild its strength, but it could never wholly escape the handicaps which any political force superimposed from the outside encounters in coming to terms with a hostile environment.

7 Control at the Grass Roots — The Outposts of Authority in the Villages

To understand the grave difficulties which the Party had to overcome in projecting its control into the countryside, one needs to catch something of the rhythm of the Russian village — its instinctive distrust of the strange and unfamiliar, its deep attachment to traditional ways of doing things, and its determination to hold on to the land it considered its own. Buried in the Smolensk Archive is an illuminating report that communicates much of the flavor of rural life in the Smolensk area in pre-collectivization days.[1] Prepared by a student at the Zinoviev Communist University (Leningrad) as his summer project, it describes his native Ilino volost (which was a part of Velizh uyezd) in a frank, unvarnished way. Although written with a hopeful eye to the future, it is notably free of Party sloganeering, and it registers what its author saw.

Rural Life before Collectivization

Ilino volost was a remote district forty-five versts away from the nearest railway station, the horse its only means of communication with the outside world; in spring when the Western Dvina overflowed it might be cut off from the uyezd center for as much as a week. Up to 1923, the author tells us, armed bands still roamed the countryside and enforced so-called "contributions" from the peasantry. During this period five Soviet workers were murdered, including the chairman of the volost executive committee, a people's judge, and the head of the volost land division. "Even in 1923 during the whole year the chairman of the volost executive committee . . . went out only once, and then was accompanied continuously by detachments to suppress banditry."

In a volost with a population of about 14,000 people the Party organization consisted of only seven members and three candidates, mostly volost officials. The Party secretary was a worker who had lived in the country until the age of twelve, had joined the Party in 1918, and had some experience "in various administrative organs and the GPU." Our student thought him deficient in leadership and in knowledge of peasant attitudes. He cited the following example:

In the spring, in May of this year, an uyezd worker . . . was sent from the uyezd committee . . . to hold peasant meetings and to deliver a report on land policy at the Barborovsk village assembly. After the report they [the Party secretary and the uyezd worker] proposed a resolution to the peasants . . . to transfer to a collective form of land tenure. In the raion all the peasants had gone out to individual farms 15 to 18 years before, and now not even the sites are visible where the villages and settlements were previously located . . . The peasants came out against the proposals of the lecturer, pointing out that they were convinced that the individual form of land tenure is better than other forms, and therefore they were against the transfer back to settlements and to the collective form of land tenure. It can be said that individual farm land tenure has entered into the flesh and blood of our peasants. They rejected the resolution . . . Such cases . . . to a significant degree undermine the authority of the [Party] organization.[2]

The student then described how the Party sought to direct the life of the volost:

The volkom guides the volost executive committee . . . and the staunchest comrades, one per village soviet, are assigned to the village soviets . . . Up to this time leadership consisted only in being present, if possible, at sessions of the village soviet and peasant meetings and in participation in the discussion of various questions.

The shortcomings are as follows: . . . they [the Party workers] strive to criticize, to command, but they do not . . . explain practically how it is necessary to work. For example . . . at the end of July I was present at the plenum of the village soviet where the account of the work of the village soviet was given. After the report the assigned comrade asked about ten different questions of the reporter, for example, how do the sections work, what has been done in the study of agriculture, etc. Then he came out with criticism, lashed into everything, saying, in general, that the sections are not working, that the work is not set up as it should be, etc., dictating in general trite phrases, but not getting down to concrete cases. The chairman, a non-Party man, listened to the criticism and blushed, and so did other members of the village soviet who are also non-Party people, including one Komsomolite. The sections under the village soviet are new organizations . . . They often do not understand where and how to begin, but they receive rather harsh criticism from the Party member who is assigned to them. Of course, such leadership yields no results, sometimes even repels one or another active peasant.[3]

The Ilino village soviet consisted of twenty members, including one woman and a Komsomol member. Much of its time was spent in resolving land disputes, which, our student tells us, were "often accompanied by a real fight."

Sometimes it takes a whole day to solve one question. Often it is necessary to travel to the spot in order to solve the problems. The chairman of the village soviet, in order to draw the members of the village soviet into the work . . . tries to send members of the village soviet to the spot to resolve various problems in dispute, but in the majority of cases no results are achieved . . . i.e., they [the peasants] do not agree with the decision . . .

and often the chairman himself must make a second trip and resolve the disputes which have arisen. There are cases where the peasants do not agree with the decision of the chairman of the village soviet and turn to the volost executive committee . . . The remainder of the time [of the village soviet] is occupied with administrative work, the issuance of information, the collection and compilation of data, etc. . . . once a month there are plenums of the volost executive committee, where the chairmen of village soviets are present . . . Rather often a member of the volost executive committee travels to the village soviets. In economic work — for example, the discussion of problems of improving agriculture, the coöperative structure, the leadership of the peasant committee, etc. — things are not quite up to standard, often because of a failure to understand the solution of these questions properly.[4]

The situation in the coöperative was particularly unsatisfactory. Both the board and the revisory commission, which checked accounts, were "semiliterate." In October 1924 the revisory commission "established that there was a shortage in the stalls of goods and money amounting to 662 rubles." In August of the same year,

A member of the board, who was going to Leningrad for goods, had his pocket cut out and 381 rubles stolen. The board was dismissed and brought to court; . . . several people were sentenced for from one to three years . . . In May of this year one member of the board (Mateyenko) went to Vitebsk for goods and there got drunk — he drank 260 rubles' worth. In Vitebsk Mateyenko was twice held for drunkenness by the militia. As a result the militia took the money away from him and sent it by telegraph to the Ilino consumers' coöperative. In the revisory committee investigation in May of this year, shortages of goods were discovered in the shops amounting to around 200 rubles.

Because of such "shortcomings," the student pointed out, "many, and especially the middle peasants, hold back from entering the coöperative." [5]

One of the student's grievances against the volost executive committee was that it had permitted the public bath in Ilino to fall into disrepair. As a result he had to patronize a privately operated bath which cost him 15 kopecks. The public bath, he solemnly reported, "is located about 200 steps from the volost executive committee, and the lack of management of the VIK is immediately apparent to every peasant and local inhabitant." "In the first place," he declared, "if we put the bath in order, we would receive income. In the second place, the local population, which needs baths, would be served (also the members of the volkom would not be obliged to visit the bath of the local priest). In the third place, the bath would not serve as an object of agitation to the effect that the local government does not know how to manage things . . ." [6]

Yet despite these and other shortcomings our student concluded that the prestige of the Soviet government in the countryside was rising.

The most important factors regulating the mood of the peasants toward the Soviet are economic relationships such as taxes and prices for industrial goods, and also the attitude of officials toward the peasants. The lowering of the single agricultural tax played an important part in [determining] the mood of the poor peasants and middle peasants. Upon receiving the tax lists, when the peasants see that the agricultural tax has been decreased in comparison with last year, they are convinced that the Soviet government is meeting the peasants half-way. The same thing is observed in regard to lowering prices for industrial goods, which convinces the peasants that the workers in the cities are doing something for them . . . Those peasants who regarded the Soviet government with hostility . . . have changed their minds in view of the destruction of banditry and the general strengthening of Soviet construction; many are beginning in various ways to adjust themselves to the Soviet government.[7]

As these quotations indicate, the picture in the villages at the height of the NEP was a confused one. In one sense, the NEP concessions served to stabilize the position of the Soviet authorities in the countryside; at least outright hostility to Soviet policy diminished. In another sense, the position of the Soviet authorities remained precarious. The weakness of the Party in the villages and the inefficiency and undependability of its governing apparatus were patent for all to see. Beneath the surface of sovietization, the life of the peasant flowed on in its accustomed way relatively untouched by the great political and social overturn which the revolution engendered in the cities. The key personage in the village, the chairman of the village soviet, more often than not, was a non-Party man far closer to the needs and aspirations of his peasant neighbors than to the demands and outlook of the far-off Soviet Power in Moscow or even Smolensk. He had to collect the taxes that higher Soviet authorities demanded, furnish recruits for the army, manage the primitive rural public services, and try, so far as was possible, to settle land quarrels and other disputes among the peasantry; but for the rest the directives which rained in from the center were largely ignored, and the village remained more or less impervious to change in the world outside.

The Impact of Collectivization

The decision to embark on a program of collectivization and dekulakization marked the beginning of the real revolution in the villages. Inevitably, it imposed a tremendous strain on rural Party organizations and on the outposts of Soviet authority in the villages — the chairmen of the village soviets and the chairmen of the newly organized kolkhozes. Within the ranks of the rural Party organizations and, to a lesser degree, among the chairmen of village soviets, there were, of course, zealots who were thoroughly committed to the new program, but there were also others who regarded collectivization and dekulakization with the most profound misgiving. The real sympathies of the latter group lay with the peasants who resisted the changes, and not infrequently these sympathies were reinforced by ties of blood, friendship, and close association.

The central leadership sought to use the village soviets and their chairmen as spearheads in the campaign for dekulakization and collectivization. But they encountered more than a little reluctance. As the 1929 report of the Western Oblast Executive Committee put it, after noting that some ninety-seven new kolkhozes had been organized:

> However, it is still impossible to note a decisive turn of the village soviets toward the kolkhoz movement. The right-opportunist reliance on laissez-faire in the field of kolkhoz construction, the inability and lack of desire to organize the activity of the masses for the fulfillment of collectivization plans, the insufficient rebuff of the kulak agitation against the kolkhozes continue to take place in the practice of the work of village soviets.
>
> In a number of village soviets we observe an insufficiently exact adherence to the general line of the Party and the government and clear opportunism in practical work. Thus, in the course of the economic and political campaigns (taxes, collection of peasant payments, grain, potato, and flax deliveries) in some of the village soviets there was revealed a "loss" of kulaks, a failure to tax kulaks and well-to-do peasants, a failure to bring the plans for deliveries to the kulak and wealthy households, clear connivance with the kulak who does not fulfill his obligations to the state within the time limit. On the other hand there were also observed "Leftist" excesses in the form of overtaxation of the middle peasants, giving heavy delivery assignments to middle-peasant and poor-peasant households . . .[8]

The Party leadership sought to rectify these "deviations" by pushing more poor peasants and farm laborers into the soviets, by drawing kolkhozniks into soviet work and using them as a soviet aktiv, by purging the ranks of village soviet chairmen of undependable elements, and by mobilizing workers from the cities for positions of responsibility in the countryside. According to the 1929 oblispolkom report, out of 616 village soviet chairmen in 26 raions, 304, or 49.8 per cent, were removed in the course of the year, and of these 102 were "brought to trial."[9] The report broke down the 304 removals as follows: "For perversion of the class line, 102; for bribery, 11; for inactivity, 113; for other reasons, 78." Of those removed, 285 were individual peasant farmers, sixteen were kolkhozniks, and three workers.

Despite this drastic effort to "purify" the ranks of village soviet chairmen, serious problems remained. As opposition to dekulakization and collectivization mounted and flared into violent resistance, the "zealots" among the village soviet chairmen and soviet activists found their lives increasingly hazardous. Some random excerpts from Western Oblast OGPU reports for 1929 may help to convey the tension of the period:

Bryansk okrug — On the night of October 1–2, this year, in Trubchevsk raion the chairman of Khmelevsk village soviet, Ivan Kokhanov, was seriously wounded by a shot through the window . . . The day before, the secretary of the same village soviet was assaulted . . .[10]

In Velikiye Luki okrug, in the village of Smorodovnik, Tsivelsk raion, on August 29 of this year, the secretary of the Tsivelsk village soviet, Kalinin, a poor-peasant public servant, who carried out the class line, was murdered . . . The kulak Novikov finally confessed and added that besides him 2 kulaks and 3 well-to-do people took part in the murder . . .[11]

On the night of August 28, this year, in the village of Kasenka, Glinkovsk raion, Smolensk okrug, the house of the former chairman of the village soviet burned down. It was established by the inquiry that the fire was set by a fellow-villager, a former landowner, in order to take vengeance on the public servant for the loss of voting rights and land. The former landowner was arrested according to Article 58 of the Criminal Code . . .[12]

On the night of September 6–7, this year, on the Borka farm, Pervomaisk village soviet, Kuninsk raion, Velikolutsk okrug, the household belonging to a non-Party peasant activist, a very poor middle peasant, was set afire. In the fire a barn containing 1200 puds of clover and rye brought from the field and a cattleyard were destroyed. This peasant is a member of the village soviet. On the day of collectivization he took an active part in dismantling individual households; setting a personal example he was the first to enter the kolkhoz, leading 13 peasant households into it . . . During the fire the victim was helpless since none of the neighboring farms would help put the fire out . . .[13]

These examples illustrate some of the dangers of zealotry when the face of the village was set against collectivization. But not all chairmen of village soviets were zealots. Despite the most strenuous efforts to purify their ranks and to transform them into dependable instruments of central policy, there were more than a few who dragged their feet, accepted bribes to protect the well-to-do peasants from liquidation, and otherwise sabotaged state policy. The OGPU records of Krasnyi raion for 1932 provide numerous examples of such practice. On February 5, the raion OGPU chief reported:

Recently in Krasnyi raion under the influence of kulaks and other counterrevolutionary and anti-Soviet elements, there has taken place mass destruction and slaughter of livestock, both in the individual sector and in the socialized sector — the kolkhozes . . . In the village of Khvorostovo, Lyubalichi village soviet . . . 22 calves and one cow were slaughtered for sale at speculative prices. The first slaughter . . . in this village was begun by the deputy chairman of the village soviet; his example was followed by other citizens, mainly the wealthy elements of the village, some of whose households were assessed with a heavy tax. The heavy assessment was removed on the initiative of the above-named deputy chairman in return for a bribe (he received bribes from two people with a heavy tax: from one, 250 rubles in money, and from the other, felt boots with galoshes). One of the formerly heavily taxed people, who is a relative of this deputy chairman, systematically engages in speculation and resale of livestock which he slaughters in the yard of the deputy chairman . . .[14]

An OGPU report of January 20 on the progress of grain deliveries noted:

In the village of Solokinovo . . . there is absolutely no control by the village soviet over the fulfillment of grain deliveries by the kulak well-to-do elements. The official of the raion executive committee in this village is a former member of a criminal band who is now a candidate of the CPSU(b), and who often gets drunk together with these heavily taxed people and conceals them. Besides, the village official in this village soviet is the son of one of the heavily taxed people. This has been reported to the raikom so that proper measures may be taken . . . The chairman of the Trigubovo village soviet in return for a bribe issued a document to two speculators of the village to the effect that they never previously engaged in speculation and do not engage in it at the present time. One of these speculators was a thief previously sentenced for murder, but in the document it was indicated that he was not sentenced. The chairman of the village soviet at the present time is being brought to criminal responsibility by the raion militia . . .[15]

Another OGPU report, undated, dealing with kulak penetration of the kolkhozes of Krasnyi raion describes the following incident:

On January 15, 1932, the Chairman of the Bukinsk village soviet, Konkov, at a general meeting in the kolkhoz *Maiskoye utro* [May Day] . . . raised the question of the purge of the kulak element from the kolkhoz. He stated, "Well comrade kolkhozniks, now there is taking place among us in the Western Oblast a purge of kolkhozes and probably your kolkhoz must pass through the purge also. You are supposed to purge seven kulaks [names listed] . . . You yourselves must purge these persons from the kolkhoz." With this he finished his speech. He was then asked this question by the teacher of the Bukinsk school, a member of the Komsomol . . . "Is this to be done as a campaign, in obligatory fashion; is it obligatory to have seven households, or may we add more or decrease them?" To this . . . Konkov replied, "No, this has been given to you as a control figure by the village soviet, and therefore it is necessary for you to fulfill this figure." To which the teacher replied, "If that is so, then this amounts to naked administration."

Konkov then put each case to the meeting, and the kolkhozniks voted unanimously to leave the kulaks in the kolkhoz. The report continued:

After this Konkov got up and stated in conclusion, "Well you yourselves decreed that we must reinstate all of them in the kolkhoz: well that's all right, I would have decreed not to purge them either." After the meeting the chairman of the village soviet, Konkov, went to spend the night with one of the kulaks designated to be purged from the kolkhoz . . . with whom he drank all night . . .[16]

As these examples perhaps illustrate, the Soviet leadership sometimes found the chairman of the village soviet a frail reed on which to rely. The problem was particularly acute during the years of dekulakization and rapid collectivization, but it remained serious even after the new collectivized order on the land had become relatively stabilized. During the thirties there was increasing pressure to fill the post of village soviet chairman with a Party member or candidate, but the thinness of Party representation in the countryside did not always make such action feasible, and even when a Party member or candidate was found to take the job, he was apt to be of peasant origin, fairly recently recruited, with many ties to the countryside, and with less than total commitment to the Communist cause.

Problems of Village Administration

With the spread of collectivization, the nature of the chairmanship underwent an important transformation. The face of the village soviet was turned toward the kolkhozes. The boundaries of the soviet usually included at least one kolkhoz, and where the kolkhozes were small, perhaps even two or three. The main task of the chairman of the village soviet was to help enforce the obligations of the kolkhoz to the state, to make certain that it met its delivery quotas, and that each kolkhoznik paid the taxes assessed against him. In addition, he, of course, enforced similar obligations on such individual peasants as remained within the jurisdiction of the soviet.

Chart VI outlines the structure of village government as it existed in the Western Oblast at the beginning of the thirties. This chart requires some explanatory comment. Members of the village soviet were elected by the adult inhabitants of the village who had not been deprived of electoral rights. In the fairly rare cases where Party cells existed in the village or in the kolkhoz, they ordinarily caucused in advance to choose the slate of village soviet members. But as an inevitable by-product of Party weakness at this level, Party "guidance" tended to be rather loose and permissive.

The authority of the village soviet in any case was rather conjectural. It was an unpaid body which met infrequently to discuss such matters as the chairman placed before it. In theory its jurisdiction embraced the whole life of the village and its sections had special responsibility for supervising particular sectors of village life. In fact the actual responsibility for village government rested in the chairman of the village soviet and the secretary, both of whom were full-time paid employees. Sometimes they might also be assisted by one or more technical workers. While the chairman and the secretary of the village soviet were formally elected by the soviet's members, their appointments required the approval of the RIK and the raikom of the Party, and in many cases both appointments and removals were actually initiated by the raion.

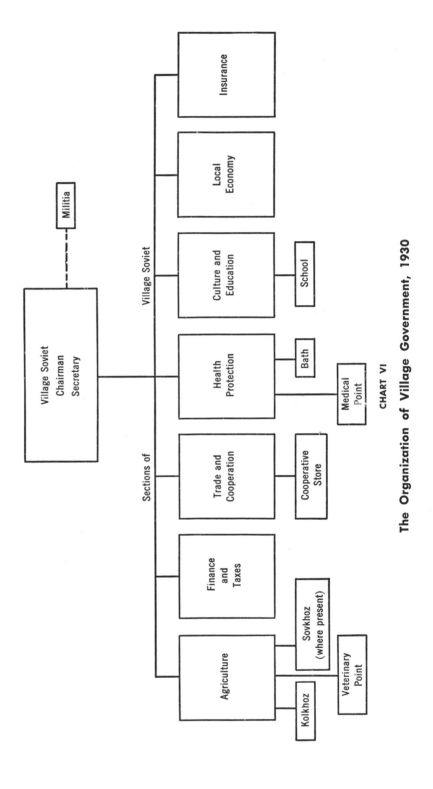

CHART VI

The Organization of Village Government, 1930

The Smolensk Archive, however, contains one instance at least where all the kolkhozniks and members of a village soviet joined in a protest to Rakitov, the chairman of the oblast executive committee, against the arbitrary removal of their chairman by a raion official. The village petition, dated October 26, 1936, read in part:

In November 1934 the chairman of the Sychevka raion executive committee, Comrade Bogdanov, recommended to us for the post of chairman of the village soviet Comrade I. N. Lotov. Comrade Bogdanov described Comrade Lotov as a worker who finished the courses of Soviet construction in the city of Rzhev in 1932, who had worked as chairman of a village soviet since 1932, and who had led a village soviet out of ruin. The voters agreed with Comrade Bogdanov and confirmed Comrade Lotov as chairman of the Bolshevsk village soviet. Comrade Lotov really justified the words of Comrade Bogdanov. He led [our] village soviet out of ruin. He strengthened the kolkhozes by [his] organizing and managing [ability]. The development of livestock breeding flourished. The economic and political campaigns were completely fulfilled within the time limit. According to the financial plan the village soviet is advanced. The kolkhozniks are well paid for their workdays. They built a good school building. They built two bridges over the river Dnieper. For the above measures Comrade Lotov received a premium of 1,000 rubles from the raion executive committee, the oblast, and the People's Commissariat of Finance. They also granted 1,000 rubles to the village soviet . . . Comrade Lotov enjoyed great authority among the kolkhozniks and also in the raion . . .[17]

The petition then described how a representative of the RIK, under the influence of local intriguers, arrived in the village, summoned the members of the soviet, "and told them that it was necessary, no matter how, to remove Lotov from work." The villagers pleaded with Rakitov to permit Lotov to remain.

Rakitov was sufficiently disturbed to feel that an investigation was in order. On November 5 he wrote a member of the obkom secretariat, "The statement is very serious since this question probably was decided by the raikom . . . I think that it is necessary to send [some one] immediately from the Obkom and the Oblast Executive Committee to investigate *on the spot*. This can be entrusted to Comrade Ivanov . . . I ask you to do this."[18] Ivanov then proceeded to Bolshevsk and on November 15, 1936, he rendered his report. In general, he confirmed the claims of the villagers. "Comrade Lotov," he noted, "produces the impression of an efficient and energetic worker. Last year the village soviet was among the advanced ones . . ." But he also pointed out:

This year the village soviet is doing poorer work. The basic trouble is that in the Party organization of the Bolshevsk village soviet there exists an unhealthy, squabbling, and anti-Party situation which was not considered on time by the raikom of the Party . . . Here are the facts: (1) The Partorg of the Bolshevsk Party organization, Comrade Pokhomov (teacher at the Bolshevsk incomplete middle school) and Party candidate Vyutnov (director of this same school) submitted a claim to the village soviet for the granting to their households . . . of a reduction in the meat and milk deliveries. The chairman of the village soviet, Comrade Lotov, on a legal basis refused them this deduction. (2) The Partorg, Comrade Pokhomov, for a long time despite the decision of the judicial organs, did not pay alimony for his child. The chairman of the village soviet, on the instructions of the raion procurator, made a list of the property of Pokhomov. (3) In 1935 the Vyutnov brothers beat the kolkhozniks after having been assessed a heavy tax for which they were given eight years in prison. The Party candidate, Vyutnov, actively came out in defense of his brothers and demanded interference by the raikom secretary in this case. Comrade Lotov helped to formulate the material on the Vyutnov brothers. As a result of all this, in September 1936, Vyutnov poured out his hatred on Comrade Lotov and struck him with a shaft bow . . .[19]

Ivanov then noted that the raion representative had taken the side of Lotov's accusers and "achieved a resolution of the village soviet to remove Comrade Lotov." At the same time "no other person was elected to the position of chairman and therefore Lotov continues work as chairman of the village soviet even at present." Ivanov then ordered the raion executive committee to transfer Vyutnov and Pokhomov from the village and to call another election, leaving it to the members of the village soviet to retain Lotov if they wished.

In view of these recommendations, the conclusion of the case was rather startling. On December 2, 1936, the village soviet was permitted to hold another election at which Lotov was unanimously affirmed as chairman. But on December 10 the raion Party organization decreed that Lotov, as well as the Party organizer Pokhomov, be transferred from the Bolshevsk village soviet.[20] One can perhaps infer from this that the raion Party was settling accounts with a village soviet chairman who had discredited it by appealing over its head to the oblast leadership.

While this case confirms the ultimate helplessness of the village in choosing its own leadership and the transcendent power of the immediately superior Party organization, it also throws some incidental light on the informal structure of authority in the village itself. In the not too frequent instances where a Party cell or a Party-candidate or Party-Komsomol group existed, power tended to concentrate in the hands of this group. Its members might embrace the chairman and secretary of the village soviet, the kolkhoz chairman, the school director or teacher, and perhaps a few other members of the so-called village intelligentsia such as the manager of the village store, the veterinarian, the feldsher in charge of the local medical point, or the accountant attached to the local kolkhoz. Where neither the Party nor the Komsomol had representatives in the villages, the initiative was likely to be taken by the raion Party authorities operating through the chairman of the village soviet, the local kolkhoz chairman, and other members of the non-Party aktiv.

During the thirties a notable change in the character of the village governing group began to be manifest. The chairman of the village soviet or the kolkhoz chairmen were more apt to be Party members or candidates, often schooled and indoctrinated in the Red Army, from which they returned to the villages to take on political responsibilities. The village school teachers of the older generation with ties to the "former people" began to be replaced by young members of the Komsomol who identified themselves with the Soviet order. A new Soviet-trained generation gradually was moving into responsible village posts.

But the process was slow and, in many rural backwaters, hardly perceptible. The more usual picture was a mixture of the old and the new — with all the strains and tensions which such a juxtaposition generated. The rural Party zealot remained a rather lonely and isolated figure — surrounded by peasant suspicion and hemmed in by resistance to change. The traditional leadership of the village did not take kindly to the Komsomol and Party activists who pointed out shortcomings in its work. The Smolensk Archive contains many tales of active rural correspondents who came to mysterious and untimely ends. The techniques of the village in dealing with these busybodies were often brutal, but occasionally rather subtle and refined. In some cases they were drawn into the family circle of village power; in others the whole village was mobilized to discredit them in the eyes of their superiors. Sometimes this worked, and sometimes it did not. In the case of one village correspondent, Natalya Kudelavskaya, who had been chosen by *Krestyanskaya Gazeta* (Peasant's Gazette) to study at a rabfak, the chairman of the village soviet, a certain Bogdanov, caused many letters to be written to the editor denouncing her as "a criminal and corrupt woman" who only quarreled and was "a burden to other people." [21] But this time the editors of the journal *Selkor* (Village Correspondent) investigated, learned that Kudelavskaya had uncovered many local "crimes," and that Bogdanov was opposed to her because, among other things, she had revealed that he had installed an incompetent drinking companion as village librarian. The result in this case was the removal of Bogdanov from his position as chairman of the village soviet.

But the busybodies and zealots also met their rebuffs. The Archive provides a particularly interesting and revealing example. During the late summer of 1936 one T. N. Sapozhenkov, a lieutenant of NKVD convoy troops, spent his vacation in his native kolkhoz "Krasnyi Gorodok," in Konononsk village, Pochinsk raion. Part of what he saw pleased him, but he also noted many "disorders," and being an energetic young man, he decided to do something about it. He started with the kolkhoz, which was run by one Semyon Zhuravlev, a Civil War veteran and Party candidate, and two fellow board members. As he later wrote to the Chief of the Political Department of his unit in the NKVD:

> This troika systematically gets drunk every day at any time of the day. They are not ashamed to appear at a kolkhoz meeting or a plenum of the village soviet drunk, and there are many cases of this. There were two cases to which I personally was a witness. These drinking bouts are known to all the members of the kolkhoz, since they are often done openly during working hours. Among the kolkhozniks the question arises: "Where do these people get the funds, and for what, they drink so often and so much?" And the kolkhozniks themselves answer that the kolkhoz board engages in abuses and plunder of socialist property . . .[22]

The lieutenant pursued his investigations and discovered many irregularities in the kolkhoz accounts and in the organization of its work. He determined to bring matters out into the open:

> On all of these problems I spoke with the members of the board of the kolkhoz, explaining to them what their actions would lead to. I spoke on individual occasions and at a general kolkhoz meeting . . . at the meeting Zhuravlev did not object to my speeches and agreed with my remarks . . . But Zhuravlev adopted another line in order to close my mouth. Taking advantage of my absence from the plenum of the village soviet, he came out openly with the statement that I, as a vacationer, do not help the kolkhoz board, but on the contrary, hamper its work, undermine the authority of the kolkhoz board . . . that I spoke against the coöperative movement . . . In other words, he compromised me.[23]

The lieutenant then requested the local Party organization to investigate his complaint. There he encountered a blank wall in the form of a partorg, named N. P. Zhuravlev, a relative of the kolkhoz chairman. The partorg, as he put it, "pacified" him but did nothing. Thereupon, being a very determined young man, he turned to the raikom, some twenty-five kilometers away. He found that the raikom secretaries were away attending a plenum of the obkom. He then went to the raion division of the NKVD, submitted a written statement, and demanded an investigation. "They promised me they would take immediate measures, but up to the end of my vacation no one came from the raion organization." Desperately intent on justice he decided nevertheless, "no matter how," to see the raikom secretary.

> On the day of my departure, I arrived in the raion at 9:00 A.M., fully convinced that during the day I would succeed in talking with the raikom secretary for 20 minutes. But things happened otherwise; both raikom secretaries were at a theoretical conference on the theme "State and Revolution" in the building of the raion executive committee. I went there and waited for a break, asked the first secretary of the raikom to receive me for 30 minutes. The first secretary refused to listen to me, explaining that he was busy, that he was going to a radio broadcast, but he informed me that he knew of my "quarrel" with the chairman and considered it a trivial problem. I told him

that it was not a trivial problem . . . and that . . . I wanted him to listen to me. Then Comrade Khokhlov, the raikom secretary, told the second secretary, Comrade Lobinsky, that he should talk with me, but Lobinsky too refused to listen to me . . . Thus I could not speak with the raion Party leaders, despite all my wishes.[24]

The lieutenant concluded his appeal by pointing out that the Party organizer, N. Zhuravlev, "surrounded himself with relatives, of whom there are many, both in the kolkhoz and also in the village soviet, in responsible and leading positions, and naturally he protects them in all their abuses . . ."

This letter was forwarded to the obkom secretary in Smolensk. The reply of the head of the agricultural department of the obkom was revealing. After pointing out that the allegations of the lieutenant were checked "on the spot" by an instructor of the department, the letter continued:

It was established by the investigation that the "Krasnyi Gorodok" kolkhoz achieved significant success in strengthening its organization and economy. All the agricultural work of the current year was completed thoroughly and on time. The kolkhoz settled accounts with the state on all types of deliveries and supplies . . . The board of the kolkhoz and its chairman, Zhuravlev, guide the kolkhoz correctly, but there are certain managerial shortcomings, and the kolkhoz board and the raikom of the Party have been ordered to eliminate them . . .[25]

What is of particular interest in this case and in others as well is the gospel of success which guided the judgment of both the raikom and obkom. Both were prepared to ignore, or at least overlook, the drunken bouts and petty defalcations of the Zhuravlevs; what counted was that they ran a successful kolkhoz, that is to say, one which met its obligations to the state. Their methods might be rather unsavory and not bear too close scrutiny, but as long as they produced results, they were safe, and as long as there were not too many kolkhozes that produced as well, they were safer still.

But the tight little family circles which the Zhuravlevs typified did not always fare so well. There remained the touchstone of performance, of deliveries of flax, of grain, and of potatoes which could be measured precisely and checked against quotas and plans. No family circle could long survive which persistently defaulted on its obligations to the state. Failures might be ingeniously concealed for a time, but ultimately there was a day of reckoning, and when it came the reckoning could be harsh indeed.

Yet even here, or perhaps especially here, there were limits to what force could do. To a not inconsiderable extent, the Party was at the mercy of the villages, of their capacity for passive resistance and **silent** sabotage. The training of new village cadres was at best a slow and painful process, and even the new cadres had roots in the countryside which made for cross loyalties and divided allegiances. Meanwhile, the Party had to work with the material at hand — the respected village leader, the occasional zealot and more frequent scoundrel, the ambitious careerist and such others as demonstrated a willingness to serve and an inclination to manage. It was a motley group, and it produced motley results. There were striking cases of devotion to duty, and many more where members of the new village aristocracy feathered their nests at the expense of their neighbors and the state. Resistant to control by their superiors and protected against too close scrutiny by distance and isolation, the village rulers sought to build their own feudal preserves only to find themselves subject to increasingly rigorous discipline as the center pressed its demands in the countryside. But try as it might, the center could never wholly succeed in preventing them from exacting a small tribute along the way.

8 The Organs of State Security

The first important reference in the Smolensk Archive to the activities of the organs of state security is to be found in a file of the Smolensk guberniya Cheka, dated January-April 1921, and containing a number of orders and protocols of the collegium of the gub-cheka.[1] This was a period when the Civil War was drawing to a close, when tensions were beginning to relax, and preparations were already underway for the full-scale launching of the New Economic Policy. The publication of the amnesty decree of the All-Union Central Executive Committee of November 7, 1920, served to signalize an easing of Cheka pressure.

The Cheka at Work

This mood of relaxation found its reflection in Cheka orders. On January 27, 1921, officials of the Investigation Section of the Smolensk Cheka were instructed to review all cases of workers and peasants under arrest and sentence and to extend preferential treatment to them in the house of detention.[2] The order provided that they were to be separated from the professional criminal and bourgeois elements, that they were to be permitted to see their relatives, to receive better food, and to enjoy other special advantages. On February 3, 1921, the collegium reviewed a large number of pending cases involving abuse of office, speculation, theft, bribery, provocation, counterrevolutionary agitation, illegal keeping of firearms, banditry, and evasion of military service.[3] Acting in accordance with the amnesty decree, the collegium ordered a substantial number of petty cases closed, chiefly those involving speculation, abuse of official position, and other minor crimes of an economic character. In these cases, as the phrase had it, "the dossier was consigned to the Archive." At the same time, the collegium acted with the greatest harshness in cases of counterrevolutionary activity, banditry, or other armed defiance of authority. A number of "bandits" were sentenced to be shot; in other cases involving counterrevolutionary activity the culprits were consigned to what the Cheka at that time frankly described as concentration camps.

The new climate to which the Cheka had to adjust was made explicit in a telegram which the Smolensk Cheka received on January 26, 1921, from Dzerzhinsky, the all-Union Cheka head. The telegram read:

The All-Union Cheka has information that the local organs of the Cheka are making arrests of qualified specialists working in the most important branches of industry of the country, accusing them of counterrevolutionary actions during their stay in the White Army. This serves to paralyze the creative work now going on. The All-Union Cheka orders that the arrest of specialists accused of "old affairs" be stopped, and also that specialists arrested for the above reasons be released immediately under the supervision of responsible Communists . . .[4]

Despite these restraints the Smolensk Cheka managed to keep busy. The Cheka house of detention was never empty. The daily reports on its occupancy indicated a high of 145 persons under arrest on February 26, 1921, and a low of fifty-eight on April 27, 1921. Meanwhile, on March 4, the collegium issued a special order to dispose of all petty cases within a two-week period.[5] This was followed by still another order on April 24 to "unburden" the house of detention.[6] The new instructions provided that no persons were to be held there for more than a week. After that, those not released were to be transferred to other prisons or to concentration camps.

The personnel of the Smolensk Cheka during this period was divided into the following five groups: (1) external intelligence, (2) counterrevolution, (3) military affairs, (4) banditry, and (5) general cases and speculation.[7] Typically, the head of each group not only directed operational activities in his bailiwick, but also presented recommendations for action at meetings of the collegium.

A brief summary of some typical cases may suggest the grist which passed through the Cheka mill at this time.[8] A person caught twice for banditry was sentenced to be shot. Two speculators were condemned to six months in a concentration camp. Three other speculators who had been dispatched to a concentration camp for a year petitioned for their release, but were refused because they were not "highly qualified workers." In a case involving seven persons who were accused of banditry and desertion, the collegium was more lenient. "In view of the fact that the arrested . . . are not malicious deserters and that all are from the poorest peasantry," it was decided "to free them from arrest and send them to the uyezd military commission" (presumably for military service). A person suspected of "counterrevolution and drunkenness" was sentenced to six months in a concentration camp. Several persons accused of agitation against the Soviet government were sent to a concentration camp for a year. Another person who had engaged in counterrevolutionary agitation during an election period was sentenced to forced labor in a concentration camp for two years. Several railroad workers who had stolen sugar from trains were ordered shot.

As these and other similar cases make clear, ordinarily sharp class lines were drawn in assessing punishment. The tendency was to be more lenient with workers and poor peasants than with persons of bourgeois origin. But this was far from being a universal rule. Workers who stole state property were subject to the most drastic penalties. On the other hand, bourgeois specialists who were hostile to the regime but badly needed in state industry had their sentences lightened and even commuted.

One of the most serious problems which the Cheka faced was that of disciplining its own workers. Cheka work attracted a motley group — careerists, opportunists, and unprincipled sadists as well as dedicated idealists and fervent zealots. On occasion the Cheka collegium made examples of its own workers who abused their authority. On February 26, 1921, for example, a number of militiamen and Cheka employees who had been found guilty of beating people whom they had arrested were sentenced to a concentration camp for varying terms — from one month to one year. On April 19 a group of Cheka workers received a year's sentence in a concentration camp for stealing meat.[9]

The problem of security safeguards within the Cheka organization also occasioned difficulties. On February 3 three Cheka members were accused by the collegium of spreading rumors about the forthcoming arrest of an engineer.[10] One received a strict reprimand and was dismissed from the Cheka; the second received only a strict reprimand; and the third was sentenced to six months in a concentration camp. On March 1 still another Cheka official was arrested for divulging information on a case. This time the collegium issued a stern warning to all members of the staff:

> Every member of the Cheka should finally realize and firmly remember that all the activities of the Chekas are based on strict secrecy, without which the work is unthinkable, and therefore those guilty of divulging [secrets] will be punished in the cruelest and most merciless manner. Every Chekist should know and always remember that, working in the organs of the Cheka, no matter what duties he fulfills, he is an advanced defender of the workers' and peasants' government on the internal front. There should be no place in the Cheka for chatterboxes, braggarts, self-seekers, and inept people who do not understand the tasks and significance of the Cheka in this period of Civil War.[11]

Among the important responsibilities of the Cheka at this time was that of censorship. The guberniya branch of ROST, the Russian Telegraph Agency, was required to submit to the Cheka in advance a daily summary of material to be published in the press and broadcast on the radio.[12] On orders from the All-Union Cheka, the Military Censorship Division of the gubcheka monitored correspondence with army units to make sure that no "illegal" or "pogrom" literature was distributed through these channels.

Flowing into the guberniya Cheka headquarters was a steady stream of reports from Cheka plenipotentiaries who were stationed in the uyezds and towns of the guberniya. The Archive contains a file of such reports from Roslavl for the period January-August 1922.[13] They touch on such topics as the political mood of the inhabitants, the sources of their dissatisfaction, the rumors that were circulating in the uyezd, strikes in the factories, the agitation of the clergy, and the activities of dissident elements. These reports make no effort to gloss over popular grievances; they report them frankly and fully. The local Chekas apparently operated under instructions to transmit their findings without embellishment.

The Roslavl Cheka gives evidence of having been well-served by its network of informers. A careful account was kept of all former members of political parties who at one time or another had opposed the Bolsheviks. Still at large in the uyezd were seventeen Socialist-Revolutionaries, sixteen Mensheviks, seven Anarchists, and four Kadets.[14] In one volost the Cheka discovered a nest of former members of the Union of the Russian People headed by a former village policeman. The group conducted agitation against the tax in kind, but its agitation in the view of the Cheka did not enjoy "much success." On January 31, 1922, there was a report on an anarchist who spoke at a conference of Soviet Workers and accused the Communists of being dictators.[15] There were also reports of scattered SR and Menshevik activity and of the posting of the following proclamation in Roslavl: "Comrades, the time of ruin has come. All mankind will perish. Therefore, let us organize in an underground manner, and destroy the bloody Communist Party, the bloodsuckers of the whole world, who agitate with selfish motives to blacken the people and to improve their own base lives. Faith in God and mankind is our victory." [16]

The Cheka made no effort to hide workers' grievances — their outspoken complaints concerning insufficient wages, delays in payment, shortages of foodstuffs, and high prices on products of prime necessity.[17] There were reports of a strike in one factory and of another strike of 350 workers at a railroad depot where "it was suspected that the leaders were anarchists." [18] Robberies of freight cars were reported almost daily. In the period June 15–30, 1922, fifteen such cases were recorded and about 20 to 30 per cent of the daily shipment of lumber simply "disappeared." [19]

The mood of the peasants was reported as "improving" as the result of the NEP, though resentment continued to be expressed against the tax in kind, the shortages and high prices of consumers' goods, and the delays in making land allotments. There were still reports of occasional banditry in the countryside; on June 12 bandits attacked and killed the chairman of a volost executive committee and wounded his secretary.[20]

One of the chief grievances of the peasantry was the Communist attitude toward the churches. The bulk of the peasants were described as "friendly toward the clergy"; the latter were said to be hostile toward the Soviet regime but cautious in expressing their hostility. The confiscation of church valuables which was taking place at that time "to aid in famine relief on the Volga" exacerbated relations with the peasants. Attempts to remove gold and silver from the churches were met by open resistance; they also served as a signal to set off anti-Semitic outbreaks. In one case, the Cheka reported, "The commission which arrived made an attempt to take the gold by armed force but the people would not let them, declaring, 'We won't give up the gold, and if it is taken away, not one Jew will remain; we'll kill them all during the night.' The clergy tried to persuade the people that the gold was not theirs, but they would not be convinced." On March 29 the Cheka reported that women and boys opposing the confiscation of church valuables roamed the streets and markets of Roslavl, attacked the Jews and beat them, shouting, "Beat the Jews, save Russia!" [22] The Cheka noted, "No one believes that the gold will aid the hungry. All think it will line the pockets of the Communists and Jews. Rumor says that the Bolsheviks, thinking there will be war with Poland, are collecting gold so that they can escape abroad." [23]

Judging by Cheka accounts, the rumor factories of Roslavl worked overtime. Stories spread like wild fire that all men of military age would be mobilized into the Red Army for ten to twenty years; that there would be a war in the spring on the Western Front and that no soldiers would go to war; that Trotsky had been shot (though some also said that he was insane); that all the workers in Moscow were on strike; that Rumania, Poland, and Japan had already begun a war against Russia; that the harvest had failed for the second year running; that the Volga, Azov, and Black Sea regions which had been punished with a drought last year were now "suffering from locusts"; and that the Bolsheviks were planning serfdom for the peasants. The Roslavl Cheka noted all these rumors faithfully and passed them on to their superiors where they may or may not have inspired corrective action. One catches a glimpse here of the startling capacity of a controlled and distrusted press to generate its own antidotes. In the informal communication channels of Roslavl, rumor displaced and blotted out much of the official propaganda which the press carried.

Recruitment Practices and Personnel

Unfortunately, the early Cheka reports provide virtually no information on the recruitment of Cheka workers. From other sources, however, notably Party records for the same period, it is apparent that Chekists were ordinarily selected through Party channels.[24] The only really detailed data the Archive offers on this subject center on the recruitment of OGPU workers in Bryansk okrug in 1929.[25] This was a period when the OGPU was rapidly expanding its forces to cope with the problems of collectivization, and the Party committees were being pressed to recommend trusted Party members for OGPU assignments. The record reveals that the recommendations of the Party okrug committee were forwarded to the chief of the okrug division of the OGPU for action. The OGPU chief could approve or reject the Party recommendation; if he approved, the appointment had still to be confirmed by the OGPU plenipotentiary for the Western Oblast before it became effective.

The Bryansk case is instructive. On September 14, 1929, the secretary of the Bryansk okrug Party committee recommended twenty-three Party members to the Okrug OGPU chief for work in the OGPU organs.[26] The recommendations listed the raikom which sponsored the candidates, the length of their Party memberships, and brief characterizations of them by the secretary of the Party cell from which they had been chosen. Of the twenty-three candidates, only four had joined the Party prior to 1921. In most cases, membership dated from the mid-twenties. An overwhelming percentage of the candidates recommended were workers. Some typical characterizations read:

Comrade M . . . is a staunch, reliable, stalwart, and devoted member of the Party. He fulfilled all the party assignments entrusted to him exactly and accurately. He has been a member of the raikom and gubkom and at the present time is secretary of the cell of the refrigeration shop.[27]

Comrade S . . . member of the CPSU(b) since 1926. A worker by social position. From 1917 to 1921 was in the ranks of the Red Army, afterwards served three years in the Navy. A staunch and capable Party member, works in the cell as technical secretary of the bureau. Has an inclination to work in the organs of the OGPU. The bureau of the cell considers it possible to recommend him for this work.[28]

All twenty-three candidates were given a medical examination, investigated, and interviewed by an OGPU representative. As a result of this sifting thirteen were accepted, four declared unfit for medical reasons, four rejected because they expressed some reluctance to enter into the service of the OGPU, and one discarded because of compromising material in his file. In the last case the OGPU okrug chief noted that investigation revealed that the candidate "was a poor manager who took a bureaucratic attitude toward his work and liked to get drunk."[29]

The reluctant recruits formed a particularly interesting group. The OGPU chief reported on one of them as follows: "In personal conversation with Comrade Ilin it was revealed that he has no special desire to work in the organs of the OGPU. He is wavering in his decisions, is burdened by [the problem of] his economic security, for which reasons the Okrug Division considered it expedient to refrain from admitting him to work in the organs of the OGPU." [30] Interviews with the three others brought out even more strongly expressed doubts which resulted in their dismissal. The fact that the candidates dared to air these doubts is not without significance, though the usual grounds cited stressed such relatively neutral themes as affinity for production work and obligations to large families. Obviously, the OGPU was anxious to enroll recruits who were thoroughly committed to the service, and thus a special effort was made to sift out waverers.

The importance of the Party role in NKVD recruitment was made even more manifest in a secret letter dated November 19, 1934, from the obkom secretariat to secretaries of all raikoms. The letter read:

With the formation of the USSR People's Commissariat of Internal Affairs, the organs of the latter have been enlarged by the addition of two very responsible divisions, Fire Protection and the Corrective Labor Administration.

Attaching exceptional significance to the problem of strengthening the cadres of the NKVD in corrective labor institutions and in fire protection, the bureau of the obkom, in its decree of November 10, 1934, ordered the raikoms of the Party immediately to occupy themselves with strengthening the cadres of these organs, both of leaders and of rank-and-file members. The present working conditions of these organs must be radically improved.

The Soviet-Trade Division of the Western Oblast Committee of the CPSU(b) orders you, upon receipt of this letter, to strengthen the organs of the NKVD in fire protection and corrective labor institutions, guiding yourselves in this work by the principle of choosing people who would be completely worthy of the lofty title of workers in the militant organ of the proletarian dictatorship — the NKVD.

In order to check upon the people presently employed (according to the NKVD materials) and to select and recruit new comrades into these organs, form a commission composed of the assistant secretary of the raikom, a representative of the raion executive committee, and the chief of the raion division of the NKVD, under the chairmanship of the raikom assistant secretary.

It is necessary to complete the work of reviewing and recruiting these cadres not later than December 15. Inform the obkom of the results in a special note, stating in detail the number of those removed, the reasons, and a list of the new comrades whom you have recruited into these organs.[31]

Further evidence of the Party's role in regulating NKVD appointments is provided by the 1936 obkom nomenklatura.[32] Listed in the nomenklatura were the chief of the oblast administration of the NKVD, the deputy chief, the assistant chief, the six chiefs of sections, the chief of the division for places of imprisonment, and eighty-one chiefs of raion and city divisions of the NKVD. Judging by the protocols of the obkom, however, the function of the Party secretariat was to confirm these appointments rather than to initiate them. In the case of appointments to the oblast NKVD apparatus, the initiative lay with higher NKVD authorities, but the appointments had to be ratified by the obkom before they could become effective. In the case of the raion NKVD chiefs, the initiative was taken by the oblast NKVD, but the appointments also had to run the gauntlet of the obkom before they became valid. A typical action noted in the protocol of the obkom bureau for January 23, 1936, reads:

Item 27. *On the Official of the Raion Division of the NKVD of Ilinsk Raion* . . .
To accept the proposal of the Oblast Administration of the NKVD:
a. on the removal of Comrade Snegirev from the office of the chief of the Ilinsk Raion Division of the NKVD;
b. on the approval of Comrade I. A. Baikov as chief of the Ilinsk Raion Division of the NKVD.[33]

While the obkom bureau protocols for 1936 contain no instance of a rejection of an NKVD proposal, they do indicate an occasional intervention by the obkom to secure the dismissal of raion NKVD personnel. In all such cases, however, the initiative in replacement was reserved by the oblast NKVD authorities.

What manner of men did the OGPU-NKVD attract to its service? The information available in the Archive is limited to lower-level employees, and even that is selective. Perhaps the richest source for analysis dates back to the 1929 purge when sixty members of the OGPU Party cell of the Western Oblast were subjected to screening and questioning in the course of which they also supplied biographical data about themselves.[34] Since all of them survived the purge, an examination of these data may provide some useful insights into the composition of the OGPU at that period.

A striking characteristic of the group was its youth. The oldest among them was thirty-seven years old; the youngest twenty-three. Of the total of sixty, thirty fell in the thirty to thirty-seven age range, while the remaining thirty were between twenty-three and twenty-nine years old. But while the group was young in age, it was not particularly junior in terms of Party status. Of the total of fifty-eight for whom the date of affiliation with the Party was available, thirty-two, or considerably more than half, had joined the Party in the years between 1917 and 1921. None was an Old Bolshevik, but as such matters went in the Soviet Union, the majority could definitely be classified as veterans of the Revolutionary and Civil War period. This generation dominated the key posts in the OGPU oblast organization.

The overwhelming majority had also served in the Red Army. Out of a total of fifty-five for whom military data were available, only fourteen had not seen Red Army service. Included among the ex-Red Army men were at least a dozen former junior commanders, political commissars, and politruks of Civil War days. While the data reveal that Red Army service was not an absolute prerequisite for work in the OGPU organs, it obviously created a favorable presumption and frequently served as a threshold to an OGPU career.

The material on the social origins of the group is also revealing. Of the total of fifty-three OGPU employees for whom such data were available, sixteen were workers, twenty-eight of peasant background, and nine of bourgeois or employee origin. The large percentage of peasant derivation may perhaps be explained by the special character of the Western Oblast with its overwhelmingly rural population. The composition of the peasant contingent in the OGPU, moreover, had its special class flavor. Of the total of twenty-eight, thirteen were classified as poor peasants and two as batraks, or farm laborers. Moreover, the remaining thirteen, who were described either as middle peasants or merely as peasants, were subjected to the closest questioning in the course of the purge. Many still had ties with the land; some had parents or other relatives who opposed collectivization. The purge commission demanded evidence of an undivided commitment to collectivization. Some members of the group promised that they would exert maximum pressure on their relatives to join the kolkhozes; others replied that they had broken completely with their families and had no contact with them. While none of the OGPU officials of peasant derivation was purged, it was clear that they were under special observation, and that the purge commission was concerned that they might not demonstrate sufficient staunchness in carrying out the collectivization program.

The nine OGPU members of bourgeois or employee origin constituted an especially interesting group. In almost every case they had washed away the sins of their social origin by serving in the Red Army during the Civil War and joining the Party early. At least four had been political commissars in Red Army units during the Civil War years, and all of them were praised as staunch Chekists in the course of the purge proceedings. One of those who survived had at one time been a Zionist and still later a Trotskyite; it is a measure of the relative lightness of the 1929 purge that both these grievous sins were overlooked in view of a record of devoted OGPU service.

As this analysis makes clear, the OGPU apparatus in the Western Oblast in 1929 was still dominated by the Civil War generation of Party members with Red Army service behind them. Their social origins were diverse, but a surprisingly large proportion came from the peasantry.

Their educational level was low, rarely extending beyond the first four grades or the seven years of the incomplete middle school. Only one member of the group of sixty was a graduate of a higher educational institution.

Unfortunately, similarly detailed data are not available for later years so that it is impossible to project comparisons into the thirties. The material cited earlier on Party recruitment of new OGPU members suggests that a determined effort was made during the years of collectivization to strengthen the worker detachment in the OGPU, but the Archive sheds no real light on the success of this effort. It is probably fair to assume that it was the OGPU generation analyzed above which both managed the Great Purge in the oblast and was ultimately consumed by it.

Security Safeguards

The documents in the Archive make clear that the OGPU-NKVD guarded its jurisdiction jealously. The sacred preserve of the organs of state security was their control of their "agenturno-osvedomitelnaya set," or agent-informer network, and their responsibility for "agenturno-operativnaya rabota," or agent-operative work. When a conflict developed in the MTS in 1933 on the respective jurisdictions of the heads of the Political Sections (the Party control organs) and their OGPU deputies, the memorandum of agreement which sought to resolve the dispute stated that the chiefs of the Political Sections had no right to "demand . . . reports on the status of the agent-informer network or agent-operative work." [35] Indeed, the circular signed by the head of the Political Administration Krinitsky and the deputy chairman of the OGPU Yagoda affirmed categorically that in this area the OGPU deputies were to "maintain complete independence." [36]

The OGPU-NKVD sought to guard its independence by enforcing the most rigid security rules on its collaborators. All those admitted to secret work had to sign a statement reading as follows: "I, the undersigned ———, give this signed statement to the effect that I pledge never and to no extent to divulge any state secrets which may be made known to me. Failure to fulfill this will make me liable to prosecution in accordance with the corresponding paragraphs of the criminal code." [37] There was a similar statement to be signed on leaving secret work. In addition to the pledge not to divulge state secrets, the collaborator was required to keep the security organs informed of his whereabouts for a two-year period. "I am aware," the pledge concluded, "that for failure to fulfill this signed statement, I am liable to prosecution by extra-legal procedure, in accordance with the decree of the Presidium of the Central Executive Committee of the USSR of May 26, 1927." [38]

Since all those who had access to any form of classified information had to be cleared by the security organs and classification embraced a large part of Soviet life, the tentacles of the security organs stretched out into virtually every office and enterprise of the Soviet Union. The scope of classification broadened early. The Smolensk Archive for 1927 contains a list of topics — classified top secret, secret, and not for publication — which was intended to guide all those who had responsibility for correspondence in the trade union organizations.

Letters had to be labeled top secret if they contained any data or photographs on defense industries or mobilization and evacuation plans; if they described "demoralization and depression" in "the mood of both the country as a whole and of individual localities, enterprises, etc."; if they constituted "correspondence with Party organizations in the nature of guidance on the part of the latter" (directives, instructions, orders, etc.); and if they contained coded and decoded correspondence, or made references to "trial cases in accordance with Articles 58–67 and 71 of the Criminal Code." [39]

Material dealing with any one of the following twenty-five topics had to be stamped secret:

1. Individual negative manifestations of a political and moral character among workers which could contribute to demoralization.

2. Materials on [Party] fractions.

3. Correspondence on issuing visas by a special procedure.

4. Recommendation materials.

5. Correspondence on work among individual trade union groups in fulfillment of the directives of higher organizations or of the Party.

6. Personnel files and correspondence on the transfer of responsible workers, especially where the fulfillment of directives of higher trade union or Party organizations was involved.

7. Correspondence on preparations for entrance of the Russian trade unions into the trade union international.

8. Correspondence on preparations for the participation of the Russian trade unions in the congresses of foreign unions.

9. Correspondence with fraternal foreign trade unions, if it bears the character of guidance or instructions.

10. Correspondence with individuals abroad involving questions of guidance.

11. Comments on moods among the unemployed.

12. Correspondence or discussion of plans and orders on immigration and colonization.

13. Organization of state or state-financed construction in industry and trade prior to the confirmation of such plans by legal organs.

14. Correspondence concerning limitations or changes in civil aviation flights.

15. Location of military and aviation factories and enterprises.

16. Mobilization correspondence other than that subject to top-secret classification.

17. Questions concerned with the mobilization readiness and preparedness of all types of transport in the mobilization plan (in accordance with the lists established periodically by the People's Commissariat of Transport and the People's Commissariat of the Army and Navy).

18. Correspondence on questions of administrative banishment and exile.

19. Correspondence on legal cases (not covered by top-secret provisions), the publication of which can harm the course of the investigations.

20. Organization of secret files, including procedures for safe-guarding secret correspondence.

21. Correspondence on violation of trade union democracy both by trade union' workers and by representatives of other organizations.

22. Correspondence on debts to workers in cases where the interference of higher organs is necessary.

23. Correspondence of a political and economic nature consisting of disagreements in principle, pending the solution of these disagreements by higher organs (congresses, plenums, etc.).

24. Instructions to local units on hospitality items, such as the reception of foreign delegations, the organization of workers' excursions, etc.

25. Correspondence on violation of trade union prerogatives, such as expenditure of trade union funds for carrying out work not related to trade unions, etc.[40]

In addition, six subjects were listed as "not for publication." They included discussion of wages and wage norms before they were confirmed by legal procedures; correspondence on strikes "if they occurred spontaneously"; correspondence "on the declining productivity of labor, the elimination of which requires the interference of higher organs"; investigation materials produced in accordance with the instructions of higher organs; White Guardist and foreign literature not subject to open sale in the USSR; and character descriptions and recommendation materials on personnel.[41] While this list was intended for the use of trade union functionaries, it can be assumed that similarly comprehensive guidance was provided for all other Soviet organs.

The 1927 instructions on secret correspondence issued by the Special Section of the OGPU specified that "no employee (including a Party member) can be allowed to work on or to handle secret correspondence without the preliminary sanction of the local division of the OGPU, to which, as a prerequisite to permission, the personal questionnaire of the employee is sent, with the attachment of two recommendations from Party members, a photographic card, and a signed statement that he will not reveal the secrets which may be made known to him." [42] The Archive contains a copy of this questionnaire; it includes a comprehensive series of twenty-seven questions covering such sensitive topics as class origins, foreign travel and contacts, relatives and friends living abroad, activities during the Revolution and Civil War period, job history, and involvement in previous investigations or arrests before the Revolution and afterwards.[43]

Meticulous and explicit rules regulated every aspect of the handling of classified documents — their storage, the procedure for obtaining and returning them, their wrapping and transmission.[44] Taking secret documents home was strictly forbidden, as was leaving them on tables, in portfolios, or in unlocked drawers of desks where secrecy could not be guaranteed. The extreme security-consciousness which pervaded the OGPU is made manifest by the instructions on wrapping and sending secret packages. The instructions read:

Secret correspondence, before being put in envelopes, is wrapped in non-transparent, light-colored paper or newsprint.

In sealing it, do not be satisfied only with the glue which is on the envelopes, but in addition smear the flap of the envelope with glue. The envelopes are sewn so that the threads include all the flaps of the envelopes. On each secret package a seal is placed.

The dispatch of secret correspondence abroad should be done through the Central Committee, and to another town, through the field communications of the OGPU, and for this purpose it is necessary to conclude an agreement through a local courier who can be trusted.

The typist or copyist who types the secret correspondence and the person who delivers the secret correspondence is placed on the rolls of the OGPU.[45]

In enforcing these rules, the OGPU made no distinction between Party and non-Party members. Both were equally liable, and a special decree of the Central Executive Committee, dated May 26, 1927, granted the OGPU the right to utilize extra-legal procedures in prosecuting persons who were lax in handling secret documents.[46]

Relationships with the Party Apparatus

The problem of relationships with the Party apparatus posed delicate and difficult problems for the security organs. In one respect, the relation was collaborative. The security organs were supposed to assist their opposite numbers in the Party hierarchy by keeping them informed of the political mood of the inhabitants, calling their attention to abuses and irregularities, and locating and rooting out opponents of the regime. But in another respect, the relation was potentially antagonistic. The Party apparatus exercised jurisdiction over OGPU or NKVD employees in their capacity as Party members, while the security officials had as one of their missions checking and reporting on the Party apparatus itself. The strains which this produced can be documented, notably in the case of the MTS and sovkhoz political sections referred to earlier.[47] Squabbles between raikom secretaries and NKVD raion chiefs were not uncommon, and they find their reflection in the protocols of the obkom bureau where efforts were made to settle them.[48] On a number of occasions, higher Party officials had to intervene to prevent raikom interference with the operations of the security organs. On October 4, 1937, for example, the obkom bureau approved the following resolution:

Noting that in a number of raions — Yekimovichsk, Belsk, and others — there are cases where NKVD workers are promoted to various Soviet and Party positions without obtaining the approval of the organs of the NKVD and the obkom of the CPSU(b), the bureau of the obkom decrees:
1. The existing practice of promoting NKVD workers to various work (not in the NKVD) without the approval of the oblast organizations, is censured as incorrect.
2. All raikoms of the CPSU(b) are ordered without fail to obtain approval from the oblast organizations on the question of promoting NKVD workers (outside the organs of the NKVD) and not to allow the promotion of NKVD workers to other work without the sanction of the obkom of the CPSU(b).[49]

As the Great Purge of the mid-thirties gathered momentum, the Party apparatus found itself increasingly subject to NKVD harassment. During the twenties and early thirties there were still some institutional protections to guard the Party member against arbitrary police action. A secret Central Committee decree of April 26, 1925, required that Party committees and the Control Commissions be immediately notified in all cases where a member of the Party was brought to trial or arrested and that the reasons for the arrest be stated. While the decree counseled against efforts to interfere with the criminal and punitive organs, it also contained the following provision:

In those cases where the Party organs and the Control Commission come to a definite conviction of the actual innocence of a Communist and of the lack of substance of the accusations leveled against him, they can, through the Gubkom, inform the guberniya procurator of their opinion. When necessary the gubkoms, obkoms, and Central Committees of the republic Parties can turn to the Central Committee and the Central Control Commission.[50]

The decree of the Central Committee and Central Control Commission of September 8, 1931, was even more explicit.

In those cases where a Control Commission after becoming acquainted with the issues, finds that the investigation and trial of Party members are incorrect, that the sentence is without grounds, and that the repressive measures being used by the court are unwarranted, the Control Commission places before the local organs of the procuracy, the court, and the OGPU, the question of correcting the mistakes which were permitted. Where the latter refuse to comply, the [local] Control Commission can carry the case to the higher instance of the Control Commission [in order to] seek a repudiation of the incorrect decisions and convictions by the highest organs of the courts and procuracy.[51]

While the right of appeal through Party channels remained on the books during the thirties, at the height of the Great Purge it became virtually meaningless. Acting under instructions from Stalin himself, the troikas of the NKVD dispensed their own brand of quick justice, and no distinctions were made between Party and non-Party members. By the time the purge reached its climax in 1937, even the once all-powerful first secretary of the Western Obkom was no longer in a position to help his friends; indeed he and his entire entourage were among its prime victims.

Insofar as the Party apparatus exercised control over NKVD officials at all, it was in their capacity as Party members. As Party members they were supposed to perform Party assignments and conform to certain standards of conduct which were enforced through the Party hierarchy. If they neglected their Party duties or violated the norms of behavior expected of Party members, they could be subjected to Party discipline, expelled from the Party, and ejected from the NKVD itself. But Party controls over NKVD Party personnel did not intrude into the inner sanctuary of secret police work itself. The NKVD network of agents and informers and the operational activities of the police were not regulated through Party channels.

The Archive contains a substantial number of protocols of Party meetings in OGPU and NKVD cells in various localities. Perhaps the longest run is a series of protocols of the NKVD cell in Tumanovo raion extending from April 1935 to April 1938, a span covering the worst of the purge excesses.[52] An analysis of these protocols may help illuminate the Party role in the NKVD during this period.

On the average, meetings of the Party cell were held at monthly intervals, but there were also long periods when no meetings were held at all. Between April 1, 1935, and July 4, 1935, there was a total of eight meetings. This was followed by an unexplained break of five months until the next meeting on December 4, 1935. At this meeting, however, the Party organizer was subjected to severe criticism for his negligence and was replaced. During 1936 twelve meetings, at more or less regular monthly intervals, were held. But in 1937, perhaps under pressure from the purge, a pattern of irregularity again emerged. There were eight meetings from January through August — and after that only one meeting during the balance of the year, on October 15, 1937. At this meeting, also, it was perhaps significant that a new Party organizer was chosen. During 1938, with the worst of the purge over, the Party cell began again to meet regularly. Six meetings were held between January 16 and April 11, when the protocols of the cell come to an end.

Over most of the period there was a total of ten members in the cell: nine members and one candidate at the beginning, and seven members and three candidates on April 1, 1937. In contrast to most other Party cells, where large-scale denunciations and mass expulsions were the rule, the NKVD in Tumanovo was apparently little affected by the sweep of the purge. Indeed, the protocols of Party meetings convey a sense of unreality. There is virtually no reference to the operative work of the NKVD itself in the district, and there is a sham quality to the meetings as if those in attendance were going through required motions while the burden of their real responsibility lay elsewhere.

A summary of the proceedings of some of the Party meetings may help to suggest their atmosphere. On April 11, 1935, for example, the meeting was devoted to an allotment of Party assignments among members — Party education, trade union work, collection of membership dues, editing the wall newspaper, and so forth.[53] It was agreed to "adopt" the Tumanovo village soviet and to help it in the spring sowing campaign. But subsequent protocols disclosed that the "adoption organization did thoroughly poor work," that the Party comrades were neglecting their Party assignments, that little attention was being paid to Party education, and that not enough Party meetings were being held. When they did take place, they were devoted largely to a discussion of various speeches, resolutions, and decrees. Some examples:

May 27, 1935: Discussion of Stalin's speech on cadres; discussion of Central Committee letter on procedure for safekeeping and issuance of Party documents. The members pledged themselves "to help unmask all hostile elements which cover themselves with Party cards and to be models of conscious discipline in the keeping of Party documents."[54] June 15, 1935: Discussion of obkom decree on work of primary Party organizations in Soviet institutions. August 26, 1935: Discussion of International Youth Day. The members agreed to "take an active part in the celebration of Youth Day, to appear at the demonstration, and to see to it that no hooligan tricks are allowed."[55] March 4, 1936: Discussion of the December Plenum of the Central Committee on carrying out the exchange of Party documents. June 5, 1956: Discussion of the decisions of the 10th Komsomol Congress and the speech of Comrade Andreyev. November 30, 1936: Discussion and questions on Stalin's report on the Draft Constitution of the USSR. January 19, 1937: Discussion on the international situation — "The task of the Party organization is to explain to its members and non-Party supporters the bestiality of Fascism." March 30, 1937: Discussion of Stalin's report at the February Plenum of the Central Committee.

As these examples perhaps illustrate and as the Party organizer of the cell frankly acknowledged in his report of April 2, 1937, the subjects for discussion were handed down from above through the raikom.[56] In effect, the members who attended cell meetings represented a captive audience, required periodically to listen to reports that reflected the current preoccupations of the center and embodied instructions which rank-and-file members were expected to execute.

These were the formalities, and the protocols of the meetings convey the impression that they were treated as such. For the most part the real cutting-edge of raion NKVD activity lay hidden behind the bland surface of general Party oratory. But there was at least one occasion when it could not be obscured. In mid-1937 the purge of Rumyantsev and other oblast leaders was followed by a purge of the raion Party organizations, including that of Tumanovo. The raion NKVD head was in danger of being compromised. Answering a charge of lack of vigilance and an effort to identify him with the discredited raion and oblast leadership, the NKVD chief lashed out in reply that he alone had been responsible for the arrest of 120 "criminal and anti-Soviet elements" in the raion in connection with the Rumyantsev affair.[57]

But such zeal was soon to prove embarrassing. In January 1938 the Party Central Committee modified its course and called upon the local Party organizations to correct the mistakes which they had made in expelling Party members unjustly. The Tumanovo NKVD Party cell made a quick adjustment to the new line. Various examples were cited at the meeting of January 22, 1938, of insensitive treatment and of incorrect actions where Communists were "expelled from the Party because a distant relative or former comrade was at one time expelled or arrested for counterrevolutionary Trotskyism, without sufficiently studying the extent to which the expelled person took part in this and what connections he maintained with this Trotskyite." "We must be merciless in the struggle against our enemies," the meeting declared, "but we must also learn to distinguish between friend and enemy and not to act without first carefully investigating." [58] At this point the record stops; we shall probably never know how the Tumanovo NKVD fulfilled its pledge.

In many respects, the most revealing feature of the protocols of the Tumanovo NKVD Party cell is what they omit. One looks in vain for a record of the day-to-day operational activities of the NKVD or of any specific Party instructions relating thereto. Clearly, this was an area into which the local Party leadership did not intrude. The Tumanovo protocols provide a striking confirmation of the absence of effective Party control of NKVD operative work at the raion level.

Even at the oblast level, the Party leadership was chary about interfering with NKVD decisions. Occasionally letters were addressed to the oblast Party authorities denouncing various NKVD officials for absconding with state funds or engaging in other high-handed or illegal activity.

In such cases, the matter was ordinarily referred to an instructor of the obkom apparatus or a representative of the oblast control commission who in turn requested the oblast NKVD authorities to conduct an investigation. The findings of the oblast NKVD investigator were usually decisive.

Two cases in the Archive illustrate the usual procedure. In one case, involving a Comrade Strigo, NKVD chief in the raion of Starodub, a letter of complaint was addressed to Yezhov, then chairman of the Party Control Commission of the Central Committee. The letter, which was written by one of Strigo's former subordinates, the chief of the prison in Starodub, charged Strigo with a variety of crimes, including the acceptance of bribes and other violations of "revolutionary legality." [59] The letter-writer pointed out that he had previously complained to the NKVD oblast authorities. He described what happened as follows: "An NKVD official, Comrade Sychev, arrived at the end of May, this year, to examine the complaints in regard to Comrade Strigo. For about five days he lived with Comrade Strigo, who was under investigation, at his expense, ate chicken, etc. And there's the result — they investigate themselves, they gloss over things . . ." A copy of this letter was forwarded by Yezhov to Rumyantsev, who referred it to an obkom instructor for further investigation. The obkom instructor then got in touch with an official of the Special Section of the NKVD oblast office, who gave Strigo a clean bill of health.[60] The obkom instructor so reported.

The second case was more complicated. Its central figure was one Vinogradov, NKVD chief in Belyi raion during the stormy years of 1936–37. Vinogradov was denounced in a letter to the oblast Party Control Commission for allegedly engaging in large-scale pilfering of state property, for accepting bribes, and for other crimes. The Party Control Commission referred the matter to the Oblast NKVD which, after investigation, cleared Vinogradov on all counts.[61] Vinogradov then sent a copy of his letter of clearance to the bureau of the Belyi raikom, undoubtedly thinking that this would be the end of the matter. But this time there was an unexpected kick-back. The Belyi raikom revolted. Renewing the accusations against Vinogradov, they excluded him from the raikom and its bureau, and then at a subsequent meeting, despite the opposition of the obkom representative present, proceeded to vote his expulsion from the Party.[62] The final victory, however, was Vinogradov's; on appeal the action of the Belyi organization was overruled, and Vinogradov was restored in accordance with the January 1938 decree of the Central Committee requiring the readmission of Party members who had been expelled unjustly.[63] In this case too, despite unexpectedly staunch opposition, the NKVD succeeded in taking care of its own.

Even such an important personage as Rumyantsev, the obkom first secretary, lacked authority to grant dispensation from NKVD justice. Buried in the files of the obkom are many appeals for help and pleas for mercy addressed to Rumyantsev, but when the NKVD was involved, the tendency was to proceed cautiously. The following letter may serve to dramatize the problem:

Comrade Rumyantsev: First of all, excuse me for taking up your precious time, but at present I have somehow lost the ground under my feet and have decided to seek help from you, dear Ivan Petrovich. I am the wife of the former chairman of the Nevlya raiispolkom, Spirin, who has been sentenced to two years' labor in accordance with Articles 109 and 110 [of the Criminal Code] and who is serving his sentence 18 kilometers from Smolensk in the agricultural colony "Astrogan." You have a family, and I am sure that you will understand me if I tell you that I am also serving this sentence with my husband, even though I am far away from him. I lived with Spirin for six years; I have seen how he worked; I have seen how dear the Party was to him. He worked without sparing his health and strength, and you know that he did his work quite well. He himself is the son of a poor peasant, and during his entire membership in the Party he was not sentenced once, and even now, while serving his sentence, he is honestly and conscientiously doing the work given him, even physical work. In the spring he works as a tractorist. He has been expelled from the Party. For him this is the highest form of punishment, and certainly his stay with thieves, bandits, and other criminal elements has redoubled his punishment. But still he is no stranger to the Party; he is not an enemy of the Soviet government. I am sure that he will be a useful member of socialist society, and maybe will show the Party his innocence in all that happened in Nevlya.

You, Ivan Petrovich, always treated Spirin very well, and therefore I decided to ask you to help me to free Spirin, who has already served more than half of his term, for I know that they free those sentenced to 8 to 10 years when half the term is over. I am sure that my husband is not socially dangerous, and he has been so cruelly punished for the mistakes which he allowed in Nevlya, and his imprisonment has significantly impaired his health.

I myself am a physician. I work as head of the Pochinkovsk Hospital. I bend all my efforts and knowledge in the struggle to maintain the health of the toilers, and the freeing of my husband will give me still more energy and power for work in the field. I beg you, Ivan Petrovich, to help me.[64]

Scrawled at the bottom of this letter was a cryptic note in Rumyantsev's hand: "In my opinion — if there are no formalities." In other words, Rumyantsev was disposed to act favorably on the appeal, but the question still remained whether the NKVD would approve. The Archive does not contain an answer.

While the available evidence in the Archive supports the view that the operational activities of the NKVD officials in the Western Oblast were largely free from control by their opposite numbers in the Party, this should not be understood as meaning that the NKVD functioned without any Party guidance. But it was Party guidance in a special sense. The Party was essentially a pseudonym for Stalin, and the Party apparatus merely communicated his wishes. The unique position of the NKVD derived from the fact that it became Stalin's special instrument to watch the Party as well as other sectors of Soviet life. The directives that regulated the activity of the NKVD came from Stalin through Party as well as NKVD channels, but they were essentially Stalin's directives no matter how transmitted. It is a curious fact that even at the height of the purge, Stalin maintained the fiction of "the leading role of the Party." Still trumpeting this theme, Stalin proceeded in 1937 to use the NKVD to decimate the ranks of the leading Party workers in the Western Oblast. This was the ultimate irony of Party control.

9 The Machinery of Justice — The Procuracy and the Courts

The materials in the Smolensk Archive on the procuracy and the courts are spotty. Consisting largely of a miscellany of reports that found their way into the Party records over the period 1924–1937, they do not readily lend themselves to systematic historical analysis. But there are other values which they do supply. On the themes which they treat and for the brief time-spans for which they are available, they provide flashes of illumination that furnish a useful corrective to the more formal institutional descriptions based on official monographs and statutory and constitutional provisions.

During the period covered by the Archive, the machinery of justice in the region was subjected to important structural changes. Until the absorption of Smolensk guberniya into the Western Oblast in 1929, the judicial system consisted of a guberniya court, a number of okrug or circuit courts, and, at the base, a large network of people's courts which were spread among the uyezds, or districts of the province. These courts were all subordinate to the RSFSR People's Commissariat of Justice, as was also the hierarchy of procurators at the uyezd, okrug, and guberniya levels. After the establishment of the Western Oblast and the subsequent abolition of the okrugs and their redivision into raions, the judicial system was reorganized. Under the new dispensation the okrug courts disappeared, and the oblast court in Smolensk presided directly over the people's courts which were located in the raions. Members of the oblast court also traveled on circuit in order to hear cases in various parts of the region.

While the courts remained subject to the People's Commissariat of Justice, the procuracy developed an increasingly independent status with respect to the judicial organs. The law of June 20, 1933, which created the office of USSR Procurator General, marked an important step in this direction. The law of July 20, 1936, and later the USSR Constitution of 1936, completed the process by separating the procuracy and the organs of investigation from the People's Commissariat of Justice and making them directly subordinate to the Procurator General of the USSR. The procurators at the oblast and raion levels thus became part of a wholly independent hierarchy paralleling that of the courts.

The procuracy, which was first established by the law of May 28, 1922, was vested by that act with a unique combination of functions. In addition to prosecuting persons accused of violating the law, the procurators were required to supervise the legality of the actions of all organs exercising public authority and to protest decrees and orders which raised legal doubts. They were also authorized to supervise the activity of agencies conducting investigations of criminal cases and to check on conditions in places of confinement.

The Work of the Procuracy at the Grass Roots

The Archive contains two reports of local procurators which were written not long after the creation of the procuracy. They provide a revealing picture of its grass-roots activities during the middle years of the NEP. The first report, by a new appointee obviously eager to make a good impression on his superiors, is an account of his stewardship as assistant procurator in Roslavl for the period January 1–July 1, 1924.[1] He began his report with a general statement on "the political situation in the uyezd." He found it "fully satisfactory"; the attitude of the population toward Soviet authority was termed "quite loyal," except for "insignificant strata." He discovered no anti-Soviet groups; there was only one counterrevolutionary case presently under investigation. He then summarized the uyezd crime statistics for the period. Of 480 cases of "property" crimes, the largest group involved horse-stealing. In struggling with this "evil," however, he reported having drawn up a plan for "the liquidation of groups of horse thieves which gave positive results," and the thievery was subsiding. There were 366 cases of so-called "economic" crimes, of which a substantial number were "home brew" cases. He noted that repressive measures were being taken to stamp out the "moonshiners." A total of 188 cases were classified as "official" crimes committed by employees of various local governmental and economic agencies. These he blamed on inadequate supervision by their distant superior organs. There were ninety-one cases of crimes against the person, involving murders and bodily injuries. These crimes, he asserted, arose out of drunkenness, family property quarrels, and gang attacks. He reported with satisfaction that five criminal gangs had been liquidated. The remaining crimes were grouped in the following categories: violations of administrative orders, eighty-eight; against public security, eighty-seven; counterrevolutionary, one; and violation of rules on separation of church and state, one.

In discharging his supervisory functions, the procurator noted that he attended all sessions of the uyezd executive committee, "entering his agreement on the projects of decrees and orders which were sent to his office." He also established a procedure by which the various government agencies in the uyezd sent their circulars and instructions to him for clearance. During the period he protested three actions of the uyezd executive committee, one of which was accepted while two others were still pending. In the course of fulfilling his supervisory responsibilities, he had discovered irregularities in various economic agencies and initiated criminal proceedings against the offending officials. He had also looked into the problem of labor inspection and visited two children's homes.

The procurator then gave a detailed account and appraisal of his relationships with the militia and the criminal investigation division. While he described "the general condition" of these organs as "satisfactory" he noted that the secret department of the criminal investigation division was handicapped by "lack of means to pay informers" and that the delay in carrying out investigations created "an unhealthy atmosphere." He reported, however, that "there were no instances of nonfulfillment of the orders of the assistant procurator."

His relations with the OGPU were described as equally satisfactory; ". . . there were no conflicts in the period of the report." The OGPU, he stated, was represented in Roslavl uyezd by a plenipotentiary and a staff of five persons, three of whom were Party members. He rated the staff, by a somewhat curious mathematical process, as "55 per cent trained and 45 per cent weak." Its transport department seemed to him to suffer from a lack of guidance on the part of those in command; he noted that the struggle with economic crime on the railroad was being carried on "weakly." He also participated in meetings with agents of the OGPU where he "made reports on Soviet legislation such as: law from the point of view of Marxist understanding, and also explained all shortcomings noted on the part of ODTOGPU [the transport department]."

The procurator also checked on the quality of the investigative apparatus which served the courts of the uyezd. He described the main shortcomings as due to inadequate training and "an insufficient supply of monetary means and . . . bad material security." In order to improve the quality of the investigation apparatus a "juridical [study] circle" was organized, defects were explained, and check-ups made of work in the localities.

He described his relations with the people's courts as "good." Of the eleven judges, nine were Party members and two non-Party; "one could consider" seven trained and three untrained (making a total of 10?). He noted that the people's judges received a monthly salary of 41 rubles, 40 kopecks, which he considered "far from satisfactory." During the reporting period he made ten appearances in open court and protested thirty-four cases, of which thirty-two were returned to the people's courts and two were carried to a higher judicial instance. Copies of verdicts of the people's courts were transmitted regularly to the procurator, and the militia also presented information monthly on sentences carried out.

Jointly with the OGPU and a plenipotentiary of the guberniya court, the procurator also supervised the activities of the bureau of judicial aid. This bureau, which consisted of five lawyers, four in the city of Roslavl and one in the uyezd, provided free legal consultations "chiefly for the working masses."

The procurator also described his inspections of the house of detention, which he visited not less than twice a month. He found conditions there "completely satisfactory"; the quarters were "quite accommodating," and the premises "clean and neat." In checking on the correctness of detentions, he noted that he had arranged to free five persons who had been illegally imprisoned. He also observed that a number of prisoners had been sentenced to forced labor, although the Roslavl Bureau of Forced Labor "in view of the lack of demand for a working force . . . does not function."

He reported no friction with the leading Party organs in the area. "In my work," he stated, "I am in close contact with the indicated organs, and I always try to come to an agreement through conversations [with them] on the usefulness of this or that line of work. I made one informational report to the secretary of the uyezd committee on work performed and future prospects." His "political work" was limited to one speech at a factory. For this he apologized because "I assumed office not long ago, and . . . I was overloaded with work." As proof of his diligence and the popularity of the procuracy he cited figures on a substantial increase in visits to his office by workers and peasants, not only with complaints, but also for judicial advice. In not unfamiliar bureaucratic fashion, he concluded his report of a very busy life with an urgent plea for additional staff assistance.

The report of the assistant procurator for Medyn uyezd on his work for the period July 1, 1925 to January 1, 1926, follows much the same pattern.[2] Indeed the subheadings of both reports correspond so precisely as to indicate the existence of a standard set of requirements. Like his Roslavl colleague, the Medynsk procurator found the political situation in his uyezd "satsfactory." Priests remained active and commanded many followers in rural areas, but they refrained from outright attacks on the Soviet regime. There were no large-scale counterrevolutionary manifestations, although the report did note the murder of one village correspondent and an attack on still another. As in Roslavl, illicit distilling of alcohol was widespread, though the Medynsk procurator claimed that the incidence of such activity was declining. On the other hand, "hooliganism" and economic crimes were on the increase. Embezzlement, bribe-taking, and other forms of misappropriation of funds in the coöperative trade network and economic agencies were particularly common.

The Medynsk procurator reported no difficulties in his relations with the ukom, the ukom executive committee, or the OGPU. Politically, he was far more active than his Roslavl colleague. He cited no less than eighteen separate lectures which he had delivered over the six months' period. He was also apparently far more vigorous in protesting the decrees and actions of the various agencies over which he exercised supervision, particularly at the volost level.

His report on the people's courts of Medyn was particularly revealing. Of the seven judges, three were Party members, two candidates for Party membership, and two non-Party. The Party contingent was obviously recruited with an eye to political reliability rather than judicial qualifications. Of the three Party judges, two were of peasant background with no legal training and no formal education. The third was of employee origin, had completed a middle school, but also lacked legal training. The two Party candidates were also of peasant origin; one had no schooling at all, while the other had attended a short-term judicial training course. Of the two non-Party judges, one was a peasant who had completed a similar course, while the last was a university law graduate whose clergy origin made him suspect. The difficulties created by a corps of ignorant and untrained judges perhaps needed no underlining. The procurator merely noted that the people's courts had been far behind in their dockets, but that as a result of pressure from him they were now current. He also observed that he had had to protest six criminal decisions and eight civil cases to the guberniya procurator.

While two scattered procuracy reports of this type hardly lend themselves to grand generalization, they give evidence of being representative of the work of the procuracy at local levels during the mid-NEP years. The range of crimes they describe — horse-stealing and home-brew manufacture, disputes over land and property, hooliganism and drunkenness, the petty and large-scale embezzlements of officialdom — was characteristic of the period. Equally significant was the decline in so-called counterrevolutionary outbreaks, a measure of the temporary truce which the regime had worked out with the peasantry. The reports also make clear that the procurators functioned as an important instrument of control in the localities. Operating within the framework of the regime's guiding directives, the procuracy helped to impose restraints on arbitrary behavior by local officials and to provide a focal point to which complaints could be directed. Within limits the activities of the procuracy epitomized one facet of the struggle to give a degree of validity to the new legal norms which the regime was developing to regularize its relationships with its subjects.

Party Controls

But above and beyond the law, as well as through the law, the procuracy and the courts continued to function as an instrument of the Party dictatorship. Party directives provided the political guide lines that regulated the scope of judicial discretion and determined the direction of the work of the procuracy. The Party leadership sought to make sure that key positions in the procuracy and the courts would be occupied by Party members. Both procurators and judges were on the nomenklatura of Party committees; in the Smolensk area appointments had to be approved by the gubkom up to 1929 and by the obkom of the Western Oblast afterwards.

The guberniya and oblast Party authorities maintained a continuous and careful check on the activities of their comrades in legal positions. The following extracts from a memorandum of the guberniya Party Control Commission dated August 20, 1928, which assesses the qualifications of various people's judges and investigators in Sychevsk uyezd, illustrates the closeness of Party control:

I. F. Fedorovich — plenipotentiary of the Smolensk guberniya court in Sychevka —

Fedorovich is a peasant from Smolensk . . . 40 years old. Member of the CPSU(b). Five years, five months in the organs of justice. Has no legal education, General education — intermediate. In Sychevsk uyezd since the end of 1926. He manages the apparatus of justice poorly. Is afraid of the officials. Can fall under the influence of the legal line, does not hold to class and punitive policy well enough . . . Before the Smolensk scandal was reprimanded for amoral actions and for carousing and card-playing . . . It is necessary to transfer Fedorovich to another guberniya.

S. A. Akimov — people's judge, city of Sychevka —

Akimov is a local peasant, member of the CPSU(b), 30 years old, in the organs of justice for two years, five months. Education — lower. Before he was in the organs of justice he worked in lower Party and coöperative work. Illiterate in legal matters. Because of insufficient supervision and guidance in the cases examined he does not at all hold to the class line, especially when he is at meetings of the land commission. Many of his sentences are confused and have no basis. Has no authority among the peasants, because of unpreparedness for this work. Weak-willed. Under the influence of his wife. Necessary to send him for requalification with a transfer to another uyezd.

P. S. Semenov — people's judge, city of Sychevka —

Semenov is a local peasant, member of the CPSU(b). In the organs of justice for three years, eleven months. Doesn't have any legal education. Political development is lower than average. Not very interested in public work. Has a close tie with the well-to-do section of the countryside. Doesn't have any authority among the peasants. In pronouncing sentences he holds neither to the class nor to the legal line. There is information on bribery [in regard to him]. He should be removed from work . . .

S. N. Smirnov — people's judge, village of Griva —

Smirnov is a local peasant, member of the CPSU (b), unmarried. Earlier did Party-soviet work. In the organs of justice for two years, five months. Has no legal education. General education — very slight. No authority among the peasants, because of his continual drinking bouts and the fact that he comes late to investigations. Has a close connection with the local peasants, which results in legal work in shortcomings in enforcement of the class line. Necessary to transfer him to another uyezd.[3]

As these excerpts perhaps make clear, the Party ideal in the legal field represented a combination of many sterling qualities — integrity, knowledge of the law, noninvolvement with the local scene, and administrative competence, but what was wanted above all was devotion to the class line of the Party.

The Role of the Procuracy and the Courts
in Collectivization and Dekulakization

The importance of such devotion became manifest as the Party launched its program of collectivization and dekulakization. The resources of the procuracy and the courts were quickly mobilized to contribute to the campaign. The Smolensk Archive contains a number of Information Bulletins of the procuracy of Smolensk guberniya and the Western Oblast and several reports of the oblast court for the period 1929–30.[4] They read like communiques from a flaming battle front.

From the beginning the procuracy drew on its full armory of legal powers to carry the battle to the kulak. It intervened to prevent fictitious land divisions and other subterfuges which well-to-do peasants utilized to divest themselves of kulak status with its attendant onerous tax obligations. It led a campaign to prevent millers from evading the grinding fees and initiated action to recapture milling enterprises for the state. It sought to ensure the enforcement and collection of taxes from the kulaks by helping to purge the tax commissions of elements sympathetic to the kulaks and by ensuring accurate inventories and assessments on kulak property.

In some cases the procuracy faced the problem of putting its own judicial house in order. The Rzhev okrug procurator reported: "the procuracy during a review of criminal cases discovered a clearly pronounced right deviation in the work of the people's court of the third raion of the city of Rhzev."[5] Cases against millers for violations of the law on the grain fee were dismissed; kulaks who engaged in speculation were permitted to escape with insignificant fines. In Klintsovsk okrug an investigation disclosed that people's judges were "violating" the class line by acquitting kulaks accused of exploiting farm laborers. The procuracy obviously faced a real problem in breaking the ties of the lower judicial organs to the countryside. The purge of "right wing" people's judges symbolized the new militancy which the times imposed.

At the same time the procuracy sought to restrain so-called "excesses." On October 26, 1929, the deputy procurator of the Western Oblast sent an order to all the okrug procurators "On the application of repressive measures with respect to kulaks and others hampering the procurement and collection of taxes and payments." [6] After noting the "positive results" achieved as a result of the decisive measures already taken, the letter pointed out that some of the punitive organs had been guilty of undiscriminating zeal. Excessive sentences had been imposed for minor infractions, and "the militia organs had seized and put in prison the first person who fell into their hands with the result that they offended, instead of the kulak, both the middle and poor peasant."

The oblast procuracy therefore proposed more discriminating treatment of poor and middle peasants. "Taking into account," the order read, "that we recently applied measures of coercion, as a result of which we have an overload of the places of detention, it is necessary immediately to switch and apply pressure along the line of economic coercion (fines, confiscation, and exile)." Prisons were to be checked to see whether it was possible to free poor and middle peasants. Militiamen were instructed to "approach the question of detention more carefully, especially in cases of counterrevolutionary agitation and propaganda where, at times, they jail a poor peasant because he somewhere shouted a phrase against Soviet authority, either through irresponsibility or through the incitement of anti-Soviet elements." In such cases, the order stated, it would be better to note the facts and transmit the protocol to the OGPU. However, those guilty of terrorist acts were to be immediately detained without regard to their social status.

In issuing this call for "revolutionary legality," the procuracy made clear that it had no intention of abating the campaign against the kulak. As kulak violence mounted, and resistance spread to middle and poor peasants, the procuracy found it increasingly difficult to enforce the distinctions in treatment of different parts of the peasantry which it had been urging. The reaction of the more zealous local authorities tended to be pragmatic in the extreme. Those who opposed collectivization, no matter what their social position, were classified as kulaks and treated accordingly. The Information Bulletins of the procuracy indicate that some efforts were made to restrain the "hot heads," but it was not until after the publication of Stalin's "Dizziness from Success" article in *Pravda* on March 2, 1930, that the procuracy was able to launch another effort to "regularize" the processes of dekulakization, deportation, and collectivization.

On April 5, 1930, Yanson, the People's Commissar of Justice for the

RSFSR, addressed the following "secret, very urgent" communication to the RSFSR Council of People's Commissars:

Thousands of complaints and complainants pouring into the Procuracy of the Republic, and likewise other materials coming in daily from the local units, reveal more and more new cases of the most varied distortions and excesses which were allowed and continue in some places to be allowed in the local units during the carrying out of collectivization and the liquidation of the kulaks as a class.

The complaints and materials coming in continue to indicate the following basic violations and distortions of revolutionary legality:

In regard to COLLECTIVIZATION: (*a*) the organization of kolkhozes through administrative pressure with violations of the principle of voluntary entry into the kolkhoz; (*b*) the practice of socializing, despite the rules of agricultural artels, the smaller livestock of the peasants who enter the kolkhozes; (*c*) the lack of economy and criminally neglectful attitude toward the preservation and keeping of the proper order of socialized equipment, etc. In regard to DEKU-LAKIZATION: (*a*) the expropriation of kulak households in raions which were not declared to be raions of complete collectivization; (*b*) abuses and violence during dekulakization; (*c*) the illegal revocation of voting rights; the levying of individual taxes on the middle peasants in order artificially to create formal grounds for dekulakization etc.

Together with this a new type of distortion and excess is observed: in some places Soviet and Party workers are not only completely demobilized in regard to the tasks of collectivization and liquidation of the kulaks as a class, but by their actions they aid departure from the kolkhozes, squandering of equipment, etc. Related to this, there are also observed cases of definite excesses in regard to bringing to trial and judgment masses of workers of the Soviet apparatus. Although they allow obvious distortions, they do this unconsciously and because of complicated objective reasons.

For swift and resolute liquidation of the excesses and distortions pointed out, the mere everyday review and resolution of the growing stream of complaints coming in (the complainants travel from the most far-distant areas) is clearly insufficient. In order to eliminate as soon as possible the distortions in the local units, it has become definitely necessary to commandeer special groups of procurators and members of the court into the most unfavorable oblasts (krais) and into the okrugs and raions, granting them broad powers and the right to resolve on the spot questions of the correction of distortions.[7]

The memorandum then proposed that some 210 workers be commandeered for two months to perform this emergency task and requested a special appropriation of 100,000 rubles from the reserve fund of the RSFSR Council of People's Commissars to finance it. On April 9 the Council made an allotment of 30,000 rubles and ordered the oblasts, krais, and autonomous republics "urgently to carry out the proper measures through the local procurators."

On the next day the RSFSR Council of People's Commissars issued a decree "On measures for regulating the temporary and permanent resettlement of exiled kulak families."[8] The decree ordered the Procurator of the Republic to organize an appeals procedure to review complaints concerning incorrect dekulakization and exile. On April 25 the People's Commissar of Justice supplemented this decree with a top-secret circular addressed to the oblasts, krais, and autonomous republics.[9] After calling attention to the provisions of the decree, the circular continued:

1. The number of complaints daily coming into the Procuracy of the Republic, both by mail and directly from the complainants themselves, testifies to the fact that up to the present time the directives of February 2 and March 14 on eliminating distortions and excesses during dekulakization have not been adopted everywhere by the jurisdiction of the procuracy. In the majority of cases they are not carried out with the proper speed and thoroughness. The complainants who have been personally present at the reception in the Procuracy of the Republic report that the procuracies on the local level (mainly the okrug and raion ones) either do not receive complaints at all or, after they receive them, direct them for investigation or disposition to the raion executive committees and village soviets. Such a procedure is completely inadmissible. The raion executive committees, promulgating decrees on dekulakization, and the village soviets, providing information for such decrees, are not and cannot be organs which can objectively investigate the correctness of the decrees previously promulgated by them. Hundreds of complaints directed to the okrug procuracies from the center are also for the most part redirected to the same raion executive committees and village soviets, which at best delays their solution, and in most cases does not bring any essential improvement.

2. Reports lately indicate that there are a great many mistakes in carrying out dekulakization. At least in a number of cases the information on the basis of which the decrees were promulgated, not only on dekulakization but also on exile in the first category [to Siberia and the northern regions], was not confirmed at all. This information was given either on the basis of unverified rumors, or because of personal quarrels of the local workers with the person exiled. A number of cases of the subsequent correction of mistakes in regard to middle peasants, rural teachers, etc., deserve special attention.

3. In connection with the decree of the RSFSR Council of People's Commissars on carrying out a complete check of kulaks classified in the fourth category [those relocated to poor land in the area in which they had previously resided], the jurisdiction of the procuracy should propose to the executive committee an immediate investigation. This should be carried out by commissions under the executive committees which travel to the spot or send their official representatives to the area. The receipt and analysis of complaints should be organized both by the commissions themselves and the procuracy. The consideration of complaints and their final solution should be done by the commissions with the necessary participation of representatives of the procuracy. If there is information on mass wrongs in one or another raion or settlement, trips should be organized to the spot by the commission or their representatives with the participation of representatives of the procuracy in order to correct the most obvious cases of distortion.

4. . . . In cases of procuracy disagreement with the decisions [of the commission] they should definitely be protested to the corresponding executive committee, and in case of refusal of the protests for invalid reasons, the question should be transferred to the next higher executive committee . . .

5. In regard to complaints sent involving the first and second category, it is proposed to the procurators of the Northern and Siberian krais:

a. Complaints sufficiently validated and supported by documents should be decided immediately on the spot in agreement with the Plenipotentiary of the OGPU;

b. complaints demanding investigation should be sent, together with the relevant documents to be checked by the okrug prosecutor in the place of primary residence of the complainant, with a designation of short time-limits for investigation and simultaneous reporting of recommendations to the corresponding krai (oblast) procuracy.

Complete investigation of complaints should be finished, if possible, not later than May 15. Inform us in a special letter by June 1 on the results of the investigation and the conclusions drawn from it.

Unfortunately, the only record of a reply to this request is a note in Information Bulletin Number 5 of the Western Oblast procuracy that on May 1, 1930, 729 cases of illegal dekulakization and 507 cases of illegal deprivation of voting rights had already been corrected in seven okrugs of the Western Oblast.[10] Even these fragmentary statistics are enough to suggest both the rough-and-ready character of the dekulakization process and the massive scale on which so-called mistakes were made. They also provide a paradoxical demonstration of the efforts of the regime to make use of the procuracy to regularize and give quasi-legal direction to a process that was fundamentally lawless and revolutionary in character.

The Archive contains some evidence of the role of the oblast court in the dekulakization and collectivization campaign. Reports of the oblast court are available only for two ten-day periods, March 1–10 and 10–20, 1930; they contain summaries of the actions of the okrug and people's courts as well as directives of the oblast court itself.[11] The March 1–10 report noted that the okrug and people's courts during the month of February had handled a total of 509 cases involving problems connected with the spring sowing campaign, dekulakization, and collectivization.[12] These cases brought before the courts 911 persons, of whom 53 were freed and 858 convicted. Of those convicted, 298 were classified as kulaks, 194 as well-to-do peasants, 230 as middle peasants, 48 as poor peasants, and 46 as officials. During the first ten days of March the pace of court business quickened. The courts disposed of 278 cases involving a total of 449 persons, of whom 407 were convicted. During the second ten days of March the number of cases mounted to 353, with 644 individuals appearing before the courts.[13]

Judicial business registered the tensions of collectivization. The largest group of cases involved illegal slaughter of cattle; the next largest group counterrevolutionary agitation against collectivization, hooliganism at meetings, and so on. During the mid-March period there was a large increase in arrests of individuals who sought to escape their obligations in connection with the lumber-delivery campaign. In these cases sentences ran from exile, forced labor, and two years' deprivation of freedom for kulaks to six months of forced labor for poor peasants. Other smaller categories of cases included crimes of officials, the nonfulfillment of obligations in connection with seed-fund deliveries, and the illegal sale of kulak property.

The reports placed considerable emphasis on various "distortions" of the class line by the lower courts which the oblast court had corrected and overruled. Basically, these "distortions" extended in two directions: excessive mildness toward kulak "crimes" and unnecessary severity in dealing with the offenses of middle and poor peasants. The report cited several cases where kulaks, who had infiltrated into leading positions in kolkhozes in order to destroy them, were brought to trial under Article 169 of the Criminal Code with its relatively mild penalties of confiscation of property and deprivation of freedom for three years instead of being charged with the much more serious crime of counterrevolutionary activity under Article 58, paragraph 9. At the same time some of the lower courts were sharply criticized for failing to distinguish in their sentences between poor and middle peasants who participated in demonstrations against collectivization and the kulaks who allegedly organized, led, and inspired them. Perhaps the most significant development was the decision of the enlarged plenum of the oblast court (obviously in accordance with central directives) to discontinue the criminal prosecution of middle and poor peasants for slaughter of cattle or mild expressions of dissatisfaction with collectivization which did not manifest a clear counterrevolutionary character. Instead, such offenses were to be dealt with administratively or by comrade courts of the kolkhozes. The nature of the penalties to be imposed by these administrative organs was, however, left unclear. This relaxation of pressure against poor and middle peasants, however, was accompanied by increasingly severe measures against kulaks.

The oblast court also reported a number of cases of malfeasance on the part of officials in connection with collectivization and dekulakization. Two chairmen of village soviets were charged with providing kulaks with fictitious documents which permitted them to slaughter their cattle and dispose of their property; a third, who was described as "closely tied with kulak elements" was sentenced to seven years deprivation of freedom by a people's court. On appeal to the okrug the sentence was reduced to four years. Members of dekulakization commissions were indicted for misappropriation of seized kulak property, and in one case a group of kolkhoz leaders were condemned to six months of forced labor for drunkenness, the sale of kolkhoz cattle, and other kindred abuses.

These scattered records indicate the extent to which problems of dekulakization and collectivization dominated the agenda of the courts and procuracy during this period. But they also reveal something more.

Both the courts and the procuracy were instruments of the Party dictatorship, and their primary obligation was to execute Party instructions emanating from the center and transmitted through both Party and governmental channels. As guardians of the Party line, both the oblast court and the procuracy had a special obligation to discipline their own subordinates, to eliminate "right-wing deviations" and "left-wing excesses," and to make certain that the machinery of justice would mirror the shifting needs and demands of the Party leadership in fulfilling the dekulakization and collectivization program.

The Struggle for Legality

In carrying out the Party line, however, both the courts and the procuracy had an additional obligation deriving from their professional role as guardians of "revolutionary legality." Theirs was the task of insuring that uniform standards were applied in choosing the victims of dekulakization, that appropriate penalties were invoked, that proper differentiations were made among various social categories in meting out punishment, and that required procedures were adhered to in executing governmental decrees. As legal spokesmen, their function was to correct errors and mistakes in applying the regime's regulations and to make certain that the administrators who were charged with executing these regulations were not abusing the discretion vested in them. The documentary evidence for 1929–30 points to the fact that the procuracy and the courts endeavored to perform this function within the limits of the possibilities open to them.

But the possibilities were limited. Perhaps the most revealing and authoritative testimonial of the ineffectiveness of the procuracy and judicial organs in checking arbitrary arrests and mass deportation of kulaks during the period 1930–1933 is contained in the secret Stalin-Molotov letter of May 8, 1933, addressed to all Party and Soviet workers and to all organs of the OGPU, the courts, and the procuracy.

The Central Committee and the Sovnarkom are informed that disorderly mass arrests in the countryside are still a part of the practice of our officials. Such arrests are made by chairmen of kolkhozes and members of kolkhoz administrations, by chairmen of village soviets and secretaries of Party cells, by raion and krai officials; arrests are made by all who desire to, and who, strictly speaking, have no right to make arrests. It is not surprising that in such a saturnalia of arrests, organs which do have the right to arrest, including the organs of the OGPU and especially the militia, lose all feeling of moderation and often perpetrate arrests without any basis, acting according to the rule: "First arrest, and then investigate." [14]

A secret joint circular issued by the Central Control Commission and the Commissariat of Workers' and Peasants' Inspection on May 25, 1933, put it even more strongly:

. . . Information coming in to the Central Control Commission from the localities still shows that mass arrests continue, that there is legal repression on an extraordinary scale, which has led everywhere to intolerable overloading of the places of imprisonment, to inordinate burdening of all organs of investigation, the courts, and the procuracy. As a result . . . the quality of the work of the organs of investigation, the courts, and the procuracy has sharply deteriorated, which in turn in the presence of complicated, masked forms of class struggle results in a number of instances in extremely misdirected legal repression.[15]

The letter of May 8, which ordered the discontinuance of arrests by unauthorized persons, had as one of its purposes a strengthening of the authority of the procuracy. The letter provided that arrests could be made only by organs of the procuracy, the OGPU, or by officials of the militia; that examining magistrates or investigators could make arrests only with the preliminary sanction of the procurator; that arrests made by the militia had to be approved or repudiated by the raion OGPU head or by the procurator not later than forty-eight hours after the time of arrest; that arrests by the OGPU had to receive preliminary approval of the procurator except in cases of terroristic acts, explosions, arson, espionage, border-crossing, political banditry, and counterrevolutionary, anti-Party groupings; and finally that the USSR procurator and the OGPU were both to guarantee undeviating fulfillment of the 1922 instructions on procuracy control of persons arrested by the OGPU.

The Stalin-Molotov letter also ordered a reduction in the number of prisoners held in places of detention and assigned the procuracy a major role in arranging releases. Under the terms of the order, the 800,000 prisoners who were at that time confined in places of detention, aside from camps and colonies, were to be reduced to 400,000 within a two-month period, and a quota of 400,000 was established as the maximum number of persons who could be kept in prisons. The Procurator of the USSR and the OGPU were given joint responsibility for allocating this quota among the separate republics and oblasts or krais. The decree envisaged the mass transfer of some categories of prisoners to forced labor camps; the mass transfer of other categories, including kulaks sentenced to a term of three to five years, to so-called labor settlements; and the release of the remaining prisoners under bail or other forms of supervision. Together with the OGPU and the People's Commissariat of Justice, the procuracy was instructed to organize a review of the cases of all prisoners in confinement in order to fit them into their appropriate classification. This work was to be supervised by special oblast commissions chaired by the oblast procurator, but including in its membership the chairman of the oblast court, the OGPU plenipotentiary, and the chief of the oblast militia administration. Where the total number of prisoners in an oblast exceeded 30,000, auxiliary

ИНСТРУКЦИЯ

всем партийно-советским работникам и всем органам ОГПУ, Суда и Прокуратуры

Отчаянное сопротивление кулачества колхозному движению трудящихся крестьян, развернувшееся еще в конце 1929 года и принявшее форму поджогов и террористических актов против колхозных деятелей, создало необходимость применения советской властью массовых арестов и острых форм репрессий, в виде массового выселения кулаков и подкулачников в северные и дальние края.

Дальнейшее сопротивление кулацких элементов, вредительство в колхозах и совхозах, вскрытое в 1932 году, широко распространившееся массовые хищения колхозного и совхозного имущества — потребовали дальнейшего усиления репрессивных мер против кулацких элементов, воров и всякого рода саботажников.

Все это говорит о том, что в областях и краях имеется еще не мало товарищей, которые не поняли новой обстановки и все еще продолжают жить в прошлом.

Все это говорит о том, что, несмотря на наличие новой обстановки, требующей перенесения центра тяжести на массовую политическую и организаторскую работу, эти товарищи цепляются за отживающие формы работы, уже не соответствующие новой обстановке и создающие угрозу ослабления авторитета советской власти в деревне.

Похоже на то, что эти товарищи готовы подменить и уже подменяют политическую работу в массах в целях изоляции кулацких и анти-колхозных элементов — административно-чекист-

---

II.

ОБ УПОРЯДОЧЕНИИ ПРОИЗВОДСТВА АРЕСТОВ

1) Воспретить производство арестов лицами, на то не уполномоченными по закону—председателями РИК, районными и краевыми уполномоченными, председателями сельсоветов, председателями колхозов и колхозных об'единений, секретарями ячеек и пр.

Аресты могут быть производимы только органами прокуратуры, ОГПУ или начальниками милиции.

Следователи могут производить аресты только с предварительной санкции прокурора.

Аресты, производимые нач. милиции, должны быть подтверждены или отменены районными уполномоченными ОГПУ или прокуратурой по принадлежности не позднее 48 часов после ареста.

2) Запретить органам прокуратуры, ОГПУ и милиции применять в качестве меры пресечения заключение под стражу до суда за маловажные преступления.

В качестве меры пресечения могут быть заключаемы под стражу до суда только лица, обвиняемые по делам: о контрреволюции, террактах, о вредительстве, о бандитизме и грабеже, о шпионаже, переходе границы и контрабанде, об убийстве и тяжелых ранениях, о крупных хищениях и растратах, о профессиональной спекуляции, о валютчиках, о фальшивомонетчиках, злостном хулиганстве и профессиональных рецидивистах.

3) Установить при производстве арестов органами ОГПУ предварительное согласие прокурорского надзора по всем делам, кроме дел о террористических актах, взрывах, поджогах, шпионаже и перебежчиках, политическом бандитизме и к.-р. антипартийных группировках.

Установленный в настоящем пункте порядок вводится в жизнь для ДВК, Средней Азии и Казахстана лишь через 6 месяцев.

4) Обязать прокурора СССР и ОГПУ обеспечить неуклонное исполнение инструкции 1922 г. о порядке прокурорского контроля за производством арестов и содержанием под стражей лиц, арестованных ОГПУ.

III.

О РАЗГРУЗКЕ МЕСТ ЗАКЛЮЧЕНИЯ

1. Установить, что максимальное количество лиц, могущих содержаться под стражей в местах заключения НКЮ, ОГПУ и Главного управления милиции, кроме лагерей и колоний, не должно превышать 400 тысяч человек на весь Союз ССР.

пересмотр личного состава следственных заключенных с тем, чтобы всем, кроме особо опасных элементов, заменить содержание под стражей другой мерой пресечения (поручительство, залог, подписка о невыезде).

5. В отношении осужденных провести следующие мероприятия:

а) Всем осужденным по суду до 3 лет заменить лишение свободы принудительными работами до 1 года, а остальной срок считать условным.

б) Осужденных на срок от 3 до 5 лет включительно—направить в трудовые поселки ОГПУ.

в) Осужденных на срок свыше 5 лет—направить в лагеря ОГПУ.

6. Кулаки, осужденные на срок от 3 до 5 лет включительно, подлежат направлению в трудовые поселки вместе с находящимися на их иждивении лицами.

7. Для разгрузки мест заключения и проведения указанных в пп. 5 и 6 мероприятий организовать в каждой республике, области (крае) специальные областные комиссии в составе: краевого (областного) прокурора, председателя краевого (областного) суда, ПП ОГПУ и начальника краевого (областного) управления милиции под председательством краевого (областного) прокурора.

8. В республиках, краях, областях, где общее количество заключенных превышает в данный момент 30 тысяч человек, разрешить областным комиссиям образовывать межрайонные подкомиссии, как вспомогательные их органы, с тем, чтобы решения межрайонных комиссий утверждались областными комиссиями.

9. Предоставить право областным комиссиям освобождать из лагерей и поселков, независимо от срока осуждения, нетрудоспособных, инвалидов, стариков, матерей с маленькими детьми, беременных женщин, заменяя им лишение свободы принудительными работами.

В отдельных случаях областные комиссии вправе направлять в лагеря особо опасные элементы, хотя бы и осужденные на срок до 5 лет.

10. Для проведения разгрузки в Средне-Азиатских республиках, Казахстане и Кара-Калпакии предложить прокуратуре СССР, ОГПУ и Верхсуду СССР направить специальные комиссии из Москвы для общего руководства работой республиканских комиссий этих республик.

⁂

Обязать НКЮ союзных республик и Наркомздравы союзных республик в месячный срок ликвидировать полностью сыпно-тифозные заболевания в местах заключения.

Председатель Совета Народных Комиссаров СССР В. МОЛОТОВ (Скрябин)

Секретарь ЦК ВКП(б) И. СТАЛИН

8 мая 1933 г.

П 6028

Parts of the secret Stalin-Molotov order calling a half to mass arrests of kulaks — May 8, 1933.

inter-raion commissions were authorized to speed action. The oblast commissions were vested with discretion to send "especially dangerous elements" to forced labor camps, even though they had been sentenced to a term of less than five years. In the case of disabled people, invalids, old people, mothers with small children, and pregnant women, the commissions were authorized to substitute lesser forms of punishment for shipment to the camps and settlements.

The Stalin-Molotov letter appeared to augur strengthened procuracy control over the activities of the OGPU, the militia, and other organs of investigation and repression. Yet such was not to be the line of development. There are scattered cases in the Archive during the mid-thirties which show the procuracy at work preventing the overexpenditure of wage funds by a city soviet, investigating the misdeeds of a chairman of a village soviet, and engaging in other similar supervisory functions with respect to administrative and judicial agencies.[16] But the procuracy proved powerless to control the OGPU, and its successor, the NKVD. Indeed, during the Great Purge all restraints on the organs of security vanished, and in the Western Oblast at least, by an ironic twist of fate, the leading members of the oblast court and procuracy ended as victims of the very organs they were supposed to control.

The Great Purge in the Oblast Court Party Cell

The Smolensk Archive contains the protocols of all Party meetings of the oblast court cell (which included workers in the oblast procuracy) for the period July 27, 1936, through December 16, 1937.[17] It is a sad record of increasing helplessness in the face of NKVD terror. The temper of the group can be illustrated by a minor incident. At a meeting on October 11, 1936, the Party cell considered the possibility of transferring one Klyutsev from the status of sympathizer to Party candidate.[18] In the course of the discussion it developed that Klyutsev's father-in-law had been arrested by the NKVD as a Trotskyite, and that Klyutsev had committed the unpardonable sin of demanding that the arresting officers produce a procurator's warrant sanctioning the arrest. Moreover, noted one speaker, "Instead of helping the NKVD, he, together with his wife, kept coming to the NKVD and arguing that his father-in-law was not a Trotskyite and that there was no evidence to substantiate the charge." The Party cell of the oblast court decided to exclude Klyutsev from the ranks of sympathizers.[19]

Beginning in March 1937 and mounting to a climax after the purge of Rumyantsev and other Party leaders of the oblast in June 1937, a flood of mutual denunciations engulfed the oblast court Party cell and virtually destroyed its leadership. The three leading figures in the oblast court prior to the purge were Andrianov, the chairman; Grachev, the head of the criminal division; and Leiman, the head of the civil cassation division. Their fate is instructive.

The first to fall under attack was Leiman, a Latvian by nationality who had joined the Party in 1919. At a meeting of the oblast court Party committee in mid-June, Leiman was accused of having delivered himself of a whole series of anti-Soviet formulations.[20] He was reported as having said that the Stalin constitution restored the right to vote to those who had been deprived of liberty and were being held in jail; that it was undesirable to appoint eighteeen-year-olds as judges and that if the constitution permitted it, it was necessary to reconsider the constitution; that, while lecturing to oblast court workers, he had observed that such appointments were forbidden by the constitution; that while reading a lecture he scribbled on Stalin's portrait; and finally that he treated his subordinates so badly that they wept. In reply Leiman admitted that he had unconsciously drawn lines over a corner of Stalin's portrait, but for the rest pleaded that he either must have been misunderstood or that his Russian must have been at fault. At this meeting the partkom contented itself with issuing a reprimand to Leiman and requested the Supreme Court to investigate his work. But Leiman was not to be let off so easily. On December 16, 1937, the Party Committee of the oblast court was informed that Leiman had been arrested by the NKVD as an enemy of the people and that clear evidence of his counter-revolutionary views had been uncovered in papers found in his desk.[21] He was thereupon expelled from the Party.

The first major attacks on Andrianov and Grachev were launched at a meeting of the oblast court cell which assembled after the "unmasking" of Rumyantsev and stretched over four days, July 1–5, 1937.[22] At this meeting Andrianov, Grachev, Leiman, and other leaders of the court were sharply criticized for various inadequacies in the work of the oblast court and an effort was made to link them with the discredited obkom leaders. Grachev at that time was absent on a Red Army assignment and therefore did not participate in the discussion. Andrianov beat his breast about his past political blindness, made the damaging admission that he had authorized the expenditure of 1,100 rubles for a portrait of Rumyantsev, but also proudly boasted that he had been severely criticized by both Rumyantsev and Rakitov. The meeting expelled Andrianov from the Party committee, and recommended to the obkom that both Andrianov and Grachev be relieved as leaders of the oblast court.

On July 14 the Party cell reassembled to consider the cases of Andrianov and Grachev.[23] The general tenor of the discussion was that both had made serious mistakes, but that they should not be accused of "wrecking" activities nor indicted as "enemies of the people." But the previous recommendation that they be removed from court leadership was allowed to stand.

The reprieve, however, proved to be temporary. On August 11–12 the Party committee of the oblast court cell met to reconsider the destinies of Grachev and Andrianov.[24] This time, it soon became clear, the partkom had gathered for the kill. Grachev pleaded in vain that he had tried to the best of his ability to carry out the orders of his superiors. He hotly denied the charge that he had once said that life was better in prison than on a kolkhoz. What had happened, he tried to explain, was that a prisoner whom he was interrogating had remarked that he was better fed in prison than on the kolkhoz. He should perhaps have found some way of preventing the prisoner from making the remark, but he argued that it was gross distortion to attribute the remark to him. He admitted that, when ordering portraits of Party leaders, he included among them a portrait of one who subsequently turned out to be an "enemy of the people." Unfortunately, he had had no advance knowledge that this would happen. While Grachev was alternately defiant and self-justificatory, Andrianov cringed before his accusers, admitted all the mistakes with which he was charged, and pleaded for mercy. At first there was some disposition on the part of those present to be more lenient toward Andrianov, but as accusation piled on accusation, the mood of the gathering hardened and both Andrianov and Grachev were expelled from the Party as agents who had fallen under the influence of the "enemies of the people" — Rumyantsev and Shilman — and had carried out their "wrecking" directives in the oblast court.

The final *coup de grâce,* which included among its victims leading officials of the oblast procuracy and the law school as well as of the oblast court, was administered by the new obkom bureau in a resolution of September 11, 1937. The resolution read in part:

> Having heard the report of the commission on the results of the investigation of the work of the oblast procuracy and the oblast court, the Bureau of the Obkom of the CPSU (b) states that the leading workers of the oblast procuracy (Yeremin) and the oblast court (Andrianov, Grachev), have pursued right-Trotskyite practices, manifested in the coarsest perversion of punitive policy; violations of revolutionary legality; the closing, glossing over, and delaying of important political cases on the control of revolutionary agitation, the beating and persecution of Stakhanovites, wrecking in the sovkhozes, kolkhozes and MTS, and plundering of socialist property.[25]

The resolution then spelled out a bill of particulars charging that the judicial and investigatory organs had been filled with "hostile and doubtful elements" and listing many cases in which the procuracy and the oblast court had allegedly carried out their "wrecking activities." The resolution concluded by confirming the expulsion of Yeremin, Andrianov,

Grachev, and numerous others from the Party and transferring the case "to the proper investigatory organs," a thinly disguised euphemism for the NKVD.

There are two footnotes to this drastic action which perhaps deserve to be recorded. One of the many disagreeable concomitants of every purge is the premium it places on irresponsible denunciation and the opportunity it creates for skillful practitioners of this highly specialized art. The purge of the oblast court and procuracy produced a particularly notorious and obnoxious practitioner in the person of one Rabinovich. His jackal-like zeal in pouncing on his colleagues and his rapid rise in oblast court Party circles as a result of his denunciations provide a peculiarly eerie insight into the fear-drenched atmosphere of the purge years. There was no accusation too wild for Rabinovich to repeat, and none so fantastic that it would not be believed. He was among the first to attack Andrianov, Grachev, and Leiman and call for blood. When one Lepin was chosen secretary of the Party cell, it was Rabinovich who caused his expulsion from the Party with the charge that Lepin was an impostor and spy and that the real Lepin was dead.[26] By October 1937 Rabinovich had managed to be elected deputy secretary of the Party cell. At this point, by a grim logic not uncharacteristic of the purge years, Rabinovich finally fell victim to his own devices. Accusations began to be directed against him. At a Party meeting on October 5, 1937, he admitted defensively there was some material on him, namely that the husband of his sister was an "enemy of the people," but he insisted that he had never seen him, "not even on a photo."[27] He flatly denied reports that he had had contact with an "unmasked" raikom secretary.

Meanwhile, apparently, the dossier on Rabinovich was accumulating. At a meeting of the Party committee on December 7 a series of charges was leveled against him: (1) that while working as a people's judge, he had had contacts with a local raikom secretary who had since been unmasked as an "enemy of the people" and that he had supported the expulsion of a Party member who criticized the raikom secretary; (2) that he had not been in favor of strengthening the village soviet; (3) that in 1935 he had received a reprimand for misuse of the bread fund; and (4) that he was a "flatterer."[28] At this meeting Rabinovich was removed from his newly won post, and further action was postponed pending reëxamination of the charges. At this point, unfortunately, the Archive stops, leaving the future fate of Rabinovich in complete suspense.

If the purge created only doubtful or temporary opportunities for the Rabinoviches, there was one group for whom it was a grim blessing in disguise. This category represented the junior workers occupying less responsible posts who were mobilized to fill the yawning gaps created by the purge not only in the top layer of the apparatus of the courts and the procuracy, but in Party and governmental work generally. The Archive contains a list, dated September 16, 1937, of comrades recommended by the Party organization of the Oblast court for leading work.[29] The list dramatizes the fact that the purge had its beneficiaries as well as its victims. Some examples may reinforce the point. A thirty-six-year-old worker with only an elementary education and no legal training became chief of the cadres division of the oblast court, that is, responsible for all court appointments. A thirty-seven-year-old woman worker of peasant origin who had attended only a primary school became a member of the special collegium of the oblast court. A young woman of twenty-seven, of peasant origin, who had supplemented an elementary education with a one-year law course and had also served as a Komsomol organizer, became a member of the oblast court. Another young man of thirty-two, of peasant origin, with a similar educational background was recommended for assignment as a people's judge. A somewhat older worker, aged forty-five, with only a primary education and a record of two Party reprimands for drinking, who had served as chief of the administrative and financial department of the oblast court since June 1937, was put forward as a candidate for appointment either to the oblast court or to leading work in the militia. One can deduce from cases such as these how desperate was the need for personnel and how unlooked for were the opportunities for those who had the good fortune to survive the purge.

The picture of the activities of the procuracy and the courts which issues from the Smolensk Archive is necessarily fragmentary. Rich as the record is for selected periods and episodes, it remains far short of comprehensive in its coverage of the wide-ranging functions of the procuracy and the judicial organs. Yet, despite these limitations, one unmistakable characteristic emerges. Both the procuracy and the courts are revealed as arms of the Party dictatorship, dedicated to carrying out its policies and reflecting its changing demands. The norms which the legal organs enforce operate from time to time as restraints on arbitrary action by administrative subordinates, but they do not restrict the Party leadership itself. The ultimate reality is one of servility and subservience rather than of an independent legal system binding rulers and ruled alike.

PART THREE

The Impact of Authority

10 Crime in Smolensk — Out of the

Police Records

The Smolensk Archive contains two sizable collections of material on crime in the region. The first, which consists of a series of monthly and special reports by the criminal investigation department of the Western Oblast for the period September 1929–May 1930, is of primary interest in connection with the resistance to dekulakization and collectivization, and will be reserved for treatment in Chapter 12 on the history of collectivization.[1] The second file incorporates numerous reports on major cases in the Western Oblast during the year 1934. Prepared by the oblast militia for the special information of Rumyantsev, the obkom first secretary, they provide a representative sample of the range and incidence of crime in the region during the period of consolidation which followed hard on the heels of the collectivization drive.[2] These militia reports provide the primary data for this chapter.

Until 1934 the militia, or uniformed police, functioned as an independent administration attached to the Council of People's Commissars at the center and to the oblispolkoms in the regions. The jurisdiction of the militia embraced ordinary, rather than political or counterrevolutionary crimes; the latter fell within the purview of the OGPU. In July 1934 the NKVD, or People's Commissariat of Internal Affairs, was established as a successor agency to the OGPU; at the same time the militia became a branch of the new organization. The activities of the militia, however, remained largely unaffected. It continued to deal with ordinary crimes while the security arm of the NKVD concentrated on counterrevolutionary offenses.

The militia reports to be analyzed here reflect this division of labor. They exclude the broad category of political crimes; they do, however, include a vast array of alleged criminal activity which can conveniently be classified under the following rubrics: banditry; arson; kolkhoz disorders and harvesting crimes; embezzlement, bribery, and procurement irregularities; abuse of power by officials; attacks on officials; and sex offenses. These will be discussed seriatim.

Banditry

The reports disclose that banditry was still a major problem in the oblast, despite the great efforts being exerted to stamp it out. On January 16, 1934, the militia officials informed Rumyantsev that they had arrested a group of eight "armed bandits" in the city of Bezhitsa. Over a period of three weeks the gang had engaged in thirteen street holdups, robbing passers-by, mostly workers, of money and clothing and shooting one person. Investigation disclosed that only two of the bandits had previous criminal records. The rest were chiefly young factory workers; indeed four of them were members of the Komsomol and one was the son of a Party member. On the same day the militia reported the capture of another bandit group of ten who had been terrorizing peasants in Novo-Duginsky and neighboring raions.[4] One of the members of the gang turned out to be the secretary of the Komsomol cell in the village of Kozhanovo in Novo-Duginsky raion. The crimes of the group included robbery of peasant homes, the theft of kolkhoz horses, and the murder of a peasant woman for refusal to hand over gold allegedly in her possession. The band was armed with a revolver, three hunting rifles, and knives. Still another report, dated January 10, noted the liquidation of a bandit group operating on the border between Pogarsky and Trubchevsky raions.[5] This band had four members, all heavily armed with rifles. In ten days they had committed eight thefts and six robberies. Their marauding activities were facilitated by a chairman of a village soviet and two village soviet members, who provided hiding places for members of the band and who shared in the spoils from the robberies. The bandits operated with impunity and even engaged openly in drinking parties with the soviet members and two female school teachers of the village. The local peasants knew of the tie with the village authorities but were "too terrorized to reveal it" or even to report cases where they had been robbed. The chairman of the village soviet, a Party member, offered the excuse that "he entered the band in order to destroy it." The explanation was not accepted since there was evidence that he had warned the bandits of the militia's plan to arrest them and that as a result several had escaped.

Beginning in May and extending through October 1934, the file contains a series of round-up reports on the state of organized banditry in the oblast. A summary of the May report will suggest the pattern.[6] The "majority" of armed robberies, according to the report, were committed by small bands of three to five men, composed mostly of "déclassé elements," runaways from prison, or persons previously prosecuted for crime. The report listed thirteen groups as liquidated, five as partly liquidated, and nine bands as still free. Altogether, the report recorded a total of thirty-four armed robberies, of which eight were accompanied by murder. The crimes included house-breaks, holdups on the roads and streets, and robberies of state stores and offices where money or goods were available.

The June report indicated a mounting crime wave with a total of seventy-five armed robberies, fourteen of which were accompanied by murder or serious wounding of the victims.[7] At the end of the month a total of twenty-three groups composed of eighty-one members remained "unliquidated." The report then described the activities of more than a dozen bands in the different raions. One of the most notorious was the eight-man Kotchenko band, whose leader Kotchenko had fled from prison while serving a ten-year sentence. This band, which was responsible for thirteen armed robberies in Pogarsky raion alone, worked hand in hand with the chairman of a village soviet and the head of a village store. The former warned the bandits of militia raids, supplied them with "various documents," hid them, and provided them with food. The latter supplied ammunition for their rifles. Protected in this fashion, the gang successfully eluded capture for a long time, but was finally cornered on June 28, and Kotchenko was killed in an exchange of gun fire.

Another typical band consisted of eight escaped convicts who were led by the Trofimov brothers. Operating in their native raion they stole food and cattle from the collective farmers and staged armed robberies in the villages. In a particularly brutal attack, they beat a peasant into unconsciousness, and after robbing his hut, raped his wife. In this case, as in many others, the militia organized a so-called "operational group" to hunt down the culprits. Finally, six, including the leaders, were caught, but two made good their escape.

During July the number of acts of banditry declined to sixty-one compared with seventy-five in June, and only seven were accompanied by murder or wounding of the victims.[8] At the end of the month, however, twenty-eight groups still remained at large. One of the bands which was roaming the countryside was said to consist of a former priest, his two sons, the son of a deacon, and two sons of a Baptist. According to the report, the band specialized in robbing churches and priests and killed the guard of a church "with the intent to rob."

The month of August saw another marked fall in the extent of banditry — only twenty-nine armed robberies compared with sixty-one in July. At the end of the month twenty-six groups with a total of eighty-one members were still listed as unapprehended. Perhaps the most dramatic case of the month involved the robbery of the Novo-Duginskaya Savings Bank by its cashier, one G. G. Rusakov, a Komsomol member, who fled with more than 460,000 rubles in bonds, stamps, and cash.[9] When caught several weeks later in Aktiubinsk, however, only 90,000 rubles in bonds were found on him. Subsequent investigation disclosed that he had been a member of a band headed by a certain Klimov, a convicted cattle thief, who had escaped from prison and led a group of runaways.[10] On August 3 these bandits killed one Bozkov, a warehouse man in an MTS, confusing him with another Bozkov, the NKVD chief in the same MTS, whom they had planned to kill in order to capture his weapons. The whole band was liquidated.

The September report registered a further decline in banditry — ten armed robberies compared with twenty-nine the previous month.[11] The militia proudly proclaimed that no "organized" bands remained on the rolls; a search for some thirteen single bandits was still going on. The final report for October again stressed the drastic decline in bandit operations.[12] During October only six new groups were reported to have been formed and only twelve armed robberies occurred. Among the bands eliminated during the month, one led by Makarov holds particular interest because it illustrates a recurrent pattern of operations. Makarov had fled from an NKVD camp, and organized a six-man band from local criminal elements. He then recruited six other helpers among the local population. One was the head of a village coöperative store who supplied the bandits with ammunition, another a bookkeeper in a village soviet who provided the band with appropriate documents, and the other four were independent peasants who kept the gang informed of developments in the village. As this and many similar examples illustrate, connections with the local population and officialdom represented an essential element in the ability of the bands to survive and flourish. But they did not guarantee immunity from arrest. By November 1, 1934, only one band was still reported as at large in the oblast. At this point, the operational reports on banditry end, apparently indicating the conclusion of a successful mop-up operation.

Arson

Arson represented another category of crime against which the militia had to wage a constant struggle. Indeed, the file opens on January 1, 1934, with the report of a large fire in an alcohol-producing factory — "causes unknown." [13] Altogether a total of ten cases was reported involving, among others, the destruction of a wood-processing plant, a flax factory, and the burning of kolkhoz property. In most cases, the causes of the fires were reported as unknown or due to negligence, but in a number of instances where the bitterness of the collectivization experience still carried over, kolkhoz property was deliberately set aflame in revenge for past confiscations. On March 5, 1934, for example, the militia reported the burning of a large warehouse of the kolkhoz "Proletariat" in the village of Topol involving damage of approximately 5,000 rubles.[14] The culprits were alleged to be members of a group that included an individual peasant who had formerly been a Cossack policeman; his nephew, the business manager of the kolkhoz; a former titled landowner who had managed to insinuate himself into the kolkhoz; and an individual peasant of kulak background. The group, according to the report, had long carried on agitation against the kolkhoz leadership. The case was handed over to the OGPU for disposition. On April 7 the militia reported a fire in the kolkhoz "Rumyantsev" in Glinkovsky raion which destroyed forty-two horses and other kolkhoz property.[15] Investigation disclosed that the fire was started by an eighty-two-year-old man who had been dekulakized in 1931 but continued living on the territory of the kolkhoz. After igniting the fire, the old man went back to his hut and hanged himself.

By 1934, however, the great majority of kolkhoz fires was attributable to negligence and carelessness. A typical report of a large fire in the kolkhoz "Politotdel" in Zubtsovsky raion has special interest because of the incidental light which it throws on the mores and social structure of the kolkhoz.[16] On November 6, the kolkhoz administration with the permission of the MTS politotdel distributed cash to the collective farmers to buy vodka to celebrate the anniversary of the Revolution. The next evening the whole village engaged in a noisy alcoholic orgy "under the guise of a public dinner." Meanwhile, the members of the kolkhoz administration and their wives had a party of their own in the home of a brigadier where especially procured red wine and "other sweets" were consumed. When the drunken kolkhozniks found out about these delicacies they gathered 200 strong around the brigadier's house and demanded that the members of the administration come out into the street. In the ensuing free-for-all the administration members and others were badly beaten up. Immediately following the "scandal," fire broke out in the cattle and horse shed of the kolkhoz, and the animals and two peasant homes were destroyed. It was impossible to save the animals since the keys to the shed were in the possession of the chief horse tender who was stretched out in a drunken stupor at the administration party. According to the militia report, the burning resulted from "careless handling of fire" by either the animal tenders or the kolkhozniks, all of whom were drunk. The militia added that the kolkhoz administration had rejected the suggestion made by the one guard on duty that the number of guards be increased during the holiday celebration. The report unfortunately contains no record of the disposition of the case; it merely notes that the matter had been referred to the criminal investigation division of the raion militia for further inquiry.

Kolkhoz Disorders and Harvesting Crimes

During the year 1934 the militia also launched a campaign to stop thefts of kolkhoz, sovkhoz, and MTS property.[17] On January 16, 1934, the oblast militia chief reported on the result of a "raid" carried on in Smolensk raion to check on arrangements for safeguarding "socialist" property. The "raiders" found that some of the guards who were supposed to be on duty were either absent or sleeping; many were overage and feeble, others unarmed or even when armed unable to handle weapons. In a number of kolkhozes the seed reserves were discovered to be rotting, due to negligence on the part of the kolkhoz leadership, and the attitude toward the upkeep and preservation of machinery and other agricultural equipment was termed "criminal." In one kolkhoz the raid revealed systematic theft of grain by the collective farmers; in another both the chairman and the bookkeeper were uncovered as "foreign elements" who had pilfered kolkhoz property. In two other kolkhozes the chairmen and their aides also systematically engaged in large-scale fraud. Everywhere the state of fire-fighting equipment was found to be alarmingly inadequate. The report recommended that strict instructions be issued to the raion agricultural division to correct the situation, and that "cavalry raids" by the militia be repeated "periodically."

As the harvesting season approached, the militia initiated still another campaign to prevent the stealing of wheat from the fields and the warehouses. On August 10, 1934, the oblast militia chief presented the first of a series of round-up reports on harvesting crimes.[18] During the second half of July, he reported, 428 persons were arrested for stealing growing wheat from the fields. Of these, 180 were collective farmers. Also listed were 116 arrests for stealing grain from warehouses. Of those arrested, fifty-six were kolkhoz members. Some astounding cases were cited, including one where a former kulak was supposed single-handedly to have harvested nine hectares of wheat (far above the norm for any kolkhoz brigade) and to have carted off his prodigious gleanings. The report also noted that 15,600 kolkhoz and sovkhoz guards had been checked over the preceding three-month period, that 1,630 had been discovered to be of "foreign" or "criminal" background, and that 534 had been arrested for various violations of regulations.

The next harvesting report, which covered developments in fifty-nine raions for the period August 1–10, 1934, listed 169 arrests for thievery of grain from the fields and 165 arrests for stealing grain from warehouses.[19] Cases were cited where collective farmers connived with brigade leaders to conceal and pilfer whole sacks of grain which should have been delivered to the warehouses. In one rather unusual instance (the kolkhoz "Krasnyi Boriets," Kamiensky raion), the women of the kolkhoz "en masse," refused to go to the fields and harvest wheat because the norm for a labor-day had been doubled. "But the chief fault," declared the militia report, "lay with the inept leadership of the kolkhoz chairman."

The harvesting report for the August 10–20 period noted a falling off in arrests for thievery from the fields to 113 persons — but an increase in arrests for thefts from warehouses to 194 persons, of whom 123 were collective farmers.[20] During this period there was also a substantial increase in arrests for "sabotaging" deliveries. The most notable case involved a kolkhoz chairman in Leninsky raion who violated the first commandment of kolkhoz life by distributing grain to the collective farmers before making his deliveries to the state. His promise "to deliver to the state after the sowing campaign," that is, to deliver what was left after the kolkhoz had satisfied its needs, resulted in a prompt threat of retaliatory action. As a result, the militia chief grimly reported that the kolkhoz chairman met his state delivery quota "100 per cent."

The report for the last ten days of August saw a further falling off of field crimes to eighty-four, and a substantial increase in warehouse thefts to 400.[21] During the first ten days of September the seasonal decline in these crimes began to set in.[22] The two categories of field and warehouse crimes were merged, and a total of 165 arrests were reported for thirty-seven raions. On the other hand, arrests for "sabotaging" deliveries increased to sixty-eight. The final report in the series — for fifty raions over the period September 15–October 1 — noted 274 arrests for field and warehouse thefts and 133 arrests for nonfulfillment or sabotage of deliveries.[23]

As this group of harvest reports makes clear, crime followed the seasons. As the grain ripened, thievery from the fields reached its peak. As the harvest was completed, stealing shifted to the warehouses. As the time for grain deliveries arrived, arrests for nonfulfillment of state obligations mounted. This was the new rhythm of collectivization as it found reflection in the criminal statistics of kolkhoz life.

Embezzlement, Bribery, and Procurement Irregularities

Large-scale embezzlement, bribery, and procurement irregularities represented still another important category of criminal activity in the oblast. The Archive contains numerous examples which illustrate some of the more ingenious methods which were developed to defraud the state. One of the simple cases reported to Rumyantsev on January 16, 1934, involved a conspiracy among a kolkhoz chairman, his bookkeeper, and the head of a warehouse of Zagotlen (the flax delivery organization).[24] For a bribe of 2,000 rubles the warehouse head gave the kolkhoz chairman and his bookkeeper a receipt for 4,158 kilograms of hemp, which were in fact not delivered. They were also paid 410 rubles, 20 kopecks and 138 kilograms of butter for the hemp which they *had not delivered*. Meanwhile, the kolkhoz leaders, equipped with a certificate that they had fulfilled their state delivery quota, took the hemp to the free market and disposed of it for 5,000 rubles. The kolkhoz chairman, who was subsequently arrested together with his fellow-conspirators, was a Party member.

A more complex black-market case, which began with pilfering and other irregularities in a meat-processing plant in Klintsy raion, took nearly three years to unravel.[25] In 1931, according to the militia report, the state nationalized several small sausage-processing plants which had formerly belonged to two private dealers and installed one Kotlikov to run them. Kotlikov entered into an arrangement with the former owners whereby both were left in leading positions and all profited by fraudulently understating the output of the shops and selling the surplus on the black market. To conceal the crime, Kotlikov hired an alcoholic as a bookkeeper and systematically feted him with vodka. The leading member of the auditing commission was also given a good job and enough alcohol to make him sign anything. Large amounts of the sausage were exported to Kharkov where they were sold at black-market prices through various contacts which Kotlikov had established there. The sums realized in Kharkov were then used to buy scarce articles which were subsequently brought back to Klintsy raion and sold locally at speculative prices. In order to obtain extra supplies of meat for his operations, Kotlikov exceeded the procurement prices fixed by the state, and made up the difference by pouring back some of his black market profits into the accounts of the enterprise. When the militia finally caught up with Kotlikov, the losses of the enterprise over which he presided had mounted to over 75,000 rubles. Ten persons involved in his machinations were arrested, including one Party member.

On January 14, 1934, the militia chief submitted a report to Rumyantsev on various financial irregularities in the apparatus of Zagotzerno, the grain procurement agency, and Soyuzplodoovoshch, which was charged with the procurement of potatoes and hay.[26] Over a five-month period the report listed twenty cases of pilfering involving the loss ("according to quite incomplete data") of 37,000 kilograms of grain, 7,800 kilograms of potatoes, and 3,071 kilograms of hay. The investigation revealed that warehouse heads, who directed the pilfering, had been hiring trusted friends and relatives to work in the warehouses and to sell produce in the black market through their own and their friends' relatives; that bookkeepers had been bribed to issue fraudulent receipts to cover up the thievery; and that receiving and weighing agents had also participated and received their cut of the loot. The pilfered produce was usually removed from the warehouses during the night, but sometimes it was also carted away in open daylight under the guise of state deliveries. In order to conceal shortages, railway cars were incompletely loaded; detection was made difficult by "arranging" signs of a robbery en route, suggested by torn-off seals, broken car doors, and other similar devices. To put an end to these practices, the militia pressed the obkom to purge the warehouses of untrustworthy personnel, if possible interspersing the procurement organizations with trained Party forces who could be trusted to keep a vigilant eye open for possible deception and fraud.

A case involving the Yartsevo branch of Plemzagottrest, the cattle procurement trust, and reported to Rumyantsev on January 23, 1934, illustrates somewhat similar pilfering practices.[27] To cover up large losses due to fraudulent manipulation, employees of the organization made bookkeeping entries indicating that they had paid 600 rubles per head of cattle instead of the 128 rubles actually paid, thus erasing the losses and "creating" a fictitious profit of 30,000 rubles. They then seized the opportunity to pocket the difference between the sum actually expended on the cattle and the price which they purported to pay. In addition cattle was fed below norms, and milk was not accurately accounted for. The accumulated "surpluses" were then sold on the black market. The top leadership of the organization winked at these practices and was in fact itself involved. As a result of the militia investigation, eight persons were indicted, including two Party members, the head of the Yartsevo branch and the chief of the procurement base.

On January 29 the militia reported two additional cases of embezzlement. The first centered on a store manager in Katyn, one Korneyev, who systematically pilfered such "deficit goods" as soap and tobacco and disposed of them in the black market through a speculator friend, Titov, who was also a candidate for Party membership.[28] Korneyev's operations were facilitated by a connection with one Kloyzner, who was the deputy commercial director of the store's supply base, and also Korneyev's companion in expensive carousing and drinking parties with local women. When store "profits" proved too small for their needs, they embarked on a whole series of machinations to divert goods from the supply base. By manipulating bills and receipts for nondelivered produce, they managed to create sufficient bookkeeping confusion to make it virtually impossible to compare receipts with the balance of produce on hand. Eventually, however, these maneuvers were unraveled, and the three central figures were arrested.

The second case involved some highly complex and ingenious machinations in the Bryansk Central Savings Bank.[29] The principals included the deputy director of the bank, the chief bookkeeper, the head of the fund department, the head of the storeroom where the funds were kept, and the controller in the same department. Utilizing their special knowledge, the group managed systematically to get hold of and to cash winning loan certificates in the state lotteries. Instead of destroying redeemed loan certificates and coupons, the group connived to turn them in again and receive payment a second time. In addition, special representatives of the group bought up loan certificates which circulated in the black market at greatly reduced rates — 5 to 15 rubles for a 100-ruble certificate — and arranged their redemption at full value. Loan certificates stolen from the office were sold through reputable factory channels on the basis of fraudulent documents. Fictitious credit accounts were set up by members of the group and later drawn on to the extent of 21,000 rubles when they were presented for payment in Orel, Moscow, Leningrad, and other cities. Similar insurance accounts were also established, and some 6,000 rubles were paid out to "beneficiaries" of the insurance policies, who were members of the group. The large-scale drinking bouts in which the band indulged ultimately led to their undoing. Altogether, fifteen persons were arrested.

Another case reported to Rumyantsev on August 14, 1934, illustrates an illegal procurement practice for which there are many precedents in the records.[30] The Yartsevo textile factory needed paper which it could not purchase through legal channels. To obtain this paper the bookkeeper of the factory entered into an "arrangement" with the chief of the Polygraphic Trust of the Western Oblast and the director of the Vyazma typography plant, both Party members. The trust director ordered the transfer of two tons of paper from the Bukharino typography plant to the Vyazma plant. The director of the Vyazma plant went to Bukharino to pick it up, but instead of bringing it back to Vyazma delivered it to the textile factory in Yartsevo. Meanwhile, the bookkeeper prepared fictitious documents to cover up the transaction and arranged for the factory to pay a speculator's price of 7,000 rubles in cash for the paper. Of this amount 2,000 rubles was to go to the Bukharino plant to settle its accounts, 1,000 rubles to the bookkeeper for his "services," and the remaining 4,000 rubles were to be pocketed by the trust director and head of the Vyazma plant. The plan came to grief when its details leaked out to the militia, and all three culprits were arrested while the sale was being consummated. All confessed.

The incidence of embezzlement and thievery, particularly in the trade and coöperative network, reached such dimensions and involved so many Party members that Rumyantsev felt compelled in July 1934 to address a special closed letter to all Party and Komsomol members, calling upon them to overcome "these disgraceful phenomena." [31] Despite this plea, bribery and embezzlement continued to flourish, suggesting perhaps that the forces which nourished them were so endemic as to be proof against even the most vehement Party admonitions.

Abuse of Power by Officials and Attacks on Officials

A few scattered cases in the crime file indicate that the militia occasionally moved into action to prevent gross abuse of authority by officials. Thus on January 9, 1934, the militia chief reported that one Yonov, a member of a village soviet, came to the home of a peasant woman, Makarova, to demand the fulfillment of flax deliveries.[32] On the woman's request to give her a little more time, Yonov beat her and her mother and took away all the raw flax, a cow, and some rye grain. Makarova, pregnant at the time, was severely hurt and had to be hospitalized. Yonov's case was transferred to the procurator for criminal prosecution. On April 21, 1934, the militia submitted a report to Rumyantsev and Yeremin, the oblast procurator, on "illegal measures" undertaken by local village soviets in Plokhinsky raion to force individual peasants to join collective farms.[33] According to the report, all independent peasants who refused to enter collective farms had had their horses and property confiscated. The confiscations were carried out by a village soviet chairman and a raion emissary. The village soviet chairman was arrested, and both he and the raion emissary were slated for criminal prosecution. There is also the case of a collective farm chairman and his brother who, while drunk, opened fire on passers-by in the village of Korolevsky, killing one and wounding two.[34] The militia report to Rumyantsev on January 16 merely announced that an investigation was proceeding.

A crime category which is more frequently represented in the Archive involves attacks on officials. Some examples follow. On January 18, 1934, Trifomov, the chairman of a village soviet, went to the home of one Leonov to check rumors that the latter was a speculator.[35] Leonov was caught red-handed. When Trifomov attempted to write a statement describing the transgression, Leonov split open his skull with an ax and fled. Trifomov, a Party member, was badly hurt and hospitalized. On February 18 the kolkhoznik, Lukashev, murdered his brigade leader, one Nikitin, because the latter had frequently accused him of poor work and evasion of his kolkhoz duties.[36] Lukashev was arrested and confessed.

A particularly brutal crime appears in a report to Rumyantsev dated May 3, 1934.[37] On March 20, the Smolensk city committee of the Komsomol commandeered one Goviazina, a young woman, to spur the sowing campaign in the village of Voznovsky. Goviazina disappeared. Her corpse, cut into pieces, was discovered by the militia. The murderer turned out to be an independent peasant who occupied himself with speculation. He had taken the same train with Goviazina from Smolensk, promised to be her guide, brought her home to his wife and family in order to rob her, and then murdered her in her sleep with an ax. To hide his crime he cut the corpse into pieces and disposed of them in a river, where they were found. His wife confirmed the story but denied participation in the murder. Both were arrested, and the militia reported that "their motives are under scrutiny."

Another case involving an official had its elements of farce as well as ultimate tragedy.[38] In early May one Nikulin, the raion head of the Vegetable Procurement Office, visited the village of Kudrenskaya to consult with the chief of the local procurement base. They had a merry evening together, and finally, Nikulin, quite drunk, mounted a horse with the intention of "visiting a female school teacher" in the village. He lost his way; the horse drowned; and he proceeded on foot in the general direction of the village. An hour before midnight he came to a peasant hut, noisily demanded entrance, and broke a window. The peasant's wife, thinking that it was a bandit attack, fled from the house and gathered together the collective farmers. A posse of ten to fifteen men under the leadership of the kolkhoz chairman sped to the house, but encountering Nikulin and thinking that he was not alone, they retreated to the kolkhoz administration building where they barricaded themselves in. Nikulin, cursing loudly, pursued them. One of the peasants called on Nikulin to identify himself; when no answer was forthcoming, the peasant shot and killed him. An autopsy revealed that Nikulin was gravely intoxicated. The peasant who shot Nikulin was a demobilized Red Army man. The militia announced that the affair was under investigation.

Sex Offenses

If the militia file can be regarded as representative, sex crimes were fairly rare in the Smolensk area. Rape was the most common sex offense. A typical report to Rumyantsev on July 21 noted that at 1 A.M. in the main park of Yartsevo a twenty-year-old female factory worker was raped by five youths who worked in the same factory.[39] All were arrested and confined. Other sex items in the Archive have perhaps more sociological and political than criminal interest. There are a number of cases of officials who compelled women subordinates to enter into sexual relations with them in order to retain their jobs. There is the piquant case of the restaurant International which was heard by the guberniya court from February 28 to March 5, 1929, and which revealed some of the more unsavory details of the so-called Smolensk scandal.[40] If the procurator's report is to be credited the restaurant was the scene of repeated drunken orgies and debauchery in which some of the highest officials in the guberniya participated. According to the testimony, on the day of the opening of the restaurant, a prostitute was called in to serve the guests, and the deputy chairman of the guberniya executive committee, an Old Bolshevik who had joined the Party in 1905, asserted his right to enjoy her favors first because of his Party seniority. At another banquet a group of responsible officials in turn had relations with the wife of one of the guests, and two of the drunken officials were cut with a knife in a fight over a woman. Reports of these scandalous goings-on eventually penetrated to the center and formed part of the background for the complete overturn of the guberniya leadership in 1928.

An Investigation of a Labor Colony

The 1934 militia file contains one final item which is rather rare — a report on conditions in a labor colony by a commission representing the obkom of the Party, the raion procurator, the contracting enterprise, and the head of the colony.[41] Under investigation was the Kletniyanskaya Open Labor Colony Number 5. To it were assigned lesser criminals who had been "deprived of their freedom" and other persons condemned to "corrective labor." The inmates served as a compulsory working force for a local lumber enterprise which was part of the Bryansk Lumber Trust. At the time of the inquiry the colony contained 431 persons, most of whom were engaged in cutting, warehousing, loading, and processing timber.

The investigation disclosed that the Bryansk Lumber Trust had failed to live up to its agreement to provide "normal" living conditions for the colonists. The barracks were overcrowded, and both imprisoned and freely hired women lived together with the men in the same barracks. There was a serious shortage of mattresses and of shoes, padded jackets, and other clothing. There was no place to dry clothing, no teapots, and no electricity. The kerosene lamps were broken, and there was very little light. Feeding norms were not observed. No meals were available in the middle of the day, and at the two feedings which did take place, bread was "not always provided, not to speak of other products." Since January 1934 practically all vegetables and potatoes had disappeared from the diet. Sanitation too was below the norm. The barracks were filthy; there was no hospital, no "delousing" centers, and only one "disinfection" point.

Nor was the service personnel in much better case. There were no separate living quarters for the guards; the chief of one of the guard units with a family which included two children of school age shared the prisoners' barracks and ate from the same boilers. Some of the guards had no shoes and walked around in "lapti," or bast sandals. The supply of weapons for twenty-five guards consisted of two rifles and five revolvers, of which two were broken. As a result, noted the report, "the prestige of the guards in the eyes of the prisoners is low." One guard had been killed while trying to detain an escaping prisoner. "Labor fluidity," the official term for prison breaks, was high; up to 40 per cent of the prisoners assigned to the camp managed to escape. In the words of the report, "all the mentioned facts could not but contribute to frequent breaks of prisoners; without an elimination of the outlined irregularities, breaks are inevitable." [42]

The investigating commission recommended a strengthening of the guard and more adequate provision of clothing, food, and living space. "As a rule," the commission declared, "prisoners must eat three times a day." Men and women were to be assigned to separate quarters; criminals to be isolated from free labor; and the guards were to be given separate quarters. The raion procurator was instructed to check on the execution of these recommendations at intervals of ten days. The first report of the procurator, submitted on April 3, 1934, noted some improvement in providing mattresses, shoes, and jackets.[43] More medical help had been made available, and the prisoners were eating three times a day. But the situation was still termed "unsatisfactory," and the report recommended that the selling of commercial bread be permitted in the camp, and that the camp administrators who were responsible for the persistence of "abnormal conditions of life" among the prisoners be brought to criminal liability.

A final memorandum in the file continued to express alarm at the growing frequency of prison breaks from "open labor colonies" in the oblast.[44] The reasons for this were stated to be (1) the lack of political-educational work in the colonies, (2) the filthy state of the barracks, (3) the brutality of the camp administrators in dealing with the prisoners, (4) the absence of medical help, and (5) the conduct of work "by bureaucratic means." "As in the spring of 1933," the report predicts, such a situation may lead "this spring also to mass banditry and criminality in the oblast." The material cited at the beginning of this chapter indicates that the prediction was fulfilled; indeed, the militia had to stage a special campaign to counteract bandit raids, and it was not until late summer that the situation was finally brought under control.

While the militia reports which have been drawn on here exclude political offenses such as counterrevolutionary agitation and other forms of anti-Soviet activity, which became of increasing importance as the Great Purge mounted to a crescendo, they nevertheless yield fresh insight into the scope and variety of criminal activity which flourished below the monolithic surface of Soviet life in the mid-thirties. Fragmentary as the reports are, they provide a vivid reminder that totalitarian controls have their limits, that they generate their own peculiar techniques of defiance and evasion, and that desperate and despairing elements in the Soviet population who found themselves squeezed and exploited by their new rulers reacted by turning to thievery, petty crime, and corruption as a way of life — and a means of meliorating the pressures of sovietization.

11 *Purges and People*

The first reference in the Smolensk Archive to a Party purge is contained in a typed copy of a 1919 Central Committee circular "On Registration" found in the files of the Yelnya Party Committee.[1] The circular, based on a decree of the Eighth Party Congress, ordered all Party organizations "to carry out a general reregistration of all Party members." Party cells were instructed to undertake "a basic investigation of the entire personnel of the Party" and to "purge the Party of . . . people who attached themselves to the Party because of its leading position and who use the title of Party member for their own personal interests." Listed as candidates for expulsion were the following categories: "(1) those convicted of behavior unworthy of a Communist (drunkenness, debauchery, violence, cruel or exceedingly coarse treatment of subordinates, the use of their position in Soviet service for personal interests, etc.); (2) deserters; (3) those who violate the decrees of the Party; (4) those who fail to attend Party meetings without valid reasons; (5) those who do not pay their membership dues."

The 1919 Central Committee circular set the pattern for what was to become a recurrent phenomenon of Communist Party life. Periodically, all Party members had to run the hazardous gauntlet of the purge — designed to weed out the passive and the unreliable, the self-seekers and the heretics, all those who in the eyes of the leadership failed "to justify the lofty title of member of the Party." Over the next years the Communists of the Smolensk area were subjected to a long succession of such "cleansings": the general Party purge of 1921, the purge of non-industrial Party cells in 1924, the investigation of rural Party cells in 1925–26, the expulsion of followers of Trotsky and Zinoviev in 1926–27, the complete overturn of the guberniya Party leadership after the Smolensk scandal of 1928, the general Party purges of 1929–30 and 1933, the purges which accompanied the post-Kirov check on Party documents in 1935 and the exchange of Party documents in 1936, and finally the climactic Great Purge of 1937 which produced an almost complete turnover in the ranks of the oblast party leadership.

For the period up to the Smolensk scandal, archival material on the purges is notably sparse. Such information as is available, as well as the story of the Smolensk scandal itself, has already been summarized in

Chapter 2, and there is no need to retrace the same ground here. From 1929 through 1937, however, the Archive contains an almost unmanageable abundance of material on the purges, and it is on this span of years that the present chapter will focus.

The Purge of 1929–30

The signal for the purge of 1929–30 was given at the Sixteenth Party Conference which met in Moscow April 23–29, 1929. It was primarily directed against the right-wing followers of Bukharin, Tomsky, and Rykov; its main purpose was to cleanse Party ranks of elements who were opposed to the new program of collectivization and industrialization to which the Party was committed. In the words of the resolution authorizing the purge, "In the period of the reconstruction of the socialist economy of the country, which is bound up with a socialist attack on capitalist elements in both city and country and with a sharpening of the class struggle, the Party must reëxamine its ranks with special care in order to strengthen resistance to the influence of petty-bourgeois moods, to make the Party more homogeneous, and better able to fight in overcoming the difficulties of the socialist reconstruction of the national economy." [2] The cutting edge of the purge was to be particularly sharply felt in rural Party cells where resistance to collectivization was most deeply entrenched; but it also reached out to embrace many members of urban Party organizations who entertained doubts about the new direction of Party policy.

The purge was launched in the Western Oblast under conditions of special difficulty. Following close on the exposure of the Smolensk scandal and coinciding with the establishment of the Western Oblast itself, it found the Party organization of the region in that state of maximal confusion which attends the initial stages of every major reorganization. These difficulties were intensified by certain peculiar characteristics of the Western Oblast which made its Party organization particularly vulnerable to the 1929–30 purge. The overwhelmingly agrarian character of the oblast, its weakly developed socialized sector in both agriculture and industry, its insignificant working-class cadres, their great dispersion among small enterprises, and the existence among them of many workers with close ties to the countryside all combined to create a significant sounding board of opposition to the new policies of collectivization and industrialization on which Stalin had embarked.

The Archive contains a detailed report by the Control Commission of the Western Oblast on the results of the 1929–30 purge which makes this unmistakably clear.[3] The report begins with an analysis of anti-Party deviations in production cells. As might be expected, right-wing deviations predominated. "I agree with Bukharin's line on the question of the development of agriculture," a Communist in the Lyudinovsk factory is quoted as saying; "we must not hurry with collectivization; we must let the kulak grow, so that we can take his superfluous puds of grain from him." [4] And the same Communist continued, "The Five Year Plan cannot be fulfilled." Many analogous statements by worker Communists are cited of which the following are typical: "There is an incorrect policy in the countryside — the sovkhozes and kolkhozes give nothing, but only take . . ." [5] "Why do you prohibit grain to be marketed freely? Let the peasant sell grain freely. It's all the same from whom we buy . . ." [6] "It is not necessary to suppress the kulak so." [7] Commenting on such expressions of sentiment, the report noted that "a significant number of workers and peasants, who often have kulak households in the country, bring into the factory petty-bourgeois, kulak attitudes." [8]

In one case, a factory in Duminichi raion, the purge authorities even discovered the existence of an organized opposition group, labeled "14" (from the number of its participants). The program of the group was vague, but one of its rallying cries was "the defense of all the peasants." [9] According to the report, "the group was disciplined and conducted all its work in a conspiratorial manner." The organizer of the group was a member of the trade union committee of agricultural workers and was himself of peasant background. The leaders of the group were expelled from the Party; the rest received a sharp reprimand.

A few cases of alleged Trotskyite sympathizers were also uncovered. A Party member in the cell of the factory "Red Sewing Worker" who had been an active Trotskyite in the past, in answer to a question about his attitude toward Trotsky's exile replied: "The Party could have been mistaken on this question, for Trotsky is nevertheless an intelligent man." [10] And pressed to comment on treatment of the issue in the Party press, he added: "It is not always possible to believe what the Party press writes." [11] In the Smolensk railroad station cell the purge authorities uncovered a Trotskyite who "continually made speeches on the impossibility of building socialism in one country, on the impossibility of realizing the Party slogan 'pursue and overtake the capitalist countries,'" and noted that his action "was not rebuffed or exposed by the cell." [12] Still another alleged Trotskyite, one Parfenov, was accused of asserting "that the position of the workers is growing worse, that the workers live in bad apartments and their 'superiors' in good ones, that all our difficulties are the result of an incorrect policy." [13] Even more serious, "during the investigation Parfenov had the support of the remaining strata of workers, who remarked that 'Parfenov is correct.'" Despite this expression of sympathy, Parfenov was purged.

The purge also revealed a number of other "unhealthy" symptoms among Communists in production cells. Indifference toward the expression of anti-Semitic sentiments by worker Communists was singled out for special censure. Together with anti-Semitism, the Control Commission also reported that "there were Communists who had not torn themselves away from religion, Communists who carried on religious observances." [14] As a "typical case" the Commission cited a Party candidate who "after going through the purge, baptized his child four days later." In the cell of the hauling service of Smolensk station, the report stated, "The Communist Titov visited church regularly; the Communist Goretsky took part in a wedding in church; the Communist Pochnovsky baptized his child. The cell of atheists does not operate at all, and the Party cell 'pays no attention' to this. Even the secretary of the cell of the League of Militant Atheists, Anushkevich, has ikons at home and has baptized his children." [15]

Still another "unhealthy symptom" disclosed by the purge was the widespread drunkenness among Party members in production cells. "In the cell of the radiator foundry shop of Lyudinovsk Factory," the report declared, "30 per cent of the Communists are continually drunk . . ." [16] In the cell of the hauling service of Smolensk station, "All drink (with the exception of some comrades) . . . The secretary of the cell himself, Comrade Vitkus, drinks, and he even got drunk during the purge of the cell." [17] In the course of the purge drunkenness was defended by Party members as a "normal phenomenon . . . necessary for the worker in view of the hard conditions of his life." The report concluded, "A conciliatory attitude toward drunkenness and the absence of a struggle against this evil . . . are common phenomena in most production cells." [18]

The report also noted numerous cases of "self-seeking" activity among worker Communists. In one case a Party member in a textile factory is quoted as saying at the time of the subscription to the industrialization loan: "Do not give money — the Communists will squander it on drink." [19] In the cell of one of the shops of the factory "Red Profintern," 85 per cent of the Communists sold their bonds in the second industrialization loan, and in the hammer shop of the same factory "all the Communists sold their bonds without exception." [20] Replying to criticism of their unpatriotic actions, they said: "Why should we help the state? It will get along without us. We ourselves need the loan; we ourselves are building." "And actually," observed the Control Commission, "they are building their own houses." [21] A study of a number of production cells in various factories disclosed that from 11.4 to 68.6 per cent of all Party members either owned or were building their own homes, and that the proportion of Communist owners was higher than that of non-Party workers.[22] Under pressure of the purge Communist home-owners were faced with the unpalatable choice of either giving up their Party membership or transferring their homes to housing coöperatives. Some chose the former alternative. Thus the Party member Pentegrina who worked in the Dzerzhinsky factory, when asked whether she would give up her house (which cost 3,000 rubles) to the coöperative, replied: "No, I won't give it up. I spent all my health and much money, and now you want me to give it to you. I'd rather give up my Party card, but I won't give up my house." [23]

Communist tolerance of the "backward attitudes" of non-Party workers also came in for condemnation. "Often," the Control Commission reported, "Communists approve the backward attitudes of workers on questions of raising the productivity of labor: 'As they pay, so shall we work.'" The Commission cited "a typical case" of such Communist passivity in the face of anti-Party declarations. At a conference of shock workers, a group of "backward" workers declaimed: "Socialist competition sucks the last juices out of the worker. It is necessary first to improve working conditions, to increase wages. Labor discipline is intolerable. There are no foodstuffs. They oppress the kulaks, and therefore there is nothing . . . exploitation is worse than under capitalism." ". . . This clearly kulak statement," the Control Commission indignantly declared, "was given no reprimand by Communists who were present at the conference; they sat 'in silence' . . . and 'hid,' not showing their faces." [24]

The Control Commission attributed a large part of the blame for the demoralized mood of Communist workers to the fact that a great many still had close connections with the villages and reflected the oppositional mood of the well-to-do peasantry. Communist workers who fell into this classification were among the first victims of the 1929 purge.

The investigation of rural Party cells disclosed an even greater concentration of "unhealthy symptoms" than was prevalent in the urban areas. The Control Commission observed "that in many cases Communists do not participate much in kolkhoz construction, and Party members sometimes even have a negative attitude toward the kolkhozes." [25] The report cited many examples. In Mglinsk raion the purge commission proposed to a Communist that he go into the kolkhoz, and on the following day his wife brought his Party card and a statement to the effect that her husband was leaving the Party.[26] In Dubrovsk volost, some Party members are quoted as having said, "You can talk as much as you want about the collectives, but it's all the same, nothing will come of them. It is not yet time to build kolkhozes. We are not yet prepared. And how do you imagine the kolkhoz, of what is it capable? The kolkhozes only breed idlers . . . We won't be the first ones to go into the kolkhoz; we'll see how it turns out for the peasants." Others stated, "The kolkhozes are punitive battalions where they put people for self-criticism." [27] In the village of Zaulyi in Sevsk raion, the poor peasants took the initiative, but not one Party or Komsomol member "expressed a desire to enter the kolkhoz. Moreover, the secretary of the [Party] cell, said to the poor peasants: 'Why the devil should I work for you?' " [28]

The report cited many remarks in the following vein: "Why force Communists to go into the kolkhoz? That is the personal affair of each Communist. Prosperous peasants must be drawn into the kolkhoz, but not the poor peasants. Our tax policy is incorrect. It makes for the ruin of the country." And one Communist, who also refused to enter a kolkhoz, daringly replied, "We would get along much better without the Party." "There is no doubt," concludes the Control Commission, "that it is impossible to carry on a reconstruction of agriculture with such Communists. The Party had to get rid of such Communists, and it did." [29]

The report revealed considerable concern over the strength of "right-deviationist" sentiments in rural Party cells.

All these cases discovered during the purge and the investigation of rural cells testify to the necessity of immediately improving future work in explaining the anti-Party essence of the right deviation and of conciliatoriness toward it. At the same time the investigation of Party ranks shows that rural Communists are especially easily subjected to the influence of petty-bourgeois, kulak elements, and very often slide down into the position of the right deviation. The work which was done in rural cells in unmasking the right deviation was clearly insufficient . . . It is necessary . . . to develop significantly the explanation, both to Communists and to the hired workers and poor-peasant masses of the country, of the entire petty-bourgeois, anti-Leninist essence of the right deviation.[30]

One of the major sources of difficulty, the Control Commission added, was "the very low political level of the Party members, not only of the rank and file, but also of the leaders of Party and Komsomol organizations . . . The decisions of the Sixteenth Party Conference and of the plenums of the Central Committee were not discussed in many cells, not to speak of extensively popularizing them among the people . . . The lack of understanding of the essence of the rightist deviation is especially apparent from all the reports." [31] As an especially glaring case, the commission cited the secretary of a volost Party committee, who when asked to give an explanation to the Purge Committee of the right deviation, replied: "The right deviation is a deviation to the right; the left deviation is a deviation to the left; but the Party itself follows a middle course."

Even more than in the urban cells, the rural purge registered widespread drunkenness and religiosity among Party members. The report spoke of drinking sprees as a "collective" Party enterprise. "At Easter, Christmas, and on church holidays Communists drink excessively. They do not hesitate to drink even on the anniversary of the October Revolution." [32] "Religiousness among the families of rural Communists" is spoken of as a "common phenomenon."

The total impact of the 1929–30 purge is perhaps best conveyed by an analysis of the purge data. Table 2 lists over-all figures and breaks them down by occupational categories and social position.[33] As this table indicates, 4,804 Party members, or 13.1 per cent of the total membership in the Western Oblast, were excluded from the Party in the course of the 1929–30 purge. The purge worked particular havoc on the peasant contingent in the Party. Among those classified as peasants, 17.6 per cent fell victim to the purge. Membership in rural Party cells declined 16.9 per cent, while the peasant element in these cells lost 19.8 per cent of its membership. By contrast the worker Communists fared best in the purge, dropping only 11.4 per cent of their members, while the category of "employees and others" fell between the peasants and workers with a loss of 13.8 per cent. On the other hand, when the table is reëxamined in terms of the impact of the purge on different types of Party cells, it becomes clear that its effects were felt least in educational and administrative institutions, more in the factories and production cells, and, as has already been noted, most of all in the rural cells where the opposition to collectivization and sympathy with the right wing of the Party was most strongly concentrated. The effect of the purge was to weaken the peasant contingent in the Party substantially.

Table 3 classifies those purged in various types of Party cells in terms of the reasons given for exclusion from the Party.[34] It should be noted that in many cases more than one ground for expulsion was cited, with the result that the sum of the percentages recorded exceeds 100 per cent of the total number purged in each of the categories listed. An analysis of this table reveals some interesting variations in the grounds for exclusion from the Party among the different types of Party cells. In the worker or production cells drunkenness, passivity in the performance of Party duties, violations of labor discipline, and the continued practice of religious rites operated as particularly important factors in contributing to the purge. In the rural cells drunkenness, passivity, and religous attachments were also important, but they were supplemented by a noteworthy increase in the proportions excluded for refusal to enter a kolkhoz, for connections with so-called "hostile elements," and for crimes committed in the performance of official duties. The administrative cells, as perhaps might be expected, revealed the highest percentage of exclusions for official crimes, but drunkenness and passivity also bulked large, and a substantial group was also purged for alleged connections with "hostile elements."

The educational cells disclosed a markedly different pattern. Judging

TABLE 2

The Purge in the Western Oblast, 1929–30

	Total no. of Communists at time of the purge	Classification by social position			No. and % purged	Of these by social position		
		Worker	Peasant	Employees and others		Workers	Peasants	Employees and others
Oblast								
Total............	36,702	22,343	8,996	5,363	4,804	2,484	1,581	739
Percentages......		60.9%	24.5%	14.6%	13.1%	11.4%	17.6%	13.8%
Workers cells								
Totals...........	18,392	15,900	1,057	1,434	2,250	1,920	152	178
Percentages......		86.4%	5.7%	7.8%	12.2%	12.1%	14.4%	12.4%
Rural cells								
Totals...........	9,045	2,278	5,718	1,049	1,532	243	1,130	159
Percentages......		25.2%	63.2%	11.6%	16.9%	10.7%	19.8%	15.2%
Administrative cells								
Totals... ..	7,715	3,349	1,726	2,640	914	285	252	377
Percentages......		43.4%	22.4%	34.2%	11.9%	8.5%	14.6%	14.4%
Educational cells								
Totals...........	1,051	585	348	118	69	23	28	18
Percentages......		55.8%	33.1%	11.2%	6.7%	3.9%	8.0%	15.3%
Post-purge								
Totals...........	31,405	19,531	7,277	4,598				
Percentages......		62.5%	23.2%	14.6%				

TABLE 3

The Purge in the Western Oblast: Reasons for Exclusion

	Hostile elements	Official crimes	Religious ties	Drunkenness	Violations of labor discipline	Violations of Party discipline	Passivity in relation to Party	Refusal to enter kolkhoz	Connections with hostile elements	Distortions of the Party line
Workers cells										
Totals..........	234	299	277	869	256	148	1033	124	179	72
Percentages........	10.0%	13.3%	12.3%	38.6%	11.4%	6.6%	45.0%	5.5%	8.0%	3.2%
Rural cells										
Totals..........	256	234	191	576	27	121	562	275	164	102
Percentages........	16.7%	21.8%	12.5%	37.6%	1.8%	7.9%	36.7%	18.0%	10.7%	6.7%
Administrative cells										
Totals..........	201	279	52	312	26	61	335	68	122	39
Percentages........	21.9%	30.5%	5.7%	34.2%	2.8%	6.7%	36.6%	7.4%	13.3%	4.3%
Educational cells										
Totals..........	20	14	2	12	3	7	11	6	25	13
Percentages........	29.0%	20.3%	2.9%	17.4%	4.3%	10.1%	15.9%	8.7%	36.2%	18.8%
Total exclusions										
Number........	711	926	522	1,769	318	337	1,941	473	490	226
Per cent........	14.8%	19.3%	10.9%	36.8%	6.5%	7.0%	40.4%	9.8%	10.2%	4.7%

by the purge data, the Party organizations in these cells provided a refuge for many "former people" of suspect social origins who previously had been tolerated because their professional qualifications rendered them indispensable. The 1929 purge hit this group particularly hard, as the large percentages excluded as "hostile elements" or for connections with "hostile elements" make strikingly evident. The educational cells also contained the highest percentage of those purged for distortions of the Party line or for violations of Party discipline, an indication that members of the Party intelligentsia at this time were not merely inwardly restive, but vocal in expressing their discontent.

The Archive includes no data on the impact of the purge on army units in the Western Oblast, but it does contain a revealing top-secret directive of the People's Commissariat of Military and Naval Affairs and Revolutionary War Council dated September 23, 1929, and signed by Unshlicht, then a Deputy People's Commissar.[35] Unshlicht noted:

> Both in the process of the preparatory campaign and in carrying out the purge itself, cases observed where former [tsarist] officers are looked upon as hostile and alien elements, subject to removal from Soviet organs only because they were formerly officers. Such a sweeping approach is absolutely incorrect and contradicts the orders of the central organs which demand that special care be used in the purge of the commanding staff of the regiment. A somewhat different attitude may be allowed in the purge toward former White officers, but even in their case a sweeping approach is inadmissible, since many of them, in subsequent active struggle in the ranks of the Red Army during the period of the Civil War, and by work during the following years, atoned for their guilt and proved their devotion to the Soviet government. However, this does not eliminate the necessity of checking on and removing from Soviet organs the really corrupt elements hostile to us, without taking into consideration whether or not they belong to the commanding staff of the regiment.

The directive declared that the release "of persons of the commanding staff" could take place "only in cases of extreme necessity and with the approval in each individual case of the military department." It also instructed lower military units that the purge should be based "on the necessity of in every way preserving for the Red Army the Commanding staff which has military experience and also the valuable technical specialists, and it is necessary to approach especially carefully the purge of such specialists of the commanding staff as machine gunners, combat men, cavalrymen, artillery men of all types, tankmen, field engineers, pontooners, chemists, radiomen, topographers, flight and engineering technical personnel of the air forces, and engineers, mechanics, and combat personnel of the navy." As this directive clearly indicates, the armed forces were determined to hold on to trained and qualified personnel, and apparently exerted maximum influence to prevent the purge from impairing military efficiency.

The effect of the 1929 purge was felt not only in Party exclusions, but also in reprimands administered to erring Party members who were permitted, at least temporarily, to remain in the ranks of the Party. A total of 5,881, or 16.2 per cent of the oblast Party membership, received Party reprimands, notably for drunkenness and passivity in the performance of Party obligations.[36] After the completion of the purge in the local Party cells, 1,788 victims, or more than a third of those who had been excluded from the Party, took appeals to the Control Commission of the Western Oblast to have their cases reëxamined. The organs of the Control Commission reaffirmed the exclusions in 1,011 instances, or 56.8 per cent of the total; replaced exclusion with a Party reprimand in 656 instances, or 36.7 per cent of the total; and reëstablished Party membership without any reprimand in 119 cases, or 6.7 per cent of the total.[37] The Archive contains voluminous protocols of the disposition of these appeals by the Troikas of the Western Oblast Control Commission which acted on them.[38] These records reveal that the oblast Party authorities reversed the actions of lower purge commissions where the latter expelled or reprimanded Party members whose primary sin consisted of passivity arising out of poor political training. On the other hand, where the offenders were deemed class-hostile or ideologically untrustworthy, the decisions of the lower purge commissions were almost invariably sustained. The final court of appeal for the victims of the purge was the Central Control Commission in Moscow, and there is evidence in the Archive that many of them journeyed to Moscow to press their cases personally on the premises of the Central Control Commission. Indeed, a circular letter of the Party Collegium of the Central Control Commission dated September 14, 1929, and addressed to lower control organs and Party members warned appellants not to waste time or money in coming to Moscow unless they were called.[39] The CCC stated that it would assume no responsibility for the expenditures involved and that "in no event would the voluntary arrival of appellants influence the order in which appeals would be heard." Whether this in fact happened the record does not disclose.

The 1933 Purge

After the purge of 1929–30 the membership rolls of the Party rose sharply to reach a new peak in 1933. At this point the Party leadership determined to launch another general Party purge. The reasons for the action were outlined in a joint decree of the Central Committee and the Central Control Commission dated April 28, 1933.[40]

. . . With mass acceptance into the Party, which in some places often occurs in a sweeping manner and without careful verification, alien elements, that use their stay in the Party for careerist and selfish objectives, penetrated into the ranks of the Party; also double-dealing elements, that pledged their loyalty to the Party in words, while trying to hamper the execution of its policy by deeds. On the other hand, because of the unsatisfactory state of Marxist-Leninist education of Party members, there has appeared in the Party not a small number of comrades, who, although honest and prepared to defend the Soviet state, were nevertheless either insufficiently firm, did not understand the spirit and demands of Party discipline, or were politically illiterate, did not know the program, rules, or basic decrees of the Party and were unable, because of this, actively to execute the policy of the Party.

The decree ordered that the following categories be purged from the Party:

1. Class-alien and enemy elements who have wormed their way into the Party by deceptive methods and have remained there in order to split the ranks of the Party;

2. Double-dealers who live on deception of the Party, concealing from it their real aspirations and who, under the cover of false oaths as to their "loyalty" to the Party, actually try to hamper the policy of the Party;

3. Open and hidden violators of the iron discipline of the Party and the state, who do not fulfill the decisions of the Party and government, who cast doubt upon and discredit the decisions and plans established by the Party by chattering about their "unreality" and the fact that they are "incapable of realization";

4. Degenerates who have their origin in bourgeois elements, who do not really wish to fight against class enemies, who do not really fight against kulak elements, self-seekers, idlers, thieves, and embezzlers of public property;

5. Careerists, self-seekers, and bureaucratic elements, who use their stay in the Party and their service to the Soviet state for their own personal, self-seeking goals, who are isolated from the masses and who ignore the needs and demands of the workers and peasants;

6. Moral degenerates, who by their improper behavior do harm to the dignity of the Party and stain the banner of the Party.

At the same time the decree made clear that devoted but politically illiterate Communists would receive gentler treatment. The decree recommended that "such Communists be transferred into candidates of the Party, not as Party punishment, but in order politically to educate them and to prepare them better so that in a year the question may be raised of transferring them back to Party membership if they succeed in raising their political literacy to the level required of a member of the Party." Similar provisions were made for demoting Party candidates into the category of sympathizers, with the proviso that in a year they could be transferred back to candidates or even membership if investigation disclosed that they were ready for promotion.

Under the leadership of a Central Purge Commission chaired by Rudzutak, purge commissions were established in the republics, oblasts, and krais. The oblast commissions in turn organized raion purge commissions, whose membership was to be composed of "authoritative, politically educated, staunch Communists, who were not previously members of other Parties, who were not in the opposition, and whose length of membership was not less than ten years." The purge was to begin on June 1 and end not later than November 30, 1933.

The decree authorizing the 1933 purge provided for open proceedings before purge commissions which could be attended by non-Party elements as well as Party members. This was the practice in Smolensk. Each Communist appearing before a purge commission gave an accounting of the salient facts of his life, described his work in production, explained how he fulfilled his Party tasks, and what efforts he had made to raise his "ideological and theoretical level." Questions were put both by the purge commissions and by auditors at the purge meetings; primary emphasis was placed on "unmasking" elements that fell into the proscribed categories.

But such data as are available indicate that the 1933 purge had a rather limited impact in Smolensk compared with other areas in the Soviet Union. Out of a total of 5,828 members and candidates in the city of Smolensk in 1933, only 109 were expelled from the Party in the course of the year, although another 909 may have left the Party for reasons connected with the purge.[41] Between 1933 and 1934 the worker contingent in the Smolensk organization fell from 4,222 to 3,431, the peasant from 1,003 to 820, while the "employee and others" category actually increased from 613 to 753. The bite of the purge was particularly felt in peasant and worker ranks, a conclusion which is consistent with evidence elsewhere in the Soviet Union that the incidence of the 1933 purge was heaviest among recent peasant and worker recruits who had not succeeded "in raising their political literacy" to the minimum level which the Party demanded.

The Assassination of Kirov and the Check of Party Documents

The assassination of Kirov in December 1934 touched off a new round of almost continuous purges which spread out in ever-widening circles and rose to a smashing crescendo in the virtual destruction of the oblast Party leadership in 1937. Immediately after the death of Kirov the Party Central Committee sent a closed letter entitled "Lessons of the Events Bound up with the Evil Murder of Comrade Kirov" to all Party organizations with the injunction that it be read and discussed at meetings of Party cells throughout the Soviet Union.[42] While the text of the letter is not available, the discussions which it evoked clearly indicate that it was a call to vigilance, that it demanded that the ranks of the Party be purged of all "alien elements," and that it placed particular stress on the necessity of immediately ousting all former followers of Zinoviev, Kamenev, and Trotsky from the Party. The Kirov meetings provided the occasion for a mass outburst of denunciations and the accumulation of long lists of suspects, many of whom were soon destined to be expelled from the Party.

A secret letter dated February 17, 1935, from the head of the Bureau of Leading Party Organs of the obkom to all raikoms conveys the concern of the Party leadership at this time.[43] Among other questions, the letter asked:

Is an account being kept of . . . cases of unmasked Zinovievites and Trotskyites, double-dealers and socially hostile elements . . . ? During the discussion of the letter, how many of the Communists were uncovered as Zinovievites, Trotskyites, double-dealers, and socially alien elements, how many were brought to Party responsibility, and how many were expelled? . . . What questions were asked during the discussion of the letter? (Cite 10 to 15 questions) . . . What did the non-Party workers (especially the old cadres), the kolkhozniks, and the students say in regard to the murder of Comrade Kirov? . . .

Despite the fact that the replies yielded a rich haul of newly unmasked oppositionists, the Central Committee was apparently dissatisfied with the results, and on May 13, 1935, dispatched another secret letter to all Party organizations "On Disorders in the Registration, Issuance, and Custody of Party Cards, and on Measures for Regulating this Matter." [44] In effect, this letter inaugurated a new purge under the guise of a check-up on Party documents. As has already been noted in Chapter 2, the Party authorities in the Western Oblast responded to this request by a rather routine and cursory reëxamination of the Party rolls, but they were brought up short on June 27, 1935, when a special resolution of the Central Committee singled out the Western Oblast Party leaders for a severe rebuke, canceled the initial check-up on Party documents, and ordered the oblast to begin all over again.[45] This time the oblast Party leadership more than made up for its earlier lack of ardor. The percentage of Party cards either taken away or challenged in the Western Oblast far exceeded that of any other Party organization in the Soviet Union.

The Archive contains many protocols of Party meetings which were held shortly after the call for the second check-up on Party documents. They register a mood of mounting hysteria. The meeting of the Party organization of the Institute of Marxism-Leninism on July 9, 1935, provides a typical example.[46] At this meeting, Comrade Kogan, the head of the obkom agitprop section, reported on the Central Committee decision criticizing the initial investigation of Party documents in the Western Oblast. As soon as he had concluded his remarks, the denunciations began.

There are rumors [observed one Comrade Davydov] that in our Institute the social composition of the students is not entirely favorable. For example: there are rumors to the effect that Strogonov is of kulak origin, that the father of Smirnov, in the first group of courses, was a merchant in Moscow and later went to Vyazma, where he married into a family of traders. Comrade Abetsunus has a very incomprehensible past. She says that she is the daughter of a worker, and at the same time she also says that her father traded in various trinkets. The Party committee should have seriously investigated all these rumors, but up to this time nothing has been done by the Party committee; on the contrary, there is some feeling of complacency.

The second speaker, Comrade Ivanov, supplied additional denunciatory material. "There is information," he stated, "that Smolov is married to the daughter of the merchant Kovalev, and that the Party organizer of the second group of the Institute is the son of a person who was given a strict reprimand." And so the discussion went, with others contributing their accusations in turn, while those denounced rose to explain away or deny the derelictions of which they were accused. The meeting ended with a resolution demanding that "every Party member should take all measures to discover and oust alien and hostile elements, no matter where they work (in other organizations, oblasts, or krais)." [47] It ordered "the Party committee to collect relevant information about all persons mentioned in the speeches . . . and where inquiries were left unanswered, to send special messengers chosen from trusted Party members in order to establish the facts in on-the-spot statements." The resolution concluded by calling on the committee "immediately to decide the question of the Party loyalty (partiinost) of persons who were [accused of being] alien and hostile to the Party . . ."

At this meeting one Party member, Comrade Prokhorenko, was expelled. Prokhorenko had served as the assistant head of the culture and propaganda department of the Smolensk gorkom before his assignment to the Institute of Marxism-Leninism. It was discovered in the course of the check-up on Party documents that his father had been "an important merchant," a fact which emerged as the result of a denunciation in the raion where his father had lived. It also transpired that Prokhorenko had intervened to help a sister obtain a passport which concealed her social origin, and that he had not informed the Party that he had once distilled liquor illegally. These accusations were enough to seal Prokhorenko's fate.

During the next months the ax of the purge swept through the Institute. [48] P. F. Smirnov, the Party organizer of one of the courses, was expelled for concealing the fact that his father was a church elder and for not "unmasking" a Trotskyite, one Smerdov, with whom he had been friendly and to whom he sent condolences and regards after questions had been raised concerning Smerdov's loyalty. A. S. Matsepuro, a student, was ejected from the Party for hiding his connections with a Menshevik uncle and in-laws who had been shot for counterrevolution. He was also accused of anti-Semitism because he had not informed the Party that his wife, a Komsomol, had written him, "The Jews do not let me live." N. I. Bocharov, another student, was purged for concealing his kulak origins. V. A. Borodulin, a former chairman of a village soviet and a raion newspaper editor, was expelled for assisting his son-in-law, "a hostile element," to slip into the Party and for not taking measures to liquidate the kulak household of his uncle, a former Socialist-Revolutionary. A. I. Volodchenkov was ousted for concealing the fact that he came from a kulak family. P. V. Vasilyev, a member of the Institute presidium, was given a severe reprimand for not having revealed the participation of his brother in the Kronstadt revolt. V. M. Bagranovsky, a professor teaching economic subjects at the Institute, received a reprimand for not informing the Party organization that his wife had formerly been an active Trotskyite and had been exiled for three years. S. A. Skotnikov was also given a reprimand because he failed to apprise the Party organization that his former wife, from whom he had been divorced in 1929 but whom he continued to see until 1935, had been the daughter of an estate manager who had been prosecuted in the "Promparty" (Industrial Party) case in 1930. And finally one P. A. Melnikov was given a strict reprimand with a proviso "to consider it inexpedient to use him in leading Party work" because of his connection with one Cherkovskaya, "an alien element."

The last case holds special interest because on July 5, 1936, Cherkovskaya took it upon herself to address a moving appeal to Rumyantsev.[49] Her letter follows:

To the secretary of the Western Oblast Committee of the CPSU(b), Comrade Rumyantsev

Ivan Petrovich:

The matter about which I have decided to write you concerns the CPSU(b) member Melnikov, who works with you in the Obkom. In the investigation of Party documents he received a reprimand because of me, and because of this my life has been completely shattered, and therefore I cannot remain silent. I feel that I should write you everything frankly and honestly.

I am the daughter of a railroad employee. My father worked on the railroad for 35 years, 25 years at Pochinok Station, Western Oblast. A few years ago, at the age of 17, I married a veterinarian, who, upon finishing the institute, was assigned to Pochinok. It may have been because he was twice as old as I, or for another reason, but from the first days of our life together it became obvious that we had nothing in common, we were different types of people, strangers. At first I did not have enough resoluteness to speak of divorce, and then a baby came and I lived for the greater part of a year with my parents in Pochinok. When my husband was transferred to the Brasov stud farm, I started to study at the Brasov technical school, and he at the same time found himself a more suitable woman and began to live with her, although unofficially. I did not finish the technical school, because I did not want to live where he was, and I went to Moscow for a half-year course, leaving my daughter with my mother. After finishing the course, I returned to Pochinok and remained

СЕКРЕТАРЮ ЗАПОБКОМА ВКП/б/ т. РУМЯНЦЕВУ.

Иван Петрович!

Дело, о котором я решила написать Вам, касается члена ВКП/б/ Мельникова, работающего у Вас в Обкоме. При проверке партийных документов ему был вынесен выговор из-за меня, а мне этим окончательно разбита жизнь, поэтому молчать нет сил, чувствую, что должна откровенно и правдиво написать Вам все.

Я дочь железнодорожного служащего, мой отец 35 лет проработал на ж.д., из них уже 25 лет на ст. Починок Зап. области. Несколько лет тому назад я 17-ти лет вышла замуж за ветврача, по окончании института назначен-

---

мой бывший муж когда-то был осужден и я не имею права быть женой человека, которого люблю, пусть он член партии, но ведь и я не чуждая, я ничего не скрывала, никого не обманывала, я не хочу быть без вины виноватой.

Вам, Иван Петрович, откровеннее чем родному отцу рассказала всю свою жизнь и все свои "преступления". Ценою жизни рада была бы доказать Вам правдивость своих слов.

Верю Вам безгранично и каково бы ни было Ваше мнение по этому вопросу оно будет для меня законом.

Зинаида Черковская.

5.УП-1936г.

Верно:

A copy of the letter of Zinaida Cherkovskaya, a victim of guilt by association, appealing to the oblast first secretary, Rumyantsev. The typed copy was prepared for Rumyantsev's perusal. The query at the end, "Is it possible that the obkom has made a mistake . . . ?" is in his hand.

Секретарю Зап. Обкома ВКП(б) т. Румянцеву

184

Иван Петрович!

Дело, о котором я решила написать Вам, касается члена ВКП(б) Мельникова, работающего у Вас в Обкоме. При проверке партийных документов ему был объявлен выговор из-за меня, а мне этим окончательно разбита жизнь, поэтому молчать нет сил, чувствую, что должна откровенно и правдиво написать Вам все.

Я дочь железнодорожного служащего, мой отец 35 лет проработал на ж.д. из них уже 25 лет на ст. Починок Зап. области. Несколько лет тому назад я 17-ти лет вышла замуж за Мельникова, по окончании института назначенного в Починок. Может быть потому, что он был вдвое старше меня или по другой причине, но с первых же дней совместной жизни стало очевидным, что у нас нет ничего общего, слишком разные, чужие. Первой заговорить о разводе не хватало решимости, потом появился ребенок и я большую часть года

there to take care of my sick mother, who died within a year. From the moment I left Brasov I had no correspondence with my former husband. He lived openly with another woman, but no one in Pochinok, except my parents, knew that we had separated. I was ashamed to talk about it. In 1932 I learned that he had been arrested for participation in a wreckers' organization and was exiled for 3 years. When things went badly with him he remembered me and our daughter and began to write, to beg forgiveness, etc. I never loved him, and after all this he didn't mean anything to me at all, but for the sake of our daughter I agreed to write him once in a while about her. After the death of my mother I continued to live with my daughter and my father in Pochinok. I began to work as a proofreader in the editorial office of the *Pochinok Kolkhoznik*. I worked enthusiastically, felt free, independent, wanted very much to live, wanted happiness, which I had never known. After a time Melnikov was appointed editor of the *P.K.* We became acquainted and liked each other. We began to see each other. On the first night I told him everything about myself, so that there would be no misunderstandings afterwards. I'm not going to begin to speak about him, but I fell head over heels in love with him. After some time we became intimate. Soon he was appointed assistant secretary of the raikom of the CPSU(b), and under the pretext that he had a great deal of work, we began to see each other less often, and after a time I was dismissed from work. It was Melnikov who did this, since there was not yet a new editor. It is impossible to express in words how I suffered. I had put my whole soul into my work, heard only approval from those around me, and the man who knew me best of all dismissed me from work. Often I was insistently pursued by the thought of suicide. This is cowardice, I know, but I felt that it was easier to die than to live without the man in whom I saw all happiness, all joy for myself. My little daughter forced me to dispel these thoughts.

I went to Smolensk and got a job as a proofreader in the House of the Press, and although I was the youngest proofreader, they soon appointed me copy editor on the kolkhoz newspaper. Soon Melnikov began to study in the Institute of Marxism-Leninism, and we met and spent our free time together, but he lived in the dormitory and I with my sister, since it was difficult to find a room in which to live together, and furthermore, it was easier and better for him to study while living with his fellow students. We lived in the hope that after he finished his studies we would finally settle things. But in the fall of 1935 I learned that they had created a whole case against Melnikov because he was seeing me. We began to see each other less frequently, and finally parted. Later I learned that they had reprimanded him because of me. I do not know to this day of what I was accused — nobody told me. But I was completely devoted to Melnikov, lived for his interests, and the fact that he had unpleasantness on account of me was painful and incomprehensible to me. My position was desperate.

After working a year in the House of the Press, I left work in August, as Melnikov had suggested. When I learned of his reprimand, I went to pieces. It seemed to me that not only had I no right to work, but that I could not live with people. I left my sister without telling her the reason, and I did not want to live with my father. I feared that there would be unpleasantness for him on account of me, although he was in the decline of life.

In January 1936 I received a letter from my former husband, in which he wrote that they had freed him before his term was up and that he had worked for a year in the system of the NKVD in Kazakhstan. At the end he wrote: if during these four years you did not get married, during your vacation come to visit me with your daughter, to see Kazakhstan. At that time I could not reason sensibly. I decided that my life was at an end anyway, and I went to him with my daughter, but I could not live with him for one day. I told him I had loved somebody else for three years now, and that only despair could have pushed me to this rash journey. He decided that I had sacrificed myself for the sake of my daughter. He really does not know the situation, and I did not want to tell him. He hopes that sometime I will "quiet down" and will be able to live with him. In April he went to a health resort and I went to my relatives in Smolensk. I am not deceived in regard to him. I am not a young girl. I am 24 years old and have lived through many adversities of life, and things were good with me only with Melnikov. I will not be able to fall out of love with him or forget him, and I never want to build my life without him. I met him accidentally in Smolensk, told him how much I had suffered without him, and he told me that I should live only in my work, but that we should not see each other.

But I think I shall go mad. I don't want to be reconciled to it. I cannot get it through my head that in our free country, where the children of kulaks are not responsible for the crimes of their parents, I should be tortured my whole life because my former husband was once sentenced, and I do not have the right to be the wife of the man I love. Though he is a Party member, I am not an alien. I have concealed nothing, I have deceived no one, and I do not want to be a criminal without a crime.

I have recounted my whole life and all my "crimes" to you, Ivan Petrovich, more frankly than to my own father. At the cost of my life I would be happy to prove to you the truthfulness of my words.

I trust you implicitly, and whatever your opinion will be on this problem, it will be law for me.

ZINAIDA CHERKOVSKAYA

At the bottom of this letter there is an enigmatic hand-written note signed "I. R." (Ivan Rumyantsev). The note reads:

Comrade Krovchik!
Is it possible that the obkom has made a mistake in regard to Melnikov? Consider the matter yourself and report to me.

Unfortunately, the Archive contains no response to the request and no record of any further action.

The Archive provides no over-all data on the impact of the 1935 purge. But some measure of its sweep is contained in a report filed with the obkom "On the Results of the Investigation of Party Documents of the Members of the Smolensk City and Raion Party Organization." [50] According to this report, a total of 4,100 Party members underwent investigation. Of these, 3,441 had their Party documents confirmed as genuine. Of the remaining 659, 455 were expelled from the Party while the rest either had their cards held back for further investigation or were awaiting action on petitions to receive Party documents confirming their membership.

The report provided the following classification of purge victims:

1. Agents of the enemy (spies and those connected with them)   7
2. White Guardists and participants in counterrevolutionary uprisings   12
3. Remnants of counterrevolutionary, anti-Party groupings of Trotskyites and Zinovievites   11
4. Those who left other parties, changing only on the surface   9
5. Swindlers who used the Party apparatus to obtain Party documents   2
6. Swindlers who procured Party cards by deceitful means   5
7. Those from a class-alien and hostile milieu who concealed their past   99
8. People who do not inspire political trust and who betray the interests of the Party   127
9. People who have a criminal past (13 of them embezzlers)   53
10. Deserters from the Red Army   12
11. Those accepted in violation of the Party rules   9
12. Those who evaded the purge of the Party in 1929 and 1933   3
13. Those who evaded the investigation of Party documents   3
14. Those corrupt in a moral and ethical sense   32
15. Those who take an anti-Party attitude toward Party documents   38
16. Those who were alienated from the Party and who violated the rules of the Party on the payment of membership dues, etc.   33
   Total   455

In achieving this grand total the report noted that the Smolensk Party authorities had enjoyed the benefit of no less than 712 oral denunciations (mainly in speeches at Party meetings) and "200 written declarations with compromising materials on members of the CPSU(b)."

The report also supplied the following breakdown of expelled Party members according to type of occupation:

1. In Party work	2
2. In soviet work	93
3. In economic work	145
4. In trade union work	11
5. Workers at the bench	98
6. Kolkhozniks	11
7. Scientific workers, teachers	17
8. Students	64
9. Pensioners	3
10. Unemployed	11
Total	455

As this list indicates, the 1935 check-up made virtually no dent on the Party apparatus itself. The brunt of the purge, at least in Smolensk, was borne by Party members engaged in economic and soviet work, workers at the bench, and students. Among the victims were eighteen persons engaged in leading oblast work and thirteen employed in leading municipal work. This group included the rector of the higher Communist agricultural school, the head of the cadres section of the NKVD, the chief of a labor colony, the chairman of the oblast social security department, the head of the planning and financial section of the oblast land administration, the director of the Smolensk post office, the head of the city communal economy department, and a number of others occupying positions of comparable responsibility. The bite of the purge was felt particularly deeply in certain organizations and enterprises, notably in the administration of a labor colony where 33 per cent of the Party members were expelled, in the Western Woodworking Trust which lost 28.6 per cent of its Party members, in the oblast trade union apparatus where 25 per cent were ejected, in the Hardware Trust where 23 per cent were purged, in the foreign trade administration where 22 per cent were removed, and in the city raion procuracy which lost 21 per cent of its Party membership. Despite this rather thorough cleansing, the leaders of the Smolensk Party organization were not prepared to rest on their laurels. "The conclusion cannot be drawn," the report noted, "that all the alien and hostile elements who mask themselves with a Party card have been exposed and ousted. Undoubtedly, in the Party organization some alien and hostile people still remain, more skillfully masked . . ."

Meanwhile, those expelled from the Party were encountering grave difficulty in finding and retaining employment. They spelled danger to anyone associated with them, and employers were loath to run the risks of contamination. The issue became so troublesome that on October 21, 1935, Shilman, the obkom second secretary, issued instructions to all raikoms on how to deal with the problem. Shilman's letter read:

In connection with the check of Party documents, many complaints reach us in the obkom from those expelled from the Party to the effect that after their expulsion from the Party they are dismissed from work and are in general not allowed to do any kind of work. Dismissal from work, without grounds, in connection with expulsion from the Party, is incorrect. Hastily dismissing from work those expelled from the Party and leaving them without work for a long time can arouse in them excessive animosity. I wish to make clear that only those expelled from the Party who are clearly unmasked enemies and socially dangerous elements should be dismissed from work. It is necessary, when possible, to isolate such people, to arrest or banish them. It is understood that it is also necessary to remove those expelled from responsible posts, based on public trust, and from especially important projects (defense enterprises, electrification stations, etc.). After removing them from responsible posts, it is necessary to use those expelled from the Party in low level or technical work. Persons who up to their expulsion from the Party worked directly in production (workers, kolkhozniks, very young service personnel, specialists) and in technical work in various organizations should not be dismissed from work if they do not seem socially dangerous. It is understood that it is necessary to organize

suitable surveillance by Party organizations over the behavior of those expelled; it is necessary to keep them in mind, to know where they are working,
in order to make it possible to spy on them . . . [51]

The continuing concern of the Party leadership with the problem of
the expelled is reflected in the following secret letter sent by Rumyantsev
on January 21, 1936, to all raikom secretaries:

When you come to the obkom on January 29 for the meeting of secretaries,
bring for me personally the following information:
1. How do you evaluate the attitude of those expelled from the CPSU(b)
in your raion . . . ?
2. What facts do you know about the counterrevolutionary work of this
or that group or of individual people who have been expelled from the Party?
3. What measures have you taken and still consider it necessary to take in
regard to those people who have been expelled in order to suppress the counterrevolutionary work of some and at the same time not to make widespread
indiscriminate use of such [repressive] measures against those who can be corrected and who can win our confidence again in the future?
4. How many people are there of those expelled, whose stay in your raion
you personally now consider politically and socially dangerous and harmful,
and for what reasons?
In assembling this information, only the second secretary and an official of
the NKVD may participate.[52]

The ominous portent of this letter was soon to become painfully evident
as the NKVD went into action.

*The Exchange of Party Documents
and the Climactic Great Purge*

The year 1936 began with still another screening of Party ranks, this
time as an accompaniment of the exchange of old Party documents for
new ones which was to take place for all Party members between the first
of February and the first of May. In its instructions of January 14, 1936,
the Central Committee stated the purpose of the exchange as follows:

While in the check-up of Party documents, the Party organizations concentrated chief attention on unmasking the enemies of the Party who penetrated into the CPSU(b) deceitfully, unmasking every kind of rogue and
swindler, in the exchange the chief attention must be paid to eliminating passive people, who do not justify the lofty title of member of the Party, and who
came into the ranks of the CPSU(b) accidentally.[53]

Again the best data on the effect of this screening are those available
for the city of Smolensk. There, according to the report of the gorkom
secretary, only 2.3 per cent of the Party membership and 1.2 per cent of
the candidates were expelled.[54] The great majority of those purged were
young workers. This, the report attributed "to the fact that actually in
1930, 1931, and 1932 there occurred the most coarse perversions in admission into the Party by whole groups on the basis of a single factor,

whether or not they worked in production, and as a result completely un-prepared people came into the Party." While the bulk of those expelled lost their Party membership because they were "passive, hopeless, not willing to work on themselves," or because they discredited the Party by their behavior (drunkenness, immorality, embezzlement, etc.), additional so-called "class-alien and hostile elements" were also uncovered. Thus the Party organizer of the Smolensk electric station, whose neighbor had been arrested as a Trotskyite and who himself had received a reprimand for leftist mistakes, was expelled because he came out with the state-ment that "the material situation of the workers is growing worse." The report revealed that a so-called Trotskyite group in the Rumyantsev fac-tory had been arrested by the organs of the NKVD "for counterrevolu-tionary work," and Party members and candidates who were either re-lated to members of this group or maintained connections with them were ejected from the Party. In addition, a small number were purged for con-cealing their social origins.

Hard on the heels of the completion of the exchange of Party docu-ments came yet another signal for the continuation and intensification of the purge. On July 29, 1936, the Central Committee dispatched a top-secret letter to all Party committees down to the raikom and gorkom level "On the Terrorist Activity of the Trotskyite, Zinovievite Counterrevolu-tionary Bloc." Designed to prepare the way for the impending trial of this group and outlining its alleged crimes in great detail, the letter also called for renewed vigilance and demanded that the Party ranks be screened once again. The letter concluded as follows:

Only the absence of Bolshevik vigilance can explain the fact that some of the arrested participants in the terrorist groups in a number of Party organiza-tions were passed in the check of Party documents and were left in the ranks of the Party.

Now when· it has been proved that the Trotskyite-Zinovievite monsters unite in the struggle against the Soviet state all the most hostile and accursed enemies of the toilers of our country — the spies, provocateurs, diversionists, White Guardists, kulaks, etc. — when all boundary lines have been wiped out between these elements on the one hand, and the Trotskyites and Zinovievites on the other, all Party organizations, all members of the Party, should under-stand that Communist vigilance is necessary in every sector and in every situ-ation.

The inalienable quality of every Bolshevik under present conditions should be the ability to recognize an enemy of the Party, no matter how well he may be masked.[55]

With the circulation of this letter, the hunt for enemies began in dead earnest. A holocaust of denunciations swept through Party ranks. The Party records of the period reflect a mood of rising panic and disarray. Some examples from the Kozelsk raion Party files suggest the atmosphere of the time.

The first secretary of the raikom, a Comrade Demenok, was a particularly diligent denouncer. Available in the Archive are the following samples of his work:

To the Western Oblast Committee of the CPSU (b)
Secret

After reading the closed letter of the Central Committee of the CPSU (b) on the . . . activity of the Zinovievite-Trotskyite bloc, I called to mind Trotskyites who actively struggled against the Party. I remember that in 1925–26, when I still worked as Secretary of the Novozybkovsk Volost Committee . . . there worked in the volost committee at that time an agitator and propagandist named Karkuzevich, whose first name was apparently Michael, a member of the CPSU (b) since 1917, and a railroad worker. Karkuzevich at that time was an active Trotskyite. He not only slandered the Party and its leader, Comrade Stalin, but things went so far that he clearly refused to carry out the decisions of the Fourteenth Party Congress in the Party network, since he did not agree with these decisions and considered them incorrect. We then dismissed him from work, and prosecution by the Party was apparently instituted, but he remained in the Party, and I do not know where he worked, but I seem to recollect that he worked in a militarized guard on the railroad in Byelorussia. It is possible that up to this time he has not been unmasked. I am offering this information so that the necessary measures can be taken.[56]

. . . I remember in 1924–1925 in the Novozybkovsk Party organization of the Western Oblast, apparently on the instructions of the Trotskyite Center, a member of the Party, Kovalev (I don't know his first name) came with the aim of disrupting the Party organization in order to aid Trotsky. He made a Trotskyite report to the aktiv. The Party organization then decisively reprimanded him, but it is possible that up to this moment he is still a member of the Party and up to this moment has not been unmasked as a Trotskyite. I give this information so that the necessary measures may be taken. Kovalev at that time studied at the Sverdlovsk VUZ [University]. He came from Klimovsk raion in the Western Oblast and was the son of a sexton.[57]

Demenok also demonstrated his zeal by constantly feeding denunciatory material to the NKVD. The following note addressed to Comrade Tsebar of the NKVD was typical:

On June 22, 1936, a portrait of Trotsky was discovered in the living quarters of the kolkhoznitsa Afanasiya Uromova (kolkhoz "Krasnyi Oktyabr" [Red October]) in Plyuskovsky village soviet. Uromova, according to information, is a corrupt kolkhoznitsa who carries on subversive work in the kolkhoz. According to the report of Vasili Ulyanov, Uromova assaulted Ulyanov's father. I request that measures be taken to investigate and bring Uromova to trial.[58]

On August 4, 1936, an enlarged session of the bureau of the Kozelsk raikom assembled to discuss the closed letter of the Central Committee on the Trotskyite-Zinovievite bloc. A summary of part of the discussion will perhaps suggest the hysteria which prevailed.[59] The first speaker, Gorokhoz, of the raion procurement organization, began with the usual call for vigilance and then launched into denunciations:

In the procurement organization, there is a Communist named Kozin. He has been censured by the Party for a conciliatory attitude toward Trotskyites. The task of the procurement organization is to follow and observe the actions of Kozin. It is known to me that in the Klintsovsk soviet-Party school there was a Trotskyite, Glazer. I personally should have come out against him immediately. I think it is necessary to inform the Obkom about him . . .

The second speaker, Kavchenko, editor of the raion newspaper, repeated the cry for vigilance and then added some "facts" of his own — about alleged embezzlements in the raion consumers' union, about financial irregularities in railroad construction, and about the slowness of the Party organization in responding to complaints. The next speaker, Fedko, the obkom instructor assigned to the raion, reiterated the by now monotonous demand for increased vigilance.

In our raion there are many people who have come from many other raions. They come here because our Bolshevik vigilance is not on a sufficiently high level. The task of our organization is in every way to develop and increase Bolshevik vigilance, decisively and daringly to expose and unmask people who have had some connection with Trotskyism in the past. It is not important whether the connection is direct or indirect. There is Natokhin, who is a kolkhoz chairman and Party organizer. He himself said that he had in his possession the platform of the Trotskyites. I must state that he should not be kept in the position of Party organizer. Such people as Kozin and Kulikova — now expelled from the ranks of the CPSU(b) — also must be treated with caution. Besides those mentioned above, it is evident that not all have been discovered.

Kutasov from the obkom sanatorium struck a fresh note. "I love the Central Committee," Kutasov pronounced. "I love Comrade Stalin, but I think that up to now the Central Committee and Comrade Stalin have taken a conciliatory attitude toward the Trotskyite-Zinovievite group. Now it is necessary to finish them off — the Trotskyites and Zinovievites — and to finish them off for good. We should give them no mercy."

The next speaker, Balobeshko, second secretary of the raikom, resumed the denunciations.

In our organization there are people who have been connected, directly or indirectly — it is not important — with Trotskyism. For example, Lyustenberg, the director of the sovkhoz "Krasnyi Kombinat" [Red Combine] was educated at the Institute of Red Professors. He has been censured by the Commission on Party Control of the Central Committee for giving a favorable character description to a Trotskyite. And now Lyustenberg is always silent and never speaks. He has never expressed his attitude toward the Trotskyite counterrevolution. Likewise he has never admitted his mistakes in the past or told how he is correcting them now. It is time finally to demand that Lyustenberg do this.

He then paid his respects to the preceding speaker.

Kutasov's speech must be considered politically disloyal and even harmful. Kutasov is incorrect in accusing the Central Committee and Comrade Stalin of being conciliatory . . . Kutasov himself is a Party organizer, but he does not give lessons in his organization. Kutasov deserves serious censure because of this. Then there is Stepanov, the director of the procurement office of the raion union. This Stepanov follows an incorrect line in his work. He does not want to go to the country, and he has brought friends and acquaintances to work for him — people who are untrustworthy . . .

And so the discussion proceeded — with one denunciation piled on another. Kutasov arose to apologize for his excessive zeal. "My statement," he admitted, "was incorrect and harmful. I myself censure it." The final speech was contributed by Comrade Demenok, the first secretary. He declared:

The letter of the Central Committee makes us rejoice to the depths of our being, makes us happy because thanks to the vigilance and sagacity of Comrade Stalin . . . the possibility of sad consequences has been averted . . . Life has become better, comrades, life has become happier. These correct words of the leader of the Party, Comrade Stalin, apply completely to our raion. We know that there are many shortcomings in our work. At the same time we will decisively and thoroughly wage a struggle to abolish them.

Then Demenok dwelt on certain questions and personalities touched on in the discussion and pledged the raion Party organization "to an irreconcilable struggle." He concluded:

We shall decisively unmask the last Trotskyite-Zinovievite counterrevolutionary remnants, and under the leadership of the Western Oblast Committee of the CPSU(b) and Comrade Rumyantsev, we shall go forward to new victories, we shall lead the toiling masses of the raion to an even better, brighter, richer, more cultured life. Long live our beloved leader, Comrade Stalin!

The last act, at least so far as the Smolensk Archive is concerned, came in 1937 when the Purge turned full circle and its sharp edge was directed against Rumyantsev himself and his leading associates in the oblast and raion Party leadership. The circumstances which surrounded the Rumyantsev purge remain obscure; such information as the Archive yields has already been summarized in Chapter 2. But one ironic and prophetic footnote remains to be added.

Buried in a file of communications addressed to Rumyantsev in 1936 is a rather incoherent letter signed by twenty-one workers of the Rumyantsev factory:

We workers in the factory which bears your name will no longer allow to go unpunished those of our leaders who trusted and permitted the accursed enemy to receive a Party card and to be in our ranks. We workers said so at the first meeting; we wrote to the secretary of the Party committee, Yegorov, but he didn't even listen, didn't want to hear about it, although he was informed when he came to us in the factory. As far as the chairman of the factory committee, Metelkova, goes, she has obstructed your eyes and ears. She, like Yegorov, didn't want to hear anything either. And because of such loafers our dear great Bolshevik tribunes will perish. So all of us, dear Comrade Rumyantsev, hope that such "Communists" who have become bureaucratized, have become puffed up with conceit, have become great magnates, have alienated themselves from the masses, who did not want to hear anything, although they knew and were informed a thousand times, we feel that those who deliberately allowed the accursed enemy into the ranks of the Leninist-Stalinist Party, will not remain unpunished.[60]

Scrawled across the bottom of this letter is a handwritten note of Rumyantsev's: "The method of the enemy, to discredit the leaders." Within the next year Rumyantsev himself was to be completely discredited and crushed. One can only wonder whom he identified as the enemy then.

12 The Story of Collectivization

Smolensk on the eve of collectivization was an overwhelmingly agricultural province in which more than 90 per cent of the population lived in the countryside. Less than 1 per cent of the land was collectivized, and the private sector accounted for 98.7 per cent of the gross agricultural output.[1] Out of a total of 393,523 peasant households registered in 1927, 5 per cent were classified as kulaks, 70 per cent as middle peasants, and 25 per cent as poor peasants.[2] In tsarist days the Smolensk area had been one of the centers of flax and hemp culture. After the Revolution, however, the cultivation of flax and hemp declined sharply; population pressure and the expanding needs of home consumption led to a considerable shift to potatoes, grain and fodder groups, and livestock breeding. The NEP years registered significant gains in food output, but population increase outraced growth in production, and the percentage of marketed produce steadily declined.

The Initial Attack on the Kulaks

The decision of the Soviet authorities to abandon the NEP and embark on a policy of agricultural collectivization and rapid industrialization had its immediate repercussions in Smolensk as elsewhere. The first victims of the new campaign in the countryside were the kulaks, who controlled a substantial part of the agricultural surplus which was essential to feed the new factory centers and who could be counted on to resist collectivization most staunchly. During 1927–28 the noose was gradually tightened around the necks of the kulaks.

The initial attack on the kulaks involved a sharp increase in their tax burden, designed to force them to disgorge their grain surpluses. At the same time up to a third of all poor-peasant households were freed from all agricultural taxes, and economic aid to poor-peasant groups in the form of agricultural credit and other assistance was increased. Measures were also taken to raise wages for hired laborers working in kulak households. Thus, the regime sought to consolidate the support of the poor peasants and hired laborers in the villages while at the same time neutralizing and weakening kulak influence. Kulaks were denied agricultural credit and equipment, deprived of lands which had allegedly been improperly distributed to them, eliminated from the rural apparatus of soviets, agricultural credit and coöperative organizations, and prosecuted for speculation in grain and concealment of grain surpluses.

The kulak reaction to this attack took a variety of forms. Official reports complained that kulaks were still "worming their way into" and "planting their own people" in leading organs of rural soviets and coöperatives, bribing soviet workers and even Party members to obtain tax concessions, and taking advantage of the grain difficulties to agitate against the Soviet system and "to dissolve the union between the poor peasants and the middle peasants."[3] As the persecution of the kulak intensified, the kulaks replied in kind. The police records of the period are filled with reports of "terrorist acts" against zealous Party and soviet workers — the beating of chairmen of village soviets and other "public workers," the killing of village correspondents, the murder of Party secretaries, the disruption of meetings of poor peasants, and so on.[4] The flare-up of violence testified to mounting kulak resistance.

The Grain Collection Campaign of 1929

As the First Five Year Plan gathered momentum, the demands on the countryside intensified. The grain collection campaign of 1929 registered the pressure, and it fell with particularly crushing force on so-called well-to-do farmers. The Western Oblast, into which Smolensk guberniya had been absorbed in 1929, lagged badly in meeting its quotas.[5] The dissatisfaction of the center was reflected in a Politburo telegram of September 20, 1929, which demanded that the targets be met immediately.[6] Pressed by the center, the oblast Party authorities embarked on shock tactics. Special emissaries, appointed by the Party and armed with full power to extract grain wherever they could find it, were dispatched to the okrugs to spur deliveries.[7] The reports of these special emissaries provide a revealing record both of the tactics employed and the difficulties to be surmounted.

In theory, the main thrust of the grain collection campaign was directed against the kulaks, and the special emissaries were under instructions to enlist the aid of poor and middle peasants in carrying the battle to the kulaks. In practice, the problem was not so simple. Many of the kulaks were village leaders respected by their fellow-villagers, frequently related by ties of blood to poor and middle peasants, and occupying positions of influence which ramified into the local soviet and even Party apparatus. The villages refused to fall neatly into categories of poor, middle, and well-to-do peasants and frequently insisted on maintaining a group solidarity that the special emissaries found frustrating and impenetrable. Even more aggravating was the extent to which the local soviet and Party apparatus identified with the peasants and even shielded the kulak against the emissaries' demands.

Some extracts from the reports of special emissaries may serve to illustrate the problems which the local officialdom presented. Thus, the chairman of a raiispolkom is quoted as saying: "Why such pressure on the kulak? We will turn him and the whole population against us. This will be fatal for NEP . . ." [8] An assistant raikom secretary complained at a raion Party conference, "We are constantly taking and taking . . . until there will be no more to take in the village." [9] The emissaries encountered responses from Party members such as "Why are you constantly yelling about the kulak? We have no kulaks here." [10] "There is no food here, and the state norms of purchase are rising." [11] Raion leaders, declared the emissary for Smolensk okrug, virtually had to be "carried by the collar" to do something.[12] Over and over again the emissaries complain of inadequate raion leadership, of the passivity of lower echelons, of the refusal of village Communists to participate in the campaign, and even of open defiance of Party directives. The "counterpressures of the countryside" even began to tell on some of the emissaries. According to one report, "They slowly fall into a system of more restrained tactics; they hesitate to squeeze everything from peasant households; they grow pacifist." [13]

The solidarity of the villages presented another formidable obstacle to the success of the grain collection campaign. Middle and even poor peasants joined the kulaks in resisting the exactions of the emissaries and openly attacked Party and soviet workers at village meetings as "thieves and bandits." [14] While some poor peasants applauded the regime's pressure on the kulaks, others were quoted as asserting, "There are no kulaks in our village. Why do we have to fight them?" [15] "Now they are confiscating bread from the kulak; tomorrow they will turn against the middle and poor peasant." [16] Cases were reported where poor and middle peasants shielded and defended the richer ones, saying, "The whole village is equal; quotas should be equally distributed." [17] Indeed, some emissaries frankly confessed that, pressed by the obkom for grain, they were sequestrating it from every one indiscriminately. "When wood is chopped," observed one of the emissaries, "chips must fly." [18] Thus the stubborn and inflexible drive to carry out the plan served to undermine the official policy of driving a wedge between the kulaks and the rest of the village.

As reliance on "voluntary" contributions failed to yield results, the tactics of the emissaries became harsher. Under the law, grain quotas were imposed on all peasant households subject to taxation with the proviso that these quotas be delivered in a period of two to five days.[19] Failure to deliver the grain quota was subject to a fivefold penalty on the first offense. The penalty for a second offense was a year of prison or forced labor. The same offense if carried out by a group with collective premeditation to resist Soviet orders was punishable by two years of prison or forced labor with deportation and seizure of all or part of the property of the convicted.[20]

The actual procedure in dealing with kulak households was more summary. If the kulak failed to fulfill his assessed quota, "workers' brigades" or village soviet forces, under the emissary's supervision, simply raided the household and confiscated any grain "surpluses" which could be located on the premises. Some emissaries were more implacable than others. Thus one Litenbrand reported a disagreement with a raikom Party secretary whom he accused of "philanthropy" because the raikom secretary insisted that enough grain be left to the kulaks for sowing and for feeding the children. This, said Litenbrand, was dangerous. "When you are attacking, there is no place for mercy; don't think of the kulak's hungry children; in the class struggle philanthropy is evil." [21] Litenbrand was accused of "warlike acts," but he was convinced that his was the only correct Bolshevik attitude.

The stern measures directed against the kulaks produced a variety of reactions. Where possible, the kulaks hid their grain, or sought to escape sequestration by bribery or other subterfuges. As repressive measures intensified, some kulaks replied in kind. The reports of the emissaries contain numerous references to kulak attacks on village "activists" who were engaged in grain seizures. A pall of terror enveloped the villages. As reports of killings and arson multiplied, Party members were warned "to stay away from the windows" when working in soviet institutions and not to walk the village streets after dark.[22] The emissaries begged for GPU reinforcements and stern measures which would paralyze kulak resistance. The procurator of the Western Oblast, meanwhile, reported a substantial increase in the number of terrorist acts as the grain delivery campaign gathered momentum. During the two-month period July-August 1929 there were thirty-four such cases; in September their number reached twenty-five, and during October mounted to forty-seven.[23] Of the forty-seven victims of attack in October, ten were chairman and eight secretaries of village soviets, eight were grain delivery officials, and the rest a variety of "activists" who participated in the campaign. Of the 122 persons who were apprehended in October for committing "terrorist" acts, approximately half were kulaks and well-to-do peasants, and another 45 per cent were middle and poor peasants. The latter group, observed the procurator, was closely allied with the kulak elements by "family and economic ties" and still manifested a "petty-bourgeois" ideology.[24]

The Liquidation of the Kulaks as a Class

The grain collection campaign of 1929, as it turned out, was merely a prelude to a far more drastic operation, the decision to liquidate the kulak as a class and to lay the groundwork for total collectivization. The signal for the all-out drive was given at the end of 1929, and soon after the turn of the year the operation was launched in various parts of the Western Oblast. The Smolensk Archive provides a particularly rich record of the execution of the operation in Velikiye Luki okrug; it will be described here in some detail.[25]

On January 28, 1930, the Party committee of Velikiye Luki okrug approved a proposal to deport kulaks from the okrug and to confiscate their property.[26] Two OGPU officials (Kolosov and Dabolin) were designated to prepare a plan of action. On January 30 the Party committee approved the following arrangements: (1) to enlarge the okrug OGPU apparatus by four more members and to mobilize an additional eleven people from the OGPU reserve; (2) to make 10,000 rubles available to the OGPU to finance the added personnel; (3) to release okrug militia forces from other duties and to use them in the dekulakization campaign; (4) to supply arms from the "mobilization reserves" to all participants; and (5) to postpone putting into effect an earlier okrug decision to take down all church bells and close churches in order not to arouse general peasant resistance.[27]

March 1, 1930, was set as a target date for the completion of the operation. On February 6 special okrug and raion troikas were designated to direct activities.[28] In each case the troika consisted of the first secretary of the Party committee, the chairman of the soviet executive committee (ispolkom) and the head of the OGPU. The okrug Party committee also arranged to dispatch twenty-six people to the raions to assist the local authorities.

On February 12, a top-secret letter was sent to all raitroikas outlining detailed instructions for the conduct of the operation.[29] Working through the raikoms and the village soviets, the raitroikas were to undertake a prompt inventory of all kulak property, meanwhile warning the kulaks that if they were caught in the unauthorized sale of any of their property, all of it would immediately be confiscated. The inventory was to be completed within a two-week period.

The letter ordered the raitroikas to divide all kulak households into three groups, according to the degree of danger which they presented to the soviet authorities and the severity of the punishment which was to be imposed on them. The first and most dangerous group, described as "the counterrevolutionary kulak aktiv," was to be arrested by the OGPU. The raitroikas were authorized to make additions to this "list" on the basis of recommendations emerging from meetings of poor peasants and agricultural laborers. Incriminating material was to be forwarded to the OGPU. The second category consisted of "certain (separate) elements of the kulak aktiv," especially from among the richest peasants and "quasi-landowners," who were to be deported to "far-off" parts of the Soviet Union. The remaining kulaks were to be removed from areas scheduled for "total collectivization," but were not to be deported from the okrug. For such kulaks the raion executive committees were to provide special land parcels carved out of "eroded" areas, "swamp-lands in woods," and other soil "in need of improvement."

Families of Group I and II kulaks were to be deported from the okrug on the approval of the okrug troika. Property of Group I households was to be confiscated immediately and handed over to neighboring collective farms either in existence or in process of organization. In the absence of such farms, the property was to be delivered to the nearest functioning kolkhoz. Property of Group II households was to be confiscated gradually, with confiscation timed to coincide with deportation schedules. In order to "guide" the raions in conducting the operation, the okrug troika supplied each raion with an "orientation number" of Group I kulaks who were to be arrested and Group II kulaks who were to be deported.

Families of Group I and II kulaks were to retain only the most "elementary" and indispensable items for survival, including some food till the next harvest (about four kilograms of grain and eight kilograms of potatoes per person per month). One cow was also to be left to a family with children, as well as necessary work implements, until the time of deportation. Kulaks scheduled for deportation were allowed to keep 500 rubles per family in order "to facilitate settlement in a new place." Otherwise, everything else was to be confiscated.

Group III kulaks were to retain an "indispensable minimum of work implements" in order to enable them to cultivate their newly assigned lands. Kulaks resettled in the okrug were also required to do service in special labor units for work in forestry, highway and rail construction, and so forth. In addition, they were required to meet production and delivery quotas on their new lands; failure to fulfill these quotas entailed criminal prosecution and property confiscation.

The letter "unconditionally prohibited" the deportation or resettlement of poor and middle peasants. In the words of the letter, "This warning is issued because in many cases emissaries dekulakize and arrest poor peasants on the ground that the latter are ideologically kulaks. A firm class line must here be prepared. A wedge must be driven between the kulaks — the class enemy — and the rest of the peasants, and the latter must be mobilized to help in annihilating the class enemy." [30] Measures of dekulakization were also forbidden against families of Red Army soldiers or officers even if such families were in the kulak category. The presence of a member of a kulak family in the Red Army, however, was immediately to be reported to the okrug troika.

Party and trade union organizations were instructed to purge factories of kulak elements. Special vigilance was to be exercised to prevent the flight of kulaks from the countryside to the cities and industry. If, however, a member of a kulak family was found to have worked in a given industrial enterprise for a long time, an "especially cautious approach" was to be used. Each case was to be considered on its own merits by the okrug troika in collaboration with the appropriate factory organizations.

The letter sought as far as possible to "regularize" and "legalize" seizures of kulak property. Confiscations were to be carried out by special representatives of the raiispolkom with the mandatory participation of village soviets, kolkhoz representatives, and groups of poor and middle peasants. Village soviets were to be responsible for a precise and complete inventory and valuation of confiscated property. The kulaks' confiscated homes were to be utilized for public and social purposes by village soviets and kolkhozes or as temporary dormitories for poor peasants entering the kolkhoz. Savings books and state-loan bonds seized in kulak households were to be transferred to the People's Commissariat of Finance for "safekeeping." The letter noted that in certain raions confiscations and deportations were occurring "without the slightest preparations." Labeling such phenomena "impermissible," the letter warned that all operations in the raions required the approval of the okrug troika and were to be preceded by preparatory work including "explanations to the poor peasant masses, complete property inventory, history of all kulak households, establishment of the locale of land parcels for kulak resettlement, etc."

The letter concluded: "There shall be no oscillation, no concessions to rightist-deviationist attitudes and no pacifism. The Party must solve the problem of liquidating the kulaks and collectivizing the villages in the shortest possible period. In all cases where anything is insufficiently clear, immediately consult the okrug." [31]

Subsequent sessions of the okrug troika disclosed that all was far from clear. At a meeting on February 19, 1930, Dabolin, the OGPU representative, complained of "deviations" in the form of arrests of "village intelligentsia," poor peasants, peasants with sons in the Red Army, etc.[32] Banditry was on the rise, and all raikoms were instructed to extend full support to the OGPU in the struggle to stamp it out. On February 20 the OGPU reported mounting arrests and dekulakization of middle peasants. Peasants were quoted as saying: "If all this is allowed from the top, then we are doomed; there is no one to turn to." [33] The same report noted that poor peasants who had been hired hands before the revolution and who now owned an extra horse or cow, were, in many cases, also being dekulakized. In this connection, peasants were commenting: "Such a fate awaits all of us; may the war come sooner, for otherwise it is impossible to build up your own household." [34]

On February 28, the okrug troika rendered an account of the progress of dekulakization to Rumyantsev, the oblast Party secretary.[35] According to still incomplete data, the okrug had 3,551 kulak households subject to liquidation, of which 947 were in Group I, 1,307 in Group II, and 1,297 in Group III. Up to that date approximately 800 persons had been "taken over" by the OGPU. Fifty fled to avoid arrest. In a "majority of raions" the property of Group I kulaks had already been confiscated and transferred to kolkhozes. Of the twenty-six raions of the okrug, sixteen were being utilized "for the resettlement of kulaks." By February 28, "appropriate land parcels" totaling 7,505 acres and consisting of "eroded land, swamps, wasteland, and bushy areas" were allocated for this purpose. "It is necessary to note," said the report, "that on the above parcels, with rare exceptions, there are no homes or structures of any kind, which makes resettlement difficult." [36]

Protocols of the okrug troika mirror the confusion and disorganization of the period. Despite apparently precise directives and instructions, many raion and village authorities went their own way, interpreting the kulak category broadly to embrace middle and even poor peasants who were opposed to collectivization, evicting kulak families with Red Army connections, and rarely bothering to supply the okrug troika with supporting data to justify their decisions. In the first flush of the dekulakization campaign, "excesses" were commonplace. An OGPU report of February 28, 1930, provides a matter-of-fact recital of some of the antics of the dekulakizers.[37] According to the report, in many villages "certain members of the workers' brigades and officials of lower echelons of the Party-soviet apparatus" deprived members of kulak and middle peasant households of their clothing and warm underwear (directly from the body), "confiscated" head-wear from children's heads, and removed shoes from people's feet. The perpetrators divided the "confiscated" goods among themselves; the food they found was eaten on the spot; the alcohol they uncovered was consumed immediately, resulting in drunken orgies. In one case a worker tore a warm blouse off a woman's back, put it on himself with the words, "You wore it long enough, now I will wear it." The slogan of many of the dekulakization brigades was: "drink, eat — it's all ours." One commune, in search of more and richer "confiscations," commenced to dekulakize kulaks of the bordering village soviet. As the kulaks in question were administratively under the "jurisdiction" of another kolkhoz, a struggle ensued between the communards and the kolkhozniks. The communards under the direction of their Party secretary absconded with much of the money and property of the kulaks before the kolkhoz could act. In the process, even eyeglasses were torn from the peasants' faces; kasha was "confiscated" straight from the oven and either eaten or used to smear the ikons. When the OGPU investigated the whereabouts of the "confiscated" property, the commune destroyed the original inventory lists and wrote new ones.

Another OGPU report, dated February 23, 1930, noted that middle and even poor peasants were being arrested by "anybody" — by raion emissaries, village soviet members, kolkhoz chairmen, and any one in any way connected with collectivization.[38] People were being transported to militia prisons without the slightest grounds or evidence. Although the raion authorities were aware of this, they were reluctant to interfere so as "not to undermine the authority of the village soviet" responsible for the arrest. Some poor peasants and "activists" were blackmailing the richer peasants, taking bribes for removing them from the confiscation or deportation lists. In many cases, confiscated cattle was not being fed and was starving to death.

Still another report pointed out that the looting in the villages had induced an atmosphere of panic among the well-to-do peasants.[39] According to this report, a wave of suicides was sweeping the richer households; kulaks were killing their wives and children and then taking their own lives. In order to prevent complete property confiscation, many kulaks and their wives were entering into fictitious divorces, in the hope that at least some property and the lives of wives and children would be spared. Sensing their impending doom, kulaks in growing numbers were fleeing to the east (Moscow, the Urals, Siberia). They dekulakized themselves by selling out all they owned, or leaving their property with relatives and friends, or simply abandoning their fields and homes.

Occasionally kulaks also found friends and protectors at court. Chairmen of village soviets were reported as befriending kulaks by exempting valuable kulak property from confiscation; some Party members defended kulaks because of their previous humanitarian behavior toward poor peasants.[40] Many poor and middle peasants considered dekulakization unjust and harmful, refused to vote approval of deportation and expropriation measures, hid kulak property, and warned their kulak friends of pending searches and requisitions. In many cases poor and middle peasants were reported as collecting signatures to petitions testifying to the loyalty and good character of kulaks, millers, and other well-to-do elements. The high-handed tactics of indiscriminate and arbitrary confiscation and deportation turned many poor and middle peasants into bitter opponents of the regime.

At this point the Party leadership decided to call a halt to the "excesses" it had set in motion. On February 20, 1930, Rumyantsev addressed a letter to all okrug Party secretaries, calling attention to the fact that, despite "exhaustive and precise instructions" from the obkom, deviations in dekulakization policy were continuing.[41] Among these he particularly condemned: (1) the dekulakization of middle peasants and the "mass-inclusion" of such peasants in kulak lists based only on "vicious rumor" and "possible provocation"; (2) the lawless actions of dekulakization brigades which "interfere with normal administrative processes"; (3) the use of Red Army units in carrying out dekulakization; (4) the spreading of the slogans of dekulakization (with the same inadmissible methods) to the city Nepmen; (5) the actions of drunken soldiers and Komsomols who "without mass preparation" were "arbitrarily closing village churches, breaking ikons, and threatening the peasants."

The Rumyantsev letter was followed by a top-secret obkom circular of March 2 reprimanding the okrug Party committees for "brutal" abuses committed by raion and village officials against the "dekulakized."[42] Brought up short by these warnings and Stalin's "Dizziness from Success" article (published in *Pravda* on March 2), the okrug troikas initiated a review of all raion decisions on dekulakization. In a typical action in Velikiye Luki okrug involving a list of 121 dekulakized households in Siebezhsky raion, the raitroika's decisions were rejected in forty-four cases, and eight cases were referred to the OGPU for further investigation.[43] The OGPU quickly adjusted to the new line and followed the lead of the okrug troikas in overruling raion decisions. The raitroikas were instructed to return confiscated property to those peasants who had been "unjustly" dekulakized. Like other posthumous efforts to render justice, the instructions proved easier to issue than to execute.

Kulak Deportations

Meanwhile, kulak deportations gathered momentum. The most detailed description of the deportations in the Smolensk Archive are to be found in OGPU reports of March 1931 dealing with the situation in the Roslavl area.[44] In the rural district of Roslavl preparations for deportation began on February 15, 1931.[45] Lists of all kulaks and well-to-do peasants were collected from the village soviets. But these lists, the OGPU emissary complained, "failed to provide the information necessary to do the impending job."[46] Consequently, personal questionnaires were circulated to 215 potential victims under the guise of checking the correctness of their tax liabilities. On March 18, the raitroika reviewed the questionnaires and condemned seventy-four households to liquidation. On the evening of March 19, the raitroika assembled its emissaries at a central point, gave them instructions, and assigned two households to each emissary. The operation was to be completed that same night. But "not all went smoothly." In a number of cases the emissaries stalled, conducted drawn-out meetings with poor peasants, and in general "failed to arrange the job in a tightly conspiratorial fashion." [47] As a result kulaks were forewarned, and the emissaries failed to find those marked for deportation. Some emissaries allowed "tearful goodbyes to be drawn out" during which many able-bodied men slipped away. A number of kulaks succeeded in smuggling their property to poorer relatives. All in all, thirty-two families were deported from the raion; the rest fled, and the OGPU head stated that measures were being taken to find them. He complained that many emissaries had made "grave mistakes"; the wife of one emissary, a Komsomol, publicly expressed grief and sympathy for the deported. "We are no longer people," she was quoted as having said; "we are animals." [48] But most Komsomols were lauded for having done an outstanding job, "better than that of responsible officials." According to the report, poor peasants were "generally pleased" with the progress of events. But middle peasants were "confused and unnerved." "Our turn will come soon," they kept repeating. [49]

Another top-secret OGPU document (March 27, 1931) reported on popular attitudes in Roslavl in connection with the deportations. [50] On that date 437 families (2,202 persons) were gathered in the city's "assembly points" being readied for deportation. The OGPU claimed that workers were "basically" well-disposed to the government's measures against the kulaks. "If they are deported," some workers were quoted as saying, "it's probably necessary to do so; [the Bolsheviks] know whom to take; they won't take us." Other workers (whom the report refers to as "workers" in quotation marks) "betray negative attitudes." They talk about the "good old times." "All this would not have happened if Lenin had been alive," they say. "Such things were unheard of in those times, people had enough to eat . . . But now . . . now it is impossible to understand what is going on." One of the workers, looking at Lenin's portrait, declared, ". . . were Lenin alive, he would have allowed free trade and eased our lot; afterwards, he would have instituted a shift toward collectivization — not by force, but by consent and persuasion." [51]

According to this report, the deportations brought an atmosphere of panic to the towns as well as to the villages. Some workers "do not sleep nights," waiting to be taken away, or expecting some of their relatives to be taken. "All my acquaintances have already been taken away," one commented, ". . . the most terrible thing is that no one knows where he is taken to; people have been brought to the verge of complete passivity; no matter what one does to them, they don't care any more; earlier an arrested man was led by two militiamen; now one militiaman may lead groups of people, and the latter calmly walk and no one flees." [52] The report cited a "characteristic" case where one citizen came

СНК СССР
Полномочное Представительство
по Западной области

Росла...кое
городское ...
27 ...рля 193 г.
№ ...
гор. Рославль

НАЧ.ПП ГПУ О ПП ОГПУ З/О - г. СМОЛЕНСК.

ДОКЛАДНАЯ ЗАПИСКА

О настроениях в связи с выселением
кулачества.-

По состоянию на 26|III-1931 года.

За отчетный период на сборных пунктах Горотделения имеется
437 семей с общим количеством людей 2202. По сборным пунктам
они распределяются следующим образом:

	Семей:	Людей:
Рославльский пункт	172	811
Стодолищенск. "	68	369
Дубровский "	79	460
Починковский "	118	562

Из коих на территорию Рославльского Горотделения падает
семей 375 и людей 1917, а 62 семьи, в коих находятся 285 чел.
падает на Монастырщинский район, который доставляет их на По-
чинковский сборный пункт.-

В настроениях основной массы рабочих гор. Рославля, мы имеем
положительные реагирования на выселение кулачества, сводящееся
к одобрению мероприятий правительства по выселению. Беднота и
колхозники единодушно поддерживают выселение кулачества.-

Большинство рабочих типографии одобряют мероприятия Правительства по выселению кулачества и ликвидации его, как класса, говоря,
что это дает большой толчек коллективизации

Рабочие выражают одобрение мероприятиям сов
власти по выселению кулачества, смеются над
осужденными выселяемыми, говоря:" раз вы-
селяют, значит надо, ведь знают кого берут,
кто не возьмут."-

The top-secret GPU reports on attitudes of the Roslavl populace toward kulak deportations — March 27, 1931. Note the seal of the OGPU in the upper left-hand corner.

to the raion procuracy and begged to be deported together with the kulaks, reasoning that he would at least have a chance to start a "less hectic life." [53]

Manifestations of sympathy for the deported were widespread, even in the cities. Groups of women watching the departure of the deported commented: "It is in vain that these poor families are so mistreated . . . they have been suffering for the last two years . . . everything was in any case taken away from them through taxes . . . this is horrifying . . . children are taken together with adults . . . with only what is on their backs . . . It is impossible to comprehend why all this is happening to the people . . ." [54] "Hearsay" is reproduced by the OGPU to the effect that "deportee-families are separated . . . with mothers in one rail-car, husbands and children in other cars. Mothers are hysterical, tearing hair from their heads." [55]

The OGPU reported the following conversation among a group of bookkeepers as indicative of the views of employees in the state service. "Even if they take away all kulaks," said one, "and there are no more kulaks to take, there will soon be new kulaks. It seems that there will have to be new kulaks until that time when everybody will be herded into kolkhozes. It is difficult to know how they will live in the kolkhozes, but one thing is sure: they won't be equal anyway; one will be earning more and the other less." [56] A second bookkeeper ("whose name, background, and working place it was impossible to determine") commented: "I saw cattle trains readied for the kulaks who are obviously to be taken to Karelia . . . the best and hardest workers of the land are being taken away (with the misfits and lazybones staying behind)." [57] A third commented that the Bolsheviks "were themselves propagandizing: 'Go to the countryside, build up cultured farms, raise good cattle, etc.' — the peasants did just that. They acquired this and that, and now they are dekulakized for having two cows and horses and for having stopped eating filth. Are these kulaks? What kind of kulaks can they be — they who have just begun to enjoy their own piece of bread. The real kulaks are sitting and looking on. Maybe all this is wrecking; maybe somewhere there sits somebody who is worse than these kulaks and who is only planning how to hunt people down. I am sure that this is wrecking, for now the peasants will stop producing any surpluses, and thus none of us will be able to buy anything at the bazaar." [58]

While the OGPU report cited such conversations as reflecting a general attitude that "certain distortions" did take place in connection with dekulakization, that "locally, things were oversalted," it nevertheless defended the behavior of the OGPU itself. It pointed to the "calm" of the deportees and the "contented" letters written by deportees from "labor colonies." Letters were quoted to the effect that "treatment" (by the guards) is good, that "needs are satisfied," that families are united, that transportation conditions are satisfactory "in every respect," that the echelon guards are "attentive and polite," and that the OGPU's attitude is "very just." [59] Nor did the report fail to note the sharp upsurge in collectivization which came in the wake of the deportations. This, in the eyes of the regime, was the ultimate rationale of the entire dekulakization program.

Problems of Kolkhoz Organization

Prior to the application of this pressure, the kolkhoz movement was slow to take root in the Western Oblast. Indeed, the First Five Year Plan for the oblast contemplated that only 8.6 per cent of the peasant households would be enrolled in kolkhozes by 1932–33. On October 1, 1928, the actual percentage of collectivization was an almost infinitesimal 0.8 per cent. By October 1, 1929, it had increased to only 2.5 per cent.[60] From that point on, in accordance with directions from the center to liquidate the kulak and intensify the organization of kolkhozes, the tempo of collectivization mounted swiftly. On March 1, 1930, the Western Oblast reported that 38.8 per cent of all hired-labor, poor-peasant, and middle-peasant households were collectivized.[61]

What happened in the intervening five months is perhaps best portrayed in the language of the peasants themselves. The Smolensk Archive contains a collection of peasants' letters (most of them unpublished) written during this period to the editors of the oblast peasant newspaper, *Nasha Derevnya* (Our Village). They vividly convey what was happening in the countryside and how the letter writers felt about it. "Dear Comrades," wrote Ivan Trofimovich Chuyunkov from the village of Yushkovo:

For a long time I have wanted to write you about what you have written on collectivization in your newspaper *Nasha Derevnya*.

In the first place I will give you my address so that you will not suspect that I am a kulak or one of his parasites. I am a poor peasant. I have one hut, one barn, one horse, 3 dessyatins of land, and a wife and three children. Dear Comrades, as a subscriber to your newspaper . . . I found in No. 13/85 for February 15 a letter from a peasant who writes about the life of kolkhoz construction. I, a poor peasant, reading this letter, fully agreed with it. This peasant described life in the kolkhoz completely correctly. Isn't it true that all the poor peasants and middle peasants do not want to go into the kolkhoz at all, but that you drive them in by force? For example, I'll take my village soviet of Yushkovo. A brigade of soldiers came to us. This brigade went into all the occupied homes, and do you think that they organized a kolkhoz? No, they did not organize it. The hired laborers and the poor peasants came out against it and said they did not want *corvée*, they did not want serfdom . . . I'll write more of my village soviet. When the Red Army brigade left, they sent us a kolkhoz organizer from Bryansk okrug. And whom do you think this Comrade signed up? Not poor peasants, not hired laborers, but kulaks, who, sensing their own ruin, enter the kolkhoz. And your organizer . . . takes to evil deeds. At night, together with the Komsomolites, he takes everything away from the peasants, both surpluses and taxes, which you fleece from the peasants. Of course agricultural taxes are necessary, self-taxation is necessary, fire taxes are necessary, tractorization is necessary. But where can the toiling peasant get this money if not from the seeds of his products? And these Party people stay up all night and rob the peasants. If he brings a pud, if he brings 5, it's all the same. I would propose that you let the peasant live in greater freedom than he does now, and then we won't beg you to get rid of such a gang, for we ourselves will eliminate them.[62]

Wrote one Pyotr Gorky:

In the first place, I, a citizen of the village of Muzhyno . . . tell you, our government and also the editors, that we toiling peasants, poor peasants, and also the middle peasants see that life is bad, but nevertheless we have endured it. But when we got to the year 1930, we saw that we were ruined. We have bad land and little of it in the village of Muzhyno, and we had grain and potato requisitions, and they took them from us by force, both from the poor peasants and from the middle peasants. Simply speaking, it was robbery . . . We ourselves do not know what to do. Every day they send us lecturers asking us to sign up for such-and-such a kolkhoz for eternal slavery, but we don't want to leave our good homes. It may be a poor little hut, but it's mine, a poor horse, but it's mine. Among us, he who works more has something to eat. We peasants are used to working, but you, our government, change the pay every day arbitrarily . . . We ourselves don't know what to do. There aren't any nails, there is nothing and life is bad. We will not be able to eat in the kolkhoz . . . Therefore we beg you to turn the rudder of the kolkhoz movement and let the peasant own property. Then we assure you that everyone will be able to put more surpluses on the market, and trade will be free. We poor peasants ask you to change everything, to give us freedom, and then we will be glad to help the state.[63]

Wrote still another peasant:

Comrades, you write that all the middle peasants and poor peasants join the kolkhoz voluntarily, but it is not true. For example, in our village of Pod-buzhye, all do not enter the kolkhoz willingly. When the register made the rounds, only 25% signed it, while 75% did not. They collected seeds by frightening [the peasants] with protocols and arrests. If any one spoke against it, he was threatened with arrest and forced labor. You are deceived in this, Comrades. Collective life can be created when the entire mass of the peasants goes voluntarily, and not by force . . . I beg you not to divulge my name, because the Party people will be angry. [Signed] POLZIKOV.[64]

Another peasant wrote:

They [the kolkhoz organizers] use force and threats against those who do not enter the kolkhoz — they take away their land and deport them out of the bounds of the village. I ask you . . . whether they can behave like that and take away the land and deport an invalid poor peasant like me?[65]

The following letter is in a similar vein:

Comrade editor . . . If, as you write, they [the peasants] join the kolkhozes voluntarily, why do you send brigades who send you to prison for the slightest resistance against the kolkhoz? Did the people think that they would live this way after they received freedom? Now it happens that freedom is not a word, but prison is a word. Say something against collectivization, and you're put in prison . . . If you took a vote, you would only find half of a per cent who joined the kolkhoz voluntarily. Each one thinks it is a terrible thing; each one wants to be a master and not a slave . . .[66]

The same hatred of the kolkhoz was expressed by Ivan Bogdanov from the village of Lodosh:

My household consists of one horse, 3 sheep, 4 dessyatins of land for 7 consumers . . . I ask you to answer the question whether it is compulsory to enter the kolkhoz. I think not, but they gave us complete collectivization in Usvyatsk raion. I am sure that if you came and took a vote that not more than 15% would be in favor of the kolkhoz. All the people destroy their livestock, saying, "It doesn't matter, you have to go into the kolkhoz against your will" . . . Do not force the people to join the kolkhoz — there isn't any sense to it . . . It's better to hang yourself than to join the kolkhoz; it's better not to be born than to join the kolkhoz . . .[67]

These extracts, which are culled largely from the letters of poor peasants, underline the role that force played in accelerating the tempo of collectivization. Nor was the opposition to collectivization confined to verbal protests. In some instances, at least, violence was met with violence, and the reports of the procurator and the OGPU for this period are replete with examples. On September 30, 1929, Lebedev, the oblast procurator, reported the following incident to the obkom: "On September 2, of this year, in the village of Lyalichi, Klintsy okrug, a mob of 200 people made an open attack on the kolkhozniks who were going out to work the fields. This attack consisted of the dispersal of the kolkhozniks from the field, the destruction of their equipment, clothes, etc. They chased after the leaders of the kolkhoz, but the latter succeeded in saving themselves by fleeing. The majority of the attackers were women, who were armed with staves, pitchforks, spades, axes, etc. On the night of September 3 a threshing floor with all the harvest, belonging to a member of the kolkhoz, was destroyed by fire." [68] Thirty-nine persons were brought to trial for their participation in this affair. According to a special Information Bulletin of the Procurator of the Western Oblast for July-October 1929, "The most widespread means of struggle against kolkhoz construction (after its organization) is arson." [69] Numerous instances are cited where barns, haystacks, and houses belonging to kolkhozes were burned. Also listed as "very typical" are "cases of mass outbursts against the kolkhozes, primarily by women, under the leadership of kulaks and wealthy people." One such incident in the village of Golshino where a kolkhoz was being organized is described as follows:

> The local priest came out as an ardent oppositionist, carrying on open agitation among the women to resist the organization of the kolkhoz. On . . . the day designated for the division of land under the future kolkhoz, a crowd of women went to the fields, armed with axes, staves, and pitchforks, to beat the kolkhozniks. Meeting the surveyor and the secretary of the village soviet on the way, they began to insult them, tried to break the surveyor's instruments, and beat the secretary. Then they went on to the field and pulled out all the posts which bounded the kolkhoz. In the investigation of this case it was found that not enough mass work had been done by the local Party organs while the kolkhoz was being organized. The local priest occupied himself with "agitation work" . . . coming out openly against the closing of the church, and he went around to the peasants in their yards and summoned the women to demonstrate against the kolkhoz. Nobody from the volost Party and soviet organs knew about the agitation, for the organization of the kolkhoz had been entrusted to the surveyor . . ." [70]

The story of the first great collectivization drive (1929–30) as it unfolds in the Smolensk Archive is a record of "storm" tactics and stubborn peasant opposition, of grandiose projects and "paper" victories. The regime in many cases could not trust its local soviet functionaries to carry the brunt of the drive, and as a result workers were mobilized from the factories to organize the kolkhozes. The "25,000'ers," as they were called, did not find their task easy. Here is a letter which a group of them wrote to their responsible superior, one Comrade Stolbov:

> We workers have been sent to the Western Oblast, Voskresensk raion, Vyazma okrug, to work in the kolkhozes. But our living conditions do not permit us to work as we should. They have placed us in kolkhozes which have only been established a month or less. They sent us into leading work in kolkhozes where there were supposed to be funds, and they told us we would be paid out of the funds of the kolkhoz, but it didn't happen that way at all. They put most of us 16 people in such conditions in Voskresensk raion that we beg for help. They put us in kolkhozes with economies where there are no funds, where property has not yet been socialized, and we workers must be the organizers of the kolkhozes. Those of us who have arrived in the small kolkhozes are not given either money or food; they receive us worse than beggars. There are no living quarters . . .
>
> In view of all these conditions, the work is not progressing; we live and do not know what the future will bring, how and what we will eat. What they told us when they sent us to work in the country is not at all so; they said that we would work in kolkhozes and would receive up to 30–40 rubles per month, but we didn't even receive 5 rubles a month, and there is not even food, and we don't eat.
>
> The local organizations take a miserable attitude toward this and do not know themselves how we will eat and do not do anything about it.
>
> Under such conditions of life as we have described above, it is impossible

to work, and there is only one way out. To work longer is impossible, and to live in such circumstances is impossible; we must flee home, and then see what will happen. We ask the okrug committee of the Party to answer this and to tell us what to do.[71]

The Archive contains no response to this letter, but there is a subsequent record of a meeting of the secretariat of the Shuiski okrug committee (March 18, 1930) which noted the flight of "wavering" workers from the kolkhozes, denounced such action as "diversionism from the front of kolkhoz work," and at the same time ordered factory managers to continue wage payments to workers assigned to the kolkhozes and also directed the Consumers' Coöperative stores to supply such workers with first-category rations.[72] Presumably, some improvement in the situation of the 25,000'ers followed; at least, there is no further record of complaints in the Archive.

Meanwhile, those responsible for kolkhoz organization at the oblast level also faced problems. On September 12, 1929, one Finogin, of the Oblast Kolkhoz Union, addressed the following letter to Comrade Rakitov, then one of the obkom secretaries:

On July 12 the Oblast Kolkhoz Union began its existence, without workers, without office, without any equipment, and with the complex work of kolkhoz construction facing it.

From the first day of its existence it filed a petition for an office, even temporarily, of one or two rooms . . . but all this was to, no avail . . . In answer to my personal message to the Chairman of the Smolensk City Soviet and the Head of the City Communal Economy Department, they promised me a month ago to furnish me with an office now occupied by the Department of Labor. After the month was up, they promised a second time to provide an office within two days, but up to the present time they have done nothing . . . and there is no hope that I will obtain an office soon . . .[73]

After pointing out that "further procrastination" would "make it impossible to carry on any kind of serious work," Finogin begged Rakitov to intervene. The appeal was successful.

With its office problem finally resolved, the tribulations of the oblast kolkhoz union did not cease. A letter of January 23, 1930, from Novobytov, the chairman of the union, to Comrade Shurmanov of the oblast Party secretariat, conveys a lively sense of the bureaucratic toils in which the kolkhoz union found itself enmeshed:

Comrade Shurmanov, despite the fact that the Oblast Kolkhoz Union is understaffed and that 85% of its employees are working directly in the lower units . . . nevertheless the oblast organizations, beginning with the Oblast Land Administration, the Trade Division, and ending with the League of Militant Atheists, pull apart the representatives of the Kolkhoz Union at various types of gatherings, sessions, commissions, meetings, etc.

As a result it happens that the above organizations' workers fulfill their work, and that we serve "at their beck and call" and must administer and plan hastily, hurriedly, and because of that we do poor work and there are various mistakes.

I have cut down the running about of my representatives by 50%, but every day they assault my apparatus more and more and simply pull us into all kinds of urgent meetings.

The day begins with uninterrupted bombardment on the telephone and special requests on paper. "We ask you at 10 o'clock to send your 'responsible' representative to the Oblast Land Administration"; "at 10 o'clock you must also go to the Oblast Trade Division and at 12 — to the same place"; "immediately send . . . to the Oblast Planning Commission, to the Consumers' Co-operative"; "we are reorganizing, your representative is necessary"; "send a representative to the League of Militant Atheists"; "send a lecturer to the soviet-Party Schools"; "immediately choose an agronomist for the Oblast Department of Public Education to travel to the local units with the culture wagon"; "send an agronomist to travel to the local units to check on the course of the month for livestock breeding," etc., etc.

When you read all this, when you listen on the phone, you feel like screaming into telephone No. 16: "Help, they assault us, they pull us apart, they deprive us of our individuality . . . and don't let us work! "

Comrade Shurmanov, I am not speaking of those organizations where I myself must appear and do appear and will appear, and to which, when it is necessary, I send and will send my representatives, but to be transferred at their beck and call during such an important demanding period . . . as collectivization, . . . I cannot, nor can the apparatus, serve as representatives from morning till night, while business stands still . . .

Flying around from one meeting to another, we cannot even compose a preliminary summary of the course of the election campaign of the kolkhozes, of the preparatory spring sowing work; we cannot summarize the results of the collection of seed funds, of deposits for tractors, etc., etc. People don't want to understand this, and they pull us anywhere they wish . . .

Making you acquainted with the above, I ask you to help me to create more normal working conditions, on which the fulfillment of Party directives in the field of total collectivization depends.[74]

While the staff of the oblast kolkhoz union fought its bureaucratic battles with its sister organizations, developments in the okrugs and raions were pursuing their own hectic course. The reports of the oblast kolkhoz union provide eloquent testimony of "paper" victories and the chaotic character of the collectivization drive. In a letter of February 28, 1930, to Rumyantsev, Novobytov complained that the kolkhoz organizers "occupy themselves with inventions, fantasies, and obsessions . . . They do not organize on the basis of the November plenum of the Central Committee . . . but think up all kinds of things in the name of the toiling masses. Kolkhoz giants, kolkhoz combines, raion communes, and various other high-sounding names without content and without productivity." [75] He cited a number of examples:

1. Kunyansk raion, Velikiye Luki okrug — where a giant kolkhoz of 45,000 hectares was organized under an orgbureau created by the raion

executive committee. When the raion officials saw that "nothing would come of the giant, they decided to divide the raion into 32 squares, each with an area of 2,500 hectares and to mark the centers of the future kolkhozes according to the squares, frightening the peasants, and paying absolutely no attention to the initiative of the poor peasants and the middle peasants in the organization of the kolkhozes." [76]

2. Komarichesk raion, Bryansk okrug — "collectivizes all the toiling population into communes with a single Board of the Commune and appoints special heads (like the managers in the old days) — of large production sectors where there are no kolkhoz boards . . ."

3. Roslavl okrug — "Dubrovski Gigant on 15,000 hectares of pasture-land is divided into 8 large sectors, in which they created production committees with a single board over the entire 15,000 hectares, assigning members of the board to each sector (go and manage)."

These "paper" organizations into which the bewildered peasants were herded did not long survive. The center soon realized that "percentage victories" in the drive for total collectivization were being purchased at the price of a complete disruption of agricultural production. On March 2, 1930, Stalin himself condemned "the bureaucratic decreeing of a collective-farm movement from above, — the formation of collective farms on paper — of farms which do not yet exist, but regarding the 'existence' of which there is a pile of boastful resolutions." In Smolensk as elsewhere this pronouncement was interpreted as a signal that peasants could withdraw from the "paper" collectives, and a mass exodus followed. On March 1, 1930, 38.8 per cent of the hired-laborer, poor-peasant, and middle-peasant households in the Western Oblast were reported as collectivized. By April 15, 1930, the proportion had declined to 10.5 per cent.[77] The picture varied widely in the different okrugs as the following tabulation, showing the per cent of collectivized households in each okrug, indicates:

Velikiye Luki 8.3
Rzhev 5.6
Vyazma 7.5
Smolensk 19.3
Roslavl 9.3
Sukhinichy 4.6
Bryansk 14.3
Klintsy 10.0

The flight from the collectives accentuated the disorganization of the countryside. In the words of an oblast kolkhoz union report, "Some okrug workers were . . . taken aback, not knowing where to begin and how actually to approach the correction of mistakes," while "the kulak, perverting the decisions of the Central Committee, carried on anti-Soviet agitation; 'And so we said not to enter the kolkhozes'; . . . 'all those who were in the collectivization brigade are being put in prison,' etc., etc." But the leaders of the oblast kolkhoz union saw or pretended to see a brighter side to their predicament. In the words of the same report, ". . . this exodus is not coming from the really organized and formulated kolkhozes, but only from the kolkhozes existing on paper and those with exaggerated percentages, where mistakes were allowed. As a result, on April 15, there is a stable situation in regard to the real kolkhozes and kolkhozniks, who, consciously, voluntarily joined the kolkhozes and began to reconstruct the small-scale individual peasant economy on the basis of the collectivization of the country . . . The mood of the kolkhozniks is healthy and cheerful . . ." [78]

The evidence from other sources fails to support this judgment. A typical report dated February 1, 1931, from the first secretary of the Roslavl raikom and addressed to the obkom, paints a much gloomier picture.[79] The report complained of great shortages of seed and fertilizer in the newly organized kolkhozes. Individual peasants before entering the kolkhozes were selling or "destroying" their cattle. The kolkhozes were "already experiencing a sharp need for cattle feed (owing to 'careless administration')." Peasants were grumbling: "We shall not enter the kolkhoz until we slaughter our last cow. How stupid it was to call oneself a poor peasant — now we are expected [by the Bolsheviks] to be the first to enter the kolkhoz . . . the kolkhozniks do nothing. Food is rotting. We will all starve to death in the kolkhoz." Even certain village soviets were protesting collectivization. The secretary noted that kulaks in a number of cases were achieving "a quiet but effective penetration of the kolkhozes. They find in the kolkhozes the calmest refuge from dekulakization, individual taxation, etc. They spread rumors of the impending war, of the coming punishment to kolkhozniks and workers, etc." The secretary saw all these elements as contributing to "the flourishing of bad economy in the kolkhozes, to the absence of labor discipline, to 'anti-moral phenomena' like drunkenness, thievery, simulation, etc. This in turn is responsible for many kolkhozniks, even of long membership, leaving the collective farms." [80] Despite these difficulties, the collectivization drive was resumed during the spring of 1931 in accordance with a telegram of February 15, 1931, signed by Stalin and urging implementation of the "decisions of the Sixteenth Party Congress" with regard to an "intensification of the kolkhoz movement." [81] By April 21, 1931, 64.8 per cent of the households of Roslavl raion had been collectivized.[82] But criticism of the poor performance of the kolkhozes continued to be voiced and Party agitators appearing at meetings were treated to bitter complaints of sharp rises in food prices and inadequacies in the food supply.[83]

The 1932 Famine

The food situation continued to deteriorate during the year 1932, and the kolkhoz movement itself showed signs of disintegration. On July 5, 1932, Rumyantsev dispatched a top-secret letter to all raikoms instructing them how to deal with "cases where kolkhozes fall apart and kolkhoz property is illegally appropriated." [84] Rumyantsev first urged that every effort be made to hold the kolkhozes together by reviewing the complaints of kolkhozniks and punishing those who "caused the economic deterioration of the kolkhozes." Should part of the membership "of the failing kolkhoz manifest a desire to continue working collectively," *all* former kolkhoz land was to become the possession of the kolkhoz, while peasants not willing to return to the kolkhoz would lose the land which they had contributed to the kolkhoz and presumably be resettled on such surplus land of inferior quality as happened to be available in the district. If, despite this pressure, the kolkhoz members decided to disband, they were to be required to complete the harvesting and threshing of the grain collectively. The division of the harvest among the withdrawing kolkhozniks was only to take place after appropriate norms had been delivered to the state, norms based on the higher taxes and deliveries required of individual households. All debts of the kolkhoz to the state were to be distributed among the individual households as their own debt and were to be collected in ten days. The indivisible capital of the failing kolkhoz was to be appropriated by the district kolkhoz union for distribution to other kolkhozes. No property could be divided without the approval of the district kolkhoz union and the village soviet, and only after such approval was given could the peasants begin their spring sowing privately on land strips of the former kolkhoz.

Despite these drastic sanctions invoked against departing kolkhozniks, the flight from the kolkhozes continued. The year 1932 was a bitter one in Soviet agriculture, and the Smolensk area had more than its share of tribulations. The failure of the Western Oblast to fulfill its grain delivery plan from the 1931 harvest had stern repercussions. In the spring of 1932 the oblast Party authorities were informed that Moscow was counting *all* undelivered grain as part of the grain available for oblast consumption, and that the supply of grain from the centralized funds would be substantially curtailed during the second quarter of 1932.[85] On March 23, 1932, the raikom secretaries were warned that the cuts threatened the supply even of basic factories and of units of the Red Army, and that the raion authorities would be left largely to their own devices in meeting local needs.[86] The situation became increasingly critical, and on June 14, 1932, Rakitov informed the raions by telegram that supplies even for basic industries would be exhausted by July 1, that no reserves were left to meet July commitments, and that no imports from other oblasts would be available.[87] Despite the critical situation in the countryside, sizable additional emergency grain-delivery quotas were imposed on each raion in a desperate effort to meet the problem of feeding the urban centers. In order to conserve and protect dwindling bread reserves, special troikas, composed of the raikom secretary, the RIK chairman, and the OGPU chief, were established in twenty-five raions where the situation was deemed "extremely dangerous." [88] In other raions the raikom secretary was made personally responsible for the preservation and distribution of the bread fund. Special controllers were assigned to watch over the milling, baking, and selling of bread, and the OGPU and procuracy were instructed to take drastic measures against pilferers.

Meanwhile, preparations for grain deliveries from the 1932 harvest proceeded apace. A secret Central Committee decree of July 7, 1932, outlined the organizational measures the republics and oblasts were expected to take.[89] The localities were warned against assessing quotas mechanically and were especially enjoined to take into account "the peculiarities of each raion, each kolkhoz, and each village," making certain that kolkhozes which were most successful in fulfilling their plans would be rewarded by having "correspondingly large amounts of grain for their own needs." At the same time an addition of 4 to 5 per cent was to be added to the plan of each raion "as insurance — in order to make it possible to cover the unavoidable mistakes in accounting and to fulfill the plan itself *no matter how.*" The decree continued, "The plan by raions should be drawn up with the obligatory participation of raikom secretaries and chairmen of raion executive committees, and the plan should be brought to the kolkhozes, and in regard to individual farmers, to the village with the participation of kolkhoz chairmen and chairmen of village soviets. The village soviets should exercise daily supervision over the fulfillment of the plan for grain deliveries throughout the whole village, both in regard to individual farmers and kolkhozes." In order to hold out greater inducements to the peasants to meet their delivery quotas, the Central Committee promised that consumers' goods "of extensive use" (cotton fabrics, threads, shawls, shoes, galoshes, etc.) would be made available to the countryside for the third quarter "in a ruble amount double the value of the amounts delivered in the preceding year . . ." At the same time the local authorities were enjoined to engage "in the most resolute struggle" to prevent the grain deliveries from falling into the hands of speculators. To help enforce this injunction, the obkom and oblispolkom ordered militia and OGPU units in the raions to prevent all sale of bread in bazaars until the peasants had fulfilled their state-delivery obligations.[90]

Despite these commands from above, the food shortage continued to be acute.[91] There were many reports of kolkhozes falling apart and kolkhozniks abandoning the kolkhozes. There were even more numerous reports of widespread pilfering of kolkhoz property and crops both by kolkhozniks and those entrusted with the management of the kolkhozes. Even the publication of the drastic governmental decree of August 7, 1932, with its proviso that embezzlement and robbery of kolkhoz and cooperative property would be subject to a maximum penalty of death by shooting and a minimum penalty of not less than ten years' imprisonment, failed to put an end to the thievery. By mid-1932 the food situation bordered on desperation. While the Archive contains no data on deaths attributable to the famine of 1932, some extracts from OGPU reports on conversations of kolkhozniks convey the temper of the period. A former poor peasant was quoted as saying (June 9, 1932): "What kind of life has this become? You work and work and there is nothing. Soon we will not even be able to drag our legs. It is necessary to go somewhere in production and save yourself from starving to death." [92] A former middle peasant commented: "This has become not life, but hell, there is no bread and such things." [93]

Even local Party officials began to echo the moods of the peasants. Thus, on August 8, 1932, Svyatchenko, the deputy secretary of the Krasnyi raikom, sent a desperate appeal to the obkom of the Western Oblast. Reporting on departures from the kolkhozes and "unhealthy attitudes" among the kolkhozniks because of "lack of bread," he wrote:

Today in the raion organizations . . . a number of demands came in from the boards of kolkhozes, the secretaries of Party cells, and also delegations of kolkhozniks themselves insisting on immediate extension of aid in bread. There are no insurance funds in the local units. The only source . . . from which it would be possible to take some grain to give help is the fee for grinding grain, but this may not be distributed.

In our opinion for the very minimum satisfaction of the needs of the kolkhozniks, 700–800 puds are NOW necessary. I beg you immediately to decide the problem of giving aid in grain, for failure to give this aid very soon may cause a number of undesirable consequences and situations.[94]

A Party member (a labor inspector by occupation), participating in the grain delivery campaign, was reported by the OGPU as saying: "Here they commandeer me into the Bukinsk village soviet for deliveries. If I were alone without a family I would shoot somebody, and then I would shoot myself. I haven't a *funt* of grain at home. I leave my family, and I myself have to go off to the raion for deliveries. What next? Things become worse and worse all the time, and now they demand the return of the seed loan from the kolkhozes, and in the spring there won't be anything to seed with. The kolkhozniks are now bringing bread to the market, but surely they themselves won't have anything to eat." [95]

As the supply problem became increasingly critical, employees in the towns were stricken from the ration lists and forced to fend for themselves on the free market. Their conversations as reported by the OGPU registered panic and bitter disillusionment.[96] A foreman of a blacksmith shop is quoted: "Today at the market they sold bread at 65 rubles [per pud]." Swearing at the top of his voice at Stalin and Kalinin, he continued, "They have finally robbed us. Their heads are dizzy with success. They do not mention the fact that the workers and employees, after they are removed from supply, come out so that they receive not 100 rubles per month, but 2 rubles." A veterinarian is reported as saying, "Yesterday on August 7 for a pud of rye flour they were asking 60 rubles, for a pud of potatoes 20 rubles — how can we poorly paid employees live from the market . . ." A hospital employee said, "If the employees of the hospital are not given flour by the coöperative, then all will submit notice that they are leaving, because none of them is able to buy bread on the market, which costs 60 rubles per pud, while the nurses receive a pay of only 40–50 rubles per month, and a physician receives 400 rubles a month, and they issue him a ration."

OGPU and Party records for the year 1932 are filled with similar complaints. Despite intense pressure from above, the grain delivery campaign of 1932 yielded worse results than that of the preceding year.[97] The food crisis in the oblast reached a climax of desperation during the bitter winter of 1932–33.

The Turning Point

The 1933 harvest marked a turning point. Perhaps the most notable step in placating discontent in the kolkhozes was the central decree of January 19, 1933, revising the procurement system to provide for fixed deliveries to the state based on acreage planted instead of the largely arbitrary quotas which had previously been assessed in the guise of "contracts." The new system provided inducements to increase production since the obligations to the state were definite and any surplus the kolkhoz accumulated could be distributed to the members in proportion to the workdays which they earned. This concession to the self-interest of the collective farmers provided an incentive to work in the kolkhoz which had previously been lacking, and its effects soon became apparent.

Soon thereafter the central leadership itself ordered that "the center of gravity" of work in the villages turn from "mass repression" to "mass political and organizational work." In a dramatic secret circular of May 8, 1933, signed by Stalin and Molotov and distributed to all Party and soviet officials and all organs of the OGPU, the courts, and the procuracy, orders went out that mass deportations and indiscriminate arrests "be immediately stopped." [98] Henceforth, said the circular, "deportation may be permitted only on a partial and individual basis and only with regard to those households whose heads are carrying on an active struggle against collective farms and are organizing resistance to sowing and state purchasing of grain." Maximum deportation quotas which could not be exceeded were assigned to a number of regions, including the Western Oblast whose quota was 500 households. Among other provisions, the circular called for the prohibition of all arrests by unauthorized persons and forbade pre-trial imprisonment for "insignificant crimes." This circular too was not without its effect in the countryside. By signaling, at least temporarily, the end of mass repressions and indiscriminate arrests, it struck a note of reassurance which contributed to the stabilization of the collective farm government.

Helped by a good harvest, grain collections mounted and the kolkhozes began to take on life. In a speech before chairmen of leading village soviets of the Western Oblast on September 5, 1933, Kalinin boasted that ". . . up to September 1 of this year . . . we have collected about three times as much as in 1932. In all previous years, during these months we collected incomparably less grain than we have this year." [99] The collectivization percentages again began to increase. While figures for the Western Oblast as a whole are not available in the Archive, the percentages in the Smolensk district reveal the trend. On December 15, 1932, 60.6 per cent of all peasant households were collectivized. By July 1, 1934, the collectivization ratio had increased to 66.2 per cent; by December 15, 1934, it mounted to 77.8 per cent.[100]

But as late as mid-1934 there were still large numbers of individual peasants who remained unregenerate despite the heavy penalties imposed on them for maintaining their individual status. In the district of Belyi, for example, over 40 per cent of the sown area was still occupied by individual households.[101] When interrogated about their reasons for not joining the kolkhozes, many responded as follows: "I hate this system — it is slavery"; "I do not want to go into the kolkhoz and I will not go — I do not like the kolkhozes"; "I want to be a home owner and not subject to any one"; "It is harder to live in the kolkhoz; it is better to live as an individual, especially on an individual farm"; "We are not being forced yet, and I won't go into the kolkhoz until such time as it is impossible to live independently." [102]

These reported responses have a ring of authenticity, but they represented the stubbornly proclaimed views of a dwindling band. As the economic pressure on the individual peasants intensified, more and more of them were forced to seek refuge in the collectives. How they felt we may guess, but so far as the Party records go, they become mere digits recording the steady triumph of collectivization in percentage terms.

13 Life on the Kolkhozes — Some Extracts

from Reports

During the period covered by the Smolensk Archive (up to 1938–39) the kolkhoz movement was still in the early stages of consolidation. If the picture of kolkhoz life that emerges from the Archive is an especially dark one, it should be remembered that the initial difficulties which attend any extensive organizational innovation were compounded in this case by widespread peasant distrust and antagonism, by a desperate shortage of trained and trustworthy managerial personnel, and by the grim determination of the regime to use the kolkhozes as an instrument of primitive capital accumulation to finance the industrialization drive.

Abuses and Inefficiency

It is difficult to exaggerate the chaotic confusion of the early kolkhoz days. The OGPU reports from the raions strike an almost monotonously repetitious note of total disorganization and inefficiency. Here are some examples from the year 1932.

In the kolkhoz "Stalin," Markovsk village soviet, Krasnyi raion, which includes more than 40 households, there exists the most complete negligence. Some members of the board of the kolkhoz systematically engage in drinking and abuses . . . The chairman of the board . . . a former middle peasant, systematically gets drunk and does not guide the work of the kolkhoz at all . . . about 20 hectares of oats lie cut down, which, as a result of the fact that they were not harvested, almost completely rotted . . . There remained unmowed 1½ hectares of oats, which were completely spoiled. The winter wheat, which was mowed on time, remained lying in the fields, thanks to which it rotted. Almost all the pulled flax is still lying in the field and is rotting, as a result of which the flaxseed is almost completely ruined. There are about 100 hectares of as yet unmown meadows, while the socialized livestock in the kolkhoz are not supplied with fodder for the winter, and according to calculations [feed] is about 4,000 puds short. With the funds of the kolkhoz 4 former kulak homes were bought for the reconstruction of a cattle yard which the kolkhoz greatly needed, but these buildings are being pilfered by the kolkhozniks and burned as firewood. The equipment and harnesses of the kolkhoz are not repaired on time, as a result of which future use has been made impossible . , , Up to the present time no income has been earned by the kolkhoz. At present, as a result of mismanagement and abuses on the part of the board of the kolkhoz, certain kolkhozniks . . . talk of leaving . . .[1]

Describing another kolkhoz in the same raion, the OGPU noted many similar abuses and a complete absence of labor accounting. The grumblings of former middle peasant members of the kolkhoz were reported as follows:

> How can you live in such a kolkhoz? Without fail it is necessary to leave. If they issue to the kolkhoz any premium funds from the village store, the board of the kolkhoz receives them, and they issue nothing to the kolkhoznik. We know how last year the chairman of the kolkhoz in return for kolkhoz honey received yard goods from the store and didn't even show them to the kolkhozniks . . . Before entrance into the kolkhoz our representatives said to us: Comrades, you have had enough of working in your individual households day and night; it is time to lighten your labor; you must go into the kolkhoz. In the kolkhoz you will work very little and will receive a great deal. But things turned out the opposite. We work day and night, have nothing, only one cow remains, and from that we have to give milk without receiving payment, and we paid less agricultural taxes in our individual households than in the kolkhoz.[2]

The "negative" attitudes of the kolkhozniks are frankly and vividly portrayed in the OGPU reports. A member of the kolkhoz "Proletarsky Put" (Proletarian Path) was overheard describing his plight as follows:

> In the present year in the kolkhoz the rye was poor; you get 0.5 kilograms per workday, which is an average of 10 puds per family . . . You cannot buy, because a pud of rye on the market costs up to 100 rubles; there is nothing to sell; probably I and others will have to perish from hunger. I will have grain for five months, and the rest of the time I will have to sit without grain; and how I'll live this year I can't imagine. Such a situation in regard to grain exists not only with me, but also with many other kolkhozniks; if we only survive this year, it means that the kolkhozes will remain; and if we do not survive, famine will begin, and the entire Soviet government will perish from hunger.

The business manager of the kolkhoz "Kommunar" moaned:

> What will we do? The rye in the kolkhoz this year has been threshed extremely poorly; the wheat also; the kolkhoznik will get for one workday not more than 1½ funt of rye, and out of this nothing will come. We will never have a good harvest if we sow flax; the whole land is being laid waste. There will never be grain in the kolkhoz; the kolkhozniks will work, and there will be nothing to eat. We will have to leave soon and go to work in industry. My soul aches when I see all this.

And a middle peasant in the kolkhoz "Krasnoye Znamya" (Red Flag) added still another despairing note:

> This year it will be very bad to live in the kolkhoz; by spring there will be no grain for the majority of the kolkhozniks, and if in the future we sow according to such plans, we will perish from hunger. If the leaders would not

give us plans, but would sow according to our plans, from experience, then things would be better; we have sown a great deal, but there is no grain and will be none. Even the grass under the rye and flax, of which there was a great deal, the board of the kolkhoz does not permit us to cut for our cows, and they themselves do not cut it. And it will turn out that the kolkhoz-nik will have nothing with which to feed his cow.[3]

Still another kolkhoznik asked:

Why are we living with our kolkhozes? The Ukraine is hungry. I went to Leningrad, and the Ukrainians come there for bread. There is no end to it, and they say that in the Ukraine they have no bread. And we in the kolkhoz also have no bread, and we will not have it, because they do not permit us to sow what we need and they give us more flax [to sow]. The working of the land is poor; they plow once and usually not on time. The working force in the village is resettling in the cities, in industrial centers, because in the kolkhoz it is not profitable to work. We work all year, and you don't know what you'll get. Things turned out badly — flax yields a loss to the kolkhozes — since payment for flax fiber is very low in comparison with those goods which are supplied by industry. Therefore I think that we are treading a definite path toward general hunger. In the entire Soviet Union according to the present situation of the kolkhozes hunger is unavoidable.[4]

The chairman of a kolkhoz in the village of Rechitsa, reaching out for an explanation, asked:

What does this mean? Industry is working at full capacity . . . but there are no products anywhere . . . What has become of light industry? I think that all this goes abroad, not one country makes a treaty without fleecing us . . . What's happened to our good things? . . . You make things and you make things, and then you give them up, and we ourselves walk barefoot and naked. As the Bolsheviks say, we are waiting for the revolution in capitalist countries. Surely we'll die while we're waiting for the revolution. We sow so much flax, but we don't see any manufactured linen. Everything must be going abroad, and the capitalists are strangling us by peaceful means, while the Bolsheviks, holding on to power, give up everything and force the Russian people to be tortured, and, as is apparent, they will hold on to this position until a general famine comes everywhere.

"And," the OGPU reported, "the members of the kolkhoz who were present agreed with him." [5]

Yet despite widespread hunger and mass flights from the kolkhozes to the new industrial centers, the kolkhoz movement somehow survived the bitter winter and spring of 1932–33, and the forced enrollment of the peasants in the kolkhozes was intensified. Here and there, moreover, a kolkhoz which was favored by a combination of fertile land, efficient management, and relatively good morale among the kolkhozniks managed to achieve a relatively high level of productivity, and was held up as a model to be admired and imitated by its less fortunate neighbors. But in the Western Oblast, at least, such models were usually few and far between, and the instances mentioned in the Archive are not brilliantly impressive. As a sample of an outstanding kolkhoz, for example, the Belyi raikom in 1934 cited the kolkhoz "Putevaya Zvezda." Its accomplishments were reported to the obkom agricultural division as follows:

This kolkhoz was organized in 1928 and up to 1932 it was one of the weak kolkhozes; always and everywhere it was pointed to as a very poor example . . . In 1932 the kolkhoz was strengthened with good leaders, and the situation improved. Correct eight-field crop rotation was introduced; the organization of labor was exemplary; all work was done and is now done on the basis of exact calculations, according to plan; calendar plans have been introduced as a system for every period. At the present time the economy of the kolkhoz [includes] 58 households. The sown area is 281 hectares, including 50 hectares of flax, which is 17.8% of the total sown area. There are 115 kolkhozniks able to work, who completely manage the work. There are 63 work horses, and for each horse there are 4.46 hectares of sown area, which is a realizable assignment. Sown grasses constitute 19% of the total sown area. Of the fertilizers, the kolkhoz uses only cow manure, 30 tons per hectare . . . The yield in rye is 13 centners and in oats 10 centners . . . There is a dairy farm of 112 head . . . The farm is supplied with a good cattle yard, built according to proper technical standards. The cattle are correctly cared for zootechnically, and the feeding takes place according to established norms. The milk yield of the cows is from 16 to 25 centners. The kolkhoz is sufficiently mechanized. It has a 25-horsepower steam engine, a mill, a threshing machine, a flax brake, 7 mowing machines, 4 harvesters, and 2 seeders. In the kolkhoz there is a primary Party organization which guides kolkhoz production quite well. Mass political work among the kolkhozniks is satisfactory . . . The wall newspaper is published regularly. Last year the kolkhozniks received 2.4 kilograms of grain per workday . . .[6]

The same Belyi Party report also cited the example of a so-called "weak" kolkhoz. (It should perhaps be added that half of the twenty-two kolkhozes of the raion were so classified.) This kolkhoz was organized in 1930 from among former hired laborers and "people who lived individually." According to the raikom report:

There was a total of 20 households in the kolkhoz. In the years 1930–31 poor management reigned in the kolkhoz, complete equalization; no account of labor was kept, and they did not keep a list of products given out . . . The property and livestock of the liquidated kulaks were transferred to the kolkhoz . . . This property was divided mainly among members of the board; the livestock was slaughtered for meat, and no one was responsible for this, since the leadership changed every month without the knowledge of either the raion organization or even of the village soviet. The raion organization supervised this kolkhoz very poorly. The state credits which were released went into the pockets of the swindler board members . . . The formerly excellent arable lands were neglected . . . More exactly, 25–30% of the arable land lies fallow. Crop rotation has not been introduced. The yield of the kolkhoz is low — rye, 7.8 centners; oats, 4.3 centners; flax-fiber, 1 centner; and potatoes, 8 centners . . . The absence of proper supervision on the part of the village soviet and the raion organizations and the presence within the kolkhoz of a criminal and alien element has made it possible for this element not only to pursue its line but to penetrate into the leadership [of the kolkhoz] . . . The aktiv of the kolkhoz has few members and is not organized. Losses and mismanagement are common phenomena in the kolkhoz. In 1933 the kolkhoz suffered losses in the harvesting of flax; more than 300 puds of flax rotted and lost its ability to produce seeds; 30 hectares of good hayfields remained unharvested . . . The raikom of the Party still has not corrected the situation in the kolkhoz, which has been in the making over a period of years. Great daily work is needed to remold the psychology of the people, to fight against idlers, to struggle against and isolate backward elements.[7]

Similar examples of kolkhoz maladministration can be cited from the Archive almost without end. And try as it might, the regime encountered the greatest difficulty in stamping them out. The problem was too complex to be resolved either by exhortation or repression. The members of the kolkhoz were, in a sense, reluctant prisoners who contributed their labor unwillingly and had little incentive to do more. The managers of the kolkhoz were generally poorly trained to discharge their responsibilities, sometimes not unsympathetic with the plight of the kolkhozniks, but at the same time under constant pressure from higher authorities to meet the delivery quotas which were imposed on them. In this setting all types of irregularities flourished: stealing by the kolkhozniks to supplement their meager earnings, exploitation of the kolkhozes by corrupt managers, and efforts to conceal failures of performance and abuses in the kolkhoz through the bribery of higher governmental and Party officials. In the words of a former kolkhoz chairman, "The over-all picture . . . was one in which illegalities and infractions of discipline were the rule rather than the exception; in which high officials tried to squeeze as much as possible out of the kolkhozes, both for the state and for themselves; in which the peasants tried to give up as little as possible, in terms both of effort and of goods; and in which people like the kolkhoz chairman were pushed to the limit of their ingenuity to strike some sort of balance between the two."[8]

Problems of Management

The pressures under which kolkhoz chairmen operated were fairly uniform, but the response to these pressures varied with the character, personality, and managerial skill of the chairman. Sometimes, though not often, the kolkhoz chairman sought to ingratiate himself with the kolkhoz members by taking an easy-going attitude in the enforcement of work norms. The Krasnyi raion OGPU chief reported a case on May 2, 1932 where the chairman, before leading the kolkhozniks out to the field for plowing, said: "Let us go out for show for about two hours, report to the raion that we worked, and then let us split up and go home."[9] Before the Easter week holiday of Radonitsa, he was reported as saying: "Let us work a little on Tuesday before supper, and then let us celebrate a little." [10] The OGPU chief reported indignantly that under such leadership "the kolkhoz will be ruined," and he urged strongly that the chairman be removed from work and brought to criminal responsibility.

The easy-going kolkhoz chairman, however, was a fairly unusual and ordinarily not a long-lasting type. The more normal case reported in the Archive ran in an opposite direction — the chairman who was hard driving and hard drinking, blustering and threatening, frequently abusive and foul of mouth. Sometimes the behavior of kolkhoz chairmen approached such extremes of indignity that the kolkhozniks were moved to protest, and the obkom itself intervened. One such case reported in the Archive involved the chairman of the "Drug Detei" (Friend of Children) kolkhoz, a rather incongruous appellation in view of the circumstances. The NKVD report on this chairman reads in part as follows: "On September 11, this year [1936], at 6 to 7 P.M., Volkov, coming to the house of the brigade leader Smolov . . . called Smolov out into the street and asked him why his brigade did not go out to work at night." As Smolov began his explanation,

Volkov flew into a rage and began right on the street to beat Smolov. The latter raised a row and began to shout to the whole kolkhoz. This is the behavior of Volkov, and all the kolkhozniks saw it . . . In the middle of May, this year, he also beat the kolkhoznik Kuprin, only because the latter tore some newspaper which Volkov had in order to roll a cigarette . . . In the same month he ran after the guard of the cattle yard with a revolver only because the latter had fallen asleep . . . On April 20 this year Volkov summoned into the office of the kolkhoz the kolkhoznitsa Kotova, 60 years old, whose son died in the Far Eastern krai where he was mobilized for construction work. On January 9, 1936, she had 400 workdays . . . And because Kotova did not go to work for one day because of illness, Volkov began to swear at Kotova with the most outrageous words, saying, "I will expel you from the kolkhoz; I'll send you to Jericho"; in a word he brought the woman to complete hysterics. The same sort of thing happened with the kolkhoznitsa Mavra Zhukova. The latter ran away to choke herself, but her relatives saw her, and did not allow her to commit suicide. The same situation with the pregnant kolkhoz woman, Filkina . . . and almost all the kolkhoz women. All these hooligan actions took place while he was drunk . . .[11]

It should be added that the charges against Volkov were not confined to abusive treatment of kolkhozniks; he was also involved in large-scale embezzlement of kolkhoz funds. In any case, on recommendation of the raikom, he was removed as chairman of the kolkhoz and expelled from the Party.

The Family Circle

Management had its perquisites, illegal and quasi-legal, and many kolkhoz chairmen sought to protect them from exposure by installing their own clique in strategic positions in the kolkhoz, by absorbing the chairman of the village soviet, the store manager, and other leading village personalities into a common network of shared privileges, and by bribing the relevant raion officials where possible to keep quiet. Sometimes the ruling clique was literally a close-knit family group. The OGPU chief of Krasnyi raion reported the existence of a kolkhoz in 1932 near the village of Vasinichi where the wife was chairman of the kolkhoz, the husband the accountant, and the father the business manager. This kolkhoz, according to the OGPU, became a refuge for kulaks and speculators; nothing was in fact collectivized, and nothing delivered to the state. The OGPU report implied that "proper measures" were being taken to "purify" it.[12]

Nor was this case an isolated exception. As late as 1935 a Komsomol rural correspondent from Dorogobuzh raion called the attention of *Krestyanskaya Gazeta* (Peasants' Gazette) to a kolkhoz (named after Voroshilov) in which the son of the chairman was the accountant, the wife the milkmaid, the mother the receiver of milk, and the father the guard of the kolkhoz.[13] Among them they apparently engaged in large-scale embezzlement of kolkhoz property, and when individual kolkhoz-niks, including the correspondent, objected, the latter were simply ousted from the kolkhoz. Appeals were taken to the raion procurator, but with no results. It was not until the oblast procurator became interested in the situation that an investigation was made and the kolkhoz chairman removed.

In most cases, however, the clique which dominated the kolkhoz was a family circle in a figurative rather than a literal sense — drinking companions and friends who occupied leading positions in the kolkhoz and supported and protected each other in covering up irregularities of various types. A not atypical case is revealed in a letter dated September 17, 1936, from a kolkhoznik from Yelnya raion to the Agricultural Department of the Central Committee of the Party. The letter read:

This is the third year of the existence of the kolkhoz "Krasnaya Gorka," but there have been no achievements in economic growth. The kolkhoz lags behind in all campaigns, dragging out a miserable existence. The fact is that in the leadership there are dishonest people, embezzlers of kolkhoz property. Thus, at the beginning the chairman was Grigori Arkhipov, class alien, a church elder. During the year of his leadership he showed himself a wrecker, an out-and-out drunkard, a breaker of the law . . . The new chairman of the kolkhoz, Yakov Avernin, is even worse. Out of the harvest of 1934 he set aside around 30 centners of seed oats (not debited) in the storehouse and kept this for his own use. And in the winter Avernin took these oats to the city and squandered them, drank up the money with friends — board members. He distributes kolkhoz funds at will, violating the kolkhoz budget. The kolkhozniks do not even know where the funds go; the accounts are confused. Avernin especially likes monetary operations with private traders, from whom he presents fictitious bills for a sum which he desires; the treasurer usually pays them; the accountant signs it and puts it on the books. And such checks are for hundreds of rubles. He chose illiterate people for the revisory commission [to check kolkhoz accounts], who often themselves are participants in glaring disorders. Not satisfied with this, Avernin placed as storekeeper his own man, Kunin, who was previously sentenced for hooliganism and with whom he keeps on warm terms. In order to avoid a shortage, he placed in the storehouse old unstamped scales which show monstrous discrepancies . . . He squandered much kolkhoz hay, and left the kolkhoz cows without fodder . . . He treats the kolkhozniks roughly, in a haughty manner. If one of the kolkhozniks calls attention to something, he orders him to keep quiet, calls him an agitator and threatens him with expulsion from the kolkhoz within 24 hours, "as a class enemy." At the meeting he is always drunk, swears at the kolkhozniks, and threatens them. I . . . once warned the Yelnya raion Party organization . . . of [these] abuses, but there was complete silence. Apparently they were occupied with more important matters. The chairman of the village soviet, Chizhikov, knows all about this, but he too displays a strange silence, considering this completely normal. It is time finally to rehabilitate the kolkhoz and to place it on the path toward a happy prosperous life.[14]

Whether a happy life was forthcoming the Smolensk Archive does not record, but as a result of the letter the director of the neighboring MTS was instructed to put the affairs of the kolkhoz in order.[15]

Another letter sent to Shilman, second secretary of the obkom, by a group of kolkhozniks points to the nature of the protection which the ruling clique in a kolkhoz was sometimes able to invoke. The letter began, "You are the head of our kolkhoz, which bears your name, the Shilman kolkhoz. The kolkhoz is essentially good and the kolkhozniks industrious. The kolkhoz is large, has 117 households, but the chairman of the kolkhoz himself, Comrade Pyalov, Party member, behaves very badly, has become addicted to alcoholism, is not sober one day, gets drunk to the point where he remembers nothing . . . On September 20 [1936] there was a general meeting in order to explain the new Constitution. The secretary of the raikom, Khoklov, attended the meeting; there were many people who spoke. The meeting ended, and then came drinking of wine." [16] The letter proceeded to describe how the raikom secretary, the chairman of the village soviet, and the chairman and leading members of the kolkhoz engaged in a prolonged drinking bout that ended in a fight in which several brigade leaders were severely beaten. It also described various financial irregularities in which the chairman was involved. "If a kolkhoznik tells Pyalov the truth," the letter continued, "he answers: 'I am the master, I do what I want; I understand you very little; but if you wish, go to Shilman or Rumyantsev, but the raion will do nothing to me; they are friends of mine; they have all been bribed.' " After providing particulars on a bribe given to the raion senior agronomist of "8 puds of cabbage and half a piglet weighing 19 kilograms" and detailing other abnormalities in the life of the kolkhoz, the letter concluded: "We, the kolkhozniks of the Shilman kolkhoz, beg Comrade Shilman to send from the oblast your own people for an inspection. Your people will find and will learn everything which is involved . . . We beg you not to make this notice known to anyone. It is secret . . ." [17] In this case an obkom instructor was sent to the spot and verified the complaints of the kolkhozniks. The raikom secretary Khoklov was instructed "to take the necessary measures to eliminate these shortcomings." What measures he took the Archive does not indicate.

The Search for Efficient Chairmen

The difficulty of finding reliable and efficient kolkhoz chairmen is emphasized over and over again in the Archive. In one perhaps extreme case, aired in a letter dated February 1, 1935, from the kolkhozniks of the kolkhoz "Batrak" to the oblast newspaper *Rabochii Put* (Worker's Path), there was a parade of five chairmen in a period of four years. The letter described a succession of three chairmen as follows: "Comrade Kireyev, sent by the raikom of the Party as chairman of the kolkhoz, was not suitable for this appointment. Under him there were many robberies . . . After this the raikom of the Party sent Comrade Komarovsky into the kolkhoz, who during one month wasted 300 rubles. After Komarovsky they sent Comrade Filatov to strengthen the kolkhoz. He sold kolkhoz grain . . . 150 kilograms of rye, and 690 kilograms of oats. This case was discovered by the procuracy; the facts were confirmed. Filatov . . . began to engage in drinking, card playing, and fighting. In the apartment of the kolkhoznik Bodokin he knocked the glass out of the windows. In justification of his action he said: 'I am a partisan and will not be punished for this case.' The raikom of the Party should send into the country well investigated people for leading positions in the kolkhozes." [18] *Rabochii Put* dispatched this letter to the Sukhinichy raikom, which replied, "the facts . . . in your note . . . were confirmed. The chairman of the kolkhoz, Filatov, for all these disorders . . . was expelled from the Party, and those guilty are being brought to criminal responsibility." [19]

Since good kolkhoz chairmen were scarce, some raikom secretaries were prepared to go to great lengths to hold on to those who produced results, even to the extent of overlooking irregularities in their behavior. The following letter dated October 21, 1936, from Demenok, the secretary of the Kozelsk raikom, to Andrianov, chairman of the oblast court, is revealing in this respect.

By the decision of the people's court of Kozelsk raion the chairman of
the kolkhoz "Bolshevik" . . . Filipp Aldonin was sentenced to 2 years' imprisonment for embezzling from the kolkhoz and for attempting to seduce two
kolkhoz women. I ask you to review carefully the accusations made against
Aldonin.

1. Aldonin in social rank is a poor peasant, a non-Party man, who since
1930 . . . has worked as a kolkhoz chairman. At the present time he works as
chairman of the kolkhoz "Bolshevik." The kolkhoz this year did all its work
well. It fulfilled on time all its obligations to the state — bread, potatoes, and
flax — and was among the advanced kolkhozes. It harvested 15.5 centners of
wheat, 11 centners of rye, etc. In every respect it was good under this
year's conditions. The kolkhozniks were well provided with bread, potatoes,
etc. The kolkhoz is really becoming stronger and it is on the correct path of
its socialist development.

2. His mistakes. Aldonin, after being transferred to the chairmanship of
another kolkhoz, "Iskra," under the influence of hard material conditions embezzled from the kolkhoz about 200 rubles. He was absolutely obliged to
return the money. But it is necessary to consider that he had not received
from this kolkhoz the products which he had earned, neither bread nor potatoes. But of course he behaved incorrectly in regard to his expenditures.

3. In regard to attempts to seduce the kolkhoznitsa Anna Zenina, former
brigade worker. We checked this matter in the raikom in March 1935 . . .
and there is no basis for accusing Aldonin of such attempts . . .

4. Considering that Aldonin has worked 6 years as chairman of a kolkhoz,
and moreover that the kolkhoz where he works as chairman is an advanced
strong kolkhoz, has a rather good yield, and honestly fulfills all its obligations,
I ask you, in reviewing the case, to make a more careful study of the accusations which were made.[20]

Again, the Archive provides no indication of what actually happened to
Aldonin, but the strong intervention of a raikom secretary in his behalf
testifies to the extent to which successful kolkhoz chairmen were prized.

In 1936 the Party and government decreed the promotion of women
to leading work in the kolkhozes. Behind this decree lay more than an
appreciation of woman's new role in Soviet life. Industrialization was
emptying the kolkhozes of men in the prime of life, and women were
being called upon in increasing numbers to fill the gap. The promotion
of women to the post of kolkhoz chairman while men still remained
in the kolkhozes was not without its accompanying tensions and problems. Some of them are portrayed in a vivid letter from a recently promoted woman kolkhoz chairman to Rumyantsev, the obkom first secretary.

At the beginning [she wrote] all the kolkhozniks helped me, but this help
did not last long. When the chairman of the village soviet, Comrade Kommissarova, returned from her studies there was no help, but only disruption.
Why did this happen? It happened only because the father and brothers of
Kommissarova are in our kolkhoz. The older brother, Comrade Mishin, on her

request was sent to study at the Vyazma soviet-Party School so that he could become chairman of our kolkhoz, but the raion committee of the Party did not allow him to be the chairman of our kolkhoz, but sent him to another kolkhoz, which position Mishin categorically refused, and from that time both the village soviet and Comrade Mishin began to badger me. In order to gain the leadership of the kolkhoz, Comrade Mishin did disruptive work during the entire summer. He seized upon the least little thing that I did and immediately criticized me, badgered the kolkhozniks, saying why would they summon a woman as chairman of the kolkhoz when there is no lack of men among us . . . But I, Ye. Appollonova, did not lose heart; I learned from my mistakes and now have corrected them, waging an irreconcilable struggle for the fulfillment of Stalinist rules. Comrade Mishin, seeing my irreconcilable staunchness in the leadership of the kolkhoz and seeing that propaganda among the kolkhozniks did not cause the kolkhozniks to eliminate me from leadership, and feeling his own helplessness, began to prepare a terrorist act. And on October 28 of this year [1936], bringing the terrorist act to fruition, he persuaded the kolkhoz storeman to go for wood without the permission of the brigade leader, despite the fact that it was a period of heavy work — digging the potatoes and threshing the rye. When the brigade leader noticed that the horses were being taken without permission, I went to Comrade Mishin and asked him to postpone today's journey, but Comrade Mishin galloped up to me and began to beat me, mumbling: "I have waited a long time for the proper moment to make short work of you." All the kolkhozniks were indignant at the behavior of Comrade Mishin. The chief of the raion militia came to investigate the case. The inquiry went full course, and I expected that the proletarian court would judge the impudent hooligan according to his merits, but things didn't turn out that way. Exactly a month and a half passed and only then did the people's court begin to analyze this case. And now on December 12 this year, the court sentenced Mishin to 6 months' forced labor, the sentence to be served in the kolkhoz, and on leaving the court, Comrade Mishin began to insult me, alleging that I did not give the chairman of the revisory commission one pound of bread for her workdays. And Comrade Mishin pursuing his course, ordered his relative, the storeman, not to issue bread to me according to the register [of workdays].

Dear Comrade Rumyantsev, I beg you immediately to protect me from hooligans who are going too far. I have more than once turned to the raion committee of the Party, to the raion executive committee, and the raion agricultural division, but there is no help there. Again I beg you to help me.

Forgive me, Comrade Rumyantsev, for my plain and awkward letter. I am semiliterate and cannot write better. With greetings, I await your answer.[21]

In this case, help was quickly forthcoming. A handwritten note of Rumyantsev is appended to Appollonova's letter stating, "It is necessary to send some one to the spot to investigate the matter." On January 2, 1937, the obkom instructor who had been dispatched to the kolkhoz reported that the persecution and beating of Appollonova by Mishin had been proven, that Mishin's main slogan was "first for myself and then for the kolkhoz," that Appollonova was hard-working and sincere, and that most of the kolkhozniks approved of her actions. Meanwhile, on

December 29, 1936, the raikom of the Party also intervened on the side of Appollonova and called on the people's court to reopen the case against Mishin and to punish him severely. The file closes on January 10, 1937, with a letter from Appollonova to Rumyantsev in which she thanks him effusively for his help and promises to do even better work in the future as chairman of the kolkhoz.

The Removal of a Chairman

Under ordinary circumstances, as most of the cases in the Archive bear witness, the members of the kolkhoz had little to say about the choice of their chairman, and it was customary for the raion authorities to designate a candidate who was more or less automatically approved by the kolkhoz meeting. But there were occasional instances where a particular kolkhoz chairman had so endeared himself to the kolkhozniks that the raion authorities encountered real difficulty in dislodging him and installing a successor. The case of P. Svishch, the chairman of the "Dzerzhinsky" Polish national kolkhoz in Smolensk raion, provides such an instance.[22] Svishch, who was a Polish worker by social origin, had joined the Party in 1923. In July 1934 he was sent by the Smolensk city committee to strengthen the Polish national kolkhoz. He apparently did an impressive job; at least the obkom instructor who later had to investigate the case reported that the kolkhoz was meeting its commitments to the state and was "economically a strong kolkhoz." In addition, the kolkhoz had more than the usual array of amenities, including electricity, a well-equipped club, a radio center, and a library of 4,000 books. Despite this record, on September 9, 1936, the Smolensk raikom expelled Svishch from the Party and ordered his removal from the chairmanship of the kolkhoz. He was charged mainly with perverting the nationality policy of the Party by carrying on a program of excessive polonization in the kolkhoz, but allegations of mismanagement, drunkenness, and weak discipline were thrown in for good measure. After his expulsion from the Party he wrote to the Central Committee denying the charges and requesting an investigation.

His description of the process by which he was ousted from the kolkhoz is especially interesting.

On September 19 [1936] a kolkhoz meeting was held at which the question of removing me from the position of chairman of the kolkhoz was discussed. The meeting lasted from 8:00 in the evening until 4:00 in the morning. Among those present at the meeting were the secretary of the raikom of the Party, Comrade Vidruchenko; the chairman of the raion executive committee, Comrade Ivanov; the head of the culture and propaganda department of the raikom, Comrade Romanov; and the chairman of the village soviet, Comrade Radchenko. While criticizing the shortcomings existing in the kolkhoz, the majority of the kolkhozniks rejected the accusations leveled against me, especially on the national question . . . Proof of this is the fact that only 7 people voted for my removal . . . After this the leading raion workers in their speeches asked the kolkhozniks how it was possible for them not to obey the resolution on removing me from work as chairman of the kolkhoz. At this there were a number of speeches by kolkhozniks to the effect that the raikom should punish me as a member of the Party, but that the kolkhozniks saw no basis for removing me from work. The question was put to the vote a second time. This time 23 people voted for the removal of the chairman. Again there were speeches. Accusations were made that the failure of the kolkhozniks to vote for the removal of the chairman bordered on crime against the Party and the government . . . When some kolkhozniks stated that nothing would intimidate them, the leaders of the raion paid no attention and called for a third vote. This time 31 people voted for removal. There were not enough votes. Again there were speeches. Again, pressure and intimidation. I begged for a word in order to explain that in view of the attitude of the raion organization, it was self-evident that I could not work any longer as chairman. They did not let me speak. Only the insistent demands of the kolkhozniks forced the leaders to allow me to speak. Finally, at 4:00 A.M. on the fourth vote 48 people voted for the removal of the chairman [still short of a majority of those present] . . . the chairman of the raion executive committee, Comrade Ivanov, then announced that the kolkhoz rules in regard to the removal of a chairman had been completely observed.

I am not raising the question of reinstating me in the position of kolkhoz chairman; I only consider it my duty to inform the Central Committee of the Party about the atmosphere which existed at the meeting, about the system of pressure and crude intimidation, about the reckless violation of the Stalinist kolkhoz rules . . . I earnestly beg the Central Committee of the Party to send its representative to check on the above facts on the spot . . .[23]

At the instigation of the Central Committee, a representative from the obkom was sent to investigate. He confirmed Svishch's story.[24] But this led to a clash with the raion leadership in which the obkom instructor was accused of having conducted a one-sided investigation and in which, he reports, "absurd accusations" were hurled against him "which did not have any relation to this case." The final outcome of the affair was summarized in a memorandum of December 29, 1936, from the head of the agricultural department of the obkom to the agricultural department of the Central Committee.

The statement of the chairman of the Dzerzhinsky national kolkhoz, citizen P. Svishch, has been investigated on the spot by the non-staff instructor of the obkom, Comrade Romanenko. A case on citizen Svishch is presently being conducted by the organs of the NKVD, and his counterrevolutionary work over a period of years is being established by the investigation. At the present time Svishch is under arrest. His removal from work as chairman of the kolkhoz was necessary, but the Smolensk raikom conducted this case tactlessly, which was pointed out to them.[25]

Checks on Maladministration

As these extracts from the record indicate, efforts were occasionally made to mitigate abuses in the kolkhozes by appeals to higher authority. Sometimes these appeals came from the kolkhozniks themselves, at other times from a zealous rural correspondent, or even, as the Svishch and Appollonova cases illustrate, from the kolkhoz chairmen themselves. Ordinarily requests for intervention were addressed in the first instance to the raion authorities, but where the raion leaders were themselves involved in the abuses or reluctant to take action, appeals were taken to the oblast and national press, to the obkom, and even to the Central Committee. Where serious abuses were indicated, the appeals were usually followed by an investigation initiated by higher authority. Although these investigations did not always sustain the complainants and indeed, in some cases, were smothered by raion leaders who had reason to fear exposure, a number were followed by drastic sanctions against collective farm chairmen who were guilty of gross administrative irregularities. The threat of investigation thus operated as a partial check to hold kolkhoz chairmen in line. But even here, a distinction needs to be drawn. The successful chairman who managed to meet his production and delivery quotas could ordinarily wriggle out of responsibility for minor irregularities and count on the support of higher authorities if he were denounced. On the other hand, the weak chairman who regularly lined his own pocket while failing to meet state quotas was a natural target for attack. Indeed, in many respects, he was almost a made-to-order scapegoat upon whom both the regime and the kolkhoznik could join in venting their dissatisfaction with the management of the collective farms.

It is not easy to summarize the experience with collectivization as it emerges from the scattered reports in the Smolensk Archive. There are many gaps in the record, including a notable dearth of data on the earnings of kolkhozniks and on methods of payment for kolkhoz work. Despite the regime's increasing emphasis during the mid-thirties on adjusting compensation to productivity and on rewarding Stakhanovite performance with premiums and bonuses, the general impression derived from the Archive is one of apathy among the rank and file and a notable lack of enthusiasm for life in the kolkhoz. So too, despite serious and even strenuous efforts by the regime to train kolkhoz chairmen, brigadiers, and other directing personnel for managerial responsibilities, the Archive is full of complaints of kolkhoz inefficiency, of lax work practices, of drunkenness, of thievery, and of even worse abuses.

And yet the regime pressed forward with collectivization until by the end of the period covered by the Archive (1938–39) more than 90 per cent of the peasants of the Smolensk area were enrolled in the collective sector. The peasants might grumble, but the Communist leadership was determined to ride the peasant nag. And, for all the patent difficulties, ride it the regime did. Through the kolkhozes it reshaped the production pattern of the Smolensk countryside to serve state needs rather than the peasant's convenience, and through the collectives it gathered in and siphoned off the output of the peasants to meet the rapidly growing demands of the new industrial centers. To read the Smolensk record is to watch this process of exploitation at work, to realize that the kolkhozniks and the kolkhoz chairmen, the raion and the oblast officials, were in different degrees agents and victims of this process, even as they sought, sometimes more and usually less successfully, to shield themselves from its consequences.

14 The MTS — Spearhead of Control

The MTS, or machine-tractor stations, were slow to penetrate the Smolensk area, but, like other centrally inspired innovations, once launched they developed a momentum of their own, and by the mid-thirties no raion in the Western Oblast was without its MTS fortress. Originally designed to bring the benefits of mechanization to the countryside, the MTS soon became one of the spearheads of the collectivization drive. They played a major role in stimulating the organization of new kolkhozes, in shaping their production plans, in enforcing kolkhoz deliveries to the state, and in projecting Party and police controls into the kolkhozes.

The Managerial Structure

The material in the Smolensk Archive on the machine-tractor stations is of a highly specialized character. It consists largely of files of the MTS political sections and necessarily reflects their particular preoccupations. The political sections, or politotdels, were Party organs deliberately introduced into the MTS in 1933 to consolidate Party control over the kolkhoz movement.[1] They represented an emergency task force mobilized largely from "specially chosen" urban Party workers who were dispatched to the MTS to direct the political and economic reorganization of the Soviet countryside. Since existing rural Party organizations were weak and considered rather untrustworthy, the MTS political sections were made independent of the raion Party organizations and given exclusive power to direct Party and Komsomol work in the kolkhozes served by machine-tractor stations.

As originally established, the technical management of each MTS was entrusted to a director and a number of key aides. A senior agronomist was responsible for the organization of kolkhoz production and for the preparation of instructions on crop rotation, depth of plowing, and agricultural practices. A senior engineer-mechanic was charged with the distribution, maintenance, and repair of tractors and other mechanical equipment. The chief bookkeeper kept MTS accounts, certified the completion of work assignments, and approved all payments of MTS obligations. The fuel chief procured fuel and lubricants and regulated their consumption in accordance with planned allocations. The field work of the MTS was performed by so-called tractor brigades, made up of kolkhozniks temporarily attached to the MTS, and directed by MTS brigadiers responsible to the MTS director.

The creation of the political sections introduced serious complications into this managerial structure. The head of the political section, who was also known as the deputy director of the MTS for political affairs, was theoretically a subordinate of the director, but in many respects his authority was at least co-equal to that of the director, and in Party status he was usually the director's superior. The head of the political section functioned as part of an independent Party hierarchy with lines of responsibility running directly to the Political Administration of the MTS in the Commissariat of Agriculture and ultimately to the Central Committee of the Party. The politotdel chief thus operated as a Party check on the director and, for the period 1933–34, was largely free from the control of the Party organization in his raion. Providing still an additional organizational complication was the presence in the political section of a "second deputy," the so-called "deputy for special work" who was in fact an agent of the OGPU, and who in his police capacity functioned more or less independently of both the MTS director and the head of the political section.

Implicit in these awkward but not atypical organizational arrangements were a whole series of potential jurisdictional conflicts — between the head of the political section and the MTS director, between the head of the political section and the raikom, and between the OGPU representative and his theoretical superiors, the politotdel chief and the MTS director. Perhaps the most useful single contribution of the MTS files in the Archive is the light which they throw on these jurisdictional conflicts and on the efforts which were made to resolve them.

Conflicts between the MTS Director and the Politotdels

The question of the relations between the MTS director and the head of the political section raised one of the perennial and still unresolved problems of Soviet political organization, the ambiguity between the Party's right of control and the director's right of one-man management. The January 1933 decree establishing the political sections stated with seeming clarity that "the political sections of the machine-tractor stations should in no event substitute in their work for the director . . . They must remember that economic guidance of the station . . . is realized by the director on the principle of one-man management . . ." [2] But in characteristic fashion the decree also instructed the head of the political section that "he bears along with the director the responsibility for fulfilling the production and procurement plans of the MTS." [3] The pressure to discharge this responsibility inevitably led to infringements upon the director's authority.

The Smolensk Archive contains a series of reports from the head of the political section of the Yelnya MTS to his oblast superior in Smolensk for the period 1933–34.[4] These reports make clear that the head of the political section played a vigilant and vigorous role in supervising the whole range of MTS operations. In a secret report dated August 1, 1933, Donskoi, the chief of the Yelnya politotdel, complained that the MTS director was inactive, that he failed to take leadership in organizing the harvest, that there were no harvest plans, and that only "intervention" by the head of the political section produced such plans.[5] During the hay-harvesting and the deliveries, he continued, the politotdel was obliged to take direction of kolkhoz work into its own hands. The program for the repair of agricultural implements was saved only by the politotdel's "direct intervention and the taking over of economic supervision." The MTS director Ustinov was described as "too soft . . . He rarely visits the fields, has no idea of what is going on in the kolkhozes, and is constitutionally incapable of effective operative supervision." Recommending the firing of the MTS director, Donskoi then pointed out that if the oblast failed to send a replacement, "it will thus force the politotdel to assume not only the political but also the economic guidance of the MTS . . ." In addition he called for a new senior agronomist. The present acting senior agronomist, he observed, "may be a good agronomist," but "he is anti-Soviet in attitude, and refuses to supervise the work of the agronomists in the field; he stays in the MTS and does only office work." Similar interferences with managerial prerogatives occurred with considerable frequency. Thus on May 8, 1934, Donskoi reported that because of the inability of the MTS director to organize tractor work and to get spare parts, the politotdel "found itself obliged in many cases to take over part of the administrative leadership." [6]

Yet it is also worthy of note that while the politotdel did not hesitate to breach the principle of one-man rule, it did feel called upon to justify its action. The reasons are apparent. On November 16, 1935, for example, Rumyantsev, the obkom first secretary, dispatched a letter to all deputy directors of MTS political units in which he warned that "some deputy directors . . . do not engage in their own functions, slide over into administration, and substitute for MTS directors . . ." [7] He called upon the deputy directors to base their activities exclusively on Party educational and Party mass work in the MTS and the kolkhozes. But despite Rumyantsev's injunctions, the line could not be drawn so neatly. Joint responsibility for results led to joint concern for management, and the compulsion of the political units to intervene when things were going badly was almost irresistible. The contradictions between one-man management and Party control generated continuing tensions.

Jurisdictional Problems between the Politotdels and the Raikoms

Relations between the politotdels and the raikoms were also fraught with difficulty. According to the January 1933 decree, the politotdels were given a special responsibility for Party and political work in the machine-tractor stations and the kolkhozes served by them. Their authority, however, was not clearly defined, and they were told that "in fulfilling their tasks, the MTS political sections should not replace local raion Party committees, but should operate in full contact with them." The raikoms in turn were instructed that the establishment of the politotdels "by no means relieved them of the tasks and responsibilities laid on them by the Party." Thus a situation of overlapping responsibility was created, where the politotdel assumed the raikom's functions in the kolkhozes while the raikom was also instructed not to restrict its normal area of operations. As a further aggravating factor, the politotdel, although a Party organization located in the raion, was outside the normal Party chain of command and not responsible to the raikom. The creation of the politotdels thus detracted from the authority and prestige of the raikoms and bred resentment and jealousy.

Signs of friction appeared early. A number of the newly established politotdels encountered extreme difficulty in obtaining adequate food and housing, despite an obkom order to the raikoms obliging them to render all possible assistance to the politotdel workers who were settling in the raions.[8] On June 13, 1933, the Yelnya politotdel chief complained that after two months of effort the politotdel was still without satisfactory quarters or food, and that it was encountering "resistance" from local soviet organizations.[9] The wives and children of politotdel officials had not been supplied with food ration cards or consumers' goods, and when criticism was voiced the raion leadership replied that "everybody is busy sowing and there is no one to deal with the matter." Meanwhile, the politotdel at its own cost had to dispatch two men to go to Smolensk to fetch rations. The chief of the politotdel of the Sukhinichy MTS indignantly reported to his superiors in Smolensk that the raion executive committee was threatening to use police to evict MTS specialists from a house in order to make room for a group of teachers. "I beg you to give me support," he wrote, "because I am not on good terms with the raion organizations — there is no peace." [10]

A Central Committee decree published in *Pravda* on June 16, 1933, made an effort to head off more serious trouble by giving the politotdels sole jurisdiction over Party activity in kolkhozes served by MTS's while reserving raikom authority over all Party groups outside the MTS-kolkhoz network. The politotdel, however, was required to keep the raikom informed of its actions and to obtain the raikom's confirmation in all cases where members were accepted into or excluded from the Party. To facilitate liaison, the head of the political section was to serve as a member of the raikom bureau.

But friction continued despite this decree. The MTS politotdels were naturally anxious to strengthen Party organization in the kolkhozes subject to their jurisdiction, and under the provisions of the CC decree of June 16, 1933, the raikoms were instructed to supply Party personnel for this purpose. But this was more easily said than done. The raion Party aktiv was usually small and used in "leading" raion work. Party members were in any case reluctant to go to the kolkhozes, and the raikom itself was even more reluctant to send them to kolkhozes in an MTS zone, since they then became subject to the jurisdiction of the politotdels and were lost to raikom control.

The Yelnya situation may serve to illustrate the problem. The Yelnya raikom had been ordered to mobilize fifty Communists for village work. Actually, according to the August 1933 report of the Yelnya MTS politotdel chief, only twenty were mobilized, chiefly for soviet and coöperative work.[11] Only four of the twenty were assigned to the politotdel for use in the kolkhozes. Of these four, two were Party candidates, one an individual farmer, and the other wholly ignorant of agriculture. The Yelnya politotdel chief termed such support pitifully inadequate. In October the politotdel chief protested again, this time because of the failure of the raikom to coöperate in the selection and dispatch of Komsomols for work in the kolkhozes.[12] Scheduled to send fifteen Komsomols, the raikom actually sent only four, two of whom had to be fired for incompetence and drunkenness. The politotdel chief termed this an "outrage" and asserted that "such a disgraceful action on the part of the raikom secretary must be evaluated as indicating no desire to strengthen the kolkhoz cells in the area for which the MTS is responsible."

The dispute was now raised to the oblast level, and on November 5, 1933, Shilman, the obkom second secretary, and Ilinsky, the chief of the oblast Political Administration of the MTS, sent a joint letter to all politotdel chiefs and raikoms which was designed to strengthen the hand of the politotdels. "Despite the very clear instructions of the Central Committee of the Party . . . ," the letter began, "some raikoms have approached the fulfillment of this very important Party directive in a formal, bureaucratic manner, have not taken the necessary measures to supply the production cells with Party forces, which would insure the strengthening of these cells. In a number of cases the raikoms of the Party either chose an extremely small number of Party people to be assigned to kolkhoz cells, or chose clearly unsuitable people." [13] The letter cited some concrete examples, including the case of the Vyazma MTS where up to October 1 the failure of the raikom to supply Party workers prevented the organization of even one cell in the eighty-four kolkhozes in the MTS district. "And when, finally," the letter continued, "the raikom chose 9 people, 4 had to be expelled from the Party for self-supply [a polite name for illegal appropriations], while the remaining five deserted."

The letter then criticized the raikoms for poaching on the jurisdiction of the politotdels and working at cross purposes with them. "Despite the instructions of the CC to the effect that Party workers operating in the MTS zone are to be sent through the politotdels and are to work under their orders, some raikoms send their officials directly to the spot, without obtaining the agreement of the politotdels, without even informing them, and these officials hold conferences without the participation of the politotdel chief, while the workers of the politotdels learn about the sending of officials by the raikoms only when they meet them on the spot in the kolkhozes. Resolutions of the raikom bureaus and raion executive committees relating to the kolkhozes are not reported to the chief of the politotdel . . ." The letter then pointed to the action of the Khavstovichy raion leadership as a horrible example. In this case the raion authorities ordered kolkhozniks and kolkhoz leaders to engage in lumber deliveries without obtaining politotdel consent, and instead of taking people and horses from kolkhozes which had already finished the harvesting and sowing, the raion leaders mobilized people from lagging kolkhozes and thus further delayed the completion of the agricultural campaign. In this same raion, the executive committee simply appropriated lumber which was to be delivered to the MTS for building sheds for agricultural machines. The letter concluded by ordering that the friction between the raion organizations and the politotdels be liquidated, that the raion committees take "resolute measures" to aid the politotdels, and threatened Party punishment against violators of the CC directive.

But there was no easy resolution of politotdel-raikom differences. Some politotdel chiefs tried to solve the problem informally by subordinating themselves to the raikom, but this too led to trouble. Thus the politotdel chief of the Kantemirskaya MTS was severely rebuked for doing nothing to stop a raikom order which permitted all kolkhozes in his MTS zone to make excessive advance payments of grain to kolkhozniks. In the words of the USSR head of the MTS Political Administration, "Being guided by the effort to 'live in peace' with the raion leadership at all costs, the chief of the politotdel of the Kantemirskaya MTS did not raise the flag of Bolshevik self-criticism in the raion Party organization . . . The chief of the politotdel gave his consent to the raikom's plundering of the politotdel, to the sending of his own workers in the capacity of raikom representatives."[14] While such subordination may have been unusual, it testified to the continuing vitality of the raikoms and their formidable capacity to sabotage the politotdels' operations. Indeed, so effective was the resistance of the raikoms that in November 1934 the Party leadership decided that the politotdels had carried out their mission and moved to dissolve them. The politotdels were transformed into MTS Party cells, and the authority of the raikoms was extended to embrace MTS Party organizations as well as all kolkhoz Party cells in the MTS area.

The Special Position of the OGPU Deputy

Still another source of friction in the MTS structure arose out of the special position of the second deputy, or OGPU representative in the political section. The original OGPU order of January 25, 1933, establishing the position of the deputy chief of the Politotdel for OGPU work is unfortunately not available, but the Archive does contain a clarifying circular of February 3, stamped "Top Secret (Guard like a Code)" and signed jointly by Yagoda, then deputy chairman of the OGPU, and Krinitsky, chief of the Political Administration in the Commissariat of Agriculture. This circular stressed that the deputy chiefs were to retain full independence in carrying out their secret "agenturno-operativnaya rabota" (agent-operative work), but at the same time were to be "wholly subordinate" to the politotdel chiefs in other respects.[15] They were required to carry out the general orders of the politotdel heads and report to them on economic and political conditions in the MTS and sovkhozes.

Despite this effort at clarification, friction and conflict between the politotdel chiefs and their OGPU deputies apparently persisted. Their struggle is well illumined in another top-secret order of July 10, 1933, which was in the nature of a treaty of peace between the OGPU and the political administration of the MTS and sovkhozes.[16] This order sought to solve the delicate problem of the proper relationship between a Party chief and his police deputy by demarcating their respective spheres of action. The order began by taking both OGPU representatives and politotdel chiefs to task for failing to adjust their relationships in accordance with the roles which had been assigned to them. The OGPU representatives were warned that they must subordinate themselves to the politotdel chiefs in carrying out the task of investigating and reporting on political and economic conditions in the kolkhozes and MTS and in ferreting out cases of organized sabotage and other activities of counterrevolutionary kulak groups. Examples were cited of OGPU deputies who failed to cooperate with the politotdel chiefs in screening MTS and kolkhoz Party organizations or in investigating cases of theft and arson and who excused themselves with the remark that they were too busy, that they had "other duties in the OGPU line," or that "they knew what to do, and they were subordinate only to the OGPU."

On the other hand, the politotdel chiefs were also reproved for assigning jobs to their OGPU deputies which had nothing to do with normal secret police duties. Among other things, the OGPU deputies had been ordered to check on kolkhoz bookkeeping, to organize the signing of contracts between an MTS and its kolkhozes, to collect information on sowing, to lead state bond drives, and to engage in political mass-work. All this, said the order, "directly impairs the second deputy's usefulness and effectiveness as an OGPU operative." When OGPU deputies protested this misuse of their office, some political chiefs were reported as having lashed back that the OGPU representatives were "superfluous."

The order again sought to block out the OGPU deputies' area of responsibility. They were instructed to report systematically to their politotdel chiefs on "counterrevolutionary groups of kulaks, on wrecking acts, and on organized sabotage and pilfering," as well as on the general politico-economic condition of the MTS and kolkhozes. The OGPU representatives were told to coördinate their planned operations with the politotdel chiefs; in the event that the politotdel chief disagreed with a given operation, he could protest to a higher OGPU echelon which retained ultimate authority to sanction the operation. The politotdel chiefs were not to burden their OGPU deputies with duties that diverted them from their fundamental police responsibilities. In their "agent-operative work," moreover, the OGPU deputies were to be "wholly independent." The politotdel chiefs were categorically forbidden to require any reports dealing with the "agenturno-osvedomitelnaya set" (agent-informer network) of their OGPU deputies.

Even this effort to spell out the precise relationship between the OGPU deputy and his politotdel chief failed to avert conflict. The independence of the OGPU deputies proved irksome to many politotdel chiefs. In a letter written in July 1934 the chief of the Roslavl politotdel complained to his superior in Smolensk that in his absence his OGPU deputy had departed on an illegal and unauthorized month's leave.[17] When reprimanded for this, the OGPU deputy explained that he was going "on a pass from the OGPU," and added, "Why should I obtain consent [from you] when I have my own boss?" — this despite the clear statement of the July 1933 order that OGPU deputies had to receive permission from the politotdel chiefs before leaving the MTS area. At the same time there were also indications that politotdel chiefs were transgressing the terms of the July 1933 agreement by requiring their police deputies to represent the politotdels in rural soviets and kolkhozes and to help in emergency efforts to meet delivery quotas. A joint decree of the oblast NKVD and the Political Section of the Oblast Land Administration dated October 31,

1934, deplored this misuse of secret police employees and warned that it led "to a weakening of the work of guaranteeing state security in all the kolkhozes of the MTS zone." [18] The balance between Party and police work was not easily righted.

It would be misleading, however, to assume that jurisdictional conflicts absorbed all of the energies of the political sections, and that no time was left for substantive activity. As a matter of fact, the political sections played a crucial role in consolidating the collective form structure in a period when its fate was still in doubt and when demoralization and disintegrative tendencies were much in evidence.

The Functions of the Political Sections

The contributions of the MTS political sections were fourfold. In the first place, they gave considerable impetus to the organization of Party and Komsomol cells in the kolkhozes, and through them supplied the steel which kept the collective farm structure intact. In the second place, they purged the kolkhozes of anti-Soviet elements and thus put an end to active sabotage of the kolkhoz movement. In the third place, they provided the political energizing force which helped to revitalize the economies of the kolkhozes and to put their affairs in some semblance of order. And fourth, and perhaps most important, they served as an instrument to enforce the obligations of the kolkhozes to the state, pressing for the tribute to supply the rapidly growing industrial centers.

One of the primary functions assigned to the politotdels was the organization of a Party and Komsomol network in the kolkhozes. Without such a network the politotdels could not really make their control of the kolkhozes effective. The permanent staff of the political sections was never very large. Typically it consisted of the politotdel chief, a deputy for OGPU work, two deputies for mass political work, a deputy for work among women, an assistant for Komsomol work, and possibly a newspaper editor and one or two secretarial workers. With as many as seventy-five kolkhozes served by a single politotdel, it soon became obvious that the opportunity for direct intervention in kolkhoz affairs was limited, and that heavy reliance would have to be placed on Party and Komsomol groups in the kolkhozes and on the non-Party aktiv.

The experience of the Yelnya MTS may be taken as typical. In June 1933 there was not a single Party cell in the seventy-five kolkhozes served by the MTS, and in all there were fourteen Party members and candidates scattered through these kolkhozes.[19] There were, however, sixteen Komsomol cells with a membership of 157. Fifty-six additional Komsomol members distributed through the remaining kolkhozes brought the total Komsomol forces at the disposal of the political section up to 213.

By the end of 1933 the situation had improved somewhat.[20] The kolkhoz Party complement totaled twenty-three members and thirteen candidates. In the seventy-five kolkhozes, there now existed one Party cell, two small Party-candidate cells, and nine Party-Komsomol groups. In addition the number of Komsomol cells had increased from sixteen to twenty. But there were still fifty kolkhozes which had neither a Party member, a Party candidate, nor a member of the Komsomol. The limitations this imposed on the politotdel are self-evident.

As might be expected, the great majority of Party members held administrative posts. Twenty-two of the thirty-six Party members and candidates served as kolkhoz chairmen. The crucial point of weakness was the absence of Party or Komsomol representation in the field brigades. The Yelnya politotdel chief noted a tendency to join the Komsomol in order to escape field work and reported that in one Komsomol cell six out of eleven members, including the secretary, had been fined for shirking field duties.[21] But under pressure from the politotdel the Komsomols were forced into the fields; at the end of 1933, 116 Komsomol members had been attached to field brigades.

An additional device employed by the politotdels to project their influence into the kolkhozes was the organization of a non-Party kolkhoz aktiv. In the Yelnya MTS area on November 15, 1933, this consisted of 304 persons. Intended as a reserve from which Party and Komsomol members might ultimately be recruited, it was more immediately utilized as part of the vanguard which the politotdel could maneuver in influencing the life of the kolkhozes.

As this accounting indicates, the forces at the disposal of the politotdel were pitifully small. But small as they were, they were growing. Under politotdel pressure, they were placed in leadership positions where they could exercise strategic leverage in influencing kolkhoz decisions. Not infrequently they were infiltrated by "opportunist" and "careerist" elements which the politotdels encountered great difficulty in eliminating. The kolkhoz vanguard on which the politotdels relied was expected to inspire other kolkhoz workers, both by example and by exhortation. Many fell short of the standards set for them. But enough responded to keep the kolkhozes together and to make them a serviceable instrument of state policy.

Another important function of the politotdels was that of rooting out anti-Soviet elements from the MTS and the kolkhozes. In performing this function the OGPU deputy played a particularly important role. Operating through his own network of informers in the kolkhozes, he collected reports on hostile conversations and activities which subsequently formed the basis for purges and arrests. Some sense of the scope of this activity can be derived from the report of the Yelnya political section for December 1933 which contained tables of the number of "class-hostile," "anti-kolkhoz" and "sabotaging" elements that had been removed from the MTS and its seventy-five kolkhozes in the first nine months of the section's operation.[22] Those purged from the MTS included three out of twelve agronomists, two mechanics, one out of six tractor brigadiers, and four tractor operators. The purge of the kolkhozes accounted for nine out of seventy-five kolkhoz chairmen, three out of seventy-five accountants, ten out of 108 brigadiers, and eighteen field workers.

Such repressive actions were supplemented by vigorous efforts to put the affairs of the kolkhozes in order. These more positive measures ranged from endeavors to raise the political consciousness and morale of the peasants to attempts to reorganize the work of the kolkhozes in the interest of greater discipline and efficiency. Various forms of agitation and propaganda were utilized to try to win the peasant to the kolkhoz cause. The Yelnya politotdel published a newspaper with a circulation of six hundred copies, one for every five households in the MTS area.[23] It claimed that "our paper has won a position of authority among the kolkhozniks, and there are many requests from kolkhozes and kolkhozniks to increase its circulation." Meetings were widely held in the kolkhozes at which politotdel workers tried to whip up enthusiasm for greater productive effort. These meetings not infrequently featured awards of premiums to outstanding workers, a device which helped draw a crowd and perhaps also spurred lagging kolkhoz members to greater efforts. At one such gathering two deserving women were presented with material for a dress; "the premium awards," reported the politotdel, "made a big impression on the kolkhozniks and have helped to raise their productive activity even more." [24] The politotdels also sought to ingratiate themselves with the kolkhozniks by presenting themselves as an agency to which the kolkhoznik could appeal for redress against the abuses of local kolkhoz officials. The Archive notes a number of instances of such intervention, though the fundamental role of the politotdels as the instrument to enforce state deliveries was hardly calculated to endear them to most of the kolkhozniks.

Political activity was supplemented by economic guidance. The politotdels tried as best they could to improve the quality of agricultural work and to raise labor discipline. In early 1933 kolkhoz labor was still badly disorganized. One of the first moves of the Yelnya politotdel was to try to establish permanent field brigades for all types of work, to introduce reliable cadres at the heads of the brigades, to enforce regular working hours, and to direct female labor away from the household plots into the kolkhoz fields.[25] Representatives of the politotdel made flying visits to the fields to check on how their orders were being executed. But the impact of their work was unavoidably uneven. The politotdel workers were too few and the area of their responsibility too vast to insure efficient coverage.

The first commandment for the politotdels was the fulfillment of procurement plans. This too was not easy. The politotdels found themselves caught between the pressure from above for larger deliveries and the resistance from below to excessive and unreasonable demands. A typical letter from the Smolensk politotdel head to his corresponding number in the Medyn MTS lashed out: "The situation with regard to the processing and delivery of flax in your district remains completely catastrophic. This is a direct result of the lack of concrete, operative direction on the part of the politotdel [which] has not displayed Bolshevik flexibility and persistence in the organization of work in each separate kolkhoz. It has not guaranteed leadership in organizing labor in the kolkhozes, in introducing labor discipline, and in supervising daily the processing and delivery of flax." [26]

Sometimes the local politotdel heads replied with excuses, pointing to bad weather or lack of machinery; but these excuses availed little in the face of the center's wrath. Reacting to the pressure to achieve plan fulfillment, most politotdel heads simply transferred the pressure to the kolkhozes which they supervised. Occasionally their methods were rough. On September 20, 1934, the Smolensk politotdel head rebuked the Baryatinsk politotdel because its assistant for Komsomol work had "twice shoved and even struck a kolkhoz chairman and two brigadiers . . . and roughly cursed and abused the kolkhozniks." [27] The politotdel chief "had made himself a party to this rudeness, tactlessness, and abusiveness, by swearing roughly at the chairman of the Baryatinsk village soviet . . ." Such behavior, the Smolensk headquarters pointed out, could only end by completely alienating the kolkhoz leadership from the politotdels.

Some political chiefs, to judge from their reports, developed a certain sympathy for the peasants with whom they dealt, which was intensified by the confusing directives and excessive demands which they had to transmit and execute. On February 27, 1934, the Yelnya politotdel chief complained to his superior that a new plan increasing the area of spring sowing by 300 hectares was forced on a kolkhoz just two weeks after a previous plan had been presented by the MTS and agreed to by all concerned. Obviously sharing the interest of the kolkhoz in receiving a manageable plan, the politotdel chief argued that the new plan would work havoc with the crop-rotation system and leave far too little fallow land. The peasants, already in a "very unhealthy mood," are quoted as saying, "You agitate for us to raise yields and to carry out crop rotation, and then you ruin it yourselves." [28]

On August 1, 1934, the same politotdel chief referred to other similar cases. In April 1934 a government order had promised that kolkhozniks who cleared certain swamps and wooded areas would be given a year's tax exemption on the crops that they planted there. Instead an emissary from Smolensk descended on the Yelnya villages demanding deliveries on the exempt land and promising that the grain would be returned later to the peasants. The politotdel chief reported that "the kolkhozes who have the right to their [government guaranteed] privileges" were now asking him to see to it that the earlier order of the government was executed. "All this is quite understandable," he comments, "because some time ago it was the politotdel and the Party that widely disseminated [the promise of tax exemption], and all kolkhozniks are well acquainted [with these promises]. Therefore it is not surprising that such dealing with the case provokes the kolkhozniks' indignation." [29] He then quoted some typical kolkhoznik comment: "Why should [people] now have to be pushed around, [grain] delivered and then received back — all for nothing? Why should there be an unnecessary loss of time, why should horses be driven [to and fro] and extra labor-days spent?" . . . When [they have to take] from us, decisions are adopted quickly, but when it is we [who are to receive something], there is always hesitation." The politotdel chief strongly urged that the earlier promise be kept.

He cited still another dangerous inconsistency. In connection with the sowing of flax the government had promised that kolkhozniks who worked on flax would be paid in bread for all workdays earned beginning with the sowing. The politotdel had widely publicized this promise. Now (July 15, 1934) the obkom had announced that bread would be paid out only for workdays earned since the pulling of flax, thus greatly limiting the quantity of bread to be issued. The politotdel chief stressed the fact that the terms of the original contract were widely known, and that it was "very important" that it be adhered to. He requested intervention with the obkom to make the latter "review" its decision, and he urged a reply "without delay." [30] The Archive provides no indication that a reply was forthcoming. Incidents such as these illustrate the unenviable position of the grass-roots Party representative who found himself forced to defend policies which he could not justify, who identified with the peasants whom he had to exploit, and who at the same time became the inevitable scapegoat for their resentments.

Crucially important though they were, the politotdels proved to be only an emergency expedient. In November 1934 their organization and scope of authority were radically altered. The politotdel head was transformed into a deputy MTS director for political affairs directly accountable to the raikom and with responsibility for Party and mass political work in the MTS and the kolkhozes which it served. But many of the old problems lingered on. The relations between the MTS director and his deputy for political affairs continued to present difficulties. The Party records of the period make clear that it was not easy to draw a precise line between their respective spheres of operation. The protocols of the obkom bureau note "unhealthy and squabbling relationships" between MTS directors and their political deputies, though such references to the problem as are available indicate a tendency to discourage the Party representative from interfering unduly in administrative decision-making.[31]

By 1937, however, the MTS appeared securely established in the countryside. A proposal to improve their operations which was circulated by Stalin to the republics and oblasts at the end of June 1937 boasted that "5,615 MTS have been created, possessing 41,000 powerful 'Stalin' caterpillar tractors, 270,000 wheeled tractors, 38,000 cultivator tractors, and 86,000 combines." [32] The same circular claimed that in 1937 "three-fourths of the plowing and almost half of the sowing and tillage of cultivated crops in the kolkhozes was being done by the tractors of the MTS." But the circular also noted that "the net cost of the work done by the MTS was extremely high, as a result of excessive use of fuel, the great expense and the unsatisfactory quality of the repair of tractors and agricultural machines, and the large administrative and management expenditures." The scheme advanced by Stalin was designed to control these costs more closely and to provide additional premiums and incentives to MTS personnel who met their plan.

While the MTS spread the benefits of mechanization over the countryside, the kolkhozes also discovered that mechanization had its price. The payments extracted from the kolkhozes for the services rendered by the MTS amounted to approximately 20 per cent of the crop. In the eyes of many kolkhozniks the MTS thus became simply one more device by which produce was siphoned from the countryside and little came back in return.

However displeasing this may have been to the kolkhozniks, it provided the ultimate rationale for the machine-tractor stations in the eyes of the regime. The MTS justified themselves as collection devices par excellence; the tribute which they exacted provided the sinews of industrialization. The MTS became the bastions of Party strength in the countryside, projecting Party controls into the last strongholds of peasant obduracy and resistance, the kolkhozes themselves.

15 The State Farms — Problems of Control and Management

When the Western Oblast was organized in 1929, the sovkhozes, or state farms, played an extremely inconspicuous role in the agricultural life of the region. The total area assigned to them was 124,000 hectares and the sown area only 11,600 hectares. The decision of the center to embark on a vast expansion of the sovkhoz sector during the First Five Year Plan had its immediate repercussions in the Western Oblast. By the end of 1930 the area allocated to the sovkhozes increased to 167,000 hectares, from which a more than fivefold increase to 910,000 hectares was planned for the end of 1931.[1] As elsewhere in the Soviet Union, the sovkhozes of the Western Oblast were organized on the basis of crop specialization. They were designed to fit in with the oblast emphasis on the development of flax and hemp culture, livestock breeding, and industrial truck farming.

Initial Organizational Difficulties

The rapid proliferation and extension of the sovkhozes during the First Five Year Plan were attended by the most serious organizational difficulties. The joint Central Committee–Sovnarkom decree of November 27, 1931, on the grain sovkhozes spoke of "appalling wastefulness and an intolerably criminal attitude toward state property. The losses in harvesting, threshing, and transportation are appallingly large."[2] The situation in the livestock kolkhozes was no better. There, according to the CC-Sovnarkom decree of March 31, 1932, investigation disclosed "wastefulness and complete disorganization of the production processes . . . entirely unsatisfactory organization of the care of stock, excessive losses of young stock, high percentages of unbred animals, absolutely inadequate increase of the stock by way of reproduction on the farms, and poor condition of the herds . . ."[3]

Beginning in 1932, steps were taken to render the sovkhozes more efficient by cutting down on their size and by greater emphasis on crop diversification and less emphasis on total mechanization. Organizationally, perhaps the most important measure was the joint decree of the Central Committee and Central Control Commission of January 11, 1933, which provided for the establishment of political sections in the sov-khozes (as well as in the MTS), which would be manned by trusted Party personnel who could be counted on to provide Party leadership in the sovkhozes, to control the administrative-technical personnel, and to apply maximum pressure for plan fulfillment.[4] The original decree made the head of the political section, who also carried the title of deputy director of the sovkhoz for political affairs, a direct subordinate of the Political Administration of the People's Commissariat for State Farms and responsible along Party lines to the obkom, kraikom, or Central Committee of the republic. As an indication of the importance of the assignment, all designations of politotdel chiefs had to be approved by the Party Central Committee. The politotdel head was not only to have full responsibility for Party-political work in the sovkhozes, but to share responsibility with the director for the fulfillment of plans, and to take "an active part" in the choice of sovkhoz cadres, including administrative-technical personnel. He was to be assisted by two deputies — one for general Party work and the other for Komsomol activities. By a separate order of the OGPU he was also provided with a deputy for OGPU affairs.

The Smolensk Archive contains a substantial number of central directives of the Political Administration of the People's Commissariat for State Farms (PUNS) stretching over the period 1933–1937 as well as scattered reports on the operations of sovkhozes in the Western Oblast.[5] From this material it is possible to capture some sense of the problems of management and control posed by the state farm.

Conflicts between Politotdel Chiefs
and Sovkhoz Directors

From the beginning, as these documents make clear, the politotdel chiefs took their watchdog function with the utmost seriousness. Indeed, as a secret order of the Deputy Chief of PUNS noted on June 27, 1933, hundreds of reports from local politotdels were arriving at the center demanding a purge of sovkhoz directors and citing as reasons the pilfering of state property, negligence, weak coöperation with the politotdels, and the failure of the directors "to follow the politotdel's orders in day-to-day work."[6] The zealousness of the politotdel chiefs led to so many casualties among sovkhoz directors that on May 21, 1933, the Central Committee issued a directive that the rapid turnover of sovkhoz directors must stop, that the minimum term of service of a director was to be three years, and that all new assignments of directors were to be made only by the collegium of the State Farm Commissariat in coöperation with the agricultural department of the Central Committee.[7] On the basis of this directive, PUNS instructed politotdel chiefs to coöperate with their directors in every way and to help create for them "an indispensable authority among the sovkhoz workers." Only in cases where the ineptness or negligence of a director became "directly" harmful and the director proved "absolutely incapable" of continuing his work were the politotdel chiefs to recommend removal. Such recommendations, the PUNS chief warned, had to be accompanied by "exhaustive material" testifying to the incapacity of the director.

Some politotdel chiefs apparently interpreted this as meaning that the sovkhoz directors should be left to their own devices in managing the state farms. But PUNS quickly explained that this was not the intention at all. In a top-secret circular to politotdel chiefs of all sovkhozes dated September 2, 1933, the deputy chief of PUNS warned that too many politotdels were simply becoming creatures of the sovkhoz administration, lowering their vigilance, and forgetting that they were "the eyes of the Party in the sovkhoz." [8] Their function was not only to coöperate with but also to watch and criticize the director.

The task of maintaining a nice balance between control and noninterference in the details of administration apparently still eluded the political sections. On October 15, 1933, came still another order from the chief of PUNS, K. Soms, again warning against politotdel encroachment on the director's jurisdiction.[9] The political sections' "immersion in economic functions within the sovkhozes," said Soms, resulted in a neglect of political and Party work, a weakening of the one-man rule of the sovkhoz director and a duplication of his work. Too many politotdels were engaging in haphazard firing or shifts of responsible administrative personnel, causing "profound disturbances" in the working processes of the sovkhozes. Some politotdels were simply "ignoring" the director, or "quite incorrectly" giving out party reprimands to sovkhoz directors and even publishing such reprimands in the press.

Despite the plethora of instructions from the center, the relations between the sovkhoz directors and their political deputies continued to create difficulties. Some examples from the Western Oblast in a somewhat later period make this clear. Thus on February 15, 1935, the politotdel chief of the hog-raising sovkhoz "Pyatiletka" (Five Year Plan) complained to his superiors that, despite the fact that the sovkhoz was not supplied with seeds, that the tractors were not repaired, and that urgent preparations for the spring sowing had still to be completed, the sovkhoz director had simply gone off without leave requiring the politotdel chief to return from his vacation before it was completed. "The attitude of the director," he declared, "is simply negligent. I have written a great deal about this, both in 1933 and 1934 . . ." [10] On March 4, 1935, the political chief of the Barbino sovkhoz reported on a dispute between the sovkhoz director and the chairman of the workers' committee of the sovkhoz.[11] The latter had brought a case against the director for failure to pay wages to the workers on time and for not taking measures to improve the living conditions of the workers. A traveling session of the oblast court sentenced the director to six months of forced labor in the sovkhoz with a deduction of 20 per cent of his salary. The chairman of the workers' committee apparently also had his faults; in the words of the politotdel chief he "discredited himself by systematic drinking." The politotdel chief recommended that both be dismissed.

Police Controls

As in the MTS, the special position of the OGPU, or NKVD, deputy also created difficulties. Just as the politotdel chief served as "the eyes of the Party in the sovkhoz," the OGPU deputy functioned as "the eyes of the police." Largely independent of both the director and his ostensible politotdel chief, he made trouble for both. The Archive contains a top-secret report by one Brichkin, the NKVD representative in the Krupskaya sovkhoz.[12] The report, copies of which were made available to higher Party authorities, read in part as follows: "The Krupskaya sovkhoz was completely unprepared for the harvesting and threshing . . . The director of the sovkhoz, Novikov, did not give and is not giving sufficient attention to the problem, and the Party organization of the sovkhoz also gave it insufficient attention." Brichkin then cited losses of up to 50 per cent of the harvest and blamed it on "the lack of concrete operative leadership" on the part of the sovkhoz director and the politotdel chief. "They do not react against mismanagement; the worker masses are not mobilized around this problem, but consider all this normal (merely trifles) and their complacency leads to mismanagement and criminal actions. This situation in the sovkhoz deserves special attention and interference on your part."

The speech of a politotdel chief to his staff in the Kalinin sovkhoz on February 13, 1935, documents both the independence of the police deputy and the strained relations which sometimes developed between him and the head of the politotdel section. In this case the politotdel chief requested his NKVD deputy to bring some workers on the dairy farm to trial because of the great loss of calves. The NKVD representative is quoted as having replied: "I am not obliged to concern myself with this matter; this is your affair. The director is a member of the Party."[13] The NKVD deputy, who lived off the sovkhoz, apparently confined his activities to occasional visits to the sovkhoz, during which, according to the politotdel head, he served in the role of an observer, "photographing" various disorders, placing these "photo shows" before the politotdel chief, transmitting them to his superiors, "and with this considering his mission finished." As the politotdel chief put it, the NKVD representative "does his work without any obedience to me or connection with me . . .

supervising in general, but not concretely." It should be added that in this case the politotdel chief was defending himself against charges of lack of "class vigilance" and that part of his defense involved the claim of lack of coöperation on the part of his NKVD colleague.

The NKVD deputy, whose business it was to denounce others, occasionally was the object of denunciation himself. An interesting case in the Dalisichy sovkhoz during 1935 may serve as an illustration.[14] There an NKVD investigation disclosed that the director of the sovkhoz, who was a Party member, had concealed the fact that he had been an active member of the Left SR's before joining the Party. As a result, he was expelled from the Party and lost his position as sovkhoz director. The director's wife, seeking revenge, then wrote a letter to the editors of *Sovkhoznaya Gazeta* (State Farm Gazette) alleging that the NKVD chief of the sovkhoz led a dissolute life, that he took bribes, that he had "protected" a thief in the bakery, and that when finally forced to arrest him, had permitted the thief to escape. The matter was submitted for investigation to the raion NKVD chief, who gave his colleague in the sovkhoz a clean bill of health. "I report," he wrote, "that Comrade Prigaro [the sovkhoz NKVD head] during his work in the sovkhoz initiated nine cases on robberies and other anti-state crimes involving 26 accused people, who were sentenced to various terms, and most of the accused were supporters of the former director, Semyonov, and in regard to a number of the accused, great arguments occurred between Prigaro and Semyonov because Semyonov defended [the accused] and sheltered them during the trial . . . [I] feel that this claim was written by the wife of Semyonov exclusively on the basis of personal antagonism, with the aim of compromising Prigaro." Prigaro subsequently received a rebuke from the sovkhoz Party organization for his "blunder" in allowing the bakery thief to escape, but otherwise he emerged unscathed. The material in the Archive makes clear that, while the position of the local NKVD representative was not sacrosanct, it was ordinarily sufficiently formidable to withstand attack.

Party Life in the Sovkhozes

A revealing glimpse of Party life in the sovkhozes is provided by a series of documents devoted to Party organization in the Larnevsk sovkhoz in the year 1935. At that time the Party organization in the sovkhoz consisted of eight members and five candidates.[15] The Party members were all top officials of the sovkhoz — the director, the politotdel chief, the assistant politotdel chief, the NKVD deputy, the chairman of the Workers' Coöperative who also served as Party organizer, a sovkhoz division head, a brigade leader, and the sovkhoz forester. The five Party candidates on the average occupied much less exalted posts — brigade leader, chairman of the workers' committee, storeman, horse trainer, and builder. The sovkhoz Komsomol organization served, partially at least, to project Party influence into the production ranks. Its twenty-three members consisted of two students, two political workers, two engineering and technical workers, four office workers, two tractor drivers, four swineherds, two milkmaids, and five other workers engaged on miscellaneous assignments. Of the fourteen udarniks, or shock-workers, in the sovkhoz, one was a Party member and five were Komsomols. The network of Party education in the sovkhoz included four circles, one devoted to Party history, two to the training of Party candidates, and one for the Komsomols.

The Archive contains two protocols of Party meetings in the Larnevsk sovkhoz which shed light on both Party and sovkhoz problems. At a meeting on September 4, 1935, the sovkhoz director, Comrade Novikov, reported on the harvest, the fulfillment of grain deliveries, and the preparation for meat deliveries.[16] After noting that the plan for grain deliveries had not been attained and that no winter wheat was available for delivery, he indicated that the seed loan and barley deliveries had been fulfilled and that the rye would be sent on the morrow. The politotdel chief, Comrade Leonov, took the lead in the discussion. He stressed that, since Larnevsk was a hog-raising sovkhoz, the fulfillment of the plan for meat deliveries would decide "the entire fate of our sovkhoz." He castigated the "general mismanagement" of hog-raising in the sovkhoz, the inadequate attention to the needs of the swineherds, and the lack of leadership on the part of Communists in the enterprise. A Comrade Kolkin, who directed one of the divisions of the sovkhoz, then asserted that fulfillment of the plan depended on an adequate supply of swineherds, and that the supply was inadequate simply because the swineherds "were not assured food." Criticism was then directed against the chairman of the workers' coöperative who replied that the coöperative was not adequately supplied, that perhaps matters would be improved if the sovkhoz administration assumed responsibility for the dining room, gave the swineherds "a special place in feeding" and provided them "with cultural and living conditions" ("there are no gramophones in the dormitories, etc."). "At almost every meeting," he continued, "we speak about this, pass a resolution about improvement in cultural and living conditions, but this remains unfulfilled."

True to precedent, the Party organization then passed a resolution which read in part:

1. The harvesting of grain is lagging behind . . . as a result of the shortage of workers and the insufficient productivity of labor.
2. The preparation of grain for delivery . . . is also lagging behind . . .

3. The progress of the sowing of winter crops is also insufficient . . .
4. The preparation for meat deliveries is progressing unsatisfactorily . . .
5. Party mass work has been insufficiently developed . . . Few production meetings are held.

The resolution ordered the sovkhoz director "to compose a concrete plan . . . to eliminate the above shortcomings" and set deadlines for the fulfillment of each part of the plan.

The meeting then listened to reports by individual Communists on their fulfillment of Party assignments. The reports were characterized by a notable absence of zeal. One comrade whose job it was to read newspapers to his fellow workers claimed that he had been faithful until August, but had then begun to slip. A second whose task it was to "liquidate" his illiteracy admitted that he had not done so, since, as he put it, "I have poor vision and do not see at night." The third who was supposed to have prepared a wall newspaper admitted that he had neglected the task, though he claimed to have done some work "on checking the membership of Osoaviakhim." Again there were indignant references in the discussion to "shortcomings," and again a resolution which began:

Having heard the personal accounts of the Communist Comrades . . . the Party meeting notes: a non-serious attitude on the part of all the comrades toward the Party assignments entrusted to them. Comrade M . . . did not regularly read newspapers with the workers, and lately has completely stopped this. Comrade U . . . did not manifest a desire to engage in raising his own general educational level. Comrade S . . . manifested a purely formal attitude toward the work entrusted to him . . . He failed completely to organize the publication of the wall newspaper in the shop. The Party meeting decrees: To leave the given assignments to the comrades named and to warn them about a more serious attitude toward the fulfillment of their tasks . . .

The meeting next listened to a report "On the anti-Party behavior of the member of the CPSU(b) I. M. Drobkov." The case against Drobkov was presented by the sovkhoz NKVD chief, who reported that Drobkov not only had defended the son of a kulak who had been dismissed by the board of the workers' coöperative, but had subsequently gone to this man's home and spent the evening drinking with him. He also cited rumors that Drobkov had embezzled more than 800 rubles from the coöperative. "Today," he concluded, "I think that we will not pass any resolution, but it is necessary for all of us Communists to talk about this." The members then pounced on Drobkov and denounced him as an incompetent embezzler who "weeps over the fate of kulaks and gets drunk with them." Drobkov's defense was weak. "It is true that we drank," he admitted, "but this does not mean that I lost my class vigilance . . . I did not embezzle 800 rubles. If there is some missing, I took not more than 200 rubles . . ." After further prolonged discussion the meeting decreed that Comrade Drobkov deserved serious punishment, "but because it is necessary to clarify this matter, the question is considered open until the next Party meeting."

On September 19 the sovkhoz Party cell assembled again.[17] This time the meeting began with a report on the verification of Party documents in the sovkhoz. "On September 18," the politotdel chief reported, "at the plenum of the raikom the question of how the check-up of Party documents was progressing was discussed. The verification in our raion was not of good quality, and this was particularly true of our Party organization. The general shortcoming in our raion is the extremely low percentage of class-alien and hanger-on elements whom we have sifted out of the Party . . . If some one knows of aliens who made their way into the Party, they must not shelter them." After paying his respects to Drobkov he then set a denunciatory example by revealing various unsavory items from the past of three of the five Party candidates in the sovkhoz cell. The first had served a term of forced labor and had later been sentenced to another year of forced labor for stealing oats from the sovkhoz. The second had allegedly concealed the property of a kulak relative in 1931, had had connections with bandits, and took a "careless attitude" toward his production duties. The third, a brigade leader, who failed to appear at the meeting, was said to have been "sentenced" several times and to have embezzled some 78 puds of grain. On the motion of the NKVD chief, Drobkov and the first two candidates were expelled from the Party; the case of the absent candidate was put over until the next meeting.

The meeting next went on to discuss the economic difficulties of the sovkhoz. The director lashed out at the "sabotaging" operations of the Klintsy Hog-Breeding Trust which supervised the sovkhoz and which, he charged, had cost the sovkhoz hundreds of thousands of rubles by locating, building, and equipping the sovkhoz camps in such bad fashion as to "lead to the death of almost all the young animals." "Pigs," observed one of those present, "are delicate animals and need skillful care. In the sovkhoz the quality of the pigs is poor because the young porkers do not have the conditions they need." He then instanced various inadequacies, such as lack of adequate feed, and litter in the pigsties. At this point the politotdel chief interrupted with a demand for self-criticism. "We are shilly-shallying . . . ," he exclaimed.

How have we ourselves fulfilled [our tasks]? . . . We have not fulfilled the plan. We have not fulfilled the norms for gain in weight per head. What are the reasons? It is necessary to say as self-criticism that we should have set up kettles to cook potatoes for feed, and we postponed the matter a very long time. It took us a whole week to set them up. And when we [finally] set up the kettles, we do not supply them with potatoes . . . Many of our lanterns are broken and lie about anywhere, and no one cares to collect them and repair them. Manure is not put out because there are no pitchforks. The pitchforks are also scattered about everywhere . . . We have many short-comings. The Communists working in hog raising show much inattentiveness toward their work . . .

Again, there was a resolution ordering the director of the sovkhoz "to insure a radical improvement in the leadership of the work of hog-raising." Not without significance, the chairman of the meeting was the NKVD chief and the secretary the head of the politotdel.

At this point, the record of the Larnevsk sovkhoz stops, but the same story of inefficiency and disorganization in the sovkhozes can be documented on every side. The Archive contains a long report on the sovkhoz "Zhukovka" which was prepared for the Party Control Commission in 1936.[18] The list of inadequacies in the sovkhoz runs a typical gamut. The planned increase of cattle was not fulfilled. The number of horses decreased from year to year. The death rate among young porkers was fantastically large — from 26 to 32 per cent of all offspring. Costs were far in excess of plan. In 1934 the sovkhoz finished the year with losses of 156,000 rubles. The final figures for 1935 had not yet been totaled, but large losses were again indicated. The feeding of the workers was extremely poor; in the absence of the cook who was on leave, the workers were obliged to eat raw pork, of which 0.2 kilograms were issued per day. Workers' pay was in arrears, and as a result labor turnover was high. Preparations for the winter had not been properly made. The plumbing did not work; the pigsty was damp; the stoves had not been repaired; and the water situation was poor. The repair of tractors was being done unsatisfactorily; spare parts for two tractors were unavailable. To add a somewhat piquant note, at a memorial meeting called to commemorate the death of S. M. Kirov, two school children had proposed that Trotsky be included in the honorary presidium! It was the last action in particular which roused the indignation of the obkom bureau.[19] As a result the assistant politotdel chief for Komsomol work was removed, and both the head of the politotdel and the raikom secretary were reprimanded.

The Sovkhoz Labor Force as a Refuge for Outlawed Elements in Soviet Society

One of the striking characteristics of the sovkhoz labor force was the extent to which it became a refuge for outlawed elements in Soviet society. Former kulaks, one-time tsarist army officers, prison officials and gendarmes, ex-bandits and others whose past was suspect apparently flocked into the sovkhozes in large numbers in order to establish a new identity in Soviet society. Since both labor and administrative personnel were badly needed in the sovkhozes during their period of stormy expansion in the early thirties, the sovkhoz administrators made little initial effort to check the background of the people whom they were hiring. With the establishment of the political sections and the appearance of the OGPU representative in the sovkhoz, controls began to be tightened. But the real impetus to a mass purge of the sovkhozes did not come until after the Kirov affair.

On April 12, 1935, the PUNS chief circulated a secret letter to all heads of politotdels "On raising revolutionary vigilance in the work of the political sections." [20] The letter began by congratulating them on having rid the sovkhozes of 100,000 enemies of the Soviet regime from the time of the establishment of the politotdels. But the letter then went on to cite cases of "lowered vigilance" where as a result of the hiring of laborers "without checking their social background," sovkhozes were penetrated by "kulaks, White Guards, and other counterrevolutionary elements." A special investigation in one sovkhoz disclosed that out of 577 employees and workers, forty-nine were White Guardists, sixty-nine kulaks, four former White officers, and six sons of atamans and priests. Some of them had even gained admittance in the Party and were "the principal cause" of anti-Soviet propaganda and wrecking. Other cases were mentioned where Trotskyites, Zinovievites, and even Socialist-Revolutionaries had managed to insinuate themselves into such responsible sovkhoz positions as directors, deputy directors, politotdel chiefs, and agronomists. One sovkhoz agronomist, who later "confessed" that he was an active wrecker and an agent of the Polish intelligence service, is quoted as having said after the assassination of Kirov: "There are still brave men who kill the leaders." One politotdel chief was accused of having allowed some sovkhoz workers "to express their satisfaction with the death of Kirov." In this sovkhoz "counterrevolutionary elements" succeeded in "mutilating portraits of the leaders" in the Lenin corner. The politotdel chief not only failed to do anything about it, but even gave aid and comfort to the counterrevolutionaries "by circulating anti-Soviet anecdotes." The politotdel chief was fired from his job and expelled from the Party. In another sovkhoz members of a tractor brigade "mutilated portraits of Lenin and Stalin" and at a meeting commemorating Kirov, one of them cried out: "So they killed him! Well, let's now collect a kopeck from every one in his memory." Although the NKVD and politotdel chiefs heard the cry, they "failed to give the matter an appropriate political evaluation."

In conclusion, the letter noted that "after initial successes" the politotdels were falling down on their job, failing to unmask class enemies and treating Zinovieties, Trotskyites, and right deviationists "with opportunistic indifference." The letter ordered a thorough screening of all sovkhoz workers and prompt action to rid the sovkhozes of remaining class enemies.

In the Western Oblast action was quickly forthcoming. The Archive contains long lists of "former people" and "socially alien" elements in various sovkhozes who were scheduled for elimination. In the sovkhoz "Zlynka," for example, it was discovered that the director was the son of a trusted stableman "of the great prince Mikhail Romanov," and that he had brought into the kolkhoz a whole host of disenfranchised people with whom he drank and was friendly.[21] The zootechnician turned out to be the son of a kulak and the veterinarian an expelled Trotskyite of kulak background. In addition, there were more than a dozen brigade leaders, tractor drivers, swineherds, guards, carpenters, and other workers who were either former kulaks, children of kulaks, "large-scale exploiters," or church elders.

As might be expected, the order to rid the sovkhozes of "socially alien elements" provided a field day for the NKVD representatives in the sovkhozes. A typical letter dated November 3, 1935, from the NKVD chief in the Barbino sovkhoz to the head of the political section of the Klintsy Hog-Breeding Trust conveys the atmosphere of the period.[22] The letter read:

We attach lists of the socially alien elements in the "Barbino" and "Krasilovka" sovkhozes. At the same time I report that despite my information on the presence of socially alien elements in the sovkhozes, the directors of the sovkhozes ignore the instructions of the Political Administration of the People's Commissariat of State Farms on ridding the sovkhozes of class-alien elements.

For example: in the "Krasilovka" sovkhoz at the end of 1934 according to my information the daughter of a kulak and the wife of a bandit, S. D. Kovaleva, was sentenced for stealing things from the dining room. On the basis of this I demanded that the director of the sovkhoz, Ponomarev, release her from the sovkhoz. But the director did not release her, and she works there to this day.

In addition on the arrival of the new politotdel chief, Comrade Usachev, I informed him of the presence of socially alien elements in the sovkhoz, after which we asked the director to release from the sovkhoz [seven persons, names listed] to which Ponomarev gave his agreement — but the persons enumerated are working there to this day.

In the Barbino sovkhoz they also take almost no measures to get rid of the kulak elements. For example: F. Ye. Voron, the son of a dekulakized kulak . . . on the insistence of the politotdel at the beginning of 1935 was released, but after a short time was reaccepted and works to this day as a carpenter on construction. Another case: despite my categorical objections, the heavily taxed person and idler, F. Shapovalov, works to this day as mechanic in the hog-raising farm.

In addition, the former accountant, I. R. Zavatsky, the son of a kulak, whose father owned a butter factory and who employed hired labor in his household, was removed from work for systematically cheating the workers and for a negligent attitude toward his work, and he was brought to trial. But the sovkhoz director did not release him, as he should have done, but put him back as accountant in the sovkhoz office, where he again cheats the workers. Zavatsky works as accountant to this day.

The lists attached to this letter contained twenty-one names, for the most part former kulaks and children of kulaks, merchants, and priests.

Between the lines of the letter, one can sense some of the problems which the purge of the sovkhozes created for sovkhoz administrators. The reluctance of the sovkhoz directors to part with so-called "socially alien elements" was ordinarily inspired, not by sympathy with them, but by the desire to retain experienced personnel who were badly needed to keep the sovkhozes running on a reasonably efficient plane. But such insistence became increasingly dangerous as the purge hysteria mounted during the mid-thirties. Sovkhoz directors who resisted the dispersal of their work force were themselves the victims of accusations of anti-Party behavior which cost them their jobs and sometimes even their lives.

As the material cited here indicates, the record of the sovkhozes in the Western Oblast through the mid-thirties was far from a glorious one. Complaints of low productivity, high cost, and inefficiency run like a monotonous refrain through the reports. As elsewhere in the Soviet Union, the disappointment with the performance of the sovkhozes led to their deëmphasis. After the first phase of stormy expansion in the early thirties, the sovkhozes settled down to a period of consolidation and slow growth in an effort to render them productive and efficient. The success of these efforts cannot be appraised on the basis of the evidence in the Archive, since there are no sovkhoz files for the years after 1936. Up to that point the Archive makes clear that their achievements were modest indeed.

16 The Grievances of Industrial Workers

The problems of industrial labor occupy a relatively subordinate place in the Smolensk Archive; the flow of documentation tends to reflect the preoccupations of the oblast leadership with issues of agrarian policy and administration. During the thirties, moreover, the trend toward increasing industrial centralization removed a substantial segment of industry from local supervision; as Rumyantsev pointed out in his speech to the Seventeenth Party Congress in 1934, "In 1930 in our oblast, all-Union industry amounted to 31%, republican to 33%, and oblast to 36%. In 1933 this percentage changed sharply; all-Union industry was 88% and oblast industry 12%. Thus our enterprises in some way imperceptibly fell under the influence of the central units, of all four [industrial] People's Commissariats, so that all the small factories were run by the central boards." [1] With the transfer of industry to central management also went responsibility for the industrial labor force.

The only systematic collection of labor data in the Smolensk Archive is contained in a lengthy document entitled "Materials for a report on the position of the working class in the Western Oblast as of October 1, 1929." [2] Yet even these data must be used with caution, since the anonymous author or authors inform us that "a characteristic phenomenon is the contradiction of the numerical data: the oblast statistical division gives one set of figures, the oblast planning organization another, the coöperatives a third, and the local trade unions — a fourth." [3] According to the report, out of an oblast population of 6,577,000, workers in census industry totaled only 70,714, or 1.15 per cent of the population.[4] If railroad, agricultural, and seasonal workers were added, the total mounted to 203,183 or 3.08 per cent of the population. The oblast trade union membership, which included many nonindustrial categories, totaled only 302,153 on July 1, 1929. Nor was the projected increase in the industrial labor force under the First Five Year Plan particularly grandiose. By the last year, 1932-33, the number of workers in census industry was expected to reach 107,292.

The largest plants in terms of employment were concentrated in the machine-building and metal-working, textile, chemical, and paper industries. In 1929 the machine-building and metal-working industry alone absorbed 27.8 per cent of the industrial labor force.[5] Next followed the textile industry with 18 per cent, the chemical industry with 16 per cent, the wood-working enterprises with 12 per cent, the paper industry with 7.8 per cent, and the construction industry with 5.3 per cent. Together they accounted for 86.9 per cent of the industrial labor force. With a few major exceptions the industries of the oblast were typically small-scale enterprises rarely employing more than several hundred workers.

The Link with the Villages

The most characteristic feature of the oblast industrial labor force was its newness to factory life, its relatively recent arrival from the countryside, and its continuing close connection with the land. The constant influx of new workers from the villages posed a variety of problems for both management and the Party. Peasants fresh from the plow adjusted with difficulty to the industrial discipline. They had to be taught and trained, and frequently their standards of literacy were so low as to make the process of training a tortuous and frustrating enterprise. Usually they were passive and indifferent to Party indoctrination, and they tended to be suspicious of the godless Commissars. Their links with the countryside induced sympathy with those who resisted dekulakization and collectivization.

The persistence of these peasant attitudes is vividly reflected in a series of OGPU reports from Yartsevo on conversations among textile workers. "On April 19 of this year [1929]," noted one report, "in the spinning section of the factory a conversation took place among the workers in which Kondratovich said that we've had 12 years of the revolution, but there isn't any grain, and there isn't any because the government doesn't give enough aid to the peasants . . ." [6] Other typical statements quoted include: "The incorrect tax policy in the country is ruining the peasants and undermining the food base of the workers . . . They don't let the strong peasant grow, and therefore there is a shortage of agricultural products . . . The majority of the poor peasants are idlers, and they are exempted from taxes." [7]

The indifference of the worker-peasants toward Party leadership is reflected in another report. "According to our information," stated the OGPU, "on May 1 near the 203rd barrack where the workers were supposed to assemble for a [holiday] demonstration, a conversation took place among the Party members where Marchenkov from the economic division said, 'It is evident that we cannot lead the mass of workers. We alone are only 50 people in the barrack, and the workers wash their linen in their rooms and some look at us from the windows and laugh. It is a shame for us Party members that with such a barrack as Number 203, where there are about 500 workers, not one went out of the barrack and joined us . . .'" [8]

"On May 4 of this year," continued the OGPU report:

in contradistinction to the May Day holiday, the workers in the barracks made feverish preparations for the Easter holidays, fixed up the barracks, baked *kulich* [Easter cakes], etc. In general on this day you could sense from the mood of the workers that they were looking forward to some great holiday. Among the workers there was a conversation in which Larchenkov, the grinder, said that today the workers begin to prepare for a holiday, feel that it is their own holiday, and not the Bolshevik holiday. You only have to go into the barracks and immediately you can see that the workers are looking forward to and preparing for their own holiday. Here, see how all in the barracks bake kulich for themselves, and if you ask any one of the workers, they say that they will bring the kulich to the church in Ulkhovo to be blessed. The cleaner Kondratovich said: "This is good; let our commissars see what the workers think is the real holiday. I am sure that today the church will be full, much more so than their club." The spinner Volchkov said: "What do you see at the club? *The Blue Blouse* [apparently a play]. People are fed up with it; they have given it 10 times, and it's all the same; we've had enough of it. Of course, the workers will go to church, because they have no other place to go . . . The worker won't go to the club, because they have made him angry, and have especially angered him because before the holidays they closed the wine shop, which left the workers without vodka, and they even played such a low trick as to forbid the sale of raisins. They think that without raisins, the workers will not bake kulich, but let them come and look around, and they will be convinced that in any stove you wish they are baking kulich without raisins."

In the evening it was observed that the workers gradually began to go to the Ulkhovo church, and a whole procession began in the direction of the church. Old people and middle-aged people went, and also some young people. Comparing this year with last year, it is necessary to point out that this year among the workers the attraction toward the church was much greater than last year and even in previous years . . . On May 5, on the day of Easter itself, in all the barracks and on the streets the workers were dressed in holiday garb; there were more drunkards about, and they sang songs with a religious content.

And the OGPU report continued:

On May 6 this year in the spinning section there was a conversation among the workers where the apprentice S. V. Arefyev said: ". . . Our Bolsheviks write in the newspapers that in many places they have closed the churches, and I think that this is simply nonsense, because among us the workers have become more religious than in the old days. Now in the church in Ulkhovo there were about 4,000 people; it was impossible to get to the church." The apprentice I. M. Grachev said: ". . . I don't even remember an Easter when there were so many people in the churches . . . I think that the Bolsheviks certainly must have pondered when they saw so many workers in church . . . The Bolsheviks spite the workers, so the workers spite the Bolsheviks. Take their May Day holiday. The little children came out to hear the music, but all the workers sat at home. But on their own Easter holiday they all went to church. The Bolsheviks do evil to the workers, so the workers do them evil."

Such conversations take place among the workers not only in the factory, but also in the barracks. Almost all the workers are delighted at the fact that this year there were many workers in church. It is necessary to note that in the current year there were more cases than ever before where the workers accepted priests among themselves into their rooms, and even those workers who did not accept priests last year accepted them this year.[9]

The Imperatives of Industrialization

The year 1929 marked something of a turning point in the history of Soviet labor. As the imperatives of rapid industrialization took hold, there occurred a marked tightening of labor discipline, a strengthening of managerial prerogatives, an atrophy in the powers of the trade unions, an increase in work norms, and a serious deterioration in the living standards of rank-and-file workers. The Smolensk Archive offers abundant evidence to document these developments.

On February 21, 1929, the Central Committee of the Party circulated a letter to all Party organizations labeled "Not for Publication." [10] The letter began by noting a "deterioration of labor discipline" in the factories, which it attributed mainly to "the attraction into production of new strata of workers, most of whom have ties with the country. Because of this, in most cases rural attitudes and private economic interests dominate these strata of workers, and therefore, since they are insufficiently connected with production, it is more difficult for them to submit to factory and mill work and they master slowly the labor discipline necessary in production. The most serious cases of breach of labor discipline concern these very cadres of workers . . ." The letter called on the trade unions and the Party to wage a "resolute struggle" to improve labor discipline and to increase productivity. "The struggle for the successful realization of the directive on lowering production costs and improving labor discipline in production," the letter stated, "is chiefly the task of the manager, the specialist, and the technical personnel. The task of the Party organs and the trade union organizations is to insure one-man rule (of the administrator, the director) in all problems of the operative leadership of the enterprise, giving to the administration all possible support in carrying out measures directed toward improving production and creating for the administrative and technical personnel a businesslike, comradely atmosphere for work in the enterprise."

"In view of the fact," the letter continued, "that up till now in enterprises it has been observed that the workers carry on various types of public duties (sessions, meetings, collections of membership dues, etc.) during working hours, all factory and plant organizations are categorically ordered to eliminate such things, timing the fulfillment of public duties to the lunch hour or the period before the beginning and after the end of work, with the exception of people who are specially released according to an established procedure."

The letter called for an end to specialist-baiting. "In the eyes of a conscious, class-loyal proletarian, the engineer, or the foreman, should be considered good who himself displays technical initiative and supports the initiative of workers, especially resourceful workers, who advances the cause of rationalization, introduces new methods, strictly and sternly carries out labor discipline, and demands unconditional discipline from all subordinates." The directive to strengthen managerial prerogatives was accompanied by a reminder to all Party organizations that they would be judged by their ability to help management improve labor discipline, root out absenteeism, and raise labor productivity.

In the course of the year a determined campaign was launched to fulfill the terms of the Central Committee letter. In the Western Oblast at least, the campaign enjoyed only qualified success. Although the 1929 report cited earlier claimed some improvement, it described the situation as still "unsatisfactory." "The number of voluntary absences was large; an increase of absences from work on account of sickness was noted; people appeared at work drunk; there was a careless attitude toward production in some cases. It is necessary to note," the report added, "that lowered labor discipline is found mainly among the unqualified, newly arrived cadres, the majority of whom are connected with agriculture." [11]

The required emphasis on one-man management was also attended by a substantial weakening of the position of the trade unions and a decline in their prestige among the workers. Again the OGPU reports for 1929 provide graphic supporting evidence. Reporting on conditions in Yartsevo, the OGPU noted:

In the mechanical shop among the locksmiths there was a conversation about elections of the factory [trade union] committees and the shop trade union bureau [tsekhprofburo] in which Prudnikov said that there was something in the newspapers to the effect that at the "Third International" Factory the workers refused to elect a tsekhprofburo. At this the worker Vorontsov said that the workers of the "Third International" Factory acted correctly. We don't need the tsekhprofburo at all; it is a superfluous overhead expense. The workers present agreed completely with Vorontsov's opinion . . . In barrack No. 156 among the workers there was a conversation along these lines: "Why the devil did we elect a factory committee and a tsekhprofburo? They have turned out to be useless organizations. We elected them so that they would defend the workers and trade union members, but they did the opposite. They help the administration fire from the factory their own workers who elected them. The factory committee and the tsekhprofburo are on our necks; they don't defend us, but only take our money in order to help the managers drive our workers out of the factory. We don't need such factory committees at all . . ." In the lavatory of the weaving section the weaver Zavitsky in the presence of other weavers made the accusation that the factory committee and the administration are one and the same thing, that they work together as one . . .[12]

In the Yartsevo textile factory as well as elsewhere the resentment of workers against the new dispensation was intensified by the decision of management to increase work norms and to introduce other measures of rationalization designed to raise labor productivity. In some cases the reaction bordered on the explosive. The OGPU describes a meeting at the Yartsevo plant at which the assistant director of the factory Gubanov and the chairman of the factory trade union committee Davydov attempted to address the weavers on the subject of lowering production costs.

As soon as the meeting opened [the OGPU reported], the weavers made their way to the exit, and, as a result, of all the weavers working in the second shift, not more than 100 remained . . . The weavers as they were leaving, shouted: "You well-fed devils have sucked the juices out of us enough. You hypocritical wall-eyes are pulling the wool over our eyes. For twelve years already you have driveled and agitated and stuffed our heads. Before you shouted that the factory owners exploited us, but the factory owners did not force us to work in 4 shifts, and there was enough of everything in the shops. Now we work in 4 shifts. Where before 4 men worked, now only one works. You are bloodsuckers, and that's not all, you still want to draw blood out of our veins. If you go to a shop now and want to buy something, the shops are empty; there are no shoes, no clothing; there is nothing the worker needs. But the [cost of] shares in the coöperative increase every day. Before we got along without any shares, and there was enough of everything. When the administration had to transfer the factory to an uninterrupted shift, they built refreshment stands, sold rolls, did everything for the worker so that he would support the proposal, but as soon as this project was put into effect what happened? They closed the refreshment stands, stopped selling rolls, again everything was as before. After 8 hours of work at the benches you are so worn out that your eyes are dimmed, and then they come to drown your senses completely. They have found a gimmick which they can keep using — you comrades are the managers of the factory. But when you look at the managers, you will see how they throw hundreds of us out of the factory onto the labor market. Here are managers for you! Before the bourgeoisie during a strike used to fire two or three participants and then let it go at that, and now not a year goes by without their cutting down . . ."[13]

On April 21, the OGPU reported another typical conversation among the spinners in the 91st barrack:

The spinner Yakov Koglov said that in India after the strike in Bombay a man became a skeleton; they wore him out completely. The unemployed person, Anton Belsky, said that our leaders see what is going on in other countries, but they don't see what is going on here. And don't they wear our workers out? Now they are planning the working-day more efficiently, and where 3 to 6 people worked previously, they are leaving one, so that they wear us out just as much as in India, only the difference is that with us, they do it gradually, but the result is the same . . .[14]

In some cases the reaction against increased norms spilled over into open strikes against the regime. Among the items found in the Smolensk Archive is an Informational Letter of the Stalino okrug Party committee dated July 10, 1929, which contains a number of references to such incidents.[15] On May 9, noted the letter, both shifts in mines 4 and 5 of the Budenovsk Mine Administration refused to go to work. An investigation disclosed that the Mine Administration had increased the norms on an average of 11.7 per cent, which led to a sharp curtailment of earnings of up to 30 to 40 per cent for nearly half the miners. In this case the increase in norms was cut back to 4.7 per cent; the miners were ordered back to work; and the mine manager, trade union committee, and bureau of the Party cell were dismissed because "they were incapable of managing the leadership of the economic and trade union organizations." On June 27 in the "Italia" mine of the Makeyevsk Mine Administration ninety-four miners struck because they had been ordered to shift from small cars to cars of larger capacity without corresponding upward adjustments in pay. Prior to the outbreak of the strike the workers had demanded a review of norms and evaluations without obtaining any satisfaction. "If you don't want to work," commented a member of the mine's trade union committee, "go ahead and leave." Thereupon a group of seven, including two Communists and a Komsomol member, took the lead in calling the strike. After persuading one shift not to go down into the mines, they appealed to the next: "Our comrades on the previous shift did not go to work, and we must not go. Let them consider us deserters, but we will not go to work until they review the norms and evaluations." The chairman of the mine's trade union committee, who was present, pleaded in vain with the miners to go down into the shafts. What happened to the strikers is not recorded; the secretary of the Stalino okrugkom attributed the trouble to "insufficient explanatory work among the workers on the tasks facing the country" and to "the alienation of the Party and trade union organizations from the mass of workers." [16]

As part of the campaign to raise labor productivity, a determined effort was made to enlist the energy and enthusiasm of the workers around the slogan of "socialist competition" as "a new form of resolute struggle for the fulfillment of the economic tasks of the Five Year Plan." But this campaign too encountered unexpected resistance. In the words of the report "On the Position of the Working Class in the Western Oblast": "Economic and political contracts were signed between enterprises, challenges were made by one enterprise to another, but the workers who thus entered into socialist competition did not know what was concretely demanded of them, what norms they should achieve." [17] As the realization dawned that "socialist competition" involved the raising of work norms without corresponding upward adjustment in wages, a number of workers developed a negative attitude toward the whole concept. The report cited above provides a frank record of these reactions.

For example, in the Kamensk Paper Factory such statements were made: "competition is being carried out so that they can wring the sweat out of the workers"; "Socialist competition is bondage for the workers and prosperity for the administration." . . . In the Pesochi Factory the workers stated: "We develop competition, and then you lower the norms." In the cement factory the factory committee wrote: "There are on the part of some groups of workers, who are connected with agriculture, such statements as: 'Socialist competition abolishes norms; we will work as we now do, but competition is not necessary for us.'" There took place the outrageous case in the "Krasnyi Gigant" Factory where a former member of the Party fell upon the worker Pirulnikov with the words: "You traitor, you bootlicker, socialist competition is bondage for the workers, the Party wrings the juices out of us!" etc. A no less outrageous event occurred in one of the enterprises of Bryansk okrug, where the shockworker Yermakov, in the interests of the enterprise, came to the conclusion that one worker in the shop could be discharged without harmful effects, and for this he was beaten by the worker who was designated to be fired.

In the Yartsevo factory there were conversations: "They began to lull the workers with various songs to the effect that if our factory fulfills the established norm, it will occupy first place. All this is done so that we will work better. But the worker is not a fool, he's breaking his back for nothing, he will not agree." In the Klintsy factories there were such statements: "They want to build mountains at one stroke, and on whom will the burden fall? — on the neck of the workers. Socialist competition is a new yoke on the neck of the workers. They want to drive the half-dead worker to the grave before his time. Socialist competition is an invention of those who sit on top."

No less typical are the cases of the negative attitude toward socialist competition among the railroad workers of Velikiye Luki okrug, where the workers of Klyastitsa Station did not accept the challenge, stating that their labor productivity was high enough, and in the main shops one worker came out against socialist competition, saying that they work well and that socialist competition is of no avail to them.

"Such attitudes," the report concludes, "can be attributed in the first place to workers who are connected with agriculture and who have recently come to the factories. This category participates least of all in productive life and to some degree influences the backward workers. It is necessary to say that at the present moment, in connection with the survey of socialist competition which has been carried out in the enterprises by the economic organs and their apparatuses, in a number of places there is exceptional apathy and sluggishness . . ." [18]

The Deterioration in Living Standards

The "apathy and sluggishness" of ordinary workers were not unconnected with the deterioration in the supply of food and consumers' goods
and the failure of real wages to keep up with increased work norms.
The 1929 report contains a variety of data on wages and the standard of
living at that period. Data cited in the report indicate that while the
average nominal monthly wage per worker increased 8.8 per cent during the first ten months of 1928–29 compared with the average for
1927–28, real wages during the same period increased on an average
only 1.3 per cent.[19] In a number of industries — textiles, tanning, wood-
working, matches, flax-processing, and distilling — real wages, however,
declined from 2.5 to more than 6.0 per cent. Between October 1928 and
August 1929 the *nabor* (the amount of money which a worker had to
pay at official prices for a typical market basket of necessary articles such
as bread, salt, etc.) increased 11.3 per cent. This increase, however, did
not measure the full extent of the inflation. In the cautious words of
the report, "The high percentage of influence of the private market
in supplying the agricultural group of goods and the 'scissors' between
the prices of the coöperatives and the free market, which has been
especially apparent lately, testify to the fact that the workers' coöperatives were unable to fulfill their tasks in preserving the real level of
wages." [20] Workers had to turn to the private traders to meet their needs,
and since food was scarce prices on the free market mounted accordingly. The price per kilogram of rye flour in the free market increased
from 12.3 rubles in 1927–28 to 33.1 rubles in 1928–29, or nearly three times
the official price in the coöperatives. The price of wheat flour increased
from 25.9 rubles to 48.4 rubles per kilo in the same period, while sugar
mounted from 75.9 rubles to 108.2 rubles per kilo. In the words of the
report, ". . . the situation with respect to food and produce supply of
the workers in industrial enterprises remains continually strained throughout the Western Oblast, and in some goods, probably, it is growing worse
(meat, milk products) . . . Up to this time the consumers' coöperatives'
share of the market for food products of agricultural origin (meat,
potatoes, vegetables, butter, milk, eggs, etc.) and the supply of the
workers with them is far from satisfactory, as a result of which the private
trader occupies almost a dominant position in these markets." [21]

The report painted a rather grim picture of factory and coöperative
dining rooms which catered to the worker. "The sanitary and hygienic
situation of the dining rooms needs to be radically improved: there is
dirt, there are swarms of flies, soiled oil cloths, dirty tablecloths on the
tables, etc. The quality of the food is not at all satisfactory. Lines at the
ticket office and endless waiting for lunches lessen the desire to frequent the

dining rooms. The prices in the dining rooms are still high." [22] Quoting one group of workers on the dining room of the Central Workers' Cooperative No. 7, the report stated: "The luncheon menu is always the same; every day *shchi* with *kasha* and cutlets. In the so-called soup it is hard to find pieces of anything. It is not soup, but vegetable water; there is no fat, and the meat is not always washed sufficiently. There were cases where they served meat with entrails. Little worms were found in the lunch. A statement was drawn up and sent to the division of public nutrition, but the workers do not know of the results." [23]

"The situation with regard to supplying the workers with goods in short supply," the report continued, "is especially acute." [24] The norms for baked bread were 600 grams per day for a worker and 300 grams for a member of his family. The supply of fat ranged from 200 grams to one liter of vegetable oil per month, "and even that not every month. These norms, of course, cannot be considered normal and sufficient." [25] The average worker received one kilogram of sugar products per month, with the exception of Rzhev and Viazma where the amounts distributed were slightly higher. "The supply of tea," the report pointed out, "has always been insufficient. The prospects for the supply of tea in 1929–30 guarantee the satisfaction of only 25–30% of the demand." [26] The supply of consumers' goods was also described as "unfavorable." In the words of the report, "The workers received roughly 30–36 meters of cotton cloth per year (there is almost no woven cloth). Linens are poor . . . Thread at the present moment must also be included in the group of goods in acute shortage . . . there were cases [during the last few months] when for . . . 2–3 spools of thread . . . lines of up to 300 people formed at the stores of the Central Workers' Coöperative . . . Leather goods continue to remain in the group of products in short supply. They are furnished only to repair shops, the work of which, by the way, is still in poor condition in the oblast . . ." [27] Summarizing, the report noted, "All these shortcomings . . . engender anti-Soviet feelings . . . and sometimes even valid dissatisfaction on the part of the workers." [28]

It was also acknowledged that the Western Oblast was suffering from "an unusually acute housing shortage." As the report put it, "The village is going to the city, the population is increasing, and, understandably, there is a shortage of living space." [29] Despite increased expenditures on housing construction, the average norm per worker was strikingly inadequate. In the Yartsevo factory, for example, for the year 1928–29 the norm in the barracks was 3.50 square meters, in houses 5.61 square meters.[30] The factory committee of the Vorovsky Cement Factory reported: "In our factory now there is an extraordinary housing crisis . . . Every day there are many complaints about apartments at the factory committee. Many workers have families of 6 and 7 people and live in one room, with an area of 12 square meters. The factory committee has about 500 applications from workers who do not have apartments." [31] The Western Glass Trust wrote: ". . . the housing fund of the factories is extremely small . . . at the present time, it satisfies roughly 5% of the demand. The housing crisis in our factories undoubtedly has a bad influence on production, since the workers are forced to live in neighboring villages around the factories. There are frequent absences due to bad weather (spring and fall slush, for example), and then work is interrupted to the detriment of production. There are workers who live a distance of 45–70 versts away from the factories . . . It is impossible to hush up the fact that although there is a housing crisis, persons who have nothing to do with the factory live in the houses of the factory. For example, in the Dyatkovo Crystal Factory up to 80 apartments are occupied by outsiders, while about 250 workers live in private apartments outside of the factory." [32] The report also noted "an unfavorable situation" in regard to dormitories. All the available materials characterize the status of the dormitories as unsanitary. For example, the factory committee of the Snezhetsky Sawmill No. 12 writes: "The housing area is poor, especially in the dormitories. It is crowded; there are not enough repairs made; bed bugs are frequent guests in the dormitories." [33] The report concluded that it would be necessary to increase expenditures on housing. "Otherwise the crying need for housing will not be eliminated. And it is difficult to carry on cultural and educational work and to raise the productivity of labor if the worker lives under difficult conditions." [34]

It is against this background that the dissatisfaction of rank-and-file workers with the course of events during the early years of the First Five Year Plan assumes concreteness and reality. Indeed, there is also evidence that worker dissatisfaction spilled over into Party ranks. The Smolensk Archive contains an interesting letter dated April 17, 1929, from one Tyavsa, a Communist, addressed to Ivanov, the secretary of the Party cell in the Yartsevo factory, which illustrates the self-doubts and tortured consciences the policies of the late twenties engendered.

Comrade Ivanov: I direct this letter to you because you, as a Communist worker, know the working class and its psychology very well, and therefore you will understand very well its complaints and dissatisfaction with our Party at the way in which some problems are being solved.

Among us in the textile industry they are now carrying on a campaign of rationalization . . . ; in this campaign we, as Communists, lead the masses, but under our leadership it proceeds as in any capitalist economy abroad. You will probably agree with me completely in this . . . If we do not change the course of rationalization . . . then we will cause a rupture with the working class which we will be unable to heal for some time. And it is certainly necessary to understand that times have changed, that the time has passed when the worker didn't understand anything. Everything revolved around him and continues to revolve around him. And we already know that he is beginning to understand — the last two meetings where we suffered a complete failure in our attempt to lead the masses. They now begin to boycott us, they begin to call us jabberers in production and speak such heresy: "You Bolsheviks, you were Bolsheviks up to the time when you were without power in torn breeches, but as soon as you seized power, you forgot what you had prophesied," etc. In some cases you don't know how to wriggle out of such questions.

Comrade Ivanov, you will say that this is a manifestation of Trotskyism, or of the right deviation, that under such conditions the Party must work. There are difficulties — nobody denies them — but if we traveled the Leninist path we would always conquer without any dissatisfaction on the part of the workers. And we as Communists should take this dissatisfaction into consideration, for it is completely justified.

Oh, what impudence do some "Party members" display, only not Leninist Communists, who assert, sitting in their offices and seeing no further than their noses, that they are following in the footsteps of the testament of the Communist leader, Lenin, in solving economic difficulties. You see that everywhere they speculate on the authority of the dead leader, even where this should not be. Ah, if he were alive, how he would thrash into us sorry Party leaders for our attempt to be at the head of the masses but not always with the masses, for the fact that we now do what previously we decried! What a disgrace for the Communists when reproaches are poured on us by non-Party people for our unjust chatter and deeds, and how demeaning for the Communists to hear their just reproaches! . . .

I write you this letter, but am certain that the Party organization will not know anything about it . . .[35]

Labor Disputes and Strikes

As might be expected under conditions of tightening pressure on the workers, the 1929 report noted a substantial increase in labor disputes.[36] In ten enterprises for which data were available, 1,865 disputes were recorded in the period from January to September. Of 449 conflicts which were more intensively studied, 49.8 per cent focused on disputes over wage rates or work norms; another 19.6 per cent involved protests against dismissals from work; 12.2 per cent arose out of administrative punishments for violation of labor discipline; 4.9 per cent concerned issues of labor protection; and the rest related to interpretations of the collective labor agreement. Ordinarily such disputes were submitted to the RKK (Rates and Conflict Commission), on which factory management and trade unions were equally represented. An analysis of disputes in the "Krasnyi Profintern" Factory, one of the largest in the oblast, revealed that 85 per cent of the dispute claims were initiated by workers and only 15 per cent by the administration. The report described this distribution as probably typical of most enterprises. Still another study of 1,252 dis-

putes in eight factories disclosed that 86.6 per cent were settled in the
RKK, 53.1 per cent in favor of the administration and 46.9 per cent in
favor of the workers. Of the appeals taken from the RKK to higher conflict organs, 33 per cent were decided in favor of the workers.

While the availability of this procedure for the resolution of disputes
undoubtedly helped to mitigate or prevent more violent outbreaks on
the part of the workers, in some instances strikes did take place. "From
January to June of this year [1929]," notes the report, "seven strikes were
recorded with 718 participants." [37] The largest strikes involved seasonal
workers. Presumably these strikes as well as the Stalino walk-outs mentioned earlier were illegal, but the Archive leaves the issue in some doubt.
The only general statement on the status of strikes in state enterprises
which was discovered in the Archive was contained in a secret directive
of January 26, 1927, from the Chairman of the Central Committee of the
Wood-Workers' Union to all central boards and oblast and guberniya
divisions of the union. The directive read:

> A strike in a state enterprise, in whose successful work we are directly con-
> cerned, is an extreme measure only and can only be the result of a clearly
> *bureaucratic approach* on the part of the economic organ or of *an unconscious
> attitude on the part of some groups of workers and trade unionists* who have
> not fully realized that we must not do damage to the state economic organiza-
> tions. Therefore the most important task of the trade union organs is to take
> preparatory measures on time in order to prohibit a strike movement in state
> enterprises.
>   In case of demands to call a strike in a state enterprise, regardless of the
> size of the enterprise and the number of workers in it, the strike must be
> sanctioned beforehand by the Central Committee of the Trade Union, with-
> out which the calling of a strike is categorically forbidden.[38]

As this directive makes clear, no strike could be considered legal without
the advance approval of the central authorities of the trade union concerned; the Archive records no instance where such central approval was
forthcoming, and indeed no further references to strikes at all.

The Rising Status of the Technical Intelligentsia

After 1929 the material on labor in the Smolensk Archive thins out
greatly, and what material there is provides hardly more than an impres-
sionistic, if still authoritative, view of trends. One striking trend which revealed itself early was the high value placed on technical training and
the readiness of the regime to abandon old slogans of proletarian egalitarianism in favor of special attention to the needs of the technical intelligentsia. The Archive makes this solicitude clear in a secret decree of the
Party Central Committee dated June 10, 1931, "On the work of the tech-

nical personnel in factories and the improvement of the living conditions of engineering and technical workers." [39] The more important provisions of the decree read as follows:

1. The leaders of enterprises and institutions, Party and trade union organs must enhance the authority of the engineering and technical personnel. It is especially necessary to support young specialists, insuring their further growth during their work.

2. Offer to the engineering and technical personnel the opportunity to display broad initiative in the rationalization and improvement of the processes of production — unsatisfactory results are to be subject to technical and economic analysis by leaders of factories and units only.

3. The leaders of enterprises and institutions must in every way encourage specialists to display inventiveness in their work, skillful leadership, energy, and initiative, through awarding them premiums, writing in the press about their achievements, and in especially outstanding cases nominating engineering-technical workers for rewards.

4. Review the cases of those specialists tried and sentenced to forced labor for defects which they allowed in work and for blunders and violations of labor legislation. In regard to sentenced specialists who have proven by their work devotion to the cause of socialist construction, annul the sentence, eliminating entries from their work papers . . .

5. In order to use to the best advantage the present engineering-technical cadres, review the work burdens of specialists working in enterprises and institutions and release them from bureaucratic and other work which is not their own, transferring it to the service personnel.

6. Increase the practice of appointing engineering and technical workers to the position of heads of shops, heads of construction, heads of technical and like divisions, and to other leading positions.

7. In order to improve the living conditions of engineering-technical workers, carry out the following measures:

a. Supply places for the children of engineering-technical workers in educational institutions on a par with children of industrial workers;

b. Insure . . . houses of rest and sanatoria equal to those of the industrial workers;

c. Give aid . . . during their illness equal to that for workers;

d. In transferring engineering-technical workers from production to work in institutions . . . do not permit lower pay for their work;

e. Make the engineering-technical workers equal to the industrial workers in the right to receive living space . . . In establishing the norms of living space . . . offer them the right to an additional area on a par with responsible workers.

8. *a.* Forbid the organs of the militia, the criminal investigation department, and the procuracy to interfere in the productive life of the factory and to investigate production matters without special permission from the director of the enterprise or higher organs.

b. Consider inexpedient the presence of official representatives of the OGPU in the enterprises.

c. Forbid the Party organizations to change, correct, or delay the operative orders of the directors of the factories.

While this decree was specifically designed to put a stop to the specialist-baiting of the early years of the First Five Year Plan and many of its provisions were subsequently honored in the breach, it nevertheless symbolized the rising influence and status of the technical intelligentsia under the conditions of rapid industrialization.

The Repudiation of Egalitarianism

Hand in hand with this development went a repudiation of *uravnilovka* (egalitarianism in wage payments), and increasing emphasis on wage differentials which were tailored to skill and productivity. The new labor hero of Communism was the udarnik, or shock-worker, the Stakhanovite who excelled his fellow-workers in production, set a standard to which they might aspire, and whose achievements were recognized by a variety of special perquisites and privileges. Worker members of the Party were under special pressure to become shock-workers and to serve as bellwethers of the working class. Some evidence of this pressure is provided by a series of protocols of Party meetings during 1935 in Factory No. 35, an enterprise primarily devoted to airplane production.[40] Of 144 Party members and candidates, ninety were listed as shock-workers. A report on shock-work in the plant noted that shock-workers were featured in the plant's newspaper, given the best rations, provided with better dinners from the factory kitchen, given preference in allocating apartments and in renovations, provided with free tickets to movies and theaters, and supplied with a variety of other favors.[41] They were also anything but popular with the rank-and-file workers, who not only failed to share in their bounty, but saw in the production records of the Stakhanovites a constant threat of increasing work norms without corresponding pay increases.

A secret letter in the Archive from Rumyantsev to all raikom secretaries in the oblast, dated March 22, 1935, registers the reality of this threat. The letter read:

> The Central Committee of the CPSU(b) and the Sovnarkom have decided to review among various categories of workers outmoded and incorrect output norms, which do not correspond either to productive and technical conditions or to potential in the area of labor productivity. With the construction of new factories, the introduction of new equipment, the growth in the skill of workers, and their acquisition of ability to operate the new equipment, the output norms of individual groups of workers in many enterprises are clearly outmoded and are a hindrance to a further rise in the productivity of labor. In accordance with the decision of the Central Committee, the selection of norms for approval by the directors should be made with careful attention to the actual speed of work and the efficient utilization of the working day, rather than merely with regard to extra earnings for the workers. The newly established norms should be set with the purpose of achieving a full working load. Furthermore, the managers should employ all organizational and technical measures to guarantee the fulfillment of the new output norms (instruction

of the workers, uninterrupted supply of materials and tools, reduction of idle periods).

The review of norms should be completed not later than May 1, 1935. In connection with this, the obkom proposes:

1. At the next meeting of the bureau the plans of directors of enterprises for the fulfillment of the decree of the CC and the SNK should be discussed.

2. In the review of output norms, systematic guidance and control over the work of factory administrators and leaders of factory trade union committees should be established.

3. Extensive preparatory work should be developed among the masses in order to insure the correct execution of the review of output norms.

4. Regularly, not less than once every ten days, the obkom should be informed of the progress of this work.[42]

The Sacrifices of the Unskilled and Semiskilled Workers

Scattered references in the Archive make clear that the burden of higher work norms and other sacrifices attendant upon rapid industrialization fell largely on the mass of unskilled and semiskilled workers. A letter dated 1936 from the workers in Shop No. 2 of the Rumyantsev factory and addressed to Rumyantsev throws light on the attitude of these groups:

We have a great request. If you do not intercede, we will all leave work. It is impossible to work further. We are greatly oppressed. We do not earn anything — from 1½ to 2 rubles [presumably per day] — since the leaders are concerned only with themselves, and they receive salaries and give themselves premiums. Metelkova, the zavkom [head of the trade union factory committee], takes their side. For them there are spas, rest homes, and sanatoria, but there is nothing for the workers. In Shop No. 2 things are very bad. A certain Yagneshko is in charge of the shop. Yagneshko does the work poorly . . . She is worse than a gendarme, treats the workers roughly, swears at them. Her husband is a White Guardist, a Kolchak supporter. Her father was a former prison employee in a tsarist prison. We beg you to remove Yagneshko from the workers, from the leadership of Shop No. 2. Then the workers will fulfill and overfulfill [the plans], but otherwise this shop will be lost. We suffering workers have decided to bother you. Intercede for us!"[43]

The letter was sent to the Zadnepr raikom secretary for investigation, and on November 2, 1936, the secretary of the factory Party committee reported to the raikom that the "rough attitude of Comrade Yagneshko, as foreman of the shift and moreover as member of the Party, is really true. The partkom pointed this out to her and warned her, and now she has corrected the situation. As far as the low wages are concerned, the complaint is untrue since salaries in the shop have significantly increased. Whoever fulfills and overfulfills the norm earns in category 5–6 from 200 to 300 rubles, and in category 3 from 140 to 185 rubles, and this category is the lowest, so that this year in this Shop No. 2 there have been no wages of 1½ to 2 rubles . . ."[44]

While the Archive provides no means of finally determining what the actual wages were, nevertheless, the sense of grievance that permeates the workers' letter remains significant as an index of labor discontent.

A striking piece of evidence of the way in which unskilled workers were treated is provided by the 1937 Party protocols of the Medgorodsk organization, a construction enterprise which operated in Smolensk. On February 14, 1937, the Party organization heard a report of its Party committee on the living conditions and mood of the workers and the state of mass work among them.[45] The discussion was unusually frank and revealing. The workers' barracks were described as overcrowded and in a state of extreme disrepair with water streaming from the ceiling "straight onto workers' beds." Heat was rarely provided in the barracks; bedding went unchanged; and sanitary work was almost nonexistent. There were no kitchens and eating halls on the construction sites; hot food could not be obtained until the evening when workers had to walk a long distance to reach the dining hall. "Many of the women," one female Party member reported, "live practically on the street. No one pays any attention to them; some of these defenseless creatures threaten to commit suicide." In addition, cases where wages were not paid on time were on the increase. All this "neglect of the elementary needs of the workers" as well as "lack of care for them as human beings" resulted in "fully justified dissatisfaction" and bitterness on the part of the workers.

The mood of some of the workers was described as "often threatening" and "directly counterrevolutionary." For example, in a discussion of the 1936 Constitution a certain Stepan Danin, a carpenter, and workers of his brigade were quoted as saying:

> We must permit the existence of several political parties in our midst — as it is in bourgeois countries; they will be able better to note the mistakes of the Communist Party.
> Exploitation in our midst has not been eliminated; communists and engineers employ and exploit servants.
> The Trotskyites Kamenev and Zinoviev won't be shot anyway — and they shouldn't be, for they are Old Bolsheviks.

To the question of an agitator as to who should be viewed as an Old Bolshevik, one worker replied, "Trotsky." During the conduct of the national census, rumors circulated among the workers to the effect that any one who admitted a religious allegiance would be persecuted. "All this shows," the report of the Party committee noted, "that there are [non-Soviet] elements among the workers and that the Party must become ever more severe" and react immediately to "incorrect attitudes of workers" by unmasking them.[46]

The state of propaganda among workers was described as "poor." Although women comprised 35 to 40 per cent of the labor force, no work was being done among them. Workers had practically to be pushed to attend study circles and even coerced to leave their barracks and participate in demonstrations. All this was blamed on the weak leadership of Party members of the cell, whose attitude toward the workers was characterized by "formality" rather than "love."

The apathy and indifference which the rank-and-file construction workers displayed toward the Party emerged clearly in the course of a discussion on July 26, 1937.[47] At this meeting three Party members assigned to agitational duties in the workers' barracks described their activities. The first reported that he had held talks among the workers on a recent speech made by Shvernik, but that "there were very few questions." The second indicated that he had encountered great difficulty in addressing his assigned barrack hall since workers in the next room "sang and played loudly and disturbed the meeting." In the course of a discussion of a speech by Yakovlev on elections to the Supreme Soviet, one of the workers, a certain Kadomtsev, after a few minutes of indecisiveness, observed. "I guess the Party guessed wrong — now that it allows secret voting, Stalin won't be elected." The third agitator reported that he had held several talks, but that there was "hardly any participation by the workers." The secretary of the Party cell scolded all three for their weak work. "Were not you reminded," he chided, "that reaction to the workers' errors must be immediate?" The talks, he explained, were designed not only to educate the workers, but also "to sound out their attitudes and thus to learn their social make-up." The workers' complaints about their living conditions had also to be adjusted in order to gain their confidence.

But there was the rub! A system which reserved its major resources for new investment in heavy industry had no margins to expend on amenities for the rank-and-file workers, and the agitators and trade union officials who confronted the workers in face-to-face discussion had little to offer them except words and promises for the future. The dilemma of the grass-roots trade union worker is strikingly exemplified in a letter dated September 6, 1936, from Metelkova, the trade union chairman in the Rumyantsev factory, to Rumyantsev himself. The letter read in part:

Ivan Petrovich: Forgive me for daring to write you and to beg you to find out from our Party organization whether or not it is true that I am a bureaucrat as *Rabochii Put* [Worker's Path — the obkom newspaper] writes.

Ivan Petrovich, I take all of this very hard; as the trade union leader of an enterprise which bears your name I shall finally become desperate in the face of the accusation that I am a bureaucrat and insensitive to the needs of the workers.

True, in our trade union work, there are still many shortcomings, still many bad aspects, but what the press writes lately concerning me is not entirely true. (This is what I write to you, but when the workers ask me, I answer all of them: "It is true, and I will take into consideration all the instructions of *Rabochii Put*.")

Ivan Petrovich, again I beg you to forgive me for taking up your time, but I am in such a serious situation, and therefore, so that you would know about it, I dare to write you about how the matter stands and why they accuse me.

It is not possible to repair the quarters of the worker Safronova, since the worker lives in a place suitable for hay and the place is rotting — the whole roof fell in, and all the timbers are rotting. Our technician and I went to see what could be done . . . and wrote a statement in which we pointed out that it was impossible to make any repairs, but we begged the proper organization to give her an apartment, since three sisters live there, all of whom work in our factory and are good workers and not bad public servants. I turned to the city soviet. Comrade Pliusnin answered that there were no rooms. Yes, I know myself that the problem of apartments is an extremely serious one . . .

Ivan Petrovich, there must be many dissatisfied people among us in the factory, since we investigated 843 workers' quarters and discovered that we have 143 workers who need quarters, who live under very bad conditions, and that 205 apartments need repairs. And we are making repairs on 40 rooms as designated by the plan, costing 10,000 rubles, and the rest of the people will remain dissatisfied.

These people come to the factory committee, beg for repairs, for apartments, and I have to refuse them. They in turn tell me that they will write to *Rabochii Put*, will write to you and to Comrade Rakitov. That is why I decided to write to you, so that you and Grigori Davydovich will not be of the opinion that I am a bureaucrat and an insensitive trade union worker.[48]

The Archive contains no response to this letter, and there could be no real reponse. The Stalinist system required its lightning rods to divert the anger of the working class. The Metelkovas who were offered up as sacrifices in the pages of *Rabochii Put* were themselves the victims of a process in which scapegoats were substituted for real concessions to the workers.

The commitment of the regime to rapid industrialization meant that the basic material needs and aspirations of the rank-and-file workers had to go unassuaged. If the Smolensk Archive does nothing else, it provides an authoritative documentation of their sacrifices as vouched for through Party eyes. It reveals a mass of unskilled and semiskilled workers as indifferent to Party appeals and smoldering with a dull resentment which they dared not or could not publicly express.

17 The Party and the Armed Forces

The scattered documents in the Smolensk Archive on the relations of the Party and the Armed Forces do not lend themselves to a systematic or comprehensive treatment of the subject. Such materials as are available relate primarily to the following topics: (1) the procedures for drafting youth into military service and the role of the district Party organizations therein; (2) the utilization of the local Party organizations in connection with recruitment for military schools; (3) the obligations of the local Party and administrative organs with respect to the families of conscripts serving in the armed forces; (4) the activities of Osoaviakhim, the para-military Society for the Promotion of Defense and Aero-Chemical Development; (5) Party work in an army unit as illustrated by a series of regimental reports of a political commissar. The discussion below will be addressed to these particulars.

The Role of the District Party Organizations in Conscription

The primary responsibility of the district Party organizations in connection with conscription was the political preparation of the youths selected for military service. The following secret letter, dated July 28, 1929, from the Yartsevo representative of the Commissariat for Military Affairs to the raikom secretary makes this clear:

I ask you, together with the raikom of the Komsomol, to hold conferences of youths undergoing pre-military training born in 1907 and those deferred, born in 1906, simultaneously conducting an agitation campaign to facilitate the conscription. In either case the basic content of the work should be the explanation of the general Party line (preservation of the rapid tempo of industrialization, socialist reconstruction of agriculture, collectivization and coöperation of the broad peasant masses, and rallying them in order to overcome the difficulties of socialist construction), arranging matters in initial agitational work so that the attention of the conscripts will be directed to the fact that the peaceful policy of the Soviet Union runs up against the stubborn resistance of the imperialist states, which are preparing for a new imperialist war, and that the Red Army should be prepared at any moment. Also see to it that in agitational work glossing over . . . the difficulties of Red Army service is decisively eliminated, and point out that the Red Army first of all demands extensive battle training, iron discipline, and fighting endurance. At the same time I beg you to consider that the anti-Soviet elements are eagerly exploiting the difficulties of our construction among the conscripts, and hence you must develop your work so that they are properly rebuffed by the conscripts . . . In working out a plan for agitational work during the next conscription, I ask you to pay attention to the identification of class-hostile elements, and in accordance with the list furnished by the raion executive committee, to make a basic investigation of the conscripts with the aid of a representative from the Young Communist League, the chief of the militia, the people's judge, and others, making notes as to those who cannot be allowed into the army, and for what reasons. I ask the . . . raikoms to do additional political work among the conscripts during their appearances and medical examinations at the draft commissions, obtaining the most extensive participation in this work of factory and shop cells, trade unions, the Osoaviakhim, and others, through the organization of agitation points attached to the draft commissions, the establishment of information departments, the organization of reading rooms, supplying them with literature and newspapers, decorating the premises, issuing wall newspapers dedicated to the conscription . . . and through establishing a commissary with a sufficient assortment of needed goods, and also a detachment of responsible people for this political work, one person to each draft commission, to be aided by consultants, heads of reading rooms, and others. You are requested to present to the uyezd War Commissariat a plan of work and the results and progress of agitational activity . . . The conscription will begin in the first days of September . . .[1]

The concern of the Party with the social composition of the conscripts received striking exemplification in a top-secret obkom and oblispolkom directive dated January 25, 1932, and addressed to all lower Party and governmental organs of the Western Oblast. The letter read:

In accordance with the directives of the government, during the period of February to March of this year a conscription will take place on the territory of our oblast of those obliged to do military service with troop units. In order not to give unnecessary publicity to this work, the conscription will be carried out under the guise of a one-day roll-call muster.

Attaching great importance to this matter, it is proposed:

1. To insure through the proper Soviet organs and the raion war commissariats the notification of those obliged to do military service and their prompt appearance at the points of muster.

2. To pay special attention to the careful social and class selection of those obliged to do military service and subject to conscription into troop units, not allowing a repetition of the mistakes of last year, when cases of conscription of clearly socially alien and dangerous elements took place and socially favorable elements were sifted out. Every Party cell and village soviet should review in good time and carefully the lists of those obliged to do military service and subject to conscription in order to eliminate social-alien and hostile elements.

3. Organize cultural and political services for the muster points, connecting this work with the economic and political campaigns being conducted.

4. Give the troop units all kinds of practical aid during the conscription, both through choosing the necessary workers, and along the lines of organizational and economic measures (supplying quarters, coöperative, and sanitation services).

5. Do not allow the conscription work to be mentioned in the press.

6. Work out a detailed plan to carry out this directive, together with the commands of the troop units and the raion war commissariats.[2]

Despite these and similar injunctions the preparations for conscription by lower Party and governmental organs frequently left much to be desired. A secret communication from Rumyantsev and Rakitov dated March 4, 1935, and addressed to the Party, governmental, and military organs of the oblast noted at least ten raions which had done poor work "in studying the social composition of the draftees and in sifting out socially alien elements," another ten which had done little to liquidate illiteracy and semiliteracy among the draftees, and at least five where the quality of pre-military training was completely unsatisfactory.[3] The raion authorities were ordered to improve their work, to "pay special attention to the question of the study of the class character of the draftees," and to assign leading raion workers to lead discussions among the draftees on current economic and political questions. "In view of the high cultural level of the fighters of the Red Army and the necessity of inculcating in good time cultural habits among the next reinforcements for the Red Army," the letter continued, "carry on mass cultural and educational work on this question among the draftees so that each draftee, when appearing in the military unit will appear completely 'cultured' (decent outer clothing, shaven, with haircuts, washed, etc.) and will have with him objects for personal use (towel, handkerchiefs, brushes — tooth brush, hat brush, shoe brush — and other items necessary for the personal use of an army man)."

The next year apparently revealed little improvement. On October 25, 1936, a secret communication of the Kozelsk raion military commissariat quoted the Commander of the Byelorussian Military District (which included the Western Oblast) as disturbed over a number of "inadmissible defects" in the registration and conscription of the class of 1914–1916.[4] These defects included:

1. Not all the youths undergoing pre-military training were included in the draft.

2. In the registration the check on literacy was superficial and incomplete.

3. There was poor work in composing character descriptions for the youths undergoing pre-military training and in studying their class origins, and, as a result, some of them had not been investigated up to the moment of the conscription.

4. Work on liquidating illiteracy and semiliteracy was not done on time. There was no real accounting, control, or active leadership of this work on the part of the raion public education departments.

5. The raion sanatoria exerted insufficient control in conducting sanitation work.

6. There was an insufficiently careful evaluation of the public service

capabilities of those undergoing pre-military training, their family positions, devotion to the Party, etc.

7. There was a complete absence of systematic educational work by the raikoms of the Young Communist League among youths undergoing pre-military training. The quality of political preparation at study centers was low, as a result of the lack of permanent politruks [political leaders].

In order to eliminate these defects the Commander of the Byelorussian Military District ordered a complete overhauling of registration and and conscription procedures. Literacy tests were to be administered to all those undergoing pre-military training; where further schooling was indicated, the military records of the draftees were to show the schools where they were registered and the date when studies began. Teachers assigned to this work were required to report progress at ten-day intervals to the raion war commissariat and the raion public education department. Attendance was to be noted on the military cards of the draftees. At the registration centers all those undergoing pre-military training were to be vaccinated and their blood groups determined. Those needing medical treatment and operations were to be assigned to medical institutes for treatment. Doctors were ordered to register each visit on the draftee's military card and to report to the raion war commissariat and the raion health department at ten-day intervals on the progress of the medical treatment.

Elaborate procedures were also prescribed to check on the political reliability and character of each draftee. With the approval of the raion war commissariat, inspectors of the raion executive committee and the commander of the political staff of the reserve were authorized to undertake individual studies of prospective draftees during the period when they were undergoing pre-military training. The person making the study was required to "compose an exhaustive characterization" of each prospective draftee. "In the characterization not only the social position, the political and moral condition of the draftee, etc., but also his personal qualities, way of life, training, inclinations, etc. should be included. Every characterization should be approved by the raion military commissariat." Especially complete information was required with respect to persons who had relatives who were in prison or who had been exiled, deported, or sentenced to forced labor.

Attached to this directive was a detailed 1937 conscription plan drawn up by the raion military commissariat of Kozelsk.[5] The plan provided for registration of prospective draftees in November 1936. At that time all youths were to be given a physical examination. Those who were clearly unfit for military service were to be removed from the register, while others who had remediable defects were to be provided with medical treatment. Draftees who were the sole support of their families were also supposed to be exempt from military service. During the registration literacy tests were to be administered in order to discover illiterates and semiliterates who required further schooling preparatory to military service.

During the ten months intervening between registration and actual induction into the armed forces, the draftees were to be "prepared" for military service. Those needing medical treatment became the special charges of the raion divisions of public health. The raion divisions of public education were required to establish special courses to "liquidate" illiteracy and semiliteracy among the draftees. The raion military commissariat had primary responsibility for premilitary training. During this period each youth was required to undergo a 120-hour training program, in the course of which he was supposed to fulfill the norms of a "Voroshilov shooter" and to earn the badge of the GTO ("Prepared for Labor and Defense"). His athletic activities during the period were to be directed by the raion council of physical culture.

The raikoms, Young Communist League, and the political divisions of the machine-tractor stations were given the mission of supervising and directing the political indoctrination of the prospective draftees. These activities embraced lessons on the history of the Party, the army, and the Soviet Union, and special efforts were to be made to enroll the youth in various public organizations such as SVB (the League of Militant Atheists) and MOPR (the International Aid Society for Revolutionary Fighters). Each youth was to be carefully "studied" in order to provide material for the characterization which would accompany him into military service. Whether in fact these methodically laid plans were executed the Archive does not reveal. The recurrent criticisms of the gap between plan and performance serve at least to raise doubts.

The Party and the Mobilization of Recruits for Military Schools

One of the important contributions of the Archive is its documentation of the Party role in mobilizing recruits for certain specialized military schools. The Party leadership was particularly insistent on maintaining a high proportion of Communists in the newer services such as the air force and the tank corps. The way in which this was done can be illustrated by a secret letter dated June 10, 1933, from Shilman, the obkom secretary in charge of cadres, to all raikom secretaries of the oblast. The letter read:

> In accordance with a decision of the Central Committee VKP(b) there is going to take place a mobilization of Communists into the flying and technical schools of the Air Force of the RKKA [the Red Army].
> The Central Committee considers it very important that this mobilization

be carried out conscientiously. This involves first of all great care in the selection of every candidate and particularly strict checking of his social background, family connections, loyalty and steadfastness with regard to the Party, etc. In order to perform this task the Central Committee has established a central commission and commissions for the oblasts. All candidates selected in the localities are to be approved by an oblast commission. The final decision will be made by the Commission of the Central Committee.

The following conditions must be met by the mobilized persons: (1) Age: between 18 and 24. (2) General education: the equivalent of the nine-year school. (3) Candidates are to be selected mainly among those who acquired military training either in the army or outside of it. Reserve officers, however, are not to be selected. (4) Mobilized persons ought to be full members of the Party. Well-tested Party candidates are to be admitted by way of exception (not more than 10%). (5) The selection process should give priority to bachelors, to persons with small families, and to those who wish to study in the Air Force school. (6) The selected individuals must be completely healthy physically and fit for service in units of the Air Force.

In the Air Force Flight Schools, the period of study is three years, in the Air Force technical schools it is two years. Those mobilized will obtain . . . remuneration in the amount of 60 rubles monthly. Families of those mobilized will be paid the difference between the average earnings of the mobilized person in his previous work and the pay of 60 rubles which he will personally receive in the school. Furthermore, families of the mobilized persons may not be deprived of apartments occupied by them in their [present] place of residence. They will also obtain products from coöperatives according to the norms for industrial workers.

According to the instructions of the Central Committee, the mobilization is to be carried out primarily among those studying at workers' faculties [rabfaks], tekhnikums, soviet-Party schools, and among the first-year students of universities. The best kolkhoznik shock-workers are also to be recruited . . .

After the selection is completed, but not later than July 1, the oblast selection commission should receive with regard to each candidate: the recommendation of the raikom, a detailed characterization signed by the raikom secretary, a certified questionnaire, information about the candidate's health, and data on his average monthly salary or stipend during the last three months.

The obkom stresses once more the importance of this mobilization. The responsibility for the selection of candidates lies personally with the raikom secretary. He will be held responsible before the Party for sending unworthy or poor Communists. It is necessary to check the social background of every selected candidate at his place of residence . . .[6]

Attached to the letter was a list of materials to be presented by the raikoms to the oblast selection commissions. The list included (1) a record of the action of the raikom; (2) a questionnaire filled in by the candidate and certified by his Party organization; (3) a detailed autobiography written by the candidate himself "confirming the social background and social position of the candidate and of his closest relatives (father, mother, wife, brothers, sisters) and the absence of disenfranchised or dekulakized relatives, or of relatives who lived abroad or who had had service in the White Army; (4) a detailed Party-political characterization signed by the raikom secretary; (5) certificates showing general educational background; and (6) information concerning health, average monthly salary or stipend for the preceding three months, and the number of dependents. As this letter illustrates, the leadership used the Party as a primary mobilization medium whenever special measures were necessary to strengthen the Party contingent in one or another especially important branch of the armed forces.

Care for the Needy Families of Conscripts

Another responsibility the Party shared with the local governmental organs was that of taking care of needy families of draftees serving in the armed forces. The state of mind of the soldiers was usually strongly influenced by letters from their families; when word reached them of difficulties at home, morale was adversely affected. Theoretically, all complaints received from soldiers and their families were supposed to be given expedited treatment by local administrative agencies. In fact, a special investigation launched by the presidium of the Western Oblast executive committee toward the end of 1936 disclosed serious short-comings in dealing with these complaints. The chairmen of the raion executive committees and city soviets were accused of having "transferred this work to second-string and third-string people," who dealt with it "in a formal and bureaucratic manner" and made many "incorrect decisions." [7] In most cases there were no special registries of soldiers' complaints, and the time limits established by the government for their review were extensively violated.

The investigation also revealed that the difficulties of soldiers' families were compounded by the failure of the raion military commissariats to take family needs into account when soldiers were drafted. According to the report, ". . . citizens are drafted in families where there are no people left who are able to work at all or else there is one person able to work and several persons unable to work; often the draftees themselves do not ask for the privilege [of exemption] when they are drafted, sometimes simply hiding the fact because they wish to serve in the Red Army." Moreover, the report continued, "the raion military commissariats do not supply the raion executive committees, the village soviets, and the kolkhozes with lists of those to whom it will be necessary to give material aid. The raion military commissariats themselves are hardly interested in these families, although if measures were taken in advance, it would significantly curtail the number of complaints from soldiers and their families."

The report then cited some typical cases where no action had been taken:

Smolensk — the wife of the soldier Frolov has a sick ten-year-old child, lives in an exceptionally poor apartment (holes in the door, no stove); the house is on the verge of caving in; and despite her many requests to the city soviet about improving her apartment, the latter has still to act on the problem. The complaint of the soldier Podinov on the repair of his apartment was sent to the city housing office on October 28, which to this day [December 31, 1936] has still to make a decision, which forced the commissar of [Podinov's] unit on December 11 to turn to the procuracy with a request to press the city soviet to resolve this complaint within the shortest possible time.

Bryansk City Soviet — . . . In the city communal economy department as a rule standard and formal bureaucratic answers are given to complaints submitted by soldiers and their families requesting apartments [such as]: "There are no apartments; when there are some we shall give them." To the complaint of the soldier Krizhishchevsky, the chairman of the Volodarsk raion office replied with a callous, formal bureaucratic resolution: "Fulfilled with an answer that there is no apartment." The wife of this soldier receives a salary of 100 rubles and pays 40 rubles for a private apartment.

Bryansk Raion Executive Committee — . . . the wife of the soldier Karavayev lives alone with a ten-month-old child, as a result of which she is unable to work; she has no heat for her apartment and as a means of subsistence she sells vodka and denatured alcohol. The chairman of the Tolmachevsk village soviet, Chuvin, instead of organizing aid for Karavayeva, said, "We cannot help her; we know about Karavayeva's selling vodka and denatured alcohol, but have decided to remain silent, since that is her only means of subsistence."

Smolensk Raion — The secretary of the Khokhlovsk village soviet, Comrade Sazonov, to the question whether he visited the families of soldiers or interested himself in how they lived, answered: "Why visit them? There isn't enough time, and if necessary they will come themselves."

To correct these defects the Presidium of the oblast executive committee ordered all chairmen of raion executive committees and city soviets to check immediately on the status of soldiers' complaints, to establish special registers for such complaints, to dispose of them within the prescribed time limits, and to arrange to have complaints reviewed personally by the chairman or his deputy.[8] Decisions on complaints were to be reported to the soldier, his family, and the political commissar of the unit in which the soldier was serving, and a "procedure" was to be established "whereby members of the raion executive committees, city soviets, raion soviets, chairmen of village soviets and kolkhozes, and leaders of trade union and other economic organizations systematically interest themselves in the life of the families of soldiers." The military commander of the region was requested "to curtail to a minimum" the drafting into the Red Army of citizens with numerous dependents and to instruct raion military commissariats to supply lists of needy soldiers' families to the raion executive committees and the city soviets. Finally, the oblast procurator was instructed to tighten control over the handling of complaints and "to bring to responsibility" those who treated them in a "formal bureaucratic and callous" manner. Whether the situation of soldiers' families improved substantially as a result of these actions the Archive does not disclose, though the urgent nature of the secret decree clearly indicates that it was intended to have and probably did have some operational significance.

The Work of Osoaviakhim

The effort of the regime to place itself on a secure war footing during the mid-thirties was also attended by a major reorganization of the work of the Osoaviakhim, the para-military organization of civilians which was designed to buttress the strength of the Red Army. Again the Party was required to play a leading role in achieving the transformation. The Archive contains a copy of a joint decree of the USSR Council of People's Commissars and the Central Committee on the Osoaviakhim, dated August 8, 1935, labeled "not for publication," and signed jointly by Stalin as Party secretary and Chubar, then deputy chairman of the Council of People's Commissars.[9] The decree was severely critical of the existing state of Osoaviakhim. Its responsible leaders were castigated for engaging in a mere race for membership, for dissipating their energy and resources over a wide variety of miscellaneous activities, for building a "bureaucratic, blustering apparatus of paid workers," and above all for "unsatisfactorily training civilians and youths undergoing pre-military training for the Red Army."

The reformulation of the tasks of the Osoaviakhim placed primary stress on military objectives. These were defined as follows:

a. The preparation of the youth undergoing pre-military training and of those outside of the army for Red Army service.

b. Aid to the commanding staff of the reserve in maintaining and improving its military qualifications without taking it away from production.

c. Mass aviation sports and training of aviation cadres (aeroclubs, glider and parachute stations, circles for aviation models).

d. Elementary military training of the toilers, especially mass shooting for sport (Voroshilov marksmen and snipers).

e. Anti-aircraft training of toilers, the provision of elementary technical information on aerial attacks, equipment of shelters, camouflage, and measures for the liquidation of destruction from bombing.

f. Chemical training of the toilers, the dissemination of elementary technical information on the methods of chemical attack, anti-chemical defense, organization of gas shelters, decontamination, first aid, and the organization of command and self-defense groups.

g. Horsemanship (riding schools, cavalry schools, study points, circles).

h. Naval training and sports (naval clubs, bases, study points).

i. [The training of] short-wave radio amateurs.

j. Raising dogs for military use.

k. Raising pigeons for military use and sport.

l. Scientific research work and service to inventors in the above-mentioned lines of the Osoaviakhim.

As this list makes clear, the decree emphasized the para-military aspects of Osoaviakhim activities. "In all its work," the decree stated, "the Osoaviakhim should pay special attention to raising the level of preparation of the fighters of the Red Army reserve by attracting them into the ranks of the society and engaging them in mass shooting for sport, educational-drill formations . . . and in fulfilling the norms of preparation for anti-aircraft and anti-chemical defense."

Instead of "indiscriminate pursuit of numerical membership," the decree demanded an organization based on active involvement, practical activity, and firm military discipline. The basic training was to be performed by a public aktiv, "educated and instructed by limited cadres of paid workers," the latter in no case to exceed 25,000 for the whole Soviet Union. The leadership of the Osoaviakhim was vested in a Central Council headed by a presidium with special administrative sections devoted to aviation, military training, anti-aircraft and anti-chemical defense, organizational mass work, and the administrative and economic activity of the organization. The heads of these sections were to be nominated by the Division of Leading Party Organs of the Central Committee Secretariat and confirmed by the Orgburo.

Party responsibility for the work of the Osoaviakhim was concentrated in the second secretaries of kraikoms, obkoms, gorkoms, and raikoms. The Party in turn was to be assisted by the Komsomol and the trade unions. Within the Komsomol responsibility was centered in the military secretary of the Central Committee and the first secretaries of kraikoms, obkoms, gorkoms, and raikoms; in the trade unions the initiative was vested in the first secretary of the all-union central council of trade unions and the chairmen of the central committees of the unions. Particular importance was attached to Komsomol activity. "It is necessary to see to it," read the decree, "that every Komsomolite actively takes part in the work of the Osoaviakhim, acting as an example in the study of military affairs and in the strengthening of discipline among members of the society." The trade unions were also ordered "to take a very active part" in the work of the Osoaviakhim, and liaison was to be maintained by introducing trade union representatives into the leading bodies of the organization.

Finally, various government departments were ordered to assist the Osoaviakhim in fulfilling its mission. The People's Commissariat of Defense was instructed "to increase aid to the Osoaviakhim, [to improve] control and instruction on the part of the commands of the okrugs and commanders of the units, and to pay special attention to raising the quality of the cadres of the Osoaviakhim themselves . . ." The People's Commissariat of Light Industry was ordered to "take immediate measures to

increase the output of parachutes . . . and decisively to improve their
. . . durability." Special allotments were made from the reserve funds of
the Council of People's Commissars to provide trucks, tractors, and military vehicles to the schools and aero-clubs of the Osoaviakhim. And "in
order more widely to push the use of small-calibre weapons among the
population," the NKVD was requested to "establish a simplified procedure" regulating the acquisition of small-calibre weapons by the Osoaviakhim, certain athletic clubs and institutes of learning, members of the
Party and the Komsomol, "and other citizens who do not have any compromising information on them."

As these provisions make clear, the obvious aim of the decree was to
transform the Osoaviakhim into an effective auxiliary of the Red Army.
Preparations for total war called for "a nation in arms," and the special
task of the Osoaviakhim was to transform concept into reality. Although
performance lagged behind plans and ambitions during the next years,
the Osoaviakhim, nevertheless, played a significant role in instilling martial spirit into the youth and in helping to prepare it for the impending
conflict.

Party Work in the Armed Forces

The final topic to be treated in this chapter — Party work in the
armed forces — is one on which the Smolensk Archive has relatively little
to offer. The available material is largely confined to several central
decrees and a series of reports by regimental political commissars dating
back to the mid-twenties. Even these fragmentary sources, however, reveal patterns of control and activity which were to retain persisting significance in later periods.

The first central directive, dated December 20, 1924, and issued jointly
by L. Kaganovich, then a Central Committee Secretary, and A. Bubnov,
Chief of the Political Administration of the Army, contained instructions
on the organization of Party cells in the Red Army and Navy.[10] Party
cells were to be established in each company, squadron, battery, and
naval vessel where there were not less than three Party members. The
organizational initiative was to be taken by the political commissar exercising jurisdiction over the unit, or by a Party member authorized by the
commissar to do so. The primary responsibility for guiding the work of
Party cells in the army and navy was placed in the Political Administration of the service.

The basic Party unit in the army was the company cell, which was required to meet at least twice a month. Where the cell numbered more
than ten members, the general meeting elected a presidium of three members and two candidates to direct Party work. Where the cell numbered

less than ten, the presidium was replaced by a secretary-organizer with at least one year's standing as a Party member. The basic tasks of the company cell involved:

> *a.* Active participation in the general work of the Party and in unit Party work.
> *b.* The execution of all directives and orders of higher Party organs.
> *c.* The effort to raise the political and cultural level of its members . . .
> *d.* Establishment of a close connection between the Party and the Red Army mass, strengthening the influence and leadership of the Party through indoctrinating the masses with Party slogans and directives.
> *e.* Carrying on work among members of the Komsomol.
> *f.* Attracting new members into the Party and training candidates for Party membership.
> *g.* Assistance to the political commanding staff of the unit [the politruk, or political leader] in educating the soldiers and sailors and improving the political and moral condition of the unit.

In addition the members of the cells were required to "take all measures toward strengthening Party discipline" and to "struggle against all unhealthy symptoms among members of the Party and non-Party people (against drunkenness, excesses, squabbling, demobilizing attitudes, etc.)." They were to assist in the organization of political schools and Marxist circles, and to order all their members to attend them. They were to maintain "very close rapprochement and contact with the Red Army masses," and carry on various types of agitational campaigns among the non-Party soldiers. With the approval of higher authorities, they were to designate candidates to Army conferences, local soviets, and other public bodies. The Party cell was also required to work closely with Komsomols in the company, to assign one of its members as a Komsomol organizer where there were less than five Komsomol members in the company, and to draw Komsomol members into participation in Party circles and various types of political educational work. Party members were also supposed to set an example by fulfilling their duties in an exemplary manner, by informing the political commissar "on the political and economic condition of the company," and by giving aid to the commissar "in the struggle against counterrevolution and abuses."

The next echelon above the company cell in the military Party hierarchy was the regimental collective which consisted of all the Party members in the regiment, met at least once a month and carried on current work through a regimental bureau, composed of five members (including the responsible secretary) and two candidates. The regimental Party secretary was ordinarily required to be a Party member of at least two years' standing. To the leading organs of the regimental collective fell the task of guiding and planning the activities of the company Party cells. "For practical, daily direction of the work," the instructions stated, "the bureau divides duties among its members in the following manner: one member of the bureau supervises work in the field of Party education and training; a second is the representative of the Party organization in the board of the [regimental] club; a third guides the work among non-Party people and supervises the work of independent army organizations; a fourth is the organizer of work among members of the Komsomol . . . The responsible secretary is the direct leader of all daily work of the regimental collective . . ." and maintains "the closest supervision over the work of secretary-organizers of company cells."

The instructions also made provisions for adjusting possible conflicts between the Party cells and the political commissars who were charged with their supervision. "The political commissar," the instruction categorically stated, "is the official representative of the Party and is responsible to it for the status of Party work in the given unit. The regimental collective and the cell do not interfere in the orders of the commissar." In the event of disagreement between the political commissar and the regimental bureau, the latter was obliged to carry out the instructions of the commissar, but could "turn for a final solution of the problem" to the political department at the next higher instance. Under wartime conditions, however, such an appeal could be deferred by the commissar for a period no longer than seven days. Moreover, no discussion of the actions of a political commissar could take place at a general meeting of a Party cell without the permission of the political department and the presence of its representative at the meeting. In case of conflict between the company Party cell and its politruk, however, the question was to be discussed by the regimental Party bureau and resolved by its political commissar.

The instructions also sought to regulate the relations between the Party cells and the command and administrative staff of the unit. The bureau of the regimental collective and individual members of the Party were instructed "to support and strengthen trust and respect for the command and administrative staff" among the soldiers and sailors. In no case was the Party cell to "interfere" with the orders of the command and administrative staff. Where the command and administrative staff deviated from the correct fulfillment of service duties, violated the rules of the Red Army, or committed other service abuses, the Party bureau was, however, obligated to inform the political commissar, who was authorized to undertake remedial action, if necessary, by appeal to higher Party organs.

A second decree entitled "One-Man Rule in the Red Army," dated March 6, 1925, and signed by A. Andreyev, then a secretary of the Central Committee, endeavored to restate the relations between commissar and commander.[11] "One of the most important steps in the reconstruction of the Red Army at the present time," read the decree, "is the practical realization of one-man rule . . . In accordance with the last resolutions of the plenum of the Revolutionary War Council of the USSR, one-man rule in military units will be carried out in two forms. In the first form, all operational, command, administrative, and managerial functions are completely concentrated in the hands of the commanding officer. The commissar, meanwhile, relieved of the duties of daily supervision of the . . . commander, maintains the leadership of political and Party work in the unit and bears the responsibility for its moral-political status. The commissar . . . exerts all his influence and authority to aid the commander to strengthen and improve the training, combat, and technical level of the unit. In the second form, those Party commanders who satisfy the demands of Party-political leadership (i.e., are able to be political commissars at the same time), will combine the functions of combat, administrative-economic and Party-political leadership." The decree provided that this second form of one-man rule would, to begin with, be tried out in the Red Army. In the army national units, however, and in the navy it was to be introduced "at a slower pace"; there, as a general rule, commissars were to be maintained as before. "There is no doubt," the decree continued, "that the transfer to one-man rule will increase the social and political weight of the commanding staff . . ." The hope was also expressed that it would draw the command "nearer to local Soviet and Party organs." At the same time, the decree called for "the maximum strengthening of political work and the reinforcement in every way of the influence of the Party in the units."

The precise impact of the decree is difficult to measure. The only evidence in the Smolensk Archive is found in a report to the podiv (Divisional Political officer) of the commissar of the 243rd Medyn Rifle Regiment for July 10, 1926, more than a year after the decree on one-man rule had been promulgated.[12] Up to that time only one company commander in the regiment had been entrusted with unity of command. It was too early to judge his performance, the commissar reported, but it appeared adequate. He also noted that a politruk was being prepared for this role. This, of course, involved the transformation of a commissar into a commander. He also stated that another company commander, a Party member since 1921, qualified for unity of command, but that so far no action had been taken. The report evidenced no disposition to hasten the process.

The Archive contains more than two dozen political reports by this same commissar stretching over the period December 11, 1925, to December 24, 1926.[13] Broadly speaking, they conform to a standard pattern. They report the political morale of the conscripts and troops, their material condition and state of discipline, Party work in the regiment, work with the Komsomols, political and educational work among non-Party soldiers, relations with the local population, and cases of insubordination and other violations of army regulations by the troops.

One of the primary concerns of the commissar was the reception and political preparation of each new class of conscripts. The Medyn Rifle Regiment drew its conscripts from neighboring uyezds, and long before the draftees were actually inducted into the regiment preparatory agitational measures were undertaken among them with the help of local Party workers. The actual leave-taking and welcome into the army was a highly organized affair with patriotic speeches and a march through a decorated gate into the camp.[14] Once in the camp, however, military discipline took hold, and the draftees faced the usual problems of adjustment to their new environment. The Medyn encampment apparently left much to be desired. On May 20, 1926, the commissar reported that because of late snows the camp was a muddy mire and not properly prepared or equipped to receive the new conscripts.[15] Their first task was to help put the camp in order, a back-breaking assignment which apparently caused discontent. By June 23, 1926, however, the commissar reported the condition of the camp as satisfactory.[16] Tents were pitched on high, dry ground, and the camp was even supplied with electricity.

Immediately on arrival in the camp the new conscripts were divided into groups for purposes of political instruction.[17] Each group, consisting of from fifteen to forty-five soldiers, was led by a politruk and was supplied with blackboards and maps, though the commissar complained that there was not enough paper. Here political education began, discussions on the history of the Red Army and the Party and lectures on topical themes in the area of both domestic and international affairs. These discussions gave the commissar an opportunity to appraise the political attitudes of the conscripts, and his reports provide conscientious notations on this theme. In a typical report of May 30, 1926, he described their "political-moral state" as generally satisfactory, but he also noted that "negative attitudes" had manifested themselves "as a result of the material shortcomings of the camp, the quality of the food, and annoyance at having received old uniforms." [18] He noted that some members "of the village intelligentsia, sons of doctors and feldshers," had even registered their complaints with the corps commander when the latter visited the regiment. As might be expected from conscripts who were recruited from the countryside, their outlook reflected peasant interests. Certain typical questions were asked.[19] Why are workers better off than peasants? Why is the Communist Party a workers' party and not a worker-peasant party? Why don't peasants have their own trade unions? Concern was expressed over the burden of the agricultural tax. But on the whole the commissar in a later report on August 5, 1926, professed to be satisfied.[20] He noted that with regard to industrialization "no mistaken views" had been expressed, and that there was a general feeling that independence from capitalist economies was desirable. With reference to relations with England, which were then tense, most expressed support for the Soviet regime, though he also conceded that there were an apathetic few who were simply afraid of a war either with England or Poland.

The commissar's reports devote much less attention to the life of the regimental Party and Komsomol organizations than to work with non-Party troops. The latter program was extensive and, at least on paper, impressive. A determined effort was made to stamp out illiteracy and semiliteracy, and special evening courses were organized to raise the educational qualifications of the troops to a minimum level.[21] Political instruction was supplemented by a variety of extracurricular activities which were also not without political content. The regimental club had its library, its sport circle, its radio circle, and its dramatic group, and the troops were also encouraged to join such public organizations as MOPR and the League of Militant Atheists. A Mutual Assistance Fund was available to assist the soldier in a financial emergency. From time to time general regimental meetings were scheduled for agitational purposes. On May 20, 1926, for example, the commissar reported that such a meeting was held "to help the striking English workers." On July 24 the regiment met to commemorate Dzherzinsky's death. "The enlightened part of the regiment," the commissar reported, "was very saddened by his death; others were apathetic." [22] Through these many-sided activities the commissar hoped not only to improve the qualifications of the rank and file and to engage their loyalty to the regime, but to identify the activists among them and to enlist them in Komsomol and Party ranks. Indeed, the reports demonstrate that the commissar served as a species of recruiting officer in the regiment for both Party and Komsomol. The regiment had its own school where political as well as military subjects were taught. Of a total of 302 Red Army men of the 1903 class, 173 attended the regimental school, and at least forty-four expressed the desire to apply for admission to a higher educational institution after completing their military service.[23] The commissar undertook some responsibility for the placement of Red Army men, and particularly officers, after demobilization. This was done through special placement commissions operating through Party channels. The Archive contains such a request, labeled "Secret — Very Urgent," which called upon the Medyn ukom to find local posts for some members of the staff who were being released from the army.[24]

The commissar also maintained a running record of important disciplinary infractions which occurred in the regiment. For the most part, these involved drunkenness, rowdyism, debauchery, desertion, and insubordination. In a round-up report of December 24, 1926, on violations of army regulations by conscripts of the class of 1905, the commissar noted a total of 432 infractions, of which more than half involved absence without leave, while the rest arose out of drunkenness, conversation in the ranks, failure to keep weapons clean, and similar offenses.[25] In most cases the offenses were punished by disciplinary penalties; only six soldiers were arrested and imprisoned. In the course of the year one suicide was reported. As one aspect of the Party-political work of the unit, occasional public trials were held of soldiers charged with infractions of regulations. On October 2, 1926, for example, the commissar noted that 300 men attended the court martial of a soldier accused of insubordination.[26]

A careful watch was also kept over the conduct of command and political personnel, as the following extract from the commissar's report of May 20, 1926, makes clear:

> During the stay of the command personnel of the third battalion in the settlement of Iznosky, the politruk of the third machine-gun company, Comrade Kolesnikov, and the local volkom [of the Party] noted frequent cases of drunkenness (during the Easter holidays) and of hobnobbing with elements which are alien to our Party (tradesmen). A number of platoon commanders were involved in these activities, such as Niskuba, secretary of the Party cell of the third machine-gun company, platoon commander Kuvalden (a non-Party man), and platoon commander Shmelev (a Party member). Their hobnobbing took the form of organizing and participating in evening drinking parties. The politruk also notes that Comrade Niskuba frequently does not fulfill his work . . . and is completely passive in his capacity as secretary of the cell. The platoon commander Kuvaldin, apart from his drunkenness, attempted to mislead the politruk and the commander of the recruiting point by concocting fictitious documents of work allegedly done by him [at the recruiting points] . . . This case is under investigation so that the guilty ones may be brought to Party and administrative responsibility . . .
>
> The plenipotentiary of the Special Section (OO-OGPU) reported drunkenness and riotous behavior on the part of commanding personnel of the Massalsk training point . . . The company commander, Kiselev, has been guilty of a number of scandalous acts. He arrested two citizens and arranged for their detention by the militia. These arrests were unfounded and were caused by quarrels about women. Whenever the detachment of trainees under Kiselev's command marched past the house of a mistress of his (a former landowner) he used as a rule to stop the detachment in front of the house for about 20 minutes exclaiming proudly "Little leg, little head, etc." . . . Sometimes he also fired revolver shots. His politruk, Golovkin, was often also involved in drinking. We are sending separately a detailed account of all the scandals of which the commanding personnel presided over by Kiselev are guilty. When the investigation is finished, the case will be sent to a revolutionary tribunal. I would like to draw the attention of the Podiv to the fact that Kiselev, who ought to be discharged from the Red Army, was allowed by the command of the regiment and of the division to go personally to Moscow to ask to be left within the ranks of the Red Army.
>
> The commander of the I Company, Party member Comrade Zvyagintsev, has also been guilty of systematic drinking . . . In a number of cases he drank

in the presence of trainees . . . Most of his drinking was done on credit. His creditor was one of the private tavern owners of the settlement of Iznosky. Zvyagintsev continues to owe him 32 rubles until the present day. Recently this tavern owner wrote to the staff asking that the debt be deducted from Zvyagintsev's pay. He enclosed a number of notes all approximately to this effect: "Sidor Ivanich, be so kind as to give me on credit, until such-and-such a day, half a bottle, two bottles, a bottle of cognac, of vodka, herring, etc." He always used to address the tavern keeper as "very highly esteemed comrade" . . . When the investigation is finished, the case will be handed over to the revolutionary tribunal. Simultaneously it is going to be decided by the Party organs.[27]

Thus in minuscule a picture of life in the Red Army and of the role of the commissar emerges. We see the commissar, with the help of the political police, spying on the command, striving to curb abuses and seeking to indoctrinate the regiment in Party values. We see the Party bending the army to its will, endeavoring to make it a school of Communism, and utilizing it as a recruiting center to prepare Party cadres to play their part in the Communist transformation of the countryside. The pattern crystallized in the mid-twenties was to project its influence over the next decade. With industrialization the Army was to become a much more formidable technical fighting force, and the problem of adjusting the Party role to military professionalism was to create continuing difficulties. But through all these transformations the Party remained in the army as the guardian of political orthodoxy. Fearful of the dangers of Bonapartism, the Party leadership sought to prevent the army from becoming an independent force by controlling its appointments, by atomizing and intimidating opposition, and above all, by constant efforts to suffuse the army with the Party's own political outlook. The ideological indoctrination implanted by the political commissar persisted as the symbol of Party authority. Indeed, it could not be repudiated without risking the Party's extinction.

18 Party Controls and Higher Education

In prerevolutionary days the area embraced by the Western Oblast had the reputation of being one of the more culturally retarded regions of European Russia. Its literacy rate in 1897 amounted to only 17.3 per cent, as against an average of 22.9 per cent for European Russia.[1] By 1927 the literacy rate rose to 41.6 per cent, but it was still below the 44.1 per cent average for the RSFSR. The first higher educational institution — Smolensk State University — was founded in 1918; overshadowed by nearby Moscow and Leningrad universities and lacking a well-developed academic tradition or high standing, it was condemned from the beginning to the role of a rather second-rate provincial center, struggling to establish itself in the intellectual backwaters of the Western Oblast. Its two faculties, Medical and Pedagogical, had as their main mission the training of doctors and teachers to serve the region around Smolensk. The university drew most of its students from the surrounding area and its faculty from such remnants of the old intelligentsia as were available. Recalling the early days of the university, its one-time dean, Professor Rovinsky, himself non-Party, noted that the faculty was filled with "reactionary" professors. "In the first days of the existence of the university in 1918 and 1919," he wrote, "there were professors of this type: a landowner of Smolensk guberniya, exiled by the Soviet government from his estate; a former chief of police of the Kerensky government, a kulak who has kept his household up to this time, who was sentenced several times for the exploitation of hired laborers of minor age, etc." [2]

The Student Body of the University

The student body too had a high proportion of individuals whose social origins were suspect. Available in the Archive is a 1924 file containing fifty-three questionnaires of third-year medical students of the university who were being checked for political reliability, as well as eight questionnaires of students of the Pedagogic Faculty who had been expelled for various reasons, had appealed to have the action reversed, and had been reinstated.[3] The questionnaire itself was designed to elicit a detailed picture of the student's work experience, his trade union affiliation, his role in the Revolution and Civil War, his social origins, his parents' occupational history and social background, and his Party standing and political outlook. Approximately half of the students accompanied their questionnaires with documents from their village soviets or other local authorities certifying that they were of proper social origin. "The bearer of this certificate," read one of them, "is indeed of proletarian origin. Her father did physical work before and after the Revolution." Another read, "This is issued to ——— to confirm that he indeed springs from the family of a poorest peasant." But there were also many students who survived the screening despite the fact that their education (gymnasia or schools for children of the clergy) and family background raised political doubts. In such cases the notation "socio-political" can be found on the questionnaire, apparently a signal that the student needed watching or that special attention was to be devoted to his "socio-political development." At this time the dearth of students with the necesary educational background to do university work was still so great as to make it necessary for the Party authorities to overlook cases of dubious class origin.

The general picture of the student body which emerges from the questionnaires is of a highly motivated, but rather apolitical group. Out of the fifty-three medical students, less than ten had Party or Komsomol connections, in some cases already broken. Few parents were members of trade unions. Many of the students were thirty years or older and had had their schooling interrupted by the Revolution or the Civil War. All had worked at least two years, sometimes as teachers, and sometimes as feldshers (doctors' assistants), pharmacists, or nurses. Many had been sent to the university by their trade unions, sometimes with a niggardly stipend that rarely exceeded 5 rubles a month. Most had to work to support themselves, giving private lessons or doing physical labor. The great majority had endured extreme privations and severe illnesses (typhus was still epidemic in 1922–23). Most of the students still had ties with the land, though not infrequently they were ambiguous about the precise social status of their parents. There were only two students of indubitable proletarian background. The rest were classified as either of peasant or employee origin.

Aside from the data derived from these questionnaires, the Archive contains virtually no information on the state of the university during the NEP. The educational material in the Archive is largely centered on the years 1929–1931 and consists in the main of a rich file of protocols of Party meetings in the university and in the Medical, Pedagogical, and Agricultural Institutes into which the university was transformed at this time. Since this period happened to coincide with the great drive to communize the university and its successor institutes, it provides a particularly interesting case study in the assertion of Party control over higher education in the Soviet Union.

The Communization of the University

The story begins on a deceptively quiet note with the report of a meeting of the university's governing board on February 4, 1929, at which the resignation of Professor N. N. Rovinsky from the rectorship of the university was accepted.[4] At this session, Rovinsky made a short speech thanking the entire collective of the university for their past support, and testimonials to Rovinsky were read by the new rector, Belkin, and other educational officials. Camouflaged by these polite ceremonials, what actually happened was that the obkom had ordered the removal of Rovinsky, a non-Party rector, and his replacement by Belkin, a trusted Party worker from Moscow. Along with Belkin a new set of Party deans was installed in the university faculties.

The new crew met a frigid reception. As Belkin later testified, when he arrived in Smolensk he called a meeting of the Party aktiv at the university.[5] Immediately he was told that rumors were being circulated to the effect that he had a record as an embezzler and that some Communists, when asked about the truth of these rumors, replied: "We'll see, we'll investigate, we'll tell you." The professors, upon hearing of his appointment, sent a delegation to the Commissariat of Education in Moscow to petition for his removal and "spread all kinds of untruths about him." The evaluation of him changed for the better after he delivered a report on a scientific theme. "Now," he declared, "the attitude of the majority of the instructors toward me is good, but far from all are sincere. Some of the professors are dissatisfied, but they do not say this openly." [6] Slutskin, the new dean of the rabfak (workers' faculty), encountered opposition even in Party ranks. At a meeting held to introduce him to the students, Party and Komsomol members raised objections to him, saying that his appointment against the wishes of the masses was a violation of democracy, and that there was no reason to replace the excellent non-Party incumbent with a Party dean of dubious qualifications.[7] Khenok, the newly appointed teacher of Party history, was at first denied membership in the Association of Scientific Workers on the grounds, first, that he was not a university graduate; second, that he had published no scholarly works; and third, that "Leninism is not a science." [8] Only after much pleading and pressure was he granted membership.

The flying wedge of Belkin and company which the obkom had inserted into the administration of the university was intended to be the instrument of a larger social transformation. The directives of the obkom ordered the new leadership to improve the social composition of the student body, to communize the leading organs and scientific workers of the university, and to create conditions "which would aid to the maximum the task of training cadres of real builders of socialism." [9] An obkom commission was appointed to report on the execution of these directives.

On May 9, 1929, the commission rendered its report.[10] It noted some improvement in the social composition of the student body as a result of the "direct intervention of the obkom." The party cadres among the newly admitted students had mounted to 15.4 per cent compared with 5.2 per cent in the previous year; the Komsomol percentage had increased from 22.1 to 38.9 per cent, and the worker-peasant category from 42 to 72.3 per cent. But the commission still professed to be dissatisfied. It deemed the percentage of Party members too small. Only fourteen of the new students came from the rabfak, and 290, or 81 per cent of the students, were graduates of second-degree schools (which prepared for the university and were then considered to be divorced from production). "This," the commission stated, "explains the large number of class-alien elements among the student body."

In the last six months, the commission reported, forty-five students had been expelled, mainly for concealing their family origin and for anti-Semitism. Of these, sixteen were subsequently reinstated, among them some who were "clearly [class-]alien." The commission concluded that the purge campaign among the students had not been extensive enough. "According to presumptive information, the obstruction of the student body [by alien elements] amounts to around 15%. If it is taken into account that there are 1,422 students in the university, it will become clear that more than 200 students should be expelled."

The commission also reported the dismissal of fifteen scientific workers. They were described as the most conservative, anti-public types, "unsuitable, harmful for a Soviet VUZ [university]." To replace them, twenty new appointments were made, of whom thirteen were Party members. The reorganized governing board of the university consisted of five Communists and three non-Party people. The report expressed satisfaction that the board had approved a Communist as secretary of the studies section and that all but one of the teachers of the social sciences were now Communists. At the same time the Party cell of the university was admonished for having committed a number of crude political mistakes, particularly for having given a positive characterization of Rovinsky, "a reactionary professor, hostile to the Soviet government." The Party fraction was also criticized for its lack of leadership of the university and for making decisions on appointments in a "narrow circle." Belkin was severely castigated for taking 800 rubles for work which he never did — "behavior absolutely unworthy of a member of the Party." The general conclusion of the report: "Smolensk State University is in a serious state of crisis."

Acting on this report, the bureau of the obkom ordered the Party

fraction of the governing board to overcome "its right-opportunist attitudes" and to press forward with the expulsion of "socially alien and
hostile students and reactionary scientific workers." [12] It also decided to
call on the Party Central Committee and the People's Commissariat of
Education to supply "a significant number of prepared Party teachers
and non-Party Marxists in order to achieve a decisive reorganization in
the teaching of the university, an improvement in the class composition of
the teaching cadres, and a strengthening of the cultural base in the Western Oblast." [13]

Faculty Purges

With the circulation of this decree, a new campaign to root out
"reactionary" professors was launched. The first victim was Professor
Rovinsky. At a meeting on July 4, 1929, the Party fraction of the Board
considered a proposal emanating from Rovinsky to establish a new chair
in regional geography.[14] The fraction approved the chair, but rejected
Rovinsky as the incumbent. At its next meeting, on July 10, it dismissed
Rovinsky from the editorial board of the university's "Scientific News,"
ordered that his article entitled "Ten Years of Smolensk University" be
removed from typesetting and that Comrade Belkin write another in its
place, and decided to bar him from membership in the delegation of
scientific workers to the Oblast Congress of Soviets.[15] It noted that the
administration had raised the question of dismissing Rovinsky from
the university. Meanwhile, Belkin, the new rector, was authorized to
go to Moscow at once to discuss the dismissal of a number of reactionary
instructors. There the matter was taken up with none other than
Vyshinsky, and permission was obtained. Meanwhile, Professor Rovinsky
apparently saw the handwriting on the wall, busied himself on his own
behalf, and arranged another post in Moscow. On August 24, 1929, the
Party fraction released Rovinsky from his position as Professor of
Political Economy and named a Party replacement.[16]

But this was not to be the end of the story. What remains to be
told was contained in a long letter from Rovinsky, dated October 22, 1929,
to one Comrade Shelekhes. The letter, stamped "Secret," read in part:

Dear Comrade Shelekhes: I turn to you as the Chairman of the Oblast
Executive Committee and as a man who, I am sure, is objectively calm and
very self-restrained, in regard to the following two problems: . . . in the
newspaper *Rabochii Put* [Worker's Path] of September 7, this year, No. 206,
there appeared an anonymous article under the title . . . "Is Rovinsky a
Professor?" which from the first word to the last was either pure lies and slander or gossip and insinuation. Leaving the latter aside, since its foolishness
speaks for itself, the main accusations are two: (1) swindling, consisting of
the fact that in my questionnaire I listed numerous published works, increasing
from year to year, which actually do not exist, and (2) that I received a false

reference from the responsible secretary of the association of scientific workers . . .

I immediately sent the editors a refutation, where I pointed out how it is possible to check on the existence of my works, quoted dates and numbers of documents which prove that I was confirmed as a professor by the collegium of the State Scholarship Council, that the reviewers were professors and members of the Party and the State Scientific Council who were known to everyone, and that my qualifications were established twice by an expert commission of the TsEKUBU [Central Commission for the Improvement of the Living Conditions of Scientists] . . . At the same time I submitted a claim to the procurator of the Western Oblast about bringing the author of the article to trial for slander.

Somewhat later this question was reviewed by the Section of Scientific Workers of Smolensk State University, and after the qualifications commission checked on all my works, it decided that all of them exist and that thus the article in this respect is definitely a lie . . . Finally, recently my qualifications were confirmed by the Central Expert Commission and the Moscow Bureau of the Section of Scientific Workers. Despite all this, the newspaper up to this time has not printed either my refutation or the protocols of the Section of Scientific Workers which were reported to it, and the procurator did not bring the author of the article to trial. These circumstances seem simply monstrous in regard to a scientific worker, specialist, and public servant from the first days of the October Revolution. This, together with subsequent events, leads me to think that this is conscious persecution, pursuing some kind of secret aim: . . . I beg you earnestly to exert influence on the organs of the Oblast Executive Committee so that a refutation is printed [to the effect] that the contents of the article were not confirmed.

. . . In No. 241, October 18, of the same newspaper my name appeared again in an article "For a Proletarian VUZ," where the newspaper not only makes me out as a swindler, but tries to depict me as some kind of reactionary die-hard who recruited "under his wings" a unit of rank Black Hundred scientific workers, selected them from the point of view of "kinship," obstructed the student body with a socially hostile element, suppressed the social sciences, and was connected by family ties with the Party part of the board (and vice versa).[17]

Rovinsky then tried to refute these charges, pointing out that admissions to the university were regulated by the Party, that the ideological weakness of the scientific staff was due to "objective conditions" (i.e., the lack of trained Party scientists), that he "waged an energetic struggle for the improvement of the social sciences" and the elimination of "Black Hundred" professors, and that much of his trouble was due to irresponsible intrigue and denunciations by "reactionary" members of the staff, who out of an instinct for self-preservation had suddenly assumed the guise of "the most advanced workers." In conclusion he requested that measures be taken to preserve the files and documents of the university during the period of his rectorship in order to enable him to protect his reputation against further besmirching. He reminded Shelekhes that, at the time of the Smolensk scandal, the representative of the Central Control Commission, after investigating the university, had "stated at a general meeting that the only bright spot in the entire dark background of activity of Smolensk guberniya is Smolensk University." [18]

The Archive contains no record of a reply from Shelekhes to this letter. Indeed the only other references to the Rovinsky affair are, first, a notation in the protocol of the meeting of the Party fraction of the governing board on October 3, 1929, that the request for the dismissal of Rovinsky contained in an earlier protocol should be stated more clearly and uncompromisingly and tied to political changes carried out at the university; and second, a resolution of the university Party cell dated October 15, 1929, which condemned the Party fraction of the board because, among other derelictions, it had earlier supported Rovinsky and given him a positive characterization. [19]

From this point on the campaign to purge "reactionary" professors from the university gathered momentum. The next victim was Professor Solosin, a linguist. "Taking into consideration . . . the absence of Marxism and the idealistic content of explanations given by Professor Solosin in his course in the Russian language and also in connection with conflicts between the students and Professor Solosin," the Party fraction voted on August 24, 1929, "to release him from the position of holder of the chair of Russian Language and Dialectology from September 1 . . ." [20] On September 6 the Party fraction, in answer to a request from the pedagogic section of the Chief Administration for Professional Education for a recommendation for Professor Solosin, ordered that the reply stress that Solosin was unsuitable for teaching in a VUZ. Still later, on October 3, 1929, the Party fraction heard that Solosin, who had been dismissed for anti-Marxism, had found another academic job and was now an assistant head of a VUZ. [21] The Party fraction resolved to file a protest with Bubnov, the People's Commissar of Education. Meanwhile, a more ominous note was introduced by the interest of the OGPU in Solosin. A top-secret memorandum of October 15, 1929, addressed by an OGPU raion official to the OGPU chief of the Western Oblast, stressed that Professor Solosin was guilty of "clear wrecking," because, among other reasons, he had spent 500 rubles of the state's money to acquire a copy of "The Lay of Prince Igor," which the memorandum described as "a memorial to the great princely chauvinism of the twelfth century." [22] The OGPU official asked for instructions as to how to proceed. The Archive contains no reply to his request.

The next victim of the purge was a historian, Professor Kudrin. On August 24 it was announced that Kudrin had been "released" from the course on the History of Trade and Industrial Capital and replaced by a graduate of the Institute of Red Professors. [23] To soften the blow the initial announcement stressed that he had been released for "reasons of health," but this did not satisfy the Party zealots. On November 6 the Party fraction ordered the administration to recast its dismissal formula and to stress that Kudrin was released because "he is not a Marxist and does not possess a special education in history courses." [24] The Party fraction again emphasized that the course in the History of Trade and Industrial Capital must be given by a Marxist.

Meanwhile, a scandal developed around the library and Professor Yefimov, the librarian. On October 9 the Party fraction heard a report that a Comrade Kostromov some time ago (the "time" is crossed out and replaced in ink by "years") had seen a forbidden monarchist magazine in the hands of a student who allegedly obtained it from the Smolensk State University library.[25] The fraction decided to appoint Comrade Kostromov and a group of Komsomols to investigate the methods used to safeguard books that had been ordered withdrawn from general circulation. Professor Yefimov, who held the chair of literature and was also a close associate of Solosin's, thereupon became frightened and sought a transfer to another VUZ, a fact which was duly noted in the OGPU report on Solosin. In the subsequent investigation it was determined that the last time forbidden literature had been issued was in 1925, before Professor Yefimov became librarian, and that he was therefore to be considered innocent of the charge of releasing a monarchist magazine.[26] But the Party fraction nevertheless decided that the characterization which was to accompany Yefimov's request for transfer was to stress that he was socially passive, had refused to subscribe to the State Loan, that he was haughty, indifferent, and an extreme individualist who stood apart from the collective and was very "formal" in his relationships with students. At the same time the library was criticized for not keeping forbidden literature under seal and apart from other books. On December 9, 1929, the Party fraction ordered the librarian to remove all "religious and moral books, books which idealize the capitalist and tsarist regimes, and books of anti-Semitic tendencies." [27] These books were to be stored in a special place, and access to them was to be limited to specially cleared persons conducting scientific research which required consultation of such material.

In December 1929 another scandal erupted around a Professor Kuzmin of the medical faculty. Students reported that the professor had made clearly anti-Soviet statements in the course of his lectures.[28] Comparing the old methods of supplying a city with present methods, he remarked that the old ladder (private profit) which had worked successfully in the past had been destroyed while a new one had not yet been built. Milk and meat which Moscow used to have in abundance were hard to get because the "private dealer is killed." He stated that a Soviet engineer tried to take his apartment from him, laying special stress on the word "sovetski." He also recommended the building of small separate houses as preferable to large communal houses from the point of view of social hygiene. These quoted remarks of Kuzmin aroused a storm of indignation in Party circles. At a meeting on December 19, 1929, the bureau of the university Party cell was particularly indignant because Komsomols and a Party member present at the lecture remained silent in the face of provocation and failed to contradict Kuzmin.[29] The Party member, Comrade Grushetskaia, who had served in the Red Army and had joined the Party in 1920, was called upon for an explanation. She replied: "At his lecture the professor spoke to us about meat supply and about some kind of a ladder; that we have destroyed the old ladder but have not built the new one; that we have destroyed the old trade but have not organized the new one, but I could not understand what his statements led to. I did not consider his statements serious, but one can attribute to his words another purpose." [30] She was promptly attacked from all directions, some denouncing her as a "political imbecile" and a supporter of right-wing policies and demanding that she be expelled from the Party; others suggesting only a strict reprimand in consideration of her long Party tenure and Red Army service. Grushetskaia protested in vain that she had been unable to understand the significance of Professor Kuzmin's demonstration. Finally, by a vote of seven to five the bureau decided to expel Comrade Grushetskaia from the Party on the ground that she had failed to react to the sallies of Professor Kuzmin against Soviet policy, and that on the contrary she had defended him and asserted that there was nothing politically incorrect in his remarks. The bureau also decided to demand the dismissal of Professor Kuzmin, to organize mass lectures to combat the misconceptions circulated by him, and to direct Komsomol and Party members to be particularly vigilant in detecting and challenging "ideological corruptions" and anti-Soviet remarks by members of the faculty.

Professor Kuzmin apparently survived this attack, for at a meeting of the bureau of the Smolensk Medical Institute (the former medical faculty of the university) on February 26, 1931, we find him being denounced again for having expressed a number of "politically incorrect opinions," such as that the mortality of children in the USSR had decreased only slightly, that food supplies were being improperly distributed, that the Malthusian law was incorrect because there were many unused food reserves such as rats, mice, locusts, etc., and that the gifts and talents which had been a particular monopoly of the former ruling classes were passed on through heredity.[31] For the second time, the Party demanded that Kuzmin be dismissed, and that articles be written and meetings held to combat his statements.

The next professor to fall afoul of the Party was Russkikh, who headed the department of nervous diseases. At a meeting of the bureau of the Party cell on December 28, 1929, a student reported that Professor Russkikh had said, "Peasants come to us with neurasthenia because they are being squashed by taxes." [32] Some students agreed with the professor, but others challenged him. The Professor was also reported to have attributed nervous illnesses to the fight against religion. The bureau resolved to press for the dismissal of Professor Russkikh. Like Kuzmin, Russkikh managed to ride out the first attack, for on May 20, 1931, we find the bureau again considering the case of Professor Russkikh.[33] At this meeting it was reported that Russkikh had apologized for remarking that the Jewish race was degenerate, but the bureau refused to accept the apology as sincere. The bureau noted that the efforts of the administration and "socially active" groups to stop Russkikh from making anti-Soviet remarks had been entirely ineffective, and that he made them more frequently than ever. Professor Russkikh was described as hostile to the training of young scientific workers. He refused to teach his assistants and clinical associates or to direct their research projects. He conducted his own researches in strict secrecy. He was opposed to "active methods" of teaching and considered that the abandonment of the lecture system was bound to lower the quality of instruction. The bureau instructed the associate dean of the institute to confer with the obkom on the time and method of removing Professor Russkikh from the chair of nervous diseases.

On March 12, 1930, the bureau of the university Party cell assembled to consider the case of another "unreliable," Professor Gurevich of the medical faculty.[34] Gurevich, it was pointed out, maintained a private practice in Moscow and as a result missed some of his university lectures. But the real burden of the complaint against him was his political attitude. He told many anti-Soviet anecdotes. He openly criticized the system of "pushing forward" proletarian students and said only capable students should be pushed forward. He made a "reactionary" speech at the funeral of Professor Prokin, observing that we do not know when life begins or ends and what happens afterwards. He had been admonished by Rector Belkin who proposed that Gurevich write a newspaper article acknowledging his "mistakes." The bureau resolved to request the dismissal of Gurevich.

The problem of political heresy continued to plague the medical faculty. On February 26, 1931, the bureau of the Party cell heard a report by one Comrade Kaplan on an article entitled "Psychoses under Conditions of Class Struggle" by Professors Brukhausky and Zhukov.[35] According to Kaplan, the authors of the article attributed the increase in cases of psychoses among peasants to collectivization. They pointed out that middle and poor peasants were susceptible to psychic illness, as well as kulaks. "It seems," they wrote, "that it is harder to understand psychologically the cases where flare-ups of psychoses took place among middle and poor peasants. The central reason here is the extreme complexity of our times, an enormous quantity of continuous irritations which stupefy by their newness and unexpectedness and which are aggravated by the 'dizziness from success' which led in some localities to perversion of the general line of the Party." The article was condemned as "politically dangerous" and as "objectively expressing the sorties of the class enemy on the scientific front." The bureau ordered that the article be withdrawn from circulation, and that Brukhausky be excluded from the Association of Scientific Workers. It also arranged for meetings of students and scientific workers at which the article was to be given an appropriate evaluation. This time Belkin came in for a special rebuke for having approved the publication of the article and for having checked it so superficially as not to notice its grave political errors. At the bureau meeting Belkin "at once" admitted his great political mistake and requested that he be permitted to make a speech to the students and scientific workers refuting the dangerous political views contained in the article.

At the same time a number of professors sought to escape the heresy hunt and perhaps to advance their careers by seeking refuge within the Party. At an open Party meeting at the university on April 13, 1930, with 500 persons in attendance, four professors and two assistants were welcomed into the Party.[36] Some of the remarks made by the professor-candidates on this occasion hold more than passing interest. Professor Sobolev commented: "Why do I enter the Party? We see increasing threat of war . . . many trials in which scientific workers are involved in counter-revolution. Some say we come to get promotions. We come but for serious, heavy duties." Professor Belousov continued, ". . . In this epoch when whole sectors of factories enter the Party, we cannot be neutral." Professor Grzhebin declared: "I first entered the All-Union Association of Scientific Workers, and now at this moment of sharpening class struggle, I give myself entirely into the hands of the Party of Lenin . . ." Professor Linberg stated, ". . . The decisions of the Party on agrarian and industrial questions demand that scientific workers show their faces." Objections were raised only to Linberg as a former Socialist-Revolutionary and a descendant of a bourgeois family who had not fought the reactionary professors. But Rector Belkin defended him on the ground that he had never concealed his social origin or SR membership and that he was now much more "left" than a year ago. All six candidates were recommended for entrance into the Party.

Despite the purge of so-called anti-Soviet elements and the assimilation of new converts into the Party, the social composition of the faculties of higher educational institutions in the Smolensk area remained unsatisfactory to the Party leadership. A report on the Smolensk Medical Institute for the year 1930 noted that 38 per cent of the academic workers were still descendants of noblemen, priests, and civil servants.[37] A similar report on the Smolensk Pedagogical Institute pointed out that its teaching staff of eighty-five included only five persons of worker origin and only thirty-two of peasant origin.[38] A fifth of the faculty were members of the Party, but at least three-fourths of this number were concentrated in lower academic ranks — instructors, assistants, and graduate students. The report distinguished three groups in the faculty: (1) the most reactionary elements, (2) a neutral or middle group, and (3) a group which was loyal to Soviet power. The latter group had grown in number in the last year and a half, but the professors belonged almost entirely to the first two groups, especially in the sciences. History was still being taught by non-Party personnel. Three notorious "reactionaries" had been expelled from the faculty, but all had found better jobs elsewhere.

The report noted a deplorable lack of Marxist and Leninist content in the curriculum. Except for economics (and there not entirely), there was no clear political line in instruction. There was no Marxist methodology or dialectical materialism in the teaching of physics and chemistry; on the contrary, idealism and religious ideas crept into their presentation. Economic geography was taught without any political content. The subject of dialectical materialism (diamat) was especially badly handled. The holder of the chair, Professor Miller, was non-Party. He managed to give a whole course on diamat while dispensing with words like "dialectics" and "class struggle." He avoided contemporary questions, talked about Aristotle by the hour, and never dropped a single word about Lenin. A group of student "rightists" used his course to develop their views, quoting from Marx, Engels, and Lenin to defend Bukharin's position. "This abnormal situation" was accentuated by the timidity of the director of the Pedagogical Institute, one Bogdanov, who, when he was asked as a philosopher to correct Professor Miller's position, replied: "But how can I influence him when I am a docent and he is a professor, and when it comes to science I must work under his leadership?"[39]

The situation in the Agricultural VUZ was no better. A report for the year 1930 noted that its staff of twenty-seven instructors and professors included only one Party member, one Party candidate, and seven persons of worker or peasant origin.[40] "It is characteristic," stated the report, "that professors who hold the chairs are all members of classes alien to us . . . Politically, the professors need very sharp supervision . . ."

As these reports make clear, the communization of the faculties was a slow process. At the beginning of the thirties the Soviet regime faced a desperate shortage of trained teaching cadres, and the old intelligentsia was still indispensable. Those who were dismissed in Smolensk usually found better positions elsewhere. But already there were signs that the new young Party intelligentsia was coming into its own. Slowly but inexorably, the older non-Party professors were being displaced from key administrative positions and subjects where political content was important. The Rovinskys were being brushed aside, while the day of the Belkins was dawning.

Efforts to Proletarianize the Student Body

Similar changes were taking place in the social composition of the student body. The effort to proletarianize the student body began to bear fruit. To hasten the process, a rabfak, or Worker's Faculty, had been established in the university to help workers with inadequate educational backgrounds prepare themselves for entrance into the university. On September 12, 1929, the bureau of the Party cell noted with satisfaction that the newly admitted students in the rabfak consisted of 70 per cent workers, 18 per cent agricultural laborers, and 12 per cent peasants.[41] A considerable improvement was also reported in the social composition of the students newly admitted to the VUZ. The worker-peasant contingent in the entering class in the Pedagogical Faculty mounted to nearly 71 per cent and in the Medical Faculty to about 77 per cent. Plans were laid to prevent newly admitted worker students from becoming discouraged or feeling lost. Outstanding senior students were assigned to help workers who were encountering academic difficulties. Such difficulties were also taken into account in assigning extracurricular tasks. Scholarships were also made available to ease the transition to university life.

Meanwhile, the purge of alien elements from the student body continued. On August 24, 1929, the Party fraction of the administration voted the expulsion of seven students who had concealed their social origins as children of clergy, landed gentry, kulaks, and merchants.[42] On January 8, 1930, Rector Belkin reported to the bureau of the Party cell that forty-five students had been expelled during the preceding months, though he also expressed his chagrin that thirteen had been reinstated by the Oblast Department of Public Education.[43] Appeals to and reversals by the oblast department posed serious problems, and on January 7 Belkin addressed the following letter to the Party unit of the oblast public education department with a copy to the obkom agitprop:

Supplementing my personal discussions with Comrade Lyubimov, I hereby report that the relationships which have lately been created between the board of the university on the one hand, and the Oblast Department of Public Education on the other, are abnormal, harm the work, and discredit both institutions in the eyes of non-Party people. The reinstatements by the Oblast Department of Public Education of students expelled by the university, without attempts to come to an agreement with the Communist leaders of the university, bring the students to the conclusion that there exist two Soviet powers in Smolensk — one, the "bad" one, in Smolensk State University, and the other, the "good" one, in the Oblast Department of Public Education . . .

In order to eliminate these disagreements and in order to prevent them in the future, on the instructions of the fraction of the board of Smolensk State University and the bureau of the cell . . . I order the following:

1. At all meetings of the board and the fraction of the board — invite the responsible leaders of the Oblast Department of Public Education.

2. Questions about students who are subject to expulsion from Smolensk State University for social reasons are to be decided in the future in conjunction with representatives of the Oblast Department of Public Education; if there are disagreements, cases are to be transferred for final decision to the agitation and propaganda department of the Obkom, and this decision is to be put into effect . . . Please certify your approval of these orders.[44]

While a measure of coördination was thus achieved, the rector in line with instructions from the center found it necessary to temper the purge. Again the shortage of trained cadres served to protect students whose social origins were suspect. On April 16, 1930, the rector informed a special university Party conference that the purge authorities in the university had been overzealous, that particular care had to be exercised in dealing with students who were nearing graduation, and that the "social worth" of the students must be taken into account as well as their social origins.[45]

Meanwhile, the university itself was undergoing a basic reorganization. On April 11, 1930, the bureau of the Party collective was informed that both the pedagogical and medical faculties were to be transformed into separate institutes during the summer.[46] In the interim, preparations for admissions for the 1930–31 academic year proceeded apace. At the Smolensk Medical Institute 169 students were accepted in the entering class, of whom 78 per cent belonged to the worker and agricultural-labor social strata.[47] At the Pedagogical Institute the statistics on new admissions for 1930–31 were equally impressive. Sixty-five per cent were classified as workers, 9.8 per cent as agricultural workers, and 13.3 per cent as kolkhozniks.[48] Students of employee origin still accounted for 37 per cent of the student body, but as the report on Party work at the institute pointed out, the bulk of the employee group were upperclassmen. In the Agricultural Institute of the Western Oblast, which opened its doors for the first time in 1930, the social composition of the student body was considered even more satisfactory. Out of a total of 148 students, 130 were classified as workers and agricultural laborers, nine as kolkhozniks, one as an individual peasant, and only eight as employees.[49]

The only data available on admissions for the academic year 1931–32 are for the Medical Institute. Meeting on June 3, 1931, the bureau of the Party cell of the Institute established the following quotas: 40 per cent, workers; 20 per cent, children of workers; 5 per cent, agricultural laborers; 7 per cent, kolkhozniks; 5 per cent, children of kolkhozniks; 8 per cent, medical workers; 7 per cent, children of specialists; 3 per cent, children of employees; 5 per cent, others.[50] The bureau also set as its goal a fifty-fifty division between men and women, a Party contingent of 30 per cent, and a Komsomol membership of 40 per cent.

The recruitment of the specified proportion of workers proved difficult. On July 12, 1931, a Comrade Levtsov reported to the bureau that, despite publicity and the dispatch of ten recruiting brigades to industrial centers in the oblast, the enrollment of workers was still far from satisfactory.[51] The major problem was that industry had an insignificant number of workers with a high-school education and that it was necessary first to draw the workers into the rabfak so that they could be properly prepared to enter the Medical Institute. He proposed the dispatch of an additional four brigades to comb the industrial centers for recruits. At a meeting on August 20, 1931, the bureau was informed that the Smolensk gorkom had ordered that 88 per cent of the new students consist of workers and kolkhozniks.[52] Doubt was expressed that this could be managed, and the bureau indicated that the quota imposed by the gorkom would not be met unless the system of voluntary recruiting was supplemented by "contracts" under which individual enterprises agreed to assign students to the institute for study. At this point the record stops, leaving us in the dark as to whether the Medical Institute actually succeeded in meeting its goals. Confronted with Party pressure to proletarianize the VUZ's, the Medical Institute, along with other higher educational institutions, did its best to adjust to the new demands made on it. By the early thirties the composition of the university student bodies was beginning to register the full impact of the social revolution ushered in by the Communist triumph.

The new admissions policy exacted its price in a temporary decline in the quality of the student body and in academic standards. The discussions in the Party cell of the Medical Institute make this clear. Although the claim was put forth at the meeting of December 2, 1930, that fewer students had failed than in the previous year, the discussion brought out that no satisfactory academic records existed, since professors feared conflicts with their students and were unwilling to differentiate among them.[53] This was still a period of brigade rather than individual work, but dissatisfaction with this method of measuring performance was already apparent. A resolution adopted by the bureau read, "Examination must be made personally of each student; under no condition must one be satisfied by checking only the knowledge of the whole brigade, since the latter . . . removes responsibility from each student." [54] The situation in the rabfaks was especially unsatisfactory. On June 3, 1931 the Bureau of the Party cell was informed that of sixty students who had entered the evening rabfak only twelve were still studying there.[55] The greater part had failed in their studies; among those who survived, social origins were not "too acceptable." There was marked restlessness in the rabfak. On February 26, 1931, it was reported that 35 per cent of the third-year class was failing. Many did not want to go to the Smolensk Medical Institute, though under the rules of admission they were "attached" or "restricted" to it.[56] One student complained: "We are not gentry or landowners. We are descendants of workers. I am against 'restrictions.' " [57] (The Russian word *prikreplenie* is used here to convey the sense of peasants attached to the land in the time of serfdom.)

The situation in the Smolensk Pedagogical Institute was, if anything, worse.[58] There the rabfak was not attached exclusively to the institute, and as a result there was a constant flight on the part of the graduates to other more desirable institutions of higher education. At one point the whole second year of the rabfak went out on strike, but was persuaded to desist as a result of an "unexpected" visit from the secretary of the gorkom. The aim of the demonstration was to draw the attention of leading organs to the unwisdom of trying to "attach" the rabfak to the Pedagogical Institute. Although three of the organizers of the strike were expelled from the Komsomol, there were many others, noted a Party report, who put personal interests first, and in answer to appeals to their Party loyalty replied: "Don't try to propagandize us. We are interested in a profession first of all." Academic work at the Institute was continuously disorganized by the practice of dispatching Party members and other activists on special assignments to the villages. Tardiness and absences from class were rife; much of it was excused because of "social work." Both the administration and the Party contributed to the disorder by holding frequent meetings during lecture hours. Discipline left much to be desired. There were instances, especially in the rabfak, of students being rude, refusing to answer instructors' questions, and so forth. Morale among students was low, since "no one knew what kind of a teacher, for what kind of a school, the institute was supposed to train."

The situation in the newly organized Agricultural VUZ was no better.[59] The preparation of the entering students was poor. Only twenty had finished high school and seventy-one elementary school. An investigation disclosed many academic failures — in one group in mathematics the failure rate hit 70 per cent. Books and equipment still remained unpacked. In general, the report concluded, "both the institute and the rabfak have much to look forward to, but now they are trailing behind."

Living Conditions of the Students

The living conditions of the students were also far from satisfactory. In this case the difficulties created by rapidly mounting enrollments were compounded by inadequate housing, overcrowding, and a general worsening in the food supply. A report on the Pedagogical Institute noted that the promise of the obkom secretariat to improve the feeding of students had not been carried out.[60] The dining room of the institute had been excluded from the meat distribution plan. In December 1930 there were only four meat servings instead of the scheduled ten. The dormitories were overcrowded and unsanitary. Stoves did not work, and there were not enough wash basins and sleeping gear. Some rooms had no locks, and there were many thefts. In all five dormitories there was only one Red Corner, which had neither newspapers nor equipment and was more like a passageway than a center of student cultural life.

The Medical Institute faced similar problems. On August 20, 1931, less than two weeks before the opening of the 1930–31 academic year, the bureau of the Party cell discovered that, even if all dining rooms and Lenin corners were used as dormitories, some 200 students would still remain without sleeping space.[61] The Party cell was solemnly informed that students would not be permitted to spend the nights at railroad stations and that efforts were being made to obtain permission for them to bed down in some workers' clubs. In the dormitories themselves there was a shortage of 100 beds and 160 mattresses, and the food situation was described as "very bad." The rabfak of the institute was in no better case; 222 students were scheduled to sleep in its dormitories, but there were only 122 beds. The dormitories were in bad condition, but two were being repaired. There was no firewood for the winter, so 150 students were dispatched to the forests to cut wood. The pious hope was expressed that the academic work of the students would not be hampered by this chore. To meet the desperate food situation, the Party cell decided to operate a pig-raising project in connection with the students' dining room.

In the midst of these hardships and inconveniences the question of student scholarships loomed large. Funds had to be found to support the workers who were being recruited for the rabfaks and institutes of the oblast. This task was not easy. It required patient negotiation and constant begging to obtain allocations both from the oblast and RSFSR budgets. At the oblast level, requests for aid were directed to the obkom and the oblast department of public education; in Moscow they went originally to the RSFSR People's Commissariat of Education, though after the division into institutes, the Medical Institute looked for support to the Commissariat of Health. Data on the latter institute indicate that

60 to 70 per cent of the entering students in the rabfak and institute for the year 1931–32 were able to receive scholarship aid.[62]

Scholarships varied in size and were tailored to need. For the year 1929–30 the oblast authorities provided the university with 240 scholarships with an average monthly stipend of 27 rubles.[63] In addition, there are references in the Party protocols to 60-ruble scholarships and even 75-ruble scholarships, which were reserved for "poverty-stricken" workers with the longest industrial records and for the poorest peasants.[64] The distribution of ordinary scholarships was in the hands of a committee representing the Party fraction of the University administration, the administration itself, and the trade union committee of each faculty. The distribution of the prize 75-ruble and 60-ruble scholarships was entrusted to a special committee representing the obkom of the Party, the oblast trade union council, and the administration of the university.

The life of the student body was both Spartan and hectic. The many-sided demands on the energies of the students left little time for reflection or for concentrated mastery of the curricula to which they were exposed. This was a period when courses were being telescoped and accelerated and as a result training was frequently superficial and incomplete. At the same time, the students were bombarded by all kinds of extracurricular claims. They were mobilized to help with collectivization in the villages, to liquidate illiteracy, to provide organizers for the League of the Godless, to prepare wall newspapers, to participate in the military training work of Osoaviakhim, to solicit subscriptions to the state loans, and to perform a multitude of other "social" duties which inevitably diverted them from the academic work at hand. This was also the era of the "pushed-forward" worker, frequently poorly trained and prepared, encountering difficulty in coping with the academic rigors of the university and institute curricula, but singled out to provide proletarian leadership in the period ahead. For some the experience was frustrating and tragic; on December 5, 1929, the Party fraction of the university administration was informed that three students of the rabfak had attempted suicide, apparently because they could not meet even the low academic standards to which they were held.[65] For others, the experience was liberating and exhilarating; pulled up from the depths, they saw limitless vistas rising before them.

With each year Party and Komsomol penetration of the student body increased.[66] In the Agricultural Institute 29 per cent of the student body in 1930 were Party members and another 50 per cent members of the Komsomol. In the Pedagogical Institute 16.3 per cent were Party members and another 36 per cent Komsomols. But the state of Party indoctrination still left much to be desired. As the collectivization campaign gathered force, the bureau of the university Party cell noted signs of "pessimism" and a "peasant point of view" even in Party and Komsomol ranks. An investigation of the Agricultural VUZ in 1930 revealed a considerable degree of "political naïveté" among the students: some tried to make a kulak join a kolkhoz, and others wondered why "we" had encouraged successful peasants and now dekulakized them.[67] At the Pedagogical Institute, a right-wing group, led by one Egorov, and composed of six or seven of the "cleverest" students, had openly defended Bukharin; all were expelled from the Party, and their continued presence at the institute was under attack.[68]

Anti-Semitism and other residues of "national chauvinism" still persisted in Party as well as in non-Party ranks. The data on the 1929 admissions to the Pedagogical and Medical Faculties of the University revealed that the Jewish group was the largest of the minority nationalities, though the Great Russians outnumbered them eight to one in the Medical Faculty and fourteen to one in the Pedagogical Faculty.[69] Occasional actions taken to suppress anti-Semitism and other chauvinistic outbursts crop up in the Party protocols. On December 28, 1929, for example, during a quarrel over a radio tube, the manager of the club in one of the dormitories called one of the Jewish students a "zhid." [70] The manager of the club was expelled from the university, but not before his action had been defended by a group of Komsomol students. In July 1930, the Party cell of the Medical Institute conducted an investigation into the alleged existence of anti-Semitism in the Eye Clinic. On June 26, 1931, two students were expelled from the Party for great-power chauvinism.[71] Their crime consisted in persecuting a Polish student who lived in the same room with them.

The Party protocols also make clear that career interests were fostered by Party membership. This was notably true in connection with the problem of promotions, transfers to other institutions, and placement after graduation. Party affiliation at this period provided a definite advantage in climbing the academic ladder. On October 29, 1929, for example, the Party fraction of the administration met to fill four clinical assistantships in the Medical Faculty.[72] Four Party members were chosen for the vacancies. On February 2, 1930, the bureau of the cell discussed three candidates for a research trip abroad.[73] The Party candidate received preference. As has already been noted, when so-called reactionary professors were purged, they were invariably replaced by younger, trusted Party members. The 1930 report on Party work at the Smolensk Medical Institute described the process very frankly.[74] It explained the increase in Party representation among the instructors from 8 to 32 per cent as arising mainly because Party members, on finishing the medical course, were kept as graduate students and clinical assistants.

The flight from the rabfaks to more desirable centers presented a continuous problem. On January 2, 1930, the bureau of the university Party cell noted that even the Party leaders in the rabfak, while conducting propaganda among rabfak students to remain at Smolensk University, were themselves pulling strings to get away to some other university.[75] On May 4, 1930, the bureau discussed what it called "disgusting occurrences" at the rabfak office in Moscow where "protection" was given to Smolensk graduates who were seeking places elsewhere.[76] The situation was at its worst in the rabfak which was supposed to feed students into the Pedagogical Institute.[77] With a clear appreciation of the drawbacks of a village teaching career, almost all its graduates did everything in their power to transfer to technical institutes in Moscow and Leningrad.

Placement after graduation from the institutes was also an occasion for maneuvering. Many students mustered such influence as they could to avoid assignments to the villages and the remote countryside. Graduates of the Medical Institute vied for the privilege of being retained at the institute for scientific work or sought an opportunity for further specialist training in the large cities. There was an obvious lack of coördination between the Medical Institute training and the needs of the oblast health department. The latter sought general practitioners who could be assigned to the localities. The pressure at the institute was in the direction of training specialists; the 1931 graduating class, for example, contained many more surgeons than the oblast health department could use.[78] Such imbalances were reinforced by the comprehensible desire of many students to acquire the kind of specialized competence which could most effectively advance their long-term careers. At the Pedagogical Institute there was the same drive to escape exile to the villages, where the conditions of work were frequently grim and the society not precisely stimulating. Indeed, as late as 1934, the plight of the village teachers remained so unenviable that Rumyantsev found it necessary to address the following letter to all raikom secretaries and chairmen of raiispolkoms:

> Complaints are still coming into the obkom and the oblast executive committee from teachers that they are being supplied extremely poorly. Such complaints come to the Central Committee and the government also. In a number of raions . . . the chairmen of Party control commissions under the Central Committee discovered glaring disorders in regard to teachers. The leaders of these raions received serious punishment and a number of heads of raion finance departments and chairmen of village soviets were brought to court. Although as a result of measures taken by the obkom, the situation in regard to paying wages to teachers has improved somewhat, in regard to supplying them, things have not changed. As a result of lack of attention and concern for teachers on the part of raikoms and raion executive committees, they continue to rob the teachers: even the meager rations of articles subject to centralized supply (flour, meal, sugar, tea) do not entirely reach the teachers. In regard to the issuance of products to the teachers which can be acquired on the spot

(milk, potatoes, vegetables, meat, confectioneries, etc.) the majority of raions do nothing. The obkom considers that this directly ignores the directives of the Central Committee on the school and the teacher.[79]

The letter then appealed for pressure on the kolkhozes to supply the teachers, particularly those "who have recently been sent to work in the villages" and who were in an "especially difficult position." It is against this background that the problems which the institutes encountered in trying to place their graduates in the villages begin to take on meaning.

As the Party protocols make clear, the years 1929–1931 represented a crucial turning point in the history of Smolensk State University and the institutes which were its offshoots. This was the period when the Party was tightening its control over the educational machinery, moving its own cadres into leading positions in the administration of higher educational institutions, purging the faculties to eliminate the obviously hostile and to make way for a new Soviet-trained generation, recruiting a student body out of the proletarian and peasant component of Soviet society, and reshaping the curriculum to serve the needs of an economy in process of rapid industrialization. These were formidable tasks which generated their own inner contradictions. The assertion of Party criteria in regulating admissions and appointments exacted a price in terms of loss of valuable intellectual capital and a marked deterioration in intellectual standards. But at least in the scientific and technical fields these losses were to prove transitory. Over the long run, the effect of the mass influx into the universities and institutes was to release surging energies from below and to ignite a new dynamism which transformed the technological, if not the political face of the Soviet Union.

19 Censorship — A Documented Record

One of the many valuable services performed by the Smolensk Archive is the insight it yields concerning the internal operations of the Soviet censorship. Although the existence of censorship in the Soviet Union has long been a matter of common knowledge, its precise organization and management have been hidden from public view. The materials in the Archive help fill this gap. They include one issue, number 8, for the year 1934 of a secret "Bulletin" sponsored jointly by the RSFSR Glavlit (the Chief Administration for Literary Affairs) and OVTs (the organs of military censorship).[1] This publication served as the house organ of the Soviet censorship apparatus and contains many frank and informative articles on the problems Soviet censors faced. There is also a rich 1934 file of secret instructions from the Zapoblit (the Chief Censor of the Western Oblast), designed to guide the work of raion or district censors.[2] In addition, there are scattered copies of central censorship directives and instructions to the press as well as a miscellaneous array of material on proscribed books and authors, on the removal of so-called counterrevolutionary publications from libraries, and allied topics. These documents provide authentic insights into the procedures and practices of the Soviet censorship staff.

The List of Censored Data

The basic charter of Soviet censorship during the mid-thirties was the so-called *perechen*. This was a detailed list of data and information which censors were charged with preventing from appearing in print or in any other publicly accessible communication medium. The list included a wide range of military, economic, and political secrets.

In the military sphere, data were withheld on the location of military forces, defense installations, armament factories, airfields, bridges, novel Soviet weapons, new operational-tactical views, and instructions on warfare. The perechen listed specific military units which could be mentioned in the press and forbade the identification of all other units. "When it is indispensable to refer to a military unit on the forbidden list," declared Circular No. 19 of May 23, 1934, "it shall be done only in the form of 'the N-unit.'"[3] In order "to prevent foreigners from drawing an analogy between Osoaviakhim [the para-military Society for the Promotion of Defense and Aero-Chemical Development] and the Red Army," read another circular, "all references to Osoaviakhim as a fully armed and rigidly trained organization are forbidden."[4] Stress was to be placed on its "voluntary character," expressing the "voluntary" surge of people to "deepen their military and military-political knowledge." No mention was to be made of military exercises under the aegis of Osoaviakhim; all references to links with the Red Army were to be deleted; and all speeches of Osoaviakhim officials were to be carefully censored before delivery and printing.

An article in the Bulletin by K. Batmanov, the USSR Council of People's Commissars' deputy plenipotentiary for the Guarding of Military Secrets, expanded on the significance of the military perechen.[5] In tsarist Russia, wrote Batmanov, military censorship was practiced only in front areas, or in matters pertaining to over-all military operational plans. In the USSR the situation was "vastly different." Military, economic, and political secrets had to be guarded "everywhere." This was made necessary by the capitalist encirclement and by the changed technical character of warfare in which the differentiation between front and rear disappears. In a future war, Batmanov declared, the capitalists would undoubtedly seek to launch a sudden attack without notice in areas where Soviet defense capacities were known. The task therefore was to deny such knowledge to the enemy. The central press, according to Batmanov, was under "adequately strong control." The same could not be said of oblast, krai, and especially raion press organs which often "babble out secrets of military value to the enemy." Particular care needed to be exercised to prevent even stray, unconnected bits of military information from appearing in the raion press and in papers of military units that circulated in large editions. He then cited various cases of transgression of the censorship, instances where "Byelorussian, Ukrainian, and other" papers spoke openly of the condition of strategic highways and railroads, published news of May Day parades which permitted the identification of military units, and even reproduced orders by army commanders which listed the forces under their command. The latter he described as no longer a mistake; "it borders on crime." The article concluded with a call for heightened awareness and vigilance on the part of all members of the censorship apparatus.

The perechen in the economic field was equally drastic. For the year 1934 no quantitative data on crop-yields in any locality were to be published unless such data first appeared in *Pravda* or *Izvestia*.[6] All numerical data pertaining to grain deliveries and purchases for the USSR as a whole as well as localities were ordered withheld. The prohibition extended to percentage as well as absolute figures, except that raions were permitted to report percentage increases in grain deliveries computed on a 1933 base.[7] Otherwise, Glavlit pronounced, deliveries could only be characterized as "good" or "bad." Specific news on railroad construction in certain areas and on the hiring of labor for these projects was also interdicted.[8] Caution was enjoined in publicizing cattle diseases: the geographical location of epidemics and the number of cattle involved were to be deleted.[9] News on sales of Soviet bonds abroad, on loans to Outer Mongolia and other Eastern countries, on export losses, and on waves of withdrawals from savings banks was also forbidden.[10]

In the political sphere, the censors were instructed to direct their fire against ideological deviations and "misrepresentations of Soviet reality." The main thrust of the campaign against ideological deviations at this time was aimed at alleged relics of the "left-wing" and "right-wing" oppositions, but even such relatively "harmless" works as A. Kiriako and G. Druzhinin's "What Does a Harvest Depend On?" or a book of poems by V. Shiskov were ordered suppressed because of their alleged "counter-revolutionary character."[11] Detailed data on court cases, crimes, and convictions were to be withheld, and descriptions of the activities of the OGPU deleted.[12] Special care was to be exercised to stop the publication of "distorted" pictures of Stalin and Lenin.[13] Censors were to guard against exaggerating the incidence of kulak terror, arson, the murder of Soviet officials, election disorders, or other phenomena calculated to emphasize "internal instability" in the USSR or the activities of anti-Soviet elements.[14] In the warning words of the Glavlit Bulletin, ". . . the *local* Soviet press sheds light on the class struggle in such a manner as to become unwittingly a supplier of illustrations for foreign agents to be placed in the bourgeois press. From these reports one may construct a picture of the extraordinary vitality of anti-Soviet elements, of their 'force' and 'heroism' as against the helplessness of Soviet organs."[15]

These examples do not exhaust the list of forbidden topics. The Smolensk Archive unfortunately does not contain a complete perechen; the items cited above are quoted in the correspondence of the Chief Censor of the Western Oblast or referred to in articles in the Glavlit Bulletin. From these sources it is clear that the perechen went through a process of constant revision; new items were added and old ones deleted as changing circumstances dictated. Every censor was expected to acquire intimate familiarity with the perechen; its guide lines gave coherence and unity to the exercise of the censorial craft.

Directives to the Press

It should, however, be stressed that the task of controlling Soviet mass communications was far broader than censorship alone. Positive guidance on news treatment was provided in the first instance through the Press Section of the Central Committee Secretariat and corresponding units in the lower Party apparatus; in addition, central and local newspapers took their tone and political lead from *Pravda,* the journal of the Party Central Committee, and a large part of their news items from TASS, the central news service, both of which operated under the general supervision of the Central Committee Secretariat.

The Smolensk Archive contains numerous directives to the press which were transmitted through Party channels. Usually, these were fairly general in character, calling upon the raion press, for example, to unmask enemy elements in the kolkhozes, to lead a campaign to raise agricultural output, and to criticize inadequacies in the work of local Party, Soviet, and economic organizations.[16] Sometimes, however, they were quite specific in their instructions. Thus on July 28, 1935, Rumyantsev dispatched the following note to all raikom and gorkom secretaries in the Western Oblast: "In connection with the check-up on Party cards, newspaper editorial offices are receiving denunciatory materials against members and candidates of the Party who are suspected of anti-state and anti-Party deeds as well as of fraudulent receipt of Party cards. The obkom orders: Newspapers shall print materials only on persons who have already been checked upon and whose Party cards have been withdrawn. All compromising materials which have been transmitted to newspapers either orally or in writing shall forthwith be forwarded to the raikom secretaries to whose organization the suspect belongs. The raikom secretaries shall take such action as is required. The raikom secretaries must acquaint all newspaper editors of their raion with the content of this letter." [17]

On November 27 of the same year, the obkom sent the following telegraphic directive to all raikom secretaries in connection with the anniversary of Kirov's assassination: "On December 1st you shall place in all raion newspapers articles devoted to the life and work of Kirov. In these articles . . . you will present Kirov's role as that of one of the greatest leaders of the Party, the Party's tribune, beloved by all toilers, fiery fighter for the Party of Lenin-Stalin against the ignoble Zinovievite-Trotskyite opposition of right-wing opportunists. It is also necessary to show the despicable role of the Zinoviev-Kamenev group, which was crushed by the Party and which ended as an agent of White Guardists and fascists . . ." [18]

Compared with the flow of positive instructions emanating from Party headquarters, the responsibility of the censorship organs was more limited; theirs was the negative function of preventing undesirable items from appearing in the communication media. In 1934 the censorial responsibility was divided between Glavlit on the civil side and OVTs on more purely military matters. Coördination of the activities of these two agencies was insured by concentrating direction of their work in the same individual. Thus B. Volin, who held the position of Chief of Glavlit, also served as the Council of People's Commissars' plenipotentiary for the Guarding of Military Secrets in the Press.[19] The Bulletin of Glavlit was also the central publication of the organs of military censorship. At lower administrative levels Glavlit censors were required to coördinate their work with OVTs representatives.

The Practice of Censorship

Censorship as it was practiced in the mid-thirties was of two types: the direct inspection and control of printed or other material over which the censor had jurisdiction, and preventive, or as it was called, prophylactic censorship.[20] The latter involved taking positive steps in advance of the production of printed or oral material to make sure that it would conform to the demands of the censorship. Thus censors were required to keep newspaper editors, supervisors of printing establishments, and directors of other media informed of changes in the perechen. Copies of the perechen were provided to Secret Sections in factories, enterprises, and administrations, and these sections were called upon to approve all references (in papers, speeches, meetings) to facts and figures of military significance or other matters involving potential violations of the perechen.[21] Thus preliminary censorship began in the Secret Sections. In the words of V. Babkin, Chief of the Gorkovsky Krailit, "This has made the censor's work easier . . . transgressions of the perechen are becoming a rarity because now *all factory* officials, before submitting any kind of material to newspapers, meetings, conferences, etc., have to clear them with their Secret Sections." [22]

The day-to-day inspection work of the censorship organs was regulated by precise rules. These rules specified that every publication — Party, governmental, trade union, and coöperative — had to be checked by a representative of the censorship before it could appear in print.[23] Checks were to be made both before final printing and after printing. Censors were required to compare the final texts with earlier changes, and they had to make certain that no record of changes would remain in the printing establishment. All material embodying the censor's changes was to be sent to higher echelons in the censorship apparatus with notations on the censor's motive for making the changes. "Control samples" of censored publications were to be dispatched systematically to the higher organs of military censorship, Oblit, the State Central Book Chamber, the Special Collection of OGIZ (the State Publishing House), and to the local OGPU (NKVD). No public lectures were to take place without a censor's check on the "thesis" and "conspectus," with the exception of lectures organized by the local kultprops (Cultural Propaganda sections) of Party committees or by the local ispolkoms, the executive committees of soviets. In the case of radio broadcasts, all material subject to censorship had to be presented for check not later than one hour before the scheduled broadcast.[24] All broadcasts were required to follow the exact text as approved or changed by the censor. All censored broadcast materials were to be filed and burned at three-month intervals. Transgressions of the censorship rules were to be reported at once to higher censorship authorities who were instructed to undertake administrative or court proceedings against the transgressors.

These rules and procedures, it should be stressed, represented goals and objectives rather than actual achievements. In practice, as the files of the Smolensk Archive make abundantly clear, the operations of censorship were seriously handicapped by a lack of trained, politically reliable cadres and the indifference of lower Party organizations to the need for this type of activity. A top-secret letter of March 20, 1934, from Shilman, one of the secretaries of the Western Oblast Committee, may serve as an example. The letter read in part:

In the Decrees of May 10, 1933, and October 1, 1933, the Western Oblast Committee of the CPSU(b) placed before the raikoms of the Party the task of strengthening in every way the political-ideological and military censorship of the press. The majority of the raikoms took a formal attitude toward the fulfillment of this directive; as a consequence in many raions the censorship situation remains unfavorable. . . . In Nevelsk and Sychevsk raions the names of military units doing secret work were allowed to be divulged. Pustoshka and Nevel allowed the mention of the construction of paved roads of a strategic character. A number of raions . . . up to now have not yet chosen censorship workers . . .[25]

The obkom called for a tightening of the censorship, and instructed the raikoms as follows: "Where the work of the raion censors is executed by people holding more than one job, consider this work their fundamental Party assignment, freeing them from all other Party assignments. Do not mix the duties of censor with the work of the editor of the raion newspaper or the head of the raion department of public education. It is more desirable to transfer the duties of censor to the raion military commissars or the directors of tekhnikums . . . The obkom warns that deputy secretaries of the raikoms will bear personal responsibility before the Party and the law for a violation of state secrets in the press . . ."[26]

Even in the Moscow region, ordinarily a model, serious deficiencies were observed. There the various raions of the oblast were divided into three categories according to their censorship significance.[27] In the first category were raions with defense installations, military units, and a developed net of printing and publishing establishments. In these raions censorship personnel was supposed to be free from all other work and thoroughly checked for political reliability. Even so, only twenty of the twenty-three raions in this category had full-time censors in 1934.

In the second category were thirty-six raions, which had relatively few printing and publishing establishments but did contain military units and defense installations. There the censors worked only on a part-time basis, and the Chief of the Moscow Oblit complained that they were of poor quality. Most of them were chiefs of the Party cabinets of district committees, employees of the raiispolkoms, and officers in district military departments. No educational personnel was employed because, reported the head of the Moscow Oblit, "experience has shown that they are the worst elements at such work. They lack discipline; they simply place the censor's seal on a document and let it go."

The third category consisted of predominantly agricultural raions, which typically had one raion paper and a small printing establishment and were without military significance. There censorial duties were vested in Party secretaries, chairmen of Soviet executive committees, newspaper editors, and directors of the raion education departments. While military secrecy was less important in these raions because of the absence of troops and defense establishments, the Moscow chief censor noted that the publications of these raions characteristically revealed the highest incidence of "political-ideological deviations," because of the inexperience and lack of political awareness of the amateur censors upon whom he had to rely.

In order to overcome these deficiencies, periodic campaigns were staged to raise the qualifications of district censors. All censors were supposed to be trained in Marxism-Leninism and Party pronouncements on the press, to have a thorough knowledge of the perechen and all directives and instructions concerning censorship, and to be acquainted with the production processes of printing establishments.[28] The "required reading" for censors included Lenin's and Stalin's writings on the press, Party decisions on the press, Stalin's *Problems of Leninism* and his article "On Some Problems in the History of Bolshevism," the reports and decisions of the Seventeenth Party Congress, the perechen, the Systematized Instructions to organs of Glavlit, *Pamiatka Railita* (the Handbook of the District Censor), and a volume by Fogolievich on "The Existing Laws of the Press." Familiarity with these publications was a *sine qua non* for censors; all were required to stand examination to test their knowledge of these documents.

The Bulletin of Glavlit, which served as the literary outlet of the censorship apparatus, provides a remarkable mirror of the censorship at work. District censors proudly boast of their success in eliminating "transgressions" of the perechen. Thus Comrade Alekseyev, the Orekhovo-Zuyevo chief censor, lists a number of triumphs in an article called "How I Overcame Difficulties."[29] First he prevented the publication of a letter to a factory newspaper which read: "We are in absolutely no need of the labor union. We pay money, but no help is forthcoming. I have been paying dues for eight years, but the benefits are not even a penny's worth. The labor union organization does not do anything — it only collects money." He stopped the same paper from printing the following about Osoaviakhim: "In the beginning of [its] activities, one of the main shortcomings was bad attendance. Of 80 members 20–25 members used to attend, but after certain concrete measures were taken, including arrests, the situation improved very quickly . . ." He cut out a sentence which read, "in *the future war, and that war is indispensable,* the use of [modern weapons] will wipe out the difference between front and rear." He also eliminated the following headline to commemorate the achievement of an udarnitsa (woman shock-brigade worker): "If you are an udarnitsa in the factory, you will also be an udarnitsa in the other world."

A long article on the work of the censorship in the Gorky region also lists some of the excisions for which it was responsible.[30] One was a letter to the editor of the *Lyskovsky Udarnik* (Lyskova Shock-Brigade Worker) reporting that "kulaks" who had been expelled from a kolkhoz were "terrorizing" and beating up members of the kolkhoz without any measures being taken to check them. Among other deletions were a report of murders of Komsomol and Red Army activists and threats against the lives of village correspondents; a story of the disruption of a newly formed kolkhoz by kulaks and priests; a tale of low morale among army recruits; and a striking headline which read "Alarm — the Village Spasskoye Goes Back to Last Year's Kulak Sabotage." Such news treatment, argued the censor, could only serve as a "boon" for foreign agents and the bourgeois press. "The whole thing is like a photograph; nothing has to be added."

In other articles there are sorrowful recitals of "transgressions" which escaped the attention of censors. A critical report on "The Activities of the Biezhetsky Gorlit" was not without its amusing sidelights.[31] Among the items the censor failed to catch were the following: (1) "The radio station broadcast questions and answers on the XVII Party Congress amid dances, foxtrots, etc." (2) "Listening to foreign stations is prohibited. We will relay Moscow." (3) "The number of illnesses in our enterprise has been substantially higher than the Control number. We have been granted 1,000 paid days for 100 workers for the whole year. We surpassed that number. Our stomach and intestinal diseases were higher by 52%, malaria by 217%."

Problems of the Censorship Apparatus

The occupational hazards of the censorship apparatus also find their reflection in the Bulletin. On the one hand, the censors were enjoined by their superiors to adhere strictly to the perechen; on the other hand, they were also condemned for "superfluous secrecy." Some censors, noted the Bulletin, "sign everything that is shoved in front of them — if only it is not straight counterrevolution." [32] But the more usual reaction was to "play it safe" and eliminate *all* news items which raised the slightest question.[33] Thus one censor refused to allow the publication of a criticism of local rail depot operations on the "pretext" that it was impermissible to provide the "Fascists" with materials for anti-Soviet campaigns. The same censor withheld an item stating that some older members of a kolkhoz had two cows. The reason given was that the possession of two cows might signify a kulak movement!

Another district censor who was overzealous in cutting materials from the press found himself the subject of a *feuilleton* in the Smolensk newspaper, *Rabochii Put* (Workers' Path).[34] Investigation revealed that the censor was completely "illiterate" in political matters, and he was removed from his job. The incident was used by the oblast censor to warn raion censors not to engage in "self-insurance deviations" (by excessive cutting of material), and they were instructed not to make actual changes in the text without consulting the newspaper editors. At the same time *Rabochii Put* was admonished for its public attack on a censor, and all censors were reminded that the perechen prohibited publication of any news pertaining to the methods and rules of censorship organs.

The unenviable dilemma of the censor faced with the need to distinguish between necessary and superfluous secrecy echoes through the pages of the Bulletin. The overriding compulsion, however, was to follow the perechen rigidly. While "distortionists" who erred on the side of excision were roundly condemned, the more serious crime was to permit secret information to leak through the press. For this "deviation" there was no forgiveness.

The trials and tribulations of the censorship apparatus included serious jurisdictional problems and inter-bureaucratic rivalries. The Glavlit Bulletin makes clear that the exercise of the censorial craft met resistance. The newspaper editor was frequently a political power in his own right and did not always take kindly to censorship. Censors complained that newspaper editors and printing establishments looked upon censorship as an "unnecessary formality." The chief of the Kuntsevsky Raigorlit reported that editors "were dissatisfied with his withholdings" and appealed to the raikom, or district committee of the Party. The censor in this instance was upheld by the raikom. When friction continued, one of the editors was fired. After that "the attitude of all editors . . . sharply changed for the better." [35]

Another censor, referred to as Y. in the Muromsky raion, also reported "great resistance" of editors to his activities.[36] The raion newspaper editor refused to admit Y. to the office when he arrived to assume his censorial duties for the first time. After a conference of editors at the raikom, there was some improvement. When Y. insisted on eliminating offensive passages from the newspaper, however, the editor again refused to obey. Y. had to resort to the help of "special organs": the latter were "very coöperative."

On occasion difficulties developed because the raion Party authorities sought to use their control of local censorship assignments to suppress criticism of the Party organization.[37] In Ivankovsky raion in the Moscow region, for example, the deputy secretary of the raikom also served as the local censor. When the newspaper editor wanted to publish the letter of a village correspondent accusing a local Communist of coöperation with kulaks, the censor refused permission, ordered that the letter be sent to the raikom, and be printed only by decision of the raikom bureau. The raikom secretary upheld the action of the censor, who was also his deputy. The matter was protested to the Moscow chief censor, who appealed to the Moscow regional Party committee. The Bulletin of Glavlit proudly noted that the latter's decision and actions "were such that it is doubtful that such a case will ever again arise in any other raion."

Still another raion censor in the Moscow region reported that the response of printing establishments to the tighter censorship controls which he had instituted had been "hasty." Employees proceeded "deliberately" to "distort" texts and engaged in "vicious misprinting" in order to discredit the censorship.[38] Instead of "socialism," they printed "capitalism"; they referred to the right deviation as the "glorious" (slavnyi) instead of "chief" (glavnyi) danger; they printed "chairman" Savinkov instead of "provocateur" Savinkov; and they described one individual as a "son of an uriadnik" (a tsarist village policeman) instead of a "son of an udarnik" (a shock-brigade worker). Although it is more than probable that these cases were owing to carelessness rather than to deliberate sabotage, the censor brought the matter to the attention of the raikom, and several printers were fired.

The sanctions available to the censor varied in severity. The various stages are described in a Bulletin article as follows: (1) "explanation"; (2) "warnings" — twice or thrice; (3) action by the raikom or gorkoms of the Party which involved summoning the culprit to the kultprop, the section of the Party secretariat that supervised publications; (4) "action through the OGPU."[39] "After these stages of action, especially the last one," reports one censor, "tampering with censorship regulations fell in frequency." In addition, the procurators were under instructions to prosecute all those responsible for breaking the rules of censorship. When such transgressions came to the attention of district censors, they were supposed "to formulate an act" and file it with the procurator, but never without the sanction of the oblast chief censor. How frequently such prosecutions occurred the Smolensk Archive does not reveal.

Library Purges

Perhaps the most dramatic censorship material in the Smolensk Archive concerns the book purges of the mid-thirties. Detailed lists of books to be confiscated were transmitted through the Glavlit hierarchy to the heads of district education departments who were ordered to confiscate the books and transfer them to the district censors. A typical order issued in June 1934 with the notation "Secret" read as follows: "All editions of all works written by authors listed shall be forthwith confiscated; the listed authors have been unmasked as counterrevolutionaries or members of nationalistic organizations." [40] There followed a list of forty-six authors, most of them with Ukrainian names. On March 7, 1935, the Lenin Library of Smolensk was ordered to confiscate all books by Trotsky, Kamenev, and Zinoviev and to segregate them under seal in a special compartment to which only the library's director had access.[41] Another order of June 21, 1935, broadened the list of "Trotskyite-Zinovievite counterrevolutionary literature." [42] Besides the works of Trotsky, Zinoviev, and Kamenev, the proscribed editions included books by such well- known Old Bolsheviks and former oppositionists as A. Shliapnikov, M. I. Yavorsky, G. Gorbachev, E. A. Preobrazhensky, V. Nevsky, B. Bulakh, B. Barden, N. Zalutsky, A. Lunacharsky, G. Safarov, A. Slepkov, V. Bolosievich, and many others. The confusion generated by these orders is reflected in the Archive correspondence.

In a memorandum dated February 19, 1935, and addressed to the Education Department of the Western Oblast, Ivanov, Director of the Smolensk Lenin Library, and Stalmakova, Senior Consultant in the Department of Bibliography, pointed out that they had been receiving urgent requests for guidance on book removals from many smaller libraries and even Party cabinets. They raised a whole series of questions.[43] What should be done with speeches by Zinoviev, Kamenev, Rykov, Bukharin, *et al.* at Party Congresses, plenums of the Central Committee, in the Comintern, the Congress of Soviets, etc.? What of anthologies on Marxism and other subjects written or edited jointly by Lenin, Zinoviev, V. Adoratsky, and others? What of Lenin's writings edited by Kamenev? What of bibliographies and memoirs about Lenin by Bukharin, Kamenev, and other banned authors? What should be done in cases where Trotsky, for example, had written an article in an issue of the *Communist International*? Should the whole number be confiscated? What of the writings of V. Bonch-Bruyevich, Sverchkov, John Reed and others, who in descriptions of the first days of the Revolution spoke "of present traitors and opportunists" as "leaders of the Revolution"? If these questions could not be immediately answered, the memorandum continued, it would be useful to receive instructions on the disposition of a long catalogue of items which were separately listed in an addendum. The addendum comprised hundreds of titles of political works, as well as books and articles by economists, technical and administrative specialists, veterinarians, agrotechnicians, and others who were involved in political difficulties. It also included various maps, slogans, postcards, music, editions of Stalin's works in Chinese and Mordvenese ("due to profound distortions in translation"), high school textbooks, books in which footnotes referred to Trotsky and other proscribed writers, and placards and propaganda leaflets with slogans and likenesses (or paintings) of opposition leaders.

The Archive contains no reply to this memorandum, but there is a report dated June 5, 1935, of a committee appointed to inspect the libraries of Smolensk. Despite repeated confiscation drives, the committee noted that it came upon scores of books by Zinoviev and Trotsky, *The Workers' Opposition Platform* of A. Shliapnikov and S. Medvedev, *The History of the Russian Social Democratic Labor Party* by the noted Menshevik, L. Martov, poems by Sergei Yessenin, and many other proscribed works.[44] These books, however, were found primarily in small factory libraries.

Evidence of the disorderly character of the purge is contained in a top-secret Glavlit order of June 21, 1935 signed by B. Volin, the RSFSR Glavlit chief and USSR plenipotentiary for the Guarding of Military Secrets. The order read:

During the removal of Trotskyite-Zinovievite literature from libraries there has simultaneously been going on a "purge" of libraries, not controlled nor directed by anyone, resulting in the pilfering and damage of the book reserves of the libraries.

I am ordering:

§ 1

The general purge and mass removal of books from libraries shall be curtailed at once.

§ 2

The removal of counterrevolutionary Trotskyite-Zinovievite literature from libraries and warehouses shall proceed strictly in accordance with the enclosed lists (see enclosure).

§ 3

The removal of listed literature is to be effected: (*a*) in krai and oblast centers — directly by the krai-oblast (or ASSR) Chief of Glavlit or his deputy in coöperation with a representative from NKVD, (*b*) in raion libraries — by emissaries of the krai or oblit (railit chiefs) in cooperation with raion emissaries of NKVD.

§ 4

Two copies of each confiscated work shall be left in the Special Departments of especially designated libraries of the Central Committee and Moscow committee of the Party, the Academy of Sciences, the Marx-Engels-Lenin Institute, the Lenin Library (Moscow), the Saltykov-Shchedrin Library (Leningrad), the Communist International Library, libraries of the Universities of Moscow and Leningrad, central libraries of main cities of union republics, krais, oblasts, and university cities as well as in the governmental library of the TsIK [the Central Executive Committee of the USSR].

§ 5

The removal of books designated in the lists shall be accompanied by the formulation of an act; the books are to be sealed and sent together with the act of removal to krai and oblast administrations of the NKVD.

§ 6

All books which had previously been removed in accord with Order No. 40 [later recalled] and which are not mentioned in the enclosed list shall forthwith be returned [with an act] to the appropriate libraries.

§ 7

Information on progress in effecting this order shall be transmitted to me on July 1st and August 1st.[45]

Despite this effort to regularize book removals from the libraries, chaos continued to prevail at local levels. The example of Kozelsk will serve to illustrate the problem. On March 16, 1936, Kogan, head of the Division of Party Propaganda, Agitation, and Press of the Western Obkom, dispatched the following secret letter to the secretary of the Kozelsk raikom:

Indications from a number of raions show that there is a bad state of affairs with regard to the removal of Trotskyite-Zinovievite counterrevolutionary literature from public libraries . . .
The obkom orders another check on the removal of this literature from all libraries of the raion without exception.
The removed literature should be transferred to the organs of the Administration of the NKVD. The list of literature subject to removal is in the possession of the latter.[46]

Prodded by this letter, the NKVD apparently took matters into its own hands and purged the library somewhat "too fundamentally." As a result the raikom secretary now found himself the object of a protest from the RSFSR People's Commissar of Education. A letter dated May 15, 1936, and signed by Rabinovich, the Deputy Chief of the Library Administration of the RSFSR, read as follows:

According to information received by the Library Administration, a large number of books have been removed from the Kozelsk Raion Library by the NKVD worker, Comrade Podyshkin, without notifying either the Chief of the

Library or the Raion Department of Public Education. How many and what books have been taken to the NKVD is not known.

In view of the fact that all removals can take place only with the sanction of the Chief of the Raion Department of Public Education (who is personally responsible for the condition of the library), we ask you to take measures to arrange beforehand the actions of all organizations in improving the library's reserve of books.[47]

As this example illustrates, the purge of the libraries operated erratically. At the grass roots where central directives had to be translated into specific action, the discretion of local officials was decisive, and their quality often left much to be desired. As a result book removals and the operations of censorship generally were conditioned by indolence and ignorance as well as excessive zeal.

Yet an analysis of the documents in the Smolensk Archive also makes clear that censorship was steadily and ominously tightening its grip during the 1930's. The processes of totalitarianization were reaching out even into the most remote rural raions. The enforced unanimity of the press and radio operated within an increasingly rigid censorial code. The libraries were becoming the repository of an official Stalinist orthodoxy. As the voices of dissent were expunged from the historical record, the way was prepared for the apotheosis of the all-powerful leader. The symbol of the censor became the intellectual hallmark of the Stalinist era.

But the documents of the Archive also reveal more. They show the censors in all their human frailty burdened with a dangerous discretion and enmeshed in a network of difficult relationships with newspaper editors, radio station directors, librarians, Party committees, NKVD representatives, and bureaucratic superiors. One sees the censorial apparatus struggling to conceal the seamy side of Soviet reality and paradoxically highlighting what it hoped to hide. And dimly perceptible, in the thrust of the censorship itself, one catches a glimpse of the forces of spontaneity which the censorship sought to contain, the aspirations toward self-expression in Soviet society which not even the most highly trained minion of Glavlit could wholly extirpate.

20 The Right of Petition — Letters to the Press and Party Headquarters

One of the least-studied aspects of Soviet political behavior is the role played by unpublished letters to the press and Party headquarters in keeping the leadership informed of the problems of its subjects and of the conduct of its local agents. The Smolensk Archive contains a vast assortment of such letters; taken together they provide a striking panorama of the friction points of Soviet existence. They also afford an insight into one of the important techniques developed by the regime to use the Soviet citizenry to spy on one another and to report on the abuses of local officialdom, to take the measure of popular grievances and to move, where necessary, toward their amelioration.

It should perhaps be stressed that virtually none of the letters sent to Party headquarters and only a small proportion of those addressed to the press were actually printed. Those singled out for publication had at the very least to meet the criteria of legitimate self-criticism; that is to say, they could expose abuse of power by officials and anti-Soviet activity of any sort, but could not challenge or reflect discredit on the policies of the regime itself. Not infrequently their publication was scheduled to fit into a campaign which the leadership had launched to focus attention on one or another pattern of disapproved conduct that the regime was eager to eliminate. The function served by letters in official publications was therefore primarily "educational" or "propagandistic." Through them the regime in effect signalled its people that it was aware of certain types of abuses, and that it was determined to stamp them out. At the same time it dissociated itself from responsibility for these abuses, and it provided approved scapegoats on whom the complaints and grievances of an outraged citizenry could vent themselves. The image of itself which the top leadership sought to project thus became one of a somewhat remote but benevolent guardian who intervened to protect his charges from arbitrary behavior on the part of local satraps who were exceeding their authority.

The great majority of letters in the Smolensk Archive belong in the unpublished category. Some of them, such as the file of peasant letters for 1930, from which extracts were quoted in Chapter 12 on collectivization, are openly critical of the regime's policies, though, except for an occasional anonymous note, letters of this type tended to fade out during the mid-thirties.[1] The reasons are fairly obvious. Such letters were usually turned over to the NKVD for investigation and disposition. The following note dated July 14, 1936, is both illustrative and self-explanatory: "To Comrade Lyakanov, Administration of the NKVD: On the instructions of Comrade Rumyantsev, an anonymous counterrevolutionary letter received by Comrade Rumyantsev is being sent to you. [Signed] Assistant Secretary of the Obkom of the CPSU(b) Kulakov."[2]

Many letters that abstained from direct criticism of the regime and even professed loyalty to it, nevertheless remained unpublished because they laid bare sore spots with a degree of frank detail which the leadership could only find embarrassing. Still others, particularly during the period of the Great Purge, were letters of denunciation where the identity of the tale-bearer had to be protected. And not a few, either directly or by implication, raised issues and problems that the regime preferred to see suppressed.

Regardless of their character, however, the letters seem to have been at least read, and, in a substantial number of cases, to have served as the jumping off point for an investigation. On this the evidence of the Archive is explicit. Many letters received by newspapers were referred to the obkom or the raikoms for comment; usually an obkom or raikom instructor was assigned to follow through on the letter, to investigate its allegations, and to draft a reply. Occasionally the raion authorities were remiss in answering, but the Archive also makes clear that the newspapers were persistent in demanding a response. The following note dated October 3, 1935, from the deputy head of the Department of Rural Correspondents and Letters of *Krestyanskaya Gazeta* (Peasant's Gazette) deals with a situation in which the raion authorities had ignored six letters, the earliest of which had been sent in January and the last toward the end of August. "Dear Comrade," read the letter to the Dorogobuzh raikom secretary:

During 1935 a number of disturbing warnings reached us on the bad situation in several kolkhozes of your raion. The letters tell of mismanagement, theft, wrecking, etc. Judging by the letters, this results mainly from the poor work of the leadership of the kolkhozes and their obstruction with hostile and criminal elements. We directed these letters to the raion organizations for investigation and the taking of proper measures. Up to this time we have not been informed about the results of these investigations, despite the fact that we sent a number of reminders . . . We hope that you will realize the great importance of this inquiry and will not delay in fulfilling our request.[3]

The prolonged dilatory tactics of the Dorogobuzh authorities were fairly unusual; in the majority of cases available in the Archive the raions responded much more quickly.

Letters to obkom Party headquarters also give evidence of fairly careful processing. Some addressed to Rumyantsev and Shilman, the first and second secretaries of the obkom, contain handwritten notations of the secretaries with instructions for their treatment. In most cases, the Archive indicates, the letters were screened by members of the secretariat and referred to an appropriate section for disposition. Where investigation seemed to be indicated, inquiries might be made at the raion level or an obkom instructor might be charged with the task. Ordinarily action was taken on the basis of the instructor's findings, but the secretaries reserved the final right of decision and sometimes overruled the recommendations of their staff.

Although the topics covered by the letters touch on almost every aspect of Soviet life, certain major categories stand out as particularly important. As might perhaps be expected in the Smolensk area, by far the largest number of letters related to kolkhoz abuses and complaints against allegedly oppressive actions on the part of village officials. Scandals in the trade network represented a second important category. The grievances of industrial workers received occasional expression in letter form, but in much diminished volume compared with the two previous categories. Since many of the letters were written as the Great Purge was approaching its climax, another important group consisted of denunciations and appeals from denunciations. Finally, there was a vast miscellany of requests for help which were addressed to the obkom in general and to Rumyantsev in particular. An examination of a sample of letters in each of these major categories may help to illuminate the role which they played in the Soviet system of governance.

Kolkhoz Abuses

Kolkhoz abuses, as has already been noted, provided the stimulus for a large outpouring of letters. Excerpts from some of them have already been given in Chapter 13 to illustrate some of the problems of kolkhoz management.[4] The discussion here will center on the use of letters as an instrument of control and discipline. The case of Yermakov may serve as an excellent first example. Early in 1935 the editors of *Kolkhoznaya Gazeta* (Kolkhoz Gazette) received from a kolkhoznik the following letter entitled "When Will Yermakov Be Brought to Trial?"

In *Kolkhoznaya Gazeta* of October 5, last year, a letter was published from a group of kolkhozniks of the "Krasnyi Lebed" kolkhoz, Pervomaisk village soviet, Dorogobuzh raion. In the letter it was reported that the chairman of the kolkhoz, Yermakov, treats the kolkhozniks roughly, suppresses self-criticism and together with the accountant, Bryzgin, continually gets drunk on kolkhoz money.

It would seem that the raion procurator, Comrade Uralova, to whom the letter of the kolkhozniks was sent, should immediately have checked on it and taken the proper measures, but actually it did not turn out that way. Eight months have gone by since that time, but the raion procurator, Comrade Uralova, up to this time has not taken any measures. This is testified to by the kolkhozniks who wrote: "After our letter was printed in *Kolkhoznaya Gazeta,* Chairman Yermakov expelled me, Drozdov, and others from membership in the kolkhoz."

Several times we turned to the raion executive committee. We also turned to the raion procurator, Uralova, but she pays no attention to our statements.

Yermakov and Bryzgin remain unpunished. Lately they have committed many new crimes . . . Receiving money from the State Bank for the purchase of fodder, Yermakov spent it on his own needs. The revisory commission discovered an embezzlement in the amount of 2,432 rubles. All the material of the revisory commission was sent to the raion procurator, but up to this time no measures have been taken. [Signed] Comrade Davydov.[5]

Having previously been ignored by the raion procurator, this time the head of the section of letters of *Kolkhoznaya Gazeta* addressed a firm note to the Dorogobuzh raikom. The letter, dated February 21, 1935, read as follows:

In sending you the correspondence coming from the rural correspondent entitled "When Will Yermakov Be Brought to Trial?" the editors ask you immediately to investigate the facts reported and to take the proper measures. The name of the author and the contents of the note, in accordance with the instructions on the press, may not be reported to anyone, except the organs of the court, on the basis of Article 121 of the Criminal Code. Inform the editor's office of the results of the investigation and the measures taken. It is necessary to return the note and to indicate our outgoing number and the date. Send the answer in duplicate. We expect an answer by March 7, 1935.[6]

There is no record of a reply by that date, but on June 21, 1935, the case was closed when the editor received the following letter from the Assistant Secretary of the Dorogobuzh raikom:

In regard to the letter which you sent from the kolkhoznik, entitled "When Will Yermakov be Brought to Trial?" the Dorogobuzh raikom reports that Yermakov, the chairman of the "Krasnyi Lebed" kolkhoz, for disorders committed in the kolkhoz was sentenced by the People's Court to five years' imprisonment and the sentence was upheld by the oblast court. In the same case the accountant of the kolkhoz, Bryzgin, was brought to trial (three years' imprisonment).[7]

Frequently, the kolkhozniks appealed to the obkom to redress their grievances. Another case in Dorogobuzh raion may serve to illustrate the process. In October 1936, Kulakov, the head of the Special Section of the Obkom, wrote to the raikom secretary as follows: "On the instructions of Comrade Rumyantsev, a statement is being sent to you from the kolkhozniks of 'Krasnyi Oktyabr' kolkhoz, Starkovsk village soviet, your raion, on the question of the drunkenness of the chairman of the kolkhoz, Volkov, and the brigade leader Zharikov, and on mismanage-

ment in the kolkhoz. Concern yourself with the request and inform the
obkom . . . not later than November 2, this year, on measures taken." [8]
Again the deadline was not met, but on November 23 the raikom secretary confirmed the fact "that the chairman of the kolkhoz, Volkov, did not
direct the kolkhoz, but only got drunk." After citing data which demonstrated the disorganization and low productivity of the kolkhoz, he went
on to describe a lively meeting of kolkhoz members which was held in
connection with the investigation.[9] "At the meeting," he wrote, "there
were unhealthy speeches. For example, the women screamed: 'We will
go naked. There is no flax, there are no yard goods. We give up everything, everything . . . we will perish from hunger.' As for the men,
Kirei Plyushchev, accusing the board, said that 'it is necessary to leave
everything and to go to Moscow.' Vasili Markitantov declared: 'We give
up everything to the workers, and now we ask the comrade workers,
where is our flax? Give us yard goods, give us everything that we need
. . . All say it's good, but Comrade Stalin should come himself, should
direct, should see what is happening. Flax should not be sown in our
land.' " The raikom secretary reported that the chairman had been removed, that the revisory commission was making a careful inspection
of kolkhoz accounts, and that the primary Party organization of the
neighboring village soviet and a raikom instructor had been designated
to organize political work in the kolkhoz. He also informed Rumyantsev
that the NKVD had been requested to investigate "the character of
Markitantov and the possibility of counterrevolutionary work by a former
Left SR" who was living in the kolkhoz.

The next letter presents a rather unusual case of a successful appeal
by a kolkhoz worker against harsh treatment by his chairman. On July
17, 1936, D. V. Gapeshin, a senior stableman in the "Perelom" kolkhoz
in Brasova raion wrote Rumyantsev to complain of the treatment he had
received from Demin, the chairman of the kolkhoz.[10] He reported that
he had been sentenced to six months' forced labor on the kolkhoz for
beating a horse, that he had paid his fine for three and a half months,
had run out of money, and was faced with the prospect of serving two
and a half months in a labor colony unless he found some way of paying
the 25 rubles which was still due. He appealed to Demin for an advance
of 25 rubles but was refused. He then turned to Demin with a second
request, to release him from the kolkhoz for five days so that he could
earn the 25 rubles elsewhere. Demin also rejected this request. With a
pregnant wife and three children to support, Gapeshin departed anyway
and earned his 25 rubles. During his absence a general meeting was
called to consider his expulsion from the kolkhoz, but the meeting postponed action and referred the matter to the kolkhoz board. On his return
he requested the chairman to allow him to use a kolkhoz horse to plow

his potato patch. Demin replied, "I don't like your personality, and there is no horse for you." Thereupon, as Gapeshin narrates it:

I lost patience, went out, and said that I would take the plow and plow with my wife [without a horse]. He answered, "That is up to you." I took the plow and plowed 8 bounds, 90 meters in length, but at that moment the director of the Brasovo Raifo, Comrade Bereznev, stopped me from plowing the potatoes. He saw me, saw that a pregnant woman with her husband was plowing the potatoes in the old-fashioned way, and he brought me into the kolkhoz and gave me a horse to plow up the rest of the potatoes. Comrade Ivan Petrovich Rumyantsev, how long will such bureaucrats, plunderers, and drunkards, such as, for example, our kolkhoz chairman, Comrade Demin, scoff and swear at an honest kolkhoz toiler? Give me an answer to my question.[11]

Gapeshin's question was referred to Tomsky, head of the agricultural department of the obkom. Tomsky was sympathetic and condemned the conduct of Demin as "outrageous." On behalf of the obkom the Brasovo raikom secretary was ordered to call a "general meeting of kolkhozniks of the 'Perelom' kolkhoz, bring those guilty to trial and inform the obkom by August 28 this year about the measures taken on this question."[12] The raikom secretary ignored the matter as such situations were usually ignored. But the obkom agricultural department was insistent and on October 23, nearly two months after the deadline had expired, it wrote to the raikom secretary as follows:

On August 23 the agricultural department informed you about the scornful attitude on the part of the chairman of the kolkhoz, Demin . . . toward the kolkhoznik, D. V. Gapeshin, and asked you to discuss this question at the raikom and in the kolkhoz. On September 9, 1936, a reminder was sent you on this question, but up to now there has been no answer. A third time I beg you to send all the materials, in accordance with our request of August 23, by October 25, 1936.[13]

Finally on November 9 came the raikom reply. "The Brasovo raikom," it read, "reports that the chairman of the 'Perelom' kolkhoz, Demin, for violation of the agricultural rules and mistreatment of the kolkhoznik D. V. Gapeshin has been removed from the leadership of the kolkhoz and is being brought to trial."[14]

A somewhat similar case of persecution of a rank-and-file collective farmer is recorded in the following letter of June 27, 1936, from Yekaterina Orlova to Comrade Shilman, for whom her kolkhoz was named:

I have worked for four years on a livestock-breeding farm, have done the work of a calf-herd during this lengthy period, and this work interested me. I have practical knowledge of this work of the birth and rearing of calves. But it happened that a person came to our farm who was in the Party, who in connection with the investigation of the Party was expelled as an undermining element. This was Vladimir Trifonov. He does not like livestock breeding at all, but only causes harm, steals milk, and arranges drunken brawls in the cattle barn. Many times the kolkhozniks caught him . . . Then there was one weak calf who got sick with an inflammation — this was in April. He gave the order to drive him into the field. I told him that the calf should not be driven into the field or he would die. He swore at me, did not listen. The calf was driven into the field and within one hour it died. They fined me 10 work days. I was very sorry and hurt that actually it came to such a thing. I wept the whole day. Then there were 3 very weak calves, who needed a stronger portion of milk. Although the veterinarian Bogoslovsky ordered the milk to be strengthened for these calves, the livestock breeder did not do it, but delayed. I insisted that the milk be strengthened. He squanders the milk. Whoever comes gets milk. For example, on May 2 people came from the raion . . . He went into the cattle yard and milked the cows in excess of the plan . . . We then had a loud altercation. I said that the Party was right not to keep such people in the Party who have become corrupt. He is very rarely in the cattle yard — either he's fishing or getting drunk. He attracted the chairman of the kolkhoz, Comrade Pyalov, with his liberal attitude, and some of the members of the board, like Kubynin, who was previously very staunch. He also attracted the brigade leader, the former candidate of the Party, who was expelled from the Party as a kulak. These people oppress the rest of the kolkhozniks and every day they arrange drunken brawls and kill the calves . . .[15]

She then described how she had been removed from work and concluded, "If the livestock breeder Trifonov continues to work, he will undermine the economy. I hope that they will investigate my letter quickly and will do something about it."

This letter was sent by the obkom to the chairman of the Shilman kolkhoz with instructions to look into Trifonov's behavior and to report the results to Comrade Shilman. At the same time a copy of the letter was sent to the secretary of the Pochinkovsk raikom requesting that the raikom send a competent person to investigate the situation on the spot and to report to the obkom. The case was closed when the raikom secretary informed the obkom that Trifonov had been dismissed from work. The raikom secretary wrote, however, that Orlova's allegation that the kolkhoz chairman had taken part in drunken brawls had not been confirmed.

The Role of the Rural Correspondents

The letters discussed above represent spontaneous complaints submitted on the initiative of the kolkhozniks themselves. While there are many such letters in the files, the Archive also makes clear that both the central and oblast agricultural press depended heavily on their regular rural correspondents to police developments in the areas which they covered. Each paper had its network of correspondents chosen from local activists, who were ordinarily but not always Komsomol or Party members. Their primary assignment was to ferret out and report any form of anti-state behavior. In theory, their anonymity was supposed to be protected; in practice, their activities were usually a matter of common knowledge in the localities in which they resided. Since the rural correspondents as a group were apt to be zealous busybodies who were constantly poking their noses into the dark corners of rural administration, they were usually a thorn in the flesh of the local officialdom. Sometimes great efforts were made to discredit or get rid of them, though ordinarily in such cases their sponsoring newspaper could be trusted to rise to their defense.

One such case involved the rural correspondent Andrei Ageyev, who worked for the oblast newspaper *Kolkhoznaya Gazeta*. On January 4, 1935, the deputy editor of *Kolkhoznaya Gazeta* addressed the following letter to the Dorogobuzh raion chief of the NKVD, with copies to the raikom secretary and to Comrade Ageyev:

> The rural correspondent of our newspaper, Comrade Ageyev, sent a warning letter in which he says that up till now the leaders of the kolkhoz are continuing to persecute him. Comrade Ageyev writes: "With tears in my eyes I beg you for your personal protection."
>
> It is apparently known to you that the chairman of the kolkhoz, Doronenkov, the Party organizer Panov, and the former livestock breeder (now leader of the truck-farming brigade) Belova — all these "Communists" have been sentenced by the people's court to forced labor for various periods. For what were they sentenced? Who exposed their criminal actions? Our rural correspondent Ageyev exposed them.
>
> To us it is completely clear that the persecution of Ageyev is being secretly organized. The people "suffering" from his rural correspondent's pen are taking revenge on him, uttering various slanders against him . . .
>
> The secretary of the raikom of the Party, Comrade Nikitin, has informed us that Comrade Ageyev has been reinstated in the kolkhoz. But actually the kolkhoz board only allows Ageyev to work and does not at all desire to put before the general meeting the question of reinstating Ageyev's rights as a member of the kolkhoz. This again confirms the fact that the rural correspondent, Comrade Ageyev, is being persecuted . . ."
>
> We beg you to consider our remarks and to take the proper measures to protect the rural correspondent, Comrade Ageyev, from the "secret" persecution which is being waged against him by the "Communists" Belova, Panov, and Doronenkov.[16]

Soon thereafter, on January 31, 1935, one of the alleged "persecutors," Comrade Belova, filed an accusation against Ageyev with the Party Control Commission of the Central Committee.[17] In her letter she charged that Ageyev was a "class enemy," a "wrecker," the son of a tsarist village policeman, who had "slipped into the aktiv of the kolkhoz and become a rural correspondent . . ." She went on to claim that she and the Party organizer Panov were the victims of persecution by Ageyev. "It is not enough," she wrote, "that the enemy of the revolution, Andrei Ageyev, attacks us, but together with him the accursed riff-raff of the Zinovievite opposition, the representative of the Dorogobuzh raion division of the NKVD (now expelled from the Party for Trotskyism), instead of unmasking the class enemy, Andrei Ageyev and his accomplices, began to threaten me and the partorg Panov with various kinds of repression." She then cited material to prove that the wrecking activities of Ageyev in livestock breeding had been scientifically established and called upon the Party Control Commission to investigate the case and "to give us the opportunity honestly and quietly to advance toward a prosperous kolkhoz life without class enemies and degenerates who are trying to put spokes in the wheels of kolkhoz construction."

Belova's letter was referred to the obkom of the Western Oblast, which apparently accepted it at face value. On March 17, 1935, the head of the agricultural department of the obkom sent a note to the secretary of the Dorogobuzh raikom demanding to know "who it was that directed the raikom . . . to reinstate Andrei Ageyev in the kolkhoz." [18] The raikom reply upheld Ageyev. After pointing out various derelictions of duty on the part of Belova, Panov, and company, the raikom reported that a thorough investigation of the situation in the kolkhoz had been made by the raion procurator, a raikom instructor, and a NKVD operative. "It was established," the letter continued, "that the rural correspondent Ageyev was not socially dangerous, that there was no harmful work on his part, and that he really reacted against all disorders, as a result of which scandals took place . . . It is true that the rural correspondent Ageyev is a quarrelsome person by nature. They insult him, and he answers back immediately. He reacts violently against all disorders in the kolkhoz and this is accompanied by swearing . . ." [19] The decision of the raikom to order the reinstatement of Ageyev in the kolkhoz apparently evoked no protest from the obkom; the Archive contains no reply to the raikom's statement.

On occasion the rural correspondents met complete frustration at the raion level. In such cases they might appeal to higher authority. The Archive contains one such letter entitled "A Rural Correspondent's Warning" which was sent to Rumyantsev in 1936 by one Dropkov, a non-Party rural correspondent from Krasnogorsk raion. [20] In substance the letter alleged: first, that Comrade Ivan Bokhmat, a member of the Party, who worked as chairman of the kolkhoz "Krasnyi Oktyabr," was continually drunk, carried on large-scale embezzlements, and had given arms to bandits; second, that the deputy editor of the raion newspaper, Comrade Trubetsky, also a Party member, had exposed the identity of rural correspondents and had also been sentenced for protecting kulaks and for beating kolkhozniks; third, that Comrade Barinov, the head of the raion agricultural department, and also a Party member, had taken products from the kolkhozes, had done nothing to stamp out kolkhoz disorders despite warnings from the rural correspondents, and that

Barinov had summoned him to his office, banged on the table, and shouted at him, "Oh, you are a vile rural correspondent, you write everything to the newspapers, but you don't want to work"; and fourth, that the Komsomolite, Comrade Gorbachev, working as deputy raion procurator, had driven out of his office a shock-worker kolkhoznik who came to him with a complaint.

In this case the letter was referred to an obkom instructor who conducted an investigation in the raion and wrote a report which supported most of Dropkov's allegations.[21] His examination of the file of the raion agricultural department, which was headed by Barinov, revealed some thirty-seven letters and complaints from kolkhozniks and rural correspondents which had not been examined; some had lain uninvestigated for two to three months. As a result of the investigation Barinov received a reprimand from the raikom bureau; Trubetsky was removed from his position as deputy editor of the raion newspaper; a letter was written to the oblast procurator suggesting that Gorbachev be replaced; and a large body of compromising material which had been assembled on Bokhmat was called to the attention of the local organs of the NKVD. Thus vindication came to the rural correspondent through obkom intervention.

There were also many letters of complaint from the kolkhozes and the villages which yielded no satisfaction to the senders. Some samples may serve to illustrate the types of situations in which the letter-writers wrote in vain. In June 1935, for example, Izvestia received a letter entitled "Tyranny or Mockery," which denounced the chairman of the Bolotonyansk village soviet, Comrade Belikov, who had allegedly summoned certain kolkhozniks to come to him at midnight, under threat that if they refused they would be fined 25 rubles apiece.[22] According to the letter, the brigade leader had to rouse the kolkhozniks from their beds, and when they came to the chairman, he shouted that they were "saboteurs, underminers, self-willed persons." He accused them of not subscribing to the loan and not fulfilling the meat deliveries, but was told that this was not true. He finally released them at 6:00 A.M. The letter added that twenty-six horses had died in Belikov's village in 1934–35 as a result of his indifference. The letter was sent by Izvestia to the Western obkom which referred it to the orgotdel (organization section) of the Western Oblast Executive Committee for investigation. The orgotdel sent an investigator to the spot who reported that the facts were not proven. Actually, he wrote, Belikov had summoned some kolkhozniks who had failed to deliver meat, but at 9:00 A.M. and not at 12:00 midnight. The investigator added that the horses had died during the administration of the previous chairman.

Another letter dated 1936 and directed to the Soviet Control Commission in Moscow complained of the use of physical force by the Zinovkinsk village soviet in carrying out grain deliveries. The letter was forwarded to Rumyantsev with instructions to investigate the facts, and "if they are confirmed, to bring those guilty of excesses and violation of revolutionary legality to responsibility." [23]

The obkom dispatched an instructor to the scene. He reported that the individual farmers of the village, despite a series of warnings, had refused to fulfill their grain delivery assignments and had hidden their grain in ditches. Thereupon the presidium of the village soviet called a meeting of individual farmers at which they were asked to explain their conduct. The Ganin brothers, Gregori and Mikhail, failed to appear, and at that very moment were burying grain. The presidium then adopted a resolution to confiscate the grain. When the grain was being taken away from the Ganin brothers, the report stated, Gregori Ganin struck the chairman of the village soviet and his deputy. For this action he was sentenced by the people's court to six years' deprivation of freedom. The investigator reported that he could find no evidence that force had been used in connection with the grain confiscations. He stated that he had questioned the signers of the letter, and that the burden of their complaint was the confiscation of the grain, and not the use of force. On September 17, 1936, Tomsky, the head of the agricultural department of the obkom, so reported to the Soviet Control Commission, adding, ". . . Sabotage in the fulfillment of state deliveries by certain individual farmers in the village of Zinovkino (and almost all of them are sectarians) is still continuing." [24]

The next case grew out of a letter written to the Central Committee by the former chairman of the "Krasnyi Dunai" kolkhoz, S. A. Saloshenko, complaining about his illegal arrest, his dismissal from work as chairman of the kolkhoz, and his expulsion as a candidate of the Party. Saloshenko was accused by the raion division of the NKVD "of counterrevolutionary agitation against members of the government, of having connections with anti-Soviet elements, of undermining activity in the kolkhoz, of using force against the kolkhozniks, of persecuting and badgering the kolkhoz aktiv, and of beating kolkhozniks." On the basis of these charges, he was expelled from the Party, removed as chairman of the kolkhoz, arrested and held in prison for four months. His letter was routed to the agricultural division of the Central Committee which assigned an instructor to investigate the case. The report of the instructor was on the whole favorable to Saloshenko.[25] It dismissed the charges of counterrevolutionary slander and connections with anti-Soviet elements, as well as various allegations of moral corruption which had been belatedly raised in the case. It described Saloshenko as "a good manager, possessing great practical experience in agriculture, concerned about the kolkhoz, [who] strove to strengthen working discipline in the kolkhoz." At the same time it also noted that Saloshenko was guilty "of crudeness in regard to the kolkhozniks, of giving illegal punishments," and that he had made "frequent use of socialized products and fodder." Although the report rebuked the NKVD raion chief for arresting Saloshenko and criticized the raikom for "failure to check carefully on the materials accusing Saloshenko," it nevertheless concluded that Saloshenko "deserved" to be expelled from his status as Party candidate because of his violations of kolkhoz regulations.

But the NKVD could not be fobbed off so easily. On August 20, 1936, Shilman informed the agricultural division of the Central Committee that additional facts had been received which made it necessary to renew the investigation, that the obkom believed that Saloshenko had been correctly expelled on the grounds of "moral corruption" and for "connections with hostile elements," that he had continually been "in the company of hostile people where all kinds of anti-Soviet conversations were carried on," and that he had himself "partially" admitted this.[26] No reply was forthcoming from the Central Committee.

As these cases illustrate, the intervention of higher authorities was usually forthcoming where kolkhoz officials were corrupt, inefficient, or engaged in other conduct which endangered the productivity of the kolkhozes. On the other hand, where the question was one of enforcing deliveries to the state, the tendency was to uphold the hand of the local officials. The NKVD provided another tender area; letters of protest against its actions were perhaps the most quixotic of all Soviet enterprises.

Scandals in the Trade Network

A second important group of letters in the Archive focused on scandals in the trade network. The large-scale incidence of embezzlement and defalcation in the trading organizations of the Western oblast has already been noted as the subject of a special circular by Rumyantsev in 1934.[27] Many letters in the Archive could be quoted to document Rumyantsev's admissions, but the details which they supply represent more or less monotonous variations on the same basic themes of thievery, bribery, and favoritism in the distribution of goods. Occasionally, however, a fresh note is heard, and a representative of Soviet trade strikes back. Thus, in reply to a leading article in *Pravda* criticizing the Western Oblast for the number of incompetent officials in the rural coöperative network, the head of the Soviet trade department of the Western obkom replied that while *Pravda* was correct with respect to some local Party committees which did not recruit trusted capable workers, it was also true that certain workers who had been mentioned unfavorably in the article had been incorrectly attacked.[28] He added, however, that the obkom and raikoms were now reviewing their cadres in the consumer coöperative system with a view to weeding out the incompetents and improving quality.

In a number of other cases, the obkom rose to the defense of local officials in the trade network who, it was believed, were the victims of false accusations. Thus in April 1935 one Ivanov, a citizen of Roslavl, wrote *Pravda* about various disorders which were alleged to have occurred in the Roslavl Raion Consumers' Union.[29] According to the letter, Slutsky, the head of the raw materials warehouse, and Reznikov, who was in charge of receiving deliveries of raw materials, took advantage of the ignorance of peasants who made deliveries by understating the quality of the goods delivered and pocketing the "savings" for their own use. The letter added that Reznikov came from a family of merchants, and that two bicycles had been purchased from the illegal profits. *Pravda* sent the letter to the Western obkom which directed the Roslavl raikom to investigate. The raikom reported that Slutsky and Reznikov had not committed any illegal acts, and that the accusation that they had lowered the qualities of delivered goods had no basis since in all cases where quality was in dispute an outside specialist made the final determination. Nor was it true that bicycles had been distributed to any workers of the raion union. The letter of Ivanov was rejected as a slanderous reflection on honest employees. In still another case in July 1935, *Pravda* forwarded a letter to the Western obkom which charged that the "Fifteenth Anniversary of October" sewing artel was headed by a criminal, S. I. Lisenko, who stole materials and surrounded himself with class-alien elements.[30] On the instructions of the obkom the charges were investigated by a special commission composed of a representative of the Western Oblast Union of Coöperatives of Invalids, an official of the oblast trade union council, and a representative of the raikom. The allegations concerning Lisenko were found to be untrue. There had been alien elements in the artel, but Lisenko removed them from work and brought them to trial.

The Archive also contains an interesting letter dated October 1935 to *Sovetskaya Torgovlya* (Soviet Trade) from a group of employees of the Western Union of Consumers' Coöperatives who had been sent to work in some recently organized raions of the Western Oblast.[31] They complained that the oblast coöperative organizations had given them no instructions as to what work to do and had not paid them any wages for two months. They also asserted that they were assigned very poor quarters and did not receive the money which had been promised them to send for their families. They described the frustration they had encountered in an effort to improve their situation and begged the newspaper to intercede on their behalf. *Sovetskaya Torgovlya* sent the letter to the Soviet trade department of the obkom, which referred it to the Western Union of Consumers' Coöperatives. The latter replied that the entire situation had been remedied and that wages had been paid up completely. Whether the employees were satisfied is not apparent from the record.

The Complaints of Factory Workers

The Archive also contains some letters from factory workers complaining of various "outrages" and "disorders" on the part of their superiors.[32] One of the more interesting was directed to the obkom by a group of workers in the Yartsevo textile factory. Its contents can be gathered from the following report submitted by the obkom instructor assigned to the case:

To . . . Comrade Shilman:
In fulfillment of your instructions on investigating the letter which came to the Western Oblast Committee from the Yartsevo Factory on outrages committed by the chairman of the factory trade union committee, Minkin, and the secretary of the Party Committee, Comrade Gerasimov, I report the following:
The first accusation, that Minkin and Gerasimov with their wives and friends of their wives on every rest day used the one-day rest home of the Stakhanovites and held drinking bouts there, was not confirmed. The rest home was opened in the middle of July. It is true that Minkin and Gerasimov with their wives took part at this opening, but in my opinion there is nothing reprehensible in this. According to the stories of the workers who were present, there was no drunkenness at this time. Then on August 1 Gerasimov was inducted into the army, where he remained until September 18. Therefore, during the entire period when the rest home functioned (it was closed on August 30), Gerasimov was absent from Yartsevo. And, in general, from conversation with individual workers who were at the rest home at that time, the very best references are given about the home, and not one mentioned any kind of drunkenness or any kind of preference for the leaders of the factory, especially Minkin.
The second accusation, however, regarding the organization of drunken brawls on the occasion of the Party for Bavshina, who was going to school, was completely confirmed. The plenum of the factory committee decided to send to higher courses of the trade union movement the Stakhanovite Bavshina and Comrade Naumenkova and to organize a going-away party for them for which 500 rubles were appropriated by the factory committee. On August 23 [1936] . . . the chairman of the factory committee, Minkin, his deputy Panasenkov, all the shop Party organizers and trade union organizers, gathered in the apartment of the Stakhanovite Bavshina, without inviting any of the Stakhanovites, and gave a send-off party for Bavshina and Naumenkova, but the latter did not take part in the party.
Thus the party, organized with public funds, instead of popularizing the best Stakhanovites, or stimulating a competition for this honorable title, was turned into a mere drunken brawl and evoked just indignation on the part of the workers. This party was organized without the permission of the Party committee and the raikom. When this question was discussed at the Party Commit-

tee upon my arrival, it was established as completely clear that this was not a party for mobilization of activity around the Stakhanovite movement, but actually a drunken brawl among a narrow circle of people in the leadership. The Party Committee with the participation of the second secretary of the raikom, Comrade Batagina, on September 27 censured this behavior of Minkin and of the shop Party organizers. They reproached Minkin and gave a warning to the shop Party organizers.

I feel that the factory committee, and especially Comrade Minkin, showed great shortsightedness and lack of comprehension of the problem of encouraging the best Stakhanovites. Besides, at the Yartsevo factory there is great stagnation among people who have worked dozens of years in various top jobs, moving around from one place to another and always in this factory and in the position of leading workers. I have in mind the Party organizers Rezimov, Maksimenkov, and others who have become too accustomed to one another and to individual administrative workers, which causes a well-known familyness, often manifested in parties within a narrow circle, visiting one another's homes, etc. This makes the workers nervous. It is necessary to take some of these people out of Yartsevo to refresh the situation.[33]

Denunciations and Appeals from Denunciations

During the purges of the mid-thirties denunciations and appeals from denunciations accounted for a substantial part of the letters to the press and to Party headquarters.

The case of Durasov offers a rare instance where a denounced person was able to win partial vindication. The newspaper *Za Kollektivizatsiyu* (For Collectivization) on August 28, 1936, published an article called "Raise Political Vigilance." "It is necessary to say directly that there are still not a few Communists who speak a lot about raising vigilance, while among themselves, in places quite near to them, they do not see the base work of the enemy," the article noted, and continued: "In the Raion Union there has worked for a long time [one] Durasov, a former kulak, whose father was shot for participation in the counterrevolutionary SR uprising in Gzhatsk. For this good-for-nothing Durasov good working conditions have been created. Taking advantage of the loss of political vigilance, this enemy carries on counterrevolutionary work. It is asked: 'Where do the Communists and the Party organization look? Why have they not yet unmasked this good-for-nothing and brought him to trial?' Certainly in the files of the Party organization there are not a few resolutions on raising vigilance!"[34]

On September 1, 1936, D. N. Durasov, who headed the raw materials warehouse of the raion union, addressed the following letter to the obkom:

In the newspaper *Za Kollektivizatsiyu* of August 28 in the leading article it was pointed out that a kulak whose father was shot works in the raion union, that Durasov carries on counterrevolutionary work and up to this time has not been brought to trial.

В газете за "Коллективизацию" от 28 августа № 115 в передовице указано что в Райсоюзе работает кулак у которого отца расстреляли что Дурасов проводит контр-революционную работу и до его времени не отдан под суд.

Я Дурасов по вопросу этой заметки пошел к секретарю Знатского Райкома тов. Большунову и стал его просить разобраться в заметкой, так-как автор заметки совершенно не знает моей биографии.

тов. Большунов выслушать меня отказался сказав: что написано Это правильно, что ты движишься не советским духом и ты нужно работать за советскую власть, подавай дело прокурору. такой ответ меня не мог удовлетворить, так как тов. Большунов меня совершенно не знал:

Поэтому я решил просить ОБКом ВКП.б разобрать мое дело ускорить предъявление мне обвинения и если я Это заслуживаю отдать меня под суд, чем смыть с меня ту грязь в которой меня обвинили на весь район и подорвали мой служебный авторитет!

A case of mistaken identity — D. N. Durasov appeals to the obkom, September 1, 1936. The notation at the top refers the matter to the NKVD for investigation.

I, Durasov, went to the secretary of the Gzhatsk raikom, Comrade Bolshunov, about this note, and asked him to investigate the note, since the author
of the note does not know my life story at all.

Comrade Bolshunov refused to listen to me, saying: "It is correct; you do
not breathe the Soviet spirit . . . submit the case to the procurator." Such
an answer could not satisfy me, since Comrade Bolshunov did not know me
at all. Then I decided to ask the obkom to investigate my case, to consider the
accusations leveled against me, and, if I deserve it, to bring me to trial, or else
to wipe away from me that mud with which they accuse me in the whole raion
and undermine the authority of my position.

Durasov then recited his life history, pointing out that he was born
in the family of a middle peasant and that his father had died in a
hospital in 1924. He continued:

From 1928 to the present I have been engaged in coöperative work. During
the whole period of my work I did not embezzle once. Neither I nor my family
and parents were ever deprived of voting rights. Nikolai and Matvei Durasov
were shot in the Gzhatsk uprising, former profiteers with whom I had nothing
in common and who only had the same name as I did, since there were five
households of Durasovs in our village.

At the present time my brother serves in the ranks of the Red Army as a
lieutenant. When he was admitted into the school for the commanding staff
in 1931, and also when he was graduated from school in 1934, our family was
investigated from all sides, and they found nothing alien in our family. Therefore, I again beg you to hasten the investigation of this case, since I have been
insulted by this to the depths of my soul.[35]

On September 26, 1936, the head of the obkom trade department forwarded Durasov's statement and the newspaper article to the chief of
the raion division of the NKVD and requested a check on Durasov and a
report "on the results by October 5." [36] On October 25 the NKVD reported as follows:

. . . citizen D. N. Durasov comes from peasants of the village of Grozdevo,
Pliskovsk village soviet, Gzhatsk raion. Before the Revolution and after, the
household of his parents was prosperous; his mother worked, they kept a
female worker, and they also periodically hired seasonal labor for field
work . . . During the period of collectivization, D. N. Durasov liquidated his
household and went to live in the city of Gzhatsk and began to work in the
raion union, where he works at present.

During the period of the Gzhatsk kulak counterrevolutionary uprising, the
uncle of Durasov, Mikhail Sobolev, a former kulak, and his uncles Nikolai and
Matvei Durasov, profiteers, actively took part in the counterrevolutionary uprising, drove the people out with weapons, and in 1918 went to the city of
Gzhatsk in order to overthrow the Soviet government, for which they were
shot by a detachment of Reds. As to the father of the accused, N. N. Durasov
. . . what was put in the note in the newspaper . . . is not true. Nikolai
Ilich Durasov was shot in the counterrevolutionary uprising, but not Nikolai
Nikolayevich Durasov, the father of the investigated. Apparently the author
of the notes confused the names. And D. N. Durasov himself did not partici-

pate in the counterrevolutionary uprising, since at that time he was living in the city of Moscow. The Raion Division has no other information.

On November 19, 1936, the case was closed with a note to Durasov summarizing the findings of the NKVD and concluding, "We have informed the editors of the newspaper *Za Kollectivizatsiyu* of the mistake they made." [37] The Archive contains no record of a retraction by the editors.

The next document is a rambling and diffuse but moving appeal from one G. E. Khaikin, head of a raion department of public education, to Rumyantsev. At a raion Party conference at the end of April 1937, Khaikin came under severe attack because he allegedly was connected with the clergy, was sheltering hostile people in the school system, and was a Trotskyite. Seeking to defend himself against these accusations, he wrote:

> . . . I was born in 1905 in a worker family . . . I was a worker before the Revolution and after it . . . The chief accusation against me [is that] while working in Suzemka raion I married a teacher and she comes from the clergy. This situation made it possible for Comrade Kovalev [the raikom secretary] to challenge me, based on the fact that I have a connection with the clergy. [He charged that] the work of the raion department of public education is progressing in a wrecking manner; in the apparatus there are hostile elements. Some said: "We do not need priests, it is necessary to oust the enemies," all this alluding to me.[38]

Khaikin then described the situation which he faced in trying to keep the schools adequately staffed:

> In Ponezovyi raion there are 47 schools, 34 of them elementary, 12 incomplete middle, and one a complete ten-year school . . . For the 1937–38 school year there is a shortage of 35 teachers for the elementary schools, 15 people for the incomplete middle schools, and we have to close the ten-year school since there are no history teachers, mathematics teachers, or literature teachers. I wrote about this to the obkom and the oblast department of public education, but as yet there has been no aid.
>
> We must consider whether in such a situation we should release and transfer the old teachers only because they are from the former people. In my opinion this is outright "Ponizovyi revolutionary vigilance." It is necessary to work with them, but not to remove them.

Khaikin went on to deal with the accusation of Trotskyism which had been hurled against him. The basis for this charge was the fact that in 1925–26 he had attended the Bryansk guberniya Soviet-Party school where there had been a nest of Trotskyites. After pointing out the seriousness of the accusation, which had already led to the suicide of one so accused, he insisted that he had struggled against the Trotskyites in Bryansk and that there had been "many good Bolsheviks" in the school, of whom he counted himself one. He concluded, "After all this, working 12 years in the organs of the Department of Public Education, I am asking either that I be transferred to another raion or best of all that you release me from work as head of the raion department of public education and send me to school. I think that you, Ivan Petrovich, will inform me of the results of my request." Khaikin's letter was dated June 7, 1937, and there is no record of a reply. Less than three weeks later Rumyantsev and his leading associates were themselves denounced as Trotskyite-Bukharinite riff-raff and disappeared forever.

The Obkom Secretary as the Dispenser of Mercy and Patronage

For many years prior to his disgrace, however, Rumyantsev, as obkom first secretary, and his deputy Shilman, functioned as the last court of appeal in the oblast, the ultimate dispensers of mercy and patronage after all other alternatives had been exhausted. Every type of petition and entreaty was addressed to them. Many involved appeals for jobs, for transfers of assignment, and even for release from assignments. Thus, on December 20, 1936, a former chairman of a raion executive committee, who had been "released" from work because of "poor" relations with his raikom secretary and who at the "advanced" age of forty-four had met frustration in the obkom apparatus in obtaining another suitable assignment, petitioned Rumyantsev as follows:

Considering that I have no specialty besides the political knowledge which the Party gave me, I feel that it is time for me to specialize in some work or other. I would like to go to work in the State Bank, where I would be able to acquire some specialty in finance and banking. I beg you to send me to work in the State Bank or in Party work. If this is impossible, where will the Party send me? For four days I have not been able to persuade the agriculture department to transfer me to the State Bank. I beg you, if possible, to decide this problem quite soon, since it is very difficult to live in the city of Smolensk, and besides I do not have a great amount of funds.[39]

The Archive records no response.

Sometimes the problem was one of avoiding transfer out of a specialty for which the job-holder was trained. Thus, on September 25, 1936, the head of the forestry department in Zizdrinsk wrote Shilman as follows: ". . . in May of this year, against my wishes and without considering my objections, they appointed me head of the Zhizdrinsk City Communal Economy Department — I went many times to the raikom, requesting that they leave me in forestry work, since I already have a forestry specialty, both theoretically and practically, but these requests of mine led to nothing . . ."[40] As a result of this appeal, the obkom assistant secretary wrote to the raikom that Shilman considered the new appointment as "inexpedient" and requested that the forester be left in forestry work.

The reply from the raikom was evasive; while not foreclosing ultimate action it replied "that it now appears impossible to transfer him to forestry work in view of the shortage of Soviet workers."

On occasion the appeal was for release from a job which the holder either disliked or felt himself unable to perform. The next letter may fairly be described as rather unusual. Dated October 10, 1936, and addressed to Comrade Shilman, it read in part:

I have been working in Baryatino raion as raion procurator for about three years. Before this I worked for a longer time in all kinds of managerial jobs, but I never worked in the organs of justice, and only from 1934 to the present time have I worked as procurator. When they put me in the position of procurator I categorically objected, because I am semiliterate and moreover a Ukrainian by nationality which makes my semiliteracy worse in the RSFSR. They answered that it is necessary to go where the Party sends you. After that I left to work as a procurator.

During my work I wrote several petitions to the Western obkom requesting them to release me from work as raion procurator in accordance with the above reasons, but Comrade Gusev kept answering me all the time: "You must work." Besides I personally went to Comrade Gusev and asked him to transfer me from the Western Oblast to the Ukrainian SSR or to transfer me to other work. I asked the Procurator of the USSR, Comrade Vyshinsky, about this, but everywhere they refuse me. Comrade Shilman, it is possible that you will consider me simply a liar, but I speak to you honestly as a member of the CPSU(b).

In the first place, I myself am a Ukrainian by nationality, was mobilized into the Western Oblast in 1931 for trade union work, at which I worked for two years, after which I petitioned for release to the Ukraine, but they did not release me. I asked to be transferred to other work where I might be of greater use, but my request was left unheeded.

I cannot work as procurator, since I am completely illiterate technically and aside from two grades in the village school in the prerevolutionary period, I have no education. I also consider myself politically illiterate since I never finished any schools.

Based on the above reasons, I must inform you that I am unable to work any longer as a procurator, since the procurator is the arm of the law and of revolutionary legality in the raion, and I do not understand many problems, and in general I do not have the capabilities for judicial work, while in other work I could be of greater use. I beg you, Comrade Shilman, to consider my request to transfer me from the Western Oblast to the Ukraine, or at least, if that is impossible, to transfer me to other work. I beg you to inform me of the results.[41]

The Archive contains no word of a reply to the unhappy procurator.

Sometimes the appeal was for relief from an unhappy work situation. The following letter dated July 27, 1936, and addressed to Rumyantsev is self-explanatory:

Excuse me for bothering you with my letter, but I can no longer endure what I am going through in my work. For two years I have worked as an official of the Oblast Trade Union Council in Yelnya, but they underestimate this work here and have even decided not to give me a place to work. Many people come to me — physicians, teachers, workers, employees, invalids of labor — but they have no place to sit and nothing can be heard, because here in one small room both the ZHAKT [the housing office] and the raion trade union council are located. I reported this to the bureau of the raikom, and they gave me an order, but everything remained on paper. I understand this only to mean that they are humiliating me and driving me from work, so that I will resign. But I can work; I want to work, if they create normal working conditions for me. But other than intriguing against fellow employees and ridiculing them, I don't see that Comrade Slovik, the second secretary of the raikom, does anything special . . . Often you hear, "You work poorly." Slovik says this. But no one from the raikom asks why, if it is bad. And thus sometimes I would go to get advice in the raikom, but they do not like me there and do not want to hear about it, and they tell me to stew in my own juice, to weep, as is my habit, and that's all. I have a family of two children, but the family does not hinder my work. I even worked during the campaign in the village soviets, and will work more, but under such conditions, it is impossible to work. I am a promoted worker from Yartsevo. For nine years I worked as a weaver, finished the Soviet-Party school, and then had to "be tormented" in Yelnya. I beg your advice on what to do and I await your answer. Good-by, dear Ivan Petrovich, and forgive me for my frankness.[42]

Appended to this letter is a handwritten note from Rumyantsev: "What kind of a neglectful attitude is this toward Adadurova? Correct this immediately. Slovik must be put in his place. Report to me on what you have done." On August 25, 1936, a letter arrived from the Yelnya raikom secretary. It read, "Your instructions have been fulfilled. Comrade Adadurova has been given a room, and the chairman of the city soviet and Comrade Slovik have been reprimanded for their incorrect attitude."

A great many pleas for help came to Rumyantsev from victims of illness and catastrophe who found themselves unable to obtain relief through ordinary channels. "I turn to you with a great request," wrote one of the supplicants in 1936, "and I hope you will not treat it as the others did, but will help me in my misfortune." The letter continued:

My husband, Pyotr Pavlovich Chernyshev, joined the Party in 1924. During the whole period of Party work he never cast a taint on the Party. He put all his health into the cause of building socialism, so that he would not lag behind. He worked hard to develop himself.

But those were ruinous years, and the salary was not large — his family obligations and his persistent correspondence studies finally ruined his health, and then in November 1934 he became ill and they sent him to the Gedeyonovka psychiatric hospital, where he stayed for 9½ months. They discharged him before he was well and he went to his mother, where he spent 3 months. He found a way out of his dead end, and stood firmly on the ground again. His illness did not influence his mental capacities. He did not forget dialectical materialism, but nervousness and a state of depression remained; he was a superfluous man, forgotten by all. No one stretched out a friendly hand to him, neither the Party organization under the Oblast Administration for State Savings Banks where he was an inspector, nor the Gorkom of the CPSU(b). I wrote to *Rabochii Put,* the Party, but everyone passed over him without noticing the forgotten man. When Chernyshev became sick, I remained with my child, turned to the administration for mothers' aid, and the administration, judging the case in a three-man commission, decided to give me 150 rubles, but about two years have passed since that time and they haven't given me the money.

In January 1936 Chernyshev, having learned that he was expelled from the Party because of sickness, went to the gorkom to Comrade Vasileyskaya and later to Comrade Morgunov, asking them to send him to a hospital, but six months have already passed and they promised everything . . . I myself went to Comrade Morgunov three times, but things are not progressing. Apparently, they'll wait three years before they do what was promised.

Now, Ivan Petrovich, there is only one hope — you. I beg you, let the man improve his health. I assure you that you'll find an honest, politically developed man for the ranks of both Soviet and Party work. To be an invalid at the age of 37 and to receive a pension in group 2, having a child — it is difficult to live. Life could be better, but it is necessary to work, and therefore again I beg you to help a man who can give much, who can be a help in our feverish building of socialism.[43]

The Archive provides no indication that this letter evoked a response.

The same fate befell another petition from a Party member addressed jointly to Rumyantsev as Party secretary and Rakitov as chairman of the presidium of the oblast executive committee. The petitioner wrote:

On June 10, 1936, I suffered a natural catastrophe — my house burned down with all my property. I was left completely naked, without shoes or clothes, and I am now living with my family in someone's damp, cold barn. We are completely famished and ill, and I am desperately ill. My mother is 78 years old and I have an 8-year-old child, and I have to support them. I turned to the secretary of the raikom for help, but he told me bluntly that the raikom is not an insurance agency and advised me to make an application to the presidium of the raion executive committee. On June 12 I appealed to the raion executive committee, but I have not received an answer. They say that they are studying the case again. I appealed to the commission of state credit under the village soviet. The commission decided to give me a loan, but the raion finance department and the savings bank delayed and ordered the chairman to review the case again, and it dragged on from June 12 to June 30 of this year. On June 30 the chief of the savings and loan bank, Comrade Konilova, sent her bookkeeper to the meeting of the commission a second time and refused to make the loan.

Honored leaders, they have made me dizzy for 20 days, prolonging the red tape . . . I beg you not to let me and my family perish. I am 32 years old and three months' pregnant. I have an 8-year-old child and a 78-year-old mother. I have no husband, and I am in sore straits. I wanted to take my life and to poison my family, but I decided to appeal to you. If you do not help me and give me assistance, I give you my Communist word of honor, I will commit suicide and will kill my family . . . I decided to appeal to you for help, for the last time, Comrade Rumyantsev. I think that our Party, under the leadership of Comrade Stalin, will not allow four people to perish . . . If our Party allows everyone to live, I beg you to expedite my petition and not to refuse my request.[44]

Still another bitter tale of woe was unfolded in a letter dated July 1, 1936, to Rumyantsev from the widow of a raion official who had died some six months earlier after a long illness. The widow, who was herself ill, was left with three children under fifteen, all of whom were also sick. She was given a pension of 176 rubles, 25 kopecks, which she found utterly inadequate for her needs. She wrote that "bread alone costs 100 rubles per month, and the apartment costs 18 rubles . . . I have nothing to live on. I now need wood for the winter; the children need shoes and clothing, and I must buy books; it is necessary to teach them. At one time I was advised to give them up to an orphanage, but it is too much for me to be deprived of such a husband and my children, and therefore I consider that my husband deserved help for his children. He always said to me: If they hurt you, then go to Ivan Petrovich and tell him about it, so I decided to write to you. It very much offends me the way people talk to me and treat me." [45]

She then described what happened when she went to the secretary of her husband's Party cell to complain about the way her husband had been buried and to ask help in connection with her pension. The secretary, she wrote, "told me that [my husband] himself should have thought about his family before he died. Then he said, 'Take your documents and run around yourself.' He should not have been buried that way — they should have bought him a suit, a wreath of flowers, a coffin, music. But the secretary of the Party cell said: 'Let them bury him without a coffin, a naked old Party man . . .' He ought to read Stalin's article on how to value a man. I am an illiterate and yet I have read how Stalin wrote to value a man. Comrade Rumyantsev, I beg you to help me in my sorrow and I beg you to let me know . . ."

This time the matter was referred to an official of the Supply Commission of the Council of People's Commissars in the Western Oblast, who wrote: "In view of the fact that the dead Koshkin, a former Red Guardsman, was in the ranks of the Party in various sectors of work, where the Party sent him, acting as a skillful leader, a capable manager, and an able Bolshevik in carrying out the directives of the Party, and taking into consideration the fact that after his death Koshkin left no money, so that the pension of 175 rubles per month established for his family cannot support the family of Koshkin, and also with the exception of the oldest daughter, all the rest of the members of the family are unable to work, the official of the Supply Commission under the Council of People's Commissars of the Western Oblast asks the Presidium of the Western Oblast Executive Committee to file a petition with the Commission under the RSFSR Council of People's Commissars to establish a personal pension for the family of the late Koshkin."

But the matter turned out to be not quite so simple. A further inquiry developed the fact that Koshkin's widow had a twenty-four-year-old son who worked in Glavzoloto (the gold administration) and received a salary of 1,200 rubles per month. The widow replied that the son gave her no help. The investigator reported: ". . . in all probability, Koshkina receives aid from her son, but conceals this in her own interests, in order to receive a personal pension." At this point the record stops.

The following letter dated June 20, 1936, and addressed to Comrade Rumyantsev tells its own story:

I decided to turn to you a second time with a request. The first time I asked you personally in 1935, when you visited our factory. The request was about my son, a 14-year-old boy who is almost deaf and dumb. I asked you to help me put him in a special school for deaf-mutes, where they would teach him some kind of a trade. You listened to me attentively and you ordered that the factory committee take my request under consideration and fulfill it. They listened, made notes, made promises, and up to now, despite my continued requests, they have done nothing. Since 1932 I have been petitioning. Many times I pleaded with the factory committee and more than once was in the Raion Department of Public Education and appealed to Comrade Baturin. For four years they have been promising me, and up to now no one has done anything. My boy has not been placed and he is growing up almost like a neglected orphan. The school all these years has done absolutely nothing. They give aid to many people in the form of clothing and shoes for the children, but I have never received anything for my children. My family and material situation have become absolutely unbearable. I have five children. The oldest is a deaf-mute; the rest are little ones. My husband is a dissolute loafer. He does not live with me. I don't know where he is, and I have never received and do not receive any alimony. It has become so difficult to live. I no longer have the physical and spiritual powers, and not seeing any help from anywhere, I become desperate, exhausted. Maybe this time you will be generous and will put my son in the special school for deaf-mutes in Smolensk. Because he has not received any education, he preys on my conscience heavily; I am disturbed about him, for he has been hurt by life.

I beg your pardon greatly for disturbing you. I remain, A. Kozlova. Weaver in the Yartsevo factory, production experience since 1931; from the old cadres, I was a shock-worker, at present am a Stakhanovite.[46]

The letter was sent to the Yartsevo raikom for disposition. On August 17, 1936, Yakovlev, the raikom secretary, informed the obkom that Comrade Kozlova had been given monetary assistance by the factory committee. Whether the son was sent to the Smolensk school for deaf-mutes the record does not disclose.

In another case, however, there is evidence of Rumyantsev's direct intervention on behalf of a deaf-mute. On August 19, 1936, Rumyantsev wrote the secretary of the Novozybkovsk raikom, "I have received a report that in your factory 'Volna Revolyutsiya,' a deaf-and-dumb youth, Aleksei Dmitrochenko, works, who was transferred to the factory from the Zlynkovsk school for deaf-mutes. The boy is in terrible condition and no one is interested in what happens to him, neither the school nor the factory organization. Check on this case yourself and report to me immediately on what has been done to improve the position of Dmitrochenko and how things stand at the factory in regard to the organization of the labor of children transferred to you from the schools."[47] The raikom secretary replied that "on August 28, 1936, the factory organization sent this youth to study at the Smolensk school for deaf-mutes, issuing clothing to him at the expense of the factory and paying for his trip." He also reported that "in investigating the boy, I found that other youths sent to work in the 'Volna Revolyustiya' factory are in need of help." He promised "that their position will be improved and they will be under our surveillance."[48]

Many of the appeals which came to Rumyantsev were a product of the acute housing shortage of the period. One of the more piquant was a letter dated July 23, 1936, "from the toiling kolkhoz children" of the kolkhoz "Novaya Zhizn" addressed to "our dear and respected Comrade Rumyantsev." The letter read:

> In the first lines of our letter we wish you a healthy, joyful and free life. Comrade Rumyantsev, we ask you for the following: our father was dekulakized and sent beyond the borders of the oblast, where he died. Our mother also died, and we came from the Urals as complete orphans. We did not have anything from their household, but the village soviet and the board of the kolkhoz admitted us into the kolkhoz, and working honestly and conscientiously we acquired everything for ourselves except a house, which we are unable to buy. Our former hut is in the kolkhoz and there are tax arrears on it, and nobody lives in it. So we children beg you, Comrade Rumyantsev, to see to it that our former hut is returned to us. We have a hut, but it is too small, it is rotting, and is falling to the ground, so that we three go to school and don't have any place to put our books. And since our former hut is empty, please see to it that they give it back to us. Please do not neglect our request. Write to the following address.[49]

The matter was referred to the Bryansk raiispolkom. The chairman investigated personally, reported that the chairman of the kolkhoz was living in the house which the "children" wanted, that it was impossible to return the house, and that the total earnings of the "children" came to 700 workdays per year which, he stated, ought to enable them to obtain a better house than the poor peasant's hut in which they were presently quartered. Despite renewed pleas from the "children," the case was closed on December 5, 1936, when the assistant secretary of the obkom informed them that the house could not be returned. "You have a large number of earned workdays in the kolkhoz," he wrote, "and like all other kolkhozniks, you are in a [financial] position to acquire a better hut for yourselves." [50]

The housing complications arising out of family separations and divorces presented another type of situation which Rumyantsev was asked to resolve. The case of Butev may serve as an illustration.[51] Butev had been the manager of the Smolensk Flax Combine. In 1935 he was accused of embezzling 28,000 rubles, but the accusation was dropped after two court trials in which no evidence of crime could be discovered. Meanwhile, however, he was expelled from the Party and dismissed from work in the combine. His new job, that of storeman in the State Transport Organization, represented a very considerable demotion. To add to his troubles, his wife decided to separate from him, but because neither could find other quarters, they continued to live in the same room until the winter of 1935, when his wife remarried. On the day of the marriage, Butev was beaten up by the newly-wedded couple. The case was brought to court, and Butev's former wife was sentenced to three months' forced labor. After the fight, she left the room which she shared with Butev, but, unable to find other quarters for her child and herself, through the intervention of the militia she was reinstalled in Butev's apartment. Butev attempted to exchange his space in the room for some space elsewhere, but was unsuccessful. He then appealed to the housing authorities to furnish him with a separate room, or at least to partition his space in the room from that of his former wife. The housing office promised to do this, but nothing happened. The situation was temporarily resolved when Butev was called for several months' military service and was subsequently hospitalized with a serious illness. The rest of the story was summarized by an obkom instructor as follows:

. . . On September 21, [1936], they took him home from the hospital . . . It turned out that his room had been given up to other inhabitants, while his wife received another room in this same house. He sat around the house until 8 o'clock at night and didn't get anywhere, and his neighbors took him to spend the night with a fellow countryman who was working as a yardman in the 13th Anniversary of October Inn, where he is up to the present time. On September 22 Butev asked the military procurator for help. They treated him well and gave him a statement to the city procurator (a woman) to the effect that she should give him a place to live and should bring the guilty people to trial. The city procurator was indifferent toward him, according to Butev, at first refused to receive him, and then took his statement, and allegedly said that the claim was accepted — we'll investigate it and you go home. . . . On September 23 he again went to the city procuracy . . . but since the question was not solved, on September 25 he sent a written claim to the oblast procurator, who also promised to furnish him with quarters. On September 26 he called the oblast procurator on the phone, and the latter promised that on that day he would summon all the necessary people and by

1 o'clock in the afternoon would decide the problem. When he called at 2 o'clock, Butev learned that the case had not yet been decided, and although the procurator had promised to send his representative to the spot on the next day, Butev decided to seek assistance from Comrade Rumyantsev . . . Butev doesn't want to be put in the same room with his [former] wife.

The Archive contains no record of the final disposition of this case. There is merely a notation in the obkom instructor's report that the investigation was proceeding.

The infinite variety and even triviality of matters which were brought to Rumyantsev's attention may be exemplified by a few samples. There is the case of the citizen I. F. Davydov, whose hunting dog the local raikom secretary and raion NKVD chief expropriated.[52] The anguished plea of the dog-owner elicited no response from the obkom secretary. There is the case of the ex-wife of a raikom secretary who appealed to Rumyantsev to make her husband pay her alimony. This time there was a sharp note to the raikom secretary from Shilman: "I feel that it is unworthy of you as a leader of the raion Party organization to bring things to such a pass, especially after the adoption of the law on increasing the punishment for failure to pay alimony. What are you waiting for — for them to drag you to court as a malicious non-payer of alimony and thoroughly to discredit you? I order you immediately to settle the question . . . Otherwise we will do it through the obkom, taking it out of your salary." [53] The alimony was paid.

There is the case of the former worker in a casting foundry who claimed to have invented a new plastering machine and was meeting difficulty in obtaining funds from the communal building organization in Ordzhonikidzegrad in order to construct a model.[54] This time Rumyantsev himself dispatched a handwritten note to the chairman of the city soviet: "Don't you have any funds to put this invention into operation, if it has been acknowledged as useful?" The answer came back that the inventor had approached the office of the communal building organization with a very rough draft of his proposed machine, that they had put him to work as a locksmith in the office to give him a chance to work out his invention, but that he had been unable to do so. They had then offered the plan to the construction bureau of the "Krasnyi Profintern" factory, but the mechanical engineer there had refused to work on it, saying that it would be impossible to use the machine. The oblast trust of the building organization then agreed to try to construct the machine, but Denisov, the inventor, refused to give his consent. "It is absolutely incomprehensible to us," wrote the chairman of the city soviet, "to know what Comrade Denisov wants, since in my opinion Comrade Denisov was given the proper technical aid and the material opportunity for realizing his invention." A later communication from the trust added that

Denisov's proposal had been investigated and found unacceptable, and that Denisov had been so informed.

Finally, there was the case of the two former gypsies, one a Party candidate and the other a member of the Komsomol, who asked Rumyantsev to help them organize a gypsy club in Smolensk and to build dormitories for the gypsies who worked in production in the city of Smolensk.[55] The letter evoked no response.

These letters to Rumyantsev convey some sense of the key role which the first secretary played in the life of the oblast. When all other local remedies were exhausted, it was to Rumyantsev that supplicants turned as their last hope in the oblast. As these letters indicate, many petitions went unanswered, but not infrequently the effect of a letter was to set an investigation into motion, and occasionally Rumyantsev intervened to untangle a bit of red tape or to right a wrong which would otherwise have been ignored.

The Oblast Leadership as Whipping Boy

All-powerful as Rumyantsev must have seemed to those who came to him on bended knees for favors, his was, after all, a precarious satrapy hedged in by constant threats and dangers. The mercy he dispensed could not transcend policies which were established by the center; the fear he inspired could not obliterate the fact that he too had to cringe before a suspicious and omnipotent despot in the Kremlin. The same apparatus of petition and redress which Rumyantsev manipulated in the oblast could be and was turned against him by Stalin; the oblast leadership too had to serve as whipping boy when the occasion dictated.

A vivid example is provided by a letter to *Pravda* dated July 15, 1936, and entitled "Plans and Reality." [56] The letter read:

> During the current year in Smolensk a large store, a hotel, a theater, a surgical clinic, a hospital lumberyard, and a four-story house on Magnitogorsk Street are being built.
> The plans are very great, but if you look at the tempos and the procedure for carrying out the work, it becomes very clear that they have begun to build everywhere and things are not progressing anywhere.
> They began to build the hotel in 1935 and up to the present they have erected only part of the building — 1 to 1½ stories; they have only laid the foundations for the movie theater; for the large store they have only dug the foundation pit and have stopped at this. The surgical clinic, the house of specialists, and the hospital lumberyard up to now have not been started. Last year they dug the foundation for the four-story house and now they have begun to erect the walls, without having enough bricks, and probably this year they will not erect the building even up to the roof.
> This is due to the fact that in Smolensk there is a special style of work — they eagerly seize upon everything, but they do not take into consideration their material and monetary resources ("it is important to begin, and then the

money will be found"), and therefore they are building a great deal, but nothing is accomplished.

Instead of concentrating all their resources on one or two projects and finishing them in the shortest possible time, they expend their energies in all directions and they accomplish nothing.

Despite this inadmissible situation in regard to buildings, the oblast executive committee decided in July to begin the immediate and out-of-order building during the current year of still another four-story house with 120 apartments . . . for the Party aktiv of the city of Smolensk.

For this purpose a whole block was designated for demolition, and about 100 families are being resettled on the outskirts of the city. They have already begun to bring in the materials for the building; they have taken the fences to pieces, are bringing in lumber, digging trenches, and slaking lime. Columns of dust fly around, the children of the inhabitants have no place to walk or to pass, and they are not demolishing the house.

They intend to resettle the toilers on the outskirts of the city, or more exactly, beyond the city, in wooden houses built at a snail's pace, without any equipment at all, without any kind of communal services; there are no street-cars, no shops, no outhouses, or sidewalks, and in the spring and fall you cannot get by because of the mud and the poor road. To go out of the house at night into the city or to work is impossible; it is far away, dark and dangerous . . .

It will be impossible to live in these houses in the wintertime. All those who are to be resettled there are nervous in expectation of this "second pogrom"; the first took place while the Flax Combine was being constructed.

In Smolensk they fear and curse new construction instead of being happy and welcoming it as in Moscow, where they furnish better-equipped apartments to those who are resettled, with good means of communication. In Smolensk there is no concern for people. A number of families do not have "living corners."

Fourteen families who were victims of fires are scattered about in club-houses, basements, etc. A number of toilers live for months in hotels, all of their apartments having been made smaller, and despite this situation, further wrecking continues . . .

Can it be that everything is so built up in Smolensk that there are no free places for building new houses? And why aren't new houses being built at the the end of the city? And if they have decided to demolish a house, why don't they build first and equip new houses and squares, and then destroy the houses, instead of getting the people angry?

It is necessary immediately to instruct a commission from the center to check on the spot on the condition of the building projects of the city of Smolensk, their tempos and the actual material and financial resources in 1936, and [to find out] when and into what houses and raions they are resettling the toilers and under what conditions many families live, who almost every day importune the city soviet, demanding rooms, and who receive answers with no results: "Tomorrow, the day after tomorrow." Thus they promise them, and they wait for years. I await aid and your answer.

[Signed] AN OBSERVER

The letter was forwarded to the Western obkom where it obviously touched a tender spot. The obkom section chief in charge of construction acknowledged that all the facts in the letter were completely correct, but he added weakly that nothing much could be done about it since the old houses which were to be torn down were all in the center of the city, and they could not be left there. What turned out to be particularly significant about this letter was not merely that it frankly aired the housing crisis in Smolensk, but that it was seized upon by the center to provide additional ammunition to weaken and discredit Rumyantsev and to support the purge of the so-called "Rumyantsev band" the next year. Whether the effect was also to relieve the housing crisis in Smolensk is less clear.

As this review of sample letters in the Archive demonstrates, the functions they performed varied with the motives which inspired them. A few were defiant challenges to the regime, bravely and foolhardily hurled despite the risk of NKVD discovery and retribution. Some sought to win the favor of the regime, by ministering to its need for spies, sentinels, and tale-bearers. But the great majority involved a primitive exercise of the right to petition for the redress of grievances. In general, the disposition of the letters depended on their relevance to state needs and purposes. Some were simply ignored because they vented private tribulations or called for a type of corrective action which ran athwart state policy. Others were given the closest attention because they exposed administrative failures or defects which the leadership itself had a strong interest in remedying. Still others might only be distantly related to public ends, yet capture the notice of a Party secretary because of some past service or personal tie and relationship.

From the point of view of the senders, the letter to the newspaper or to the obkom usually represented the last desperate act after all other local remedies had been exhausted. The bulging letter files in the Archive indicate that this final right of petition was vigorously exercised. And it is also clear that most letters received some form of scrutiny and a few at least inspired corrective action.

A reading of the letters and the investigatory reports which some of them induced helps to emphasize their role in the Soviet system of governance. The letters provided one of the few direct links which the leadership had with grass-roots experience; the outpourings of the letter-writers and the responses they elicited represented the nearest approximation to a spontaneous dialogue between the leaders and their subjects which the Soviet system afforded. Through the flow of correspondence, the leadership was provided with a partial measure of the impact of its policies, of the problems which they created, and of the dissatisfaction which they inspired. The letters frequently served to alert the leadership to the local scandals, the tight little family circles that were insulating themselves from central surveillance, and the arbitrary and high-handed actions of officials whose pattern of conduct was discrediting the regime.

With the help of the letters both the central and regional leadership were able to leap-frog the formal administrative hierarchy and to maintain a check on their own agents in terms of the reaction from below. Moreover, the knowledge on the part of local officials that their excesses and mistakes might be reported operated as an inhibitory restraint. From the point of view of the regime, the ultimate rationale for keeping these channels of communication open was not merely that they operated as a prod and control over the bureaucracy, but that they diffused and localized expressions of discontent, whose bolts of lightning might otherwise have been directed at the center itself.

21 The Komsomols

The Komsomol movement was slow to take root in the Smolensk area. The first report by the guberniya Komsomol organization, which was rendered to a plenum of the Smolensk gubkom on February 23–24, 1920, was discouraging.[1] Tseitlin, who spoke on behalf of the Komsomol, complained that the organization had no cadres to organize the youth, and that it was receiving little or no coöperation from the uyezd Party committees. The latter, pressed for personnel themselves, withdrew instructors from the Komsomol and even sabotaged its work by refusing to provide it with office space and by denying it the right to institute a Komsomol page in the local press. Tseitlin warned that unless the Party gubkom was prepared to equip the Komsomol with organizers, there would be nothing left for the Komsomol gubkom to do "except lock its door and temporarily suspend activity." The Party gubkom responded by promising five workers and ordered the uyezd committees to make additional organizers available and to supply the local Komsomol organizations with a weekly newspaper page to be entitled "Young Communist," which would be edited by them.

Early Recruiting Difficulties

During the next months the Komsomol claimed a vast upsurge in membership. At a Party gubkom meeting on April 23, 1920, the quoted figure for the guberniya was 12,000.[2] But the discussion made clear that the figure had to be treated with reserve. Newly enrolled peasant youths accounted for a large part of the gain, but they were described as the least reliable part of the Komsomol, primarily loyal to their families and villages, uninterested in studies, and preoccupied with field work. The gubkom solemnly discussed tactics to wean them away from their traditional attachments. Remizov, the Party secretary, strongly urged that successful "bourgeois" and "monarchical" practices be borrowed and adapted; he especially cited the appeal of "grandiose festivities" for peasant youth, the desirability of combining music, marching, and pageantry with political speeches. Such "festivities," he argued, should be held not only on the first of May, but on traditional religious holidays in order to prevent the youth from flocking to the churches. Some of the gubkom members strongly objected to scheduling Komsomol fetes on church holidays, but Remizov's analysis of peasant psychology persuaded the waverers, and his suggestion was adopted. In addition, it was agreed that clubs be organized for peasant youth and that its members be enlisted for voluntary work on their free days (*subbotniki*) to aid families of soldiers who were serving in the Red Army.

Despite these ingenious maneuvers to enlist peasant youth in the ranks of the Komsomol, the early efforts were not notably successful. The first effect of the adoption of the NEP was a notable decline in Komsomol membership; in the Smolensk region, which was preponderantly agricultural, it was manifested in large-scale defections among rural recruits. By March 1923 there were only 2,792 members and 493 candidates in the guberniya Komsomol organization, substantially less than a third of the 1920 total.[3]

Alarmed by these losses, the Party made strenuous efforts to reverse the tide. In Smolensk, as elsewhere, these efforts were attended with considerable success. The accompanying tabulation indicates the rapid growth of the guberniya Komsomol organization in the mid-twenties.[4]

	Members	Candidates	Totals
March 1924...................	3,498	977	4,475
November 1, 1924.............	7,451	928	8,379
December 1, 1925.............	15,703	1,058	16,761

Of the total membership on December 1, 1925, 62.4 per cent were classified as peasant, 31 per cent as worker, and 6.6 per cent as belonging to the "employees and other" category. This distribution reflected the predominantly rural character of the guberniya. At the same time the proportion of peasant youth enrolled in the Komsomol was much smaller than the corresponding percentage among the workers. In the guberniya as a whole peasants outnumbered workers by more than twenty to one; within the Komsomol the ratio of peasant to worker was approximately two to one.

Meanwhile, the Party sought to use the Komsomol as a primary spearhead in projecting its influence into the countryside. The number of rural Komsomol cells increased from 296 on November 1, 1924, to 631 on December 1, 1925. The following account, dated August 4, 1925, of the growth of the Komsomol organization of Ilino volost in Velizh uyezd conveys something of the flavor of the period:

> The Komsomol organization began in 1919 and had 12 members. Because of banditry the cell was dissolved at the beginning of 1920. In 1923 in the summer the cell was organized again. In the beginning there were about 10–12 members. Within a year the organization increased to 70 people, but no work was done among the members. In general, the educational and organizational work among the Komsomol members began in 1924 in connection with the arrival of several members who had finished the guberniya Soviet-Party school . . .

There is a strong inclination to enter the organization. Beginning in January of this year [1925], every month from 10 to 12 people have entered the organization. It cannot be said that all enter out of a definite conviction. For many, the main attraction is the desire to be in the circles where the organized part of the youth already belong. Some of those who have recently entered still have not yet entirely broken their ties with religious loyalties. After staying some time in the organization, their earlier convictions are dispelled; gradually they are drawn into public work, and thereby are developed.

About 75% have been attracted into public and economic work. For example, 10 people have been elected to the village soviets, 4 to the peasant committees, 4 people work among the hired laborers in recording and concluding labor contracts, and the others in various organizations and in Red Corners and village reading rooms. Many took part during the winter in political and agricultural circles. Almost all the members of the Red Corners are Komsomolites . . .

The volost center is a real center; there are many trained people, while in the rural raions in some cells there is not one trained person . . . in the Barborovsk [rural] cell, there are 26 people and there is not one trained member of the Komsomol.[5]

As this account makes clear, the burden of Komsomol leadership in the countryside was carried by a small nucleus of members who were trained in the soviet-Party schools. They tended to congregate in the uyezd and volost centers, leaving the more remote rural cells without effective guidance and direction. Under the impetus of this group, nevertheless, rural cells increased in number, and young people who joined the Komsomols were advanced and pushed forward into leading positions in local public and economic organizations. Thus the Komsomol served to extend the network of Party controls. Moreover, the rank-and-file Komsomolites were themselves both objects and carriers of Party agitation and propaganda. To the local Komsomol leaders fell the formidable task of undermining traditional village loyalties and transforming the peasant youth into believing instruments and effective transmission belts of Party policies in the countryside.

The report of the Party gubkom for the period 1923–24 conveys some sense of the scope of Komsomol activities during the mid-NEP period.[6] Work in rural areas loomed as one of the Komsomol's prime responsibilities. Great stress was placed on Komsomol participation in local election campaigns and penetration of local organs of government. The report proudly noted that 161 Komsomols had been elected members of village soviets, forty members of volost executive committees, fifty members of land commissions, and sixty-three members of peasants' mutual aid societies.[7] Some 200 village reading rooms had been established, ninety of which were headed by Komsomols who conducted readings and discussions for the villagers on agricultural as well as general political themes. During the year some ninety "Red Komsomol teachers" had been dispatched to village schools, where they served as links between the Party and the rising generation. Some twenty-five full-time paid Komsomol staff members were employed in organizing the volosts.

While political education work in the Komsomol cells was considered far from satisfactory, some progress was noted. Antireligious demonstrations were held on village holidays. Club work was improving and included political discussions. Attacks were launched on the problem of illiteracy. Political instructors chosen from the Komsomol helped to train those about to be drafted for military service. Sports were being developed, and a guberniya-wide Olympiad for youth was held in September 1923. During the summer there were excursions of rural cells to the cities and even to Moscow. During this period, detachments of young Pioneers also began to be organized. The children were kept busy with games, gymnastics, excursions to the cities and factories, campaigns of various types, and political conversations designed to make them loyal to the regime. The report complained, however, that there were not enough equipment, sports items, and literature to take care of the children's needs. A newspaper, "Young Comrade," was published to minister to the special interests of the young, but its circulation too was limited, and relatively few copies reached the more remote rural areas.

Despite these strenuous efforts to engage the energies and loyalties of the youth, the overwhelming proportion of young peasants in the age group eligible for Komsomol membership remained outside the fold. Less than one out of thirty was a Komsomol member. And even in the Komsomol itself only a small fraction of the peasant recruits could be counted on as zealous and devoted adherents of the Communist cause. In the measured words of the gubkom report for 1923–24, "cases of drunkenness, gambling, deviations, careerism, the persistence of religious prejudices, and other negative features cannot be counted as isolated incidents." [8]

The level of political sophistication in Komsomol ranks was generally low. The Smolensk Archive contains a list of questions asked at Komsomol meetings on the results of the Fourteenth Party Congress (December 1925) at which Zinoviev and Kamenev were decisively defeated by Stalin.[9] A few of the questions were sharp and pointed, but many more revealed a considerable degree of naïveté or even ignorance. For example:

What did N. K. Krupskaya mean when she referred to the Stockholm Congress?

In his book "Philosophy of the Epoch," Comrade Zinoviev writes about some kind of "equality." What does this "equality" mean?

If the views of the opposition were censured as mistaken at the Congress, why did not the opposition reject them?

Doesn't even greater discussion threaten the Party in the future?

Why is it that the Leningrad, and not another organization, turned out to be in the opposition?

Hasn't the Comintern considered the question of where the revolution should take place first? If it has, then which country is it?

Many of the questioners consciously identified with peasant interests and resisted the efforts of the Party to discriminate among kulaks, middle peasants, and poor peasants. Thus, for example:

Why does the opposition continuously condemn Comrade Bukharin's slogan "enrich yourselves"? What is dangerous about this slogan?

The resolution on the report of the Central Committee talks about the stricter admission into the Party of the semiproletarian element. Who is meant by this? Does this mean the peasants? Didn't Comrade Molotov in his report say that it is necessary to increase the number of peasants in the Party?

Won't the organization of groups of poor peasants again inflame the class struggle in the country, and if so, won't this reflect negatively on the development of productive forces in agriculture?

What is the danger in the organization of circles of non-Party peasant youth around the Young Communist League?

The gubkom report on the Fourteenth Party Congress discussions also noted the prevalence of "peasant moods" among Komsomols in the army units. "On the part of some comrades," the report declared, "there was an underestimation of the kulak danger." One Komsomol was quoted as saying, "You won't find kulaks in the country; there are very few of them, and in my opinion they are not dangerous." Another declared that "it is necessary to equalize the political rights of the workers and the peasants." Still another "expressed doubt that the Party would be able to lead the peasants, since it is a workers' party." The sizable contingent of middle peasants in the rural Komsomol organization proved refractory material as Party policy shifted toward special concern with the interests of poor peasants and batraks, or hired agricultural workers.

The Party-inspired antireligious campaigns were also a source of tension. In rural areas particularly there were still many Komsomols who attended church, sang in the choirs, and celebrated church marriages. The Komsomol leadership did everything in its power to prevent such "deviations" by agitation and by offering the counterattractions of the Red Wedding, but habit was strong. Some extracts from a 1927 report on a Komsomol rural cell in Velikiye Luki disclose the appeal which religion still offered. One Komsomol is quoted as saying, "On April 13 I cannot come to the Komsomol evening . . . since I have to prepare for Easter." [10] Another declared, "We will eat Easter eggs and go to church; it isn't such a great offense since on Easter they have an excellent service." [11]

Collectivization, Industrialization, and the Agenda of
Komsomol Activities

As the NEP drew to a close, the ties which bound Komsomol members to their parents were still close, and the solidarity of the villages presented a formidable barrier to Communist penetration. The decision of the Party to launch its campaign to squeeze out the kulaks had powerful repercussions, not only in the villages, but in the Komsomol cells which served them. One of its effects was to bring Komsomol poor peasants and batraks to the fore, since they now became both the favorite beneficiaries of state agricultural policy and a prime reliance in enforcing the program of dekulakization. Komsomols of poor-peasant derivation were maneuvered into leading positions in the rural Party organizations; in a typical reorganization of rural Komsomol cells in Velikiye Luki in 1927 the proportion of Komsomol secretaries of poor-peasant origin increased from 48.3 to 53.7 per cent, of batraks from 3.0 to 8.6 per cent, while the percentage of secretaries of middle peasant origin declined from 33.1 to 24.4.[12] This effort to install reliable cadres in key positions in the rural Komsomol organizations reflected a justified concern on the part of the Komsomol leadership at the probable reactions of its middle-peasant membership to dekulakization. For at least some of the latter, the attack on the kulak must already have seemed a portent of a broader assault on the peasantry. At its meeting of February 9, 1928, the bureau of the Smolensk gubkom acknowledged sharp differences of view between Komsomol middle peasants and poor peasants, noted that the former were not always following a correct class line, and condemned some who had openly opposed the organization of "committees of poor peasants."[13] The resolution of the bureau called for a further strengthening of the worker and poor-peasant contingent in the Komsomol.

The story of dekulakization and collectivization has been told elsewhere.[14] Perhaps it is enough here to note that the Party leadership relied heavily on the Komsomol to carry the process forward. The least reliable Komsomol cadres were those of middle-peasant origin, and a substantial number were expelled for weakness and unreliability in a cleansing of the ranks which was the Komsomol equivalent of the Party purge of 1929–30. When middle-peasant Komsomols balked at the new assignments thrust upon them, the reply, not infrequently, was one used in a Velikiye Luki rural cell: "You do not wish to work. We give you a mission, and if you will not work then we know what to do — we will expel you — as a class alien."[15] "Class alien" expanded into a broad and vague category to embrace all those who resisted collectivization. Meanwhile, the Komsomol emphasized proper social extraction in recruiting new members; the primary targets were young workers and poor peasants.

The Komsomol aktiv which was recruited for the collectivization brigades consisted predominantly of poor peasants and batraks from the country-side and worker and student Komsomols who were mobilized from urban proletarian centers.

During the early years of collectivization and the First Five Year Plan a marked shift took place in Komsomol activities. In the mid-twenties the Komsomol aktiv had occasionally been enlisted in emergency economic campaigns, but economic missions were still considered subsidiary to educational and propagandistic activities. Now economic assignments attendant on the collectivization and industrialization drive claimed the center of the stage, and Komsomolites began to be judged by their success or failure as soldiers of production.

The Smolensk Archive contains the resolutions approved by the second plenum of the Western Oblast committee of the Komsomol on April 10-12, 1931.[16] They underline the new economic and administrative orientation. The first resolution called for Komsomol participation in the collectivization drive, universal Komsomol enrollment in kolkhozes, and active leadership in preparation for the spring sowing. The second resolution outlined the responsibilities of Komsomol cells in fulfilling the control figures for industrial production during the year. The third called for an intensified campaign to enlist industrial and farm workers in the Komsomol and to establish a Komsomol cell in every kolkhoz and sovkhoz. The fourth expounded the duties of the Komsomol to prepare for military service, to help liquidate illiteracy among draftees, and to provide political instructors for them. The final resolution summoned the Komsomols to participate in the loan campaigns and to organize brigades to popularize savings so that the lagging financial plan of the oblast could be fulfilled.

The Archive also contains a large number of protocols of sessions of the bureau and secretariat of the Western Oblast Komsomol Committee for the period September 1932 to December 1933.[17] They too provide a vivid illustration of the production orientation of the Komsomol at this time. The flow of directives from the Komsomol obkom encompassed the whole economic life of the oblast. Agriculture, as might be expected, was very much in the forefront, and the seasonal rhythm of sowing and weeding, of harvests and state deliveries dominated the agenda. At a meeting of the obkom bureau on February 6, 1933, for example, raikom Komsomol secretaries were informed that they should pay particular attention to the repair of machines, and that they would be required to file reports at ten-day intervals on the progress of preparations for the sowing campaign in their districts.[18] At the same time representatives of the obkom went into the field to check on the status of tractor repair shops and to spur on the larger cells in the sovkhozes and MTS. On April 13, after visits to the districts, bureau members reported that progress was unsatisfactory.[19] The bureau thereupon scheduled a Komsomol subbotnik, a mobilization of oblast Komsomol forces to aid in the sowing. Special brigades of Komsomol and non-Party youth were organized to complete the cleaning of the seed, and "the best" Komsomol members were dispatched to make sure that the sowing norms were being observed, to check on the fodder supplies and the condition of the horses and their harnesses, to organize competition among the tractor drivers, and to mobilize the Komsomol aktiv in the struggle against kulaks and kolkhoz thievery.

Similar tactics were employed in connection with the harvest and the state deliveries.[20] "Light Cavalry" groups, consisting of Komsomol stalwarts, were mobilized to help in the harvest, to check on its storage and protection, to verify the accounts of collective farms with the state, with the MTS, and with the collective farmers, to insure that provisions were made for seed and insurance funds, and to see to it that proper preparations for winter were made in the cattle barns and in the storage of machines and implements. Since flax was the most important crop of the oblast, particularly strenuous efforts were directed toward meeting the plan in this area. On September 13, 1933, the obkom bureau voted to throw the whole Komsomol organization into the struggle for flax.[21] "The obkom bureau," read the resolution, "demands that every Komsomol organization struggle decisively with the kulak agitation to the effect that one ought to await good weather." The next five days were declared "a period of shock work" to bring in the flax. Despite this clarion call, results apparently fell far short of expectations, and *Komsomolskaya Pravda* singled out the flax districts of the Western Oblast for special criticism. At its meeting on November 17, 1933, the obkom bureau acknowledged the criticism as justified.[22] It noted that "the struggle for early beginning and late ending of the working day" had been neglected, and that "the struggle against idlers among Komsomol members" had not been intensive enough.

Efforts to strengthen the collective farms were not confined to special mobilizations and Light Cavalry raids. Komsomol members were assigned to collective farms and strategically placed within the kolkhozes to maximize their influence and leadership. A 1933 investigation in thirteen raions revealed that out of a total 6,796 rural Komsomol members, 164 Komsomols were either heads of collective farms or members of their governing boards, another 359 served as brigadiers, and 205 served as accountants.[23] Recruitment in rural areas sought to attract leadership elements into the Komsomol. The raion committees were instructed to assist Komsomol cells in distributing their forces among the field brigades in order to provide leadership within them and competition among them.

In order to strengthen Komsomol work in the villages, the obkom bureau on July 14, 1933, ordered the raikoms to shift their best Komsomol activists working in raion organizations into rural Komsomol cells, village soviets, and the collective farms.[24] Quotas were assigned to each raion with a deadline of August 10 for the completion of transfers. The obkom bureau discovered, however, that it was easier to issue orders than to enforce them. On September 25 it noted that many of the raikoms had approached the problem "in a purely formal manner" and that the quotas assessed by the obkom had not in fact been fulfilled.[25] Through one subterfuge or another the Komsomol raion workers eluded reassignment, and the raion leadership itself proved far from eager to disband the apparatus on which it relied.

The Komsomol members were also called upon to serve as pacesetters in industry and transport. They were required to enroll in technical courses to improve their qualifications, to organize shock brigades, and to popularize socialist competition. Again efforts were made to assign Komsomol activists to strategic positions in factories and enterprises in order to make their leadership effective.[26] They were also expected to conduct campaigns to shame the laggards and to discourage loitering on the job.[27] Among the means suggested were educational work, publicizing the names of offenders, and public trials by comradely courts.

Komsomol mobilizations to deal with emergencies were the order of the day. Merely to list some of those mentioned in the protocols is to suggest how various were the demands. There was the mobilization of the "300" to work in the villages as secretaries of Komsomol cells; of the "50" to serve as Komsomol raikom secretaries; of an unspecified number to work on construction enterprises in the Far East; of the "70" to serve as assistant politotdel directors of the MTS for Komsomol affairs; of the "600" for assignment to teacher training courses; and of the "200" to serve as brigadiers for lumber work.[28]

The Komsomol also had an important role to play with respect to military and physical training. Twenty-four Komsomol raikoms in the Western Oblast had paid military organizers on their staff.[29] Their task was to supervise Komsomol military activities and to assist in the annual preparations for conscription. The raikoms were forbidden to use these workers on any assignment not connected with their military duties. All Komsomols were required to participate in the military training program of Osoaviakhim, including the summer camps which provided pre-military training. The local cells were also expected to liquidate illiteracy among recruits, to conduct political agitation among them, and to report on the social and political outlook of those called up for military service. In addition, the Komsomols had a special patronage relationship with the military units stationed in their localities; they were counted upon, among other things, to assist in educational work and in political instruction.[30]

Physical culture also figured largely on the agenda of Komsomol activities, though the obkom bureau expressed itself as extremely dissatisfied with the quality of supervision in the field. The lower-echelon workers assigned to this area apparently posed a particularly difficult problem; at its meeting of December 29, 1933, the obkom bureau noted "painful phenomena — drunkenness, hooligan excesses, self-seeking, laxity, intrigues, and embezzlements . . ."[31] Nevertheless, the popularity of sports was increasing, and on October 14 the bureau approved an olympiad to celebrate the fifteenth anniversary of the Komsomol.

The obkom bureau also exerted constant pressure to strengthen Komsomol representation in the schools and higher educational institutions. The mobilization of 600 Komsomols to serve as teachers in rural schools has already been noted; the bureau also sought to use such influence as it possessed to improve the wretched living conditions of rural teachers.[32] Particularly close attention was paid to the FZU's (factory schools) and tekhnikums of the oblast, and to some extent at least, the Komsomol leadership tended to identify with the complaints of the students and to intervene in situations where the state of the schools was particularly deplorable. On September 21, 1932, for example, the bureau sharply criticized the Lyudinovo FZU because it lacked books, paper, and technical equipment, and the living conditions of the students were totally unsatisfactory.[33] On November 20, 1933, it issued a sweeping condemnation of conditions in the agricultural tekhnikums of the oblast.[34] Again it pointed to an absence of books and equipment, bad living conditions in the dormitories, the low scholastic performance of the students, and the flight of students from the tekhnikums. The Komsomol membership was enjoined to take the leadership in eliminating these defects.

While antireligious work was supposed to play an important role in Komsomol activities, the protocols of the obkom bureau reveal considerable dissatisfaction with progress on this front. On November 17, 1933, for example, the secretariat of the obkom heard a report by the head of the League of the Godless (SVB) and the director of its kultprop (culture and propaganda) department.[35] The report noted a sharp decline in antireligious work and the disintegration of a number of SVB cells, which was attributed to the prevalence among Komsomols of "a right-wing opportunistic view" that religion had been entirely eliminated. In challenging this view the reporters pointed to a considerable increase in the frequency of all kinds of religious celebrations which were causing delays in agricultural work. The secretariat resolved again to stamp out these stubborn relics of the past by launching a campaign for the revival of SVB cells and the activization of Komsomol antireligious agitation.

As might be expected, great stress was placed on work with Pioneers — on the organization of Pioneer detachments, clubs, and summer camps. These were intended to be the center of children's activities outside the school; through games, dances, singing, stage plays, hobby circles, and social work the Pioneers were supposed to be inducted into the values of Soviet society and taught to become pillars of its future strength. The role of the Komsomol was one of patronage and leadership; it was expected to supply the initiative and organizing talent to mold the children into loyal and devoted subjects of the regime.

Here too conception outran performance, and the protocols of the obkom bureau record many inadequacies in work with Pioneers. Some Komsomols were apparently reluctant to serve as leaders of Pioneer groups, and the turnover among them created serious problems.[36] There were great difficulties in obtaining adequate equipment and financial support for Pioneer clubs and summer camps.[37] During the summer of 1932 there was a mass exodus from the Pioneer camps as the result of atrocious conditions, and while members of the secretariat reported that this experience was not repeated in 1933, they also noted that in two of the camps children had to sleep on the floor for a whole month and that necessary equipment was still lacking.[38]

Among its many other responsibilities, the obkom bureau supervised the Pioneer press of the oblast. On January 17, 1933 it took the editors of *Yunii Pioner* (Young Pioneer) to task for a gross political error. The editors, it seemed, had allowed a sentence to pass which stated: "On the foundation of ferrous metallurgy we are quietly reaching the approaches to socialism." This sentence, stated the bureau, "although confused and ununderstandable, contained two opportunistic mistakes — we do not go quietly toward socialism but under conditions of class struggle; we have already entered the period of socialism, so we cannot find ourselves on its approaches." [39] A number of "gross mistakes" were also uncovered in another article. The editor received a reprimand, and the bureau decided that the staff of the newspaper needed strengthening.

Internal Organizational Problems

During this period the oblast Komsomol organization also faced a variety of internal organizational problems. The paid oblast staff consisted of seventeen responsible and four technical workers; they were overburdened by the multiplicity of their responsibilities.[40] Like their opposite numbers in the Party, they took their cue from the center, moving from one emergency to another, depending on which was of uppermost concern at the time. Their organization paralleled that of the Party, and they functioned through the Komsomol raikoms which in turn supervised the primary Komsomol cells. The raikom secretaries who were harassed and bombarded by a constant flow of directives from the oblast not infrequently either ignored them or went through the motions of compliance. Occasionally, the obkom bureau made an example of raikom secretaries who took refuge in such tactics. Thus, on August 28, 1933, the bureau administered a rebuke to the Kozelsk secretary who had forwarded fictitious figures on the number of non-Party youth who had been drawn into Komsomol work.[41] The turnover among raikom secretaries was high, and given the heavy load of responsibilities which was heaped on them, it is easy to understand why.

Relations with the Party were not always smooth and easy, despite the fact that it was clearly understood that the Komsomol was the subordinate organization. Eager Komsomol leaders sought to take the initiative, and their senior Party colleagues occasionally reacted contemptuously and bureaucratically by overruling the actions of the Komsomol. One such situation found its way into the obkom bureau protocol of September 17, 1932, when the Komsomol bureau decided to request the Party obkom to inform a Party raikom that such a relationship was "intolerable." [42] To avoid such conflicts, efforts were made to draw Party members into Komsomol work, and by December 1932, 5.1 per cent of the oblast Komsomol organization consisted of Party members.[43] But this was considered too small to be satisfactory, and an energetic campaign was launched both to accelerate the entrance of Komsomols into the Party and to "attach" Party members to Komsomol work. The latter was described as "one of the most important conditions for strengthening proletarian leadership in the Komsomol."

Membership policies represented another problem area. During this period the local Komsomol organizations were being urged to increase their numbers, to attract leaders among the youth into their ranks, and to put special emphasis on recruiting young people of proper proletarian social origin. At the same time, for reasons which are obscure, the membership rolls of the oblast Komsomol dropped sharply. During the first quarter of 1933, for example, the oblast organization lost 4,203 members.[44] In Smolensk alone, the loss was 2,236 members, of whom 1,811 were industrial workers. Pressed to fill the gap, a number of the raion organizations apparently began to recruit indiscriminately. This too proved unacceptable. At a meeting on August 3, 1933, the obkom bureau rebuked the Komarichsky raikom for accepting 64 members out of 71 applicants. To make matters worse, of the 64 accepted, 32 were middle peasants, while only one was a worker, 14 were poor peasants, and 17 were collective farmers.[45] At subsequent meetings similar rebukes were administered to a large number of raikoms for recruiting too many white-collar workers and employees.[46] Worker indifference was manifest in the difficulties which the local Komsomol organizations encountered in meeting their proletarian quotas.[47]

One of the interesting curiosities that emerges from the protocols is the apparent unreliability of Komsomol membership data during this period. Membership accounting was careless in the extreme, and hundreds and even thousands of so-called members who were on the rolls simply could not be located. Thus when the membership lists of certain local Komsomol cells were turned over by the raikoms to the newly established Railroad Political Sections losses of hundreds of "paper" members were disclosed.[48] The situation was denounced by the obkom bureau as "intolerable," but the discussion tended to suggest that the situation was so common as almost to be considered normal.

A central concern of the obkom bureau was the shaping of the rank-and-file membership into a loyal amalgam. All Komsomols were supposed to engage in political studies, and from time to time the bureau reviewed progress in this field. The plans approved by the bureau included courses in the history of the Party, study circles in Marxism-Leninism, and periodic lectures and reports on current political themes.[49] Enrollees in courses were graded; certificates were issued on completion of the courses, and premiums were awarded to the best students. In addition, there were special courses for the training of Komsomol cell secretaries, who were expected to provide ideological leadership in the groups to which they were assigned.[50] Indeed, Komsomol members were expected to teach as well as study. In rural areas, where illiteracy was still rife, great stress was placed on having Komsomols read newspapers and magazines aloud to the illiterate; reading was organized within collective farm brigades and took place during pauses of work in the fields.

But in rural areas especially, performance fell far short of plan. Reviewing the work of a political school in a collective farm cell, the obkom bureau noted on November 17, 1933, that the propagandist in charge of the school had himself never read a history of the Party or Stalin's *Problems of Leninism*, that the students did not bother to prepare their lessons, that there were few books, pencils, or equipment, that students sat through the classes in boredom and saw little or no connection between the classroom work and the problems of the collective farm.[51]

The rural Komsomol cells apparently presented an especially difficult problem, and "pathological phenomena" abounded. At a meeting of the secretariat on July 19, 1933, for example, these "shortcomings" were frankly aired.[52] In a number of raions, Komsomols were reported as abandoning the collective farms in large numbers, plundering socialist property, and violating labor discipline on a mass scale. While these difficulties were undoubtedly intensified by the objective hardships of the period, they also point to a very considerable gulf between the pretensions of the oblast leadership and actual practice at the grass roots. The closing of the gap was no easy matter.

The Impact of the Purges on the Komsomol

In the period after 1934 the Smolensk Archive is particularly illuminating on the impact of the purges on the Komsomol. In the aftermath of the Kirov affair a hunt began to eliminate so-called "class-hostile elements" from the Komsomol, as well as from the Party. The report of Kogan, the obkom Komsomol secretary, on the Komsomol discussion of the closed letter on the Kirov assassination revealed a surprising amount of ferment within Komsomol ranks.[53] Youth and rashness combined to produce a degree of plain-speaking which older and more experienced Party members had learned to avoid. Anti-Stalinism was much in evidence. It was manifested in such student acts as scrawling over a portrait of Stalin and inscribing beneath, "The Party blushes for your lies." [54] There were reports of rural Komsomols in a number of raions singing counterrevolutionary verses which ran: "When Kirov was killed they allowed free trade in bread; when Stalin is killed, all the kolkhozes will be divided up." [55] A Komsomol school director, serving as a propagandist, declared: "Lenin wrote in his will that Stalin could not serve as leader of the Party." [56] Another teacher accused Stalin of having transformed the Party into a gendarme over the people.[57] A nine-year-old Pioneer was reported to have shouted, "Down with Soviet Power! When I grow up, I am going to kill Stalin." [58] An eleven-year-old student was overheard saying, "Under Lenin we lived well, but under Stalin we live badly." [59] And a sixteen-year-old student was said to have declared, "They killed Kirov; now let them kill Stalin." [60] There were even occasional expressions of sympathy for the opposition. A worker Komsomol was quoted as saying, "They have slandered Zinoviev enough; he did a great deal for the Revolution." [61] A Komsomol propagandist in answer to a question denied that Zinoviev had any hand in the Kirov affair and described him as an "honored leader and cultivated man." [62] An instructor of a raion Komsomol committee came out in open support of the views of Zinoviev.[63]

Trenchant criticism of Komsomol and Party policies circulated within Komsomol ranks. One student in the Smolensk Pedagogical Institute described the Komsomol as "a worthless organization to which come those who have nothing to do." [64] Another observed, "I am a Komsomol and nothing will come of it." [65] Still another described the collective farms as not "profitable" and "leading the peasants to ruin." [66]

As late as 1935 such voices of dissent were still to be heard in Komsomol ranks, though already many were seeking protection in denunciations and tale-bearing. Indeed, the Archive reveals many an unsavory case of denunciation of friends, relatives, and even husbands and wives.[67] But there were also those who remained loyal to their friends or to their own standards of truth and justice, even at the cost of their careers and sometimes their lives. The obkom Komsomol secretary Kogan reported the case of one Fedorov who rushed to defend a fellow-student who had been excluded from the Komsomol as a counterrevolutionary, declaring, "Vasya is not a counterrevolutionary; like Trotsky, he only wants to become famous in the Institute." [68] And when Federov in turn came under fire, the director of the Institute rose to his defense, and by way of reward lost his job. Cases such as these intimidated the brave and frightened the fearful, though they did not prevent one anonymous group of students from writing to Stalin that "bandits were passing judgment on good people." [69] But as the number of those charged with counterrevolution multiplied, there were fewer and fewer defenders, since those who protested usually discovered that the assumed guilt of the accused merely carried over to those who were foolhardy enough to come to his aid.

As the hysteria of the Great Purge mounted, the Komsomol, like the Party, found itself caught up in a holocaust of mutual denunciations. Many Komsomols lost their jobs with the loss of their Komsomol cards; some lost their lives when their records were turned over to the NKVD. Desperation accelerated the suicide rate, and the pall of suspicion which enveloped the organization stifled hope and enthusiasm. The heaviness of the atmosphere led one student to write in 1937, "Everything is closed in, stuffy, and repugnant; one wants to destroy everyone, or simply kill oneself." [70]

The Komsomol purge reached its climax in 1937 when the central leadership was decimated and the Western Oblast apparatus in turn was largely destroyed in the wake of the purge of Rumyantsev and the group which surrounded him. The mood of the period is perhaps best conveyed by some extracts from a report to an oblast Komsomol conference held on October 11, 1937.[71] The report was delivered by one Comrade Manayev who succeeded the discredited Kogan as first secretary of the oblast Komsomol. After praising the Stalin Constitution and the Five Year Plans, he turned to the damage being done to the Soviet Union by Fascist spies and diversionists. "Train wrecks with loss of human lives, poisoning of workers, terror, wrecking of factories, arson, and diversion — these are the paths traveled by our enemies, who are trying . . . on the instructions of the German and Japanese intelligence service to undermine the might of the first socialist state of workers and peasants in the world." "These Fascists," he charged, "penetrated even into the Central Committee of the Komsomol — trying to restore the rule of the landowners and capitalists, trying to undermine the Communist educa-tion of the youth. They have been able to do this undermining work be-cause most Komsomol organizations are not vigilant enough. Moral cor-ruption, bribery, and obsequiousness are sown by our enemies." But these enemies will be overcome. "The glorious Chekists will always receive support from the Komsomolites."

For a long time, Manayev continued:

Trotskyite-Bukharinite spies and traitors established themselves in the leader-ship of the Komsomol organization of the Western Oblast. The enemies of the people Kogan and Prikhodko [previously in charge of Komsomol work] tried to undermine political education, propaganda, and agitation work among the youth. The hostile leadership of the obkom pursued the line of the enemy-of-the-people Rumyantsev, who stated directly, "It is not necessary to teach the youth politics, science; let them guess riddles and organize dances!" Rumyan-tsev said this in a speech before the Smolensk city aktiv.

In the last two years Kogan and Prikhodko undermined 700 kolkhoz Komsomol organizations. They slowed down the development of the Stakhano-vite movements, corrupted the kolkhoz Komsomol cadres. All this went on with the permission of the head of the obkom bureau of peasant youth of the Komsomol, Nikolayev, who went from one organization to another and concealed the bourgeois origin of his father.

The defense training of the oblast Komsomol organization was undermined by the spy Uborevich. Osoaviakhim work was ruined, mainly by Vorobyov, who corrupted the youth morally and encouraged drunkenness. Various ene-mies of the people arranged mass drinking parties for the youth.

The enemies of the people, Rumyantsev, Kogan, Reznikov, and others brought special harm to the Pioneer movement of the oblast in the schools. They filled the pedagogical institutes, the tekhnikums, the intermediate schools, the houses of Pioneers, with hostile people. They ignored the resolutions of the Central Committee of the Party and the Council of People's Commissars on the school . . . In the Smolensk and Novozybkov pedagogical institutes, and in a number of tekhnikums and intermediate schools whole nests of hostile people appeared. The Pioneer organizations are infested with hostile people. Recently up to 17 former White Guardists have been discovered.

The Smolensk city organization of the Komsomol is especially infested with hostile people. Political education was disrupted throughout the organiza-tion. Out of 7,000 Komsomolites, only 4,000 have been included in studies. In Krasnogorsk raion, out of fifty political schools only ten conduct lessons — the rest conduct none . . . In Andreyevsk raion, the raikom Komsomol secre-tary is a drunkard, corrupt, has close ties with the enemies of the people, especially a certain bandit . . . In Kholm-Zhirkovsky raion the raikom secre-tary was an enemy of the people, morally corrupt, who placed his drinking companions at the head of the primary Komsomol organizations . . .

The plenum of the obkom is greatly to blame for such a bad state of affairs . . . After the Central Committee of the Party unmasked the band of Trotskyite-Bukharinite spies in the Western Oblast headed by Uborevich, Rumyantsev, and Shilman, the plenum of the obkom unmasked some enemies of the people and ousted them from leading positions, but they left in existence a bureau composed of old workers who were not a firm support in the struggle against enemies of the people. I myself am guilty of this kind of laxity . . .

Manayev then offered some statistical data which testified to the bite of the purge. During the preceding year 5,500 people had been expelled from the Komsomol. Membership in Smolensk oblast had declined to a total of 47,423 members and candidates.[72] Of these only 14,703 were kolkhozniks, and seven out of every eight kolkhozes lacked primary Komsomol organizations. From one-half to two-thirds of the members of committees and secretaries of primary Komsomol organizations were newly elected; a large percentage of the new people were very young, aged nineteen or younger. At the raion level there had been a similar turnover; at least fifty per cent of "the leading staff of the raikoms" consisted of new people.

The speeches of delegates at the plenum echoed the feverish tone of Manayev's keynote address. Manayev himself came under sharp attack because he had distributed money for medical treatment to "enemies of the people" under arrest; he replied weakly that he had made the distribution before the recipients had been "revealed" as enemies of the people. He was bitterly criticized for "criminal slowness in uprooting enemies"; the representative of the Komsomol Central Committee who was present at the plenum struck an even more ominous note when she suggested that "possibly" the bad work of the oblast Komsomol organization could be "explained by the fact that people sit there who have not been unmasked, enemies sit there who have not been exposed."

The delegates took the hint and obliged with a new torrent of denunciations.[73] A delegate from Vyazma mentioned in passing that the Vyazma raikom had lost five secretaries in the last few years and then proceeded to attack the present incumbent "as completely corrupt, a polygamist" who did not choose workers according to political and technical qualifications. She charged that the Komsomol organization was "full of hostile people"; that, though a number had been expelled, "we have only scratched the surface." The delegate from Yelnya raion added that there were many "hostile elements" among the teachers. "Out of 402 teachers, 180 are by origin priests, landowners, and in general alien." A representative of the Stalinsk raikom, after pointing to numerous expulsions in the organization, claimed that the Pedagogical Institute was still full of "enemies of the people," and that at least twenty-one out of sixty propagandists at the institute should be removed. A delegate from Yartsevo declared, "My organization should be an exemplary one, but it is not. The secretary of the committee himself is corrupt, drinks continually. The Komsomolites join him in this." And so it went with one denunciation heaped on another, while delegates vied for the privilege of identifying new victims to add to the many already destroyed. It was almost as if the Komsomol had literally become a monster devouring its young.

The Aftermath of the Great Purge

But the madness had its limits, and the signal for a change of policy came in a resolution of the January 1938 plenum of the Party Central Committee entitled, "Concerning the mistakes of Party organization in excluding Communists from the Party, concerning formal bureaucratic attitudes toward the appeals of excluded members of the VKP(b), and concerning measures to eliminate these deficiencies." The Smolensk Komsomol organization quickly took its cue from this Party action and on February 11, 1938, the obkom bureau approved its own resolution "On mistakes permitted by [certain] raikoms in connection with exclusions from the ranks of the Komsomol." [74] In condemning what it now described as "intolerable arbitrariness" in expulsion from the ranks, the bureau noted that many individuals had been "expelled as Trotskyites, accomplices of the enemy, alien, and morally decayed elements" despite the fact that "there was no concrete evidence of hostile activity" and without any discussion in Komsomol primary organizations. The bureau now called upon the lower Komsomol organizations to correct these mistakes. It enjoined them to "fight slander and . . . expose slanderers and careerists . . . to finish with unfounded mass expulsions, to establish an individualized and differentiated approach toward expulsions and restorations [of membership], to collect all the appeals of the expelled . . . to review [them], and to restore to membership all those who were expelled for insufficient reasons."

What followed had a bitter irony all its own. For such ex-Komsomols as survived the 1937 purge, restoration to membership was almost automatic and on a mass scale. The Smolensk Archive contains short case histories of over a thousand readmissions approved by the bureau of the obkom.[75] The false accusations are unblushingly recorded: "justice" takes the form of wiping the slate clean. Some samples from the record may help to convey both the thrust of the purge and what subsequent investigation disclosed:

The case of B. I. Vainer[76] — expelled for concealing from the Komsomol connections of the family abroad and the fact that his father kept hired workers. Investigation disclosed that his father did not use hired labor, and that Vainer's only connection abroad was with a brother, who worked in a USSR embassy, and with whom he corresponded.

The case of Pokhomova[77] — expelled because she tore a brochure containing the report of Comrade Stalin at the February-March plenum of the Central Committee. Investigation disclosed that the brochure was not torn maliciously, but in an argument with a Komsomolite who was trying to take it away from her.

The case of O. M. Kovaleva[78] — expelled because she allegedly came from a kulak family and her father was under arrest by the NKVD. Investigation disclosed that the household of her father was not de-kulakized.

The case of I. T. Soldatenkov[79] — expelled for expressing Trotskyite views. Investigation disclosed that he was so charged because, while in the Red Army at a political lesson he asked the leader of the circle the question: "On what front was Comrade Stalin at first, the northern or the eastern, in 1918?" Furthermore, while reading newspapers to the soldiers, the listeners asked him, "Why do enemies of the people always occupy the leading posts?" He could not answer. It was decided that he had been expelled without a basis.

The case of A. V. Gordetskaya[80] — expelled for concealing the fact that her father engaged in trade before the Revolution and had been disfranchised. Investigation revealed that her father had been a hired worker since 1917 and an invalid since 1924.

The case of L. A. Maretskaya[81] — expelled for concealing the fact that her father was a tsarist officer and her mother came from the nobility. Investigation disclosed that her father had been a private in the tsarist army, and that, while her mother came from the nobility, she had worked as a nurse in a hospital, and after the death of her first husband, had married a locksmith.

The case of Ya. K. Sinelnikov[82] — expelled because he wrote a review of a book by Voronsky who was subsequently unmasked as an enemy of the people.

The case of S. B. Mints[83] — expelled for a connection with an enemy of the people who was a fellow-worker in the same school and whom he entertained in his own house, drinking together. Investigation disclosed that there were no connections and the drinking had been done at a general school banquet.

The case of A. I. Zubov[84] — expelled because he concealed the fact that his grandmother came from a landowner family. Investigation disclosed that the grandmother, who did come from a landowner family, had married a hired laborer who worked for her father and had lived as a peasant for many years.

The case of M. Pavlenko[85] — expelled for insincerity because she denied that her father was a Polish spy. Her father was under investigation by the NKVD, but there was no evidence to implicate her in the case.

The case of L. Ye. Beininaya[86] — expelled because her father, a Jewish butcher, was deprived of voting rights as a member of a religious cult. Investigation disclosed that Beininaya did not conceal this and was an "active and disciplined Komsomolite."

In these and many hundreds of similar cases, the original accusations were annulled, and the victims were reinstated in the Komsomol. But while the bulk of appeals were acted on favorably, there were also a few that were denied. Usually, these were situations in which the NKVD had a stake. The case of A. D. Shakar may serve as an illustration.[87] Her father and brother, Latvians, had been arrested by the NKVD in Irkutsk for disseminating nationalistic views. She thereupon went to Irkutsk to intercede for them without the permission of the raion educational authorities for whom she worked. On being expelled from the Komsomol, she expressed the view that the Russians were persecuting national minorities, and especially Latvians. She was alleged to have said, "Russians are not touched but Latvians are all put in prison." The obkom bureau refused her petition for reinstatement. In still another case involving one V. M. Poladino, who was under arrest by the organs of the NKVD and had been expelled from the Komsomol because of a connection with an "enemy of the people," the obkom bureau, too, refused to intervene.[88]

Except for such occasional grim reminders, the note which the oblast Komsomol leadership now struck was one of reconciliation and forgiveness, of relief that the worst of the purge was over, and that a fresh start could be made. A vigorous campaign was launched to attract youth into the ranks of the Komsomol, and it was attended with considerable success. At the third plenum of the obkom, on June 29, 1938, Comrade Lomonosova, the representative of the Komsomol Central Committee, noted with pride that the oblast had added 30,000 new members between January and the end of May.[89] She warned, however, that the newcomers posed a difficult problem of assimilation, that they needed to be educated and assigned specific tasks. ". . . In judging a man, admitting him into the Komsomol," she declared, "we should not only be interested in his autobiography, whether he drinks, whether he reads newspapers, but we should study the man, study his inclinations, his desires, his abilities, and in admitting him into the Komsomol, at the bureau of the raikom or the primary organization come to an agreement on what work he will do, what he wants to do, and right there at the bureau of the raikom, tell the primary organization how work should be organized with those Komsomolites whom the bureau of the raikom admitted."

After the debilitating effect of the purge, the Komsomol faced a massive task of reconstruction. The speakers at the obkom plenum made this clear. The great majority of raikom secretaries were new to their jobs, with little training or experience. As a result of the influx of newcomers, a large part of the membership consisted of Komsomols who had still to be made aware of their responsibilities. Some of the newly formed primary organizations had not even been formally sanctioned by the raikoms. The new obkom first secretary, Nosov, referred to one kolkhoz, which reported the existence of a Komsomol organization. On investigation, it was discovered that no one was in charge and that not even a secretary had been provided.[90] Nor was this the only case of its kind. One speaker noted that only five of the twenty-seven kolkhoz organizations in his raion had political circles. Mass recruitment left its impact in a dilution of political indoctrination.

In important respects the July 1938 obkom plenum offered striking contrasts with earlier Komsomol assemblies. While there was still an occasional reference "to the work of the enemy," on the whole the gathering was free of the hysterical denunciations which had marked the 1937 plenum. So far as the Komsomol was concerned, it was clear that the purge had passed its peak, and that the forces of rehabilitation were in full command. Another notable characteristic of the plenum was its deëmphasis of emergency economic campaigns as a prime Komsomol responsibility. The primary stress of the plenum was on political indoctrination, on defense work, on sports, and other so-called "cultural" activities. Komsomolites were expected to do "public work," to serve as pace-setters in industry and agriculture, but the special mobilizations and drafts of the late twenties and early thirties were, for the moment at least, a thing of the past. After the hurly-burly of the First Five Year Plan and the convulsive eruption of the purge, the life of the Komsomol seemed to be settling into a more even routine.

At this point the record of Komsomol activities in the Smolensk Archive stops, but one not unimportant footnote remains to be added. Scattered through the Archive for the year 1938 are long lists of names of young people, some Party members and some Komsomols, who were recommended by Party organizations to fill the vacancies in oblast public life created by the Great Purge. For those who were chosen the purge meant rapid advancement at an undreamed-of rate. They marched to power over graves that were still fresh. But for them at least there was grim truth in the Soviet adage that the future belongs to the Komsomols.

22 The Godly and the Godless

The vantage point which the Smolensk Archive affords for a study of religious activity in the area is a peculiarly distorted one; the available material is largely contained in reports of the League of the Godless and Party documents that provide guide lines for the conduct of antireligious work. Essentially what the Archive provides is a grudging evaluation of the strength of a redoubtable enemy and a detailed statement of plans and actions to destroy his influence and all his works.

Religious Life in Smolensk Guberniya during the Mid-NEP Period

Such an evaluation is contained in an informational letter dated November 17, 1925, stamped "Secret," and prepared by the Smolensk guberniya council of the USSR League of the Godless.[1] According to this report, there were still 548 Orthodox churches and 736 priests active in the guberniya. At this time the Orthodox in Smolensk, as elsewhere, were still split between the followers of the Patriarch Tikhon and the Renovationists; of the 736 priests 301 were classified as Tikhonites, 344 as Renovationists, and 91 had not declared themselves. The Tikhonites in Smolensk guberniya were headed by Bishop Ilarion, the Renovationists by Archbishop Aleksei, who in his effort to come to terms with the Communist revolution, openly proclaimed: "The atheists do divine work, and the commune is the ideal of Christianity." The Renovationist movement was declared to be "especially strong in Dorogobuzh, Yartsevo, Yelnya, and parts of Sychevsk, Vyazma, and Smolensk uzeyds." In addition, there was a small "leftist" group of believers who affiliated themselves with Metropolitan Antonin's League of the Regeneration of the Church, which called for the use of the Russian language in the Church service, the elimination of iconostasis, the use of a medical lancet during Holy Communion (to prevent poisoning), and in general stressed the spiritual rather than the ritualistic side of religion. "The chief mistake of the church," Antonin is quoted as having said, "is the fact that she did not greet the October Revolution with the ringing of bells." He dismissed both Tikhonites and Renovationists as "crabs, able by their nature to crawl backward only . . . the difference between them is that the Tikhonites are 'black' crabs, while the Renovationists are scalded ones (reddened by the Revolution)."

Despite the strength of Renovationism among the parish clergy, explained largely by the fact that it sought to eliminate the caste privileges of the "black" or monastic clergy, the mass of the Orthodox in Smolensk remained faithful to Tikhon, and the informational letter made clear that the Tikhonites were winning the struggle for the parishes. The letter also sought to differentiate between the attitudes of the peasants, artisans, and "petty-bourgeois" strata of the population, who, by and large, continued loyal to the traditional ritual and ceremonies of the church, and the "semi-proletarian" elements in the towns who, under the influence of the Revolution, were losing their faith in the "priestly" church. Appraising the latter group, the report noted: "They take a critical attitude toward the objects of the church cult, but they cannot become atheistic Communists. These strata strive to replace [the church ritual] with a more perfect faith. Their ritual no longer satisfies them, and they are drawn to the creation of a Christian philosophy. Hence the attempts of the Renovationists, of the League of the Regeneration of the Church, and of the sectarians to begin church reforms. Hence the continual growth of sectarianism in the guberniya (evangelism, Stundism, Baptism, and Adventism), which tries to substitute an evangelical philosophy of nonresistance to evil for church ritualism . . ." [2]

The letter expressed alarm at the spreading influence of sectarianism in the guberniya. Official figures listed some 2,300 sectarians who were spread over twenty-seven evangelical communes and two other groups. Actually, the report noted, the sects attracted much greater numbers, and they were increasing at the rate of at least 200 per year. "The sincere members of evangelical sects," the letter stated, "are often attracted by their sober life of mutual aid, doing good, and singing." At the same time sectarianism presented a real danger to the Soviet government because of its pacifist flavor. Sectarian influence, the letter noted, was responsible "at territorial mobilization points for many cases of a demonstrative refusal to enter military service in the Red Army."

The letter also pointed to a significant concentration of Old Believers in Smolensk and Gzhatsk uyezds, where there were sixteen churches with sixteen instructors, enrolling about 11,000 peasants. In their ranks were some of the wealthiest peasants and also former merchants and manufacturers. The more fanatical refused to send their children to school and "considered it the greatest sin to have anything to do with 'tobacco smokers' and heterodox people."

Also listed in the report were some thirty synagogues and eleven prayer houses which ministered to the Jewish believers of the guberniya.

"During the period of the Revolution," the letter declared, "the foundations of the Jewish religion were severely shaken, especially among the workers, the youth, and the artisans. The influence of the rabbis was weakened. However, in general, the religion is still strong, mainly among the petty bourgeoisie, the *déclassé* element, and the small producers . . . It must be noted that often the synagogue serves as the only social center for the Jewish population, especially in the villages . . ."[3]

The persisting strength of religious attachments in the Smolensk region had its roots in the overwhelmingly agricultural character of the area. During the early twenties the villages were still isolated and remote from the revolutionary impulses which radiated from the great urban centers. Both the Party and the Komsomol had only scattered outposts in the countryside, and the weakness of their rural organizations necessarily muffled the effect of their propaganda drives. Theoretically, at least, the struggle against religious prejudices was an inseparable part of the Communist program, but given the many pressing demands on the tiny vanguard of rural Party and Komsomol members, the energy which was at first devoted to antireligious campaigns was not great. Indeed, a careful reading of the report of the Smolensk gubkom for the period March 1, 1923, to March 1, 1924, leaves the impression that antireligious propaganda hardly figured in its activities at all.[4]

The League of the Godless

The establishment of the USSR League of the Godless in 1925, as a successor to ODGB, the Society of Friends of the Newspaper *Bezbozhnik* (Godless), provided a fresh impetus to organized antireligious work in the Smolensk area. Prior to that time, such activity was conducted in a spontaneous and unorganized fashion largely under the aegis of the Komsomol; a contemporary report described it as both "weak" and "unskillful."[5] Not infrequently the Komsomols "concerned themselves with simple rioting (persecution of priests, pulling out crosses in cemeteries, and similar 'art work')" — conduct which both outraged and stiffened the resistance of the believers.[6]

The new League of the Godless was designed to eliminate these crudities. Its rules condemned "mass antireligious agitation which by its contents and form sharply insults and ridicules the feelings of the sincerely believing part of the population, especially the peasants."[7] Citing Lenin's slogan that "the struggle against religion should be waged skillfully," it called for primary emphasis on propaganda which would explain the contradictions between religion and natural science and which would expose "the class content" of religion. Cells of the League of the Godless were to be organized in factories and shops, in villages, and in Red Army units. Working closely with the Party and Komsomol, these cells were to sponsor antireligious circles, lectures, and seminars, and disseminate publications directed toward inculcating "an atheistic way of life." Membership was to be open to "every citizen of the USSR who has the right to vote, who openly and sincerely severs his connection with a cult or religious society, with faith in God and with utopian forms of religion, and who actively works in a cell of the League of the Godless . . ."

The Archive contains an interesting set of instructions drafted by the guberniya council of the League for the use of cell organizers.[8] "The first task of the organizer," read the instructions, "is to communicate with the local Party, Soviet, trade union," and other organizations in the locality and to arrange through them for the choice of a cell bureau and secretary. "One must be especially careful and vigilant in signing up new atheists," the instructions declared, "for if the admissions are not careful enough our entire society could be discredited because of the presence of members who are not staunch enough in their atheism, or, on the contrary, who know only one, the worst aspect of antireligious propaganda — the method of crude attacks upon and ridicule of faith."

"The first task of the organized cell," the instructions continued, "should be to achieve where possible, a collective subscription to the newspaper *Bezbozhnik*." Each cell was to establish an antireligious reading room or library and an atheist corner, for which fittings in the form of placards and slogans could be ordered from the center. In addition to collective readings of *Bezbozhnik*, antireligious circles were to be organized to discuss such themes as "how the world began, how man began, the origin of life, faith and knowledge, the use and development of religious beliefs, religion and morality, Christianity and its history, church and state, Lenin and religion, methods of religious work, etc." In rural cells especially, propagandists were instructed "to discuss the Bible, according to the Bible of Comrade Yaroslavsky, to dwell on the first chapters, contrasting the Biblical legends on the origin of the world, the sun and man, with scientific facts on agronomy and the natural sciences." In addition, antireligious lectures were to be organized for the masses on similar themes. Members of the League were to encourage the development of a new revolutionary ritualism to replace the ritualism of the church; they were to take the lead in ceremonies directed by the Komsomol such as "Harvest Holidays" and "Komsomol Christmases," while at the same time refraining from provocatory actions which might have the effect of sharpening religious fanaticism. Strong efforts were to be made to attract non-Party workers and peasants, and particularly women, into the cells. "Otherwise," the instructions noted, "the atheist Communists and Komsomolites will stew in their own juice." The instructions also sought to differentiate between propaganda to be conducted in the cities and the villages. "While in the city straightforwardness and some sharpness in stating the problem is allowed, in the village a scientific and agricultural method of struggle against the evil of religion for the peasants is essential. It is necessary to draw into this work the village teacher, agronomist, and physician."

Each cell was also required to choose a worker or peasant correspondent for the newspaper *Bezbozhnik*. Directives were provided to guide their contributions. The following were typical:

> Such information as the closing of churches, mosques, etc., should be described only in exceptionally interesting cases . . . It is useful from time to time to give summaries of priestly and sectarian "taxes which touch the pocket of the peasant" . . . It is necessary to point out to the peasants the income of ministers of cults, drawing comparisons between expenditures for the priest and for the volost, or rural budget. These figures will strike a sharp blow against religion . . . It is necessary to contrast the healthy village with the semi-cultured village, which believes in holy healers and quacks . . . often the negative aspects of the peasant economy are closely connected with religion, while the positive aspects are connected with atheism. Pay special attention to this — our general task is systematically, without stopping, to spread our newspaper among the peasant masses.

Despite this effort to build a powerful antireligious movement, the League of the Godless fared badly in Smolensk. At the end of 1925 it claimed a total guberniya membership of only 2,500.[9] During the next few years its growth was far from impressive. A resolution "On stimulating and developing antireligious propaganda in the countryside," adopted by the bureau of the Smolensk gubkom on November 17, 1927, pointed out that the church and sects were still very powerful, that they had been putting forward their own candidates in soviet and cooperative elections in the villages, and that they were even collecting funds among believers for the construction of new churches.[10] The resolution condemned the League of the Godless for its inactivity and called upon Party, Komsomol, and educational authorities to intensify their propaganda on the antireligious front. As long as the NEP persisted, however, the activities of the League remained in low gear.

The Frontal Assault on Religion

The abandonment of the NEP marked a new turn in Soviet policy toward religious organizations. In the eyes of the regime the church interposed an obstacle to the successful fulfillment of the new program of collectivization and rapid industrialization, and a frontal assault was launched to diminish the power and influence of all forms of religious organization. The campaign took the form of discriminatory penalties against the clergy, of tightening restrictions on religious activity, and most important, of the closing of the churches on a mass scale.

The decision to close the churches represented state and Party policy, though almost invariably it was presented as an expression of the wishes of the people in the area. An example from the Party Archive of the Vyazma okrug committee may serve to make this clear.[11] On October 30, 1929, the antireligious commission of the okrug Party committee met to consider the closing of a church in Bukharino raion. It decreed, first, that all back taxes be collected from the believers; second, that a check be instituted on church property; and third, that an investigation be launched to determine whether the existence of the parish was legal. At the same time, the committee decided to launch an intensive agitational campaign in favor of closing the church and using the premises for "cultural" purposes. This campaign was to last two weeks, and at the end of the period the church was to be closed. On December 9, 1929, actually more than a month later, the bureau of the Vyazma okrug committee resolved that two churches would be closed, as the formula had it, on the "insistent demands" of the workers of the village.[12] The Party fraction of the okrug executive committee was then ordered to close the churches and to make them available for the "cultural" needs of the village. While the local Party leaders resorted to an appearance of consent in appropriating church properties, the formalities employed could not conceal the fact that these measures were administratively inspired. The resentment such tactics generated among the more devout peasants and the additional barriers they interposed to enrollment in the kolkhozes led the Sixteenth Party Congress (1930) to condemn such "excesses." The congress voted "to stop the closing of churches in an administrative manner fictitiously disguised as the public and voluntary wish of the population" and "to permit churches to be closed only in accord with the wishes of the predominant majority of the peasants and only with the confirmation by the provincial executive committees of the rulings of the village meetings . . ."[13]

This call for restraint and a more careful approach to the closing of churches found quick reflection in the actions of the Presidium of the Executive Committee of the Western Oblast.[14] The protocols of the presidium after the Sixteenth Party Congress contain a number of cases in which the decisions of lower governmental organs to close churches were overruled and the premises were restored to groups of believers. The pattern of resolutions of the presidium makes clear, however, that no wholesale reversal of the previous policy was involved.[15] The actions of local governmental bodies in closing churches were still upheld in the great majority of cases. The justifying reasons usually cited were that the religious needs of the believers could be met in another church which was open and not too far distant (for example, three to seven kilometers away); that the group of believers had violated their contract with the state by failing to pay taxes or to keep the premises of the church in good repair; and that "the overwhelming majority" of the population in the area had "petitioned" that the church be used to serve the "cultural" needs of the community. How truly spontaneous these petitions were the protocols of the presidium do not disclose.

During the early years of the First Five Year Plan the campaign against religious organizations attained new heights of intransigence and bellicosity. A resolution "On the tasks of antireligious work in the Western Oblast" approved by the secretariat of the Western obkom on December 16, 1929, provides an excellent illustration.[16] The resolution condemned "all religious organizations without exception" as "counter-revolutionary agents of the kulaks and Nepmen" engaged in "direct sabotage of socialist construction." It went on to state:

> The counterrevolutionary work of church and sectarian organizations in the oblast takes on the most varied forms. The church people and sectarians actively organize the disruption of the most important political campaigns and measures of the Party and Soviet government in carrying out socialist con-struction (the struggle against kolkhoz construction, against grain deliveries, undermining of cultural construction, etc.); they create illegal groupings whose aim is the struggle for the overthrow of the Soviet government and the reëstablishment of the monarchy. There is observed an attempt of the church people and sectarians to mask the kulak-Nepman leadership of the religious organizations by, on the one hand, drawing the workers and hired-laborer and poor-peasant strata of the peasants into church councils and other elected organs of religious bodies, and, on the other hand, by insinuating the church and sectarian aktiv into soviet, trade union, coöperative organizations, and their elected organs, with the aim of undermining the activity of these organizations in the task of socialist construction.

The resolution noted a considerable decline in the influence of the Renovationists and a tendency to establish a single church front under the leadership of the Tikhonites. But no kind words were spared for the Renovationists; their innovations were dismissed as merely "one of the forms of masquerade for a bitter struggle against the Soviet govern-ment." The resolution also observed that the activity of the sectarian movement, especially the Baptists and the Evangelists, had "noticeably increased." This growth was described as "the more dangerous because the sectarian movement, as well as the Renovationist, is the most adapt-able, refined, and flexible form of deception, enslavement, and oppression by the bourgeoisie of the broad toiling masses." "It is a militant weapon against the Soviet government and socialist construction." The resolution went on to note that the "sectarian aktiv consists mostly of kulaks, former merchants, policemen, gendarmes, etc. Their percentage in some raions of the oblast is as high as 70–80% . . . Developing agitation in the oblast against service in the Red Army, the sectarians attract into their com-munes some of the youth of draft age. Taking advantage of the growing attraction of the poor-peasant and middle-peasant masses of the peasantry into the kolkhozes, the sectarian organizations create their own fictitious kolkhozes and artels, organizing their own mutual aid in them."

To combat these "unhealthy" developments, the oblast Party leadership called for a vigorous intensification of antireligious propaganda. The work of the League of the Godless, now renamed the SVB, or League of Militant Atheists, was described as "very weak" and "insufficient"; "the failure to appreciate the significance of the antireligious front" was evaluated "as a direct manifestation in practice of rightist and conciliatory tendencies." Again Party, Komsomol, and educational authorities were called upon to achieve an "upsurge" of activity on the antireligious front.

Despite these exhortations, traditional religious loyalties continued to exert their influence, even among the Communist rank and file. Thus a 1930 investigation of the Party cell in the radiator foundry shop of the Lyudinovo Factory revealed that many Communists in the shop still attended church, that 70 per cent had ikons in their houses, that 11.5 per cent had baptized their children after joining the Party, and that one Party candidate had celebrated his successful passage of the purge by baptizing his child four days later.[17] One of the more piquant scandals was occasioned by the discovery that the secretary of the cell of League of Militant Atheists in the Smolensk railroad station both baptized his children and hung ikons at home.[18]

The Persistence of Religious Attachments

Authoritative testimony to the stubborn persistence of religious attachments in the Western Oblast is provided by a secret memorandum dated December 22, 1936, and circulated by the obkom secretary Rumyantsev to all raikom secretaries as a prelude to a renewed antireligious campaign.[19] The memorandum indicated that there were still 836 priests and ministers and 852 houses of religious worship in the oblast (including churches, synagogues, and all varieties of chapels). In the city of Smolensk alone there were four Orthodox churches, a synagogue, a Roman Catholic church, and a sect of evangelical Christians. In some raions the number of churches in operation was particularly large; Pochep raion listed thirty-five churches and Velizh fifteen. "Attendance at church, especially in the villages," the memorandum noted, "is still very extensive, especially on religious holidays. In many raions . . . the activity of religious organizations has noticeably increased. This is manifested in increased church attendance, especially of young people, the baptism of children, even of school age, and the establishment of magnificent public church services." Then the memorandum cited some examples: "In Usvyaty on June 12, the local priest organized a feast day on which a huge number of people left the village. On the same day 50 children were baptized. In Sukhinichi and Brasovo there were cases of baptism of children of school age. In Khvastovichi in the Buyanovsk church before Easter there were more than 300 children at confession. In Karachevsk raion in the summer the priest organized a service on 'the falling of the rain' . . . In Velizh itself 4 churches and 2 synagogues still are in operation. Cases of baptism of children and church weddings are frequent. In one of the churches the choir consists primarily of young people. In Velizh there is still a chapel with some kind of 'curative, divine' source — the fountain springs from the ground."

Special concern was again expressed over the power of the sectarians, of whom the most widespread were the Baptists and evangelists, and who numbered more than 6,000 believers in the oblast. The memorandum contains the following account of their activity:

It is necessary to describe especially the work of the Smolensk sect of "Evangelical Christians." The sect meets regularly on Sundays from 6:00 to 8:00 P.M. in Zadnepr raion, Nizhni-Profinternovskaya Street, No. 11. This house belongs to a certain invalid. It is an old, dark, dirty, sooty hut. The furnishings — a table and benches. The leader of the sect is a certain Vaseichenkov. He does not work anywhere and lives only by this "work." The sect includes up to 80 people, not less than half of whom are women. There are also a number of young people. The majority of the people are middle-aged. We did not succeed in defining the membership exactly, but apparently they are working people — builders, unskilled laborers, peasants — but there are also kolkhozniks.

The "service" of the sect on Sundays consists of reading and singing various prayers from the Gospel. At the "service" Vaseichenkov first places a tablecloth on the table into which the sectarians "sacrifice" money — three, five, and ten rubles. One such "service" gives a decent profit to Vaseichenkov . . . Vaseichenkov himself is connected with the Moscow center of "Evangelical Christians" and sometimes goes to Leningrad and Moscow. He also "leads" sects in the provinces around Smolensk. He makes trips to Yelnya very often. In Yelnya raion this sect numbers up to 150 people. Its center is in the village of Danino, Daninsk village soviet. The kolkhoznik Vasili Gerasov "leads" the sect. Kolkhozniks and individual farmers come from Glinkovsk and Yekomovichsk raions to the "service" in Danino.

A large sectarian nest is Velizh raion . . . which has a sectarian group of up to 150 people. This year the sectarians came out against conscription into the Red Army . . . Groups of sectarians work actively in Bryansk, Safonovo, Dorogobuzh, Nevlya, Kardymovo, Krasnaya Gora, and other raions.

All these religious organizations do counterrevolutionary work, incorrectly interpret to the rest of the "believing" groups of the population the events in our country and abroad, and spread various counterrevolutionary rumors. For example, speaking of the needlessness of increasing the harvest in the kolkhozes, they base this on the fact that "a good harvest leads to gluttony." Coming out against studies, they say that "science obscures the truth." Speaking of the Constitution, the sectarians in Krasnogorsk raion agitate that "the Bolsheviks are against religion, but in the Constitution they themselves wrote what is written in the Gospel." The counterrevolutionary activity of the church people and sectarians is noticeably increasing.

Lately the activity of various religious communes has increased. The church *dvadstatka* in Gordeyev petitioned for the opening of the earlier closed church, pointing to "religious freedom." In Prechistensk raion the leader of the sect, the evangelist Savchenkov (village of Lomonosovo) recruits new sectarians into the sect and he seeks a special hut for prayer meetings . . . It is necessary to note that the Party organizations on the local levels very often do not attach any significance to this work. In the raions they usually say "only the old people are believers," but they do not note that very often the sects and religious communes attract young people — girls and boys — and remold them along the necessary lines. In the Smolensk sect of evangelists — girls and boys "visit" the services, say prayers, and all of them either work somewhere or even study. But no one, either in the Zadnepr raion organizations (Party and Komsomol) or in the city organizations, knows who they are and why they joined the sect.

A similar situation prevails in other raions, where the raion organizations sometimes know only that the sect exists, but do not know who belongs to it . . . The leaders of the raion usually say that the organization of atheists should do antireligious work. But the League of Atheists is such a weak organization in regard to cadres, apparatus, and funds, that it is clearly unable to manage antireligious work. In addition, in the majority of raions up to this time there are no organizations of the League of Atheists . . . The active participation of all Party and Komsomol organizations in antireligious work is necessary. Antireligious work should be a component of all mass political agitation and propaganda of Party and Komsomol organizations . . .

Circulating this memorandum to the raikoms, Rumyantsev noted that "from these data you will see how great the hostile work of various religious organizations still is and to what extent the Party organizations have neglected antireligious work and the struggle against the counterrevolutionary influence of the church and the sectarians on the remaining strata of our population." And he continued, "The Obkom orders you":

1. To read these materials at a meeting of the aktiv with the participation of secretaries of Party committees and Party organizers of the primary Party organizations and to discuss the status of antireligious work in the raion.

2. In conformity with the decree of the Bureau of the Obkom on mass political work in the village, see to it that especially those groups of the population in enterprises, kolkhozes, towns, and villages which least of all have been attracted into public work and which until recently were not extensively drawn into our cultural and political work will be included in this work.

3. Antireligious work should be a component of the mass work of Party and Komsomol organizations and should be included in the program of all our Party and Komsomol circles and courses.

4. It is necessary to organize mass antireligious work so that without hurting the feelings of the believers, through explanations and persuasion, we can prove to the believers the counterrevolutionary essence of every kind of religion. Decisively prohibit any tricks in regard to the believers, and demand

of all primary Party and Komsomol organizers increased daily work in eliminating the old religious survivals among the remaining believers.[20]

The documents in the Archive suggest that this directive had only a limited effect. Rumyantsev's instructions were transmitted to the primary Party cells, which included the item in the agenda of Party meetings, made gestures by way of fulfillment, and passed on to other matters. The Party committee of the First Oblast Clinical Hospital provides a typical case. On January 4, 1937, it listened to a report that the religious sects were increasing their activity, especially among the youth.[21] The presence of sectarians on the hospital staff was duly noted. The committee decided to create a cell of atheists in the hospital and to discuss antireligious questions in all political study circles. A meeting was scheduled at the hospital club for the evening of January 6 to hear a report "On the Class Essence of Christmas." Solemn resolutions were made to devote more time to antireligious agitation. It may be that these resolutions were put into effect, though more than an element of doubt is aroused by the fact that no protocols of Party committee meetings for the rest of the year 1937 carried any references whatsoever to antireligious work. The speech of Manayev, the first secretary of the Komsomol obkom, at a Komsomol conference on October 11, 1937, only serves to reinforce such doubts.[22] In forthright fashion he described the oblast League of Militant Atheists as practically defunct, though like Rumyantsev before him, he also called for its revival in order to combat "the counterrevolutionary propaganda" of the priests.[23]

The Smolensk Archive thus provides little in the way of evidence to indicate that the League of Militant Atheists justified its title. Indeed the disparaging references to it in Party pronouncements suggest that, in the Smolensk area at least, it was not much more than a paper organization. In Smolensk, as elsewhere, the pressures of Soviet life tended to discourage religiosity and church attendance, particularly on the part of the younger generation. Yet, if the grudging tributes of the Party are to be credited, the Smolensk Archive provides a surprising testimonial to the persisting vitality of the religious appeal under conditions of persecution and oppression. The strength of the sects was particularly striking; what made them especially obnoxious to the regime was their apparent attraction for young people on whom the Party laid special store as the key to the future.

The Situation of the Jews

The Jews of the Western Oblast presented a special problem. According to the 1926 census figures, there were approximately 94,445 Jews in the oblast, of whom 12,887 were concentrated in the city of Smolensk and the rest largely scattered among the small towns of the oblast.[24] During the tsarist period, the effect of occupational restrictions upon the Jews was to force most of them into petty trade. In the Smolensk area they tended to settle in the market towns, making their living as merchants, peddlers, middlemen, and artisans. The great majority were devoutly orthodox, and the synagogue formed the center of communal life.

The impact of the October Revolution on these Jewish communities was profoundly disruptive, both in a religious and in an economic sense. The Smolensk Archive contains a report on one of these communities in the village of Lyubavichi, Smolensk uyezd, which was prepared in 1925 at the instance of the Smolensk gubkom and which is particularly interesting because of its exposure of the plight of the village Jews.[25]

According to the information of the Volost Executive Committee [noted the report], the population of the village of Lyubavichi consists of 1,931 people, including 967 Jews. If these figures are compared with the figures for the population census of 1921, it immediately becomes evident that while the non-Jewish population of the village is gradually increasing (by 20 people), the Jewish population, on the contrary, is declining sharply (it decreased by 355 people). It is easy to explain the reasons for this decline by the economic status of the Jewish population in the village.

Before the Revolution, the economy of the population of the village of Lyubavichi rested on two bases: flax and . . . the rabbi. This was an important center for the preparation of flax, which was processed here and shipped by rail. It was also the residence of the famous Rabbi Shneyerson, and a center of Chasidim [an ultra-orthodox Jewish sect]. Chasidim poured into the village of Lyubavichi every day from all sides, including a number of merchants, who supplied the local population. Artisanry and handicrafts flourished, despite the scornful attitude toward productive work on the part of the "court" (the rabbi and his clique).

The imperialist and civil wars undermined the economic foundation of the village. Flax did not appear at the markets. The court of the rabbi and the nest of Chasidim were destroyed. Most of the population were deprived of their former sources of subsistence. The impoverishment of the population began . . .

The reporter noted, however, that some relief was provided by the American Society of Emigrants from the village; through it help was extended both to relatives and to the village as a whole.

At the time the report was written, there were 205 Jewish families still in the village, of whom forty-three were classified as farmers, eighty as artisans and handicraftsmen, twenty-seven as merchants, and the rest as without definite occupation. The Jewish farmers represented a new social group who made their appearance after the Revolution. In 1918 they seized the nearby estate of "Gonorovo" with more than 400 dessyatins of land and organized it into an agricultural collective called "Pakhar" (the Plowman). But their success was short-lived. Neighboring peasants laid claim to much of the estate, and their claims were upheld by the Uyezd Land Commission. As a result the new collective decayed, though individual Jewish farmers were able to hold onto some limited strips of land which were insufficient for their needs, and which made it necessary for them to supplement their incomes by outside wage-earning. Some supported themselves by trading in samogan (illegal home-distilled liquor); others engaged in carting, handicrafts, and trade.

Of the eighty artisans, twenty were shoemakers, nine blacksmiths, and six tailors. There was very little work, and most of the artisans were poverty-stricken. Because of the heavy tax burden, the report observed, "a new type of artisan has been created — the underground artisan who hides his tools and conceals himself from the vigilant eyes of the finance agent." Trade in the village was also poorly developed, and a significant number of families had no occupation at all. Some were supported by their relatives abroad or by children in other cities of the USSR.

Since Lyubavichi had been a traditional Chasidic stronghold, "religious fanaticism" was strong. The synagogue was well attended, and the Sabbath was generally observed by the closing of shops and even artisans' coöperatives. On Friday night candles burned in most of the houses. Two ritual slaughterers ministered to the needs of the community. Children attended "cheders," Jewish religious schools which were forbidden by law. But the report also noted some signs of religious disaffection. "Some of the 'advanced' artisans have formed a separate group. They violate the Sabbath rest, work on Saturdays, eat non-kosher meat, and do not attend synagogues."

The attitude toward the Soviet government and the Communist Party was predominantly negative. In the words of the report, "The Jews fear the government and also the Communists. They do not speak aloud about the defects of the Soviet apparatus and of individual workers; but, fearing punishment, they do it among themselves, joking surreptitiously in Yiddish. There seems to be a feeling among them that they are without rights. The militiaman is feared as was the tsarist gendarme." There were no Jewish Communists in Lyubavichi volost and only ten members of the Komsomol. Most of the children still used Yiddish as their mother tongue and spoke only a broken Russian. The report observed, "In the Pioneer detachment the work suffers in view of the fact that among the Jewish children work is also done in Russian, which they cannot master. Completely different results may be expected if the educational work, both among the Komsomols and the Jewish Pioneers, were to be conducted in Yiddish."

Finally, the report noted that Jewish "nationalists and chauvinists" had "built themselves a nest" in the village. Originally the activity focused in a club organized by the Hehalutz where Hebrew was spoken and secret meetings were held. The club was dissolved on the initiative of the volost Party committee. After the closing of the club the Hehalutz organized an agricultural commune, "Teil-tsur," on land rented from the Uyezd Land Administration. The commune, which numbered thirty-two people, chiefly from the "petty bourgeoisie" and the "intelligentsia," had as its goal the preparation of agricultural workers for immigration to Palestine. Of the members of the commune, the report observed, "In politics they give the impression of being children, but they lie like adults. They conceal their membership in and connection with the Hehalutz." The Hehalutz was accused of conducting underground work among the youth of the village.

In miniature form, Lyubavichi mirrored the problems of most of the "market-town" Jewish communities in the Smolensk area and perhaps elsewhere. The economic foundations of these communities were crumbling, and orthodoxy came under increasingly severe attack. Some built their hopes on an escape to Palestine; the great majority of the youth saw no alternative except to come to terms with the Revolution and to find a niche in the new society which was sweeping all before it. In the process, many fled to the cities, divorced themselves from their old religious attachments, and sought assimilation in the stream of Soviet life. By and large, it was the elderly and the middle-aged who clung tenaciously to orthodox practices, and even they confronted increasing difficulty in maintaining their traditional ties.

During this period, Communist organizational and propaganda activity among the Jewish population was carried out under the direction of the Guberniya Evsektsia, or Jewish section of the Smolensk gubkom. A report of the Smolensk Evsektsia for 1926 estimated that the Jewish population of the guberniya numbered about 30,000, of whom, however, only 732 were Party members or candidates.[26] The Evsektsia operated in the localities through plenipotentiaries, who, where possible, were recruited from Jewish Party members or candidates to work with the local Jewish communities. Where no Party members were available, the work was entrusted to members of the Komsomol. The report noted the existence of seven Komsomol and an unspecified number of Pioneer detachments which had been authorized to use Yiddish in order to attract the Jewish youth who had difficulty speaking Russian.

The primary mission of the Evsektsia was to destroy the power of orthodoxy and to attract the Jewish "masses" into the Communist fold. In the words of a 1926 resolution of Smolensk Evsektsia workers, "Komsomols, Pioneers, teachers, reading-room and library personnel, leading organs of associations of Jewish artisans — all these are called upon to wage a struggle against the rabbi, the religious school (cheder), the religious singer (Khasan), the ritual slaughterer, Hehalutz, Zionism, etc." [27]

The Evsektsia workers were urged to intensify their activity in the small towns, to organize craftsmen clubs, reading rooms and libraries in order to eliminate the influence of clericalism on the Jewish toilers.

At the same conference of workers of the Evsektsia, held on October 29–30, 1926, the question of settling the Jewish population on the land also came in for extended consideration.[28] A report to the conference noted that approximately one hundred Jewish families from the Smolensk area had been resettled in the Crimea, but that OZET, the Society for Agricultural Settlement of Jewish Toilers, worked very poorly in Smolensk. The Evsektsia workers resolved that OZET be activized, that a guberniya convention be called, that an explanatory campaign be launched, and that Jews who desired to settle on the land be promptly registered and carefully selected to insure against failure of the experiment.

During the next years the Jewish land resettlement program began to show some results. A report to the executive committee of the Western Oblast dated August 1, 1929, noted that forty-five Jewish kolkhozes embracing 3,000 persons had been established in the oblast, and that an additional 2,180 Jews from the Western Oblast had been resettled on the land in other parts of the Soviet Union.[29] Subsequently, in the wake of the famine in the Ukraine in 1932–33, when a number of the Jewish kolkhozes in that area were decimated, a sizable group of Jewish kolkhoz families from the Western Oblast were resettled in the Ukraine by a ukaze from the center. The Smolensk Archive contains a secret order dated December 28, 1933, from the chairman of the Resettlement Commission to the Pesochensk raion authorities requiring them to dispatch twenty-four Jewish kolkhoz families from the raion to help fill the depopulated Jewish kolkhozes of the Ukraine.[30]

The efforts of the Evsektsia to settle Jews on the land was paralleled and supplemented by attempts to organize Jewish artisan artels and to draw Jews into factory work. The 1929 report to the executive committee of the Western Oblast took note of these efforts, but it concluded that much still remained to be done. The "déclassé" elements from the Jewish villages did not find the readjustment easy, and the local authorities did little to smooth the transition. As former traders, many of the Jews were deprived of voting rights, and this carried occupational disabilities for parents and children alike. The 1929 report pointed out that in Nevlya the Jews constituted 80 per cent of all those who were deprived of the franchise, in Klintsy 76 per cent, in Starodub 72 per cent, and in Pochinok 77 per cent.[31] The barrier of disfranchisement was not easily hurdled.

The persistence of anti-Semitism created still another difficult problem. While this lively relic of tsarist days was officially condemned by the Party leadership, in practice popular anti-Semitism remained strong and even penetrated Party and Komsomol circles. A not untypical example was described in 1929 by A. Chemerisky, the secretary of the Central Board of the Evsektsia, as follows:

In the Mechanical Works No. 13 in Bryansk, a gang of young workers constantly baited a young Jewish worker, Furmanov. In the gang there were six Komsomols, of whom two were members of the bureau of the cell. The cell paid no attention to these goings on . . . A general anti-Semitic feeling runs very high in this plant. Recently an informal discussion was held with workers on the subject, and this is what Comrade Ilenkov, who conducted the forum on behalf of the Bryansk raikom, writes about it:

"The workers who attended the discussion may be divided into three groups of different strength: (1) Those strongly contaminated with anti-Semitic prejudice. This is an active group — they asked questions, objected, made speeches, wisecracked, etc. (2) The bulk of the audience, who tacitly agreed with the arguments and speeches of the former. (3) A tiny minority, who timidly tried to reason with the first group. Party and Komsomol people in the audience kept silent. The secretary of the Komsomol cell behaved as if the cat had got his tongue. The impression was obtained that they were all in agreement with the anti-Jewish statements . . ."[32]

Many similar experiences could be cited from the Smolensk Archive; indeed there is a whole folder which contains nothing else.[33] The Evsektsia made it its major business to track down and expose such incidents; letters in the Archive addressed to the Evsektsia indicate that it served as a clearing house to which victims of anti-Semitism complained.[34]

In 1930 the Evsektsia was dissolved, a victim itself of the charge of "Jewish nationalism" which it had so ostentatiously combated. Anti-Semitism continued to be officially condemned, but in the words of a resolution of the executive committee of the Western Oblast, "At the same time [it is necessary] to intensify the struggle against any manifestation of Jewish nationalism, which is the other side of anti-Semitism, and therefore likewise a counterrevolutionary phenomenon." [35] After 1930, the Smolensk Archive ceases to yield any significant data on the situation of the Jews in the Western Oblast. The campaign to close the churches had its counterpart in a similar drive against the synagogues; at the end of 1936 only one synagogue remained open in the city of Smolensk.[36] By that time the old orthodox communities of the "market towns" had been largely dissolved, and the younger generation of Jews appeared well on the way toward being lost to the faith. A consciousness of separateness persisted, but the Godly had been reduced to a tiny band.

23 Conclusion — Smolensk as a Mirror of Soviet Reality

If the subject of history is, as Tolstoy once defined it, "the life of humanity," the Smolensk Archive can properly be described as an important source. Its files and documents are peopled with ordinary human beings trying desperately to lead normal lives in the midst of extraordinary and abnormal events. The history that they made or had made for them is now neatly periodized in the familiar chronology of Revolution, Civil War and War Communism, NEP, and the era of the Five Year Plans. The convulsive social, economic, and political transformations through which they passed have been fitted into equally tidy categories. The stately procession includes urbanization, industrialization, collectivization, secularization, bureaucratization, and totalitarianization. These generalizing concepts have their obviously important uses, but somehow the people who inhabit the Archive make them seem rather pallid and abstract.

The Struggle between the Old and the New

In the most fundamental sense what the Smolensk experience offers is a vivid and poignant case study of people caught up in the turmoil of the struggle between the old and the new. The forces of tradition were powerfully entrenched in the Smolensk region. Relatively untouched by modern industrialism, its population at the time of the Revolution was predominantly peasant in character, and its outlook was largely circumscribed by the narrow horizons of village existence. Until almost a decade after the 1917 Revolution, the life of the countryside was little affected by the Bolshevik innovators who had seized state power. The peasants tilled the soil in a time-honored way, celebrated religious holidays and harvest festivals, adjudicated their disputes in terms of customary law, and regulated their lives by the immemorial rhythm of the seasons. Like peasants everywhere, they grumbled at the exactions of the tax collector and at the high price of city goods, but (except for the requisitioning of goods during the Civil War), Soviet power remained something distant and peripheral, a somewhat unreal menace which had still to touch their lives in an intimate and comprehensive fashion. Even in the towns and cities, where representatives of the Soviet regime were much more thoroughly entrenched, the effect of the New Economic Policy was to muffle contradictions between the old and the new. To be sure, the regime nationalized the larger industrial enterprises of the region, but the life of the average factory worker was little affected by the change. The majority of workers in the Smolensk area continued to be employed in small private enterprises, and for them the great transformation which the Revolution purported to have ushered in was, if anything, even less real. New Bolshevik cadres displaced the old ruling strata, but even the consequences of this profound overturn were mitigated by the dependence of the new rulers on the skills of the old non-Communist intelligentsia who were frequently retained to perform important functions, though not usually in leading posts.

The full innovating thrust of the Bolshevik Revolution did not really begin to register until the program of collectivization and rapid industrialization was launched. Even so, in the Smolensk area at least, its first impact was muted and subdued. Smolensk, in contrast to many other regions, was slow to feel the effects of industrialization and collectivization. When the collectivization drive took hold, however, it produced a cataclysmic upheaval in the countryside and had a shattering effect on established social relationships. But it also revealed how stubborn and resistant the peasants were to change.

Like a slow-motion camera, the documents in the Archive reveal a tale of infinite complexity. The inhabitants of the villages refused to fall into convenient categories of kulaks, middle peasants, and poor peasants; instead they usually maintained a front of solidarity which was cemented by family relationships, communal ties, and a common hatred of the collectivizers who had come to rearrange their lives. The worker in the factory often turned out to be not a class-conscious proletarian at all, but a peasant still fresh from the village, with an ikon on his wall, with an aversion for the Godless Communists, and with connections and sympathies that bound him to the countryside. The employee in the office or trade enterprise, as often as not, was one of the "former people," perhaps a one-time shopkeeper abominating the new masters whom he was compelled to serve, but forced to serve them nonetheless.

Even the agents of State and Party power presented their contradictory faces. Not many approximated the model of the iron-willed and incorruptible Bolshevik who sacrificed everything for the cause. The village Communists and Komsomols had their links with the countryside, and their obligations as representatives of authority could not altogether obliterate their concern with the plight of their neighbors. The rank-and-file Party members in the factory shared the tribulations of their fellow-workers at the bench; the Archive makes clear that they also frequently echoed their sense of grievance. The district and village officials who operated close to the grass roots confronted a constant problem of reconciling central demands with local capacities; the attrition and rapid turnover in their ranks testify to the fact that the adjustment was not easy.

When one reflects on the formidable handicaps that the Bolsheviks shouldered in an area like Smolensk — the hostility of the villages, the dubious loyalty of the small contingent of factory workers, the antagonism of the remnants of the old intelligentsia, the thinness of Communist and Komsomol membership, and the undependable character of part of their apparatus — the wonder is, not merely that the Bolsheviks were able to win power, but that they were able to hold the power which they had won. To this question, as to many others, history has given its own seemingly clear answer, but the factors which explain the Bolshevik triumph in Smolensk remain both elusive and complex.

Why Did the Bolsheviks Triumph in Smolensk?

The Archive provides some hints. For all of the opposition of the countryside to collectivization, the resistance never assumed really organized form. It exhausted itself in sporadic acts of violence; and the villages failed to demonstrate a capacity for united action. The isolation of the peasant communities gave the Bolsheviks their opportunity, and they marshaled their forces skillfully and ruthlessly. The swift move against the kulaks robbed the countryside of much of its natural leadership, and an occasional display of force intimidated peasants whom the Bolsheviks could not otherwise persuade. At the height of the collectivization drive, all pretense of voluntarism was in effect abandoned; the Bolshevik collectivizing squads marched into the villages like an army invading enemy territory; the kulaks were deported, and the bulk of the peasants who remained behind were herded into the kolkhozes.

The problem of disciplining the industrial workers was resolved by less stringent means. At the beginning of the First Five Year Plan strikes, work stoppages, and open protests against increases in work norms were not uncommon; but after 1929, judging by the Archive, they became quite rare. Here again the explanation appears to be many-sided. The pruning of trade union prerogatives and the purge of the old trade union leadership in 1929 eliminated an organizing focus for the expression of labor's discontents. Malcontents and "trouble-makers" in the industrial labor force became the special objects of attention by the OGPU. Punishment for violations of factory discipline increased in harshness and severity. At the same time the carrot supplemented the stick. The old system of "uravnilovka," of equality of wages, was repudiated. Special incentives were held out to encourage the shock-brigade workers, and the system of wage payments was reorganized to penalize backwardness and sloth and to reward productivity and industry. There is abundant evidence in the Archive to demonstrate that the rank-and-file workers chafed in their new harness, but there is little to indicate that their expressions of discontent extended beyond the grumblings among themselves which are recorded in the reports of the OGPU and NKVD.

The antagonism of the members of the old intelligentsia presented a relatively minor challenge to the Smolensk Communist authorities. At no point did they represent an organized oppositional force. Some changed their stand toward the Soviet regime and were even absorbed into the Party itself. Others, while remaining privately hostile, neverthe-less placed their skills at the disposal of the new order and sought pro-tection in serving a regime which, for the time being, they were powerless to displace. The attitude of the Communist authorities toward them was in its turn ambivalent. They did not trust the old intelligentsia, but they were prepared to use it — at least until more dependable instruments be-came available. Meanwhile, the Communist rulers took precautions to insure that the members of the old intelligentsia were kept under surveil-lance, that they did not penetrate into posts of strategic political signifi-cance, and that they were eliminated from important positions as soon as adequately trained and politically reliable replacements could be found. The displacement of the old intelligentsia by a new Soviet-trained intelli-gentsia eventually completed the rout.

In reading through the Archive one is struck time and again by a curious anomaly. The documents provide unimpeachable evidence of widespread mass discontent with Soviet rule. Yet, except for scattered outbreaks of violence during the period of collectivization, oppositional moods never come to a focus in any form of organized challenge to the regime. Peasants, workers, and employees grumble and complain, but they are inert and apathetic so far as action is concerned. It is as if the will to resist were paralyzed, the conditions of conspiratorial combat sus-pended, and every organizational alternative to Bolshevism had faded from the scene.

The usual theories advanced to account for these phenomena stress the efficiency of the Communist terror apparatus and the perfection of the totalitarian machine. These explain much, but they do not explain all. The terror apparatus was undoubtedly efficient, and one cannot come away from a reading of the OGPU or NKVD reports in the Archive with-out realizing that there was little that went on in even the most obscure corner of Smolensk that the secret police did not know. The fear and sus-picion which such surveillance inspired no doubt contributed greatly to disarm and atomize the potential opposition.

But the totalitarian machine, at least in the Smolensk area, was far from perfect. The Party organization had a certain strength in the cities and towns, but its membership and influence thinned out perceptibly in the countryside. The average Party member was far from being the dedicated zealot which the Party rules demanded. The Party functionaries operated with a far greater degree of discipline, but even they had their share of human weaknesses and frailties. The quality of the state apparatus could hardly be described as high, and its standards deteriorated markedly as one approached the grass roots. In the districts and outlying villages drunkenness, bribery, and self-serving behavior were endemic, and they persisted despite repeated efforts to stamp them out.

Paradoxically, it was the very inefficiency of the state machine which helped make it tolerable. Had the Smolensk proconsuls functioned as a perfect instrument of the center and been able always to exact the heavy tribute which Moscow demanded, the price in terms of suffering and the possible dangers to the regime in terms of stiffening resistance would have been far greater than they actually were. The failures of the local representatives of state power provided an escape valve which did much to insure that mass indignation would not boil over. Thus the imperfections of the regional control system helped to alleviate tension.

With the passing of time controls were tightened and perfected. The imperatives generated by the commitment to rapid industrialization drove the center to intensify its pressure on the regions. In a certain sense, this involved a war with the peasants and workers in order to mobilize their full energies for the industrialization drive. It also involved a subsidiary running battle between the center and its own regional and local agents, since the voracious requirements of the center could not be met without increased demands on and by the regional and local authorities. The Smolensk experience illustrates the range of problems such demands created. Regional and district officials were driven to despair by the difficulties of their task. Many failed, and while their failures brought at least temporary relief to their constituents, they also meant the quick end of some promising careers. Some resorted to ingenious and dangerous expedients to conceal inadequacies of performance; eventually they too had to face an accounting. Others fought and bulldozed their way through to success, though the price at which it was purchased brought little joy to the victims. Slowly but surely, under unrelenting pressure from the center, the regional organizations were welded into more pliant creatures of central rule.

The Communist authorities in Smolensk enjoyed one incomparable advantage which, in moments of crisis, could be counted on to intimidate their scattered opponents. This was the monopoly of organized force at the regime's disposal. Weak as the Party might be in the countryside, the knowledge that it could readily mobilize an overwhelming force was usually enough to avert trouble. Whatever criticism may be directed against the Communist leaders, it cannot be said that they cherished any illusions on the score of the dispensability of armed might. From the beginning they anchored their power firmly on a strong military and police establishment. The care and attention they lavished on the police and the army revealed a realistic appreciation of the importance of monopolizing the instruments of force. The military power at the disposal of the regime cast its shadow before. The widespread recognition of its existence served to minimize the necessity of its use and gave the regime a capacity of maneuver which it might not otherwise have been able to enjoy.

The organizational discipline of the Communists also served to maximize their power. In a region such as Smolensk where Communist and Komsomol forces were relatively weak, their authority was greatly magnified by the unity and solidarity with which they confronted their potential opponents. The Communist leadership deployed its cadres like soldiers in an army; they were allocated and distributed where they could have maximum effect. They were projected into all the strategic power positions of the society, and the leverage which this afforded gave Communist orders added weight. To be sure, the unified front the Party presented was sometimes deceptive; the Party too had its internal rifts. There were occasions, as the Archive makes clear, when local Party organs were defiant and rebellious, but with the consolidation of Stalinist power such outbursts became increasingly rare. On the whole, the Party maintained its discipline, and its cohesiveness operated as a source of strength.

But important as force, terror, and organization were, they cannot alone explain the regime's capacity to survive and entrench itself despite a high margin of mass discontent. The search for an explanation must take into account the tradition of servility toward central authority inherited from the Russian past. It must also concern itself with the deeper social forces which the Revolution unleashed. Revolutions begin with the defeat and elimination of an established ruling group. But they also create fresh opportunities for social categories that had previously been suppressed and inert. They make it possible for the abler and more ambitious members of the newly activated groups to rise in the social scale and to attain previously undreamed of heights of authority and influence. In a fundamental sense, a Revolution only begins to consolidate itself when it calls forth new energy from below to defend its conquests.

In many respects, the Bolshevik Revolution followed this classic pattern. It dethroned an established ruling caste and set a profound social revolution in motion. It tapped fresh talent from the lower depths of society and harnessed it to the revolutionary chariot. It gradually welded together a new governing apparatus, drawn substantially from social elements that had previously been political ciphers. It built its own network of revolutionary beneficiaries with vested interests in the perpetuation of the new order.

The Creation of a New Class of Beneficiaries

The Smolensk Archive provides many vivid illustrations of this process at work. Even in the villages, where suspicion of the Bolsheviks was most intense, individuals here and there began to separate themselves from their neighbors and align their futures with the Communist cause. The Red Army functioned as a particularly important school for the preparation of rural Communists and Komsomols. The period of military service isolated the peasant soldiers from the influence of the villages and exposed them to Communist indoctrination. Those who returned from the army as Komsomols or Party members were frequently rewarded with appointments to leading village posts or were launched on careers as members of the district governmental, Party, or police hierarchy. Their assimilation into the local governing apparatus was not without its strain; it nevertheless provided the regime with a nucleus of local support without which the task of controlling the countryside would have been rendered infinitely more difficult.

The same processes went on in intensified degree in the towns and cities. One of the important symbols of the first revolutionary decade was the "pushed-forward" worker, so named because he was deliberately singled out for advancement to responsible work and there placed because it was thought that he could be counted on to be politically reliable. Frequently he had to be specially tutored in order to be able to fulfill his obligations, and not infrequently even this did not avail. Nevertheless, in the early days the Party heaped large responsibilities on its "pushed-forward" worker Communists, since trained cadres were scarce and the majority of the specialists who survived from the old regime were not deemed sufficiently dependable to be entrusted with leading posts.

As the new regime began to stabilize its position, the allure of affiliation with it extended well beyond the circle of the true believers. Membership in the Komsomol and the Party was the open sesame to power and influence under the new dispensation, and energetic and ambitious elements from all eligible, and sometimes, ineligible social strata began to flock to the Communist banner. Despite periodic efforts to weed out careerist, socially alien, and other undesirable elements, the Komsomol and the Party inevitably became a focal point of attraction for all those who sought advancement under the new system. The Party guarded the gates of opportunity, and those who joined its ranks were not only rewarded with preferment, but developed a vested interest in stabilizing a regime of which they were becoming an essential part. An imposing edifice of bureaucratic, Party, and police controls was erected with their support.

During the first postrevolutionary decade the Soviet leadership had to draw heavily on the talents of the technical specialists whom it had inherited from the old order. In the early phases of the industrialization drive, despite periodic bouts of specialist-baiting and intermittent persecution of the old intelligentsia, this dependence was, if anything, accentuated. The regime had still to resolve the problem of building its own trustworthy technical cadres. The vast educational program which the Soviet leadership launched to meet the needs of industrialization helped to fill this gap. The Soviet-trained technical intelligentsia that emerged became one of the pillars of the new order.

In many respects the revolution ushered in by industrialization and collectivization carried consequences fully as important as the Bolshevik seizure of power in 1917. Industrialization and collectivization exacted a high price in suffering and deprivation for the mass of the population. But it is sometimes forgotten that the accent on growth embodied in the Five Year Plans also spelled expanding vistas for many members of the younger generation and fresh opportunities for those who grasped them. The rush of young people to the universities and technical institutes finds graphic exemplification in the Smolensk Archive, and the same processes were at work on an all-Soviet scale. Industrialization unleashed an almost insatiable demand for factory managers, engineers, technicians, foremen, and skilled workers. On a smaller scale, collectivization inspired a similar need for managers and trained specialists to serve the new machine-tractor stations, state farms, and kolkhozes. Those who qualified themselves to discharge these new managerial and technical tasks were appropriately rewarded; industrialization and collectivization created a whole new class of beneficiaries of the regime's largesse. Essential to the regime, they nevertheless remained dependent on it for their privileges and perquisites.

By the end of the 1930's a formidable combination of vested interests had become involved, in one way or another, in the regime's survival. In the Party and Komsomol sphere the core of strength was provided by the apparatchiki, or full-time Party officialdom who manned the various rungs of the Party secretarial ladder. In the governmental sphere the most deeply committed groups were the responsible officials in the central ministries and the bureaucrats who exercised similar authority in the republics, oblasts, cities, and districts. In industry and trade the category of those specially indebted to the regime included factory directors and heads of other key enterprises, the engineers and technical élite, the shop heads and foremen, the Stakhanovites, and the better-paid skilled workers. In agriculture it comprised the chairmen of collective farms, the directors of machine-tractor stations and state farms, and their leading technical and managerial assistants. In the military and police it counted the officer corps and the corresponding posts in the police hierarchy. In the cultural area, it embraced a well-kept élite of academicians, privileged writers, journalists, theater and movie directors, actors, singers, musicians, and other "engineers of the human soul."

The coalescence of these groups around the regime contributed a basic source of strength which helped to make totalitarian controls ultimately effective. The terrible purges of the middle and late 1930's weakened but did not disrupt the combination. The yawning gaps in the ranks left by the purges were rapidly filled by new recruits whose indebtedness to the regime was emphasized by their purge-accelerated promotions.

The Smolensk Archive provides a record in miniature of these profound social and political changes. It registers the gradual consolidation of Communist power in a region where the underlying disposition of economic forces offered formidable barriers to Communist control. It reveals the capacity of the regime to manipulate and discipline the new social forces which its grandiose experiment in social engineering released. But it also lays bare the vast human costs and bitter resentments which Communist rule entailed. The Archive may serve to remind us, if reminder is needed, that the totalitarian façade concealed a host of inner contradictions, that the yoke which Communism imposed left its legacy of smoldering grievances, and that the suppressed aspirations of yesterday may yet become the seedbed of tomorrow's fierce debates.

Bibliographical Note

Almost all the references in this volume are to items in the Smolensk Archive. This collection of documents, under the title "Records of the All-Union (Russian) Communist Party, Smolensk District, Record Group 1056," is now in the custody of the Military Records Branch, Federal Records Center, Region 3, General Services Administration. A master microfilm copy of the collection is available for purchase as National Archives Microfilm publication no. T 87, National Archives, Washington, D. C.

A few explanatory remarks about the character of the Smolensk Archive and the method of identifying the files which it contains are in order. All told, the Archive contains 536 files, of which 527 bear the prefix WKP and run from WKP 1 through WKP 527, seven are in a separate series labeled respectively 116/154e, 116/154f, 116/154g, 116/154h, 116/155, 116/156, and 116/171, and two are identified as RS 921 and RS 924. In most cases the documents within each file are numbered, and in all such instances the notes below trace the source to the page of the file in which the reference occurs, as in WKP 228, p. 41. In a few cases, however, the files were found in an unpaginated state, and in such instance the reference is to the sequence in which the document occurs in the file, as in WKP 266, sequence 45, or the document is identified by its character or date, as in Protocol No. 45, December 15, 1936. The order of the documents remains in the state in which they were discovered, and each file is prefaced with a brief, but alas, frequently inaccurate description of its contents. In order to facilitate research, a general index was prepared which classifies the content of the files according to the categories used in this volume. Although this index has proved too bulky to be reproduced here, it is available for consultation in Cambridge by qualified scholars who wish to pursue further research in the Archive.

Notes

Chapter 1. Smolensk — Land, People, and History

1. See WKP 290, pp. 2–25, and *Bolshaya Sovetskaya Entsiklopedia,* XXVI (1933), 181–211.
2. *BSE,* LI (1945), 477–486.
3. *Ibid.*
4. The material for this historical sketch is largely drawn from D. P. Makovski and V. S. Orlov, *Goroda Smolenshchiny — Smolensk s drevnikh vremen do XX veka* (OGIZ, Smolenskoye Gosudarstvennoe Izdatelstvo, 1948).
5. See *Entsiklopedicheski Slovar,* 7th ed., XXXIX, 631.
6. See Donald Mackenzie Wallace, *Russia* (London: Cassell and Co., 1905), II, 202–203.
7. See *Entsiklopedicheski Slovar,* 7th ed., XXXIX, 634.
8. *Ibid.*, 1900, XXX, 551.
9. See Peter I. Lyashchenko, *History of the National Economy of Russia to the 1917 Revolution* (New York: Macmillan, 1949), p. 743.
10. *Entsiklopedicheski Slovar,* 7th ed., XXXIX, 632.
11. *Ibid.*, p. 633.
12. *Ibid.*, p. 631.
13. *Ibid.*, 1900, XXX, 551.
14. *Ibid.*
15. See Makovski and Orlov, p. 223.
16. *Ibid.*, p. 214.
17. *Ibid.*
18. *Ibid.*, pp. 223ff.
19. WKP 307. The materials in this folder form the basis for the following account of the background and events of the 1905 revolution in Smolensk.
20. Unless otherwise indicated, the material on developments during 1917 are drawn from WKP 1.
21. Leon Trotsky, *The History of the Rusian Revolution* (New York: Simon and Schuster, 1932), III, 23–25.
22. See Oliver H. Radkey, *The Constituent Assembly* (Cambridge: Harvard University Press, 1950), p. 78 (Appendix).
23. This description of Smolensk is Trotsky's. See his *History of the Russian Revolution,* III, 83.

Chapter 2. The Smolensk Party Organization

1. WKP 275, p. 18.
2. *Izvestia TsK,* no. 8, December 2, 1919, p. 4.
3. *Ibid.*, no. 15, March 24, 1920, p, 1.
4. *Ibid.*
5. *Ibid.*, no. 4. (40), March 1922, pp. 20ff.
6. WKP 1, p. 33.
7. WKP 205, p. 58.
8. *Ibid.*, p. 63.
9. *Ibid.*, p. 66.
10. WKP 2, sequence 25.
11. *Ibid.*, sequence 22.
12. *Ibid.*, sequence 33–34.
13. WKP 6 and WKP 7.
14. WKP 6, p. 11.
15. *Ibid.*, p. 78.
16. *Ibid.*, p. 13.
17. *Ibid.*, pp. 26, 32, 34.
18. *Ibid.*, p. 95.
19. WKP 7, sequence 1.
20. For examples see WKP 6, pp. 15, 92.
21. WKP 6, p. 113.
22. *Ibid.*, pp. 74, 76.
23. *Ibid.*, p. 76.
24. WKP 7, sequence 1.
25. WKP 6, p. 44.
26. WKP 7, sequence 1.
27. WKP 6, p. 115, and WKP 7, sequence 1.

NOTES

28. WKP 6, p. 105.
29. WKP 7, sequence 1.
30. WKP 6, p. 36.
31. *Ibid.*, p. 8, and WKP 7, sequence 1.
32. WKP 7, sequence 1.
33. WKP 6, p. 103.
34. *Ibid.*, pp. 87–89.
35. *Ibid.*, p. 11.
36. *Ibid.*, p. 27.
37. *Ibid.*, p. 78.
38. *Ibid.*, p. 87.
39. *Ibid.*, pp. 88–92.
40. *Ibid.*, p. 95.
41. *Ibid.*, p. 26.
42. *Ibid.*, p. 64.
43. *Ibid.*, p. 67.
44. WKP 275, p. 3.
45. WKP 273, p. 24.
46. *Ibid.*, pp. 38–39.
47. *Ibid.*, pp. 74–76.
48. *Ibid.*, p. 109.
49. *Ibid.*, pp. 141–142.
50. *Ibid.*, p. 50.
51. *Ibid.*, p. 59.
52. *Ibid.*, pp. 196–197.
53. *Ibid.*, pp. 283–285.
54. WKP 275, p. 10.
55. *Izvestia TsK*, no. 4 (40), March 1922, pp. 20ff.
56. *Ibid.*, no. 3 (51), March 1923, pp. 162–164.
57. WKP 275, p. 15.
58. *Ibid.*
59. *Ibid.*, p. 16.
60. *Ibid.*, p. 17.
61. *Ibid.*
62. *Ibid.*, p. 18.
63. *Ibid.*
64. *Ibid.*, p. 25.
65. *Ibid.*, p. 30.
66. WKP 290, pp. 2–25.
67. *Ibid.*
68. WKP 134, pp. 69–75.
69. *Ibid.*
70. *Ibid.*
71. WKP 33, p. 298.
72. WKP 29, pp. 42–43.
73. WKP 134, pp. 69–75.
74. WKP 290, pp. 2–25.
75. WKP 33, p. 153.

76. *Ibid.*, p. 229.
77. *Ibid.*, p. 60.
78. See WKP 29, pp. 46–80.
79. See WKP 144.
80. WKP 33, p. 361.
81. *Ibid.*
82. *Ibid.*, p. 365.
83. *Ibid.*, p. 361.
84. WKP 291, pp. 1, 11.
85. WKP 33, p. 408.
86. *Ibid.*, p. 451.
87. *Ibid.*
88. *Ibid.*, p. 462.
89. See WKP 33, p. 393, and WKP 296, p. 19.
90. WKP 40, p. 13.
91. WKP 61, pp. 98–168.
92. See pp. 238–264.
93. WKP 61, pp. 98–168.
94. See File 116/154f.
95. See Chapter 11 for many more examples.
96. See *Partiinoye Stroitelstvo*, nos. 113–114, July 1930.
97. *Ibid.*, no. 21, November 1932.
98. *Ibid.*, no. 8, April 1936.
99. *Ibid.*, no. 19, October 1, 1937.
100. See WKP 226 for text of decree.
101. See WKP 384, p. 231.
102. WKP 186, pp. 66–70.
103. *Ibid.*, pp. 85–88.
104. WKP 316, p. 1.
105. See WKP 316, *passim.*
106. See WKP 499 for text.
107. See WKP 93, pp. 41–42.
108. See File 116/154e.
109 See WKP 54, p. 203.
110. For text see WKP 499, pp. 322–328.
111. For examples see WKP 499 and WKP 516, *passim.*
112. See File RS 924.
113. WKP 238, pp. 155–161.
114. WKP 103, p. 126.
115. WKP 109, p. 66.
116. *Ibid.*
117. *Partiinoye Stroitelstvo*, no. 19, October 1, 1937.
118. For example see WKP 323.
119. For example see WKP 117.

Chapter 3. Party Organization and Controls at the Oblast Level

1. File RS 924, Supplement to point 38, Protocol No. 156 of the Bureau of the Obkom of the CPSU(b). (Decision of October 19, 1936.)
2. *Ibid.*
3. *Ibid.*, Point 133, Protocol 156.

4. *Ibid.*, Supplement to Point 38, Protocol No. 156.

5. *Ibid.*

6. *Ibid.*

7. *Ibid.*

8. *Ibid.*

9. *Ibid.*

10. *Ibid.*

11. WKP 40, p. 3.

12. File RS 924.

13. *Ibid.*, Protocol No. 123.

14. Two such obkom plans for 1936 are available, one covering the period May to August inclusive (Protocol No. 135) and the other October to December inclusive (Protocol No. 191).

15. See File RS 924, Protocol 157.

16. E.g., Protocol No. 125, two groups, one of 110 and the other of 166, expelled.

17. Of the 2,980 expelled in 1936, 2,064 were members, 916 candidates. During the year 564 members and candidates were reinstated, resulting in a net loss of 2,416 members and candidates for the year.

18. E.g., Protocol No. 126.

19. Protocol No. 132.

20. Protocol No. 133.

21. *Ibid.*

22. E.g., Protocol No. 137.

23. References to such telegrams as well as to harvesting losses appear in a number of protocols — No. 145, July 25; No. 147, August 8; and No. 151, September 4.

24. E.g., Protocol No. 154, October 7.

25. Protocol No. 159.

26. See Protocols Nos. 155, 160, 162.

27. See Protocols Nos. 140, 144.

28. See Protocol No. 135.

29. See WKP 215, p. 97.

30. See Chapters 8 and 14, pp. 165–166, 286–288.

31. WKP 228, pp. 14–15.

32. See WKP 178, pp. 134–135, and WKP 499, pp. 322–328.

33. See WKP 213.

34. WKP 176, pp. 101–102.

35. WKP 162, pp. 36–37.

36. WKP 176, p. 181.

37. *Ibid.*, p. 140.

38. *Ibid.*, pp. 128–131.

39. *Ibid.*, pp. 126–127.

40. *Ibid.*

41. *Ibid.*, pp. 136–137.

42. *Ibid.*, p. 155.

43. See File RS 924, Protocol No. 156, item 133.

44. *Ibid.*, item 38.

45. WKP 192, p. 69.

46. WKP 186, p. 133.

47. WKP 239, p. 86.

48. *Ibid.*, p. 87.

49. File RS 924, Protocol No. 156, item 133.

50. *Ibid.*

51. *Ibid.*, Protocol No. 140.

52. *Ibid.*, Protocol No. 157, item 46.

53. *Ibid.*, Protocol No. 160, item 23.

Chapter 4. Governmental Organization and Problems of the Oblast

1. File RS 921, p. 207.

2. WKP 235, p. 1.

3. WKP 65.

4. *Ibid.*, Protocol No. 66.

5. Adapted from data in WKP 65 and File RS 924, Supplement to Point 38, Protocol No. 156.

6. See WKP 65, Protocol No. 65 and succeeding protocols.

7. *Ibid.*

8. WKP 61, pp. 98–168.

9. WKP 40, pp. 1ff.

10. See File RS 924, Supplement to Point 38, Protocol No. 156.

11. WKP 65, *passim*.

12. WKP 61, pp. 98–168.

13. *Ibid.*

14. *Ibid.*

15. *Ibid.*

16. See WKP 65, Protocol No. 74.

17. *Ibid.*, Protocol No. 75.

18. WKP 61, pp. 98–168.

19. *Ibid.*

20. *Ibid.*

21. *Ibid.*

22. *Ibid.*

23. WKP 65, Protocol 68.

24. WKP 238, pp. 155–161.

25. WKP 61, pp. 98–168.

26. See Chapter 2, pp. 48–52.

27. WKP 186, pp. 66–70.

28. *Ibid.*, pp. 85–88.

29. *Ibid.*

30. *Ibid.*

31. WKP 235, pp. 58–62.

Chapter 5. The Role of the Raion in the Soviet Control System

1. See pp. 52–53.
2. WKP 176, p. 12.
3. See File RS 924, Supplement to Point 38, Protocol No. 156.
4. WKP 321, p. 55.
5. WKP 172, p. 12.
6. WKP 312, pp. 52–56.
7. WKP 355, pp. 178–179.
8. *Ibid.*
9. See pp. 105–108.
10. See WKP 79.
11. *Ibid.*, p. 8.
12. *Ibid.*, p. 10.
13. *Ibid.*, p. 16.
14. *Ibid.*, p. 19.
15. *Ibid.*, p. 30.

Chapter 6. Belyi — A Case Study of a Raion Party Organization

1. WKP 313, p. 147.
2. *Ibid.*
3. *Ibid.*
4. WKP 249, p. 202.
5. *Ibid.*, p. 203.
6. *Ibid.*, p. 16.
7. For protocol of meeting see WKP 249, pp. 65ff.
8. See WKP 249, p. 219.
9. *Ibid.*, p. 258.
10. *Ibid.*, p. 219.
11. *Ibid.*, p. 71.
12. *Ibid.*, p. 72.
13. *Ibid.*, p. 95.
14. *Ibid.*, pp. 230, 247.
15. *Ibid.*, p. 230.
16. *Ibid.*, p. 256.
17. *Ibid.*, p. 167.
18. *Ibid.*
19. See Chapter 12.
20. WKP 313, p. 147.
21. *Ibid.*, pp. 57–62.
22. See WKP 313, pp. 70–74, 130–131, and WKP 385, pp. 352–368.
23. WKP 385, pp. 352–368.
24. WKP 313, pp. 70–74.
25. *Ibid.*, pp. 130–131.
26. WKP 385, pp. 352–368.
27. *Ibid.*
28. See File RS 924, Protocol No. 153, item 155.
29. WKP 321, p. 89.
30. WKP 111, pp. 2–66.
31. WKP 321, p. 112.
32. WKP 111, p. 228.
33. WKP 321, p. 117.
34. *Ibid.*, p. 163.
35. WKP 111, p. 151.
36. *Ibid*, p. 177.
37. *Ibid.*, p. 193.
38. *Ibid.*, p. 92.
39. *Ibid.*, p. 207.
40. *Ibid.*, p. 117.
41. *Ibid.*

Chapter 7. Control at the Grass Roots

1. WKP 331, pp. 108–136.
2. *Ibid.*
3. *Ibid.*
4. *Ibid.*
5. *Ibid.*
6. *Ibid.*
7. *Ibid.*
8. WKP 61, pp. 98–168.
9. *Ibid.*
10. WKP 215, p. 162.
11. *Ibid.*, p. 69.
12. *Ibid.*, p. 155.
13. *Ibid.*, p. 154.
14. WKP 166, pp. 3–5.
15. *Ibid.*, pp. 10–13.
16. *Ibid.*, pp. 31–38.
17. WKP 195, p. 315.
18. *Ibid.*, p. 316.
19. *Ibid.*, pp. 318–321.
20. *Ibid.*, p. 322.
21. WKP 132, pp. 196–204.
22. WKP 195, pp. 92–96.
23. *Ibid.*
24. *Ibid.*
25. *Ibid.*, p. 98.

Chapter 8. The Organs of State Security

1. WKP 271.
2. *Ibid.*, Order No. 17.
3. *Ibid.*, Protocol No. 6.
4. *Ibid.*, Order No. 23.
5. *Ibid.*, Order No. 48.
6. *Ibid.*, Order No. 92.

7. *Ibid.*, Order No. 46.
8. See WKP 271, Protocols Nos. 9, 13, and 17.
9. WKP 271, Order No. 87.
10. *Ibid.*, Protocol No. 9.
11. *Ibid.*, Order No. 45.
12. *Ibid.*, Protocol No. 18.
13. WKP 273.
14. *Ibid.*, pp. 1–4.
15. *Ibid.*, p. 50.
16. *Ibid.*, pp. 101–103 and 404.
17. *Ibid.*, pp. 1–4.
18. *Ibid.*, pp. 109 and 223.
19. *Ibid.*, pp. 189–191 and 328–329.
20. *Ibid.*, p. 309.
21. *Ibid.*, p. 130.
22. *Ibid.*, p. 154.
23. *Ibid.*, p. 410.
24. WKP 6 and 7.
25. WKP 215, pp. 119–121.
26. *Ibid.*
27. *Ibid.*
28. *Ibid.*
29. *Ibid.*
30. *Ibid.*
31. WKP 176, p. 172.
32. See File RS 924, Supplement to Point 38, Protocol No. 156.
33. *Ibid.*, Protocol No. 123, item 27.
34. See WKP 36 and WKP 49.
35. WKP 253, pp. 3–4.
36. *Ibid.*, p. 6.
37. WKP 138, p. 6.
38. *Ibid.*, p. 7.
39. *Ibid.*, pp. 22–23.
40. *Ibid.*
41. *Ibid.*
42. *Ibid.*, p. 21.
43. *Ibid.*, pp. 3–4.
44. *Ibid.*, pp. 24–25.
45. *Ibid.*
46. *Ibid.*, p. 1.
47. See above, pp. 286–288, 297–298.
48. For example see File RS 924, Protocol No. 157, item 46.
49. WKP 238, p. 178.
50. WKP 129, p. 11.
51. WKP 178, pp. 31–32.
52. WKP 106 and WKP 322.
53. WKP 106, Protocol No. 2.
54. *Ibid.*, Protocol No. 3.
55. *Ibid.*, Protocol No. 7.
56. *Ibid.*, Protocol No. 4.
57. WKP 322, Protocol No. 6, October 15, 1937.
58. *Ibid.*, Protocol No. 2.
59. WKP 355, pp. 9–10.
60. *Ibid.*, pp. 12–14.
61. WKP 362, pp. 512–513.
62. WKP 111, p. 177.
63. *Ibid.*, p. 92.
64. WKP 355, p. 307.

Chapter 9. The Machinery of Justice

1. WKP 282 (no page numbers).
2. WKP 130, p. 376.
3. WKP 143, pp. 77–78.
4. See WKP 250, WKP 261, and WKP 525.
5. WKP 261, Information Bulletin No. 2, September 1929.
6. WKP 261, pp. 22–23.
7. WKP 525, pp. 195–196.
8. *Ibid.*, pp. 191–195.
9. *Ibid.*
10. *Ibid.*, pp. 199–201.
11. *Ibid.*, pp. 89–92 and 107–114.
12. *Ibid.*, pp. 107–114.
13. *Ibid.*, pp. 89–92.
14. WKP 178, pp. 134–135.
15. *Ibid.*, pp. 137–138.
16. For examples see WKP 354 and WKP 383.
17. WKP 103.
18. *Ibid.*, p. 15.
19. *Ibid.*, p. 21.
20. *Ibid.*, p. 120.
21. *Ibid.*, p. 212.
22. *Ibid.*, p. 126.
23. *Ibid.*, p. 166.
24. *Ibid.*, p. 174.
25. WKP 238, pp. 302–305.
26. WKP 103, p. 198.
27. *Ibid.*, p. 202.
28. *Ibid.*, p. 207.
29. WKP 323, pp. 99–100.

Chapter 10. Crime in Smolensk

1. WKP 525.
2. WKP 351.
3. *Ibid.*, p. 4.
4. *Ibid.*, p. 5.
5. *Ibid.*, p. 8.
6. *Ibid.*, p. 73.
7. *Ibid.*, p. 89.
8. *Ibid.*, p. 106.

9. *Ibid.*, p. 94.
10. *Ibid.*, p. 134.
11. *Ibid.*, p. 123.
12. *Ibid.*, p. 145.
13. *Ibid.*, p. 6.
14. *Ibid.*, p. 40.
15. *Ibid.*, p. 64.
16. *Ibid.*, p. 139.
17. *Ibid.*, p. 27.
18. *Ibid.*, p. 96.
19. *Ibid.*, p. 109.
20. *Ibid.*, p. 115.
21. *Ibid.*
22. *Ibid.*, p. 117.
23. *Ibid.*, p. 137.
24. *Ibid.*, p. 11.
25. *Ibid.*, p. 14.
26. *Ibid.*, p. 20.

27. *Ibid.*, p. 22.
28. *Ibid.*, p. 32.
29. *Ibid.*, p. 34.
30. *Ibid.*, p. 110.
31. WKP 186, pp. 66–70.
32. WKP 351, p. 9.
33. *Ibid.*, p. 59.
34. *Ibid.*, p. 3.
35. *Ibid.*, p. 30.
36. *Ibid.*, p. 39.
37. *Ibid.*, p. 62.
38. *Ibid.*, pp. 63, 65.
39. *Ibid.*, p. 90.
40. WKP 250, pp. 3–11.
41. WKP 351, p. 55.
42. *Ibid.*
43. *Ibid.*, p. 56.
44. *Ibid.*, p. 57.

Chapter 11. Purges and People

1. WKP 205, p. 60.
2. For the text of the resolution, see *KPSS v Rezoliutsiyakh*, 7th ed. (Moscow, 1953), Part II, pp. 485–494.
3. See File 116/154f.
4. File 116/154f, p. 41.
5. *Ibid.*, p. 40.
6. *Ibid.*, p. 41.
7. *Ibid.*
8. *Ibid.*
9. *Ibid.*
10. *Ibid.*, p. 42.
11. *Ibid.*
12. *Ibid.*
13. *Ibid.*, pp. 42–43.
14. *Ibid.*, pp. 43–44.
15. *Ibid.*, p. 44.
16. *Ibid.*
17. *Ibid.*, p. 45.
18. *Ibid.*
19. *Ibid.*, p. 46.
20. *Ibid.*
21. *Ibid.*
22. *Ibid.*, p. 47.
23. *Ibid.*, p. 49.
24. *Ibid.*, p. 46.
25. *Ibid.*, p. 52.
26. *Ibid.*
27. *Ibid.*, p. 54.
28. *Ibid.*, pp. 54–55.
29. *Ibid.*, pp. 55–56.

30. *Ibid.*, p. 58.
31. *Ibid.*, p. 59.
32. *Ibid.*, pp. 60–61.
33. WKP 296, p. 114.
34. *Ibid.*
35. WKP 215, p. 183.
36. WKP 296, p. 115.
37. *Ibid.*
38. See WKP 511.
39. WKP 150, p. 50.
40. See WKP 226.
41. WKP 384, p. 231.
42. See WKP 316, p. 1.
43. See WKP 189, p. 17.
44. See WKP 499 for text.
45. WKP 93, pp. 41–42.
46. *Ibid.*, pp. 36–39.
47. *Ibid.*, pp. 41–42, for text.
48. *Ibid.*, pp. 71–74.
49. WKP 197, p. 187.
50. WKP 384, pp. 144–157.
51. WKP 186, p. 157.
52. See File RS 921, p. 131.
53. WKP 54, pp. 203–208.
54. WKP 384, pp. 270–314.
55. WKP 499, pp. 322–328.
56. File RS 921, p. 124.
57. *Ibid.*, p. 123.
58. *Ibid.*, p. 271.
59. *Ibid.*, pp. 277–283.
60. WKP 355, p. 114.

Chapter 12. The Story of Collectivization

1. WKP 290, pp. 2–25.
2. *Ibid.*
3. WKP 44, pp. 41–48.

4. *Ibid.*
5. WKP 215, p. 132.
6. WKP 250, p. 93.

7. WKP 215, p. 133.
8. WKP 223, p. 1.
9. *Ibid.*
10. *Ibid.*
11. *Ibid.*
12. *Ibid.*
13. *Ibid.*, p. 54.
14. WKP 234, p. 3.
15. WKP 223, p. 18.
16. *Ibid.*, p. 19.
17. *Ibid.*, p. 43.
18. *Ibid.*, p. 31.
19. *Ibid.*, p. 107.
20. *Ibid.*, p. 110.
21. *Ibid.*, p. 53.
22. *Ibid.*, p. 50.
23. WKP 261, pp. 31–42.
24. *Ibid.*
25. See WKP 53.
26. *Ibid.*, p. 4.
27. *Ibid.*, p. 1.
28. *Ibid.*, p. 3.
29. *Ibid.*, pp. 6ff.
30. *Ibid.*
31. *Ibid.*
32. *Ibid.*, p. 9.
33. *Ibid.*, p. 3.
34. *Ibid.*
35. *Ibid.*, p. 13.
36. *Ibid.*
37. WKP 260, p. 34.
38. *Ibid.*, p. 29.
39. *Ibid.*, p. 12.
40. *Ibid.*
41. *Ibid.*, p.1.
42. *Ibid.*, p. 7.
43. WKP 53, p. 23.
44. See WKP 159.
45. *Ibid.*, sequence 20.
46. *Ibid.*
47. *Ibid.*
48. *Ibid.*
49. *Ibid.*
50. *Ibid.*, sequence 19.
51. *Ibid.*
52. *Ibid.*
53. *Ibid.*
54. *Ibid.*
55. *Ibid.*

56. *Ibid.*
57. *Ibid.*
58. *Ibid.*
59. *Ibid.*
60. WKP 61, pp. 98–168.
61. WKP 151, pp. 191–196.
62. WKP 261, p. 101.
63. *Ibid.*, p. 96.
64. *Ibid.*, p. 88.
65. *Ibid.*, p. 87.
66. *Ibid.*, p. 83.
67. *Ibid.*, p. 82.
68. WKP 153, p. 10.
69. WKP 261, pp. 31–42.
70. *Ibid.*
71. *Ibid.*, p. 59.
72. *Ibid.*, WKP 261, pp. 62–63.
73. WKP 151, p. 23.
74. *Ibid.*, p. 71.
75. *Ibid.*, pp. 115–118.
76. *Ibid.*, pp. 191–196.
77. *Ibid.*
78. *Ibid.*
79. WKP 159, sequence 1.
80. *Ibid.*
81. WKP 162, p. 26.
82. WKP 159, sequence 23.
83. *Ibid.*, sequence 28.
84. WKP 162, p. 102.
85. WKP 167, pp. 37–39.
86. *Ibid.*
87. WKP 221, p. 39.
88. WKP 162, p. 105.
89. WKP 231, pp. 163–164.
90. WKP 162, p. 107.
91. See WKP 166, *passim.*
92. *Ibid.*, p. 340.
93. *Ibid.*
94. *Ibid.*, p. 809.
95. *Ibid.*, p. 828.
96. *Ibid.*, pp. 509–538.
97. WKP 221, pp. 63–64.
98. WKP 178, p. 134.
99. See WKP 226.
100. See WKP 234, material on collectivization.
101. WKP 313, p. 147.
102. *Ibid.*, pp. 57–62.

Chapter 13. Life on the Kolkhozes

1. WKP 266, pp. 209–214.
2. *Ibid.*
3. *Ibid.*
4. WKP 166, pp. 509–538.
5. *Ibid.*

6. WKP 313, pp. 57–62.
7. *Ibid.*
8. See Fedor Belov, *The History of a Soviet Collective Farm* (New York: Praeger, 1955), p. 116.

9. WKP 167, pp. 54–55.
10. *Ibid.*
11. WKP 195, pp. 51–56.
12. WKP 166, pp. 10–13.
13. WKP 190, pp. 131–134.
14. WKP 195, p. 164.
15. *Ibid.,* p. 175.
16. *Ibid.,* pp. 333–335.
17. *Ibid.*

18. WKP 188, p. 3.
19. *Ibid.*
20. See File RS 921, pp. 204–205.
21. WKP 355, pp. 277–278.
22. WKP 195, pp. 200–213.
23. *Ibid.*
24. *Ibid.,* pp. 211–213.
25. *Ibid.,* p. 215.

Chapter 14. The MTS

1. For the text of the 1933 decree establishing the political sections, see *KPSS v Rezolyutsiyakh,* 7th ed. (1953), Part II, pp. 730–741.
2. *Ibid.*
3. *Ibid.*
4. See WKP 315.
5. *Ibid.,* pp. 22–23.
6. *Ibid.,* p. 102.
7. WKP 189, pp. 161–164.
8. WKP 271, p. 117.
9. WKP 315, p. 14.
10. WKP 169, p. 13.
11. WKP 315, p. 19.
12. *Ibid.,* p. 36.
13. WKP 231, pp. 211–212.
14. WKP 251, p. 45.
15. WKP 253, p. 6.

16. *Ibid.,* p. 3.
17. WKP 173, pp. 3–5.
18. WKP 172, p. 8.
19. WKP 315, p. 85.
20. *Ibid.*
21. *Ibid.,* p. 35.
22. *Ibid.,* pp. 82–83.
23. *Ibid.,* p. 10.
24. *Ibid.,* p. 102.
25. *Ibid.,* p. 8.
26. WKP 251, p. 126.
27. WKP 172, p. 5.
28. WKP 315, p. 99.
29. *Ibid.,* p. 109.
30. *Ibid.*
31. For an example see File RS 924, Protocol No. 160, item 23.
32. WKP 238, pp. 253–255.

Chapter 15. The State Farms

1. WKP 61, pp. 98–168.
2. See Naum Jasny, *The Socialized Agriculture of the USSR* (Stanford University Press, 1949), p. 250.
3. *Ibid.,* p. 251.
4. See *KPSS v Rezoliutsiiakh,* 7th ed. (1953), Part II, pp. 730–741.
5. See especially WKP 253.
6. WKP 253, p. 5.
7. *Ibid.*
8. *Ibid.,* p. 9.
9. *Ibid.,* p. 13.
10. WKP 185, p. 19.

11. *Ibid.,* p. 24.
12. *Ibid.,* pp. 69–70.
13. *Ibid.,* pp. 16–18.
14. *Ibid.,* pp. 27, 80–81, 84–85.
15. *Ibid.,* pp. 53–54.
16. *Ibid.,* pp. 76–79.
17. *Ibid.,* pp. 72–75.
18. WKP 390, pp. 168–175.
19. See File RS 924, Protocol No. 124, item 43, February 4, 1936.
20. WKP 253, p. 37.
21. WKP 185, pp. 60–63.
22. *Ibid.,* p. 91.

Chapter 16. The Grievances of Industrial Workers

1. *XVII Syezd VPK(b), stenograficheskii otchyot* (Moscow, 1934), p. 145.
2. See WKP 300.
3. WKP 300, p. 2.
4. *Ibid.,* p. 3.
5. *Ibid.,* p. 5.
6. WKP 150, pp. 8–9.
7. *Ibid.,* pp. 74–87.

8. *Ibid.,* p. 27.
9. *Ibid.*
10. WKP 44, p. 84.
11. WKP 300, p. 15.
12. WKP 150, pp. 8–9.
13. *Ibid.*
14. *Ibid.*
15. WKP 250, pp. 38–47.

16. *Ibid.*
17. WKP 300, p. 48.
18. *Ibid.*, pp. 49–50.
19. *Ibid.*, pp. 17–21.
20. *Ibid.*, p. 28.
21. *Ibid.*, p. 32.
22. *Ibid.*, p. 34.
23. *Ibid.*
24. *Ibid.*, p. 35.
25. *Ibid.*
26. *Ibid.*
27. *Ibid.*, p. 36.
28. *Ibid.*
29. *Ibid.*, p. 37.
30. *Ibid.*
31. *Ibid.*, p. 38.
32. *Ibid.*, pp. 38–39.

33. *Ibid.*, p. 39.
34. *Ibid.*
35. WKP 150, p. 58.
36. WKP 300, pp. 45–48.
37. *Ibid.*, p. 47.
38. WKP 138, pp. 12–13.
39. WKP 162, p. 63.
40. See WKP 89.
41. WKP 89, p. 159.
42. WKP 235, p. 170.
43. WKP 195, p. 142.
44. *Ibid.*, p. 183.
45. WKP 109, pp. 18–25.
46. *Ibid.*
47. *Ibid.*, p. 80.
48. WKP 355, pp. 133–134.

Chapter 17. The Party and the Armed Forces

1. WKP 150, p. 64.
2. WKP 166, pp. 1–2.
3. WKP 189, p. 21.
4. See File RS 921, pp. 276–278.
5. *Ibid.*
6. WKP 225, pp. 67–69.
7. WKP 195, pp. 300–309.
8. *Ibid.*, pp. 308–309.
9. WKP 186, pp. 210–219.
10. WKP 248, p. 12.
11. *Ibid.*, p. 33.
12. WKP 130, p. 239.
13. See WKP 130, *passim.*
14. *Ibid.*, p. 203.

15. *Ibid.*
16. *Ibid.*, p. 229.
17. *Ibid.*, p. 203.
18. *Ibid.*, pp. 101, 206.
19. *Ibid.*, p. 424.
20. *Ibid.*, p. 261.
21. *Ibid.*, pp. 229, 261, 408.
22. *Ibid.*, p. 258.
23. *Ibid.*, p. 239.
24. *Ibid.*, p. 326.
25. *Ibid.*, p. 424.
26. *Ibid.*, p. 313.
27. *Ibid.*, p. 208.

Chapter 18. Party Controls and Higher Education

1. See *Bolshaya Sovetskaya Entsiklopedia,* XXVI (1933), 181–211 (article on Western Oblast).
2. WKP 215, pp. 218–222.
3. See WKP 330, *passim.*
4. See WKP 51, excerpt from protocol of the board of Smolensk State University, unnumbered.
5. WKP 51, pp. 8ff.
6. *Ibid.*
7. *Ibid.*
8. *Ibid.*
9. *Ibid.*
10. *Ibid.*
11. *Ibid.*
12. *Ibid.*, pp. 2–4.
13. *Ibid.*
14. WKP 309, p. 253.
15. *Ibid.*, p. 284.
16. *Ibid.*, p. 252.

17. WKP 215, pp. 219–222.
18. *Ibid.*
19. See WKP 309, p. 249, and WKP 51.
20. WKP 309, p. 252.
21. *Ibid.*, p. 249.
22. WKP 215, pp. 200–202.
23. WKP 309, p. 252.
24. *Ibid.*, p. 243.
25. *Ibid.*, p. 247.
26. *Ibid.*, p. 245.
27. *Ibid.*, p. 237.
28. *Ibid.*, p. 274.
29. *Ibid.*
30. *Ibid.*
31. *Ibid.*, p. 88.
32. *Ibid.*, p. 264.
33. *Ibid.*, p. 59.
34. *Ibid.*, p. 214.
35. *Ibid.*, p. 88.

36. *Ibid.*, p. 197.
37. *Ibid.*, p. 109.
38. *Ibid.*, p. 111.
39. *Ibid.*, p. 115.
40. *Ibid.*, p. 119.
41. *Ibid.*, pp. 287–296
42. *Ibid.*, p. 252.
43. *Ibid.*, p. 235.
44. WKP 155, p. 22.
45. WKP 309, p. 193.
46. *Ibid.*, p. 200.
47. *Ibid.*, p. 141.
48. *Ibid.*, p. 111.
49. *Ibid.*, p. 119.
50. *Ibid.*, p. 51.
51. *Ibid.*, p. 15.
52. *Ibid.*, p. 7.
53. *Ibid.*, p. 157.
54. *Ibid.*, p. 3.
55. *Ibid.*, p. 51.
56. *Ibid.*, p. 88.
57. *Ibid.*, p. 94.

58. *Ibid.*, p. 111.
59. *Ibid.*, p. 119
60. *Ibid.*, p. 111.
61. *Ibid.*, p. 7.
62. *Ibid.*, p. 15.
63. *Ibid.*, p. 242.
64. *Ibid.*, pp. 239, 281.
65. *Ibid.*, p. 237.
66. *Ibid.*, p. 119.
67. *Ibid.*, p. 282.
68. *Ibid.*, p. 111.
69. See WKP 51.
70. WKP 309, p. 264.
71. *Ibid.*, p. 29.
72. *Ibid.*, p. 244.
73. *Ibid.*, p. 230.
74. *Ibid.*, p. 109.
75. *Ibid.*, p. 257.
76. *Ibid.*, p. 131.
77. *Ibid.*, p. 111.
78. *Ibid.*, p. 45.
79. WKP 312, p. 38.

Chapter 19. Censorship

1. See File 116/154g.
2. See WKP 230.
3. *Ibid.*, p. 3.
4. *Ibid.*, pp. 6, 47.
5. File 116/154g, p. 4.
6. WKP 230, p. 48.
7. *Ibid.*, p. 64.
8. *Ibid.*, p. 32.
9. *Ibid.*, pp. 13, 29.
10. *Ibid.*, p. 21.
11. *Ibid.*, p. 67, and File 116/154g,
p. 14.
12. WKP 230, p. 64.
13. *Ibid.*, p. 7.
14. File 116/154g, p. 15.
15. *Ibid.*
16. WKP 237, p. 272.
17. *Ibid.*, p. 186.
18. *Ibid.*, p. 289.
19. File 116/154g, p. 3.
20. *Ibid.*, p. 18.
21. *Ibid.*
22. *Ibid.*
23. WKP 230, p. 9.

24. *Ibid.*, p. 8.
25. WKP 176, pp. 55–56.
26. *Ibid.*
27. File 116/154g, p. 10.
28. *Ibid.*, p. 8.
29. *Ibid.*, p. 12.
30. *Ibid.*, p. 15.
31. *Ibid.*, p. 22.
32. *Ibid.*, p. 3.
33. *Ibid.*, p. 4.
34. WKP 230, p. 10.
35. File 116/154g, p. 13.
36. *Ibid.*, p. 23.
37. *Ibid.*, p. 10.
38. *Ibid.*, p. 14.
39. *Ibid.*, p. 20.
40. WKP 230, p. 28.
41. WKP 265, pp. 12–16.
42. WKP 237, pp. 169–171.
43. WKP 265, p. 28.
44. *Ibid.*, pp. 12ff.
45. WKP 237, p. 170.
46. File RS 921, p. 43.
47. *Ibid.*, p. 106.

Chapter 20. The Right of Petition

1. See Chapter 12, pp. 251–253.
2. WKP 197, p. 155.
3. WKP 190, pp. 225–226.
4. See Chapter 13, pp. 271–278.
5. WKP 190, p. 85.

6. *Ibid.*, p. 84.
7. *Ibid.*, p. 83.
8. WKP 195, p. 63.
9. *Ibid.*, p. 64.
10. *Ibid.*, pp. 76–77.

11. *Ibid.*
12. *Ibid.*, pp. 84–85.
13. *Ibid.*, p. 86.
14. *Ibid.*, p. 87.
15. WKP 355, pp. 99–100.
16. WKP 190, pp. 27–28.
17. *Ibid.*, pp. 23–26.
18. *Ibid.*, p. 22.
19. *Ibid.*, p. 21.
20. WKP 355, pp. 219–220.
21. *Ibid.*, pp. 221–224.
22. WKP 454, pp. 69–77.
23. WKP 195, pp. 326–327.
24. *Ibid.*, p. 329.
25. WKP 355, pp. 47–52.
26. *Ibid.*, p. 55.
27. See Chapter 2, p. 56.
28. WKP 454, pp. 78–79.
29. *Ibid.*, pp. 1–20.
30. *Ibid.*, pp. 65–68.
31. *Ibid.*, pp. 86–87.
32. For other examples, see Chapter 16, pp. 316–317, 321–322.
33. WKP 355, pp. 188–189.
34. WKP 195, p. 72.
35. *Ibid.*, p. 69.
36. *Ibid.*, p. 70.
37. *Ibid.*, p. 71.
38. *Ibid.*, pp. 252–253.
39. *Ibid.*, pp. 160–161.
40. WKP 355, p. 166.
41. WKP 195, p. 179.
42. WKP 355, p. 45.
43. *Ibid.*, pp. 304–305.
44. WKP 197, p. 170.
45. WKP 355, pp. 315–316.
46. *Ibid.*, p. 107.
47. *Ibid.*, p. 226.
48. *Ibid.*, p. 27.
49. *Ibid.*, p. 126.
50. *Ibid.*, p. 131.
51. *Ibid.*, pp. 323–325.
52. WKP 195, p. 262.
53. *Ibid.*, pp. 58, 60.
54. WKP 355, p. 270.
55. *Ibid.*, p. 320.
56. *Ibid.*, pp. 209–210.

Chapter 21. The Komsomols

1. WKP 7, sequence 1.
2. WKP 6, p. 36.
3. WKP 275, p. 78, table 1.
4. *Ibid.*, and WKP 40, pp. 46–80.
5. WKP 331, pp. 108–136.
6. WKP 275, pp. 78–88.
7. *Ibid.*, p. 81.
8. *Ibid.*, p. 79.
9. WKP 29, pp. 48–60.
10. WKP 405, p. 80.
11. *Ibid.*
12. *Ibid.*, p. 6.
13. WKP 33, p. 142.
14. See Chapter 12.
15. WKP 408, p. 80.
16. WKP 409, pp. 101–106.
17. See WKP 72, *passim.*
18. *Ibid.*, pp. 39–40.
19. *Ibid.*, pp. 80–82.
20. *Ibid.*, p. 138.
21. *Ibid.*, pp. 140–143.
22. *Ibid.*, p. 123.
23. *Ibid.*, pp. 87–89.
24. *Ibid.*, pp. 104–106.
25. *Ibid.*, pp. 145–147.
26. *Ibid.*, pp. 9–10.
27. *Ibid.*, pp. 15–17.
28. *Ibid.*, pp. 11ff, 34, 40, 116, 165.
29. *Ibid.*, pp. 153–155.
30. *Ibid.*, p. 148.
31. *Ibid.*, pp. 26–27.
32. *Ibid.*, pp. 11ff.
33. *Ibid.*, pp. 7ff.
34. *Ibid.*, pp. 160–162.
35. *Ibid.*, pp. 121–123.
36. *Ibid.*, pp. 75–78.
37. *Ibid.*, pp. 50–54.
38. *Ibid.*, pp. 112–115.
39. *Ibid.*, pp. 46–48.
40. *Ibid.*, pp. 140–143.
41. *Ibid.*, p. 138.
42. *Ibid.*, p. 6.
43. *Ibid.*, pp. 19–21.
44. *Ibid.*, pp. 50–54.
45. *Ibid.*, pp. 126–127.
46. *Ibid.*, p. 138.
47. *Ibid.*, pp. 83–86.
48. *Ibid.*, pp. 171–174.
49. *Ibid.*, pp. 80–82.
50. *Ibid.*, pp. 87–89.
51. *Ibid.*, p. 124.
52. WKP 110, p. 111.
53. WKP 415, pp. 18–25.
54. *Ibid.*, p. 8.
55. *Ibid.*, p. 22.
56. *Ibid.*, p. 21.
57. *Ibid.*, p. 20.
58. *Ibid.*, p. 22.
59. *Ibid.*
60. *Ibid.*, p. 21.

61. *Ibid.*
62. *Ibid.*
63. *Ibid.*
64. *Ibid.*, p. 20.
65. *Ibid.*, p. 23.
66. *Ibid.*
67. For examples see WKP 415, *passim.*
68. WKP 415, p. 20.
69. *Ibid.*, p. 142.
70. WKP 199, p. 83.
71. See WKP 113.
72. *Ibid.*, pp. 57–58.
73. See WKP 113, *passim.*
74. WKP 416, Protocol No. 11, February 11, 1938.
75. See WKP 416, *passim.*
76. *Ibid.*, Protocol No. 14, March 14, 1938.
77. *Ibid.*, Protocol No. 16, March 26, 1938.
78. *Ibid.*
79. *Ibid.*, Protocol No. 17, March 28, 1938.
80. *Ibid.*, Protocol No. 14, March 14, 1938.
81. *Ibid.*
82. *Ibid.*, Protocol No. 16, March 26, 1938.
83. *Ibid.*
84. *Ibid.*
85. *Ibid.*
86. *Ibid.*
87. *Ibid.*
88. *Ibid.*
89. See WKP 115.
90. WKP 116, p. 72.

Chapter 22. The Godly and the Godless

1. WKP 458, pp. 58–60.
2. *Ibid.*
3. *Ibid.*
4. See WKP 275.
5. See WKP 458, pp. 58–60.
6. *Ibid.*
7. For the text of the rules, see WKP 458, pp. 31–34.
8. WKP 458, pp. 28–34.
9. *Ibid.*, p. 52.
10. WKP 33, pp. 163–164.
11. WKP 460, p. 18.
12. *Ibid.*, p. 15.
13. John S. Curtiss, *The Russian Church and the Soviet State* (Boston: Little Brown, 1953), p. 244.
14. See WKP 65, *passim.*
15. For examples, see WKP 65, Protocol No. 59, August 6, 1930.
16. WKP 460, pp. 7–11.
17. WKP 483, p. 1.
18. *Ibid.*
19. WKP 499, pp. 295–297.
20. *Ibid.*, p. 294.
21. WKP 109, Protocol No. 1.
22. See WKP 113.
23. See also resolution of obkom bureau, July 19, 1937, WKP 238, pp. 175–177.
24. See WKP 483.
25. See WKP 14, pp. 120–124.
26. See WKP 303, pp. 62–65.
27. *Ibid.*, p. 61.
28. *Ibid.*, p. 71.
29. WKP 483, p. 4.
30. WKP 231, pp. 222–223.
31. WKP 483, p. 6.
32. See Solomon M. Schwarz, *The Jews in the Soviet Union* (Syracuse University Press, 1951), p. 245.
33. See WKP 335.
34. See WKP 303, p. 12.
35. WKP 483, p. 20.
36. WKP 499, pp. 295–297.

Glossary of Russian Words and Abbreviations

agenturno-operativnaya rabota: the operative work of agents of the security police (OGPU-NKVD).

agenturno-osvedomitelnaya set: the agent-informer network of the security police.

agitprop: the agitation and propaganda section of the Party apparatus; also used to describe the activities which this section sponsors.

aktiv: the activist nucleus of the Party and other Soviet mass organizations.

apparat: the Party apparatus.

apparatchik: a full-time Party functionary employed in the Party apparatus.

arshin: measure of length, 2.33 feet.

artel: association for common work.

ASSR: Autonomous Soviet Socialist Republic.

batrak: farm laborer.

bednyak: poor peasant.

Bezbozhnik: the newspaper "Godless"; *bezbozhnik,* atheist.

cadre: the staff or personnel of an organization.

CC: Party Central Committee.

CCC: Party Central Control Commission.

centner: measure of weight, 220.46 pounds (100 kilograms).

Chasidim: members of an ultra-orthodox and devout Jewish sect.

cheder: Jewish religious school.

Cheka: The Extraordinary Commission to Combat Counterrevolution and Sabotage.

collegium: a board or collective body exercising administrative responsibilities.

Comintern: The Communist International.

comrade court: an informal court composed of fellow workers and vested with authority to impose mild administrative penalties for infractions of discipline and other lesser offenses.

CPSU: The Communist Party of the Soviet Union.

dessyatin: land measure, 2.70 acres.

diamat: dialectical materialsm.

Duma: representative state assembly.

Evsektsia: Jewish section of the Party secretariat.

feldsher: medical worker, but without doctor's training.

FZU: factory school.

Glavlit: The Chief Administration for Literary Affairs responsible for censorship.

Glavzoloto: Main Administration of the Gold and Platinum Industries.

gorkom: city or town Party committee.

gorlit: city or town censor.

GORPO: city or town consumers' society.

gorsoviet: city or town soviet, or assembly.

GORT: city or town trade administration.

Gosplan: State Planning Commission.

GPU: State Political Administration.

GTO: literally "Prepared for Labor and Defense"; a badge awarded to Osoaviakhim members meeting prescribed physical, military, or other requirements of the organization.

Gubcheka: the guberniya, or provincial, Cheka.

guberniya: province.

gubispolkom: the executive committee of the provincial soviet.

gubkom: the Party committee of a guberniya, or province.

hectare: land measure, 2.471 acres.

Hehalutz: A Jewish nationalist organization dedicated to the preservation of Hebrew culture and the preparation of Soviet Jews for immigration to Palestine.

ispolkom: executive committee of a soviet.

Istpart: Party history; used to describe a section of the Party secretariat charged with responsibility for Party history.

Kadet: member of the Constitutional Democratic Party.

kasha: porridge.

katorga: exile.

khutor: individual farm separated from the mir.

kilogram: measure of weight, 2.2046 pounds.

kolkhoz: collective farm.

Kolkhoznaya Gazeta: "The Kolkhoz Gazette."

kolkhoznik: member of a collective farm.

Komsomol: Young Communist League.

kopeck: a small coin.

krai: territory.

kraikom: territorial Party committee.

krailit: territorial censor.

Krestyanskaya Gazeta: "Peasant's Gazette."

krugovaya poruka: the mutual support of Soviet officials in covering up deficiencies or illegalities in work.

kulak: literally fist; a well-to-do peasant.

kulich: Easter cakes.

kultprop: cultural propaganda sections of Party committees.

lapti: bast shoes.

lisheniets: person deprived of the voting privilege.

mir: communal form of land tenure.

MOPR: International Aid Society for Revolutionary Fighters.

MTS: machine-tractor station.

nabor: the amount of money which a worker had to pay for a typical market basket of necessary articles of consumption.

Narkomtorg: People's Commissariat for Trade.

NEP: New Economic Policy.

NKVD: People's Commissariat of Internal Affairs.

nomenklatura: list of appointments subject to Party initiation or ratification.

obkom: oblast Party committee.

oblast: region.

oblispolkom: executive committee of oblast soviet.

oblit: oblast censor.

ODGB: Society of Friends of the Journal "Godless."
ODTOGPU: Special Road Transport Department of the GPU.
OGIZ: United State Publishing Houses.
OGPU: Unified State Political Administration.
okrug: circuit.
orgbureau: organization bureau.
orgotdel: organization section.
Osoaviakhim: Society for the Promotion of Defense and Aero-Chemical Development.
otdel: section.
otkhodniki: migratory workers.
OVTs: the organs of military censorship.
OZET: Society for Agricultural Settlement of Jewish Toilers.
Pamiatka Railita: Handbook of the District Censor.
partiinost: devotion to the Party cause.
partkom: Party committee.
partorg: Party organizer.
Party cabinet: Party study center.
perechen: detailed list of data and information subject to censorship.
Plemzagottrest: cattle procurement trust.
plenum: a general or full assembly.
Podiv: head of the Political Department of an army division.
Politburo: The Political Bureau; leading organ of the Party.
politotdel: political section.
politruks: political leaders in lower army units.
Promparty: Industrial Party; its alleged leaders were tried in December 1930 for conspiring to overthrow the Soviet regime.
pud: measure of weight, 36.113 pounds.
PUNS: The Political Administration of the People's Commissariat for State Farms.
rabfak: Workers' Faculties established to help badly prepared workers qualify for higher education.
Raifo: raion, or district, finance section.
Raigorlit: District-town censor.
raiispolkom: executive committee of a district soviet.
raikom: Party district committee.
Railit: district censor.
raion: district.
raitroika: a three-man district commission charged with responsibility for dekulakization.
raivoyenkomat: raion military department.
RaiZO: raion agricultural section.
RIK: raion executive committee.
RKI: Commissariat of Workers' and Peasants' Inspection.
RKKA: The Red Army.
ROST: Russian Telegraph Agency.
RSFSR: Russian Socialist Federated Soviet Republic.
samogan: illegal home-distilled liquor.
selkor: village correspondent.
selpo: village coöperative store.
Selpromsoiuz: Agricultural-Industrial Credit Union.

selsoviet: village soviet.

shchi: cabbage soup.

SNK: Council of People's Commissars.

SR: member of Socialist-Revolutionary Party.

sokha: wooden plow.

Sovetskaya Torgovlya: the newspaper, "Soviet Trade."

soviet: elected assembly.

sovkhoz: state farm.

Sovnarkom: (See SNK) Council of People's Commissars.

Sovtorgotdel: Soviet-Trade Division of Party secretariat.

Soyuzplodoovoshch: agency charged with procurement of potatoes and hay.

SSR: Soviet Socialist Republic.

stakhanovite: a shock-worker who produces in excess of quota.

subbotnik: a gathering for collective work on free evenings or rest days.

SVB: The League of Militant Atheists.

tekhnikum: technical school.

torgsin: stores in which goods were sold for gold or foreign currency.

troika: from the three-horsed sleigh, a three-man commission.

tsekhprofburo: shop trade union bureau.

TsEKUBU: Central Commission for the Improvement of the Living Conditions of Scientists.

TsIK: The Central Executive Committee of the USSR.

udarnik: shock-worker.

udarnitsa: woman shock-worker.

ukom: uyezd, or district, Party committee.

uravnilovka: egalitarianism in wage payments.

uriadnik: tsarist village policeman.

uyezd: district.

verst: measure of length, 0.66 English mile.

VIK: executive committee of volost or township soviet.

VKP(b): All-Union Communist Party (Bolsheviks).

volkom: volost, or township, committee of the Party.

volost: township.

VUZ: university and other higher educational institutions.

yamstchik: driver.

Yunii Pioner: the newspaper "Young Pioneer."

Zagotlen: Association for the Procurement and Marketing of Flax, Hemp, and Clover Seeds.

Zagotzerno: grain procurement agency.

Za Kollektivizatsiyu: the newspaper "For Collectivization."

Zapoblispolkom: executive committee of the Western Oblast Soviet.

Zapoblit: the chief censor of the Western Oblast.

Zavkom: head of the trade union factory committee.

zemstvo: agency of rural self-government in prerevolutionary Russia.

ZHAKT: Housing Coöperative Society.

zhid: a term of contempt for Jews.

Index

To Riga

WESTERN OBLAST

ADMINISTRATIVE DIVISIONS · June 1, 1932

RAION LIST

1 Sebezhsky	31 Yartsevsky	61 Kozelsky
2 Pustoshkinsky	32 Prechistensky	62 Sukhinichsky
3 Novosokolnitsky	33 Dukhovshchinsky	63 Duminichsky
4 Loknyansky	34 Demidovsky	64 Lyudinovsky
5 Kholmsky	35 Rudnyansky	65 Dyatkovsky
6 Toropetsky	36 Smolensky	66 Dubrovsky
7 Leninsky	37 Krasninsky	67 Kletnyansky
8 Penovsky	38 Monastyrshinsky	68 Zhukhovsky
9 Ostashkovsky	39 Pochinkovsky	69 Bryansky
10 Kamensky	40 Glinkovsky	70 Zhizdrinsky
11 Lukovnikovsky	41 Dorogobuzhsky	71 Plokhinsky
12 Selizharovsky	42 Izdeshkhovsky	72 Khvostovichsky
13 Nelidovsky	43 Vyazemsky	73 Karachevsky
14 Oktyabrsky	44 Gzhatsky	74 Shablykinsky
15 Velikolutsky	45 Temkinsky	75 Brasovsky
16 Nevelsky	46 Medynsky	76 Navlinsky
17 Usvyatsky	47 Bukharinsky	77 Pochepsky
18 Velizhsky	48 Yukhnovsky	78 Mglinsky
19 Ilinsky	49 Znamensky	79 Unechsky
20 Belsky	50 Mosalsky	80 Surazhsky
21 Oleninsky	51 Spas-Demensky	81 Gordeevsky
22 Rzhevsky	52 Yelninsky	82 Krasnogorsky
23 Staritsky	53 Stodolishchensky	83 Novozybkovsky
24 Pogor.-Gorodishchensky	54 Khislavichsky	84 Klintsovsky
25 Zubtsovsky	55 Slumyachsky	85 Klimovsky
26 Karmanovsky	56 Roslavlsky	86 Starodubsky
27 Sychevsky	57 Ekimovichsky	87 Pogarsky
28 Novodugynsky	58 Pesochensky	88 Trubshevsky
29 Kholi-Zhirkovsky	59 Baryatinsky	89 Suzemsky
30 Safonovsky	60 Meshchovsky	90 Komarichsky
		91 Sevsky

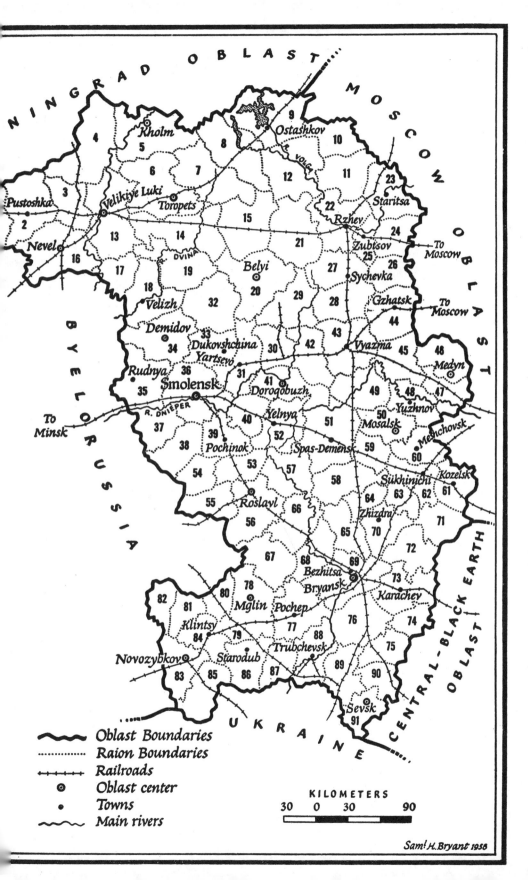

NINGRAD OBLAST

OBLAST

MOSCOW

4

Kholm

5

8

9

Ostashkov

10

MOSCOW OBLAST

6

7

12

11

23

VOLGA

Staritsa

3

Velikiye Luki

Toropets

22

Pustoshka

2

15

21

Rzhev

24

13

14

Zubtsov

To Moscow

Nevel

25

26

16

17

DVINA

19

Belyi

27

Sychevka

18

20

28

Gzhatsk

To Moscow

Velizh

32

29

43

44

Demidov

33

42

45

46

34

Dukovshchina

30

Vyazma

Medyn

Yartsevo

31

Rudnya

36

41

49

48

47

35

Smolensk

Dorogobuzh

50

Yuzhnov

R. DNIEPER

Mosalsk

Meshchovsk

To Minsk

37

40

Yelnya

51

60

39

52

59

Kozelsk

38

Pochinok

57

58

63

62

61

53

64

54

Roslavl

66

65

70

Zhizdra

71

55

56

72

67

68

69

Bezhitsa

73

78

Bryansk

Karachev

82

80

74

81

Mglin

Pochep

76

Klintsy

77

88

75

84

79

Trubchevsk

Novozybkov

Starodub

87

89

90

83

85

86

Sevsk

91

UKRAINE

CENTRAL-BLACK EARTH OBLAST

BYELORUSSIA

Oblast Boundaries
Raion Boundaries
Railroads
Oblast center
Towns
Main rivers

KILOMETERS

30   0   30   90

Sam! H.Bryant 1958

SMOLENSK GUBERNIYA

JANUARY 1, 1927

UYEZD LIST

Smolensky	chief town	*Smolensk · Gubern. center*
Belsky	" "	*Belyi*
Vyazemsky	" "	*Vyazma*
Gzhatsky	" "	*Gzhatsk*
Demidovsky	" "	*Demidov*
Dorogobuzhsky	" "	*Dorogobuzh*
Yelinsky	" "	*Yelnya*
Roslavlsky	" "	*Roslavl*
Sychevsky	" "	*Sychevka*
Yartsevsky	" "	*Yartsevo*

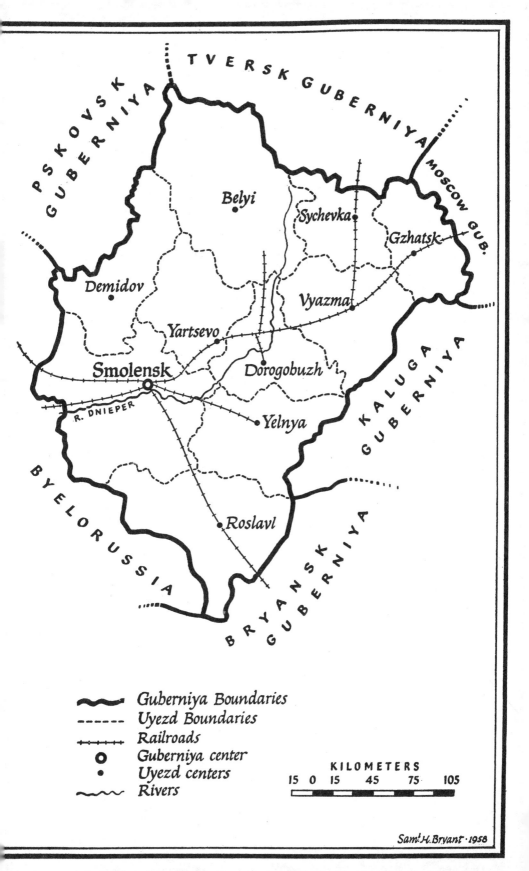

PSKOVSK GUBERNIYA

TVERSK GUBERNIYA

MOSCOW GUB.

Belyi

Sychevka

Gzhatsk

Demidov

Vyazma

Yartsevo

Dorogobuzh

Smolensk

R. DNIEPER

Yelnya

KALUGA GUBERNIYA

BYELORUSSIA

Roslavl

BRYANSK GUBERNIYA

〰 Guberniya Boundaries
---- Uyezd Boundaries
┼┼┼ Railroads
◦ Guberniya center
• Uyezd centers
〜 Rivers

KILOMETERS
15 0   15   45   75   105

Saml. H. Bryant · 1958